A

COMMENTARY

ON THE

ORIGINAL TEXT

OF THE

ACTS OF THE APOSTLES.

BY

HORATIO B. HACKETT, D. D.

PROFESSOR OF BIBLICAL LITERATURE IN NEWTON
THEOLOGICAL INSTITUTION.

A NEW EDITION,

REVISED AND GREATLY ENLARGED.

BOSTON:
GOULD AND LINCOLN,
59 WASHINGTON STREET.
NEW YORK: SHELDON, BLAKEMAN & CO.
CINCINNATI: GEORGE S. BLANCHARD.
1858.

Stereotyped and Printed by
W. F DRAPER, ANDOVER, MASS.

THE AUTHOR

Is permitted to Inscribe this Volume

TO

AUGUSTUS THOLUCK, D. D.,

WHOSE WRITINGS IN ILLUSTRATION OF THE SACRED WORD, AND WHOSE PERSONAL INSTRUCTIONS, HAVE CAUSED HIS INFLUENCE TO BE FELT AND HIS NAME TO BE HONORED IN FOREIGN COUNTRIES AS WELL AS HIS OWN.

PREFACE

TO THE

FIRST EDITION.

It has been the writer's endeavor to present to the reader in this volume the results of the present state of biblical study, as applied to the illustration of the Acts of the Apostles. Although our language contains already some valuable works devoted to the same general object, it is hoped that the dependence of the work here offered to the public on the original text, and the advantage taken of the latest investigations in this department of criticism, will render it not superfluous.

Of the importance of an acquaintance with the contents of the Acts, it must be unnecessary to speak. A single reflection will render this sufficiently obvious. No person can be prepared to read the Epistles of the New Testament with the greatest advantage until he has made himself familiar with the external history of the Apostle Paul, and with his character and spirit, as Luke has portrayed them in his narrative. Those portions of the Acts, constituting the greater part of the whole, which relate to the great Apostle, must be thoroughly mastered before any proper foundation is laid for the exegetical study of the Epistles. It is the object of these Notes to assist the reader in the acquisition of this knowledge and discipline; to enable him to form his own independent view of the meaning of the sacred writer in this particular portion of the New Testament, and, at the same time, furnish himself to some extent with those principles and materials of criticism which are common to all parts of the Bible. If the plan of the work and the mode in which it is executed are such as to impart a just idea of the process of biblical interpretation, and to promote a habit of careful study and of self-reliance on the part of those who may use the book, it will be a result much more important than that all the opinions advanced in it should be approved; it is a result beyond any other which the writer has been anxious to accomplish. The grammatical references and explanations will enable the student to judge of the consistency of the interpretations given with the laws of the Greek language. The authorities cited will show the state of critical opinion on all passages that are supposed to be uncertain or obscure. The geographical, archæological, and other information collected from many different sources, will unfold the relations of the book to the contemporary history of the age in which it was written, and serve to present to the mind a more vivid conception of the reality of the scenes and the events which the narrative describes.

No single commentary can be expected to answer all the purposes for which a commentary is needed. The writer has aimed at a predominant object; and that has been, to determine by the rules of a just philology the meaning of the sacred writer, and not to develop the practical applications, or, to any great extent, the doctrinal implications of this meaning. With such a design, no one will object to the use which has been made of the labors of foreign scholars; it would have been a matter of just complaint not to have used them, although with a different aim it would be equally inexcusable not to have brought into view more frequently the connections which exist between the Acts and the practical religious literature contained in our own language.

* * * * * * * *

I am indebted to various friends for advice and coöperation in the performance of this labor. Among these it becomes me to mention in particular the Rev. B. B. Edwards, D. D., Professor at Andover. It is doubtful whether I should have undertaken the work, or persevered in it, had it not been for his generous sympathy and encouragement.

* * * * * * * *

The author can recall no happier hours than those which

he has spent in giving instruction on this book of the New Testament to successive classes of theological students. May the fruits of this mutual study be useful to them in the active labors of the sacred work to which they are devoted. They are now sent forth into a wider sphere;—and, here also, may God be pleased to own them as a means of contributing to a more diligent study and a more perfect knowledge of his Holy Word.

NEWTON THEOLOGICAL INSTITUTION,
October 31, 1851.

PREFACE TO THE REVISED EDITION.

THE present edition as compared with the former has been in parts rewritten, and, also, enlarged by the addition of about a hundred pages. In the interval since the work was first published, the writer has continued to study the Acts both in a private way and occasionally as the teacher of theological classes. As the result of this further labor, the view on some passages has been modified; expressions that were found to be obscure have been made plainer; new points in the text have been elucidated; former explanations of a debatable character, according to the apparent evidence in the case, have been placed in a stronger light, or advanced with less confidence; and, in general, pains have been taken in this revised form to render the notes not less critical than before, and yet freer and more varied in their contents. The last six years, too, have been signally fruitful in the appearance of valuable works relating to the Acts, either directly exegetical or subsidiary to that end. The reader will find ample proof in the following pages of the extent of my indebtedness to these contributions to biblical literature, and at the same time, will appreciate the difficulty of using the abundant material with independence and judgment.

It has been of some service to me that since the publication of the first edition, I have been enabled to visit the countries in which the Saviour and the apostles lived, and the cross gained its earliest victories. The journey has made it ten fold more a labor of love to trace again the footsteps of Paul and his associates, and should add something to the interpreter's power to unfold the history of their sufferings and their triumphs.

Not to render the Commentary too heterogeneous, it has seemed best to discard the idea of a supplement for the discussion of certain miscellaneous topics, as was proposed at first. As a substitute for such an appendage, the points which it was designed to embrace have been enlarged upon more fully in the present notes, and references have been given to appropriate works in which the student who desires will find more complete information. I will only add that the Greek text has been reviewed more carefully in this edition, and, unless I have erred through some inadvertence, all the variations which affect the sense materially have been brought to the reader's notice. At the suggestion of various friends, the Greek words in the notes have been translated in all cases where the remarks might otherwise be obscure to the English reader, and thus the explanations will be readily understood by all into whose hands the work may fall.

May the Divine blessing rest upon this renewed endeavor to illustrate this portion of the Holy Scriptures.

NEWTON CENTRE, March 1, 1858.

INTRODUCTION.

§ 1. The Writer of the Acts.

The evidence that the book of Acts was written by Luke, to whom the Christian world are accustomed to ascribe it, is of a three-fold character. It will be sufficient for the object here in view merely to indicate the line of argument which establishes the correctness of that opinion. A more complete and systematic view of the evidence must be sought in works which treat professedly of the formation and transmission of the Canon of the Scriptures.

In the first place, we have the explicit testimony of the early Christian writers, that Luke wrote the Acts of the Apostles. Irenæus, who became bishop of Lyons in A. D. 178, and who was born so early that he was intimate with those who had seen the apostles, says expressly that Luke was the author of the Acts; he quotes from him various single passages, and, in one place, gives a distinct summary of the last twelve chapters of the book (Adv. Hæres. 3. 14. 1). He treats this authorship of the work as a matter which he had no occasion to defend, because no one of his contemporaries had called it in question. From the generation which separated Irenæus from the age of Luke, we have only a few scanty remains; but these, although they contain expressions[1] which, according to the admission of nearly all critics, pre-suppose an acquaintance with the Acts, are silent respecting the writer. To have mentioned him by name would have been at variance with the informal mode of citing the Christian Scriptures, which distinguishes the writings of that

[1] See the passages, in Kirchhofer's Sammlung zur Geschichte des N. T. Canons, p. 161 sq., in Lardner's Credibility, and similar works.

early period. The next witness is Clemens of Alexandria, who flourished about A. D. 190. This father not only speaks of Luke as having composed the Acts, in his Stromata (Lib. 5), but is known to have written a commentary on it, which has not been preserved. Tertullian, who lived about A. D. 200, offers the same testimony. He has not only quoted the Acts repeatedly, but named Luke as the author, in such a way as makes it evident that he merely followed in this the universal opinion of his age (De Jejun. c. 10; De Præscript. Hæret. c. 22; De Bapt. c. 10, etc.). Eusebius wrote about A. D. 325. He has recorded both his own belief and that of his time, in the following important statement: "Luke, a native of Antioch, by profession a physician, was mostly Paul's companion, though he associated not a little with the other apostles. He has left us examples of the art of healing souls, which he acquired from the apostles, in two divinely inspired books; first, in the Gospel which he testifies to have written according to what eye-witnesses and ministers of the word delivered to him from the beginning, all which, also, he says that he investigated from the first;[1] and, secondly, in the Acts of the Apostles, which he composed, not from report, as in the other case, but according to his own personal observation." (Hist. Eccl. 3. 4.)

It would be superfluous to pursue this testimony further. It may be proper to add, that no trace of any opposition to it, or dissent from it, has come down to us from the first ages of the church. Some of the early heretical sects, it is true, as the Marcionites, Manicheans, Severians, rejected the religious authority of the Acts; but as they did this because it contradicted their peculiar views, and as they admitted without question the source from which their opponents claimed to receive it, their rejection of the book, under such circumstances, becomes a conclusive testimony to its genuineness.

In the second place, the relation in which the Acts of the Apostles stands to the Gospel which is ascribed to Luke, proves that the author of the two productions must be the same individual. The writer introduces his work as a continuation or second part of a previous history, and dedicates it to a certain Theophilus, who can be no other than the person for whose special information the Gospel was written. As to the identity of the writer of the Acts with the writer of the Gospel attributed to

[1] As the relative may be neuter or masculine, many take the sense of the Greek to be, *all whom he accompanied;* but the manifest allusion to Luke 1, 2. 3 renders the other the more obvious translation.

Luke, no well-founded question has been, or can be, raised. Consequently, the entire mass of testimony which proves that Luke the Evangelist wrote the Gospel which bears his name, proves with equal force that he wrote also the Acts of the Apostles. Thus the Acts may be traced up to Luke, through two independent series of witnesses. And it may be confidently asserted, that, unless the combined historical evidence from this twofold source be admitted as conclusive in support of Luke's claim to the authorship of the Acts, there is then no ancient book in the world, the author of which can ever be ascertained by us.

In the third place, the literary peculiarities which distinguish the Gospel of Luke mark also the composition of the Acts, and show that it must have come from the same hand. The argument here is founded on a different relation of the Gospel to the Acts from that to which we have just adverted. Luke being acknowledged as the author of the Gospel, we know from that source what the characteristics of his style are; and it is maintained that these re-appear in the Acts to such an extent, that we can account for the agreement only by referring the two productions to the same writer. The reality of the resemblance here asserted is conceded by critics of every name. It will be necessary to restrict the illustration of it to a few examples.[1] In Luke's Gospel, verbs compounded with prepositions are more numerous than in the other Evangelists; they are found in the same proportion in the Acts. Matthew has σύν three times, Mark five times, John three times, or, according to another reading, but twice; while Luke employs it in his Gospel twenty-four times, and in the Acts fifty-one times. Luke has used ἅπας in his two books thirty-five times; whereas it occurs in all the others but nine times. πορεύεσθαι is found in the Gospel forty-nine times, and in the Acts thirty-eight times, but is rarely found in other parts of the New Testament. The construction of εἰπεῖν and λαλεῖν with πρός, instead of the dative of the person addressed, is confined almost exclusively to Luke. No other writer, except John in a few instances, ever says εἰπεῖν πρός, and λαλεῖν πρός occurs out of Luke's writings only in 1 Cor. 14, 6; Heb. 5, 5 and 11, 18. As in Luke's Gospel, so in the Acts we

[1] They are drawn out, more or less fully, in Gersdorf's Beitraege, p. 160 sq.; Credner's Einleitung in das neue Testament, p. 130 sq.; Ebrard's Kritik der evangelischen Geschichte, p. 671, ed. 1850; Guericke's Gesammtgeschichte des N. T., p. 166 sq.; Lekebusch's Composition und Entstehung der Apostelgeschichte, p. 37 sq.; and Dr. Davidson's Introduction to the New Testament, Vol. I. p. 190, and Vol. II. p. 8.

have a characteristic use of δὲ καί to express emphasis or gradation, a similar use of καὶ αὐτός or αὐτοί, the insertion of the neuter article before interrogative sentences, the omission of δέ after μὲν οὖν, the uniform preference of Ἱερουσαλήμ to Ἱεροσόλυμα, and still others. Credner, in his Introduction to the New Testament, has enumerated not fewer than sixty-five distinct idioms which he considers as peculiar to Luke's diction as compared with that of the other New Testament writers; and nearly all these he points out as occurring at the same time both in the Gospel and the Acts. It is impossible, then, to doubt, unless we deny that any confidence can be placed in this species of criticism, that, if Luke wrote the Gospel which we accredit to him, he must have written also the Acts.

§ 2. Biographical Sketch of Luke.

According to Eusebius, as already quoted, and Jerome, who may be supposed to represent the opinion of their times, Luke was a native of Antioch. As he appears in the Acts to have spent so much time at Philippi, some modern writers have conjectured that he may have been a native or inhabitant of that city. The historical testimony deserves more regard than an inference of that nature. That he was a Gentile by birth appears to be certain from Col. 4, 11. 14, where Paul distinguishes him from those whom he denominates οἱ ὄντες ἐκ περιτομῆς. His foreign extraction is confirmed also by the character of his style, which approaches nearer to the standard of classical Greek than that of any other writer of the New Testament, with the exception of the apostle Paul. This feature of his language renders it probable that he was of Greek origin. Some have inferred this also from his Greek name; but it was not uncommon for Jews, as well as Romans and other foreigners, to assume such names at this period. Whether he was a proselyte to Judaism before his conversion to Christianity, or not, is a question on which critics differ. The supposition that he adopted first the Jewish religion, and had done so perhaps in early life, accounts best for his intimate acquaintance with the opinions and customs of the Jews, his knowledge of the Septuagint, and the degree of Hebraistic tendency which shows itself in his style. It appears from Col. 4, 14, that Luke was a physician; and the general voice of antiquity, in accordance with that passage, represents him as having belonged to the medical profession. The effect of his following such an employment can be traced, as many critics think, in various passages of Luke's writings; comp. the Note on 28, 8. The fact that he was trained to such a pursuit, that he was a man, therefore, of culture and observing habits of mind, is an important circumstance. It has been justly remarked, that, as many of the miracles which the first promulgators of the gospel wrought in confirmation of its truth were cases of the healing of maladies, Luke, by virtue of his medical skill and experience, was rendered peculiarly competent to judge of the reality of such miracles.[1]

Of the manner in which the writer of the Acts was brought to a knowledge of the gospel, we have no information. The suggestion of some of the later fathers, that he was one of the seventy disciples, is not only without ground, but opposed to his own statement in the introduction of his Gospel, where he distinguishes himself from those who had been personal attendants on the ministry of Christ. It is evident that, after his conversion, he devoted himself to public Christian labors, for the most part in connection with the apostle Paul, whom he accompanied from place to place, and aided in his efforts for the extension of the gospel. The first explicit allusion which he makes to himself occurs in 16, 10 sq., where he gives an account of the apostle's departure from Troas to Macedonia. In that passage Luke employs the first person plural, and thus shows that he was one of the companions of Paul on that occasion. He goes with the apostle from Troas to Philippi, and speaks of himself again in 20, 6, as one of the several individuals who sailed with Paul from the same city on his last journey to Jerusalem. Whether Luke had been separated from Paul during the interval, or remained with him, cannot be certainly known. It is eminently characteristic of the sacred writers, that they keep themselves out of view in their narratives. Hence some have argued that we are not to infer that Luke was necessarily absent when he employs the third person, but rather that it was a sort of inadvertence, as it were, against his design, that he has now and then disclosed his personal connection with the history. The other opinion is the surer one. We cannot be certain that Luke was in the company of Paul, except at the times when his language shows that he was personally concerned in what he relates. It is clear, even according to this view, that Luke, in addition to his accompanying Paul on his first journey from Troas to Philippi,

[1] I have made no allusion in the text to 2 Cor. 8, 18; for it is barely possible that the author of our narrative can be meant there as "the brother whose praise is in all the churches." See De Wette's note on that passage in his Exegetisches Handbuch zum N. Testament.

remained with him, without any known interruption, from the period of his leaving Philippi the second time to the end of his career. He goes with the apostle to Jerusalem, where the latter was apprehended and given up to the custody of the Romans (20, 6 sq.; 21, 1 sq.); he speaks of himself as still with him at the close of his imprisonment at Cæsarea (27, 1); proceeds with him on his voyage to Rome (27, 1 sq.); and, as we see from the Epistles which Paul wrote while in that city, continued to be associated with him down to the latest period of his life of which any record remains. The apostle mentions Luke as residing with him at Rome in Col. 4, 14; Phil. v. 24; and in 2 Tim. 4, 11. Of his subsequent history, nothing authentic has been preserved. The traditions which relate to this period are uncertain and contradictory. According to Gregory Nazianzen, whom several later writers follow, he suffered martyrdom; according to others, and those whose testimony has greater weight, he died a natural death.

§ 3. Authenticity of the Acts.

The foregoing sketch shows us how ample were Luke's means of information in regard to the subjects of which his history treats. Of most of the events which he has recorded, he was an eye-witness. The materials which compose the body of the work lay within the compass of his own personal knowledge. The particulars which he communicates respecting Paul's life and labors before his own acquaintance with him, he could have learned, at a subsequent period, in his intercourse with that apostle. His extensive journeyings could hardly fail to have brought him into connection with most of the other persons who appear as actors in the history. Some of his information he derived, no doubt, from written sources. The official documents which he has inserted (15, 23 sq.; 23, 26 sq.) were public, and could have been copied. We assume nothing at variance with the habits of antiquity in supposing that the more extended discourses and speeches, which Luke himself did not hear, may have been noted down by others at the time of their delivery, or soon afterwards, while the impression made by them was still vivid. If the writer of the Acts had any occasion for the use of such reports, his travels from one country to another must have given him access to the persons who could furnish them.[1]

[1] Some critics, as Schleiermacher, Bleek, De Wette, have thrown out the idea that Luke may have derived those parts of the Acts in which the narrator em-

We are to recollect, further, that the declaration which Luke makes at the commencement of his Gospel applies equally to the Acts. It was his habit, as we learn there, to avail himself of every possible source of inquiry, in order to ascertain the certainty of what he wrote. With such opportunities at his command, and with such a character for diligence in the use of them, the writer of the Acts, considered simply in the light of an ordinary historian comes before us with every title to confidence which can be asserted in behalf of the best accredited human testimony.

But this is not all. We have not only every reason to regard the history of Luke as authentic, because he wrote it with such facilities for knowing the truth, but because we find it sustaining its credit under the severest scrutiny to which it is possible that an ancient work should be subjected.

First. This history has been confronted with the Epistles of the New Testament; and it has been shown as the result, that the incidental correspondences between them and the Acts are numerous and of the most striking kind. They are such as preclude the supposition of their being the result either of accident or design. It is impossible to account for them, unless we admit that the transactions which Luke records really took place in the manner that he has related. It is the object of Paley's Horæ Paulinæ to develop this argument; and the demonstration of the truth of the Acts, and of the New Testament in general, which he has furnished in that work, no objector has ever attempted to refute.

Secondly. The speeches in the Acts which purport to have been delivered by Peter, Paul, and James, have been compared with the known productions of these men; and it is found that they exhibit an agreement with them, in point of thought and expression, which the supposition of their common origin would lead us to expect. The speeches attributed to Peter contain peculiar phrases and ideas, which impart a characteristic similarity to them as compared with the other speeches, and which appear again in his Epistles, but in no other portion of the New Testament. In like manner, the speeches of Paul evince an affinity both to each other and to his Epistles, in the recurrence of favorite words, modes of construction, and turns of thought, such as belong to no other writer. We have but one address

ploys the first person plural from a history of Paul's missionary labors written by Timothy; see the note on 20, 6. Among the writers who have shown the untenableness of that hypothesis, are Ebrard, Kritik, u. s. w., p. 732 sq.; Lekebusch, Composition, u. s. w., p. 131 sq.; and Davidson, Introduction, Vol. II. p. 9 sq.

from James, but even here we discover striking points of connection with the Epistle which bears his name. Occasion will be taken, in the course of the Commentary, to illustrate this peculiar feature of the history.

Thirdly. We have a decisive test of the trustworthiness of Luke in the consistency of his statements and allusions with the information which contemporary writers have given us respecting the age in which he lived and wrote. The history which we read in the Acts connects itself at numerous points with the social customs of different and distant nations; with the fluctuating civil affairs of the Jews, Greeks, and Romans; and with geographical or political divisions and arrangements, which were constantly undergoing some change or modification. Through all these circumstances, which underlie Luke's narrative from commencement to end, he pursues his way without a single instance of contradiction or collision. Examples of the most unstudied harmony with the complicated relations of the times present themselves at every step. No writer who was conscious of fabricating his story would have hazarded such a number of minute allusions, since they increase so immensely the risk of detection; and still less, if he had ventured upon it, could he have introduced them so skilfully as to baffle every attempt to discover a single well-founded instance of ignorance or oversight. It adds to the force of the argument to remark, that in the pages of Luke every such allusion falls from him entirely without effort or parade. It never strikes the reader as far-fetched or contrived. Every incident, every observation, flows naturally out of the progress of the narrative. It is no exaggeration to say, that the well-informed reader, who will study carefully the book of the Acts, and compare the incidental notices to be found on almost every page with the geography and the political history of the times, and with the customs of the different countries in which the scene of the transactions is laid, will receive an impression of the writer's fidelity and accuracy, equal to that of the most forcible treatises on the truth of Christianity.

The objections which sceptical writers have urged against the authenticity of the Acts relate chiefly to the supernatural character of its narrations. It does not belong to the province of Biblical criticism to reply to such objections. They have adduced also a few instances of alleged offence against history, or chronology, or archæology; but these result from an unnecessary interpretation. We may understand the passages which are said to contain the inconsistency in a different manner, and thus remove entirely the occasion for it.

§ 4. Object and Plan of the Book.

The common title of the Acts — πράξεις τῶν ἀποστόλων — is ancient, but is supposed generally to have been prefixed, not by the author, but by some later hand. It is read differently in different manuscripts. It is too comprehensive to describe accurately the contents of the book. The writer's object, if we are to judge of it from what he has performed, must have been to furnish a summary history of the origin, gradual increase, and extension of the Christian church, through the instrumentality chiefly of the apostles Peter and Paul. In fact, we have not a complete history, but a compendium merely of the labors of these two apostles, who were most active in their efforts to advance the gospel, while the other apostles are only referred to or named incidentally in connection with some particular occurrence. It is not to be supposed that Luke has recorded all the facts which were known to him respecting the early spread of Christianity. On what principle he proceeded in making his selection from the mass of materials before him, we cannot decide with certainty. He may have been influenced in part by the personal relation which he sustained to the individuals introduced, and the events described by him. It is still more probable, that the wants of the particular class of readers whom he had in view may have shaped, more or less consciously, the course of his narrative; and these readers, in the absence of any surer indication, we may consider as represented by Theophilus, who was, in all probability, a convert from heathenism. (See note on 1, 1.)

In writing for such readers, we should expect that Luke would lean towards those aspects of the history which illustrated the design of God in reference to the heathen; their right to participate in the blessings of the gospel without submitting to the forms of Judaism; the conflict of opinion which preceded the full recognition of this right, and the success more particularly of those apostolic labors which were performed in behalf of heathen countries. It cannot be denied that the contents of the Acts exhibit a predilection for this class of topics; and to that extent the book may be said to have been written in order to illustrate the unrestricted nature of the blessings of the gospel. On the other hand, it should be observed that this predilection is merely such as would spring naturally from the writer's almost unconscious sympathy with his Gentile readers, and is by no means so marked as to authorize us, according to the view of some writers, to impute to him any thing like a formal purpose to trace the relation of Judaism to Christianity.

In accordance with this trait of the Acts here alluded to, we have a very particular account of the manner in which Peter was freed from his Jewish scruples. The reception of the first heathen converts into the church is related at great length. The proceedings of the council at Jerusalem, with reference to the question whether circumcision should be permanent, occupy one of the leading chapters of the book. And the individual of the apostles who preached chiefly to the Gentiles, and introduced the gospel most extensively into heathen countries, is the one whom the writer has made the central object of his history, and whose course of labor he has described in the fullest manner.

Luke has pursued no formal plan in the arrangement of the Acts. The subject of his history, however, divides itself naturally into two principal parts. The first part treats of the apostolic labors of Peter, and hence particularly of the spread of Christianity among the Jews, occupying the first twelve chapters; the second, of the labors of Paul, and hence the promulgation of the gospel in Syria, Asia Minor, Greece, and Rome, occupying the remaining chapters. But the book contains other topics which are related to these only in a general way. The following division marks out to view the different sections more distinctly. 1. Outpouring of the Spirit on the day of Pentecost, and the antecedent circumstances. 2. Events relating to the progress of the gospel in Judea and Samaria. 3. The transition of the gospel to the heathen, in the conversion of Cornelius and others. 4. The call of the apostle Paul, and his first missionary tour. 5. The apostolic council at Jerusalem. 6. The second missionary tour of Paul. 7. His third missionary tour, and his apprehension at Jerusalem. 8. His imprisonment at Cæsarea, and voyage to Rome.

§ 5. Time and Place of Writing the Acts.

The time when the Acts was written could not have been far distant from that of the termination of Paul's imprisonment at Rome, mentioned at the close of the history. The manner in which Luke speaks of that imprisonment implies clearly, that, at the time when he wrote, the apostle's condition had changed; that he was no longer a prisoner, either because he had been liberated, or because he had been put to death.

It does not affect the present question whether we suppose

that he was imprisoned twice, or only once (see note on 28, 31). If we suppose that he was set at liberty, we have then a most natural explanation of the abrupt close of the book, in the fact that Luke published it just at the time of the apostle's release; or so soon after that event, that the interval furnished nothing new which he deemed it important to add to the history. On the other hand, if we suppose that Paul's captivity terminated in his martyrdom, it is not easy to account for the writer's silence respecting his death, except on the ground that it was so recent and so well known in the circle of his readers, that they did not need the information. Thus, in both cases, the time of writing the Acts would coincide very nearly with the end of the Roman captivity of which Luke has spoken.

The question arises now, Do we know the time when that captivity ended, whether it may have been by acquittal or death. Here we must depend upon the surest chronological data which exist, though it is not pretended that they are certain. According to a computation which has received the assent of most critics, Paul was brought as a prisoner to Rome in the year A. D. 61 or 62. In the year 64 followed the conflagration in that city, which was kindled by the agency of Nero, but which, for the sake of averting the odium of the act from himself, he charged on the Christians. This led to the first Christian persecution, so called, which is mentioned by Tacitus (Annal. 15. 44), Suetonius (Ner. 16), and possibly Juvenal (Serm. 1. 146 sq.). If now Paul was set at liberty after his confinement of two years, it must have been just before the commencement of Nero's persecution, that is, in the year A. D. 63, or near the beginning of 64. But if, according to the other supposition, the two years were not completed until the persecution commenced, he must, in all probability, as the leader of the Christian sect, have soon shared the common fate, and so have been put to death about the year 64. Hence we may consider this date, or the close of A. D. 63, as not improbably the time when Luke wrote, or at least published, the Acts of the Apostles.

But if Luke wrote the book thus near the expiration of the two years that Paul was a prisoner at Rome, it is most natural to conclude that he wrote it in that city. This was also the opinion of many of the early Christian fathers. The probability of this conclusion is greatly strengthened by the fact, that Luke makes no mention of Paul's liberation, or martyrdom, as the case may have been. At Rome, every reader of the apostle's history knew of course what the result of his captivity there was; and if Luke wrote it at that place, the absence of any allusion to his fate would not seem to be so very surprising. On the contrary, if Luke wrote it at a distance from the scene of the apostle's captivity, the omission would be much more extraordinary.

§ 6. Chronology of the Acts.

The subject of the chronology of the Acts is attended still with uncertainties, which no efforts of critical labor have been able wholly to remove. "After all the combinations," says Schott,[1] "which the ingenuity of scholars has enabled them to devise, and all the fulness of historical learning which they have applied to the subject, it has been impossible to arrive at results which are satisfactory in all respects." The source of the difficulty is, that the notations of time are for the most part entirely omitted; or, if they occur here and there, are contained in general and indefinite expressions. We must content ourselves, therefore, with endeavoring to fix the dates of a few leading events, which may be ascertained with most certainty; and must then distribute the other contents of the book with reference to these, on the basis of such incidental intimations as may be found to exist, or of such probable calculations as we may be able to form.

1. *The Year of Paul's Conversion.*

The date of this event is very uncertain; but an attempt has been made to approximate to it by means of the following combination. In Gal. 1, 15–18, it is stated that Paul went up to Jerusalem from Damascus three years from the time of his conversion; and we learn from 2 Cor. 11, 32, that Damascus, when Paul made his escape from it on that occasion, was in the hands of Aretas, king of Arabia. As this city belonged to the Romans, it is remarkable that it should have been, just at that time, wrested from them; and the circumstances under which such an event took place must have been peculiar. It is conjectured that a juncture like this may have led to that occurrence. Josephus relates that an army of Herod Antipas had been defeated about this time by Aretas, king of Arabia. Upon this, the Emperor Tiberius, who was a friend and ally of Herod, directed Vitellius, Roman Governor of Syria, to collect an adequate force, and to

[1] Erörterung einiger chronologischen Punkte in der Lebensgeschichte des Apostel Paul, § 1.

take Aretas prisoner, or slay him in the attempt. Before Vitellius could execute this order, news came that the emperor was dead, and as a consequence of this, the military preparations on foot were suspended. This sudden respite afforded Aretas an opportunity to march upon Damascus, and reduce it to his possession. The city, however, supposing him to have become master of it, could not have remained long in his power. We find that the difficulties with Arabia were all adjusted in the first years of the reign of Caligula, the successor of Tiberius, i. e. within A. D. 37–39; and the policy of the Romans would lead them, of course, to insist on the restoration of so important a place as Damascus. If now we place the escape of Paul in the *last* of these years (so as to afford time for the incidental delays), and deduct the three years during which he had been absent from Jerusalem, we obtain A. D. 36 as the probable epoch of the apostle's conversion. It is in favor of this conclusion, says Neander, that it gives us an interval neither too long nor too short for the events which took place in the church between the ascension of Christ and the conversion of Paul. Among others who fix upon the same year, or vary from it but one or two years, may be mentioned Eichhorn, Hug, Hemsen, Schott, Guericke, Meyer, De Wette, Anger,[1] Ebrard, Alford, Howson.[2] This date determines that of Stephen's martyrdom, which took place, apparently, not long before Paul's conversion, and also that of Paul's first journey to Jerusalem, and his subsequent departure to Tarsus.

2. *The Death of Herod Agrippa.*

This occurred at Cæsarea in the year A. D. 44. The statements of Josephus are decisive on this point. He says that Agrippa, who, under Caligula, had reigned over only a part of Palestine, received the entire sovereignty of his grandfather, Herod the Great, on the accession of Claudius, viz. in the year A. D. 41 (Antt. 19. 5. 1); and further, that at the time of his death he had completed the third year after this extension of his power (Antt. 19. 8. 2). This date fixes the position of several other important events; such as the execution of James the elder, the arrest and deliverance of Peter, the return of Paul to

[1] De temporum in Actis Apostolorum ratione, p. 121 sq.

[2] Wieseler (Chronologie des Apostolischen Zeitalters, pp. 175–213) assigns Paul's conversion to A. D. 40. It was gratifying to me to find that, with this exception, all his other dates agree with those which I had been led to adopt before consulting his able treatise.

Antioch from his second visit to Jerusalem, and his departure on his first missionary excursion.

3. *The Third Journey of Paul to Jerusalem.*

In Gal. 2, 1, the apostle speaks of going up to Jerusalem *after fourteen years,* which are to be computed, in all probability, from the time of his conversion. It has been made a question, whether this journey is to be understood as the second or third of the several journeys which Paul is mentioned in the Acts as having made to Jerusalem. The general opinion is, that it should be understood of the third; first, because the object of that journey, as stated in 15, 1 sq., coincides exactly with that which occasioned the one mentioned in the Epistle to the Galatians; and, secondly, because the circumstances which are described as having taken place in connection with the journey in 15, 1 sq., agree so entirely with those related in the Epistle.[1] Supposing, then, the identity of the two journeys to be established, we add the fourteen years already mentioned to the date of Paul's conversion, viz. 36, and we have A. D. 50 as the year when he went up to Jerusalem the third time after he had become a Christian.[2] With this year coincides that of holding the Council at Jerusalem. Paul departed on his second missionary tour soon after his return to Antioch from this third visit to Jerusalem; and hence we are enabled to assign that second tour to the year A. D. 51.

4. *The Procuratorship of Felix.*

The time of this officer's recall, on being superseded by Festus (see 24, 27), is assigned by most critics to the year A. D. 60 or 61. The names of both these men are well known in secular history; but it so happens that we meet with only indirect statements relating to the point which concerns us here. It is gen-

[1] The reasons for this conclusion are well stated by Hemsen, in his Der Apostel Paulus, u. s. w., p. 52 sq., translated by the writer in the Christian Review, 1841, p. 66 sq. Dr. Davidson has discussed the question with the same result in his Introduction, Vol. II. pp. 112–122. See, also, Conybeare and Howson, Life and Epistles of St. Paul, Vol. I. p. 539 sq., (2d ed.) and Jowett on Galatians, p. 252.

[2] It is proper to apprise the reader that some reckon the fourteen years in Gal. 2, 1, from the apostle's first return to Jerusalem (Gal. 1, 18); and in that case his third journey to that city would be dated three years later. But few comparatively adopt this view. The apostle's conversion is the governing epoch, to which the mind of the reader naturally turns back from Gal. 2, 1, as well as from Gal. 1, 18.

erally agreed that these statements justify the following opinion. It is certain that Felix could not have been recalled later than the year 62. Josephus states (Antt. 20. 8. 9) that Felix, soon after his return to Rome, was accused before the emperor, by a deputation from the Jews in Palestine, of maladministration while in office, and that he would have been condemned had it not been for the influence of his brother Pallas, who stood high at that time in the favor of Nero. This Pallas now, according to Tacitus (Ann. 14, 65), was poisoned by Nero in the year 62. The only circumstance which impairs the certainty of this conclusion is that Tacitus states (Ann. 13. 14) that Pallas had lost the favor of Nero some time before this, and had been entirely removed from public business. Hence some have placed the appointment of Festus as successor of Felix several years earlier than A. D. 61. But there is reason to believe that the disgrace of which Tacitus speaks may have been only temporary, and that Pallas may afterwards have recovered his influence with the emperor. Since it is certain, according to Tacitus himself, that the death of this favorite did not occur till A. D. 62, it can be more easily supposed that Nero was again reconciled to him than that this revengeful tyrant should have suffered him to live several years after he had become odious to him. De Wette, Anger, Meyer, Wieseler, and others, admit this supposition, under the circumstances of the case, to be entirely natural.

It is less easy to fix the limit on the other side. The general belief is that Festus could not have succeeded Felix earlier than A. D. 60 or 61. Josephus relates (Antt. 20. 8. 11) that Festus, after having entered on his office, permitted a deputation of the Jews to repair to Rome, in order to obtain the decision of Nero in a controversy between himself and them; and that Poppæa, the wife of Nero, interceded for them, and enabled them to gain

[1] Some, as Neander, Wieseler, object to the stricter sense of γυνή in the passage of Josephus, but it is defended by Schrader, Meyer, and others, as the more obvious sense, whether we consider the historical facts or the usage of the word. Neander (Pflanzung, u. s. w. Vol. I. p. 493) expresses himself with much hesitation respecting this date of the succession of Felix and Festus. It is important, for the purpose of laying up in the mind a connected view of the history, to settle upon the precise years as nearly as possible; and we ought not to deprive ourselves of this advantage, merely because some of the conclusions, or the grounds of them, cannot be placed entirely beyond doubt. It is admitted that of the dates proposed in the above scheme of chronology, the second (that of Herod's death) and the last in a lower degree (that of Paul's arrival at Rome) are the only ones that can be brought to a state of comparative certainty. In regard to the others, I have not meant to claim for them anything more than the character of an approximation to the truth.

their object. But this woman did not become the wife[1] of Nero until the year 62 (Tac. Ann. 14. 49; Suet. Ner. 35); and hence, as Festus must have been in Judea some time before this difficulty with the Jews arose, and as, after that, some time must have elapsed before the case could be decided at Rome, Festus may have received his appointment in the year 60 or 61. The best recent authorities, as Winer, De Wette, Anger, Meyer, Wieseler, adopt one or the other of these years.

We reach very nearly the same result from what Josephus says of his journey to Rome in behalf of the Jewish priests whom Felix had sent thither for trial before his removal from office. He informs us in his Life (§ 3), that he made this journey in the twenty-sixth year of his age, and as he was born in the first year of the reign of Caligula, i. e. A. D. 37 (Life, § 1), he visited Rome on this occasion about 63. His narrative, without being definite, implies that Felix, at this time, had not only been recalled, but must have left Palestine two or three years earlier than this. Festus was the immediate successor of Felix.

It is the more important to settle as nearly as possible some epoch in this portion of the apostle's history, since there would be otherwise so much uncertainty as to the mode of arranging the events in the long interval between this and Paul's third journey to Jerusalem. Upon this date depends the year of the apostle's arrest in that city on his fifth and last visit thither, before he was sent to Rome. His captivity at Cæsarea, which followed that arrest, continued two years, and must have commenced in the spring of A. D. 58 or 59.

5. *The Arrival of Paul in Rome.*

The extreme limit beyond which we cannot place this event may be regarded as certain. It could not have been later than the year 62; for after 64, when the Christians at Rome began to be persecuted by the Roman government, their situation was such that the apostle could not have remained there and preached the gospel for two years without molestation, as stated by Luke at the end of the Acts. It is impossible to obtain a more definite result than this from secular history.[1] But the date in question follows as a deduction from the one considered in the last paragraph. It is evident from the Acts, that Paul proceeded to Rome almost immediately after the entrance of Festus on his office; and if this took place in A. D. 60 or 61, he must have arrived in

[1] Whether this result is confirmed by τῷ στρατοπεδάρχῃ in 28, 16, depends on the explanation of the article; see the note on that passage.

Rome early in the spring of 61 or 62. Hence, if he arrived even in A. D. 62, he could have remained two years in captivity, and then have regained his freedom (if we adopt that opinion), since Nero's persecution of the Christians did not commence till the summer of A. D. 64.

§ 7. The Contents in Chronological Order.

A. D.

33. Ascension of Christ. Appointment of Matthias as an apostle. Outpouring of the Spirit at Pentecost. The gift of tongues conferred. Discourse of Peter. Three thousand are converted. — Pilate, under whom the Saviour was crucified, is still procurator of Judea. Tiberius continues emperor till A. D. 37.

33–35. Peter and John heal the lame man. They are arraigned before the Sanhedrim, and forbidden to preach. Death of Ananias and Sapphira. The apostles are scourged. Deacons appointed. Apprehension and martyrdom of Stephen. Saul makes havoc of the church.

36. Persecution scatters the believers at Jerusalem. Philip preaches the gospel in Samaria. Hypocrisy of Simon the Magian. Baptism of the Eunuch. The word is made known in Phœnicia, Cyprus, and at Antioch in Syria. Christ appears to Saul on the way to Damascus. Conversion of Paul.

37–39. Paul spends these three years at Damascus and in Arabia. During the same time other laborers spread the gospel in Judea, Galilee, and along the coast of the Mediterranean. — Caligula becomes emperor in A. D. 37.

39. Paul escapes from Damascus, and goes to Jerusalem for the first time since his conversion. Barnabas introduces him to the disciples. He remains there fifteen days, but is persecuted and departs thence to Tarsus.

40–43. During this period Paul preaches in Syria and Cilicia. Churches are gathered there. Barnabas is sent to search for him, and conducts him to Antioch. In the mean time Peter visits Joppa, Lydda, and Cæsarea. Dorcas is restored to life. Cornelius is baptized. Peter defends himself for visiting the heathen. — Claudius becomes emperor in the beginning of A. D. 41. On his accession he makes Herod Agrippa I. king over all Palestine.

44. Paul labors "a whole year" with Barnabas at Antioch. Agabus predicts a famine in Judea. James the elder is beheaded at Jerusalem. Peter is cast into prison; his liberation and flight. — Herod Agrippa dies at Cæsarea in the summer of this year. Judea is governed again by procurators.

45. Paul goes to Jerusalem the second time, on the alms-errand, accompanied by Barnabas. He returns to Antioch, and under the direction of the Spirit, is set apart by the church to the missionary work. In the same year, probably, he goes forth with Barnabas and Mark on his first mission to the heathen.

46, 47. He was absent on this tour about two years. He proceeds by the way of Seleucia to Salamis and Paphos in Cyprus; at the latter place Sergius Paulus believes, and Elymas is struck blind. Crossing the sea, he lands at Perga, where John Mark abruptly left him. He preaches in the synagogue at Antioch. Labors with success at Iconium. At Lystra he is about to be worshipped as a god, and afterward is stoned. Escapes to Derbe. Retraces his way to Perga; sails from Attaleia and comes again to Antioch in Syria.

48, 49. Here he abode, it is said, "a long time." We may assign these two years to that residence. He extended his labors, no doubt, to the neighboring regions.

50. Apostolic council at Jerusalem. Paul makes his third journey to that city, in company with Barnabas and others, as delegates from the church at Antioch. Returns to Antioch with the decrees. Paul and Barnabas separate.

51–54. The apostle's second missionary tour. Silas, Timothy, and Luke are associated with him. Paul revisits the churches in Syria and Cilicia. Plants the churches in Galatia. At Troas he embarks for Europe, and, among other places, visits Philippi, Thessalonica, Berea, Athens, Corinth. In this last city he remained at least a year and a half. Labored with Aquila at tent-making. Left the synagogue and preached to Greeks. He is arraigned before Gallio. In this city Paul wrote the First and Second Epistles to the Thessalonians.[1] In the spring, probably,

[1] The reasons for assigning the different Epistles to the times and places mentioned are stated in the body of the Commentary.

of A. D. 54, he leaves Corinth, embarks at Cenchrea, touches at Ephesus, lands at Cæsarea, and from there goes for the fourth time to Jerusalem, and thence to Antioch. We may allot three years, or three and a half, to this journey. — Felix became procurator of Judea in A. D. 52. In A. D. 53, Claudius bestowed on Herod Agrippa II., the former tetrarchy of Philip and Lysanias, with the title of king. In A. D. 54, Nero succeeded Claudius as emperor.

54–57. In the autumn of A. D. 54, according to some, or early in A. D. 55, according to others, Paul entered on his third missionary tour. He goes through Galatia and Phrygia to Ephesus, where he spends the greater part of the next three years. Just before his arrival, Apollos left Ephesus for Corinth. Certain disciples of John are baptized. Nearly all Asia hears the Gospel. The Exorcists defeated. An uproar at Ephesus. The Asiarchs befriend Paul. During this sojourn here, Paul wrote the Epistle to the Galatians, and the First Epistle to the Corinthians. Within the same time he made, probably, a short journey to Corinth, either directly across the Ægean, or through Macedonia. While on this excursion, some suppose that he wrote the First Epistle to Timothy, and after his return to Ephesus, that to Titus.

58, 59. In the spring of A. D. 58, or perhaps A. D. 57 (if this tour began in 54), the apostle leaves Ephesus, and proceeds to Macedonia, where he writes his Second Epistle to the Corinthians. He spent the summer in that region, and travelled probably as far west as Illyricum. In the autumn or early winter of this year, he arrives at Corinth, and remains there three months. The Jews plot his destruction. At this time he wrote the Epistle to the Romans. In the ensuing spring, he returns through Macedonia to Troas, where he preached and "broke bread." Miraculous recovery of Eutychus. At Miletus he addressed the Ephesian elders.. Landing at Ptolemais, he proceeded to Cæsarea, and thence to Jerusalem, which is his fifth and last visit to that city. This journey occupied about four years.

58 or 59. At Jerusalem Paul assumes a vow, to conciliate the Jewish believers. He is seized by the Jews in the temple, but is rescued by Lysias the chiliarch. Speech to

the mob from the stairs of the castle. His Roman citizenship saves him from the torture. He stands before the Sanhedrim and narrowly escapes with his life. Forty Jews conspire against him. Lysias sends him as a state-prisoner to Felix at Cæsarea.

59–61. His captivity here continues two years. He pleads his cause before Felix, who detains him in the hope of a bribe. The Jews renew their charge against him before Festus. Paul is compelled to appeal to Cæsar. He speaks in the presence of king Agrippa, and is pronounced innocent. — Felix was superseded by Festus in A. D. 60 or 61.

62–64. In the autumn of A. D. 60 or 61, Paul embarked at Cæsarea for Rome, and arrived there early in the following spring. He remains in custody two years. During this period he wrote the Epistles to the Ephesians, Colossians, Philippians, Philemon, and, if he suffered martyrdom at this time, the Second Epistle to Timothy, just before his death. The Epistle to the Hebrews was written, probably, in this latter part of the apostle's life. Most of those who maintain that Paul was imprisoned twice at Rome, suppose (the correct opinion, as it seems to me) that he wrote the First Epistle to Timothy, and that to Titus, in the interval between his first and second captivity, and his Second Epistle to Timothy in the near prospect of his execution, after his second arrest.

COMMENTARY.

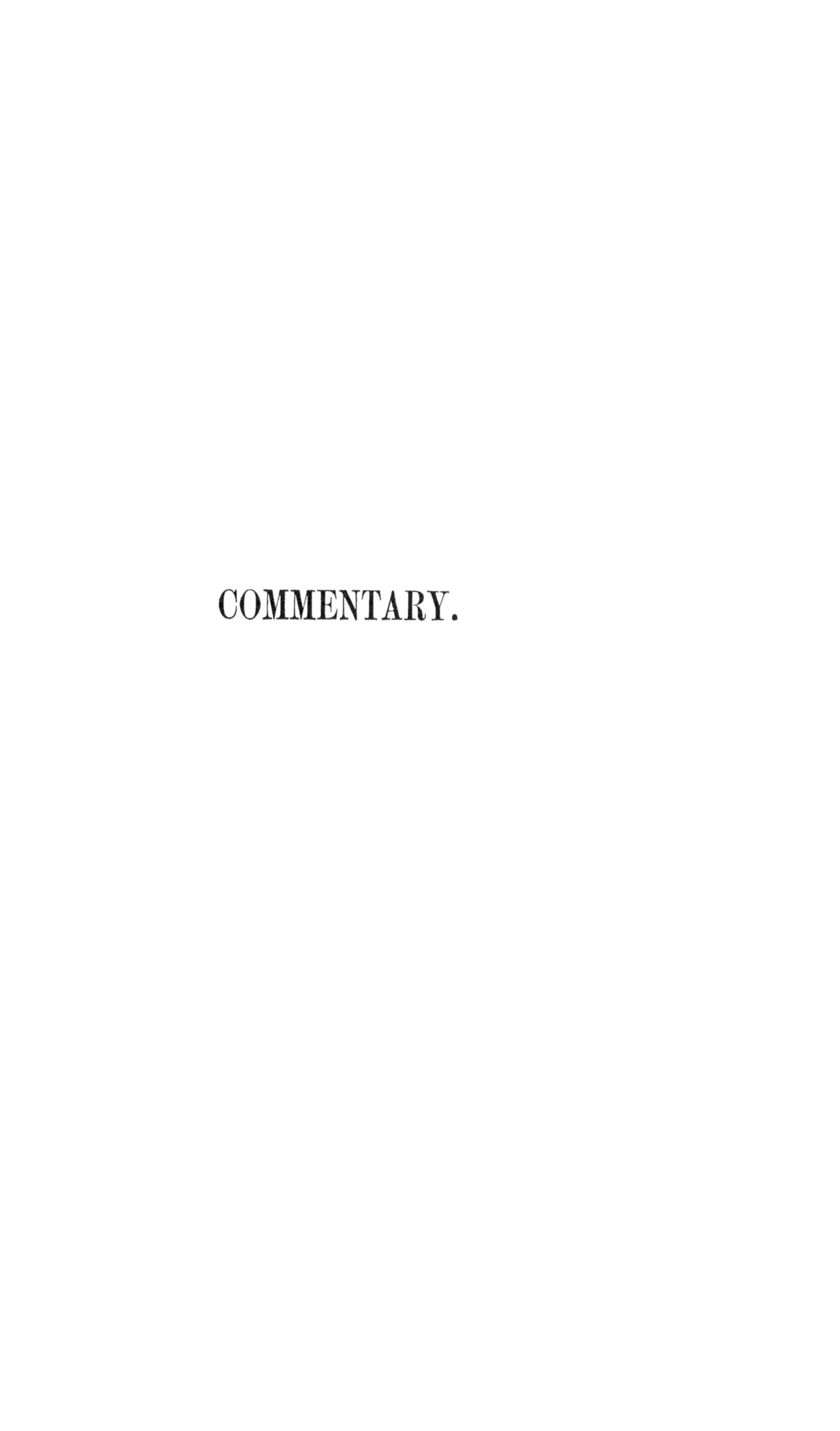

COMMENTARY.

FOR THE READER.

THE works on the Greek language to which most frequent reference has been made, are the following: —

W., WINER'S *Grammatik des neutestamentlichen Sprachidioms*, sixth edition, 1855 (the divisions in the English Translation, fourth edition, sometimes differ).

S., PROF. STUART'S *Grammar of the New Testament Dialect*, second edition.

K., KUEHNER'S *Greek Grammar*, translated by Edwards and Taylor.

C., CROSBY'S *Greek Grammar*.

B., BUTTMANN'S, Robinson's Translation.

Mt., MATTHIÆ'S, third edition of the original, or Blomfield's Translation.

Green's Gr., *Grammar of the N. T. Dialect* by T. S GREEN (London 1842).

Bernh. Synt., BERNHARDY'S *Wissenschaftliche Syntax*.

Hart. Partkl., HARTUNG'S *Lehre von den Partikeln, u. s. w.*

Kl. Devr., DEVARIUS *de Gr. Ling. Particulis* edidit KLOTZ.

Lob. Phryn., *Phrynichi Eclogae Nominum* edidit LOBECK.

Tittm. Synm., TITTMANN *de Synonymis* in *N. Testamento*.

Pape Lex., *Handwörterbuch der Griechischen Sprache*, von DR. W. PAPE (Braunsschweig 1842).

R. and P. Lex., *Passow, Handwörterbuch der Gr. Sprache*, neu bearbeitet, u. s. w., von DR. ROST und DR. PALM (Leipzig 1841–56).

Some other names, especially those of commentators or critics, mentioned often, as well as titles of books quoted often, have been abbreviated. A list of such contractions will be found at the end of the volume.

COMMENTARY.

CHAPTER I.

Verses 1–3. *Relation of the Acts to the Gospel of Luke.*

V. 1. *μέν, solitarium*, i. e., without any following δέ. This omission, which occurs in the best writers, is very common in this book; see v. 18; 3, 13; 19, 4; 26, 4, etc. K. § 322. R. 4; W. § 63. I. 2. e. The writer frames the clause in which he refers to his first history (μέν), as if he had intended to add here (δέ) that he would now relate how extensively the name of Jesus had been made known, and by what means. Being led by the allusion to the ascension of Christ to state the circumstances of that event, he drops the proposed antithesis, and leaves the subject of the book to unfold itself from the course of the narrative.— πρῶτον stands for the stricter πρότερον, like the interchange of *first* and *former* in English; comp. John 1, 15, 30; 15, 18; and perhaps Luke 2, 2.—λόγον, *history*, as in Herod. (6. 19), and thence onward.—Θεόφιλε. He appears from Luke 1, 3 to have been a man of rank, since κράτιστε, when prefixed in the Acts to the name of a person, refers not to character, but to station; see 23, 26; 24, 3; 26, 25. From the fact that Luke wrote his Gospel confessedly for Gentile readers, and that both there and here he has uniformly supplied such information respecting Jewish customs and places as they would need, we may conclude that Theophilus belonged to that class of readers, and that he was not, therefore, a Jew, or a resident in Palestine. The manner in which the book terminates (see Introduct., p. 21), favors the supposition that he may have lived at Rome, or in Italy. Some have urged it as an argument for that opinion, that Luke has merely enumerated the names of places in Italy as if his readers were familiar with them; but the proof is not conclusive. He takes for granted a similar knowledge of the geography of Asia Minor and Greece. He inserts no explanatory notices in this part of the history, unless we are to except 16, 12; 27, 12. — ὧν ἤρξατο, κ. τ. λ., *which Jesus both did and taught from the beginning*, viz. of his career. — ὧν stands by attraction for ἅ. ἤρξατο carries back the mind to the commencement of the Saviour's history, and is equivalent in sense to ἐξ ἀρχῆς. Hence this verb marks the limit of the narrative in one direction, as ἄχρι ἧς ἡμέρας does in the other. This adverbial sense belongs usually to the participle (Mt. § 558), but may be admitted also in the verb. (Hmph.[1] adopts this analysis in his 2d ed.) It gives the same result, though less directly, if we consider the expression as elliptical: *which he began* and proceeded *both to do*, etc.; comp. v. 22; Matt. 20, 8; Luke 23, 5. See W. § 66. 1. c. Other explanations have been proposed. Meyer finds in it an implied contrast between the labors of Christ and those of the apostles; he laid the foundation — they were to build upon it and finish what he began. This seems to me far-fetched. (But in his last edition Meyer retracts this opinion, and says justly that Ἰησοῦς with that contrastive force would naturally precede the verb.) Olshausen thinks that Luke intended to suggest by ἤρξατο, that Christ only commenced his work on earth — that he still continues, and will complete it in heaven. Baumgarten[2] (p. 8 sq.) contends for the same view, and deduces from it what he supposes to be Luke's special design in writing the Acts, viz. to represent the Saviour after his ascension as still acting through the apostles, and thus carrying forward, by their agency, the merely incipient labors of his life on earth. Of course this activity of Christ, who is ever present with his people (Matt. 28, 20), could not fail to be recognized in the history (as in 3, 26; 4, 30; 19, 13; etc.); but it is impossible that the writer, with that object in view, should have left it to be so obscurely intimated. This alleged contrast between Luke's Gospel as simply a beginning, and the Acts as a continuation of Christ's personal work, so far from being put forward with prominence, as we should expect, is not distinctly drawn out in a single passage. The truth is, as Lekebusch remarks (Composition, u. s. w., p. 203), the narrative

[1] A Commentary on the Acts of the Apostles, by W. G. Humphrey, B. D., late Fellow of Trinity College, Cambridge, etc. (London 1854.)

[2] Die Apostelgeschichte oder der Entwickelungsgang der Kirche von Jerusalem bis Rom, von M. Baumgarten (1852).

contains no hint of any such relation of the two histories to each other, unless this be found in ἤρξατο; and even this word, as we have seen, admits much more naturally of a different explanation. A caution against regarding this verb as superfluous here, or in any passage, can hardly be needed. See W. § 65. 7. d.

V. 2. ἧς ἡμέρας = τῆς ἡμέρας ᾗ, as in Matt. 24, 38; Luke 1, 20. — ἐντειλάμενον, I understand, with Meyer and others, as referring to Christ's command to preach the Gospel to all the world, as recorded in Matt. 28, 19; and which, from its memorable character, Luke could assume as well known to his readers. De Wette supposes it to be the command in v. 4; but we have then an unnecessary repetition of the same thing, and, contrary to the natural order, the allusion first, and the fuller notice last. Some have proposed to extend the meaning of the word so as to embrace all the instructions which Christ gave to the apostles in relation to their future work; but the term is too specific for so general an idea, and, besides, the obvious implication is that the giving of the command was something almost immediately antecedent to the ascension. — διὰ πνεύματος ἁγίου, *through the Holy Spirit*, his influence, guidance. This noun, as so used, may omit the article or receive it, at the option of the writer, since it has the force of a proper name. W. § 19. 1. See also Ellicott's note on Gal. 4, 5. These words attach themselves naturally to the participle which they accompany, and it is forced, as well as unnecessary, to connect them with the verb in the next clause. This passage, in accordance with other passages, represents the Saviour as having been endued abundantly with the influences of the Spirit, and as having acted always in conformity with its dictates; see 10, 38; Luke 4, 1; John, 3, 34, etc. That subjection was one of the laws of his dependent nature. That he revealed the command *through the Holy Spirit* cannot be meant, for the history shows that he gave this direction to them in person. — οὓς ἐξελέξατο, *whom he had chosen*. The aorist stands often for our pluperfect after a relative or relative expression. W. § 40. 5. — ἀνελήφθη, *was taken up*, sc. εἰς τὸν οὐρανόν; comp. Mark 16, 19; and Luke 24, 51. The abbreviation shows how accustomed the early disciples were to recur to this event.

V. 3. οἷς καὶ παρέστησεν. καί joins παρέστησεν to οὓς ἐξελέξατο. The persons whom Christ had selected as his apostles were the same *to whom also he showed himself*, etc. Thus they not only received their office directly from Christ, but were able to testify from their own personal knowledge to the reality of his resurrection; comp. 2, 32, and 3, 15. See note on v. 22. — μετὰ τὸ παθεῖν αὐτόν, *after he had suffered*, viz. the death of the cross; see Heb. 13, 12; and 1 Pet 3, 18. The term occurs thus absolutely in 3, 18 and 17, 3; (comp. also 26, 23), and is a striking usage. It arose probably out of the impression which the painful nature of Christ's sufferings had made on the first disciples. — ἐν πολλοῖς τεκμηρίοις, *in many proofs;* or if, as De Wette suggests, the idea of the verb mingles with that of the noun, *in many convincing manifestations.* τεκμήριον does not occur elsewhere in the New Testament, and is a very expressive term. Plato uses it to denote the strongest possible logical proof, as opposed to that which is weaker, and Aristotle employs it to signify demonstrative evidence. The language seems to show that the first Christians had distinctly revolved the question whether the Saviour's resurrection was real or not, and had assured themselves of its reality by evidence which did not admit in their minds of the shadow of a doubt. Our "infallible signs" (E. V. Gen. V.: *infallible tokens,* — both founded on Beza's *certissimis signis*), does not express the sense too strongly. Compare the idea with 1 John 1, 1. — δι' ἡμερῶν, κ. τ. λ., *during forty days appearing to them,* (as in all the earlier E. Vv.), i. e. from time to time, as related by the Evangelists; not pass., *seen by them* (E. V.). ὀπτανόμενος, (not elsewhere in N. T.), agrees best as middle, with the active sense of the other verbs, and with 1 Kings 8, 8 (Sept.); see Tromms's Concord. s. v. Wahl (Clav. Apocr. s. ὁράω) should not have put down the use in Tob. 12, 9, as certainly passive. Some have argued too positively from this word, that Christ rose from the grave with a glorified body. It represents his appearing to the disciples perhaps as occasional and sudden (comp. ὤφθη in 7, 26); but does not decide whether the state out of which he appeared was a spiritual and invisible one, or merely some place of retirement after a temporary absence. The Saviour had accomplished the great end of his earthly work, when he rose from the dead, and after that, until his ascension, appears to have mingled only at times with his followers. Some mystery rests, no doubt, on the last days of his life; but the idea that he possessed a spiritual body before his return to heaven, appears to me irreconcilable with Luke 24, 39, and John 20, 27. See the article on our Lord's resurrection body, in Bibl. Sac. Vol. II. p. 405 sq.

VERSES 4. 5. *The Promise of the Saviour to send the Spirit.*

V. 4. συναλιζόμενος, sc. αὐτοῖς, *being assembled,* (E. V.), as mentioned in Luke 24, 49; not sc. αὐτούς, *assembling them* (Kuin.

Olsh. and earlier E. Vv.). Nearly all the later critics reject the middle sense as unproved. — περιμένειν τὴν ἐπαγγελίαν, *to await the promise*, its fulfilment, realization, comp. Gal. 3, 14; not ἐπαγγελίαν = τὸ ἐπαγγελλόμενον, i. e. the promised Holy Spirit (Rob. N. T. Lex.), which is less congruous with the following verb. See W. § 34. 3. It is said to be the promise of the Father, because it was foretold in the Old Testament that he would bestow it. See 2, 16; Joel 3, 1. 2. — ἥν ἠκούσατέ μου, *which you heard from me*, as recorded in Luke 24, 49; see also John 15, 26; 16, 13. For the verb with the accusative and genitive, see K. § 273. R. 18; W. § 30. 7. c. The style of discourse changes suddenly from the indirect to the direct, as in 17, 3; 23, 22, and often. W. § 63. II. 2.; S. § 196. 2.

V. 5. ὕδατι, *with water* as the element by which, ἐν πνεύματι ἁγίῳ, *in the Holy Spirit*, as the element in which the baptism is performed. The insertion of ἐν may be slightly localizing with reference to a copious impartation of the Spirit's gifts and influences. — οὐ μετὰ, κ. τ. λ., *not after these many days*, after not many, a few. This mode of inverting the signification of an adjective is frequent in Luke's style. If this assurance was given on the day of the ascension, only ten days were now to pass before the promised effusion of the Spirit (comp. v. 3, with 2, 1.) But if, as maintained below, we are to distinguish the meeting in v. 4 from that in v. 6, we cannot decide exactly how long the interval was, not knowing on which of the forty days (v. 3) the earlier interview took place. ταύτας, being the pronoun which points out what is near at hand (ἐκεῖνος what is more remote), represents the days as closely connected with the present. It is not superfluous, therefore, but strengthens the idea of the brevity of the interval.

VERSES 6–11. *His Last Interview with the Disciples, and His Ascension.*

V. 6. οἱ μὲν οὖν συνελθόντες, *They therefore* (the αὐτοῖς in v. 4) *having come together* on a subsequent occasion (Calv. Olsh. E. V. and earlier E. Vv. except Wicl. and Rhem.); or *they who came together* at the time spoken of in v. 4 (Vulg. Mey. DeWet. Alf.). I incline to the first view, because, as Olshausen suggests, Luke in his Gospel (24, 49 as compared with v. 50) appears to assign the direction to remain at Jerusalem to an earlier interview than the one which terminated in Christ's ascension (as even DeWette admits in his Synop. Evang. p. 298), and because συνελθόντες when understood of the same assembling becomes so nearly tautological after συναλιζόμενος in v. 4. οὖν depends naturally on v. 3. The kingdom of God having been the subject of so much discourse between Christ and the apostles, they *therefore*, in this last interview, *asked him*, etc. Hence no necessary inference can be drawn from this particle (as Alf. urges) against supposing a separation after the coming together in v. 4.— εἰ ἐν τῷ χρόνῳ, κ. τ. λ. *if in this time thou dost restore?* Their inquiry indicates an established faith in him as the Messiah, but betrays at the same time an expectation that his kingdom would be to some extent a temporal one; that it would free the nation from their dependence on the Romans, and restore to them their ancient prosperity and power. This worldly view may have been the preponderant one in the question which they ask, though we are to suppose, of course, that, after having been so long associated with Christ, they had far more intelligent views respecting the spiritual nature of the Messiah's mission than the great mass of the Jews entertained. εἰ introduces a direct question, which is contrary to classical usage, though not uncommon in the New Testament and the Septuagint. K. § 344. 5. i.; W. § 57. 2. Originally εἰ may have involved a suppressed thought in such cases: *saying* we desire to know *if*, etc. See Meyer on Matt. 12, 10. ἀποκαθιστάνεις is present for an immediate future. W. § 40. 2; K. § 255. R. 4.

V. 7. χρόνους ἢ καιρούς, *times or occasions.* See Tittm. de Synon. N. T. p. 39. It is one thing to know the general period of an event; another, to know the precise time of its occurrence.— οὓς . . . . ἐξουσίᾳ, *which the Father arranged,* or *fixed in his own power*, i. e. in the sovereign exercise of it; comp. Matt. 21, 23 (DeWet. Mey. Hmph.). The implied inference is, that he may be expected to reserve the knowledge of such decisions to himself. All the E. Vv. (as far as I know) render *hath put* (defended also by Alf. as = *hath kept*). The perfect would be the more obvious form with that meaning, though the aorist, *put*, placed, may imply the same. The question of the disciples, as Bengel observes, relates merely to the time when Christ would establish his kingdom; and his answer, as here given, he confines to the same point. Their remaining misconceptions as to the nature of that kingdom were soon to be removed more effectually than by any formal instruction.

V. 8. ἀλλά marks the opposition between what was denied to the disciples on the one hand, and what was to be granted to them on the other.— δύναμιν, *efficiency*, i. e. every needful qualification to render them efficient in their apostolic sphere; see Luke 24, 49. The power of working miracles is included, but does not exhaust the idea. — ἐπελθόντος . . . . ἐφ' ὑμᾶς. This clause designates the time when they should receive this power, as well as the source of it. The construction is that of the genitive absolute. The dependence of πνεύματος on δύναμιν (we miss the article in that case) is less easy, but is preferred by some. — Read μοῦ for ἐμοί after ἔσεσθε. — ἐσχάτου, sc. μέρους. Compare the language here with Matt. 28, 19; Mark 16, 15. It is impossible that the disciples should not have understood from it that their sphere of labor was to be coextensive with the world. See the remarks on 2, 39. The foregoing conversation may have taken place on Olivet (see v. 12), or during the walk thither.

V. 9. ταῦτα εἰπών, *saying these things*, and still others (Luke 24, 51). His last accents were those of love and benediction. — ἐπήρθη, *was taken up*, i. e. into the air, not yet into heaven, on account of the next verb; hence different, also, from ἀνελήφθη in v. 2, which represents the act as completed. — ὑπέλαβεν, *received up*, (lit. *under*, with the cloud as it were beneath him), and at the same time by a pregnant construction, *away*, hence followed by ἀπό. See W. § 66. 2. This verb describes the close of the scene, as far as it was visible to the spectators.

V. 10. ὡς ἀτενίζοντες, κ. τ. λ., *as they were gazing towards heaven.* This compound imperfect is stronger than the simple, both as to the duration of the act, and the prominence given to it. The student should note this usage; though not rare in the classics, it is still more common in the New Testament. See Green's Gr. p. 103. K. § 238. R. 7. Kuinoel refers εἰς τὸν οὐρανόν to πορευομένου, which separates the words from their natural connection, and leaves ἀτενίζοντες without any indirect object, as in 3, 4. 12; 14, 9, and elsewhere. — καὶ ἰδού, *then behold*, = וְהִנֵּה; comp. Matt. 9, 10; Luke 2, 15; 24, 4. This Hebraistic use of καί in the apodosis of a sentence, after an expression or idea of time, is frequent in the New Testament. See Brüd. Gr. Concord. p. 456; W. § 53. 3. f. — ἄνδρες, *men* in form, really angels; see Mark 16, 5; Luke 24, 4. — παρειστήκεισαν, *were standing* while the disciples gazed; pluperf. = imperf. in this verb.

V. 11. οἳ καὶ εἶπον, *who also said* as well as appeared to them; see on v. 3. — τί ἑστήκατε, κ. τ. λ., *why stand ye*, etc. The precise import of this address of the angels is not certain. As compared with such passages as Luke 24, 5. 25. 26, and others, it may suggest that the apostles should have been prepared in some measure for the event which had filled them with such astonishment. They had been distinctly apprized by Christ (see John 6, 62; 20, 17) that he must ascend again to God from whom he came; and the wonders which they had seen in their intercourse with him should have diminished their surprise at what had taken place. The inquiry, as so understood, leads naturally to the announcement which follows. It should abate the astonishment of the disciples at what had taken place, to know that it was not the only event of the kind which was to enter into the history of the Saviour; he whom they had seen ascend into heaven was destined to come again in like manner. According to Calvin, the disciples linger on the spot, distressed at the Saviour's sudden departure from them, and still gazing upward, not without a hope that possibly he might reäppear. The address of the angels reproves them for this expectation, and at the same time consoles them with the assurance of his return at some future time. Meyer's view is nearly the same. — ὃν τρόπον, *in what manner*, i. e. visibly, and in the air (Bng. DeWet. Mey. Olsh.). The expression is never employed to affirm merely the certainty of one event as compared with another. The assertion, that the meaning is simply, that, as Christ had departed, so also he would return, is contradicted by every passage in which the phrase occurs; see 7, 28; Matt. 23, 37; Luke 13, 34; 2 Tim. 3, 8.

VERSES 12–14. *Return of the Disciples to Jerusalem.*

V. 12. ἀπὸ ὄρους, κ. τ. λ., *from the mount* (definite from the annexed clause, though τοῦ could be used; see Luke 19, 29) *which is called Olivet.* We are indebted for this beautiful name to the Latin *Olivetum* (in Vulg.), i. e. a place set with olives, hence the exact import of ἐλαιών. This word is so accentuated also by Lchm. Tsch. Mey., even in Luke 19, 29, and 21, 37, instead of ἐλαιῶν in the common editions. In Matt. 21, 1, we have ὄρος τῶν ἐλαιῶν, *mount of the olives.* Josephus employs the designation which occurs here in Antt. 7. 9. 2. Olive trees still grow on the mount of ascension, and thus vindicate the propriety of the ancient name. On their return to Jerusalem the disciples must have passed Gethsemane. What new thoughts would crowd upon their minds as they gazed at the spot after the scene just witnessed! — ἔχον, *having*, amounting to; not = ἀπέχον, *distant*, as often represented. A Sabbath day's journey was the distance — about three quarters of a mile — to which "the traditions of the elders" restricted the Jews in travelling on the Sabbath. In Luke 24, 50. 51, it is said that our Saviour led the disciples as far as to Bethany, and that there, while in the act of blessing them, he was parted from them and carried up into heaven. It was at Bethany, therefore, or in the vicinity of Bethany, that the ascension took place. That account is entirely consistent with this. Bethany was on the eastern declivity of the Mount of Olives; and, as appears from Mark 11, 1, and Luke 19, 29, was reckoned as a part of it; so that the disciples, in returning from that place to the city, took their way naturally across the mountain. See Rob. Bibl. Res. Vol. II. p. 100; or p. 431 in ed. of 1856. Luke specifies here the distance of Olivet from the city, instead of that of Bethany, which was about two miles (comp. John 11, 18), because the former was better known to most of his readers, and conveyed a sufficiently definite idea of the scene of the ascension.

V. 13. εἰσῆλθον, *had entered* (tense as in v. 2) into the city probably, not the house. What precedes suggests the place, rather than what follows. — εἰς τὸ ὑπερῷον, *into the upper room* of some private house, not of the temple. The opinion that it was the latter some have supposed to be required by Luke 24, 53. But διαπαντός, as used there, need not signify any thing more than a frequent resort; they were in the temple *always* on the occasions when men in their state of mind would naturally repair thither; see 2, 46; Luke 2, 37. Even De Wette allows that the passages involve no discrepancy. As the disciples must have been well known as the followers of Christ, we cannot well suppose that the Jewish rulers would have allowed them to occupy an apartment in the temple. The upper room, either directly under the flat roof, or upon it with a roof of its own, was retired, and hence convenient for private or social worship. The Hebrews were accustomed to use it for such purposes; see 20, 8, and Dan. 6, 10 (Sept.). Travellers describe such rooms at the present day as airy and spacious. See Bibl. Res. Vol. II. p. 229 ed. 1856. On the formation of ὑπερῷον, see W. § 16. 2. — οὗ ἦσαν καταμένοντες, *where were abiding*; weakened in E. V. (*abode*), as if it were the simple imperf.; see on v. 10. We could understand this of constant residence, but more naturally here of frequent resort for religious conference and prayer (De Wet.). — Ἰάκωβος Ἀλφαίου, sc. υἱός, *James the son of Alphæus*; but after Ἰούδας we supply ἀδελφός, *Judas the brother of James* (see Jude, v. 1). The nature of the relationship in such a case is not determined by the construction, but is left to the knowledge of the reader. W. § 30. 3; C. § 389. — ὁ ζηλωτής = κανανίτης in Matt. 10, 4, from the Hebrew קַנָּא. He is supposed to have received this epithet on account of his former zeal as a supporter of Judaism. As there was another Simon among the apostles, he appears to have retained the name after he became a disciple, as a means of distinction, though it had now ceased to mark the trait of character from which it arose. It has been said, that he took the appellation from his having belonged to a political sect known as the zealots, who are mentioned by Josephus; but the party distinguished by that name in Jewish history did not appear till a later period.

V. 14. ὁμοθυμαδόν, *with one mind.* The term characterizes the entire harmony of their views and feelings; comp. Rom. 15, 6. — τῇ προσευχῇ, *unto the* (work of) *prayer*, where τῇ points out that as the appropriate way in which they were occupied. καὶ τῇ δεήσει, the best editors regard as an addition to the text. It serves merely to strengthen the expression; comp. Phil. 4, 6. — σὺν γυναιξί, *with women.* Among them may have been those who fol lowed Christ from Galilee; see Luke 23, 55; 24, 10. It is incorrect to suppose that they are meant exclusively. The absence of the article forbids that restriction. — καὶ Μαρίᾳ, *and* (among them especially) *Mary.* καί combines often a part with its whole for the sake of prominence. This is the last time that the mother of Jesus is named in the New Testament. — ἀδελφοῖς αὐτοῦ may mean *his brethren* in a strict sense, or more generally, his *kinsmen*, relatives. The same question arises in regard to Matt. 13, 55, though the closer relationship there, as well as here, is the more obvious one, and finds very strong support from Matt. 1, 25. The brethren of Jesus had not believed on him at first (see John 7, 5); but we discover here that they had now joined the circle of his followers.

VERSES 15–22. *The Address of Peter on the choice of a new Apostle.*

V. 15. ἐν ταῖς ἡμέραις ταύταις is indefinite as a notation of time. The same language in Matt. 3, 1, marks an interval of thirty years; comp. also Exod. 2, 11. Here a short time only could have elapsed, as the ascension of Christ forms the limit on one side, and the day of Pentecost on the other. — τε. It is worth remarking, that this particle rarely occurs in the New Testament, out of the Acts and the writings of Paul. — ὀνομάτων = ἀνθρώπων, as in Rev. 3, 4; 11, 13. The term may have acquired this sense from the practice of taking the census by registration or enrolment, inasmuch as the names on such a record are equivalent to persons. — ἐπὶ τὸ αὐτό, lit. *unto the same place*, implying an antecedent motion. It means, not that they were so many collectively, but that so many came *together* at this time; see 2, 1; 3, 1; 1 Cor. 11, 20; 14, 23. — ἑκατὸν εἴκοσιν. We are to understand these *hundred and twenty* as the number of the disciples at Jerusalem, not as the entire number of those who had believed; see 1 Cor. 15, 6.

V. 16. ἄνδρες is not superfluous, but renders the address more respectful. It is a compliment to be recognized as men; see 2, 29; 37; 7, 2; 13, 15, and often. — ἔδει, *was necessary*. The tense is past, because the speaker has his mind on the part of the prediction already accomplished. — ταύτην refers to the double citation in v. 20. The parenthetic character of vs. 18. 19, accounts for the distance of the antecedent, which in this case follows the pronoun. See K. § 332. 8. — ἣν προεῖπε, κ. τ. λ., *which the Holy Spirit spake beforehand*, etc. We have a similar testimony to the inspiration of the Scriptures from the same apostle in 2 Pet. 1, 21. — περὶ Ἰούδα belongs both by position and construction to προεῖπε, not to πληρωθῆναι. ἐν or ἐπί would have followed the latter verb. — τοῦ γενομένου ὁδηγοῦ, *who became* (not *was*, E. V.) *guide*, who acted so base a part, though professedly a friend. See Matt. 26, 47; John 18, 2 sq.

V. 17. Here the second passage in v. 20 was before the speaker's mind. That passage contemplates the case of an office transferred from one person to another; and since forfeiture implies previous possession, it is the object of ὅτι . . . . ἐν ἡμῖν to remind us that Judas had fulfilled that condition of the passage: *for he was numbered among us*, i. e. the apostles. For that limitation of ἡμῖν, see the next clause, and also v. 26. The full connection, therefore, is this: The prophecy speaks of an ἐπισκοπή which another shall take; Judas held such an office, *for he was numbered*, etc., so that the words apply to him. To render ὅτι, *although* (Hmph.), is not allowable. — τὸν κλῆρον . . . . ταύτης, *the lot*, or *office, of this ministry* which we possess, i. e. the apostleship, comp. Rom. 11, 13. κλῆρον loses often its figurative sense, so as to denote a possession without any reference to the mode of its attainment. Our word *clergy* comes from this term, being founded on the idea of the order as one divinely appointed.

V. 18. This verse and the next are considered by most critics as an explanatory remark of Luke (Calv. Kuin. Olsh. Hmph.), not as a part of Peter's address. The reader might need this information, but those who listened to the apostle may be supposed to have been familiar with the fate of Judas. It is evident that ὥστε κληθῆναι . . . . αἵματος, though appropriate to the history, could hardly have belonged to the discourse. γάρ in v. 20 appears to demand this view of the intervening verses. μὲν οὖν does not forbid this supposition (Alf.); since Luke certainly could adjust his own words to the context, as well as those of Peter, reported by him. Some such horrible end of the traitor was to be inferred (οὖν, *therefore*) from the γραφὴν ταύτην (see on v. 20); and it was not at all unnatural that Luke should interrupt the speech at this point, and inform us how remarkably the death of Judas agreed with this prediction. Further, it is strange that the citation in v. 20 should be kept back so long after ταύτην in v. 16, except on the view that Luke inserted what intervenes. Bengel restricts the parenthesis to the explanation respecting Aceldama. μέν stands alone, as in v. 1. — ἐκτήσατο, *purchased*, or *caused to be purchased*, gave occasion for it, i. e. it was in consequence of his act, and with the money gained by his treachery, that the field was purchased, as related in Matt. 27, 6 sq. The great body of critics adopt this view of the meaning (Bez. Bretsch. Kuin. Frtz. Thol.[1] Olsh. Ebr. Mey. Rob.). This briefer mode of expression is common in every language, and may be employed without obscurity where the reader is presumed to be familiar with the facts in the case, or when the nature of the act itself suggests the proper modification. The following are analogous examples in the New Testament. Matt. 27, 60; "And Joseph laid the body of Christ in his own new tomb, which he had hewn out in a rock," i. e. caused to be hewn out for him; John 4, 1: "And when the Lord knew that the Pharisees heard that Jesus made more disciples than John," i. e. through his disciples; for he himself baptized not. See further, 7, 21; 16, 22; Matt. 2, 16; 1 Cor. 7, 16; 1 Tim. 4, 16, etc. These cases are plain; and no one refuses to admit the causative sense (not directly expressed, but implied) which belongs to the verb in such passages. The principle which this mode of speaking involves, the law recognizes even in regard to actions in its well-known maxim, *Qui facit per alium facit per se.* It is only by refusing to extend this usage to ἐκτήσατο that such writers as Strauss make out their allegation of a want of agreement between this passage and Matt. 27, 5. Fritzsche's suggestion[2] as to the reason why Luke expressed himself in this unusual manner deserves notice. He finds in it a studied, significant brevity, a sort of *acerba irrisio*, bringing the motive and the result into pointed antithesis to each other: This man thought to enrich himself by his treachery, but all that he gained was that he got for himself a field where blood was paid for blood. — πρηνής is strictly the opposite of ὕπτιος, i. e. *on the*

[1] In unpublished Notes on the Gospels.

[2] Evangelium Matthæi recensuit et cum Commentariis perpetuis edidit Carol. Fr. A. Fritzsche, p. 799.

face. His falling in that position may have occasioned the bursting asunder; that view agrees well with γενόμενος, though πρηνής admits also of the vaguer sense *headlong.* — ἐλάκησε is the first aorist from λάσκω. W. § 15; K. § 230. — In Matt. 27, 5, it is said that Judas, after having brought his money and thrown it down in the temple, went and hanged or strangled himself. Objectors have represented that account also as inconsistent with this, but without reason. Matthew does not say that Judas, after having hanged himself, *did not* fall to the ground and burst asunder; nor, on the contrary, does Luke say that Judas *did not* hang himself before he fell to the ground; and it is obvious that the matter should have been so stated, in order to warrant the charge of inconsistency. We have no certain knowledge as to the mode in which we are to combine the two accounts, so as to connect the act of suicide with what happened to the body. It has been thought not improbable that Judas may have hung himself from the limb of a tree, on the edge of a precipice near the valley of Hinnom, and that, the rope breaking by which he was suspended, he fell to the earth and was dashed to pieces.[1] It will be observed that Luke's statement is entirely abrupt, and supposes some antecedent history. In this respect Matthew's account, instead of involving any contradiction, becomes in fact confirmatory of the other. It shows, first, that Luke was aware that something preceded which he has omitted to mention; and, secondly, it puts us in the way of combining events so as to account better for the incomplete representation in the Acts, than would otherwise have been possible.

V. 19. καὶ γνωστὸν ἐγένετο, *and it became known,* viz. that he came to so miserable an end. — Ἀκελδαμά = חֲקֵל דְּמָא belongs to the Aramæan or Syro-Chaldaic spoken at that time in Palestine. On that language, see Bibl. Repos., Vol. I. p. 317 sq. It was for a twofold reason, therefore, says Lightfoot, that the field received this appellation: first, because, as stated in Matt. 27, 7, it had been bought with the price of blood; and, secondly, because it

[1] As I stood in this valley on the south of Jerusalem, and looked up to the rocky terraces which hang over it, I felt that the explanation proposed above is entirely natural. I was more than ever satisfied with it. I measured the precipitous, almost perpendicular walls, in different places, and found the height to be, variously, forty, thirty-six, thirty-three, thirty, and twenty-five feet. Trees still flourish on the margin of these precipices, and in ancient times must have been still more numerous in the same place. A rocky pavement exists, also, at the bottom of the ledges; and hence on that account, too, a person falling from above would be liable to be crushed and mangled, as well as killed. The traitor may have struck, in his fall, upon some pointed rock, which entered the body, and caused "his bowels to gush out."

was sprinkled with the man's blood who took that price. This is the common view, and so in the first edition; but I incline now to doubt its correctness. First, πρηνὴς γενόμενος, in v. 18, does not define at all where Judas fell; secondly, χωρίον ἐκεῖνο here recalls naturally χωρίον above, merely as the field purchased with "the reward of iniquity;" and, thirdly, if Judas fell into the valley of Hinnom, no spot there at the foot of the rocks could well have been converted into a place of burial. Nor does the conciliation with Matt. 27, 7, demand this view. Luke may be understood here as saying that "the field of blood" which the priests purchased with the money paid to Judas, whether situated in one place or another, was called Aceldama, because the fact of the traitor's bloody end was so notorious. Matthew (27, 6) mentions another reason for the appellation, which was, that the money paid for the field was the "price of blood;" not a different but concurrent reason, showing that the ill-omened name could be used with a double emphasis. Tradition has placed "the potter's field" (Matt. 27, 6) on the side of the hill which overlooks the valley of Hinnom. It may have been in that quarter, for argillaceous clay is still found there, and receptacles for the dead appear in the rocks, proving that the ancient Jews were accustomed to bury there.[1]

V. 20. The writer returns here to the address. γάρ, *for*, specifies the prophecy to which ταύτην points in v. 16, hence *namely* (as in Matt. 1, 18). See B. § 149; K. § 324. 2. The first passage is Ps. 69, 25, slightly abridged from the Septuagint, with an exchange of αὐτῶν for αὐτοῦ. Its import is, Let his end be disastrous, his abode be desolate, and shunned as accursed. It is impossible to understand the entire Psalm as strictly Messianic, on account of v. 5: "O God, thou knowest my foolishness, and my sins are not hid from thee." It appears to belong rather to the class of Psalms which describe general relations, which contain prophecies or inspired declarations which are verified as often as individuals are placed in the particular circumstances which lay within the view, not necessarily of the writer, but of the Holy Spirit, at whose dictation they were uttered. When Peter, therefore, declares that this prophecy which he applies to Judas was spoken with special reference to him (see v. 16), he makes the impressive announcement to those whom he addressed, that the conduct of Judas had identified him fully with such persecutors of the righteous as the Psalm contemplates, and hence it was necessary

[1] I have taken the liberty to repeat a few sentences here, already published in another work. See Illustrations of Scripture suggested by a tour through the Holy Land, p. 266. I have taken a similar liberty in a few other passages.

that he should suffer the doom deserved by those who sin in so aggravated a manner. — The other passage is Ps. 109, 8, in the words of the Seventy. We are to apply here the same principle of interpretation as before. That Psalm sets forth, in like manner, the wickedness and desert of those who persecute the people of God; and hence, as Judas had exemplified so fully this idea, he too must be divested of his office, and its honors be transferred to another.

V. 21. οὖν, *therefore;* since, as foretold, the place of the apostate must be filled. — τῶν συνελθόντων . . . . ἀνδρῶν depends properly on ἕνα, in v. 22, where the connection so long interrupted is reässerted by τούτων. — ἐν παντὶ χρόνῳ, *in every time.* The conception divides the period into its successive parts. — ἐν ᾧ . . . . ἐφ' ἡμᾶς, *in which he came in unto us, and went out,* i. e. lived and associated with us. The entire life or course of life is described by one of its most frequent acts. It is a Hebrew mode of speaking (comp. Deut. 28, 19; 31, 2, etc.), and is used properly of those who sustain official relations, or perform public labors. See 9, 28. An exact construction of the Greek would have placed ἐφ' ἡμᾶς after the first verb, and inserted ἀφ' ἡμῶν after the second. W. § 66. 3.

V. 22. ἀρξάμενος . . . . ἕως, *beginning* and continuing *unto,* etc. The supplementary idea was too obvious to need to be expressed. See W. § 66. I. c. — ἀπὸ τοῦ βαπτίσματος, *from the baptism of John,* i. e. from its beginning as a well-known epoch. The history shows that he had been baptizing a few months before our Lord made his public appearance, and continued to do so for a time afterwards (see John 3, 27); but that difference for the purpose of so general a designation was unimportant. Not from the close of John's baptism (Hmph.), since Jesus called the other apostles earlier, and not from his own baptism by John (Kuin.), since the phrase does not admit of that restriction (comp. 18, 25; Mark 11, 30; Luke 7, 29, etc.). — μάρτυρα . . . . γενέσθαι. The resurrection is singled out as the main point to which the testimony of the apostles related, because, that being established, it involves every other truth in relation to the character and work of Christ. It proves him to be the Son of God, the Justifier and Redeemer of men, their Sovereign and Judge. See 4, 33; John 5, 22; Rom. 1, 4; 4, 24; 10, 9; Gal. 1, 1, etc. Hence Paul mentions it as one of the proofs of his apostleship, and of his qualifications for it, that he had seen Christ after his resurrection. See 1 Cor. 9, 1.

VERSES 23–26. *The Appointment of Matthias as an Apostle.*

V. 23. The act here is that of those addressed (see v. 15), not that of the apostles merely. — ἔστησαν δύο, *they placed two*, i. e. before them, in their midst (see 5, 27; 6, 6); or according to some, *appointed two* as candidates (De Wet.). — Ἰοῦστος, *Justus.* It was not uncommon for the Jews at this period to assume foreign names. See on 13, 9. Barsabas is mentioned only here. Some have conjectured, without reason, that he and Barnabas (4, 36) were the same person. *Matthias* also appears only in this transaction. The traditional notices of him are not reliable; see Win. Realw., Vol. II. p. 61.[1]

V. 24. προσευξάμενοι εἶπον, *they prayed, saying.* The participle contains the principal idea. It may be supposed to be Peter who uttered the prayer, since it was he who suggested the appointment of a successor to Judas. — σὺ, κύριε, κ. τ. λ. Whether this prayer was addressed to Christ or God has been disputed. The reasons for the former opinion are that κύριος, when taken absolutely in the New Testament, refers generally to Christ;[2] that Christ selected the other apostles as stated in v. 2; that the first Christians were in the habit of praying to him (see on 7, 59; 9, 14); and that Peter says to Christ in John 21, 17, "Lord, thou knowest all things," which is the import exactly of καρδιογνῶστα. The reasons for the other opinion do not invalidate these. That καρδιογνώστης is used of God in 15, 8, shows only that it does not apply exclusively to Christ. The call of Peter in 15, 7, which is ascribed to God, was a call, not to the apostleship, but to preach the gospel to the heathen; and even if that case were parallel to this, it would be an instance only of the common usage of referring the same or a similar act indiscriminately to Christ or God. This latter remark applies also to such passages as 2 Cor. 1, 1; Eph. 1, 1; 2 Tim. 1, 1. To deny that Peter would ascribe omniscience to Christ because in Jer. 17, 10, it is said to be the prerogative of God to know the heart, contradicts John 21, 17. Some have supposed the apostle intended to quote that passage of the prophet, but the similarity is too slight to prove such a design; nor, if the idea of καρδιογνῶστα were drawn from that source, would the application of it here conform necessarily to its application there. — ἕνα (omitted in E. V. after Cranm.) belongs to ὅν,

[1] Biblisches Realwörterbuch, von Dr. Georg Benedict Winer (3d ed. 1848).

[2] See Professor Stuart's article on the meaning of this title in the New Testament, Bibl. Repos., Vol. I. p. 733 sq.

which one, or perhaps in apposition, *whom*, viz. *one that he*, etc. Tynd. and Gen. render *that the one may take*, etc.

V. 25. For κλῆρον, see on v. 17. — διακονίας . . . . ἀποστολῆς, *this ministry and* (that) *an apostleship.* καί adds a second term explanatory of the first, i. e. essentially an instance of hendiadys (Mey. De Wet.), *the ministry of this apostleship.* — ἐξ ἧς παρέβη, *from which he went aside*, as opposed to the idea of adhering faithfully to the character and service which his apostleship required of him; "ad normam Hebr. סוּר sq. מִן = deserere munus" (Wahl). — πορευθῆναι . . . . ἴδιον, *that he might go unto his own place.* The clause is telic, depending on παρέβη. So long as Judas retained his office, he was kept back, as it were, from his proper destiny. He must relinquish it, therefore, in order to suffer his just deserts. In this way the apostle would state strongly the idea, that the traitor merited the doom to which he had been consigned. The following comment of Meyer presents the only view of the further meaning of the passage which has any respectable critical support: "What is meant here by ὁ τόπος ὁ ἴδιος is not to be decided by the usuage of τόπος in itself considered (for τόπος may denote any place), but merely by the context. That requires that we understand by it *Gehenna*, which is conceived of as the place to which Judas, in virtue of his character, properly belongs. Since the treachery of Judas was in itself so fearful a crime, and was still further aggravated by self-murder (which alone, according to Jewish ideas, deserved punishment in hell), the hearers of Peter could have had no doubt as to the sense to be attached to τόπος ἴδιος. This explanation is demanded also by the analogy of Rabbinic passages, e. g. Baal Turim on Numb. 24, 25 (see Lightfoot, Hor. Hebr. ad loc.): Balaam ivit in locum suum, i. e. in Gehennam." De Wette assents entirely to this interpretation. τόπος ἴδιος, therefore, "is a euphemistic designation of the place of punishment, in which the sin of Judas rendered it just that he should have his abode." (Olsh.)

V. 26. καὶ ἔδωκαν κλήρους, *and they placed* (probably = נָתַן as often in New Testament) their *lots* in a vase or something similar; or perhaps *gave them* to those whose business it was to collect them. αὐτῶν (T. R.) or αὐτοῖς (Lch. Tsch.), *for them*, refers to the candidates because the lots pertained to them. The two names were written probably on slips of parchment, perhaps several duplicates of them, and then shaken up; the one first drawn out decided the choice. The idea of throwing up the lots agrees better with βάλλειν κλήρους than with this expression. — ἔπεσεν *fell*, came out, without reference to any particular process. — ὁ κλῆρος, *the lot,* definite because it was the decisive one. — συγκατεψηφίσθη .... ἀποστόλων, *was numbered together with the eleven apostles,* i. e. was recognized as one of their order, and had the character of an apostle henceforth accorded to him. Hesychius sanctions this sense of the verb, though it means properly *to vote against, condemn,* which is out of the question here. De Wette renders *was chosen, elected,* which not only deviates from the classic usage, but ascribes the result to their own act, instead of a divine interposition. The subsequent appointment of Paul to the apostleship did not discredit or abrogate this decision, but simply enlarged the original number of the apostles. See Guericke's remarks on this point in his Church History (Prof. Shedd's translation), p. 47.

CHAPTER II.

VERSES 1–4. *Descent of the Holy Spirit.*

V. 1. ἐν τῷ συμπληροῦσθαι, κ. τ. λ., *when the day of Pentecost was fully come,* arrived. See Luke 9, 51. The action of the verb (lit. *to be completed*) refers not to the day itself, but to the completion of the interval which was to pass before its arrival (Olsh. Bmg.). Some translate *while it is completed,* i. e. in the course of it, on that day (Mey. De Wet.). The present infinitive is consistent with this view or that. — τῆς πεντηκοστῆς the Greek Jews employed as a proper name. See 20, 16; 1 Cor. 16, 8; 2 Macc. 12, 32. ἡμέρα or ἑορτή determined the form. This festival received its name from its occurring on the fiftieth day from the second day of the Passover; so that the interval embraced a cycle of seven entire weeks, i. e. a week of weeks. It is usually called in the Old Testament, with reference to this circumstance, the festival of weeks. Its observance took place at the close of the gathering of the harvest, and was no doubt mainly commemorative of that event. See Jahn's Archæol. § 355. According to the later Jews, Pentecost was observed also as the day on which the law was given from Sinai; but no trace of this custom is found in the Old Testament, or in the works of Philo or Josephus. It is generally supposed that this Pentecost, signalized by the outpouring of the Spirit, fell on the Jewish Sabbath, our Saturday. According to the best opinion, our Lord celebrated his last Passover on the evening which began the fifteenth of Nisan (Num. 33, 3), and hence as he was crucified on the next day, which was our Friday, the fiftieth day or Pentecost (beginning, of course, with the evening of Friday, the second day of the Passover) would occur on the Jewish Sabbath. See Wiesl. Chronologie, u. s. w. p. 19. — ἅπαντες, *all* the believers then in Jerusalem; see 1, 15. — ὁμοθυμαδόν = ὁμοψύχως, *with one accord.* Its local sense, *together*, becomes superfluous, followed by ἐπὶ τὸ αὐτό. See on 1, 15.

V. 2. ὥσπερ . . . . βιαίας, *as of a mighty wind,* (lit. *blast*), *rushing along;* not genit. absolute, but dependent on ἦχος, (see v. 3). πνοή = πνεῦμα. The more uncommon word is chosen here perhaps on account of the different sense of πνεῦμα in this connection, e. g. v. 4. As used of the wind, φέρεσθαι denotes often rapid, violent motion; see the proofs in Kypke's Obss. Sacr. Vol. II. p. 11, and in Kuin. ad loc. — ἐπλήρωσεν, sc. ἦχος, which is the only natural subject furnished by the context. — οἶκον is probably the *house* referred to in 1, 13; not the temple, for the reasons there stated, and because the term employed in this absolute way does not signify the temple or an apartment of it.

V. 3. καὶ ὤφθησαν, κ. τ. λ., *And there appeared to them tongues distributed,* i. e. among them, *and one* (sc. γλῶσσα), *sat upon each of them.* So Bng. Olsh. Wahl, De Wet. Bmg. Hmph. Rob. and most of the later critics, as well as some of the older. (Meyer comes over to this view in his last ed.). The distributive idea occasions the change of number in ἐκάθισε. W. § 58. 4. αὐτοῖς belongs strictly to the verb, but extends its force to the participle. According to this view the fire like appearance presented itself at first, as it were, in a single body, and then suddenly parted in this direction and that, so that a portion of it rested on each of those present. It could be called a tongue, in that case, from its shape, as extended, pointed, and may have assumed such an appearance as a symbol of the miraculous gift which accompanied the wonder. This secures to διαμεριζόμεναι its proper meaning; see v. 45; Matt. 27, 35; Luke 23, 34, etc.; and explains why the first verb is plural, while the second is singular. Calvin, Heinrichs, (also Alf.), and many of the older commentators, render the participle *disparted, cleft* (as in the E. Vv. generally), and suppose it to describe the flame as exhibiting in each instance a tongue-like, forked appearance. The objection to this view is, that it rests upon a doubtful sense of the word, and especially that it offers no explanation of the change from the plural verb to the singular. De Wette, after others, has adduced passages here from the Rabbinic writers to show that it was a common belief of the Jews that an appearance like fire often encircled the heads of distinguished teachers of the law. To this it has been added, that instances of a similar phenomenon are related by the Greek and Roman writers. We are directed by such coincidences to an important fact in the history of the divine revelations, and that is, that God has often been pleased to reveal himself to men in conformity with their own conceptions as to the mode in which it is natural to expect communications from him. The appearance of the star to the Magians may be regarded as another instance of such accommodation to human views.

V. 4. ἐπλήσθησαν, κ. τ. λ., *were all filled with the Holy Spirit* (anarthrous, as in 1, 2); a phrase referring usually to special gifts rather than moral qualities, and to these as transient rather than permanent; comp. 4, 8. 31; 13, 9. etc. — ἤξαντο λαλεῖν, *began* (like our "proceeded") *to speak* as soon as the symbol rested on them. This use of ἄρχομαι as introducing what is next in order has not been duly recognized in the New Testament. — ἑτέραις γλώσσαις, *with other tongues*, i. e. than their native tongue. That Luke designed to state here that the disciples were suddenly endued with the power of speaking foreign languages, before unknown to them, would seem to be too manifest to admit of any doubt. It is surprising that such a writer as Neander should attempt to put a different construction on the text. He objects that the miracle would have been superfluous, inasmuch as the apostles are not known to have employed this gift of tongues in preaching the gospel. It may be replied, first, that we have not sufficient information concerning the labors of the apostles, to affirm that they may not have employed the endowment for that purpose; and, secondly, that we are not obliged to regard such a use of it as the only worthy object of the miracle. It may have been designed to serve chiefly was an attestation of the truth of the gospel, and of the character of the apostles as divine messegers. It is certain, at least, that Paul entertained that view of the γλῶσσαι spoken of in 1 Cor. 14, 22: "Wherefore tongues are for a sign, not to them that believe, but to them that believe not." The effect produced on this occasion (see v. 12) shows how well suited such a miracle was to impress the minds of those who witnessed it. A miracle, too, in this form, may have had a symbolic import, which added to its significancy. It was necessary that even the apostles should be led to entertain more enlarged views respecting the comprehensive design of the new dispensation. This sudden possession of an ability to proclaim the salvation of Christ to men of all nations (even if we allow that it was not permanent), was adapted to recall their minds powerfully to the last command of the Saviour, and to make them feel that it was their mission to publish his name to the ends of the earth. Such a mode of conveying instruction to them was not more indirect than that employed in the vision of Peter (10, 9 sq.), which was intended to teach the same truth. But we are not left to argue the question on grounds of this nature; the testimony of Luke is explicit and decisive. Even critics who would explain away the reality of the miracle admit that it was the writer's intention to record a miracle. Thus Meyer says: "The ἕτεραι γλῶσσαι are to be considered, according to the text, as absolutely nothing else than languages which were different from the native language of the speakers. They were Galileans, and spoke now Parthian, Median, Persian, etc.; therefore, foreign languages, and those too — the point precisely wherein appeared the wonderful effect of the Spirit — *unacquired languages* (γλώσσαις καιναῖς, in Mark 16, 17), i. e. not previously learned by them. Accordingly the text itself defines the sense of γλῶσσαι as that of languages, and excludes as impossible the other explanations different from this, which some have attempted to impose on the word." — καθώς, *according as*, in respect to manner; since the languages were diverse.

VERSES 5–13. *Impression of the Miracle on the Multitude.*

V. 5. δέ, *now*, transitive. — κατοικοῦντες, *dwelling*, whether for a season or permanently; hence more general than ἐπιδημοῦντες (v. 10; 17, 21); but not excluding the sojourners there. No doubt many of the Jews in question had fixed their abode at Jerusalem, as it was always an object of desire with those of them who lived in foreign countries to return and spend the close of life in the land of their fathers. The prevalent belief, that the epoch had now arrived when the promised Messiah was about to appear, must have given increased activity to that desire. The writer mentions this class of Jews in distinction from the native inhabitants, because the narrative which follows represents that many were present who understood different languages. The number of these strangers was the greater on account of the festival which occurred at that time. — εὐλαβεῖς, *devout*, God-fearing; see 8, 2; Luke 2, 25. This sense is peculiar to the Hellenistic Greek The term is applied to those only whose piety was of the Old Testament type. — τῶν, sc. ὄντων. The strong expression here is a phrase signifying *from many and distant lands.* A phrase of this kind has an aggregate sense, which is the true one, while that deduced from the import of the separate words is a false sense.

V. 6. γενομένης . . . . ταύτης. These words are obscure. The principal interpretations are the following. (1.) φωνῆς ταύτης refers to ἑτέραις γλώσσαις in v. 4, and the implication is, that the voices of those who spoke were so loud as to be heard at a distance, and in this way were the occasion of drawing together the multitude. This interpretation secures to ταύτης a near antecedent, but has against it that φωνῆς is singular, and not plural, and that the participle is hardly congruous with the noun in that sense. Neander, who adopts this view, regards φωνή as a collective term. (2.) φωνή has been taken as synonymous with φημή: *now when this report arose,* i. e. the report concerning this. The meaning is good, but opposed to the usage of the noun, while it puts ταύτης in effect for περὶ τούτου, which is a hard construction. Many of the older critics and the authors of nearly all the E. Vv. understood the expression in this way. (3.) We may regard φωνῆς as repeating the idea of ἦχος in v. 2: *now when this sound* — that of the descending Spirit — *occurred.* For that signification of φωνή, comp. John 3, 8; Rev. 1, 15; 9, 9; 14, 2, etc. γενομένης appears to answer to ἐγένετο in v. 2, and favors this explanation. The objection to it is that ταύτης forsakes the nearer for a remoter antecedent; but that may occur, if the latter be more prominent, so as to take the lead in the writer's mind. See W. § 23. 1. This meaning agrees with the context. The participial clause here may involve the idea of cause as well as time, and we may understand, therefore, that the sound in question was audible beyond the house where the disciples were assembled; that it arrested the attention of those abroad, and led them to seek out the scene of the wonder. So Hess,[1] Schrader, Meyer, De Wette, Alford, and others. The house (v. 2) may have been on one of the avenues to the temple, thronged at this time by a crowd of early worshippers (v. 15). — ἤκουον, (imperf.), *were hearing.* — ἕκαστος alone (v. 8) or with εἷς distributes often a plural subject; see 14, 29; Matt. 18, 35; John 16, 32. K. § 266. 3. — ἰδίᾳ, *his own;* usually emphatic. W. § 22. 7. — διαλέκτῳ = γλῶσσα. See v. 11. The term in its narrower sense here would be too narrow; for though some of the languages differed only as dialects, it was not true of all of them. — λαλούντων αὐτῶν. We are not to

[1] Geschichte und Schriften der Apostel Jesu, Vol. I. p. 24 (Zürich 1820).

understand by this that they all spoke in the languages enumerated, but that one of them employed this, and another that. In so brief a narrative, the writer must have passed over various particulars of the transaction. We may suppose that at this time the apostles had left the room where they assembled at first, and had gone forth to the crowd collected in the vicinity.

V. 7. οὐκ, which leads the sentence, belongs properly to εἰσίν; comp. 7, 48. W. § 61. 4. — πάντες (T. R.) was inserted here probably from v. 12. — οὗτοι, *these*, emphatic. — Γαλιλαῖοι. They were known as Galileans, because they were known as the disciples of Christ. Had the different speakers belonged to so many different countries, the wonder would have been diminished or removed.

V. 8. πῶς, *how*, since they were all Galileans. The object of ἀκούομεν follows in v. 11; but the connection having been so long suspended, the verb is there repeated. — ἕκαστος, as in v. 6. — ἐν ᾗ ἐγεννήθημεν, *in which we were born*. This remark excludes the possibility of Luke's meaning that the tongues were merely an ecstatic or impassioned style of discourse.

V. 9. In the enumeration of the countries named in this verse and the next, the writer proceeds from the northeast to the west and south. — Πάρθοι. *Parthia* was on the northeast of Media and Hyrcania, and north of Aria, surrounded entirely by mountains. — Μῆδοι. *Media* bordered north, on the Caspian Sea, west on Armenia, east on Hyrcania, and south on Persia. — Ἐλαμῖται, i. e. the inhabitants of *Elymais* or *Elam*, which was east of the Tigris, north of Susiana, (annexed to it in Dan. 8, 2), and south of Media, of which Ptolemy makes it a part. — Ἰουδαίαν. It has excited the surprise of some that *Judea* should be mentioned in this catalogue, because, it is said, no part of the wonder consisted in hearing Aramæan at Jerusalem. But we need not view the writer's design in that light. It was rather to inform us in how many languages the disciples addressed the multitude on this occasion; and as, after all, the native Jews formed the greater part of the assembly, the account would have been deficient without mentioning Judea. It has been proposed to alter the text to Ἰδουμίαν, but there is no authority for this. — The catalogue now passes from Cappadocia and Pontus on the east and northeast to the extreme west of Asia Minor. — τὴν Ἀσίαν. Phrygia being excluded here, Kuinoel and others have supposed *Asia* to be the same as Ionia; but Winer says it cannot be shown that in the Roman age Ionia alone was called Asia. He thinks, with an appeal to Pliny, that we are to understand it as embracing

Mysia, Lydia, and Caria, with Ephesus as the principal city. See his Realw. Vol. I. p. 96. Others, as Böttger,[1] whom De Wette follows, understand Mysia, Æolis, Ionia, Lydia, Caria. All admit that the term denoted not so much a definite region as a jurisdiction, the limits of which varied from time to time according to the plan of government which the Romans adopted for their Asiatic Provinces.

V. 10. Φρυγίαν. *Phrygia* was separated by the Taurus from Pisidia on the south, with Bithynia on the north, Caria, Lydia, and Mysia on the west, Gallacia, Cappadocia, and Lycaonia on the east. — *Pamphylia* was on the Mediterranean, adjacent on other sides to Cilicia, Caria, and Pisidia. — τὰ μέρη, κ. τ. λ., *the parts of Lybia towards Cyrene.* Lybia was an extensive region on the west of Egypt. One of the principal cities there was Cyrene, (now Grenna,) on the sea, originally a Greek colony, but where at this time the Jews constituted a fourth part of the population. See Jos. Antt. 14. 7. 2. It was the native place of Simon, who bore the Saviour's cross to Golgotha (Luke 23, 26). This part of Africa comes into view in making the voyage from Malta to Alexandria. — οἱ ἐπιδημοῦντες Ῥωμαῖοι, *the Romans sojourning* at Jerusalem; comp. 17, 21. — Ἰουδαῖοί τε καὶ προσήλυτοι, *both Jews and proselytes* a few critics restrict to Ῥωμαῖοι merely, but most (De Wet. Mey. Wiesl.) refer them to all the preceding nouns. The Jews generally adopted the languages of the countries where they resided. The *proselytes* were originally heathen who had embraced Judaism. The words sustain the same grammatical relation to Κρῆτες καὶ Ἄραβες, or, at all events, are to be repeated after them. The last two names follow as an after-thought, in order to complete the list.

V. 11. The declarative form which the English version assigns to the sentence here (*we do hear*) is incorrect. The question extends to θεοῦ. See on v. 8. — τὰ μεγαλεῖα τοῦ θεοῦ, *the great things of God,* done by him through Christ for the salvation of men (comp. v. 38).

V. 12. ἐξίσταντο describes their astonishment at the occurrence in general; διηπόρουν, their perplexity at being unable to account for it. — τί ἂν θέλοι, κ. τ. λ., *What may this perhaps mean.* ἂν attaches a tacit condition to the inquiry: if, as we think, it must import something. See W. § 42. 1; K. § 260. 4. This is the question of the more serious party. The hesitating form of it indicates

[1] Schauplatz der Wirksamkeit des Apostels Paulus, u. s. w., p. 23.

the partial conviction which the miracle had wrought in their minds.

V. 13. ἕτεροι . . . . ἔλεγον. Among those who scoffed may have been some of the native inhabitants of the city, who, not understanding the foreign languages spoken, regarded the discourse of the apostles as senseless because it was unintelligible to them. — χλευάζοντες is not so well supported as διαχλευάζοντες, and expresses the idea less forcibly. Calvin: "Nihil tam admirabile esse potest, quod non in ludibrium vertant, qui nulla Dei curâ tanguntur." — ὅτι, *that*, declarative. — γλεύκους, *sweet wine*, not *new*, as in the E. V. after all the earlier E. Vv. The Pentecost fell in June, and the first vintage did not occur till August. It is true, γλεῦκος designated properly the sweet, unfermented juice of the grape; but it was applied also to old wine preserved in its original state. The ancients had various ways of arresting fermentation. One of them, in use among the Greeks and Romans, was this: "An amphora was taken and coated with pitch within and without; it was filled with *mustum lixivium*, i. e. the juice before the grapes had been fully trodden, and corked so as to be perfectly air-tight. It was then immersed in a tank of cold fresh water, or buried in wet sand, and allowed to remain for six weeks or two months. The contents, after this process, were found to remain unchanged for a year, and hence the name ἀεὶ γλεῦκος, i. e. *semper mustum*." Dict. of Antt., art. *Vinum*.[1] Jahn says that *sweet wine* was produced also from dried grapes, by soaking them in old wine, and then pressing them a second time. See his Archæol. § 69. This species of wine was very intoxicating.

VERSES 14–36. *The Discourse of Peter.*

The address embraces the following points, though interwoven somewhat in the discussion: — first, defence of the character of the apostles (14, 15); secondly, the miracle explained as a fulfilment of prophecy (16–21); thirdly, this effusion of the Spirit an act of the crucified, but now exalted Jesus (30–33); and, fourthly, his claim to be acknowledged as the true Messiah (22–29, and 34–36).

V. 14. σὺν τοῖς ἕνδεκα, *with the eleven*, i. e. in their name, and with their concurrence in what he said. As the multitude was so great, it is not improbable that some of the other apostles ad-

[1] Dictionary of Greek and Roman Antiquities, edited by W. Smith, London. The abbreviation in the text refers always to this work.

dressed different groups of them at the same time; see on v. 6. On such an occasion they would all naturally pursue a very similar train of remark. — ἄνδρες Ἰουδαῖοι are the Jews born in Jerusalem; οἱ κατοικοῦντες are the foreign Jews and Jewish converts. See on v. 5. — ἐνωτίσασθε = הַאֲזִין, a Hellenistic word.

V. 15. γάρ justifies the call to attention. It brings forward a refutation of the charge which had been made against them. — οὗτοι, *these* whom they had heard speak (see v. 4 sq.), and who were then present; not the eleven merely with Peter (Alf.) — ὥρα τρίτη, *the third hour*, i. e. about nine o'clock, A. M., according to our time. This was the first hour of public prayer, at which time the morning sacrifice was offered in the temple. During their festivals the Jews considered it unlawful to take food earlier than this, still more to drink wine. See Light. Hor. Hebr. ad loc. The other hours of prayer were the sixth, (10, 4,) and the ninth (3, 1.)

V. 16. ἀλλὰ τοῦτο, κ. τ. λ., *but this* (which you witness) *is that which was said.* The Greek identifies the prophecy with its fulfilment. — διὰ τοῦ προφήτου, *through the prophet,* because he was the messenger, not the author of the message. The expression recognizes the divine origin of the book which bears his name. See the note on 1, 16. — Tischendorf has no adequate reason for omitting Ἰωήλ after προφήτου.

V. 17. The citation which follows from Joel 3, 1–5 (2, 28–32 in E. V.) runs for the most part in the words of the Seventy. The two or three verbal deviations from the Hebrew serve either to unfold more distinctly the sense of the original passage, or to enforce it. It is the object of the prophecy to characterize the Messianic dispensation under its two great aspects, — that of mercy and that of judgment. To those who believe, the gospel is "a savor of life unto life;" but to those who disbelieve, it is "a savor of death unto death;" see 2 Cor. 2, 16. Under its one aspect, it was to be distinguished by the copious outpouring of the Divine Spirit on those who should acknowledge Christ; and under its other aspect, it was to be distinguished by the signal punishment awaiting those who should disown his authority and reject him. — καὶ ἔσται . . . . ἡμέραις stands for וְהָיָה אַחֲרֵי־כֵן, rendered more closely in the Septuagint by καὶ ἔσται μετὰ ταῦτα. Peter's expression denotes always in the New Testament the age of the Messiah, which the Scriptures represent as the world's last great moral epoch. The prophet designates the same period under a more general phrase. Again, Peter places λέγει ὁ θεός at the beginning of the declaration, the prophet at the close of it.

The position of the words here fixes attention at once upon the source of the prophecy, and prepares the mind to listen to it as God's utterance. — ἐκχεῶ is future, a later Greek form. W. § 13. 3; K. § 154, R. 1. — καὶ (consequential) προφητεύσουσιν, *and thus they shall prophesy.* This verb in the New Testament signifies, not merely to foretell future events, but to communicate religious truth in general under a divine inspiration. It corresponds in this use to נִבָּא in the original passage; see Gesen. Lex. s. v. The order of the next two clauses in the Hebrew and Septuagint is the reverse of that adopted here; viz., first, οἱ πρεσβύτεροι .... ἐνυπνιασθήσονται, then οἱ νεανίσκοι .... ὄψονται. Hengstenberg[1] suggests that the change may have been intentional, in order to place the youth with the sons and daughters, and to assign to the aged a place of honor. — ἐνυπνίοις ἐνυπνιασθήσονται, *shall dream with dreams,* the dative, as in 4, 17; 23, 24. W. § 54. 3. Some authorities have ἐνύπνια, which was probably substituted for the other as an easier construction.

V. 18. καίγε = וְגַם annexes an emphatic addition, *and even* (Hart. Partik. Vol. I. p. 396.). — μου, which is wanting in the Hebrew, is retained here from the Septuagint. The prophet declares that no condition of men, however ignoble, would exclude them from the promise. The apostle cites the prophet to that effect; but takes occasion from the language — δούλους μου — which describes their degradation in the eyes of men, to suggest by way of contrast their exalted relationship to God. Bengel: "Servi secundum carnem .... iidem servi Dei." Similar to this is the language of Paul in 1 Cor. 7, 22: "For he that is called in the Lord, *being* a servant, is the Lord's freeman; likewise also he that is called, *being* free, is Christ's servant." If we cast the eye back over this and the preceding verse, it will be seen that the effusion of the Spirit was to be universal as to the classes of persons that were to participate in it; in other words, it was to be without distinction of sex, age, or rank. — The modes of divine revelation and of the Spirit's operation, which are specified in this passage, were among the more extraordinary to which the Hebrews were accustomed under the ancient economy. These, after having been suspended for so long a time, were now, at the opening of the Christian dispensation, renewed in more than their former power. The prophecy relates chiefly, I think, to these special communications of the

[1] Christology of the Old Testament, and a Commentary on the Predictions of the Messiah by the Prophets, Vol. III. p. 140 (Dr. Keith's Translation).

Spirit, which were granted to the first Christians. The terms of the prophecy direct us naturally to something out of the ordinary course; and when we add to this that the facts recorded in the Acts and the Epistles sustain fully that view of the language, it must appear arbitrary, as well as unnecessary, to reject such an interpretation. Yet the prophecy has indirectly a wider scope. It portrays in reality the character of the entire dispensation. Those special manifestations of the Spirit, at the beginning, marked the economy as one that was to be eminently distinguished by the Spirit's agency. They were a pledge, that those in all ages who embrace the gospel should equal the most favored of God's ancient people; they enjoy a clearer revelation, are enlightened, sanctified by a Spirit more freely imparted, may rise to the same or higher religious consolations and attainments.

V. 19. The apostle now holds up to view the other side of the subject. He adduces the part of the prophecy which foretells the doom of those who reject Christ and spurn his salvation. Having appealed to the hopes, the apostle turns here to address himself to the fears of men; he would persuade them by every motive to escape the punishment which awaits the unbelieving and disobedient. See v. 40 and 43 below. In the interpretation of the passage before us, I follow those who understand it as having primary reference to the calamities which God inflicted on the Jews in connection with the overthrow of Jerusalem, and the destruction of the Jewish state and nation. The reasons for this opinion are briefly these: — (1) The law of correspondence would lead us to apply this part of the prophecy to the same period to which the other part has been applied, i. e. to the early times of the gospel. (2) The expression, *the day of the Lord*, in v. 20, according to a very common use in the Hebrew prophets, denotes a day when God comes to make known his power in the punishment of his enemies, a day of the signal display of his vengeance for the rejection of long-continued mercies, and the commission of aggravated sins. The subversion of the Jewish state was such an occasion. It appropriates fully every trait of that significant designation. (3) Part of the language here coincides almost verbally with that in Matt. 24, 29; and if the language there, as understood by most interpreters, describes the downfall of the Jewish state,[1] we may infer from the similarity that the subject of discourse is the same in both places. (4)

[1] This view is defended in the Bibliotheca Sacra, 1843, p. 531 sq., and controverted in the same work, 1850, p. 452 sq.

The entire phraseology, when construed according to the laws of prophetic language, is strikingly appropriate to represent the unsurpassed horrors and distress which attended the siege and destruction of Jerusalem, and to announce the extinction of the Jewish power and glory of the Jewish worship which that catastrophe involved. Yet here too (see on v. 18) we are to recognize the wider scope of the prophecy. The destruction of the Jews is held forth by the apostle, as a type of the destruction which is to come upon every rejecter of the gospel; see v. 21. — For the sake of contrast, Peter inserts the words *ἄνω, σημεῖα, κάτω*, which are not in the Hebrew. *τέρατα ἐν τῷ οὐρανῷ, σημεῖα ἐπὶ τῆς γῆς*, means prodigies celestial and terrestrial, such as may appear in the air or on the earth; in other words, prodigies of every sort, and of the most portentous kind. The idea is, that calamities were to ensue, equal in severity and magnitude to those which the most fearful portents are supposed to announce. The mode of speaking is founded on the popular idea, that, when great events are about to occur, wonderful phenomena foretoken their approach. Hence what the prophet would affirm is, that disasters and judgments were coming such as men are accustomed to associate with the most terrific auguries; but he does not mean necessarily that the auguries themselves were to be expected, or decide whether the popular belief on the subject was true or false. — *αἷμα, πῦρ, ἀτμίδα καπνοῦ*, stand in apposition with *τέρατα καὶ σημεῖα*, and show in what they consisted: *blood*, perhaps, rained on the earth (De Wet.), or, as in Egypt (Ex. 7, 17), infecting the streams and rivers (Hng.); *fire*, i. e. appearances of it in the air, *and vapor of smoke*, dense smoke, hence = תִּימְרוֹת עָשָׁן, *pillars* or clouds *of smoke*, which darken the heavens and earth. Many have supposed these terms to signify directly slaughter and conflagration, but their grammatical relation to *τέρατα καὶ σημεῖα* decides that they are the portents themselves, not the calamities portended. That view, too, confounds *the day of the Lord* with the precursors of the day.

V. 20. *ὁ ἥλιος . . . . εἰς σκότος*, *the sun shall be turned into darkness.* Its light shall be withdrawn; the heavens shall become black. A day is at hand which will be one of thick gloom, of sadness, and woe. For the frequency and significance of this figure in the prophets, see Ezek. 32, 7; Is. 13, 10; Am. 5, 18. 20, etc. — *ἡ σελήνη*. Repeat here *μεταστραφήσεται*. The moon, too, shall give forth signs of the coming distress. It shall exhibit an appearance like blood. Men shall see there an image of the carnage and misery which are to be witnessed on earth. — *ἐπιφανῆ*, *illustrious*, signal in its character as an exhibition of divine justice. It conveys the idea of נוֹרָא, *fearful*, but is less definite.

V. 21. πᾶς ὃς ἄν, *every one whosoever*. For ἄν with this expansive effect, comp. v. 39; 3, 22. 23; 7, 3, etc. The mercy is free to all who fulfil the condition; see the note on v. 39. — ἐπικαλέσηται, *shall have called upon*; subj. aor. after ἄν = fut. exact. in Latin. The act in this verb must be past before the future in σωθήσηται can be present. See W. § 42. 1. 3. b. — τὸ ὄνομα κυρίου, *the name of the Lord*, i. e. of Christ, comp. v. 36; 9, 14; 22, 16; Rom. 13; not simply upon him, but upon him as possessing the attributes and sustaining to men the relations of which his *name* is the index. Compare the note on 22, 16. — σωθήσεται, *shall be saved* from the doom of those who reject Christ, and be admitted to the joys of his kingdom.

V. 22. Ἰσραηλῖται = Ἰουδαῖοι in N. T., here both the native and foreign Jews. — Ναζωραῖον = Ναζαραῖος. The former was the broader Syriac pronunciation, as heard especially in Galilee. Hence Peter's rustic λαλιά (Matt. 26, 73) betrayed him in the very words of his denial. See Win. Chald. Gr.[1] p. 12. The epithet is added for the sake of distinction, as Jesus was not an uncommon name among the Jews. — ἄνδρα . . . . εἰς ὑμᾶς, *a man from God* (as the source of the approval) *accredited unto you* (not as in E. V., *among you*); ἀποδεδειγμένον, lit. *shown forth*, confirmed (25, 7) viz. in his Messianic character. The meaning is, that in the miracles which Christ performed he had God's fullest sanction to all that he did and taught, that is, to his claim to be received as the Son of God, the promised Saviour of men. Some put a comma after θεοῦ, and render *a man* (sent) *from God, accredited* as such *by miracles*, etc. The ultimate idea remains the same, since to sanction his mission as from God was the same thing as to sustain his truth as to what he claimed to be. But the first is the more correct view, because it renders the ellipsis (*sent*, not apt to be omitted) unnecessary, and because (as Alf. suggests) the point to be established was that the Messiah was identical with a man whom they had seen and known. We have ἀπό after the participle, instead of ὑπό, because the approbation was indirect, i. e. testified through miracles. See W. § 47. 4; Bernh. Synt. p. 223. — δυνάμεσι καὶ τέρασι καὶ σημείοις form obviously an intensive expression, but they are not synonymous with each other. Miracles are called δυνάμεις, because they are wrought by divine power; τέρατα, *prod-*

[1] Grammar of the Chaldee language as contained in the Bible and the Targums, translated from the German by the writer (Andover 1845).

igies, because they appear inexplicable to men; and σημεῖα, *signs*, because they attest the character or claims of those who perform them (2 Cor. 12, 12). See Olsh. on Matt. 8. 1. It cannot be said that the terms are used always with a distinct consciousness of that difference. — οἷς is attracted into the case of its antecedent. — καί after καθώς good authorities omit. If retained, it must connect οἴδατε with ἐποίησε, what *he did ye also know;* or else strengthen αὐτοί, *also yourselves* as well as we.

V. 23. τοῦτον is both resumptive and emphatic; see Matt. 24, 13; 1 Cor. 6, 4. W. § 23. 4. — τῇ ὡρισμένῃ βουλῇ, *according to the established* (firmly fixed, see Luke 22, 22) *counsel*, plan; the dative is that of rule or conformity. W. § 31. 6. b.; K. § 285. 3. βουλή and πρόγνωσις may differ here as antecedent and consequent, since God's foreknowledge results properly from his purpose. — ἔκδοτον, *delivered up* to you, i. e. by Judas. — λαβόντες the best editors regard as an addition to the text. — διὰ χειρῶν ἀνόμων, *by the hands* or *hand* (if after Grsb. Lchm. Tsch., and others, we read χειρός) *of lawless ones* (partitive, hence without the article, see on 5, 16), i. e. of the heathen, as Pilate and the Roman soldiers; comp. Wisd. 17. 2; 1 Cor. 9, 21. The indignity which Christ suffered was the greater on account of his being crucified by the heathen. See 3, 13. ἀνόμων may agree with χειρῶν, *lawless hands;* but as the adjective must refer still to the heathen, it is not so easy a combination as the other. — προσπήξαντες, sc. τῷ σταυρῷ, *having fastened* to the cross, i. e. with nails driven through the hands and feet (John 20, 25. 27). See Bynæus de Morte Christi, L. III. c. 6, and Jahn's Archæol. § 262. He imputes the act of crucifixion to the Jews because they were the instigators of it; comp. 4, 10; 10, 39. — ἀνείλατε is first aorist, an Alexandrian form. W. § 13. 1; S. § 63. 11. R.

V. 24. ἀνέστησε, *raised up*, not into existence, as in 3, 22, but from the dead. The context demands this sense of the verb; see v. 32. — τὰς ὠδῖνας τοῦ θανάτου, *the pains of death;* quoted apparently from the Sept., for חֶבְלֵי־מָוֶת in Ps. 18, 5, *cords of death.* λύσας, *having loosed*, agrees better with the Hebrew idea; but taken less strictly, *having ended*, it is not inappropriate to ὠδῖνας. We may conceive, in the latter case, of the pains of death as not ceasing altogether with the life which they destroy, but as still following their victim into the grave. Hence though the Greek expression as compared with the Hebrew changes the figure, it conveys essentially the same thought, and may have been adopted because it was so familiar to the foreign Jews. Some contend that ὠδῖνας means *cords* in the Hellenistic Greek

(Kuin. Olsh.); but the assertion is destitute of proof. In that case, too, Luke would have said αὐτῷ at the end of the sentence instead of αὐτοῦ, out of regard to the figure. Others have found an allusion in the word to the resurrection as a birth (see Col. 1, 18), and hence to death as enduring (so to speak) the pangs inseparable from giving back the dead to life. It is strange that Meyer should revive this almost forgotten interpretation. — καθότι .... δυνατόν, *because it was not possible*, since the Divine purpose cannot fail. The confirmatory γάρ shows that to be the nature of the impossibility in the writer's mind.

V. 25. The quotation is from Ps. 16, 8–11, in accordance with the Septuagint. It will be observed that in v. 29–31 Peter takes pains to show that the portion of the Psalm under consideration there could not have referred to David, but had its fulfilment in Christ. In 13, 36, Paul too denies the applicability of that passage to David, and insists on its exclusive reference to the Messiah. We may conclude, therefore, that they regarded the entire Psalm as Messianic; for we have in it but one speaker from commencement to end, and in other respects such a marked unity of thought and structure, that it would be an arbitrary procedure to assign one part of it to David and another to Christ. See Prof. Stuart's Interpretation of this Psalm in Bibl. Repos., 1831, p. 51 sq. — εἰς αὐτόν, *in reference to him.* — προωρώμην, κ. τ. λ., *I saw the Lord before me* (where πρό is intensive merely), looked unto him as my only helper and support; not *foresaw* (E. V. after the Genv. V.), or *saw beforehand* (Tynd.). The verb answers to שִׁוִּיתִי, *I placed*, except that this marks more distinctly the effort made in order to keep the mind in that posture. — ὅτι, *because*, states why the eye is thus turned unto Jehovah. — ἐκ δεξιῶν describes one's position as seen off from the right. A protector at the right hand is one who is near and can afford instantly the succor needed. — ἵνα is telic, *in order that.*

V. 26. εὐφράνθη. On the augment in verbs which begin with εὖ, see W. § 12. 1. 3; K. § 125. R. 1. — ἡ γλῶσσά μου stands for כְּבוֹדִי, *my glory*, i. e. *soul*, whose dignity the Hebrews recognized in that way. The Greek has substituted the instrument which the soul uses in giving expression to its joy. We may render both verbs as present if we suppose them to describe a permanent state of mind. K. § 256. 4. — ἔτι δὲ καί, *but further also*, climacteric, as in Luke 14, 26. — ἡ σάρξ μου, *my flesh*, body as distinguished from the soul. — κατασκηνώσει, *shall rest*, viz. in the grave, as defined by the next verse. — ἐπ' ἐλπίδι, *in hope*, = לָבֶטַח, *in confidence*, i. e.

of a speedy restoration to life. The sequel exhibits the ground of this confident hope.

V. 27. ὅτι . . . . εἰς ᾅδου, *because* (not *that*) *thou wilt not abandon my soul unto hades.* ψυχήν μου = נַפְשִׁי, *my soul,* according to Hebrew usage, an emphasized pronoun. ᾅδης = שְׁאוֹל, denotes properly the place of the dead, but also, by a frequent personification, death itself, considered as a rapacious destroyer. See Gesen. Heb. Lex. s. v. The sense then may be expressed thus: Thou wilt not give me up as a prey to death; he shall not have power over me, to dissolve the body and cause it to return to dust. On the elliptical ᾅδου, see K. § 263. b. Later critics (Lchm. Tsch.) read ᾅδην, after ABCD, and other authorities. — ἰδεῖν, *to see,* experience, as in Luke 2, 26.

V. 28. ἐγνώρισας, κ. τ. λ., *thou didst make known to me the ways of life,* i. e. those which lead from death to life. The event was certain, and hence, though future, could be spoken of as past. The meaning is, that God would restore him to life, after having been put to death and laid in the grave. Kuinoel, De Wette, Meyer, concede that this is the sense which Peter attached to the words; and if so, it must be the true sense. The Greek here expresses the exact form of the Hebrew. — μετὰ τοῦ προσώπου σου, *with* (not = διά, *by*) *thy presence,* i. e. with thee where thou art, viz. in heaven. The Redeemer was assured that he would not only escape the power of death, but ascend to dwell in the immediate presence of God on high. It was for that "joy set before him, that he endured the cross, despising the shame, and is set down at the right hand of the throne of God." (Heb. 12, 2).

V. 29. The object of the remark here is to show that the passage cited above could not have referred to David. — ἐξόν, sc. ἐστί, not ἔστω, *it is lawful,* proper. — μετὰ παῤῥησίας, *with freedom,* without fear of being thought deficient in any just respect to his memory. His death was recorded in the Old Testament; no one pretended that he had risen, and the Psalm, therefore, could not apply to him. — David is called πατριάρχης, as being the founder of the royal family. This title in its stricter use belonged to the founders of the nation. — ἐν ἡμῖν, *among us,* here in the city. The sepulchre of David was on Mount Zion, where most of the kings of Judah were buried; see on 5, 6. The tomb was well known in Peter's day. Josephus says, that it was opened both by Hyrcanus and Herod, in order to rifle it of the treasures which it was supposed to contain. The Mosque, still shown as Neby Dauid, on the southern brow of Zion, cannot be far from the true site.

V. 30. προφήτης, *a prophet*, i. e. divinely inspired (see on v. 17), and so competent to utter the prediction. — οὖν, *therefore;* since, unless David meant himself, he must have meant the Messiah. — καὶ εἰδώς, *and knowing*, viz. that which follows. This knowledge he received from the prophet Nathan, as related in 2 Sam. 7, 12. 16; see also Ps. 132, 11; 89, 35-37. The resurrection of Christ in its full historical sense involved two points: first, his restoration to life; and, secondly, his elevation to permanent regal power. Peter inserts the remark made here to show that David, in predicting the main fact, had a view also of Christ's office as a Sovereign. — καθίσαι, sc. τινά, *to cause one to sit*, place him, comp. 1 Cor. 6, 4 (Whl. Mey. De Wet.); or (intrans. oftener in N. T.) *that one should sit* (Rob.). This descendant was to occupy the throne as ruler in Zion, as Messiah; comp. Ps. 2, 6. The Greek omits τινά often before the infinitive. K. § 238. R. 3. e. — After ὀσφύος αὐτοῦ, the received text adds τὸ κατὰ σάρκα ἀναστήσειν τὸν Χριστόν, viz. *that he would raise up the Messiah after the flesh*. Sholz retains the words, but most editors omit them, or mark them as unsupported.

V. 31. προϊδών repeats the idea both of προφήτης and εἰδώς. Having the knowledge derived from the sources which these terms specify, David could speak of the Messiah in the manner here represented. — τοῦ Χριστοῦ is the official title, not a proper name. — οὔτε ἐγκατελείφθη (Tsch.) κ. τ. λ., *neither was left* or οὐ κατελείφθη (T. R.), *was not left behind* (given up) *unto hades;* aorist here (note the fut. in v. 27), because the speaker thinks of the prediction as now accomplished. ἡ ψυχὴ αὐτοῦ (T. R.) should probably be dropped after the verb.

V. 32. τοῦτον τὸν Ἰησοῦν, *This* (looking back to v. 24) *Jesus*, the subject of such a prophecy. — οὗ κ. τ. λ., *whose* (masc. as Wicl. after Vulg., comp. 5, 32; 13, 31); or, as the verb suggests a natural antecedent (neut.), *of which*, viz. his resurrection, *we all are witnesses* (Mey. and E. V.). See note on 1, 22.

V. 33. The exaltation of Christ appears here (οὖν, *therefore*) as a necessary consequent of the resurrection; see on v. 28. 30. — τῇ δεξιᾷ, κ. τ. λ., *having been exalted to the right hand of God* (Neand. De Wet. Olsh. Bmg. Whl. Rob.); *not by the right hand* (Calv. Kuin. Mey. Alf. E. Vv.). The connection (see especially v. 34. 35, and comp. 5, 31) directs us quite inevitably to the first sense; and though the local dative *whither* may not occur in the New Testament out of this passage and 5, 31, yet all admit that it is one of the uses of the later Greek generally, and was not unknown to the earlier Greek poetry. See Bernh. Synt. p. 94.

Winer says (§ 31. 5) that we may translate here *to the right hand*, without any hesitation. — τὴν ἐπαγγελίαν, κ. τ. λ., *having received the promise* (i. e. its fulfilment in the bestowal) *of the Holy Spirit;* genit. of the object. See on 1, 4. — ἐξέχεε, *poured out.* The effusion of the Spirit which is ascribed to God in v. 17 is ascribed here to Christ. — βλέπετε refers to the general spectacle of so many speaking in foreign tongues, or possibly to the tongues of fire, visible on the speakers. ἀκούετε refers both to the languages spoken, and to what was spoken in them.

V. 34. γάρ confirms ὑψωθείς. The exaltation was not only incident to the resurrection, but was the subject of an express prediction, and that prediction could not apply to David; *for he did not ascend to heaven,* i. e. to be invested with glory and power at the right hand of God. The order of thought, says De Wette, would have been plainer thus: *For David says, Sit at my right hand,* etc.; *but he himself did not ascend into heaven,* i. e. he says this not of himself, but the Messiah. — λέγει, viz. in Ps. 110, 1. In Matt. 22, 43, and Mark 12, 36, the Saviour recognizes David as the author of the Psalm, and attributes to him a divine inspiration in speaking thus of the Messiah. He cites the same passage as proof of David's acknowledged inferiority to himself. — κάθου (imper.) is for the purer κάθησο. W. § 14. 4; Mt. § 236. — ἐκ δεξιῶν μου, *on my right hand* (see on v. 25) i. e. as the partner of my throne. The following remarks of Professor Stuart[1] are pertinent here. "In the New Testament, when Christ is represented as sitting at the right hand of divine majesty, Heb. 1, 3; or at the right hand of God, Acts 2, 33, and Heb. 10, 12; or at the right of the throne of God, Heb. 12, 2; participation in supreme dominion is most clearly meant. Compare 1 Pet. 3, 22; Rom. 8, 34; Mark 16, 19; Phil. 2, 6–11; Eph. 1, 20–23. At the same time, the comparison of these passages will show most clearly that Christ's exaltation at the right hand of God means *his being seated on the mediatorial throne* as the result and reward of his sufferings (see particularly Phil. 2, 6–11, and comp. Heb. 12, 2); and that the phrase in question never means the *original* dominion which Christ as Logos or God possesses. The sacred writers never speak respecting the Logos, considered simply in his *divine* nature, as being seated at the right hand of God; but only of the Logos *incarnate*, or the Mediator, as being seated there. So in Heb. 1, 3, it is *after* the expiation made by the Son of God, that he is represented as seating himself at the right

[1] Commentary on the Epistle to the Hebrews, p. 559 sq. (1833).

hand of the divine majesty. And that this *mediatorial* dominion is not to be considered simply as the dominion of the *divine* nature of Christ as such, is plain from the fact, that, when the mediatorial office is fulfilled, the kingdom of the Mediator as such is to cease. Moreover, that the phrase, *to sit* at the *right hand of God*, or *of the throne of God*, does not of itself mean *original divine* dominion, is clear from the fact, that Christ assures his faithful disciples they shall sit down with him on his throne, even as he sat down with the Father on his throne, Rev. 3, 21. It is exaltation, then, in consequence of obedience and sufferings, which is designated by the phrase in question."

V. 35. ἕως ἂν, κ. τ. λ. The dominion here, which Christ received, belonged to him as Mediator; and it is to cease, therefore, when the objects of his kingdom as Mediator are accomplished. Compare 1 Cor. 15, 23-28. This verse recognizes distinctly that limitation.

V. 36. πᾶς . . . . Ἰσραήλ, *all the house*, race, *of Israel.* οἶκος appears to omit the article, as having the nature of a proper name. W. § 17. 10. — ὅτι καί, κ. τ. λ., *that God made him both Lord and Christ*, to wit, *this one the Jesus, whom*, etc. τοῦτον τὸν Ἰησοῦν is in apposition with αὐτόν.

VERSES 37-42. *Effect of the Discourse in the Conversion of Three Thousand.*

V. 37. Not all but many of those addressed must be understood here. This necessary limitation could be left to suggest itself. κατενύγησαν τῇ καρδίᾳ, *were pierced in the heart;* dative of the sphere in which (Rom. 4, 20; 1 Cor. 14, 20). W. § 31, 3. Some editions have καρδίαν, accusative of the part affected. The verb expresses forcibly the idea of pungent sorrow and alarm. — τί ποιήσομεν, *What shall we do?* The answer to the question shows that it related to the way of escape from the consequences of their guilt. — For ἄνδρες, see on 1, 16.

V. 38. ἐπὶ τῷ ὀνόματι Ἰησοῦ Χριστοῦ, *upon the name of Jesus Christ* as the foundation of the baptism, i. e. with an acknowledgment of him in that act as being what his name imports (see on v. 21), to wit, the sinner's only hope, his Redeemer, Justifier, Lord, final Judge. For ἐπί with this force, see W. § 48. c. We see from v. 40, that Luke has given only an epitome of Peter's instructions on this occasion. The usual formula in relation to baptism is εἰς τὸ ὄνομα, as in 8, 16; 19, 5. It may have been avoided here as a matter of euphony, since εἰς follows in the next clause (De Wet.). — εἰς ἄφεσιν ἁμαρτιῶν, *in order to the forgiveness of sins* (Matt. 26, 28; Luke 3, 3), we connect naturally with both the preceding verbs. This clause states the motive or object which should induce them to repent and be baptized. It enforces the entire exhortation, not one part of it to the exclusion of the other.

V. 39. τοῖς τέκνοις ὑμῶν, *unto your descendants* (see 13, 33); not *your little ones* (Alf.) with an appeal to v. 17; for the sons and daughters there are so far adult as to have visions and to prophesy.—πᾶσι τοῖς εἰς μακράν, *to all those afar off*, i. e. the distant nations or heathen. So, among others, Calvin, Bengel, Olshausen, Harless,[1] De Wette, Neander, Lange.[2] The expression was current among the Jews in that sense; comp. Zech. 6, 15; Is. 49, 1; 57, 19; Eph. 2, 13. 17 (where see Dr. Hodge in his recent Commentary). Even the Rabbinic writers employed it as synonymous with *the heathen.* (Schöttg. Hor. Heb. Vol. I. p. 761.) It has been objected, that this explanation supposes Peter to have been already aware that the gospel was to be preached to the Gentiles; whereas, it is said, he afterwards hesitated on the subject, and needed a special revelation to point out to him his duty; see 10, 10 sq. But the objection misstates the ground of the hesitation; it related to the terms on which the Gentiles were to be acknowledged as Christians, not to the fact itself. On this point how is it possible that he should have doubted? The Jews in general, who expected a Messiah at all, believed in the universality of his reign. The prophets foretold distinctly that the Gentiles under him should form one people with the Jews, that they should both acknowledge the same God, and be acknowledged of him; see, e. g. Mich. 4, 1 sq.; Am. 9, 12; Is. 2, 2 sq.; 40, 5; 54, 4 sq., etc. Add to this, that the Saviour himself before his ascension had charged his disciples to go into all the world and preach the gospel to every creature. The relation in which the Gentile believers were to stand to Judaism, how far they were to practise its rites, and in that respect assimilate to the Jews, was not so well understood. On that question, it is true, they needed and received further instruction as to the course to be pursued. Those who reject the foregoing explanation suppose πᾶσι τοῖς εἰς μακράν to denote the foreign Jews. But they are included already in ὑμῖν, since many of those addressed were pilgrims who had come to Jerusalem to celebrate the present feast. This sense of the phrase

[1] Commentar über den Brief Pauli an die Ephesier, p. 213 sq.
[2] Das apostolische Zeitalter, zweiter Band, p. 42 (1853).

renders it superfluous. — ὅσους ἄν, κ. τ. λ., *whomsoever the Lord shall have called.* For the verbal form, see the note on v. 21. The expression imports, that as many would secure a part in the promise as it should prove that the divine purpose had embraced.

V. 40. Copies fluctuate between διεμαρτύρετο and διεμαρτύρατο. The imperfect agrees best with the next verb — σώθητε, *save yourselves.* For this middle sense, see W. § 39. 2. — ἀπὸ τῆς γενεᾶς, κ. τ. λ., *from this perverse* (Phil. 2, 15) *generation,* i. e. from participation in their guilt and doom; comp. 1 Cor. 11, 32; Gal. 1, 4.

V. 41. οὖν, *therefore,* viz. in consequence of Peter's exhortation. — οἱ μὲν, κ. τ. λ., *they* (who were mentioned as penitent in v. 37) *having received his word,* viz. that in v. 38 sq. (De Wet. Mey.). Many adopt the substantive construction: *they who received* (Bng. Kuin. E. Vv.). The first view identifies those who believe here more distinctly with those in v. 37, who evince such a preparation for the exercise of faith, and may be preferable on that account; but the use of the participle in other respects (as we saw on 1, 16) involves an ambiguity. ἀσμένως, *gladly,* elicits a correct idea, but is hardly genuine. — ψυχαί, *souls,* persons, see v. 43; 3, 23; 7, 14; 27, 37. The frequency of this sense may be Hebraistic, but not the sense itself.—ἐβαπτίσθησαν, *were baptized,* not necessarily at once after the discourse, but naturally during the same day, if we unite the next clause (τῇ ἡμέρᾳ ἐκείνῃ, see on 8, 1) closely with this. But the compendious form of the narrative would allow us with some editors to place a colon between the two clauses; and then the baptism could be regarded as subsequent to προςετέθησαν, taking place at such time and under such circumstances as the convenience of the parties might require. It is proper to add (against Alf.) that the pools so numerous and large which encircled Jerusalem, as both those still in use and the remains of others testify at the present day, afforded ample means for the administration of the rite. The habits of the East, as every traveller knows, would present no obstacle to such a use of the public reservoirs.

V. 42. προσκαρτεροῦντες, κ. τ. λ., *constantly applying themselves unto the teaching of the apostles;* they sought to know more and more of the gospel which they had embraced. — καὶ τῇ κοινωνίᾳ (comp. εἶχον κοινά in v. 44), *and unto the communication,* distribution, i. e. of money or other supplies for the poor (Heinr. Kuin. Olsh. Bmg. Hmph.); *the fellowship,* i. e. the community, oneness of spirit and effort which bound the first Christians to each other (Bng. Mey. Rob.); *the communion,* meals in common, ἀγάπαι, which were followed by the Lord's supper (Bez. Grot. De Wet.);

the Sacrament itself (Lightf. Est. Wlf.) I prefer the first sense of this doubtful word, because all the other nouns denote an act, not a state of mind or feeling; because the participle applies to an act rather than an abstract quality (which are objections to the second sense); because this use of the term is justified by Rom. 15, 26; 2 Cor. 8, 4; especially Heb. 13, 16; and because, as the contributions would naturally be made at their meetings, the several nouns relate then to a common subject, viz. their religious assemblies. It may be added, that their liberality towards the poor was so characteristic of the first Christians, that this sketch of their religious habits might be expected to include that particular. κοινωνία in the sense of our *communion*, the Lord's Supper, appears not to have prevailed before the fourth century (Suicer Thesaur. s. v. as cited by Hmph.), and hence the last of the meanings given above may be laid out of the account here. The meals in common or ἀγάπαι were known to be a part of the κλάσις τοῦ ἄρτου (see below), and consequently would not need to be specified in this connection by a separate term. The E. V. unites ἀποστόλων with both nouns: *the apostle's doctrine and fellowship* (also Tynd. Cranm. Gen.) With that combination we should have had regularly the genitive after the second noun, without a repetition of the article. See W. § 19. 3. c. Some assume a hendiadys: *the communion in the breaking of bread* (Vulg. Wicl. Blmf.). The analysis is not only awkward, but opposed by τῇ before κλάσει. — τῇ κλάσει τοῦ ἄρτου denotes *the breaking of the bread* as performed at the Lord's Supper. See 20, 7. 11; 1 Cor. 10, 16. The expression itself may designate an ordinary meal, as in Luke 24, 35; but that here would be an unmeaning notice. There can be no doubt that the Eucharist, at this period, was preceded uniformly by a common repast, as was the case when the ordinance was instituted. Most scholars hold that this was the prevailing usage in the first centuries after Christ. We have traces of that practice in 1 Cor. 11, 20 sq., and, in all probability, in v. 46 below. The *bread* only being mentioned here, the Catholics appeal to this passage as proving that their custom of distributing but one element (the cup they withhold from the laity) is the apostolic one. It is a case obviously in which the leading act of the transaction gives name to the transaction itself.

VERSES 43–47. *Benevolence of the First Christians; their Joy, their Increase.*

V. 43. πάσῃ ψυχῇ, *unto every soul* of those who heard of the events just related, viz. the descent of the Spirit, the miracle of tongues, the conversion of such a multitude; comp. 5, 5. — φόβος, *fear*, religious awe; see Luke 1, 65. — πολλά in this position belongs to both nouns, see 17, 12. W. § 59. 5. — διὰ τῶν ἀποστόλων, *though the apostles* as instruments, while the power was God's; see v. 22 and 15, 12. — ἐγίνετο, *were wrought* (imperf.), during this general period.

V. 44. ἐπὶ τὸ αὐτό, not *harmonious* (Calv. Kuin.), but *together*, i. e. they met daily in one place, as explained in v. 46; see on 1, 15. — καὶ εἶχον . . . . κοινά, *and they had all things common*, looked upon their possessions not as their own, but held them as subject to the use of the church as they were needed. The next words refer to the act of disposing of their property, and hence these describe the antecedent principle or spirit which prompted the act. The remark is defined by οὐδὲ εἷς . . . . ἔλεγεν . . . . εἶναι in 4, 32: *neither did any one say*, etc.

V. 45. τὰ κτήματα καὶ τὰς ὑπάρξεις, *their estates*, lands, *and* other *possessions*. — αὐτά, *them*, i. e. the proceeds of the sale. W. § 22. 3. — καθότι . . . . εἶχε, *as any one from time to time had need.* ἄν with the indicative in a relative sentence denotes a recurring act. W. § 42. 3. a. As this clause qualifies also ἐπίπρασκον (imperf. as done again and again), it shows that they did not alienate their property at once, but parted with it as occasion required.

V. 46. ὁμοθυμαδόν, as in v. 1. — κατ' οἶκον, *from house to house*, comp. κατὰ πόλιν in Tit. 1, 5; i. e. in different houses, some in one, some in another, or perhaps in different houses successively (E. V. Kuin. Neand.); or *at home*, in private, see Phil. v. 2 (Olsh. De Wet. Mey. Gen. V.). Even in the latter case we may suppose that they met in separate parties at different places; not necessarily (as Mey.), all in a single place at once. Both renderings are justifiable. The latter may be more exact in form, since it brings out more strongly an apparent contrast between the public worship and their more private services. ἐν in the place of κατά would have removed the ambiguity. Neander (Pflanzung, u. s. w., Vol. I. p. 36), observes that a single room would hardly have contained the present number of converts. He supposes that, in addition to their daily resort to the temple, they met in smaller companies, at different places; that they here received instruction from their teachers or one another, and prayed and sang together; and, as the members of a common family, closed their interview with a repast, at which bread and wine were distributed in memory of the Saviour's last meal with his disciples. In conformity with this view, κλῶντες ἄρτον may refer to their *break-*

ing bread in connection with the Sacrament, and μετελάμβανον τροφῆς to their reception of food for ordinary purposes. — ἀφελότητι καρδίας, *with simplicity of heart,* with child-like affection towards God and one another.

V. 47. χάριν, *favor,* approbation, (Luke 2, 52.) — τοὺς σωζομένους, *those who are saved,* or more strictly *are becoming saved* from day to day, since the present tense denotes a process going on. See 1 Cor. 1, 18 and 2 Cor. 2, 15. The Greek should have been τοὺς σεσωσμένους (perf.), to signify that they had already secured their salvation; and τοὺς σωθησομένους (fut.) to signify that they were certain of its completion. See Green's Gr. p. 28. The expression implies a certainty resulting not so much from God's purpose, as from human conduct. The doctrine is that those who embrace the gospel adopt the infallible means of being saved. — προςετίθει, *added,* (imperf. with reference to καθ' ἡμέραν,) brings to view God's agency in that acceptance of the gospel which ensures salvation.

CHAPTER III.

VERSES 1–10. *Healing of the Lame Man by Peter and John.*

V. 1. ἐπὶ τὸ αὐτό, *together,* in company, see 1, 15. — ἀνέβαινον, *were going up;* because the temple was on Mount Moriah, and even from the gate where the miracle occurred (v. 3), a flight of steps led to the court of the Israelites. — τὴν ἐννάτην, *the ninth.* This was our three o'clock, P. M., at which time the evening sacrifice was offered; see on 2, 15. The apostles and other believers at Jerusalem had not yet withdrawn from the Jewish worship (see also, 21, 23 sq.), and it is probable that most of them continued to adhere to the services of the temple, until the destruction of the temple abolished them. But the spirit with which they performed these services was no longer the Jewish spirit. Instead of regarding their compliance with the ordinances of the law as an act of merit, they recognized Christ as "the end of the law for righteousness to every one that believeth." They viewed the sacrifices which continued to be offered, not as having any efficacy to procure the remission of sin, or as typical of an atonement still to be made, but as realized already in the death of

Christ, and hence as mementos, as often as they beheld them or participated in them, of the "one sacrifice for sins" effected "through the offering of the body of Jesus Christ." As in the case of circumcision, so undoubtedly the Jewish Christians relinquished the other rights of Judaism only by degrees. They were brought fully to this, in part by obtaining a clearer insight into the relation of the ancient economy to the new, and in part by the occurrence of national circumstances which hastened the result. From the Jewish synagogues, on the contrary, they must have separated at once, as soon as their distinctive views became known. It was impossible to avow the Christian faith, and remain connected with those communities. Compare the note on 9, 2. We have seen in the second chapter, that, in connection with the worship of the temple, the believers at Jerusalem maintained separate religious worship among themselves.

V. 2. ἐβαστάζετο, *was carried along* (relative imperf.) just then as the apostles arrived. — ἐτίθουν is imperf. with reference to the custom of placing the cripple here. — τὴν λεγομένην ὡραίαν, *the one called Beautiful.* Most interpreters think that this was the gate described by Josephus (Bel. Jud. 5. 5. 3; Antt. 15. 11. 3), as composed chiefly of Corinthian brass, and as excelling all the other gates of the temple in the splendor of its appearance, though it is not mentioned by him under this particular appellation. If this be so, the gate then was on the east side towards Olivet (ἡ ἀνατολική says Jos.), and was an inner gate (πύλη τοῦ ἐνδοτέρου χαλκῆ οὖσα), leading from the court of the Gentiles into the court of the Israelites. It is not against this that Josephus speaks also of this gate as ἡ ἔξωθεν τοῦ νεώ; for he must mean (the term is not ἱερόν) *the one exterior to the temple* strictly so called, the sanctuary; not (as Mey.) opening from without into the enclosure of the sacred precincts. The folds of this brazen gate were fifty cubits high and forty broad, and were covered with plates of gold and silver. Luke's epithet — ὡραίαν — could not have had a more pertinent application. Some have thought that the gate to which he refers must have been one of the outer gates, because what is related in v. 11 sq. took place in Solomon's porch, which was in the court of the Gentiles. But we may suppose, as Lightfoot suggests, that, the apostles having been with the lame man into the temple, i. e. the court of the Israelites (see v. 8), were returning, and had reached the court of the Gentiles, when the concourse of the people there spoken of took place. — τοῦ αἰτεῖν, telic, *in order to ask.* This use of the infinitive with τοῦ to denote the object for which an act is performed (comp. 18, 10; 26, 18; Mark 4, 3, etc.), results naturally from the nature of the genitive as the *whence-case.* The older writers supplied ἕνεκα or χάριν; but the construction is neither elliptical nor Hebraistic. W. § 44. 4. b.; S. § 165. 3. 2; K. § 308. 2. b. — τῶν εἰσπορευομένων εἰς τὸ ἱερόν, *those entering into the temple*, i. e. the court where the Jews worshipped; if, as suggested above, the lame man sat at the gate of that court. τὸ ἱερόν here too may be *the temple* in its aggregate sense; not perforce the outer court (Mey.). If a noun follows an intransitive verb compounded with a preposition, it is common to repeat the preposition before the noun; see v. 3. 8; 22, 6; Matt. 7, 23, etc. W. § 56. 2.

V. 3. ὅς, *who*, stands often where οὗτος, *this one*, would be the ordinary connective. K. § 334. 3. — λαβεῖν (omitted in v. 2) is not strictly pleonastic, but expands the idea of ἠρώτα. W. § 63. 4. d. It is left out of some copies, but is genuine.

V. 4. βλέψον εἰς ἡμᾶς, *look upon us*. Their object appears to have been to gain his attention more fully to their words; so that, as they said, " In the name of Jesus Christ," etc. (v. 6), he might understand to whom he was indebted for the benefit conferred upon him.

V. 5. ἐπεῖχεν αὐτοῖς sc. τὸν νοῦν (comp. Luke 14, 7), *fixed his mind upon them.* The man's eager expectation looked through his countenance. — τι, *something* in the way of alms. We have no evidence that he recognized Peter and John as the disciples of Christ, and expected that they would heal his infirmity. Their address to him in the next verse precludes that supposition.

V. 6. ἐν τῷ ὀνόματι, κ. τ. λ., i. e. we speaking *in his name*, by virtue of his authority; comp. 16, 18. The language of Christ, on the contrary, when he performed a miracle, was, σοὶ λέγω, or to that effect; see Luke 5, 24. — τοῦ Ναζωραίου is added for the sake of distinction, as in 2, 22. — περιπάτει is imperative present, and not aorist, like ἔγειραι, because it denotes a continued act; comp. 8, 26; 13, 8, etc. W. § 43. 3. b.; S. § 141, 5.

V. 7. πιάσας, κ. τ. λ., *having taken him by the right hand*, and thus encouraged him to obey their command. See Mark 9, 27. αὐτοῦ exemplifies the rule that a genitive which belongs to two or more nouns usually precedes them. W. § 30. 3. 4. — βάσεις, *feet*; σφυρά, *ankles*. This particularity has been reckoned among the traces of a professional habit, for which Luke is distinguished. See on 28, 8.

V. 8. ἐξαλλόμενος, *leaping forth* from the place where he sat, and *up* only as involved; not from his bed (Mey., but dropped in his last ed.) since καθήμενος (v. 10) shows that he was not reclining. — ἔστη, *stood* for the first time since he was born (v. 2). — περιεπάτει, *walked to and fro*, as if to make trial of his newly found strength. — εἰς τὸ ἱερόν, *into the temple*, its inner part beyond the gate where the lame man had been healed (see on v. 2). — In περιπατῶν, κ. τ. λ., Luke writes as if he were giving the recital of some eye-witness.

V. 10. ἐπεγίνωσκον . . . . ὅτι οὗτος, *they recognized him* (upon attentive scrutiny, hence imperf.) *that this one*, etc. The subject of the subordinate clause is attracted here into the principal clause, and then repeated in οὗτος. So in 4, 13; 9, 20; 13, 32; 16, 3, etc. The subject of the second clause becomes in this way more prominent. W. § 66. 5; B. § 151 I. 6. 7. The ordinary construction would omit αὐτόν after ἐπεγίνωσκον, and make the sentence after ὅτι the object of the verb. — πρὸς τὴν ἐλεημοσύνην, *for the alms* which he solicited.

VERSES 11–26. *The Testimony of Peter after the Miracle.*

V. 11. κρατοῦντος αὐτοῦ, *while he is holding them fast*, or *keeping near to them*. This latter signification, says De Wette, has not been fully proved, but arises naturally out of the other. Meyer adheres more correctly to the first meaning: the man in the ardor of his gratitude clung to his benefactors, and would not be separated from them. αὐτοῦ is considered the correct reading, instead of τοῦ ἰαθέντος χωλοῦ in the common text (Grsb. Mey. Lchm.). The addition has been transferred to the English version. — στοᾷ . . . . Σολομῶνος. See John 10, 23. This hall or porch was on the eastern side of the temple, in the court of the heathen. The general opinion is that it was called *the porch of Solomon*, because it occupied the site of a porch which had been connected with the first temple. Lücke[1] thinks that it may have been a structure built by Solomon himself, which had escaped the destruction of the first temple. Tholuck[2] expresses the same belief. It accords with this view that Josephus (Antt. 20. 9. 7) calls the porch ἔργον Σολομῶνος. In popular speech, says Lightfoot, the Jews sometimes meant the entire court of the Gentiles when they spoke of Solomon's porch. — ἔκθαμβοι agrees with λαός as a collective term; comp. 5, 16.

V. 12. ἰδών, *seeing* their astonishment. — ἀπεκρίνατο, κ. τ. λ., *proceeded to speak* (Hebraistic, see 5, 8), or perhaps *answered unto the people* (De Wet. Mey.), since their looks of wonder

[1] Commentar über das Evangelium des Johannes, Vol. II. p. 361.
[2] Commentar zum Evangelium Johannis, p. 256 (sechste Auflage).

seemed to ask for some explanation of the miracle (see v. 11). — ἐπὶ τούτῳ may be neuter, *at this thing*, see v. 10 (E. Vv.); but more probably masculine, *at this one* (Mey. De Wet.), which prepares the way for αὐτόν, like the succession of τοῦτον and αὐτῷ in v. 16. — ἡμῖν, *upon us*, emphatic, as distinguished from Christ or God, to whom the miracle ought to have turned their thoughts. — ἀτενίζετε takes its object in the dative (see also 10, 4; 14, 9); or in the accusative with εἰς (comp. v. 4; 1, 10; 6, 15). — ὡς ἰδίᾳ, κ. τ. λ., *as by our own* (inherent or self-acquired) *power, or* (since power had been exerted) *piety* as the reason of its being conferred on them. — πεποιηκόσι . . . . αὐτόν, *having effected* (ecbatic infinitive) *that he should walk*. W. § 44. 4; S. § 165. 3.

V. 13. ἐδόξασε, *glorified*, honored, not by the miracle at this time (Mey.), but by all the mighty works which attested his mission; see 2, 22. — παῖδα, not *son* = υἱός, but *servant* = עֶבֶד, which was one of the prophetic appellations of the Messiah, especially in the second part of Isaiah. See Matt. 12, 18, as compared with Is. 42, 1 sq. The term occurs again in this sense in v. 26; 4, 27. 30. — μέν as in 1, 1. The antithetic idea may have been that in v. 17. — παρεδώκατε, *ye delivered up*, viz. to Pilate. — ἠρνήσασθε, *denied*, refused to acknowledge as Messiah. — αὐτόν. It will be seen that the writer drops here the relative structure of the sentence. — κρίναντος . . . . ἀπολύειν, *when*, or *although he decided*, viz. that it was just *to release him;* see Luke 23, 16; John 19, 4. ἐκείνου refers here to the nearer noun, and performs the proper office of τούτου. W. § 23. 1. It is not uncommon for Greek writers to interchange these pronouns.

V. 14. δέ, *but*, contrasts their conduct with that of Pilate. — τὸν ἅγιον is a Messianic title, as in Luke 4, 34. τὸν δίκαιον, *the Just one*. The epithets mark the contrast between his character and that of Barabbas. — ἄνδρα φονέα, i. e. not merely *a man*, but a man who was *a murderer;* see Matt. 27, 16 sq.; Mark 15, 7 sq.

V. 15. τὸν δὲ ἀρχηγὸν τῆς ζωῆς, *but the author of life*, i. e. as De Wette remarks, *of life* in the fullest sense in which the Scriptures ascribe that property to the Saviour, viz. spiritual or Christian life (comp. John 1, 4; Heb. 2, 10), and also natural or physical life (comp. John 5, 26; 11, 25). Olshausen and Meyer suppose the main idea to be that of spiritual life; but the evident relation of ζωῆς to ἀπεκτείνατε shows that the other idea is certainly not to be excluded. A terrible aggravation in this murder was that he whom they deprived of life was himself the one who gives life to all. — ἐκ νεκρῶν, *from the dead;* the article usually omitted after ἐξ, but inserted after ἀπό. W. § 19. — οὗ . . . . ἐσμέν, *of whom* (13, 31), or *of which we are witnesses;* see note on 2, 32.

V. 16. ἐπὶ τῇ πίστει, κ. τ. λ., *upon the faith in his name* entertained by us, i. e., on account of their faith as the ground or condition God had performed this act. Some construe ἐπί as telic: *upon the faith* as the object, i. e. in order to produce faith in the lame man and in others (Olsh. Hmph.). This latter meaning not only strains the preposition, but overlooks the manifest parallelism in sense between this clause and the following καὶ ἡ πίστις, κ. τ. λ. — ὀνόματος is the genitive of the object, and the expression is like πίστις Θεοῦ in Mark 11, 22 and πίστις Ἰησοῦ in Rom. 3, 22. W. § 30. 1. — ὅν . . . . οἴδατε, *whom you see* entirely restored now to bodily vigor, *and know* as a person who was formerly infirm, helpless. — τὸ ὄνομα, κ. τ. λ., *his name*, i. e. he invoked by an appeal to him as that which *his name* represents (see on 2, 21), *made strong* (a definite past). The reason for expressing the idea in this manner is evident from v. 6. — ἡ πίστις ἡ δι' αὐτοῦ, *the faith that* is wrought in us *through him* (De Wet. Mey. Win.). The apostles here, it will be observed, ascribe the origin, as well as the efficacy, of their faith to Christ. Compare 1 Pet. 1, 21. This second clause of the verse repeats essentially the idea of the first, in order to affirm more emphatically that it was not their own power, but the power of Christ, which had performed the miracle. — ἀπέναντι πάντων ὑμῶν, *in the presence of you all;* and hence they must acknowledge that no other means had been used to effect the miracle.

V. 17. Having set before them their aggravated guilt, the apostle would now suggest to them the hope of mercy. ἀδελφοί, *brethren*, Peter says here because he would conciliate his hearers; but in v. 12, where the object is reproof, crimination, he says more formally, though courteously, ἄνδρες Ἰσραηλῖται. One of the marks of truth would be wanting without this accordance between the style and the changing mental moods of the speaker. — ὅτι . . . . ἐπράξατε, *that ye acted in ignorance*, i. e. of the full criminality of their conduct. They had sinned, but their sin was not of so deep a dye that it could not have been still more heinous. The language of Peter concedes to them such a palliation of the deed as consisted, at the time of their committing it, in the absence of a distinct conviction that he whom they crucified was the Lord of life and glory (see 13, 27, and 1 Cor. 2, 8); but it does not exonerate them from the guilt of having resisted the evidence that this was his character, which had been furnished by his miracles, his life, doctrine, and resurrection. The Saviour himself, in his dying prayer, urged the same extenuation in behalf of his murderers: "Father, forgive them, for they know not what they do." Compare also the language of Paul in 1 Tim. 1, 13: "Who was before a blasphemer, and a persecutor, and injurious; but I obtained mercy because I did it ignorantly in unbelief. — ὥσπερ καὶ οἱ ἄρχοντες ὑμῶν, *as also your rulers*, who were not present, and hence are distinguished from those addressed.

V. 18. δέ, *but*, i. e. while they did this they accomplished a divine purpose. — πάντων τῶν προφητῶν, instead of being taken strictly, may be viewed as a phrase: *the prophets as a whole.* For this restricted use of πᾶς in such general expressions, see Matt. 3, 5; Mark 1, 37; John 3, 26. Most of the books of the Old Testament foretell distinctly the sufferings and death of the Messiah. Compare Luke 24, 27. Olshausen regards the entire history of the Jews as typical, and in that view maintains that all the ancient prophets prophesied of Christ. — παθεῖν τὸν Χριστόν, *that the Christ* (who was to come) *would*, or *must suffer* (De Wet.). After verbs which signify to declare, believe, and the like, the infinitive implies often the idea of necessity or obligation. W. § 45, 3. b. — οὕτω refers to the previous verse: *thus*, in this way, viz. by their agency; comp. 13, 27. It is incorrect to understand it of the accordance between the fulfilment and the prediction.

V. 19. μετανοήσατε οὖν, *repent therefore*, since your guilt is not such as to exclude you from the mercy procured by the Saviour whom you have crucified. — ἐπιστρέψατε, *turn*, i. e. from your present course or character unto Christ (9, 35; 11, 21); or unto God (14, 15; 15, 19). What is required here includes faith as a constituent part of the act to be performed. — εἰς . . . . ἁμαρτίας, *that your sins may be blotted out*, obliterated as it were from the book or tablet where they are recorded; comp. Col. 2, 14; Is. 43, 25. — ὅπως ἄν, κ. τ. λ., *in order that* (telic, comp. Matt. 6, 5) *the times of refreshing may come*, i. e. to you personally, that you may have part in the blessings of the Messiah's kingdom, for which men can be prepared only by repentance and the pardon of their sins. ἄν after ὅπως followed by the conjunctive represents the act of the verb as dependent, i. e. in this case, on their compliance with the exhortation. W. § 42. 6; Hart. Partik. Vol. II. p. 289. ὅπως as a particle of time, *when* (as in E. V.) is foreign to the New Testament idiom. See Green's Gr. p. 77. We must discard that translation here. Scholefield (Hints,[1] etc., p. 40) pleads

[1] Hints for Improvements in the Authorized Version of the New Testament, by the late Rev. James Scholefield, Professor of Greek in the University of Cambridge, England (4th ed. 1857).

faintly for retaining it, but admits that the weight of evidence is against it. It is not entirely certain whether *καιροὶ ἀναψύξεως* refers to the present consolations of the gospel, or to the blessedness which awaits the followers of Christ at the end of the world, when he shall return and receive them to himself in heaven. The expression, in itself considered, would very aptly describe the peace of mind and joy which result from a consciousness of pardon and reconciliation to God. So one class of commentators understand it. Others think that the time here meant must coincide with that in the next verse; and hence suppose the apostle to have in view Christ's second coming, when those who have believed on him shall enter upon their eternal rest in heaven. Compare Heb. 4, 9–11. Taken thus, the image of the future state in ἀναψύξεως is that of relief or refreshment of the wearied soul after toils and sorrows, and is strikingly similar to Paul's ἄνεσις, *relaxation, rest* which God allots to the afflicted in the day of final recompense; see 2 Thess. 1, 7. This is the interpretation of Chrysostom, Olshausen, De Wette, Meyer, and others. The order of the clauses decides nothing against the latter opinion, since it may be as natural in this instance to think first of the effect, and then to assign the cause or occasion, as the reverse. It is in favor of this opinion that it refers ἔλθωσι and ἀποστείλῃ to the same period or event, as the close succession of the verbs would lead us to expect. — ἀπὸ προσώπου τοῦ κυρίου, *from the presence of the Lord*, since the blessings in question (a Hebrew idiom) are laid up where he is (see 2, 28), and must be received thence. κυρίου, which may refer to Christ or God (see on 1, 24), applies to the latter here, since it prepares the way for the subject of the next verb.

V. 20. καὶ ἀποστείλῃ, κ. τ. λ., *and that* (dependent still on ὅπως) *he may send forth*, viz. from heaven, see v. 21; comp. δείξει ὁ μακάριος καὶ μόνος δυνάστης, κ. τ. λ., in 1 Tim. 6, 15. — προκεχειρισμένον ὑμῖν, *before appointed* or *prepared for you*, i. e. from eternity, see 1 Pet. 1, 20. προκεκηρυγμένον, *announced before*, is a less approved reading. Nearly all critics understand this passage as referring to the return of Christ at the end of the world. The similarity of the language to that of other passages which announce that event demands this interpretation. The apostle enforces his exhortation to repent by an appeal to the final coming of Christ, not because he would represent it as near in point of time, but because that event was always *near to the feelings and consciousness* of the first believers. It was the great consummation on which the strongest desires of their souls were fixed, to which their thoughts and hopes were habitually turned. They lived with reference to this event. They labored to be prepared for it. They were constantly, in the expressive language of Peter, *looking for and* (in their impatience as it were) *hastening the arrival of the day of God* (2 Pet. 3, 12). It is then that Christ will reveal himself in glory, will come "to take vengeance on them that obey not the gospel, and to be admired in all them who believe" (2 Thess. 1, 8), will raise the dead (John 5, 28. 29), invest the redeemed with an incorruptible body (Philip. 3, 21), and introduce them for the first time, and for ever, into the state of perfect holiness and happiness prepared for them in his kingdom. The apostles as well as the first Christians in general, comprehended the grandeur of that occasion. It filled their circle of view, stood forth to their contemplations as the point of culminating interest in their own and the world's history, threw into comparative insignificance the present time, death, all intermediate events, and made them feel that the manifestation of Christ, with its consequences of indescribable moment to all true believers, was the grand object which they were to keep in view as the end of their toils, the commencement and perfection of their glorious immortality. In such a state of intimate sympathy with an event so habitually present to their thoughts, they derived, and must have derived, their chief incentives to action from the prospect of that future glory. As we should expect, they hold it up to the people of God to encourage them in affliction, to awaken them to fidelity, zeal, perseverance, and on the other hand appeal to it to warn the wicked, and impress upon them the necessity of preparation for the revelations of the final day. For examples of this habit, the reader may see 17, 30. 31; 1 Tim. 6, 13 sq.; 2 Tim. 4, 8; Tit. 2, 11 sq.; 2 Pet. 3, 11 sq., etc. Some have ascribed the frequency of such passages in the New Testament to a definite expectation on the part of the apostles that the personal advent of Christ was nigh at hand; but such a view is not only unnecessary, in order to account for such references to the day of the Lord, but at variance with 2 Thess. 2, 2. The apostle Paul declares there, that the expectation in question was unfounded, and that he himself did not entertain it or teach it to others. But while he corrects the opinion of those at Thessalonica who imagined that the return of Christ was then near, neither he nor any other inspired writer has informed us how remote that event may be, or when it will take place. That is a point which has not been revealed to men; the New Testament has left it in a state of uncertainty. "The day of the Lord so cometh as a thief in the night;" and men are exhorted to be always prepared for it. It is to be acknowledged that most Christians, at the present day, do not give that prominence to the resurrection and the judgment, in their thoughts or discourse, which the New Testament writers assign to them; but this fact is owing, not necessarily to a difference of opinion in regard to the time when Christ will come, but to our inadequate views and impressions concerning the grandeur of that occasion, and the too prevalent worldliness in the church, which is the cause or consequence of such deficient views. If modern Christians sympathized more fully with the sacred writers on this subject, it would bring both their conduct and their style of religious instruction into nearer correspondence with the lives and teaching of the primitive examples of our faith.

V. 21. ὅν . . . . δέξασθαι, *whom the heavens, indeed, must* (according to the divine plan) *receive;* not *retain*, which the usage of the verb forbids. Though the ascension had taken place, we have δεῖ and not ἔδει, because the necessity of the event is a permanent fact. Meyer explains δεῖ as in effect an imperfect, an instance merely of the rhetorical present for the past. De Wette shifts the peculiarity of the expression from δεῖ to δέξασθαι, and renders *whom it is necessary the heavens should receive.* He alleges for this future sense that the ascension could be viewed as still incomplete because it was so recent. But the apostle having just referred to Christ as already in heaven, whence he is to appear again (v. 20), would not be apt to speak in the very next words as if he thought of him as still lingering on the earth. Many of the Jews believed that when the Messiah appeared, he would remain permanently among men, see John 12, 34. Peter corrects here that misapprehension: the Saviour must return to heaven and reign there for a season, before his final manifestation. The μέν (which no δέ follows) has its antithesis in ἄχρι χρόνων, κ. τ. λ. (De Wet.): Christ would not be absent always, but for a certain time only; not in the preceding ἀποστείλῃ, κ. τ. λ. (Alf.), since that would make this the δέ clause, not the μέν as it is now. — ἄχρι . . . . πάντων, *until* (*during* is incorrect) *the times of the restoration of all things*, i. e. to a state of primeval order, purity, and happiness, such as will exist for those who have part in the kingdom of Christ, at his second coming. The expression designates the same epoch as καιροὶ ἀναψύξεως (Olsh. Mey. De Wet.). — ὧν, κ. τ. λ., *which God spake of*, announced; comp. v. 24. The relative refers to χρόνων as the principal word, and stands by attraction for οὕς or περὶ ὧν. It does not refer to πάντων, *the accomplishment of all things which*, etc., for ἀποκαταστάσεως will not bear that meaning. — ἀπ' αἰῶνος, *from the beginning*, from the earliest times of prophetic revelation. Such a period of restoration to holiness and happiness is the explicit or implied theme of prophecy from the beginning to the end of the Old Testament. Some omit the expression, or put it in brackets, but the evidence for it preponderates.

V. 22. γάρ here (T. R. and E. V.) should be left out. πρὸς τοὺς πατέρας, also, is supposed to be a gloss. — μέν here responds to δέ in v. 24 : Moses on the one hand as well as all the prophets on the other. — εἶπεν, *said*, viz. in Deut. 18, 18 sq. The translation is partly that of the Seventy, partly new. In 7, 37, Stephen cites this passage as having the same import which Peter ascribes to it here. Their mode of applying it shows that the Jews were agreed in referring it to the Messiah. That this was the current interpretation may be argued also from John 4, 25; see Hengstenberg's remarks in his Christol. Vol. I. p. 67 sq. — ἀναστήσει = יָקִים, *will raise up*, cause to appear. — ὡς ἐμέ, *like me*. The context of the original passage (comp. v. 15, 16 with v. 17, 18) indicates that the resemblance between them was to consist chiefly in their office as mediator. The meaning is: Since the Israelites had been unable to endure the terrors of the divine majesty, God would, at some future time, send to them another mediator, through whom he would communicate with them, as he had done through Moses (Heng.). See also Gal. 3, 19; Heb. 9, 15. — ὅσα ἄν, *whatsoever*, see 2, 21.

V. 23. Peter interrupts the sentence here to insert ἔσται δέ, which is not in the Hebrew. It serves to call attention more strongly to what follows. — ἐξολοθρευθήσεται ἐκ τοῦ λαοῦ, *shall be utterly destroyed from the people*. This expression occurs often in the Pentateuch, where it denotes the sentence or punishment of death. The apostle uses it here evidently to denote the punishment which corresponds to that, in relation to the soul, i. e. as De Wette explains it, exclusion from the kingdom of God. Peter has substituted this expression here for אֶדְרֹשׁ מֵעִמּוֹ = ἐκδικήσω ἐξ αὐτοῦ, as rendered in the Septuagint: *I will exact vengeance from him*. The only difference is that the Hebrew affirms the purpose of God to punish, while the Greek employed by Peter defines at the same time the nature or mode of the punishment.

V. 24. πάντες . . . . τῶν καθεξῆς stands concisely for *all the prophets from Samuel, both he and they who followed*. The appositional clause is here merged in the genitive. ἀπὸ Σαμουήλ shapes the construction, instead of the remoter προφῆται. Compare Luke 24, 27. W. § 67. 2. The literal translation, *from Samuel on, and those who followed*, involves a tautology, the second clause being comprehended in the first. Samuel is mentioned next after Moses, because so few prophets appeared in the interval between them, or so few whose names are recorded. They stand in the same proximity to each other in Ps. 99, 6. We have no record of all that the prophets taught, and the apostle's assertion here that Samuel also bore testimony to Christ, does not need to be confirmed by specific passages. — ὅσοι ἐλάλησαν, κ. τ. λ., *as many as spake*, prophesied, shows as related to the next clause (note καί), how uniformly the theme of a coming Messiah had been held forth in the instructions of the ancient messengers of God. Yet the object may be to characterize the teaching of the prophetic order as such, and not of every single individual. See note on v. 18.

V. 25. οἱ υἱοὶ . . . . τῆς διαθήκης, *Ye are the sons of the prophets, and of the covenant*, i. e. are those in the first case to whom the predictions respecting the Messiah especially appertain, and in the second are those to whom God would first (v. 26) offer the mercies which he covenanted to bestow on Abraham's spiritual seed, viz. such as believe, and thus "walk in the steps of his faith;" see Rom. 4, 12. υἱοί in this sense of participation, appurtenance, is a common Hebraism; see Matt. 8, 12; John 4, 22; Rom. 9, 4, etc. Its ordinary signification, *sons*, descendants, would be incongruous with διαθήκης, and should not be retained, therefore, in connection with προφητῶν. — λέγων, κ. τ. λ., viz. in Gen. 12, 3. God repeated the promise to Abraham and the other patriarchs, at various times; see Gen. 18, 18; 22, 18; 26, 4, etc. — ἐν τῷ σπέρματί σου, *in thy seed*, viz. the Messiah (v. 26) as one of his posterity; agreeably to Paul's view in Gal. 3, 16.

V. 26. ὑμῖν, *unto you*, dependent on ἀπέστειλεν (see 13, 26; 28, 28); not *for you*, dat. comm. (Mey.), dependent on ἀναστήσας. — πρῶτον, *first* in the order of time, comp. 13, 46; Luke 24, 47; Rom. 1, 16. Here, too, Peter recognizes the fact that the gospel was to be preached to the heathen; see on 2, 39. — ἀναστήσας, *having raised up*, as in v. 22. — παῖδα, *servant*, as in v. 13. — The E. V. follows the common text, which inserts Ἰησοῦν after αὐτοῦ, but contrary to the best authorities (Grsb. Tsch. Mey.). — εὐλογοῦντα, *blessing*, applies the idea of the preceding ἐνευλογηθήσονται to the Jews, and requires ὑμᾶς to be read with emphasis. — ἐν τῷ ἀποστρέφειν κ. τ. λ., states how he blesses them: *in that he turns away each one from your sins*, to wit, by his gospel, which secures the pardon and sanctification of those who accept it (see on 2, 47). This verb has elsewhere an active sense in the New Testament. Some (Kuin. De Wet.) disregard that usage and render, *in that each one turns away*, etc. This is opposed also to εὐλογοῦντα, which represents Christ here as the actor, men rather as recipients.

CHAPTER IV.

VERSES 1–4. *The Imprisonment of Peter and John.*

V. 1. ἐπέστησαν implies commonly a hostile purpose, see 6, 12; 17, 5; Luke 20, 1. The arrest appears to have taken place while the apostles were still speaking. — οἱ ἱερεῖς, *the priests* who officiated in the temple at the time, or some of their number. The priests were divided into twenty-four classes, each of which had charge of the temple service for a week at a time. See 1 Chron. 24, 3 sq.; 2 Chron. 8, 14; and also Jos. Antt. 7. 14. 7. The particular duties from day to day were assigned to individuals by lot, see Luke 1, 9. During the observance of the festivals, the number of priests was increased, as the labors to be performed were greater. Win. Realw. Vol. II. p. 273. It is possible that the feast of Pentecost (2, 1) had not yet terminated. — ὁ στρατηγὸς τοῦ ἱεροῦ, *the commander of the temple*, was an officer having a body of Levites under his command, who preserved order about the temple, and in that respect performed a sort of military service. See Jahn's Archæol. § 365. In 5, 26, the Levites so employed are called his ὑπηρέται, *servants*. Josephus speaks repeatedly of this guard (e. g. Bell. Jud. 6. 5. 3), whose commander he designates in the same manner. In 2 Macc. 3, 4, he is termed ὁ προστάτης τοῦ ἱεροῦ, *the guardian of the temple*. We read of στρατηγοὺς τοῦ ἱεροῦ, *commanders of the temple*, in Luke 22, 52, which is best explained by supposing that the temple guard was divided into several companies, each of which had its στρατηγός, though this title belonged distinctively to the chief in command. — οἱ Σαδδουκαῖοι, the *Sadducees* as a sect, since those who acted in this instance represented the spirit of the party; comp. Matt. 9, 11; 12, 14; Mark 8, 11; John 8, 3. Meyer supposes the article to point out those of them who were present at this time. It was probably at the instigation of this class of men that the apostles were now apprehended.

V. 2. διαπονούμενοι, *being indignant;* restricted by some (Mey.

De Wet.) to the nearest noun, since the motive assigned for the interference in καταγγέλλειν, κ.τ.λ., applies only to the Sadducees, who denied the doctrine of a resurrection; see 23, 8; Matt. 22, 23. But perhaps we may regard διὰ τὸ διδάσκειν αὐτοὺς τὸν λαόν as more comprehensive than καταγγέλλειν, κ. τ. λ., instead of being merely defined by it, and in that case may refer the participle to the priests as well as the others. The priests, though they might not share the hostility of the Sadducees to the doctrine of a future state (see on 23, 8) would naturally be indignant that their office as teachers should be assumed by men like Peter and John (see Matt. 21, 23), and especially that the Jesus whom they themselves had crucified should be proclaimed as the Messiah (see 5, 28). — καταγγέλλειν ἐν τῷ Ἰησοῦ, *are announcing in Jesus the resurrection*, i. e. in his example, in the fact of his alleged restoration to life; comp. ἐν ἡμῖν in 1 Cor. 4, 6. This is the best and the generally approved interpretation (Bng. Kuin. De Wet. Mey.). Others render *are announcing the resurrection in virtue of Jesus*, by his power; see 1 Cor. 15, 22. The E. version, *through Jesus*, while the earlier E. Vv. have *in him*, appears to express that meaning. But it was not so much the general resurrection as that of Christ himself which the apostles proclaimed at this stage of their ministry; see 1, 22; 2, 24; 3, 15, etc. The single concrete instance, however, as the Sadducees argued, involved the general truth, and, if substantiated, refuted their creed.

V. 3. εἰς τήρησιν, *into prison*; comp. ἐν τηρήσει δημοσίᾳ, in 5, 18. This word denotes a place of custody (see Pape Lex. s. v), as well as the act; though the latter is the proper force of such a termination. K. § 233. b. a. — εἰς τὴν αὔριον, *unto the morrow* as the limit; see Matt. 10, 22; 1 Thess. 4, 15. — ἦν γὰρ, κ. τ. λ., *for it was already evening*, and hence no judicial examination could take place until the next day. It was three o'clock when the apostles went to the temple; comp. 3, 1.

V. 4. τὸν λόγον, *the word*, the well-known message of Christ. — ἐγενήθη = ἐγένετο, *became*, i. e. in consequence of the present addition. The use of this form is peculiar to the later Greek. W. § 15; Lob. ad. Phryn. p. 108. — ὁ ἀριθμὸς τῶν ἀνδρῶν, *the number of the men* who had embraced the gospel up to this time (Kuin. Mey. De Wet. Alf.); see 1, 15; 2, 41. A retrospective remark like this was entirely natural after having spoken of the many who believed at this time. Some suppose the new converts alone to have amounted to *five thousand*; but that is less probable, as the apostles could hardly have addressed so great a multitude in such a place. ἀνδρῶν comprehends probably both men and women, like ψυχαί in 2, 41; comp. Luke 11, 31. An emphasized or conscious restriction of the term to men would be at variance with that religious equality of the sexes so distinctly affirmed in the New Testament; see Gal. 3, 28.

VERSES 5–7. *Their Arraignment before the Sanhedrim.*

V. 5. αὐτῶν before ἄρχοντες refers to the Jews as implied in vv. 1 and 4 (De Wet. Win.); not to the believers as if to contrast their conduct with that of their rulers (Mey. formerly, but now as above), and certainly not to the apostles (Stier).[1] — τοὺς ἄρχοντας, κ. τ. λ. The Sanhedrim is here described by an enumeration of the three orders which composed that body, viz. *the chief priests*, who are mentioned last in this instance, *the elders* or heads of families, and *the scribes* or teachers of the law; comp. 5, 21; Matt. 2, 4; 26, 59. ἄρχοντας designates the Sanhedrists in general, since they were all rulers, while καί annexes the respective classes to which they belonged: *and* (more definitely, comp. 1, 14) *the elders*, etc. It was unnecessary to repeat the article, because the nouns have the same gender. W. § 19. 4; S. § 89. 9. — εἰς Ἱερουσαλήμ, *unto Jerusalem*, as some of the rulers may have lived out of the city (Mey. De Wet.), especially at that season (see 2, 1) when the heat had begun to be severe. εἰς is not put loosely for ἐν (Kuin.); for the distinctive force of the prepositions may always be traced, and the notice merely that they assembled in Jerusalem would be unnecessary. The substitution of ἐν for εἰς in the text (Lchm. Tsch.) is unwarranted.

V. 6. Those named here are prominent individuals among the rulers (v. 5), not a separate class. Ἄνναν τὸν ἀρχιερέα. The actual high-priest at this time was Caiaphas, see John 11, 49; but Annas, his father-in-law, had held the same office, and, according to the Jewish custom in such cases, retained still the same title. He is mentioned first, perhaps, out of respect to his age, or because his talents and activity conferred upon him a personal superiority. See John 18, 13. It is entirely unnecessary to charge Luke with committing an error here, as Zeller so confidently affirms.[2] It is a familiar usage in every language to speak of "the

[1] Die Reden der Apostel nach Ordnung und Zusammenhang ausgelegt, von Rudolf Stier, Zwei Bände.

[2] Theologische Jahrbücher, Jahrgang 1849, p. 60. It is due to the reader to place before him some examples of this writer's style of criticism. His articles on the Composition and Character of the Acts, published in different numbers of the Periodical named above, are considered as remarkable for the industry and acuteness which they display in setting forth the internal difficulties that are supposed to

governor," "the president," "the senator," and the like, though the person so termed is no longer in office. — Ἰωάννην καὶ Ἀλέξανδρον. We know nothing positive of these men beyond the intimation here that they were priests, and active at this time in public affairs. *Alexander* is another instance of a foreign name in use among the Jews, see 1, 23. It is improbable that he was the Alexander mentioned in Jos. Antt. 18. 8. 1, who was a brother of Philo, and alabarch of the Jews at Alexandria. In that case he must have been visiting at Jerusalem, and hence was present in the council as a guest only, or else had not yet removed to Egypt. — καὶ ὅσοι . . . . ἀρχιερατικοῦ, *and as many as were of the pontifical family*, i. e. those nearly related to the ἀρχιερεῖς = ἀρχιερατικοῦ, embracing, as that title was applied among the Jews, the high priest properly so called, his predecessors in office, and the heads of the twenty-four sacerdotal classes (see on v. 1). Many points relating to the organization of the Sanhedrim are irretrievably obscure; but it is generally agreed that the twenty-four priestly orders were represented in that body. See Win. Realw. Vol. II. p. 271. The attendance of so many persons of rank on this occasion evinced the excited state of the public mind, and gave importance to the decisions of the council. This is Meyer's view of the meaning. But a narrower sense of ἀρχιερατικοῦ may be adopted. It appears to me more simple to understand, that John and Alexander were related to Annas and Caiaphas, and that the ὅσοι, κ. τ. λ., were the other influential members of the same family. That the family of Annas was one of great distinction appears in the fact that five of his sons attained the office of high-priest. See on 9, 1. Some vary the meaning of γένους, and translate, *as many as were of the class of the chief priests.* This sense renders the description of the different branches of the Sanhedrim more complete, but assigns a forced meaning to the noun.

V. 7. αὐτούς, *them*, viz. the apostles last mentioned in v. 3. — ἐν μέσῳ, *in the midst*, before them so as to be within the view of all; comp. John 8, 3. It is said that the Jewish Sanhedrim, sat in a circle or a semi-circle; but we could not urge the expression here as any certain proof of that custom — ἐν ποίᾳ δυνάμει, *by what power*, efficacy; not *by what right*, authority, which would require ἐξουσία as in Matt. 21, 23. See Tittm. Synm. p. 158. — ἢ ἐν ποίῳ ὀνόματι, *or* (in other words) *in virtue of what* uttered *name.* This appears to be a more specific form of the same in-

embarrass Luke's history. The articles have been thrown into a volume, but I have not seen them in that form.

quiry. — τοῦτο, *this*, viz. the cure of the lame man. Olshausen understands it of their teaching, which is not only less appropriate to the accompanying words, but renders the answer of the apostles in v. 9. 10 irrelevant.

VERSES 8–12. *Testimony of Peter before the Council.*

V. 8. πλησθεὶς πνεύματος ἁγίου, *filled with the Holy Spirit*, i. e. anew, see v. 31; 2, 4. Peter was thus elevated above all human fear, and assisted at the same time to make such a defence of the truth as the occasion required. The Saviour had authorized the disciples to expect such aid under circumstances like the present; see Mark 13, 11; Luke 21, 14. 15. For the absence of the article, see on 1, 2.

V. 9. εἰ ἀνακρινόμεθα, *if we are examined*, as is confessedly the case. εἰ in the protasis with the indicative, affirms the condition, and is logically equivalent to ἐπεί, *since*. K. § 339. I. a; W. § 41. b. 2. The occasion for the present defence was a reproachful one to the Jews, and hence the speaker alludes to it thus dubiously, in order to state the case with as little offence as possible. The apodosis begins at γνωστὸν ἔστω. — ἐπὶ εὐεργεσίᾳ, κ. τ. λ., *in respect to a good deed*, benefit conferred *on an infirm man;* comp. John 10, 32. Observe that neither noun has the article. ἀνθρώπου is the objective genitive; comp. 3, 16; 21, 20; Luke 6, 7. S. § 99. 1. c; K. § 265. 2. b. — ἐν τίνι, *whereby*, how (De Wet. Mey.), not *by whom* (Kuin.). The first sense agrees best with the form of the question in v. 7. — οὗτος, *this one*. The man who had been healed was present, see v. 10, 14. He may have come as a spectator, or, as De Wette thinks, may have been been summoned as a witness. Neander conjectures that he too may have been taken into custody at the same time with the apostles. — σέσωσται, *has been made whole*. The subject of discourse determines the meaning of the verb.

V. 10. ἐν τῷ ὀνόματι Ἰησοῦ Χριστοῦ, *by the name of Jesus Christ* (the latter appellative here), through their invocation of his name. The question *how* (v. 9) is here answered. — τοῦ Ναζωραίου identifies the individual to whom the apostle applies so exalted a name; see on 2, 22. — ὃν . . . . ἐκ νεκρῶν is an adversative clause after ὃν ἐσταυρώσατε, but omits the ordinary disjunctive. For this asyndetic construction, see W. § 60. 2; K. § 325. It promotes compression, vivacity of style. For the anarthrous νεκρῶν, see on 3, 15. — ἐν τούτῳ may be neuter, sc. ὀνόματι (Mey.); or masculine, *in this one* (Kuin De Wet.), which is more natural, since ὃν is a nearer antecedent, and οὗτος follows in the next verse (and so also Mey. at present). παρέστηκεν, *stands* (E. V.); perf. = present (see on 1, 10).

V. 11. οὗτος, *this one*, viz. Christ, who is the principal subject, though a nearer noun intervenes; see 7, 19. W. § 23. 1; S. § 123. N. 1. Compare the note on 3, 13. For the passage referred to, see Ps. 118, 22. The words, as Tholuck[1] remarks, appear to have been used as a proverb, and hence are susceptible of various applications. The sense for this place may be thus given: the Jewish rulers, according to the proper idea of their office, were the builders of God's spiritual house; and as such should have been the first to acknowledge the Messiah, and exert themselves for the establishment and extension of his kingdom. That which they had not done, God had now accomplished in spite of their neglect and opposition. He had raised up Jesus from the dead, and thus confirmed his claim to the Messiahship; he had shown him to be the true author of salvation to men, the corner-stone, the only sure foundation on which they can rest their hopes of eternal life. Compare Matt. 21, 42; Luke 20, 17.— The later editors consider οἰκοδόμων more correct than οἰκοδομούντων.— ὁ γενόμενος . . . . γωνίας, *which became the head of the corner;* predicated, like ὁ ἐξουθενηθείς, of ὁ λίθος as identical with οὗτος. κεφαλὴν γωνίας is the same as λίθος ἀκρογωνιαῖος in 1 Pet. 2, 6; comp. Is. 28, 16. It refers, probably, not to the copestone, but to that which lies at the foundation of the edifice, in the angle where two of the walls come together, and which gives to the edifice its strength and support. See Gesen. Heb. Lex. s. רֹאשׁ. 4.

V. 12. ἡ σωτηρία, *the salvation* which the gospel brings, or which men need; comp. John 4, 22. For the article, see W. § 18. 1. The contents of the next clause render it impossible to understand the term of the cure of the lame man. It was not true that the apostles proclaimed the name of Christ as the one on which men should call in order to be healed of their diseases.— οὔτε γὰρ, κ. τ. λ., *for neither is there any other name.* It has just been said, that Christ is the only Saviour. It is asserted here that he is such because no other has been provided.— τὸ δεδομένον, *which is given,* since the gospel is the fruit of mercy.— ἐν ἀνθρώποις, *among men* as the sphere in which the name is known; not dat. comm., *for men.* See W. § 31. 6. The latter is a resulting idea, but not the expressed one.— ἐν ᾧ . . . . ἡμας, *in which we* (as men, and hence true of the human race), *must be saved.* δεῖ

[1] Uebersetzung und Auslegung der Psalmen, p. 496.

is stronger than ἔξεστι, and means not *may*, but *must*, as the only alternative, since God has appointed no other way of salvation. The apostle would exclude the idea of any other mode of escape if this be neglected. See Heb. 2, 3.

VERSES 13–18. *Decision of the Sanhedrim.*

V. 13. θεωροῦντες is the appropriate word here. It denotes not *seeing* merely, like βλέποντες (v. 14), but seeing earnestly or with admiration. Tittm. Synm. p. 121. — καταλαβόμενοι, *having perceived*, from intimations at the time, such as their demeanor, language, pronunciation (Str.), comp. Matt. 26, 73; or *having ascertained* by previous inquiry (Mey. Alf.). Meyer in his last edition prefers the first meaning to the second. The tense, it will be observed, differs from that of the other participle. — ἀγράμματοι καὶ ἰδιῶται, *illiterate*, i. e. untaught in the learning of the Jewish schools, see John 7, 15; *and obscure*, plebeian (Kuin. Olsh. De Wet.). It is unnecessary to regard the terms as synonymous (E. V. Mey. Rob.). Their self-possession and intelligence astonished the rulers, being so much superior to their education and rank in life.[1] — ἐπεγίνωσκον . . . . ἦσαν, *and they recognized them that they were with Jesus* during his ministry, were among his followers (Wicl. Tynd.); not *had been* (E. V.). Their wonder, says Meyer, assisted their recollection, so that, as they observed the prisoners more closely (note the imperf.), they remembered them as persons whom they had known before. Many of the rulers had often been present when Christ taught publicly (see Matt. 21, 23; Luke 18, 18; John 12, 42, etc.), and must have seen Peter and John. That the latter was known to the high-priest is expressly said in John 18, 15.

V. 14. The order of the words here is admirably picturesque. — σὺν αὐτοῖς, *with them*, viz. the apostles, not the rulers; comp. αὐτούς just before. — ἑστῶτα, *standing* there, and by his presence, since he was so generally known (see 3, 16), uttering a testimony which they could not refute. Bengel makes the attitude significant: *standing firmo talo*, no longer a cripple. — οὐδὲν, κ. τ. λ., *had nothing to object*, against the reality of the miracle, or the truth of Peter's declaration.

V. 15. κελεύσαντες, κ. τ. λ., *having commanded them to depart out of the council.* The deliberations of the assembly were open to others, though the apostles were excluded; and hence it was

[1] Walch maintians this distinction in his Dissertationes in Acta Apostolorum, p. 59 sq., (Jena 1766).

easy for Luke to ascertain what was said and done during their absence. Some of the many priests who afterwards believed (see 6, 7) may have belonged to the council at this time, or, at all events, may have been present as spectators. It is not improbable that Saul of Tarsus was there, or even some of the Christian party who were not known in that character.

V. 16. ὅτι μὲν, κ. τ. λ., *for that a notorious miracle*, a deed undeniably of that character, *has been done.* γνωστόν in the sense of *widely known* adds nothing to the text, since it merely repeats the subsequent φανερόν.—δι' αὐτῶν, *through them*; and hence accredited (see on 2, 22) as the agents of a higher power. — φανερόν agrees with ὅτι . . . . αὐτῶν, and is the predicate nominative after ἐστί understood. — οὐ δυνάμεθα, κ. τ. λ., *we are not able to deny it.* See 3, 9. 11. They would have suppressed the evidence had it been possible.

V. 17. ἵνα . . . . διανεμηθῇ, *that it* (sc. τὸ σημεῖον) *may not spread.* With a knowledge of the miracle the people would associate inevitably the doctrine which the miracle confirmed. The subject of the verb involves the idea of διδαχή, but it would be arbitrary to supply that word as the direct nominative. Some have supposed the last clause in the verse to require it. — ἀπειλῇ . . . . αὐτοῖς, *let us severely* (lit. *with a threat*) *threaten them.* Winer (§ 54. 3) regards this combination of a verb and noun as an expedient for expressing the infinitive absolute with a finite verb in Hebrew. See Gesen. Heb. Gr. § 128. 3. But we meet with the idiom in ordinary Greek; see Thiersch de Pent. Vers. p. 169. The frequency of the construction in the New Testament is undoubtedly Hebraistic. — ἐπὶ τῷ ὀνόματι τούτῳ, *upon this name* as the basis of their doctrine or authority; comp. v. 18; 5, 28. 40. W. § 48. c.

V. 18. τό before φθέγγεσθαι points that out more distinctly as the object of the prohibition. It is not a mere sign of the substantive construction. W. § 44. 3. c. — μηδὲ διδάσκειν, κ. τ. λ., *nor to teach upon the name of Jesus*, specifies the part of their preaching which the rulers were most anxious to suppress. The other infinitive does not render this superfluous.

VERSES 19–22. *The Answer of Peter and John.*

V. 19. ἐνώπιον τοῦ θεοῦ, *in the sight of God* (Hebraistic), whose judgment is true, and which men are bound to follow as the rule of their conduct. — ἀκούειν, *to obey*, see Luke 10, 16; 16, 31; John 8, 47. — μᾶλλον, not *more*, but *rather*; see 5, 29. The question was, whether they should obey men at all in opposition to God, not whether they should obey him more or less. See further, on 5, 29.

V. 20. οὐ δυνάμεθα γὰρ, κ. τ. λ., confirms the answer supposed to be given to their appeal in εἰ δίκαιον, κ. τ. λ. We must obey God; *for we cannot* (morally, i. e. in accordance with truth and duty) *not speak*, i. e. withhold, suppress our message. The double negation states the idea strongly. The impossibility which they felt was that of refraining from giving publicity to their knowledge; it was not sufficient that they taught no error. To be silent would have been treachery. — ἃ εἴδομεν, κ. τ. λ., *which we saw and heard*, i. e. during the life of the Saviour when they beheld his mighty works, and listened to his instructions. The verbs are in the aorist, not perfect (as in E. V.).

V. 21. προσαπειλησάμενοι αὐτούς, *having threatened them further*, i. e. than they had done already, see v. 18. — μηδὲν εὑρίσκοντες, *finding nothing*, no means, opportunity. — τὸ πῶς, *namely, how*, on what pretence; comp. 22, 30; Luke 1, 62; 9, 46, etc. This use of the article before single clauses distinguishes Luke and Paul from the other writers of the New Testament. It serves to awaken attention to the proposition introduced by it. See W. § 20. 3. — διὰ τὸν λαόν belongs to the participle (Mey.), rather than ἀπέλυσαν. The intervening clause breaks off the words from the latter connection. The idea, too, is not, that they were able to invent no charge against the apostles, but none which they felt it safe to adopt, because the people were so well disposed towards the Christians.

V. 22. ἐτῶν, κ. τ. λ., *for he was of more years*, etc. The cure wrought was the greater the longer the time during which the infirmity had existed. ἐτῶν depends on ἦν as a genitive of property. K. § 273. 2. c.; C. § 387. — τεσσαράκοντα, sc. ἐτῶν, *than forty years*, governed by πλειόνων as a comparative; comp. 25, 6. De Wette assumes an ellipsis of ἤ, which puts the numeral in the genitive, because that is the case of the preceding noun. But most grammarians represent ἤ as suppressed only after πλεόν, πλείω, and the like; comp. Matt. 26, 53, as correctly read. K. § 748. R. 1; Mt. § 455. A. 4. — τῆς ἰάσεως, *the healing*, the act of it which constituted the miracle; genitive of apposition. W. § 48. 2.

VERSES 23–31. *The Apostles return to the Disciples, and unite with them in Prayer and Praise.*

V. 23. πρὸς τοὺς ἰδίους, *unto their own friends* in the faith;

comp. 24, 23; Tit. 3, 14. Nothing in the context requires us to limit the term to the apostles. — οἱ ἀρχιερεῖς καὶ οἱ πρεσβύτεροι, *the chief priests* (those of the first class) *and the elders.* This is another mode of designating the Sanhedrim, see v. 5.

V. 24. ὁμοθυμαδόν must denote as elsewhere (1, 14; 2, 46; 7, 57 etc.) a concert of hearts, not of voices. If they all joined aloud in the prayer, the proof must not be drawn from this word or from ἦραν φωνήν, which could be said though but one uttered the words while the others assented, but rather from the nature of the service. The prayer on this occasion was chiefly praise, and as the words quoted were so familiar to all, it is quite possible that they recited them together. See 16, 25, and the remarks there. Baumgarten's view (Apostelgeschichte, u. s. w. p 93) may be near the truth: the whole company sung the second Psalm, and Peter then applied the contents to their situation in the terms recorded here. — δέσποτα is applied to God as absolute in power and authority. It is one of the titles of Christ, also, see 2 Pet. 2, 1; Jude v. 4. — σὺ ὁ θεός, sc. εἶ, *thou art the God;* or, *thou the God,* nominative of address. The latter, says Meyer, accords best with the fervid state of their minds.

V. 25. ὁ διὰ στόματος, κ. τ. λ., viz. in Ps. 2, 1. 2. By citing this passage the disciples express their confidence in the success of the cause for which they were persecuted; for it is the object of the second Psalm to set forth the ultimate and complete triumph of the gospel, notwithstanding the opposition which the wicked may array against it. The contents of the Psalm, as well as the other quotations from it in the New Testament, confirm its Messianic character. See 13, 33; Heb. 1, 5 and 5, 5. — ἵνα τί, *why,* is abbreviated for ἵνα τί γένηται. W. § 25. 1; K. § 344. R. 6. The question challenges a reason for conduct so wicked and futile. It expresses both astonishment and reproof. — ἐφρύαξαν, *raged;* or, which is nearer to the classic sense, *showed themselves restive,* refractory. The aorist may be used here to denote a recurrent fact. K. § 256. 4. b. The active form is used only in the Septuagint (Pape Lex. s. v.). The application to this particular instance does not exhaust the prophecy. The fulfilment runs parallel with the history of the conflicts and triumphs of the cause of truth. — λαοί, *peoples,* masses of men, whether of the same nation, or of different nations. Hence this term includes the Jews, whom ἔθνη would exclude. — κενά, *vain,* abortive; since such must be the result of all opposition to the plans of Jehovah.

V. 26. παρέστησαν, *stood near* with a hostile design; which results, however, from the connection, not the word itself. — συνήχθησαν, *assembled;* in Hebrew, *sat together*, with the involved idea in both cases that it was for the purpose of combination and resistance. — τοῦ Χριστοῦ αὐτοῦ, *his Christ*, his Anointed one, answering to מְשִׁיחוֹ in the Psalm. The act of anointing was performed in connection with the setting apart of a prophet, priest, or king to his office, and, according to the Hebrew symbology, denoted his receiving the spiritual gifts and endowments which he needed for the performance of his duties.[1] Compare the note on 6, 6. The act accompanied consecration to the office assumed, but was not the direct sign of it, as is often loosely asserted. It is with reference to this import of the symbol that the Saviour of men is called ὁ Χριστός, i. e. *the Anointed*, by way of eminence, because he possessed the gifts of the Spirit without measure, was furnished in a perfect manner for the work which he came into the world to execute. See on 1, 2.

V. 27. γάρ illustrates the significance of the prophecy. It had been spoken not without meaning: *for in truth*, etc. — After ἀληθείας we are to read ἐν τῇ πόλει ταύτῃ, *in this city.* The words are left out of the E. V., and I believe of all the earlier translations into English, except the two made from the Vulgate. They are to be retained. They are "found in A B D E, and more than twenty others, supported by the unanimous voice of ancient versions, and many ecclesiastical writers." See Green's Developed Criticism,[2] etc., p. 94. — ἐπὶ τὸν ἅγιον παῖδά σου, *against thy consecrated servant;* see on 3, 13. — ἔχρισας, *didst anoint*, with that rite inaugurate as king. — καὶ λαοῖς Ἰσραήλ, *and peoples of Israel* (see on v. 25), either because the Jews who put the Saviour to death belonged to different tribes, or because so many of them had come to Jerusalem from distant lands (comp. 2, 5), and so represented different nationalities (Mey.). It is not at all probable that the singular and plural are confounded here (Kuin.).

V. 28. ποιῆσαι, *in order to do* in reality, though not with that conscious intention on their part. — ἡ χείρ denotes *the power*, ἡ βουλή *the counsel*, purpose, of God. προώρισε adapts itself *per zeugma* to both nouns. The verbal idea required by the former would be *executed.*

V. 29. κύριε, *Lord*, i. e. God, which is required by θεός in v. 24, and παιδός σου in v. 30; comp. on 1, 24. — ἔπιδε . . . . αὐτῶν, *look*

[1] Bähr's Symbolik des Mosaischen Cultus, Vol. II. p. 171 sq.

[2] A Course of developed Criticism on passages of the New Testament materially affected by various Readings. By Rev. Thomas Sheldon Green, late fellow of Christ's College, Cambridge, etc. (London 1856).

upon their threats, in order to see what grace his servants needed at such a crisis. They pray for courage to enable them to preach the word, not for security against danger. — πάσης, *entire*, the utmost, see 13, 10; 17, 11, etc. In that sense πᾶς does not require the article. W. § 18. 4; K. § 246. 5.

V. 30. ἐν τῷ . . . . ἐκτείνειν σε, *in that thou dost stretch forth thy hand for healing*, the effect of which as a public recognition of their character on the part of God would be to render them fearless; or as some prefer, the construction may denote time, *while thou dost stretch forth*, etc.; so that in the latter case they ask that they may declare the truth with power as well as with courage. — καὶ σημεῖα, κ. τ. λ., *and that signs and wonders may be wrought* (Kuin. Mey. De Wet.). The clause is telic and related to ἐκτείνειν, like εἰς ἴασιν. Some make it depend on δός, which is too remote, and others repeat ἐν τῷ after καί. — παιδός σου, *thy servant.*

V. 31. ἐσαλεύθη ὁ τόπος, *the place was shaken.* They would naturally regard such an event as a token of the acceptance of their prayer, and as a pledge that a power adequate to their protection was engaged for them. — ἐπλήσθησαν, κ. τ. λ., *were all filled with the Holy Spirit*, etc. They were thus endued both with courage to declare the word of God, and with miraculous power for confirming its truth. They had just prayed for assistance in both respects.

VERSES 32–37. *The Believers are of one Mind, and have all Things common.*

V. 32. δέ, slightly *but*, turns our attention from the apostles (v. 31) to the church at large. — τοῦ πλήθους τῶν πιστευσάντων, *the multitude of those who believed*, like τὸ πλῆθος τῶν μαθητῶν in 6, 2. This description of the union of heart and the liberality which distinguished the disciples, applies to all of them, as the unqualified nature of the language clearly intimates. Meyer supposes those only to be meant who are mentioned as new converts in v. 4;[1] but the mind does not recall readily so distant a remark. — οὐδὲ εἷς, *not even one.* — ἔλεγεν ἴδιον εἶναι, *said that it was his own*, i. e. insisted on his right to it so long as others were destitute, see v. 34. — κοινά, *common* in the use of their property, not necessarily in the possession of it. Compare the note on 2, 44 sq. "It is proper to remark," says Bishop Blomfield,[2] "that although an ab-

[1] I am not surprised to find that Meyer has corrected this opinion in his new edition.

[2] Lectures on the Acts of the Apostles, third edition, p. 28.

solute community of goods existed, in a certain sense, amongst the first company of believers, it was not insisted upon by the apostles as a necessary feature in the constitution of the Christian church. We find many precepts in the Epistles, which distinctly recognize the difference of rich and poor, and mark out the respective duties of each class; and the apostle Paul, in particular, far from enforcing a community of goods, enjoins those who were affluent to make a contribution every week for those who were poorer (1 Cor. 16, 2. 3). Yet the *spirit* of this primitive system should pervade the church in all ages. All Christians ought to consider their worldly goods, in a certain sense, as the common property of their brethren. There is a part of it which by the laws of God and nature belongs to their brethren; who, if they cannot implead them for its wrongful detention before an earthly tribunal, have their right and title to it written by the finger of God himself in the records of the gospel, and will see it established at the judgment day."

V. 33. μεγάλῃ δυνάμει, *with great power*, with convincing effect on the minds of men, see Matt. 9, 29; Luke 4, 32. Among the elements of this power we are to reckon, no doubt, the miracles which the disciples performed; but the singular number forbids the supposition that δυνάμει can refer to miracles except in this indirect manner. — χάρις some understand of the *favor* which the Christians enjoyed with the people in consequence of their liberality; see 2, 47 (Grot. Kuin. Olsh.). It is better, with De Wette, Meyer, Alford, and others, to retain the ordinary sense: *divine favor*, grace, of which their liberality was an effect; comp 2 Cor. 9, 14.

V. 34. οὐδὲ γὰρ, κ. τ. λ., *For* (a proof of their reception of such grace) *there was no one needy*, left to suffer *among them*. — χωρίων, *estates*, landed possessions, see 5, 3. 8; Matt. 26, 36; Mark 14, 32. — πωλοῦντες ἔφερον, *sold and brought*. This combination illustrates the occasional use of the present participle as an imperfect. W. § 45. 1. a.; S. § 173. 2.

V. 35. ἐτίθουν .... τῶν ἀποστόλων, *placed them at the feet of the apostles*, see v. 37; 5, 2. The frequency of the act is determined by that of the previous verb. This appears to have been a figurative expression, signifying to commit entirely to their care or disposal. It may have arisen from the Oriental custom of laying gifts or tribute before the footstool of kings. — διεδίδοτο, *distribution was made*. The verb is impersonal. — καθότι .... εἶχεν occurs as in 2, 45.

V. 36. δέ subjoins an example in illustration of what is said in v. 34. 35. — *Barnabas* is the individual of this name who became subsequently so well known as Paul's associate in missionary labors; see 13, 2 sq. The appellation which he received from the apostles describes a particular trait in his style of preaching. Most suppose it to be derived from בַּר נְבוּאָה, (Syro-Chaldaic), i. e. son of prophecy, but in a more restricted sense of the phrase as equivalent to υἱὸς παρακλήσεως, *son of consolation*, since προφητεία includes also hortatory, consolatory discourse; comp. 1 Cor. 14, 3. For other conjectures, see Kuinoel ad loc. —Λευΐτης. He was probably a *Levite*, in distinction from ἱερεύς, *a priest*, i. e. a descendant of Levi but not of the family of Aaron. — Κύπριος τῷ γένει describes him as a Jew born in Cyprus; comp. 18, 2. 24.

V. 37. ὑπάρχοντος αὐτῷ ἀγροῦ, *he having land.* It is not said that this estate was in Cyprus, but that is naturally inferred. The Levites, as a tribe, had no part in the general division of Canaan (see Num. 18, 20); but that exclusion did not destroy the right of individual ownership[1] within the forty-eight cities and the territory adjacent to them, which were assigned to the Levites (Num. 35, 1–8); comp. e. g. Lev. 25, 32; Jer. 32, 8. After the exile they would naturally exercise the same right even out of Palestine. — τὸ χρῆμα, *the money*, which is the proper sense of the plural; comp. 8, 18. 20; 24, 26.

CHAPTER V.

VERSES 1–11. *The Falsehood of Ananias and Sapphira, and their Death.*

V. 1. We enter on a new chapter here in a two-fold sense of the expression. As Olshausen remarks, "the history of the infant church has presented hitherto an image of unsullied light; it is now for the first time that a shadow falls upon it. We can imagine that a sort of holy emulation had sprung up among the first Christians; that they vied with each other in testifying their readiness to part with every thing superfluous in their possession, and to devote it to the wants of the church. This zeal now bore away some, among others, who had not yet been freed in their hearts from the predominant love of earthly things. Such a person was Ananias, who, having sold a portion of his property, kept back a part of the money which he received for it. The root

[1] See Saalschütz, Das Mosaische Recht, Vol. I. p. 149.

of his sin lay in his vanity, his ostentation. He coveted the reputation of appearing to be as disinterested as the others, while at heart he was still the slave of Mammon, and so must seek to gain by hypocrisy what he could not deserve by his benevolence." — δέ puts the conduct of Ananias in contrast with that of Barnabas and the other Christians. — κτῆμα, *a possession* of the nature defined in v. 3.

V. 2. ἐνοσφίσατο ἀπὸ τῆς τιμῆς, *kept back*, reserved for himself, *from the price*. The genitive, which in classical Greek usually follows a partitive verb like this (K. § 271. 2), depends oftener in the New Testament on a preposition. W. § 30. 7. c. — συνειδυίας, *being conscious of it to herself*, aware of the reservation just mentioned (comp. v. 9.); not sc. αὐτῷ, *knowing it as well as he*, since it is the object of καί to hint the collusion of the parties. — μέρος τι, *a certain part*, which he pretended was all he had received.

V. 3. διατί, *why*, demands a reason for his yielding to a temptation which he ought to have repelled. The question recognizes his freedom of action. Compare James 4, 7. The sin is charged upon him as his own act, in the next verse. — ἐπλήρωσεν τὴν καρδίαν σου, *has filled*, possessed, *thy heart;* comp. John 13, 27. — ψεύσασθαι . . . . ἅγιον, *that thou shouldst deceive the Holy Spirit*, i. e. the apostles, to whom God revealed himself by the Spirit. The infinitive is telic (Mey. De Wet.), and the purpose is predicated, not of Ananias, but of the tempter. Satan's object was to instigate to the act, and that he accomplished. Some make the infinitive ecbatic, and as the intention of Ananias was frustrated, must then render *that thou shouldst attempt to deceive*. This is forced and unnecessary. — τοῦ χωρίου, *the estate*, field; see 4, 34.

V. 4. οὐχὶ μένον, sc. κτῆμα, κ. τ. λ., *Did it not, while it remained* unsold, *remain to you* as your own property? *and when sold was it not*, i. e. the money received for it, *in your own power?* This language makes it evident that the community of goods, as it existed in the church at Jerusalem, was purely a voluntary thing, and not required by the apostles. Ananias was not censured because he had not surrendered his entire property, but for falsehood in professing to have done so when he had not. — τί ὅτι stands concisely for τί ἐστιν ὅτι, as in v. 9; Mark 2, 16; Luke 2, 49 (Frtz. Mey. De Wet.). It is a classical idiom, but not common. — ἔθου, κ. τ. λ., *didst thou put in thy heart*, conceive the thing; comp. 19, 21. The expression has a Hebraistic coloring (comp. שִׂים עַל־לֵב in Dan. 1, 8 and Mal. 2, 2), though not unlike the Homeric ἐν φρεσὶ θέσθαι. The aorist (not perf. as in E. V.) represents the wicked thought as consummated. — οὐκ ἐψεύσω . . . . θεῷ is an intensive way of saying that the peculiar enormity of his sin consisted in its being committed against God. David takes the same view of his guilt in Ps. 51, 6. Ananias had attempted to deceive men as well as God; but that aspect of his conduct was so unimportant, in comparison with the other, that it is overlooked, denied. Compare Matt. 10, 20; 1 Thess. 4, 8. See W. § 59. 8. b. It is logically correct to translate οὐκ .... ἀλλά, *not so much .... as*, but is incorrect in form, and less forcible. ἐψεύσω governs the dative here, as in the Septuagint, but never in the classics. W. § 31. 5.

V. 5. ἐξέψυξε, *expired.* — καὶ ἐγένετο, κ. τ. λ., *and great fear came upon all*, etc. Luke repeats this remark in v. 11. It applies here to the first death only, the report of which spread rapidly, and produced everywhere the natural effect of so awful a judgment. Some editors (Lchm. Mey. Tsch.) strike out ταῦτα after ἀκούοντας. It is wanting in A B D, Vulg. et al., and may have been inserted from v. 11. If it be genuine, however, it may refer to a single event, especially when that is viewed in connection with its attendant circumstances. The plural does not show that the writer would include also the death of Sapphira, i. e. that he speaks here proleptically, which is De Wette's view.

V. 6. οἱ νεώτεροι = νεανίσκοι in v. 10. They were probably *the younger men* in the assembly, in distinction from the older (Neand. De Wet. Alf.). It devolved on them naturally to perform this service, both on account of their greater activity and out of respect to their superiors in age. So also Walch decides (Dissertationes, etc. p. 79 sq.). Some have conjectured (Kuin. Olsh. Mey.) that they were a class of regular assistants or officers in the church. That opinion has no support, unless it be favored by this passage. — συνέστειλαν is less certain than has been commonly supposed. The E. V. renders *wound up*, shrouded or covered, which is adopted also by Kuin. De Wet. Alf. and others. Rost and Palm (Lex. s. v.) recognize this as the last of their definitions, but rely for it quite entirely on this passage and Eurip. Troad. 382. Walch (Dissertationes, etc., p. 79 sq.) argues in favor of this signification, and with success, if it be true, according to his assumption that περιστέλλειν and συστέλλειν denote the same thing as used of the rites of burial. The Vulgate has *amoverunt*, which the older E. Vv. appear to have followed: thus, *moved away* (Wicl.); *put apart* (Tynd. Cranm.); *took apart* (Gen.); *removed* (Rhem.). This sense is too remote from any legitimate use of the verb, to be defended. A third explanation which keeps nearer both to the etymology and the ordinary meaning, is *placed together*, laid out or composed his stiffened limbs, so as to enable the bearers to take up and carry the body with more convenience. Meyer insists on this view, and contends that πέπλοις συνεστάλησαν in Eurip., as referred to above, can be translated only *were laid out* (dressed at the same time,) *in robes*. It is certain that no mode of preparing the body, which was formal at all, requiring delay, could have been observed in an emergency like the present. — ἐξενέγκαντες, *having carried forth* out of the house and beyond the city. Except in the case of kings or other distinguished persons, the Jews did not bury within the walls of their towns. See Jahn's Archæol. § 206. This circumstance accounts for the time which elapsed before the return of the bearers. It was customary for the Jews to bury the dead much sooner than is common with us. The reason for this despatch is found partly in the fact that decomposition takes place very rapidly after death in warm climates (comp. John 11, 39), and partly in the peculiar Jewish feeling respecting the defilement incurred by contact with a dead body; see Numb. 19, 11 sq. The interment in the case of Ananias may have been hastened somewhat by the extraordinary occasion of his death; but even under ordinary circumstances, a person among the Jews was commonly buried the same day on which he died. See Win. Realw. Vol. II. p. 16. Even among the present inhabitants of Jerusalem, says Tobler,[1] burial, as a general rule, is not deferred more than three or four hours.

V. 7. ἐγένετο . . . . καί, *Now it came to pass,* — *an interval of about three hours,* — *then*, etc. ὡς . . . . διάστημα is not here the subject of ἐγένετο, but forms a parenthetic clause, and καί (see on 1, 10) introduces the apodosis of the sentence (Frtz. De Wet. Mey.). For the same construction, comp. Matt. 15, 32; Mark 8, 2 (in the correct text); Luke 9, 28. See W. § 62. 2. The minute specification of time here imparts an air of reality to the narrative. — εἰσῆλθεν, *came in*, i. e. to the place of assembly.

V. 8. ἀπεκρίθη αὐτῇ, *addressed her;* Hebraistic after the manner of עָנָה, see on 3, 12. De Wette inclines to the ordinary Greek sense: *answered*, i. e. upon her salutation. — τοσούτου is the genitive of price: *for so much*, and no more, pointing, says Meyer, to the money which lay there within sight. Kuinoel's better view is that Peter named the sum; but, it being unknown to the writer, he substitutes for it an indefinite term, like our "so much," or "so and so." This sense is appropriate to the woman's reply.

[1] Denkblätter aus Jerusalem, von Dr. Titus Tobler, p. 325 (St. Gallen 1853).

V. 9. τί ὅτι, κ. τ. λ., *Why is it that it was agreed*, concerted, *by you?* The dative occurs after the passive, instead of the genitive with ὑπό, when the agent is not only the author of the act, but the person for whose benefit the act is performed. K. § 284. 11. — πειράσαι τὸ πνεῦμα, *to tempt*, put to trial, *the Spirit* as possessed by the apostles, whether he can be deceived or not; see on v. 3. — ἰδοὺ οἱ πόδες, κ. τ. λ., *behold, the feet of those who buried thy husband*. ἰδού directs attention to the sound of their footsteps as they approached the door. What occurred before their entrance occupied but a moment.

V. 10. παραχρῆμα, *immediately* after this declaration of Peter It is evident that the writer viewed the occurrence as supernatural. The second death was not only instantaneous, like the first, but took place precisely as Peter had foretold. The woman lay dead at the apostle's feet, as the men entered who had just borne her husband to the grave.

V. 11. See note on v. 5. — φόβος μέγας, *great fear came*, etc. To produce this impression both in the church and out of it was doubtless one of the objects which the death of Ananias and Sapphira was intended to accomplish. The punishment inflicted on them, while it displayed the just abhorrence with which God looked upon this particular instance of prevarication, was important also as a permanent testimony against similar offences in every age of the church. "Such severity in the beginning of Christianity," says Benson,[1] "was highly proper, in order to prevent any occasion for like punishments for the time to come. Thus Cain, the first murderer, was most signally punished by the immediate hand of God. Thus, upon the erecting of God's temporal kingdom among the Jews, Nadab and Abihu were struck dead for offering strange fire before the Lord. And Korah and his company were swallowed up alive by the earth, for opposing Moses, the faithful servant of God; and the two hundred and fifty men, who offered incense upon that occasion, were consumed by a fire, which came out from the Lord. And, lastly, Uzzah, for touching the ark, fell by as sudden and remarkable a divine judgment, when the kingdom was going to be established in the house of David, to teach Israel a reverence for God and divine things. Nay, in establishing even human laws, a severe punishment upon the first transgressors doth oft prevent the punishment of others, who are deterred from like attempts by the suffering of the first criminals."

[1] History of the First Planting of the Christian Religion, etc., Vol. I. p. 105

VERSES 12-16. *The Apostles still preach, and confirm their Testimony by Miracles.*

V. 12. δέ, *now*, continuative.— πολλά in this position qualifies the two nouns more strongly than when joined with the first of them, as in 2, 43. The first and last places in a Greek sentence may be emphatic. K. § 348. 6. — καὶ ἦσαν, κ. τ. λ., *and they were all with one mind in Solomon's porch*, i. e. from day to day. It was their custom to repair thither and preach to the people whom they found in this place of public resort. ἅπαντες refers to the apostles mentioned in the last clause (Kuin. Olsh. Alf.). Some understand it of all the believers (Bng. De Wet. Mey.); in disregard both of the natural antecedent and of the improbability that so many would assemble at once in such a place. The apostles or individuals of them are meant certainly in v. 42; and from the similarity of that passage to this, we naturally infer that Luke speaks of the same class of persons here as there.

V. 13. τῶν δὲ λοιπῶν, *but of the rest* who did not belong to the party of the apostles, who were not Christains, the same evidently who are called ὁ λαός just below. — οὐδείς, κ. τ. λ., *no one ventured to associate with them* (see 9, 26; 10, 28), viz. the apostles; lit. *join himself to them*. So deeply had the miracles wrought by the apostles impressed the Jewish multitude, that they looked upon those who performed them with a sort of religious awe, and were afraid to mingle freely with them. λοιπῶν, taken as above, need not include any but unbelievers, even if we confine ἅπαντες to the apostles. If we extend ἅπαντες to the disciples generally, the notion that *the others* are believers as well as unbelievers (Alf.), falls away still more decisively. That the apostles should have inspired their fellow Christians with a feeling of dread, disturbs all our conceptions of their relations to each other, as described or intimated elsewhere. — A comma is the proper point after αὐτοῖς. — ἀλλά, *but*, as opposed to what they refrained from doing. — ἐμεγάλυνεν αὐτούς, *magnified them*, regarded them with wonder and extolled them.

V. 14. This verse is essentially parenthetic, but contains a remark which springs from the one just made. One of the ways in which the people testified their regard for the Christians was, that individuals of them were constantly passing over to the side of the latter. — μᾶλλον δέ, *and still more*, comp. 9, 22; Luke 5, 15. — τῷ κυρίῳ, *the Lord*, here Christ, many connect with πιστεύοντες: but a comparison with 11, 24 shows that it depends rather on the verb. — πλήθη, κ. τ. λ., *multitudes both of men and women.* The additions were so great that Luke counts them no longer (see 1, 15; 2, 41 and 4, 4).

V. 15. ὥστε binds this verse to v. 13. We have here an illustration of the extent to which the people carried their confidence in the apostles. — κατὰ τὰς πλατείας, *along the streets.* W. § 49. d. — ἐπὶ κλινῶν καὶ κραββάτων, *upon beds and pallets.* The latter was a cheaper article used by the common people. See Dict. of Antt. art. *Lectus;* and R. and P. Lex. s. σκίμπους. The rich and the poor grasped at the present opportunity to be healed of their diseases. Instead of κλινῶν, many read κλιναρίων, *little beds,* with reference to their portable size. We may adopt that reading, and yet distinguish the terms as before; for these couches need not have been larger than the others in order to be more valuable. — ἐρχομένου Πέτρου, *as Peter was passing.* The genitive does not depend on σκιά, but is absolute. — κἂν = καὶ ἐάν, *at least,* so much as (vel certe); comp. Mark 6, 56; 2 Cor. 11, 16. The separate parts can hardly be traced in this idiom. Some evolve them from an ellipsis: in order that, if Peter came, he might touch some of them, *even if* it were only his shadow (Mey.). See Klotz ad Devar. Vol. II. p. 139 sq.

V. 16. ἀσθενεῖς omits the article here, but has it in v. 15. It is there generic, here partitive: *sick,* sc. persons. K. § 244. 8. ὀχλουμένους, κ. τ. λ., being added to ἀσθενεῖς, distinguishes the possessed or demoniacs from those affected by ordinary maladies; comp. 8, 7. — ἀκαθάρτων, *unclean,* i. e. morally corrupt, utterly wicked, comp. 19, 12.

VERSES 17–25. *Renewed Imprisonment of the Apostles, and their Escape.*

V. 17. *But* (δέ) this success (v. 16) calls forth persecution. — ἀναστάς, *rising up,* not from his seat in the council (for the council is not said to have been in session), but as it were mentally, *becoming excited,* proceeding to act. Kuinoel calls it redundant. See further, on 9, 18. — The ἀρχιερεύς is probably Annas, who was before mentioned under that title. Some suppose Caiaphas, the actual high-priest, to be intended. See on 4, 6. — οἱ σὺν αὐτῷ are not his associates in the Sanhedrim (for they are distinguished from these in v. 21), but, according to the more obvious relation of the words to αἵρεσις τῶν Σαδδουκαίων, *those with him* in sympathy and opinion, i. e. members of the religious sect to which he belonged; comp. 14, 4. Josephus states that most of the higher class in his day were skeptics or Sadducees, though the mass of the people were Pharisees. — ζήλου, *indignation* (13, 45), not *envy;* a Hebraistic sense.

V. 18. ἐπὶ τοὺς ἀποστόλους, *upon the apostles*, viz. Peter (v. 29) and others of them, but probably not the entire twelve. They were lodged *in the public prison*, so as to be kept more securely. It is far-fetched to suppose that δημοσίᾳ was meant to suggest that they were treated as common malefactors.

V. 19. The account of a similar escape is more fully related in 12, 7 sq. — διὰ τῆς νυκτός, *during the night*, and not far from its close, as the two next verses seem to indicate. Fritzsche[1] concedes this sense of διά here, also in 16, 9 and 17, 10, but pronounces it entirely abnormal. Classic usage, it is true, would require *through the night*, its entire extent, and it would then follow strangely enough that the doors of the prison must have stood open for hours, before the apostles went forth from their confinement. Meyer insists on that as the true meaning here. It is more reasonable to ascribe to Luke a degree of inaccuracy in the use of the preposition. See W. § 47. i. An extreme purism in some cases is one of Meyer's faults as a critic. — ἤνοιξε τὰς θύρας, *opened the doors* (see 12, 10), which were then closed again; see v. 23. — ἐξαγαγὼν αὐτούς, *having brought them forth*, while the keepers were at their post (v. 23), but were restrained by a divine power from seeing them (see on 12, 10), or at all events from interposing to arrest them.

V. 20. πορεύεσθε and λαλεῖτε are present because they denote acts already in progress. The prisoners were to proceed on their way to the temple, and to persist there in proclaiming the offensive message. See on 3, 6. — τὰ ῥήματα τῆς ζωῆς ταύτης, *the words of this life*, eternal life which you preach, comp. 13, 26. W. § 34. 2. b. Olshausen refers ταύτης to the angel: *this life* of which I speak to you; Lightfoot to the Sadducees: *this life* which they deny. According to some ταύτης belongs to the entire expression, *these words of life;* agreeing as a Hebraism with the dependent noun, instead of the governing one. See Green's Gr., p. 265. An adjective may be so used, but not the pronoun.

V. 21. ὑπὸ τὸν ὄρθρον, *at early dawn*. The temple had already opened its gates to the worshippers and the traffickers (John 2, 14 sq.) accustomed to resort thither. Hence the apostles could begin their work of instruction, as soon as they arrived. The people of the East commence the day much earlier than is cus-

[1] Fritzschiorum Opuscula Academica, p. 165.

tomary with us. The arrangements of life there adjust themselves to the character of the climate. During a great part of the year in Palestine, the heat becomes oppressive soon after sunrise, and the inhabitants, therefore, assign their most important duties and labors to the early hours of the day. Nothing is more common at the present time than to see the villagers going forth to their employment in the fields, while the night and the day are still struggling with each other. Worship is often performed in the synagogues at Jerusalem before the sun appears above Olivet. — παραγενόμενος, *having come*, i. e. to the place of assembly, which was probably a room in the temple (see 6, 14; Matt. 27, 3 sq.), and whence apparently the chief priest and his coadjutors sent out a summons (συνεκάλεσαν) to their colleagues to hasten together. On some occasions the Sanhedrists met at the house of the high-priest, see Matt. 26, 57. — καὶ πᾶσαν τὴν γερουσίαν, *and all the eldership*, senate connected with the Sanhedrim; comp. 4, 5; 22, 5. The prominence thus given to that branch of the council exalts our idea of its dignity. The term reminds us of men who were venerable for their years and wisdom. Kuinoel would emphasize πᾶσαν, as if the attendance of that order was full at this time, but was not always so. Some (Lightf. Olsh. Str. Mey.) think that this was not an ordinary session of the Sanhedrim, but that the elders of the nation at large were called upon to give their advice in the present emergency.

V. 22. οἱ ὑπηρέται, *the servants* who executed the orders of the Sanhedrim, see v. 26. Some of the temple guard may have acted in this capacity. See on 4, 1.

V. 24. ὁ ἱερεύς, *the priest* by way of eminence (1 Macc. 15. 1; Jos. Antt. 6. 12. 1), hence = ἀρχιερεύς, as the same functionary is termed in v. 17, and 4, 6. — On οἱ ἀρχιερεῖς, see 4, 6. — διηπόρουν περὶ αὐτῶν, *were perplexed concerning them*, i. e. the words reported, not the apostles (Mey. Alf.). λόγους is the more obvious antecedent, and, besides, nothing would embarrass the rulers so much as the circulation of such reports at this precise moment. — τί ἂν γένοιτο τοῦτο, *what this would become*, how it would affect the public mind in regard to the Christians and their doctrine. τοῦτο refers to the miraculous liberation, and confirms what was said of αὐτῶν.

VERSES 26–28. *They are arrested again and brought before the Council.*

V. 26. For στρατηγός, see on 4, 1. — ἵνα μὴ λιθασθῶσιν we are to connect probably with οὐ μετὰ βίας: *They brought them without vio-*

lence that they might not be stoned. ἐφοβοῦντο γὰρ τὸν λαόν, *for they feared the people*, forms a parenthetic remark, the logical force of which is the same as if it had stood at the close of the sentence. The E. versions generally (also Mey.) attach the last clause to ἐφοβοῦντο instead of ἤγαγεν, but the proper connectives after verbs of fearing are μή, μήπως, and the like, and not ἵνα μή. See W. § 56. 2. R. Tischendorf puts a comma after βίας, instead of a colon, as in some editions.

V. 28. παραγγελίᾳ παρηγγείλαμεν. See the note on 4, 17. — ἐπὶ τῷ ὀνόματι τούτῳ, *upon* (as their authority, see 4, 18) *this name*, which they left unspoken as well known, or perhaps disdained to mention. — ἐπαγαγεῖν . . . . αἷμα, i. e. fix upon us the guilt of having shed his blood as that of an innocent person; comp. Matt. 23, 35. — τοῦ ἀνθρώπου τούτου, *this man*, is not of itself contemptuous (comp. Luke 23, 47; John 7, 46), but could have that turn given to it by the voice, and was so uttered probably at this time.

VERSES 29–32. *The Answer of Peter, and its Effect.*

V. 29. καὶ οἱ ἀπόστολοι, *and the* other *apostles.* Peter spoke in their name, see 2, 14. — πειθαρχεῖν . . . . ἀνθρώποις. The Jews, though as a conquered nation they were subject to the Romans, acknowledged the members of the Sanhedrim as their legitimate rulers; and the injunction which the Sanhedrim imposed on the apostles at this time emanated from the highest human authority to which they could have felt that they owed allegiance. The injunction which this authority laid on the apostles clashed with their religious convictions, their sense of the rights of the infinite Ruler, and in this conflict between human law and divine, they declared that the obligation to obey God was paramount to every other. The apostles and early Christians acted on the principle, that human governments forfeit their claim to obedience when they require what God has plainly forbidden, or forbid what he has required. They claimed the right of judging for themselves what was right and what was wrong, in reference to their religious and their political duties, and they regulated their conduct by that decision. It is worthy of notice that, in 4, 19, they propound this principle as one which even their persecutors could not controvert, i. e. as one which commends itself to every man's reason and unperverted moral feelings.[1] In applying this princi-

[1] Socrates avowed this principle, when in his defence he said to his judges πείσομαι δὲ μᾶλλον τῷ θεῷ ἢ ὑμῖν (Plat. Apol. 29 D): and unless the plea be valid, he died as a felon and not as a martyr. See other heathen testimonies to the same effect in Wetstein's Novum Testamentum, Vol. II. p. 478.

ple, it will be found that the apostles in every instance abstained from all forcible resistance to the public authorities. They refused utterly to obey the mandates which required them to violate their consciences, but they endured quietly the penalties which the executors of the law enforced against them. They evaded the pursuit of their oppressors if they could (2 Cor. 11, 32. 33), secreted themselves from arrest (12, 19), left their prisons at the command of God, yet when violent hands were laid upon them, and they were dragged before magistrates, to the dungeon, or to death, they resisted not the wrong, but "followed his steps, who, when he suffered, threatened not, but committed himself to Him that judgeth righteously" (1 Pet. 2, 22. 23).

V. 30. τῶν πατέρων recalls to mind the series of promises which God had made to provide a Saviour, comp. 3, 25. — ἤγειρεν, *raised up*, sent into the world; comp. 3, 22; 13, 23. So Calvin, Bengel, De Wette, and others. Some supply ἐκ νεκρῶν, *raised up from the dead;* but that idea being involved in ὕψωσε below, would introduce a repetition at variance with the brevity of the discourse.— ὃν ὑμεῖς, κ. τ. λ., *whom ye slew* (26, 21) *by hanging;* not *slew and hung* (E. V.).— ξύλου = σταυροῦ, a Hebraism. It occurs especially where the Jews are spoken of as having crucified the Saviour (10, 39; 13, 29).

V. 31. ἀρχηγὸν καὶ σωτῆρα belong as predicates to τοῦτον: *this one* (as, who is) *a prince and a Saviour;* not to the verb: *exalted to be a prince*, etc., (E. V.). — τῇ δεξιᾷ αὐτοῦ, *to his right hand;* see note on 2, 33. — δοῦναι μετάνοιαν, *to give repentance*, i. e. the grace or disposition to exercise it; comp. 3, 16; 18, 27; John 16, 7. 8. Some understand it of the opportunity to repent, or the provision of mercy which renders repentance available to the sinner (De Wet.). The expression is too concise to convey naturally that idea, and τόπον μετανοίας is employed for that purpose in Heb. 12, 17. In both cases the exaltation of Christ is represented as securing the result in question, because it was the consummation of his work, and gave effect to all that preceded.

V. 32. μάρτυρες governs here two genitives, one of a person, the other of a thing; see Phil. 2, 30; Heb. 13, 7. W. § 30. 3. R. 3; K. § 275. R. 6. Since their testimony was true, they must declare it; no human authority could deter them from it, comp. 4, 20. — καὶ .... ἅγιον, *and the Holy Spirit* (δέ) *too* (sc. αὐτοῦ μάρτυρ) is his witness. — τοῖς πειθαρχοῦσιν αὐτῷ, *to those who obey him*, i. e. by receiving the gospel, comp. 6, 7. Many suppose the apostle to refer chiefly to the special gifts which the Spirit conferred on so many of the first Christians, in order to confirm their faith as the truth of God. What took place on the day of Pentecost was a testimony of this nature, and that or some equivalent sign was repeated on other occasions; comp. 10, 45; 19, 6; Mark 16, 20. But to that outward demonstration we may add also the inward witness of the Spirit, which believers receive as the evidence of their adoption; comp. Rom. 8, 16; Gal. 4, 6; 1 John 3, 24. Neander interprets the language entirely of this internal manifestation. Since the Holy Spirit testified to the gospel in both ways, and since the remark here is unqualified, we have no reason to consider the expression less extensive than the facts in the case.

V. 33. διεπρίοντο, *were convulsed with rage,* lit. *were sawn asunder,* torn in pieces. The E. V. supplies "to the heart," after the verb (see 7, 54), but the Greek text has no such reading. Some render *sawed their teeth,* gnashed them; which would require τοὺς ὀδόντας as the expressed object of the verb.—ἐβουλεύοντο, *resolved,* determined, see 27, 39, and John 12, 10; but on the representation of Gamaliel they recalled their purpose. The issue was averted, and hence the tense is imperfect. Instead of passing a formal vote, it is more probable that they declared their intention by some tumultuous expression of their feelings. The verb may denote the act as well as the result of deliberation, *took counsel,* consulted; but men exasperated as they were would not be likely to pay much regard to parliamentary decorum.

VERSES 34–39. *The Advice of Gamaliel.*

V. 34. τίμιος governs λαῷ as allied to words denoting judgment, estimation. See W. § 31. 6. b.; Mt. § 388. The character which Luke ascribes to *Gamaliel* in this passage agrees with that which he bears in the Talmud. He appears there, also, as a zealous Pharisee, as unrivalled in that age for his knowledge of the law, as a distinguished teacher (see 22, 3), and as possessing an enlarged, tolerant spirit, far above the mass of his countrymen. He is said to have lived still some fifteen years or more after this scene in the council. See Hertz. Encyk. Vol. IV. p. 656.[1]—βραχύ refers evidently to time (in Wicl., *for a while*), not to space (E. V.).

V. 35. εἶπε. What follows is probably an outline of the speech.—ἐπὶ τοῖς ἀνθρώποις τούτοις some join with προσέχετε, *take heed unto yourselves in respect to these men* (E. V.); others

[1] Hertzog's Real-Encycklopädie für die protestantische Theologie und Kirche.

with τί μέλλετε πράσσειν, *what ye are about to do in respect to these men* (Kuin. De Wet. Mey.). Both constructions are admissible (W. § 55. 4), but as πράσσειν τι ἐπί τινι is not uncommon in Greek (see examples in Wetst. N. T.), it is better to recognize an instance of that expression here.

V. 36. πρὸ τούτων τῶν ἡμερῶν, *Before these times.* This is not the first time that zealots or seditionists have appeared; they may have come forth with great pretensions, but ere long have closed their career with defeat and ignominy. For the sake of effect (observe γάρ), Gamaliel puts the case as if the prisoners would turn out to be persons of this stamp; but before closing he is careful to remind his associates that there was another possibility; see v. 39. — Θευδᾶς. Josephus mentions an insurrectionist, named *Theudas*, who appeared in the reign of Claudius, some ten years after the delivery of this speech. Gamaliel, therefore, must refer here to another man of this name; and this man, since he preceded Judas the Galilean (v. 37), could not have lived much later than the reign of Herod the Great. The year of that monarch's death, as Josephus states, was remarkably turbulent; the land was overrun with belligerent parties, under the direction of insurrectionary chiefs, or fanatics. Josephus mentions but three of these disturbers by name; he passes over the others with a general allusion. Among those whom the Jewish historian has omitted to name, may have been the Theudas whom Gamaliel has here in view. The name was not an uncommon one (Win. Realw. Vol. II. p. 609); and it can excite no surprise that one Theudas, who was an insurgent, should have appeared in the time of Augustus, and another, fifty years later, in the time of Claudius. Josephus gives an account of four men named Simon, who followed each other within forty years, and of three named Judas, within ten years, who were all instigators of rebellion. This mode of reconciling Luke with Josephus is approved by Lardner, Bengel, Kuinoel, Olshausen, Anger, Winer, and others.[1] Another very plausible supposition is, that Luke's Theudas may have been identical with one of the three insurgents whom Josephus designates by name. Sonntag, who agrees with those who adopt this view, has supported it with much learning and ability.[2] He maintains that the Theudas

[1] Jost, the Jewish historian (Geschichte der Israeliten, Band II. Anh. p. 76) assents to this explanation, and admits the credibility of Luke as well as of Josephus.

[2] In the Theologische Studien und Kritiken, 1837, p. 622 sq., translated by the writer in the Bibliotheca Sacra, 1848, p. 409 sq.

mentioned by Gamaliel is the individual who occurs in Josephus under the name of Simon, a slave of Herod, who attempted to make himself king, in the year of that monarch's death. He urges the following reasons for that opinion: first, this Simon, as he was the most noted among those who disturbed the public peace at that time, would be apt to occur to Gamaliel as an illustration of his point; secondly, he is described as a man of the same lofty pretensions (*εἶναι ἄξιος ἐλπίσας παρ' ὀντινοῦν* = *λέγων εἶναί τινα ἑαυτόν*); thirdly, he died a violent death, which Josephus does not mention as true of the other two insurgents; fourthly, he appears to have had comparatively few adherents, in conformity with Luke's *ὡσεὶ τετρακοσίων*; and, lastly, his having been originally a slave accounts for the twofold appellation, since it was very common among the Jews to assume a different name on changing their occupation or mode of life. It is very possible, therefore, that Gamaliel speaks of him as Theudas, because, having borne that name so long at Jerusalem, he was best known by it to the members of the Sandedrim; and that Josephus, on the contrary, who wrote for Romans and Greeks, speaks of him as Simon, because it was under that name that he set himself up as king, and in that way acquired his foreign notoriety. (Tacit. Hist. 5. 9.) — There can be no valid objection to either of the foregoing suppositions; both are reasonable, and both must be disproved before Luke can be justly charged with having committed an anachronism in this passage. — *εἶναί τινα*, *was some one* of importance. *τὶς* has often that emphatic force. W. § 25. 2. c.

V. 37. Ἰούδας ὁ Γαλιλαῖος, κ. τ. λ. Josephus mentions this *Judas the Galilean*, and his account of him either confirms or leaves undenied every one of the particulars stated or intimated by Luke. See Bell. Jud. 2. 8. 1; Antt. 18. 1. 6; 20. 5. 2. He calls him twice ὁ Γαλιλαῖος, though he terms him also ὁ Γαυλονίτης in Antt. 18. 1. 1., from the fact that he was born at Gamala, in lower Gaulonitis. He was known as the Galilean, because he lived subsequently in Galilee (De Wet.), or because that province may have included Gaulonitis. The epithet served to distinguish him from another Judas, a revolutionist who appeared some ten years earlier than this. — *ἐν ταῖς ἡμέραις τῆς ἀπογραφῆς*, *in the days of the registration*, i. e. in this instance, of persons and property, with a view to taxation (Jos. Antt. 15. 1. 1). The *ἀπογραφή* in Luke 2, 2, which is so carefully distinguished from this tumult and which took place at the birth of Christ, is supposed generally to have been a census merely of the population. We learn from Josephus, that soon after the dethronement of

Archelaus, about the year A. D. 6 or 7, the Emperor Augustus ordered a tax to be levied on the Jews. The payment of that tax Judas instigated the people to resist, on the ground of its being a violation of their allegiance to Jehovah to pay tribute to a foreign power; comp. Matt. 22, 17. He took up arms in defence of this principle, and organized a powerful opposition to the Roman government. — κἀκεῖνος, κ. τ. λ. Josephus relates that this rebellion was effectually suppressed, and that many of those who had taken part in it were captured and crucified by the Romans. He says nothing of the fate of Judas himself. διεσκορπίσθησαν, *were dispersed,* describes very justly such a result of the enterprise. Coponius was then procurator of Judea, and Quirinus, or Cyrenius (Luke 2, 2), was proconsul of Syria.

V. 38. καὶ τὰ νῦν, *and now,* in the light of such examples. — ἐάσατε αὐτούς, *let them alone;* not sc. ἀπελθεῖν, *suffer them to depart.* — ἐξ ἀνθρώπων, *from men* in distinction from God (v. 39), comp Matt. 21, 25. — ἡ βουλὴ .... τοῦτο, *this plan,* enterprise, *or* (more correctly) *work,* since it was already in progress. — καταλυθήσεται, *will be frustrated,* i. e. without any interference on your part.

V. 39. In εἰ .... ἐστίν (comp. ἐὰν ᾖ just before), the speaker reveals his sympathy with the prisoners. See on 4, 9. Without declaring the truth to be on their side, he at least argues the question from that point of view. — μήποτε .... εὑρεθῆτε. Critics differ as to the dependence of this clause. Some supply before it ὁρᾶτε or an equivalent word (see Luke 21, 34): *Take heed lest ye be found* (in the end) *also fighting against God,* as well as men (Grot. Kuin. Rob.). Others find the ellipsis in οὐ δύνασθε καταλῦσαι αὐτούς, thus: *Ye cannot destroy them* (more correct than αὐτό) and therefore, I say, should not attempt it, *lest ye also,* etc., (Bng. Mey.). καί, in both cases, includes naturally the idea both of the impiety and the futility of the attempt. De Wette assents to those who connect the words with ἐάσατε αὐτούς, in the last verse. This is the simplest construction, as μήποτε follows appropriately after such a verb, and the sense is then complete without supplying anything. In this case some editors would put what intervenes in brackets; but that is incorrect, inasmuch as the caution here presupposes the alternative in εἰ δὲ ἐκ θεοῦ ἐστιν. — The advice of Gamaliel was certainly remarkable, and some of the early Christian fathers went so far as to ascribe it to an unavowed attachment to the gospel. The supposition has no historical support; and there are other motives which explain his conduct. Gamaliel, as Neander remarks, was a man who had discernment enough to see that, if this were a fanatical movement, it would be rendered more violent by opposition; that all attempts to suppress what is insignificant tend only to raise it into more importance. On the other hand, the manner in which the apostles spoke and acted may have produced some impression upon a mind not entirely prejudiced, and so much the more, since their strict observance of the law, and their hostile attitude towards Sadduceeism, must have rendered him favorably disposed towards them. Hence the thought may have arisen in his mind that, possibly, after all, there might be something divine in their cause.

VERSES 40-42. *The Apostles suffer joyfully for Christ, and depart to preach him anew.*

V. 40. ἐπείσθησαν αὐτῷ, *were persuaded by him*, i. e. to spare the lives of the apostles, whom they had (see v. 33) resolved to put to death. They could not object to the views of Gamaliel, they were so reasonable; they were probably influenced still more by his personal authority. Still their rage demanded some satisfaction; they must punish the heretics, if they could not slay them. — δείραντες, *having scourged.* The instrument frequently used for this purpose was a whip, or scourge, consisting often of two lashes "knotted with bones, or heavy indented circles of bronze, or terminated by hooks, in which case it was aptly denominated a *scorpion.*" Dict. of Antt., art. *Flagrum.* The punishment was inflicted on the naked back of the sufferer; comp. 16, 22. A single blow would sometimes lay the flesh open to the bones. Hence, to scourge a person (δείρω) meant properly to excoriate, flay him. Paul says that he suffered this punishment five times (2 Cor. 14, 24.). It is affecting to remember that the Saviour was subjected to this laceration.

V. 41. οἱ μέν. The antithesis does not follow. — οὖν, illative, i. e. in consequence of their release. — ὅτι, *because*, appends an explanation of χαίροντες, *rejoicing*, not of the verb. — ὑπὲρ τοῦ ὀνόματος, *in behalf of the name*, i. e. of Jesus, which is omitted, either because it has occurred just before, or more properly because "the name" was a familiar expression among the disciples, and as such required no addition (comp. 3 John v. 7). It is a loss to our religious dialect that the term in this primitive sense has fallen into disuse. The common text, indeed, reads αὐτοῦ after ὀνόματος, but without sufficient authority. — κατηξιώθησαν ἀτιμασθῆναι, — a bold oxymoron, — *were accounted worthy to be disgraced.* For an explanation of the paradox, see Luke 16, 15. The verbs refer to different standards of judgment.

V. 42. κατ' οἶκον, *from house to house*, or *at home*, refers to their

15

private assemblies in different parts of the city as distinguished from their labors *in the temple.* Those who reject the distributive sense in 2, 46, reject it also here. — οὐκ ἐπαύοντο διδάσκοντες, *ceased not to teach,* in defiance of the prohibition which blows as well as words had just now enforced on them (v. 40). The Greek in such a case employs a participle, not the infinitive, as the complement of the verb. K. § 310. 4. f.; W. § 45. 4. — εὐαγγελιζόμενοι, κ. τ. λ., *announcing the glad tidings of the Christ* (first as emphatic) *Jesus;* the latter the subject here, the former the predicate (comp. 9, 20. 22). This clause defines the preceding one.

CHAPTER VI.

VERSES 1–7. *Appointment of Alms-Distributers in the Church at Jerusalem.*

V. 1. ἐν ταῖς ἡμέραις ταύταις, *in these days.* See on 1, 15. We may assign the events in this chapter to the year A. D. 35. They relate more or less directly to the history of Stephen, and must have taken place shortly before his death, which was just before Paul's conversion. — πληθυνόντων, *becoming numerous.* — τῶν Ἑλληνιστῶν should be rendered, not Greeks = Ἕλληνες, but *Hellenists.* They were the Jewish members of the church who spoke the Greek language. The other party, the *Hebrews,* were the Palestine Jews, who spoke the Syro-Chaldaic, or Aramæan. See Win. Chald. Gr. p. 10 sq. — παρεθεωροῦντο, *were overlooked,* is imperfect, because the neglect is charged as one that was common. — διακονίᾳ, *ministration,* distribution of alms, i. e. either of food or the money necessary to procure it. Olshausen argues for the former from τῇ καθημερινῇ.

V. 2. οἱ δώδεκα, *the twelve.* Matthias must have been one of them, and the validity of his choice as an apostle is placed here, beyond doubt. See on 1, 26. — τὸ πλῆθος τῶν μαθητῶν, *the multitude,* mass, *of the disciples.* It has been objected, that they had become too numerous at this time to assemble in one place. It is to be recollected, as De Wette suggests, that many of those who had been converted were foreign Jews, and had left the city ere this.— ἡμᾶς καταλείψαντας, κ. τ. λ., *that we, forsaking the word of God,* etc. It is not certain, from the narrative, to what extent this labor of providing for the poor had been performed by the apostles. The following remarks of Röthe present a reasonable view of that question. "The apostles, at first, appear to have applied themselves to this business; and to have expended personally the common funds of the church. Yet, occupied as they were with so many other more important objects, they could have exercised only a general oversight in the case, and must have committed the details of the matter to others. Particular individuals may not have been appointed for this purpose at the beginning; and the business may have been conducted in an informal manner, without any strict supervision or immediate direction on the part of the apostles. Under such circumstances, especially as the number of believers was increasing every day, it could easily happen that some of the needy were overlooked; and it is not surprising that the Hellenistic Christians had occasion to complain of the neglect of the widows and other poor among them."[1] The complaint, therefore, implied no censure of the apostles, but was brought naturally to them, both on account of their position in the church, and the general relation sustained by them to the system under which the grievance had arisen.— διακονεῖν τραπέζαις, *to serve tables,* provide for them, comp. Luke 4, 39; 8, 3. Some render the noun *money-tables,* counters, as in John 2, 15; but the verb connected with it here forbids that sense. The noun is plural, because several tables were supported. "Locutio indignitatem aliquam exprimit; antitheton *ministerium verbi*" (Bng.).

V. 3. ἐπισκέψασθε, κ. τ. λ., *look ye out,* etc. The selection, therefore, was made by the body of the church; the apostles confirmed the choice, as we see from καταστήσομεν, *we will appoint,* and from the consecration in v. 6. καταστήσωμεν (T. R.), *we may appoint* (E. V.), is a spurious form. — μαρτυρουμένους, *testified to,* of good repute, see 10, 22 and 16, 2. — χρείας, *business,* lit. an affair which is held to be necessary.

V. 4. τῇ προσευχῇ, *the* (service of) *prayer.* The article points out the importance of the duty (1, 14). Prayer, evidently in this connection for the success of the word, is recognized as their legitimate work, as much as preaching. — προσκαρτερήσομεν, *we will give ourselves.* This remark does not imply that they had been diverted already from their proper work, but that they wished to guard against that in future, by committing this care to others. They now saw that it required more attention than they had bestowed upon it.

[1] Die Anfänge der Christlichen Kirche und ihrer Verfassung, p. 164.

V. 5. ἄνδρα, κ. τ. λ., *a man full of faith and of the Holy Spirit.* We may retain ἁγίου, but the word is uncertain. The same terms describe the character of Barnabas in 11, 24. — Of *Philip*, we read again in 8, 8 sq.; 21, 8. The others are not known out of this passage. That Nicolaus was the founder of the sect mentioned in Rev. 2, 6, is a conjecture without proof. Many have supposed that the entire seven were chosen from the aggrieved party. Gieseler thinks that three of them may have been Hebrews, three Hellenists, and one a proselyte. Ch. Hist. § 25. Their Greek names decide nothing; see on 1, 23. The distributers would be taken naturally from both sides, but in what proportion we cannot tell. It would depend on their personal traits, after all, more than on their nationality, whether they were able to satisfy the disaffected. — Luke does not term the men διάκονοι, though we have an approach to that appellation in v. 2. In 21, 8, they are called *the Seven.* Some of the ancient writers regarded them as the first deacons; others, as entirely distinct from them. The general opinion at present is, that this order arose from the institution of the Seven, but by a gradual extension of the sphere of duty at first assigned to them.

V. 6. ἐπέθηκαν, viz. the apostles. The nature of the act dictates this change of the subject. The imposition of hands, as practised in appointing persons to an office, was a symbol of the impartation of the gifts and graces which they needed to qualify them for the office. It was of the nature of a prayer that God would bestow the necessary gifts, rather than a pledge that they were actually conferred.

V. 7. The prosperity related here is a proof that harmony had been restored, and that the prayers and labors of the apostles had suffered no interruption. — ὁ λόγος, κ. τ. λ., *the word of God grew*, spread and strengthened itself as a system of belief or doctrine. The next clause repeats the idea concretely by stating how rapidly the recipients of this faith were multiplied. See note on 12, 24.— πολύς τε, κ. τ. λ., *and a great multitude of priests.* According to Ez. 2, 36–38, the priests amounted to 4,289 at the time of the return from Babylon. They must have been still more numerous at this period. Such an accession of such converts was a signal event in the early history of the church. — τῇ πίστει, *the faith*, faith-system, i. e. the gospel; comp. Rom. 1, 5; Gal. 1, 23, etc. This mode of epitomizing the plan of salvation confirms the Protestant view of it, in opposition to that of the Catholics. See Rom. 11, 6.

VERSES 8–15. *The Zeal of Stephen and his Violent Apprehension.*

V. 8. πλήρης χάριτος, *full of grace*, i. e. by metonymy, of gifts not inherent, but conferred by divine favor, see v. 3. This is the correct word rather than πίστεως, which some copies insert from v. 5. — δυνάμεως, *power*, efficiency (1, 8) which was one of the gifts, and as indicated by the next words, included an ability to work miracles. — ἐποίει (imperf.) shows that he repeated the miracles.

V. 9. τινες . . . . Λιβερτίνων, *certain from the synagogue so called of the Libertines*, i. e. *libertini, freed-men*, viz. Jews, or the sons of Jews, who having been slaves at Rome, had acquired their freedom, and, living now at Jerusalem, maintained a separate synagogue of their own. When Pompey overran Judea, about B. C. 63, he carried a vast number of the Jews to Rome, where they were sold into slavery. Most of these, or their children, the Romans afterwards liberated, as they found it inconvenient to have servants who were so tenacious of the peculiar rites of their religion. The Jews usually named their synagogues from the countries whence those who attended them had come, and hence Luke inserts here τῆς λεγομένης, *the so called*, in order to reconcile the ear as it were to this almost unheard of designation. Some contend that Λιβερτίνων is also a patrial name, *Libertinians*, i. e. Jews from a place named Libertum. Not only has the participle no apparent force in this case, but the existence of such a town is altogether uncertain. — καὶ Κυρηναίων, κ. τ. λ. The construction here is doubtful. The simplest view is that which repeats τινὲς before each of the genitives with the implication that the Cyreneans, Alexandrians, Cilicians and Asiatics formed so many distinct synagogues, i e. including the *Libertines*, five different assemblies in all (De Wet. Mey.). The Rabbinic writers say, with some exaggeration, no doubt, that Jerusalem contained four hundred and eighty synagogues. τῶν would be proper before Κυρηναίων and Ἀλεξανδρέων, but as they refer to towns well known, could be omitted as before Αἰγυπτίων in 7, 22 and Θεσσαλονικέων in 20, 4. — τῶν ἀπὸ Κιλικίας may be simply = Κίλικες, and the article does not arise, necessarily, out of a different relation to τινὲς. Some repeat ἐκ τῆς συναγωγῆς as well as τινὲς before the successive genitives with the same result, of course, as to the number of synagogues. It is awkward to supply so many words, and also to shut up τῆς λεγομένης to the first clause, as we must in that case, since it is so plainly inappropriate to the other names. According to others we are to connect Κυρηναίων καὶ Ἀλεξανδρέων with Λιβερτίνων, understanding these three classes to constitute one synagogue, and the Cilicians and Asiatics to constitute another. See W. § 19. 5, marg. It may be objected to this, (though no interpretation is wholly unencumbered) that it unites λεγομένης too closely (for the reason given above) with the second and third noun, and also that so large a number of foreign Jews as the populous cities referred to would be likely to send to Jerusalem, could not meet conveniently in a single place of worship. Wieseler, (Chronologie, p. 63) in support of his opinion that Paul acquired his Roman citizenship (22, 28) as *libertinus* or the descendant of a *libertinus*, would take καί before Κυρηναίων as explicative, *namely, to wit;* so that they were all *libertini*, and belonged to one synagogue. This is extremely forced and arbitrary. — Among the *Cilicians* who disputed with Stephen may have been Saul of Tarsus, see 7, 58. For the extent of *Asia*, see on 2, 9.

V. 10. τῷ πνεύματι, *the Spirit*, see v. 5. — In ᾧ ἐλάλει, *with which he spake*, the relative belongs in sense to both nouns, but agrees with the nearest; comp. Luke 21, 15. Stephen experienced the truth of the promise recorded in that passage.

V. 11. ὑπέβαλον, *secretly instructed*, suborned. It was concerted between them what should be said, and to what point it should be directed. — βλάσφημα, *blasphemous* in the judicial sense, which made it a capital offence to utter such words. Contempt of Moses and his institutions was contempt of Jehovah, and came within the scope of the law against blasphemy as laid down in Deut. 13, 6–10. It was on this charge that the Jews pronounced the Saviour worthy of death; see Matt. 26, 60 sq.

V. 12. τοὺς πρεσβυτέρους καὶ τοὺς γραμματεῖς, *the elders and the scribes*, i. e. those of these classes who belonged to the Sanhedrim. The appeal was made more especially to them, because, in addition to their influence, they were mostly Pharisees, and the present accusation was of a nature to arouse especially the spirit of that sect. Hence they take the lead at this time, rather than the Sadducees. — συνήρπασαν. The subject here is strictly τινές (see v. 9), but we think of them naturally as acting in concert with those whom they had instigated to join with them.

V. 13. ἔστησαν, *placed* before them, introduced (see 4, 7); others, *set up*, procured. — μάρτυρας ψευδεῖς, *false witnesses.* They accused Stephen of having spoken contemptuously of the law and the temple, and of having blasphemed Moses and God. Their testimony in that form was grossly false. It was opposed to every thing which Stephen had said or meant. Yet, as Neander and others suggest, he had undoubtedly taught that the

Christian dispensation was superior to that of Moses; that the gospel was designed to supersede Judaism; that the law was unavailing as a source of justification; that, henceforth, true worship would be as acceptable to God in one place as another. In the clearness with which Stephen apprehended these ideas, he has been justly called the forerunner of Paul. His accusers distorted his language on these points, and thus gave to their charge the only semblance of justification which it possessed. — For ἄνθρωπος οὗτος, see 5, 28. — οὐ παύεται, *does not cease*, betrays the exaggerating tone of a "swift witness." — τοῦ τόπου τοῦ ἁγίου, *the holy place*, is the temple (21, 28; Ps. 24, 3, etc.), in some part of which they were assembled, as appears from τοῦτον in the next verse.

V. 14. λέγοντος, κ.τ.λ. They impute to Stephen these words, as authorizing the inference in v. 13. — οὗτος, *this one*, repeats Ἰησοῦς, with a tone of contempt. — καταλύσει, *will destroy*, etc. It is not impossible that he had reminded them of the predictions of Christ respecting the destruction of the city and the temple. — τοπόν τοῦτον, *this place*, because the present session was held in some room or court of the temple. — ἔθη, *customs* required to be observed, hence laws, as in 15, 1; 21, 21, etc. — παρέδωκεν may apply to what is written as well as what is oral (R. and P. Lex. s. v.).

V. 15. ἀτενίσαντες εἰς αὐτόν, κ. τ. λ. They were *all gazing upon him*, as the principal object of interest in the assembly, and so much the more at that moment in expectation of his reply to so heinous a charge. The radiance, therefore, which suddenly lighted up the countenance of Stephen, was remarked by every one present. That what they saw was merely a natural expression of the serenity which pervaded his mind, can hardly be supposed. ὡσεὶ πρόσωπον ἀγγέλλου, *as if the face of an angel*, seems to overstate the idea, if it be reduced to that; for the comparison is an unusual one, and the Jews supposed the visible appearance of angels to correspond with their superhuman rank; comp. 1, 10; Matt. 28, 3; Luke 24, 4; Rev. 18, 1, etc. The countenance of Stephen, like that of Moses on his descent from the mount, shone probably with a preternatural lustre, proclaiming him a true witness, a servant of Him whose glory was so fitly symbolized by such a token. The occasion was worthy of the miracle.

CHAPTER VII.

Discourse of Stephen before the Sanhedrim.

The speaker's main object may be considered as twofold; — first, to show that the charge against him rested on a false view of the ancient dispensation, — not on his part, but on that of his accusers; and, secondly, that the Jews, instead of manifesting a true zeal for the temple and the law in their opposition to the gospel, were again acting out the unbelieving, rebellious spirit which led their fathers so often to resist the will of God, and reject his greatest favors. It appears to me that the latter was the uppermost idea in Stephen's mind, both because it occupies so much space in the body of the address (v. 27. 39–44), and because, near the close of what is said (v. 51 sq.), it is put forward very much as if he regarded it as the conclusion at which he had been aiming. It may be objected, that this view renders the discourse aggressive, criminatory, in an unusual degree; but we are to remember that Stephen (see on v. 54), was interrupted, and but for that, in all probabilty, after having exposed the guilt of his hearers, he would have encouraged them to repent and believe on the Saviour whom they had crucified. (Bmg. has a remark to the same effect.) Yet both parts of the speech, as so understood, converge to one point, viz., that the speaker was not guilty of maligning the ancient economy; first, because even under that dispensation the divine favor was bestowed independently of the law; and, secondly, because the teachers of that economy held up the same view of its spiritual nature, and encountered a similar opposition.

In the interpretation of the speech, I proceed on the principle that most of Stephen's hearers were so well acquainted with his peculiar views, with his arguments in support of them, and his mode of illustration, that they had no occasion to be distinctly reminded of his doctrine at this time. See the Note on 6, 13. Hence Stephen could assume that the bearing of the different remarks or occurrences brought forward in the address would suggest itself to the minds of his judges; without pausing to tell them *this* means that, or *that* means this, he could leave them to draw silently the conclusions which he wished to establish. Stephen illustrates his subject historically. That mode of argument was well chosen. It enabled him to show the Jews that their own history, in which they gloried so much, condemned them; for it taught the inefficacy of external rites, foreshadowed a more perfect spiritual system, and warned them against the example of those who resist the will of God when declared to them by his messengers. Stephen pursues the order of time in his narrative; and it is important to remark that feature of the discourse, because it explains two peculiarities in it; first, that the ideas which fall logically under the two heads that have been mentioned are intermixed, instead of being presented separately; and, secondly, that some circumstances are introduced which we are not to regard as significant, but as serving merely to maintain the connection of the history.

But the address is so discursive and complex, and the purport of it has been so variously represented, that it is due to the subject to mention some of the other modes of analysis that have been proposed.

The following is Neander's view of it. Stephen's primary object was certainly apologetical, but as he forgot himself in the subject with which he was inspired, his apologetic efforts relate to the truths maintained by him, and impugned by his adversaries, rather than to himself. Hence, not satisfied with defending, he developed and enforced the truths he had proclaimed; and at the same time reproved the Jews for their unbelief and their opposition to the gospel. Stephen first refutes the charges made against him of enmity against the people of God, of contempt of their sacred institutions, and of blaspheming Moses. He traces the procedure of the divine providence, in guiding the people of God from the times of their progenitors; he notices the promises and their progressive fulfilment to the end of all the promises, — the advent of the Messiah, and the work to be accomplished by him. But with this narrative he blends his charges against the Jewish nation. He shows that their ingratitude and unbelief became more flagrant in proportion as the promises were fulfilled, or given with greater fulness; and their conduct in the various preceding periods of the development of God's kingdom was a specimen of the disposition they now evinced towards the publication of the gospel.[1]

According to Olshausen,[2] the speaker recapitulated the Jewish

[1] Quoted from Ryland's Translation of The Planting and Training of the Christian Church.

[2] Commentar über das Neue Testament, Vol. II. p. 719.

history at such length, simply in order to testify his regard for the national institutions, to conciliate his hearers, and show indirectly that he could not have uttered the *blasphemous words* imputed to him. (See 6, 11.) That those addressed saw their own moral image reflected so distinctly from the narrative results from the subject, not from the speaker's intention.

Luger develops the course of thought in this way. Stephen is accused of blaspheming the temple and the law. He vindicates himself by exhibiting the true significance of the temple and the law. The main points are, first, that the *law* is not something complete by itself, but was added to the promise given to Abraham, yea, contains in itself a new promise, by the fulfilment of which the law is first brought to completion. Secondly, the temple cannot be exclusively the holy place; it is one in a series of places which the Lord has consecrated, and by this very act foreshadowed that future completion of the temple, to which Solomon and the prophets point. Thirdly, it being a cause of special offence to the Jews that the Jesus rejected by them should be represented as the Perfecter of the law and the temple, Stephen showed that no objection against him could be derived from that fact, since the messengers of God had been treated with the like contempt at all periods. Fourthly, these three topics are presented, not *after* each other, but in each other. The history of Israel forms the thread of the discourse, but this is related in such a manner that examples of the different points come into view at every step.[1]

Baur's exposition of the plan has been highly commended. The contents of the discourse divide themselves into two parallel parts: on the one side are presented the benefits which God from the earliest times conferred on the Jewish nation: on the other side is exhibited in contrast their conduct towards him. Hence the main thought is this: the greater and more extraordinary the favors which God from the beginning bestowed on the Jews, the more unthankful and rebellious from the beginning was the spirit which they manifested in return; so that where a perfectly harmonious relation should have been found, the greatest alienation appeared. The greater the effort which God made to elevate and draw the nation to himself, the more the nation turned away from him. In presenting this view of the Jewish character, the speaker defended indirectly his own cause. He

[1] Ueber Zweck, Inhalt und Eigenthümlichkeit der Rede des Stephanus. Von Friedrich Luger.

was accused of having spoken reproachfully, not only against the law, but in particular against the temple. Hence the direction which he gave to the speech enabled him to show that the idolatrous regard of the Jews for the temple exemplified in the highest degree that opposition between God and themselves, which had been so characteristic of them from the first.[1]

It may be added, that the peculiar character of the speech impresses upon it a seal of authenticity, for no one would think of framing a discourse of this kind for such an occasion. Had it been composed ideally, or after some vague tradition, it would have been thrown into a different form; its relevancy to the charge which called it forth would have been made more obvious. As to the language in which Stephen delivered it, opinions are divided. His disputing with the foreign Jews (6, 9) would indicate that he was a Hellenist (comp. 9, 29), and in that case he spoke probably in Greek. The prevalence of that language in Palestine, and especially at Jerusalem, would have rendered it intelligible to such an audience.[2] The manner, too, in which the citations agree with the Septuagint, favors this conclusion.

VERSES 1–16. *History of the Patriarchs, or Age of the Promises.*

V. 1. δέ, *then*, binds this verse to 6, 14. — εἰ . . . . ἔχει, *Are then these things so*, as the witnesses testify? Hence this was the question to which Stephen replied, and must furnish the key to his answer. We must construe the speech so as to find in it a refutation of the charge in 6, 13. εἰ is direct here, as in 1, 6. ἄρα = "rebus ita comparatis," under these circumstances. See Klotz ad Devar. Vol. II. p. 176. The question is asked in view of the accusation. The particle is not to be struck out of the text, as in some editions.

V. 2. ἀδελφοί are the spectators, πατέρες the members of the council, like our "civil fathers;" comp. 22, 1. ἄνδρες qualifies both nouns; see on 1, 16. The English version makes three distinct classes, instead of two. — ὁ θεὸς τῆς δόξης, *the God of the glory* (τῆς, because peculiar to him) = הַכָּבוֹד in the Old Testament, or among the later Jews הַשְּׁכִינָה, i. e. the light, or visible splendor amid which Jehovah revealed himself, the symbol, therefore, of his presence (Mey. De Wet. Blmf.). Compare Ex. 25, 22; 40, 34; Lev. 9, 6; Ezek. 1, 28; 3, 23; Heb. 9, 5, etc.

[1] Paulus, Sein Leben und Wirken, seine Briefe und seine Lehre, p. 42.

[2] In proof of this, see Hug's Einleitung in das Neue Testament, Vol. II. p. 27 sq., fourth edition; and the Biblical Repository, 1832, p. 530.

ὤφθη points to that sense here; see also v. 55. Paul speaks of this symbol in Rom. 9, 4 as one of the peculiar distinctions with which God honored the Hebrew nation. Those miss the sense who resolve the genitive into an adjective = ἔνδοξος, *the glorious God* (Kuin. Hmph.). — ὄντι ἐν τῇ Μεσοποταμίᾳ, *when he was in Mesopotamia;* imperf. as often in narration. W. § 46. 6. Abraham resided first in Ur of the Chaldees (Gen. 11, 28), which lay probably in the extreme north of Mesopotamia, near the sources of the Tigris. The Chaldee branch of Peleg's family, to which Terah and his sons belonged, spread themselves originally in that region.[1] Xenophon found Chaldeans here in his retreat from Babylonia with the Ten Thousand. See further, on v. 4.— ἐν Χαῤῥάν. *Charran* = חָרָן (Gen. 11, 31), was also in the north of Mesopotamia, but south of Ur. It was the later *Carræ* of the Greeks and Romans, where Crassus was defeated and slain by the Parthians. Its position tallies remarkably with the sacred narrative. The ruins have been identified a few miles south of Urfa, on a road from the north to the southern ford of the Euphrates. It is a perversion of the text to suppose Stephen so ignorant of the geography here, as to place Charran on the west of the Euphrates. His meaning evidently is that Abraham's call in that city was not the first which he received during his residence in Mesopotamia. We have no account of this first communication to the patriarch in the Old Testament, but it is implied distinctly in Gen. 15, 7 and Neh. 9, 7. Philo and Josephus relate the history of Abraham in accordance with the statement here, that he was called twice.

V. 3. εἶπε πρὸς αὐτόν, *said unto him* in Ur before the migration to Charran. — ἔξελθε, κ. τ. λ., *go forth from thy country,* etc. This is quoted from Gen. 12, 1 sq., where it appears as the language addressed to Abraham when God appeared to him at Charran. But his earlier call had the same object precisely as the later; and hence Stephen could employ the terms of the second communication, in order to characterize the import of the first. — δεῦρο, *hither*, with an imperative force; the term adapted to the speaker's position, like ταύτην in v. 4. — ἣν ἄν, *whichever* (see on 2, 21); since he "went forth not knowing whither he goes" (Heb. 11, 8).

V. 4. τότε, *then,* after this command. — ἐξελθὼν, κ. τ. λ., *having gone forth from the land of the Chaldees;* which, therefore, did not extend so far south as to include Charran. It is barely pos-

[1] For the ethnography of the subject, see Knobel's Völkertafel der Genesis, p. 170 sq.

sible that ἐξελθὼν may reach forward to μετῴκισεν (the change of subject there is against it), and in that case the second removal would have been a part of the journey from Chaldea. Compare Gen. 11, 31. The early history of the Chaldees is too obscure to allow us to define the limits of their territory. See Hertz. Encyck. Vol. II. p. 617.—γῆς Χαλδαίων suggests a region rather than a city, and Ur (for which the Sept. renders "country" in Gen. 11, 28) was probably the name of a district among the steppes of northern Mesopotamia. Some would identify Ur with the modern Urfa, the Edessa of the Greeks; but though the name (dropping the last syllable) may seem to favor that combination, the surer etymology derives Urfa (as a corruption) from the Syriac Urhoi, and thus destroys all connection between Ur and Urfa. See Tuch (p. 284) and Delitzsch (p. 407) über die Genesis. Had Ur either as a city or region been in Babylonia as some conjecture, Charran, so far to the west, would have been out of the way in a migration to Canaan.—μετὰ τὸ ἀποθανεῖν, κ. τ. λ., *after his father was dead.* According to Gen. 11, 32, Terah died at Haran, at the age of two hundred and five; and, according to the usual inference drawn from Gen. 11, 26, he was only seventy years old at the birth of Abraham; so that since Abraham left Charran at seventy-five (Gen. 12, 4), Terah instead of being dead at that time, must have lived (205—70+75=) sixty years after his son's departure from Charran. Here again some writers insist that Stephen has shown a gross ignorance of the patriarchal history. But this apparent disagreement admits of a ready solution if we suppose that Abraham was not the oldest son, but that Haran, who died before the first migration of the family (Gen. 11, 28), was sixty years older than he, and that Terah, consequently, was one hundred and thirty years old at the birth of Abraham (130+75=205). The relation of Abraham to the Hebrew history would account for his being named first in the genealogy. We have other instances entirely parallel to this. Thus, in Gen. 5, 32, and elsewhere, Japheth is mentioned last among the sons of Noah; but, according to Gen. 9, 24 and 10, 21, he was the oldest of them. Lightfoot has shown that even some of the Jewish writers, who can be suspected of no desire to reconcile Stephen with the Old Testament, concede that Abraham was the youngest son of Terah. The learned Usher founds his system of chronology on this view. The other explanations are less probable. It appears that there was a tradition among some of the Jews that Terah relapsed into idolatry during the abode at Haran, and that Abraham left him on that account, i. e. as the Talmudists express it, after his spiritual death. Kuinoel, Olshausen, and others, think that Stephen may have used ἀποθανεῖν in that sense; so that the notice of Terah's natural death in Gen. 11, 32 would be proleptic, i. e. in advance of the exact order of the history. The tradition of Terah's relapse into idolatry may have been well founded. Bengel offers this suggestion: "Abram, dum Thara vixit in Haran, domum quodammodo paternam habuit in Haran, in terra Canaan duntaxat peregrinum agens; mortuo autem patre, plane in terra Canaan domum unice habere coepit." The Samaritan Codex reads one hundred and forty-five in Gen. 11, 32, which would remove the difficulty, had it not been altered probably for that very purpose. The Samaritan text has no critical authority when opposed to the Masoretic.[1] — μετῴκισεν, sc. θεός, *caused him to remove*, to migrate by a renewed command, see Gen. 12, 1 sq. — εἰς ἥν, *into which*, because κατοικεῖτε implies an antecedent motion. — ὑμεῖς, *you*, instead of ἡμεῖς, *we;* because as a foreign Jew Stephen excludes himself.

V. 5. καὶ οὐκ . . . . ἐν αὐτῇ, *and he gave to him* (during his life) *no inheritance in it*, no actual possession, but a promise only that his posterity should occupy it at some future period. It is not at variance with this that he subsequently purchased the field of Ephron as a burial-place (Gen. 23, 3 sq.); for he acquired no right of settlement by that purchase, but permission merely to bury "his dead," which he sought as a favor because he was "a stranger and a sojourner" in the land. Lest the passage should seem to conflict with that transaction, some (Kuin. Olsh.) would render οὐκ as οὔπω, *not yet*, and ἔδωκεν as pluperfect. De Wette agrees with Meyer in restricting the remark to the period of Abraham's first arrival in Canaan. He purchased the field of Ephron near the close of his life. — οὐδὲ βῆμα ποδός, *not even a foot-breadth*, a single foot, comp. Deut. 2, 5. — αὐτῷ . . . . αὐτήν, *that he would give it to him for a possession*, not necessarily in his own person, but in that of his descendants. The country might be said to be Abraham's in prospect of that reversion. So in Gen. 46, 4, God says to Jacob on his descent into Egypt: "I will bring thee up again," i. e. him *in* his posterity. Others understand κατάσχεσιν of Abraham's own residence in the land of promise. — οὐκ ὄντος αὐτῷ τέκνου, *when he had no child.* This clause as well as the general connection, recalls to mind the strength of Abraham's faith. It was in that way that he pleased God and

[1] See Gesenius de Pentateuchi Samaritani Origine, Indole, et Auctoritate.

obtained the promise, and not by legal observances; for circumcision had not yet been instituted, or the law given. Paul reasons in that manner from Abraham's history, both in Rom. 4, 9 sq. and in Gal. 3, 17 sq. Stephen may have expanded his speech at this point so as to have presented distinctly the same conclusion; or, as remarked in the first analysis, most of his hearers may have been so familiar with the Christian doctrine on the subject, that they perceived at once that import of his allusions.

V. 6. The speaker quotes here the passage to which he had merely alluded. — δέ, *now*, subjoins this fuller account of the promise; not *but*, although he was childless (Mey., taken back in his last ed.). — οὕτως, *thus*, to this effect, viz. in Gen. 15, 13–16. — ἔσται, *shall be*; not *should* (E. V.). The citation mingles the indirect form with the direct. — δουλώσουσιν, strangers *shall enslave*, sc. ἀλλότριοι as the subject, involved in ἐν γῇ ἀλλοτρίᾳ. See W. § 64. 3. b. — ἔτη τετρακόσια, *four hundred years*, in agreement with Gen. 15, 13; but both there and here a round number, since in Ex. 12, 40 "the sojourning of Israel who dwelt in Egypt" is said to have been four hundred and thirty years. But here arises a chronological question, to which it is necessary to advert. In Gal. 3, 17, Paul speaks of the entire period from Abraham's arrival in Canaan until the giving of the law as embracing only four hundred and thirty years; a calculation which allows but two hundred and fifteen years for the sojourn in Egypt; for Isaac was born twenty-five years after that arrival, was sixty years old at the birth of Jacob, and Jacob was one hundred and thirty years old when he went to reside in Egypt (430—25+60+130=215). The Seventy, in Ex. 12, 40, and Josephus, in Antt. 2. 15. 2, follow the same computation. There are two solutions of this difficulty. One is, that the Jews had two ways of reckoning this period, which were current at the same time; that it is uncertain which of them is the correct one, and for all practical purposes is wholly unimportant, since, when a speaker or writer, as in this case of Stephen, adopted this mode or that, he was understood not to propound a chronological opinion, but merely to employ a familiar designation for the sake of definiteness. The other solution is, that the four hundred and thirty years in Ex. 12, 40 embrace the period from Abraham's immigration into Canaan until the departure out of Egypt, and that the sacred writers call this the period of sojourn or servitude in Egypt *a potiori*, i. e. from its leading characteristic.[1] They could describe it in this manner with so

[1] Baumgarten in common with others inclines to this view in his Theologischer Commentar zum Pentateuch, Vol. I. p. 190.

much the more propriety, because even during the rest of the time the condition of the patriarchs was that of exiles and wanderers. The current chronology, Usher's system, adopts 215 as the number of years during which the Hebrews dwelt in Egypt.

V. 7. κρινῶ ἐγώ, *I* (emphatic as one able to punish) *will judge* (Hebraistic), implying the execution of the sentence. — μετὰ ταῦτα, *after these things*, after both so long a time and such events. ταῦτα refers to κρινῶ, as well as to the other verbs. — καὶ λατρεύσουσι . . . τούτῳ, *and shall worship me in this place.* This clause is taken from a different passage; viz. Ex. 3, 12, which records the declaration that God would bring the Israelites where Moses then was. But as the words there also relate to the deliverance from Egypt, Stephen could use them to express more fully the idea in Gen. 15, 16. In the communication to Moses, τόπῳ refers to Sinai or Horeb, but is applied here very properly to Canaan, since the worship in the desert was a pledge of its performance in the promised land. λατρεύσουσι may intimate that God accepted their worship before they had any temple in which to offer it.

V. 8 διαθήκην περιτομῆς, *the covenant of circumcision*, i. e. the one of which circumcision is the sign; comp. σημεῖον περιτομῆς in Rom. 4, 11. — καὶ οὕτως, *and thus*, i. e. agreeably to the covenant God gave the promised child, and Abraham observed the appointed rite. Such briefly were the contents of the covenant (see Gen. 17, 2 sq.), and ἐγέννησε and περιέτεμε very naturally recall them here. οὕτως as merely *then* (Mey.), in lieu of δέ or καί in this speech elsewhere, expresses too little in such a place. — τῇ ἡμέρᾳ, κ. τ. λ. See Gen. 21, 4.

V. 9. ἀπέδοντο, *sold* (5, 8) *into Egypt*, i. e. to be carried thither; thus concisely in Gen. 45, 4 (Heb. and Sept.). — ὁ θεὸς μετ' αὐτοῦ, *God was with him*, though he was exposed to such envy and injustice. It was a memorable instance in which the rejected of men was approved of God and made the preserver of his people; see on v. 37. The analogy between Joseph's history in this respect and that of Christ must have forced itself on Stephen's hearers.

V. 10. χάριν καὶ σοφίαν, *favor* (with the king) *and wisdom;* both the gifts of God, but the latter helping in part to secure the former. Meyer, contrary to his first opinion, understands χάριν of the divine favor towards Joseph; but the two nouns belong alike to ἐναντίον Φαραώ, and associate themselves readily as cause and effect. The *wisdom* was that which Joseph displayed as an interpreter of dreams, as the king's counsellor and minister. — τὸν οἶκον αὐτοῦ, *his house;* the palace of the sovereign, from which, in the East, all the acts of government emanate. In other words, Joseph was raised to the office of vizier, or prime minister.

V. 12. For the history, see Gen. 42, 1 sq. — *ὄντα*, instead of the infinitive after ἀκούσας, represents the plenty in Egypt as indubitable, notorious. K. § 311. 1. The place of the abundance was well known, and ἐν Αἰγύπτῳ after the participle (T. R.) is a needless corruption for εἰς Αἴγυπτον, which belongs to the next verb. — *ἐξαπέστειλε κ. τ. λ.*, *sent our fathers first*, while Jacob himself remained still in Canaan. See v. 15.

V. 13. ἀνεγνωρίσθη, *was recognized by his brethren* (De Wet. Mey.), on declaring his name to them; comp. Gen. 45, 1. The reflexive sense, *made himself known* (Rob.), would be exceptional, and is not required here. — καὶ φανερὸν . . . . Ἰωσήφ, *and the race of Joseph was made known to Pharaoh*, i. e. the fact of their presence, their arrival. See Gen. 45, 16. It does not mean that the king ascertained now Joseph's Hebrew origin, for he knew that already (Gen. 41, 12); nor that Joseph's brethren were presented to him. The introduction took place at a later period; see Gen. 47, 2.

V. 14. ἐν ψυχαῖς ἑβδομήκοντα πέντε, (consisting) *in seventy-five souls.* For ἐν, see W. § 48. 3. From so feeble a beginning the Hebrews soon grew to a mighty nation; see v. 17. Stephen would suggest to the mind that contrast. According to Gen. 46, 27, Ex. 1 5, and Deut. 10, 22, Jacob's family at this time contained seventy persons; but the Septuagint has changed that number in the first two passages to seventy-five. In Gen. 46, 26, the Hebrew says that Jacob's descendants, on his arrival in Egypt, were sixty-six, and in the next verse adds to these Jacob himself, Joseph, and his two sons, thus making the number *seventy.* On the other hand, the Septuagint interpolates, in v. 27, υἱοὶ δὲ Ἰωσὴφ οἱ γενόμενοι αὐτῷ ἐν γῇ Αἰγύπτῳ ψυχαὶ ἐννέα, and adding these nine to the sixty-six in v. 26 makes the number *seventy-five.* It is evident from this interpolation that the Seventy did not obtain their number by adding the five sons of Ephraim and Manasseh (1 Chron. 7, 14-23) to the seventy persons mentioned in the Hebrew text. That mode of accounting for their computation has frequently been assigned. If υἱοί be taken in its wider sense, those sons and grandsons of Joseph may have been among the *nine* whom they added to the sixty-six, but it is not known how they reckoned the other two. They may have included some of the third generation, or have referred to other sons of

17

Joseph, of whom we have no account. But in whatever way the enumeration arose, its existence in the Greek version shows that it was current among the Jews. That it was an *erroneous* one, is incapable of proof; for we do not know on what data it was founded. At all events, Stephen could adapt himself to the popular way of speaking with entire truth as to the idea which he meant to convey; for his object was to affirm, not that the family of Jacob, when he went down to Egypt, consisted of just seventy-five persons, in distinction from seventy-six, or seventy, or any other precise number, but that it was a mere handful compared with the increase which made them in so short a time "as the stars of heaven for multitude;" see Deut. 10, 22. That among those whom Joseph is said to have called into Egypt were some who were already there, or were born at a subsequent period, agrees with Gen. 46, 27; for it is said that "the sons of Joseph" were among "the souls of the house of Jacob that came into Egypt" with him. That representation springs from the Hebrew view, which regarded the descendants as existing already in their progenitor; comp. Gen. 46, 15; Heb. 7, 9. 10. It is equivalent here to saying, that the millions to which Israel had grown on leaving Egypt were all comprised in some seventy-five persons at the commencement of the residence there.[1]

V. 16. It is mentioned in Gen. 50, 13, that Jacob was buried in Abraham's sepulchre, at Hebron (see Gen. 23, 19), and in Josh. 24, 32, that the bones of Joseph were laid in Jacob's tomb at Shechem, or Sychem; as to the burial of Jacob's other sons, the Old Testament is silent. In this passage, therefore, οἱ πατέρες ἡμῶν may be taken as the subject of μετετέθησαν without αὐτός. Such brevity was natural in so rapid a sketch, and not obscure where the hearers were so familiar with the subject in hand. That Joseph's brothers were buried with him at Sychem rests, doubtless, on a well-known tradition in Stephen's time. "According to Josephus (Antt. 2. 8. 2) the sons of Jacob were buried at Hebron. According to the Rabbins (Light. Wetst.), the Israelites took the bones of their fathers with them to Palestine, but say nothing of Sychem; since, however, they do not include the eleven patriarchs among those who were buried at Hebron, they probably regarded Sychem as the place of their burial." (De Wet.). Jerome, who lived but a day's journey from Sychem, says that the tombs of the twelve were to be seen there in his time.—ἐν τῷ μνήματι, κ. τ. λ., *in the tomb*, etc., presents a more serious dif-

[1] See Hengstenberg's Authentie des Pentateuches, Vol. II. p. 357 sq.

ficulty. It is clear from Gen. 33, 19, that Jacob purchased the family tomb at Sychem, and from Gen. 23, 1 sq., that Abraham purchased the one at Hebron. On the other hand, according to the present text, Stephen appears to have confounded the two transactions, representing, not Jacob, but Abraham, as having purchased the field at Sychem. It is difficult to resist the impression that a single word of the present text is wrong, and that we should either omit Ἀβραάμ or exchange it for Ἰακώβ. — ὠνήσατο without a subject could be taken as impersonal: *one purchased = was purchased.* See W. § 58. 9. That change would free the passage from its perplexity. It is true, manuscripts concur in the present reading, but this may be an instance where the internal evidence countervails the external. The error lies in a single word; and it is quite as likely, judging *a priori*, that the word producing the error escaped from some early copyist, as that so glaring an error was committed by Stephen; for, as a Jew, he had been brought up to a knowledge of the Scriptures, had proved himself more than a match for the learned disputants from the synagogues (6, 10), and is said to have been "full of the Holy Spirit" (6, 5). Some attribute the difficulty to the concise, hurried style of the narrative. Biscoe states that opinion in the following terms: — "The Hebrews, when reciting the history of their forefathers to their brethren, do it in the briefest manner, because it was a thing well known to them. For which reason they made use of frequent ellipses, and gave but hints to bring to their remembrance what they aimed at. This may be the case here; and as nothing is more easy than to supply the words that are wanting, so, when supplied, the narration is exactly agreeable to history delivered in the Old Testament: 'And were carried into Sychem, and were laid,' i. e. some of them, Jacob at least, 'in the sepulchre that Abraham bought for a sum of money,' and others of them 'in that (bought) from the sons of Emmor, the father of Sychem.' Here we repeat merely καὶ ἐν τῷ (or ἐκείνῳ) before παρὰ τῶν υἱῶν; which words were easily understood and supplied by those to whom Stephen addressed himself."[1] Again, some have deemed it sufficient to say that Stephen was not an *inspired* teacher, in the strict sense of the expression, and that, provided we have a true record of the discourse on the part of Luke, we may admit an error in the discourse itself, without discrediting the acccuracy of the sacred writers. Dr. Davidson thinks that Luke must have been aware

[1] The Acts of the Apostles, confirmed from other Authors, p. 395, ed. 1840.

of the discrepency, and has exhibited his scrupulous regard for the truth by allowing it to remain, instead of correcting it. Calvin sanctions a still freer view: "In nomine Abrahæ erratum esse palam est; quare hic locus corrigendus est." — Ἐμμώρ, sc. τοῦ πατρός, *Emmor*, the father *of Sychem*. See on 1, 13.

VERSES 17–46. *The Age of Moses, or the Jews under the Law.*

V. 17. καθώς, not *when*, but *as*, in the degree that; hence ἤγγιζεν, *was approaching.* — ὁ χρόνος, κ. τ. λ., *the time of the* (fulfilment of the) *promise* (v. 7); see on 1, 4. — Instead of ὤμοσεν (T. R.), *sware*, we are to read probably ὡμολόγησεν, *declared*. (Lchm. Tsch. Mey.). — ηὔξησεν and ἐπληθύνθη represent the growth in power as consequent on the increase of numbers; not a citation, but reminiscence probably of Ex. 1, 7. 20.

V. 18. ἄχρις οὗ, *until;* for this signal prosperity had its limit. Though baffled in his first scheme, Pharaoh tried other means more effectual; see on v. 19. — ὃς . . . . Ἰωσήφ, *who knew not Joseph,* had no regard for his memory or services; not was ignorant that such a person had lived (Mey.). How could the author of such important reforms have been forgotten among a people addicted like the Egyptians to recording their national events! It has been supposed that a new dynasty may have ascended the throne at this time. According to Sir J. G. Wilkinson,[1] this "new king" was Amosis, or Ames, first of the eighteenth dynasty, or that of the Diospolitans from Thebes. Some hold (e. g. Heeren, Jost) that the Hyksos or shepherd kings had just been expelled from Egypt, and that the oppressor of the Hebrews was the first native prince who reigned after that event. The present knowledge of Egyptian history is too imperfect to admit of any positive conclusion on such a point. For the later views and literature, see on Ancient Egypt in Hertz. Encyck. Vol. I. p. 138 sq.

V. 19. κατασοφισάμενος τὸ γένος ἡμῶν, *treating subtly our race*, see Ex. 1, 10; Ps. 115, 25. His policy is characterized in this manner, because his object, without being avowed, was to compel the Hebrews to destroy their children, that they might not grow up to experience the wretched fate of their parents. — ἐκάκωσε, κ. τ. λ., *oppressed our fathers in order that they should cast out their infants, that these might not be preserved alive.* Both infinitives are telic; the first states the king's object in the oppression, the second the object of the exposure on the part of the parents. It

[1] Manners and Customs of the Ancient Egyptians, Vol. I. p. 42 sq., 2d ed.

was using the parental instinct for destroying the child; it was seething the kid in the mother's blood. For τοῦ ποιεῖν, see on 3, 2. The plan of the Egyptians failed; for "the more they afflicted the Hebrews, the more they multiplied and grew" (Ex. 1, 12); i. e. they spared their children, instead of putting them to death, and continued to increase. Pharaoh, after this, took a more direct course to accomplish his object; he issued a decree that all the male children of the Hebrews should be killed at birth, or thrown into the Nile; see Ex. 1, 16. 22. The sense is different if we make τοῦ ποιεῖν ecbatic: *so that they cast out their infants,* etc. According to this view, the king's policy was in part successful; the Hebrews exposed their children of their own accord, that they might not see them doomed to so hopeless a bondage. But the infinitive construction with τοῦ is rarely ecbatic; and, further, had the Hebrews destroyed their children as a voluntary act, a subsequent decree for murdering them would have been unnecessary (Ex. 1, 16. 22). It is harsh to make τοῦ ποιεῖν epexegetical: *oppressed them* (viz. by a decree) *that they must cast out,* etc. It is difficult with this sense to see the force of κατασοφισάμενος. Besides, the history shows that the Egyptians were to execute the inhuman order (Ex. 1, 22), not the Hebrews. The object of putting Moses in the ark was to save, not destroy him.

V. 20. ἐν ᾧ καιρῷ, *in which time,* viz. this season of oppression. — ἀστεῖος τῷ θεῷ, *fair for God,* i. e. in his view, who judges truly; comp. πόλις μεγάλη τῷ θεῷ in Jon. 3, 3 (Sept.). It is a form of the Hebrew superlative. W. § 36. 3; Green's Gr. p. 277. For the dative, see on 5, 34. Josephus (Antt. 2. 9. 7) speaks of the extreme beauty of Moses. See also Heb. 11, 23. — τοῦ πατρός, *his father,* named Amram (Ex. 6, 20).

V. 21. αὐτόν, with the participle, is not an accusative absoluto, but depends on the verb, and is then repeated; comp. Mark 9, 28. It is changed in some of the best copies to αὐτοῦ. — ἀνείλατο, *took up,* not from the water or the ark, but like *tollere liberos, adopted.* This use both of the Greek and the Latin word is said to have arisen from the practice of infanticide among the ancients. After the birth of a child, the father took it up to his bosom, if he meant to rear it; otherwise, it was doomed to perish. — εἰς υἱόν, *as a son,* appositional like לְ before that which a person or thing becomes (W. § 32. 4. b.); not telic, *to be a son* (Mey.), since the relation was an immediate one and not prospective merely.

V. 22. ἐπαιδεύθη πάσῃ σοφίᾳ, *was instructed in all the wisdom,* made familiar with it; dative of the respect or manner. Tischendorf reads ἐν before σοφίᾳ. Some render *was trained by the wisdom* as the means of culture; dative of the instrument (De Wet. Mey.). This may be easier grammatically, but looks like modernizing the idea. The accusative would be the ordinary case after this passive (*was taught the wisdom*); but it could be interchanged with the dative. See W. § 32. 4. — δυνατὸς ἐν λόγοις, *mighty in words*. In point of mere fluency, he was inferior to Aaron (Ex. 4, 10), but excelled him in the higher mental attributes on which depends mainly the orator's power over the minds of others. His recorded speeches justify Stephen's encomium. — For ἔργοις, comp. v. 36.

V. 23. αὐτῷ, *by him*, dative of the agent; see on 5, 9. — τεσσαρακονταετὴς χρόνος, *a fortieth annual time*, i. e. when he was forty years old. See the note on v. 30. — ἀνέβη ἐπὶ τὴν καρδίαν = עָלָה עַל־לֵב, see Jer. 3, 16. — ἐπισκέψασθαι, κ. τ. λ., *to visit his brethren* in order to show his sympathy for them and minister to their relief. The Hebrews lived apart from the Egyptians, and Moses as a member of the royal family may have had hitherto but little intercourse with his countrymen.

V. 24. ἀδικούμενον, *wronged*, injured, viz. by blows, which the Hebrew was then receiving, as stated in the history; see Ex. 2, 11. — ἐποίησεν ἐκδίκησιν, *wrought redress*, avenged; see Luke 18, 7. — τῷ καταπονουμένῳ, *the one overpowered*, lit. exhausted, worn out; implying a hard contest, and (the participle is present) a rescue just in time to ward off the fatal blow. — πατάξας τὸν Αἰγύπτιον, *by smiting the Egyptian* (who did the wrong) so as to kill him, see v. 28.

V. 25. ἐνόμιζε, *was supposing* in this interposition, and as the reason for it. This use of δέ, *for* (E. V.), is one of its metabatic offices. Hart. Partkl. Vol. I. p. 167. On what ground Moses expected to be known so readily, we are not informed. He may have thought that his history, so full of providential intimations, had pointed him out to the Israelites as their predestined deliverer. Stephen makes the remark evidently for the purpose of reminding the Jews of their own similar blindness in regard to the mission of Christ; comp. v. 35. — δίδωσιν, not *would give* (E. V.), but *gives*; present either because the event was so near (see on 1, 6), or because the deliverance begins with this act (Mey.).

V. 26. ὤφθη, *appeared*, showed himself, with the involved idea, perhaps, that it was unexpected. — αὐτοῖς, *to them*, i. e. two of his countrymen (Ex. 2, 13). The expression is vague, because the facts are supposed to be familiar. — συνήλασεν, κ. τ. λ., *urged them unto peace*, reconciliation. — ὑμεῖς after ἐστέ should be left out. —

For ἱνατί, see on 4, 25. — ἄνδρες belongs to ἀδελφοί, *men* related as *brethren are ye* (comp. 1, 16; 2, 29. 37); not = κύριοι as the nominative of address (E. V.). The relationship aggravated the outrage. It was more unseemly than when the combatants, as on the day before, had been Hebrew and Egyptian. With the same appeal Abraham says to Lot, "Let there be no strife, I pray thee, between thee and me, and between my herdmen and thy herdmen; for we are men brethren" (Gen. 13, 8 in Heb. and Sept.).

V. 29. ἐν τῷ λόγῳ τούτῳ, *at this word*, which showed that his attempt to conceal the murder had failed; see Ex. 2, 12. His flight was now necessary to save his life; for "when Pharaoh heard this thing, he sought to slay Moses." — ἐν γῇ Μαδιάμ, *in the land of Madiam*, or *Midian*. "This would seem," says Gesenius, "to have been a tract of country extending from the eastern shore of the Elanitic Gulf to the region of Moab on the one hand, and to the vicinity of Mount Sinai on the other. The people here were nomadic in their habits, and moved often from place to place." It is common for γῇ to omit the article before the name of a country; see v. 36; 13, 19. W. § 19.

V. 30. πληρωθέντων, κ. τ. λ., *forty years having been completed.* Stephen follows the tradition. It was said that Moses lived forty years in Pharaoh's palace, dwelt forty years in Midian, and governed Israel forty years. That he was one hundred and twenty years old at the time of his death, we read in Deut. 34, 7. — ἐν τῇ ἐρήμῳ . . . . Σινᾶ, *in the desert of the mount Sinai*, in the desert where this mount was situated. According to Ex. 3, 1, this appearance of the angel took place at Horeb. Both names are given in the Pentateuch to the same locality. Of this usage the common explanation has been, that Sinai designated a range of mountains, among which Horeb was the particular one from which the law was given. Dr. Robinson assigns reasons for thinking that Horeb was the general name, and Sinai the specific one. See his Bibl. Res. Vol. I. p. 120, ed. 1856. Hengstenberg, Winer, Ewald, and others, reject the old opinion. — ἐν φλογὶ πυρὸς βάτου, *in the fiery flame of a bush.* — πυρός supplies the place of an adjective; comp. 9, 15; 2 Thess. 1, 8. W. § 34. 3. b; S. § 117. 6.

V. 31. κατανοῆσαι, *to observe*, contemplate viz. the vision (see v. 32); not *to understand*, learn the cause, which would be unsuitable in the next verse. — φωνὴ κυρίου, *the voice of the Lord.* It will be seen that the angel of Jehovah in v. 30 (comp. Ex. 3, 2) is here called Jehovah himself. Examples of a similar transition from the one name to the other occur often in the Old Testament.

It has been argued from this usage, as well as on other grounds, that the Revealer, under the ancient dispensation, was identical with the Revealer or Logos of the new dispensation.[1]

V. 32. *ἐγὼ ὁ θεός, κ. τ. λ.* In this way Jehovah declares himself to be the true God, in opposition to the idols of the heathen, and especially the author of those promises to the patriarchs which were now on the eve of being fulfilled. — *οὐκ ἐτόλμα κατανοῆσαι*, sc. *τὸ ὅραμα.* In Ex. 3, 6, it is said further, that "Moses hid his face;" an act prompted by his sense of the holiness of Him in whose presence he stood; comp. 1 Kings 19, 13.

V. 33. *λῦσον, κ. τ. λ.*, *loose the sandal of thy feet.* *ὑπόδημα* is a distributive singular, for the plural. W. § 27. 1. It was a mark of reverence in the East to take off the shoes or sandals in the presence of a superior, so as not to approach him with the dust which would otherwise cleave to the feet. On this principle the Jewish priests officiated barefoot in the tabernacle and the temple. Hence, too, none enter the Turkish mosques at present, except with naked feet, or, in the case of foreigners, with slippers worn for the occasion. — In *γῆ ἁγία ἐστίν*, Luger finds a special reference to vv. 30. 32. The God of Abraham, Isaac, and Jacob was present, and where he appears the place is holy, though it be in the wilderness.

V. 34. *ἰδὼν εἶδον* = רָאֹה רָאִיתִי, *Truly I saw;* and so in the following verbs the tense is aorist: *I heard* when they groaned and *came down* (not *am come*) when I saw and heard. In Hebrew the infinitive absolute before a finite verb denotes the reality of the act, or an effect of it in the highest degree; after the verb, it denotes a continuance or repetition of the act. See Gesen. Heb. Gr. § 128. 3; W. § 45. 8. The easier Greek construction for this idiom is that noticed on 4, 17. For *ἀποστελῶ* (T. R.), read *ἀποστείλω* (Tsch. Mey.), but with a future sense. See W. § 13. 1.

V. 35. *τοῦτον* is here emphatic. *οὗτος* introduces the next three verses with the same effect. — *ἠρνήσαντο*, *denied.* The verb is plural, because, though the rejection was one person's act (v. 27), it revealed the spirit of the nation. — *ἄρχοντα καὶ λυτρωτήν*, *as a ruler and redeemer;* comp. 5, 31. Stephen selects the words evidently with reference to the parallel which he would institute

[1] The subject is an interesting one; but does not fall properly within our present limits. The reader will find it discussed in Smith's Scripture Testimony to the Messiah, Vol. I. p. 482 sq., and in Hengstenberg's Christology, Vol. I. p. 165 sq. Valuable supplementary matter (for the object is to deal only with the later objections) will be found in Kurtz's article, "Der Engel des Herrn," in Tholuck's Litterarischer Anzeiger, 1846, Nos. 11-14, and inserted for substance, in the author's Geschichte des alten Bundes, Vol. I. pp. 121-126.

between Moses and Christ. — ἐν χειρί stands for בְּיַד, *by the hand*, agency (comp. Gal. 3, 19), since it was through the angel in the bush that God called Moses to deliver his people. Tischendorf reads σὺν χειρί (unusual but well supported), *with the hand*, i. e. attended by the angel's aid and power, an adjunct of τοῦτον rather than the verb. — τῇ βάτῳ is feminine here and in Luke 20, 37, but masculine in Mark 12, 26.

V. 36. ἐξήγαγεν αὐτούς, *led them forth* out of Egypt. Hence we cannot render ποιήσας, *after he had shown*, performed (E. V.), because the miracles in the desert were not antecedent to the exodus. The participle expresses here an accompanying act of ἐξήγαγεν, *performing* (Vulg., *faciens*); since the leading forth formed a general epoch with which the associated events, whether historically prior or subsequent, could be viewed as coincident in point of time. On the force of the participle in such a case, see on 21, 7. — For the difference between τέρατα and σημεῖα, see on 2, 22. Lachmann inserts τῇ before γῇ, but on slight evidence. — Αἰγύπτῳ is more correct than Αἰγύπτου (T. R.).

V. 37. προφήτην, κ. τ. λ. For the explanation of this prophecy, see on 3, 22. No one can doubt that Stephen regarded Christ as the prophet announced by Moses; yet, it will be observed, he leaves that unsaid, and relies on the intelligence of his hearers to infer his meaning. Here is a clear instance in which the speech adjusts itself to those *suppressed* relations of the subject, on which, as I suppose, its adaptation to the occasion so largely depended. By quoting this prediction of Moses, Stephen tells the Jews in effect that it was *they* who were treating the lawgiver with contempt; for while they made such pretensions to respect for his authority, they refused to acknowledge the prophet whom he foretold, and had commanded them to obey. — κύριος before and ἡμῶν after θεός (T. R.) are doubtful. — αὐτοῦ ἀκούσεσθε, *him shall ye hear*, was inserted probably from 3, 22 (Lchm. Tsch. Mey.).

V. 38. ὁ γενόμενος . . . . τῶν πατέρων ἡμῶν, *who was* (lit. *became*, entered into connection) *with the angel and with our fathers*. The meaning is, that he brought the parties into association with each other, acted as mediator between God and the people; see Gal. 3, 19. This fact is mentioned to show how exalted a service Moses performed, in contrast with the indignity which he experienced at the hands of his countrymen. He was a type, Stephen would say, of the Jesus despised, crucified by those whom he would reconcile unto God. — ἐν τῇ ἐκκλησίᾳ, *in the congregation*, i. e. of the Hebrews assembled at Sinai at the time of the promulgation of the law. So all the best critics and the older E. versions (Tynd. Cran. Gen. Rhem.) translate this word. It is evident that ἐκκλησία here affords no countenance to the idea that the Hebrew nation as such constituted the church under the ancient economy. — ζῶντα characterizes λόγια with reference, not to their effect (comp. Rom. 8, 3; Gal. 3, 21), but their nature or design: *life-giving oracles*, commands; comp. Rom. 7, 12. The inadequacy of the law to impart life does not arise from any inherent defect in the law itself, but from the corruption of human nature.

V. 39. ἐστράφησαν . . . . εἰς Αἴγυπτον, *turned with their hearts unto Egypt*, i. e. longed for its idolatrous worship, and for the sake of it deserted that of Jehovah (Calv. Kuin. De Wet. Mey.). The next words are epexegetical, and require this explanation. Some have understood it of their wishing to return to Egypt; but that sense, though it could be expressed by the language, not only disregards the context, but is opposed to Ex. 32, 4 and Neh. 9, 18. The Jews are there represented as worshipping the golden calf for having brought them out of Egypt, and not as a means of enabling them to return thither.

V. 40. θεοὺς, οἳ προπορεύσονται ἡμῶν, *gods who shall go before us*, to wit, as guides, protectors. This is a literal translation from Ex. 32, 1. The plural is best explained as that of the *pluralis excellentiæ*, since Aaron made but one image in compliance with this demand of the people (called θεοί, אֱלֹהִים in Ex. 32, 8), and since the Hebrews would naturally enough transfer the name of the true God to the object of their idolatrous worship. De Wette hesitates between this view and that of θεούς as abstract, *deity*, divine power. The latter is better perhaps than Meyer's categorical plural: *gods* such as the calf represented. — ὁ γὰρ, κ. τ. λ., *for as to this Moses who led us forth*, etc. οὗτος is contemptuous, like *iste*. The nominative absolute strengthens the sarcasm. W. § 29. 1. γάρ alleges the disappearance of Moses as a reason why they should change their worship; possibly, because it freed them from his opposition to their desires, but more probably because, whether he had deserted them or had perished, it showed that the God whom he professed to serve was unworthy of their confidence.

V. 41. ἐμοσχοποίησαν is elsewhere unknown to the extant Greek. They selected the figure of a calf, or more correctly bullock, as their idol, in imitation, no doubt, of the Egyptians, who worshipped an ox at Memphis, called Apis, and another at Heliopolis, called Mnevis. Win. Realw. I. p. 644; Hertz. Encyck. Vol. VII.

p. 214. Mummies of the animals so worshipped are often found in the catacombs of Egypt. — εὐφραίνοντο, *rejoiced*, made merry, refers doubtless to the festive celebration mentioned in Ex. 32, 6. — τοῖς ἔργοις is plural, because the idol was the product of their joint labors. Meyer supposes it to include the various implements of sacrifice, in addition to the image; (in his last edition: *works* such as this.)

V. 42. ἔστρεψε, *turned away*, withdrew his favor. — παρέδωκεν, *gave up* (Rom. 1, 24), = εἴασε in 14, 16; he laid for the present no check upon their inclinations. In consequence of this desertion they sunk into still grosser idolatry. — τῇ στρατιᾷ τοῦ οὐρανοῦ, *the host of heaven*, i. e. the sun, moon, and stars. This form of worship is called Sabaism, from צָבָא, as applied to the heavenly bodies. — ἐν βίβλῳ τῶν προφητῶν, *in the book of the prophets*, i. e. the twelve minor prophets, whom the Jews reckoned as one collection. The passage is Amos 5, 25–27. — μὴ σφάγια, κ. τ. λ. This sign of a question requires a negative answer, and that answer is to be understood in a relative sense. See W. § 57. 3. *Did ye offer unto me sacrifices and offerings?* i. e. exclusively. The reply is left to their consciences. Even during the eventful period in the wilderness, when the nation saw so much of the power and goodness of God, they deserted his worship for that of other gods, or, while they professed to serve him, united his service with that of idols. The question ends here.

V. 43. καὶ ἀνελάβετε, κ. τ. λ. The tacit answer precedes: No, — ye apostatized, *and took up the tabernacle of Moloch*, i. e. to carry it with them in their marches, or in religious processions. This tabernacle was intended, no doubt, to resemble the one consecrated to Jehovah. Stephen follows the Septuagint. Μολόχ stands there for מַלְכְּכֶם, i. e. the idol worshipped as *your king*, which was the Moloch of the Amorites. The Seventy supply the name of the idol as well known from tradition. But there is almost equal authority, says Baur,[1] for reading מִלְכֹּם, *Milkom*, a proper name. That variation would bring the Greek into still closer conformity with the Hebrew. — τὸ ἄστρον τοῦ θεοῦ, *the star of the god*, i. e. an image resembling or representing a star worshipped by them as a god. — By Ῥεμφάν (also written Ῥεφάν, Ῥεμφά, Ῥομφᾶ) the Seventy express כִּיּוּן, which, like most of the ancient translators, they took to be a proper name. Some of the ablest modern scholars defend the correctness of that transla-

[1] Der Prophet Amos erklärt, von Dr. Gustav Baur, p. 362.

tion.[1] In this case the Greek name must have sprung from a corrupt pronunciation of the Hebrew name; see Gesen. Lex. p. 463. According to others, כִּיּוּן should be rendered *statue*, or *statues*, and the idol would then be unnamed in the Hebrew. So Gesenius, Robinson (N. T. Lex. s. v.), and others. Admitting that sense, it was unnecessary for Stephen to correct the current version; for he adduced the passage merely to establish the charge of idolatry, not to decide what particular idol was worshipped. Whether the star-god to which they paid their homage was Saturn, Venus, or some other planet, cannot be determined. — τοὺς τύπους, *the figures*, in apposition with σκηνήν and ἄστρον. The term was so much the more appropriate to the tabernacle, as it contained probably an image of Moloch. — μετοικιῶ is the Attic future. — ἐπέκεινα Βαβυλῶνος, *beyond Babylon*, where the Hebrew and Septuagint have *beyond Damascus*. The idea is the same, for the prediction turned not upon the name, but the fact, viz. that God would scatter them into distant lands. The Babylonian captivity was the one best known, and, besides, in being exiled to the remoter place the Jews were transported beyond the nearer.

V. 44. ἡ σκηνὴ τοῦ μαρτυρίου = אֹהֶל הָעֵדֻת (Numb. 9, 15; 17, 23), *the tabernacle of the testimony*, or law, so called, because it contained the ark in which the tables of the decalogue were kept. The law is termed a *testimony*, because it testifies or declares the divine will. Bähr's explanation (Symbolik, Vol. I. p. 80) is different: the tabernacle was a testimony or witness of the covenant between God and his people. — ποιῆσαι . . . . ἑωράκει, *that he should make it according to the pattern which he had seen*, viz. on Mount Sinai; see Ex. 25, 9. 40. By this reference, Stephen reminds the Jews of the emblematical import, consequently the subordinate value, of the ancient worship. Moses, under the divine guidance, constructed the *earthly* tabernacle so as to have it image forth certain *heavenly* or spiritual realities that were to be accomplished under "the better covenant of which Jesus is the Mediator." Here we have the rudiments of the view which pervades the Epistle to the Hebrews; see especially Heb. 8, 5 What was true of the tabernacle was true also of the first and the second temple; they were built after the same model, and were in like manner ἀντίτυποι, or σκιαὶ τῶν ἐπουρανίων. That application of the remark could be left to suggest itself.

[1] See especially Movers über die Phönitzier, Vol. I. p. 289 sq. He maintains that כִּיּוּן may be traced as a proper name in various Oriental languages.

V. 45. καί adds εἰσήγαγον to ποιῆσαι. — διαδεξάμενοι, *having received* (the tabernacle), viz. from Moses or his contemporaries, since those who entered Canaan were a later generation; not *inherited* (Alf.), a false meaning; and not *who came after*, successors (E. V., retained from Cranm.), since that substantive construction would require the article (see Pape s. v.). — μετὰ Ἰησοῦ, *with Joshua* as their leader, under his guidance. — ἐν τῇ κατασχέσει τῶν ἐθνῶν, *into the possession of the heathen*, the territory inhabited by them; comp. δοθήτω ἡ γῆ ἡμῖν ἐν κατασχέσει, in Numb. 32, 5. ἐν shows that the idea of rest predominates over that of motion. Meyer and De Wette translate *on taking possession of the heathen*, on their subjugation. The other meaning is better, because it supplies an indirect object after εἰσήγαγον, and adheres to the prevalent passive sense of κατάσχεσις; see Rob. Lex. s. v. — ἕως τῶν ἡμερῶν Δαυίδ belongs to εἰσήγαγον, employed suggestively: *brought* the tabernacle into the land, and retained it *until* (inclusive) *the days of David.* Some join the words with ὧν ἔξωσεν, which exalts a subordinate clause above the principal one, and converts the aorist into an imperfect: *was expelling* from Joshua until David.

V. 46. ὃς . . . . τοῦ θεοῦ, *who found favor*, etc. Compare 13, 22. The tacit inference may be, that, had the temple been so important as the Jews supposed, God would not have withheld this honor from his servant. — ᾐτήσατο, *asked for himself* as a privilege. We have no record of this prayer, though it is implied in 2 Sam. 7, 4 sq., and in 1 Chron. 22, 7. In the latter passage David says: "As for me, it was in my mind to build an house unto the name of the Lord my God." In that frame of spirit he indited the hundred and thirty-second Psalm. — εὑρεῖν . . . . Ἰακώβ coincides with Ps. 132, 5 (Sept.). To express the object of David's request, Stephen avails himself of the language contained in that passage. Translate, *a habitation* (= οἶκον in v. 48, place of abode, temple) *for the God of Jacob*; not *tabernacle* (= σκηνή in v. 44), as in the E. version. The tabernacle existed already, and it was not that structure, but a temple, which David was anxious to build. The confusion arises from rendering the different Greek terms by the same word.

VERSES 47–53. *Period of the Temple and the Prophets.*

V. 47. δέ, adversative. What was denied to David was granted to Solomon; see 2 Chron. 6, 7. 8. Yet even the builder of the temple acknowledged (2 Chron. 6, 18) that God is not confined to any single place of worship. The tenor of the speech would be apt to remind the hearers of that admission.

V. 48. ἀλλ' οὐχ . . . . κατοικεῖ. The temple was at length built; but was never designed to circumscribe the presence of the infinite Architect (see v. 50), or to usurp the homage that belongs to him alone. The remark here was aimed, doubtless, at the superstitious reverence with which the Jews regarded the temple, and at their proneness in general to exalt the forms of religion above its essence. For οὐχ in this position, see on 2, 7. ναοῖς is probably a gloss from 17, 24.—καθὼς, κ. τ. λ. To give greater effect to his reproof, Stephen quotes the testimony of the prophet, viz. Is. 66, 1. 2.

V. 51. There is no evidence that Stephen was interrupted at this point. Many critics assume that without reason. The sharper tone of reprehension to which the speaker rises here belongs to the place; it is an application of the course of remark which precedes. We have no right to ascribe it to Stephen's irritation at perceiving signs of impatience or rage on the part of his hearers.—ἀπερίτμητοι . . . . ὠσίν, *uncircumcised*, etc., i. e. destitute of the disposition to hear and love the truth, of which their circumcision should have been the sign; comp. Lev. 26, 41; Jer. 6, 10; Rom. 2, 29. For τῇ καρδίᾳ see 2, 37.—ὑμεῖς ἀεὶ, κ. τ. λ., *Ye do always resist the Holy Spirit*, under whose influence the messengers of God, e. g. Christ and the apostles, spoke to them. To reject their testimony was to reject that of the spirit himself. What follows appears to restrict the language to that meaning.—καὶ ὑμεῖς, *also you*, where οὕτως would state the comparison more exactly. See W. § 53. 5.

V. 52. τίνα τῶν προφητῶν, κ. τ. λ., *whom of the prophets*, etc. Stephen would describe the general conduct of the Jews towards their prophets; he does not affirm that there were no exceptions to it. Other passages, as 2 Chron. 36, 15. 16; Matt. 23, 37, and Luke 13, 33. 34, make the same representation.—τοὺς προκαταγγείλαντας, κ. τ. λ., *those who announced beforehand*, etc., designates the prophets with reference to the leading subject of their predictions. See on 3, 21. 24.—τοῦ δικαίου, *the Just one*, (3, 14) slain by them as a malefactor.—νῦν, *now*, as the climax of the nation's guilt.—προδόται, *traitors*. See 3, 13.

V. 53. Those who were thus guilty (v. 52) acted in the character of *those who* (οἵτινες, *such as*) *received*, etc.—τὸν νόμον . . . . ἀγγέλλων, *the law as* (εἰς predicative sign, see on v. 21) *ordinances* (plural with reference to νόμον as an aggregate of single acts) *of angels;* the latter not as the authors of them, in which sense they were God's, but as communicated through them; comp. ὁ δι' ἀγγέλων λαληθείς in Heb. 2, 2, *the word spoken through angels*, and especially διαταγεὶς δι' ἀγγέλων in Gal. 3, 19, *ordained* on the part of God *through angels*. The elliptical explanation, reckoned *unto ordinances*, as of that rank or class, affords the same meaning, but is not so simple. See W. § 32. 4. b. Some translate *upon the ministrations*, agency of; but that both strains the use of the preposition (not necessary even in Matt. 12, 41) and employs the noun differently from Rom. 13, 2 (not elsewhere in N. T.). The presence of angels at the giving of the law is not expressly stated in the Old Testament, but is alluded to in Gal. 3, 19, and Heb. 2, 2. Philo and Josephus testify to the same tradition. The Seventy translate Deut. 33, 2 in such a manner as to assert the same fact. It is implied perhaps in Ps. 68, 18. The Jews regarded this angelic mediation as both ennobling the law, and as conferring special honor on themselves, to whom the law was given. For a striking proof of this Jewish feeling, see Jos. Antt. 15. 5. 3. From another point of view, viz. that of Christ's superiority to angels, this angelic intervention showed the inferiority of the law to the gospel; which is the view taken in Heb. 2, 2, and probably in Gal. 3, 19. — καὶ οὐκ ἐφυλάξατε, *and yet ye kept it not*. νόμον as the principal word supplies the object, and not διαταγάς (E. V.). In this verse, therefore, we have the apostle's idea in Rom. 2, 23, where he says that the Jews gloried in the law, while they dishonored God by their violations of it.

VERSES 54–60. *The Death of Stephen.*

V. 54. It is disputed whether Stephen finished his speech or not. The abrupt manner in which he closes, and the exasperation of the Jews at that moment, render it probable that he was interrupted. ἀκούοντες as present favors the same view, but is not decisive (see 5, 5; 13, 48).— For διεπρίοντο, see on 5, 33.

V. 55. πλήρης πνεύματος ἁγίου. The Spirit revealed to his soul this scene in heaven. It was not a vision addressed to the senses. It is needless, therefore, to inquire, as Meyer now admits, whether our martyr could see the opened sky through the roof or a window. — For δόξαν θεοῦ, *the glory of God*, see on v. 2. — ἑστῶτα, *standing*, instead of sitting, as at other times. The Saviour had risen in order to intimate his readiness to protect or sustain his servant (Bng. Kuin. Mey.). It appears to me doubtful whether we are to attach that or any other significancy to the particular attitude in which he appeared.

V. 56. ἰδοὺ, κ. τ. λ. This declaration would tend to exasperate them still more. They are now told that He whom they had crucified, and whom they were ready to slay anew in the person of his followers, was exalted to supreme dominion at the right hand of God. See remarks on 2, 34.

V. 57. κράξαντες, *crying*, among other things, perhaps that he should be silent, or that he should be put to death; comp. 19, 32; Matt. 27, 23; John 19, 12. — συνέσχον τὰ ὦτα αὐτῶν. They affected to regard his words as blasphemous, and *stopped their ears* as an expression of their abhorrence. — καὶ ὥρμησαν, κ. τ. λ. Under the Roman laws, the Jews had no power to inflict capital punishment without the sanction of the procurator or his proxy; see John 18, 31. Nearly all critics, at present, concur in that view. Hence the stoning of Stephen was an illegal, tumultuous proceeding. The Roman governors connived often at such irregularities, provided the Roman interest or power suffered no detriment. As Pilate was deposed in A. D. 35, or 36, some have thought that his office may have been still vacant (see on 6, 1), and that the Jews took greater liberty on that account.

V. 58. ἔξω τῆς πόλεως, *out of the city*, because a place so holy was not to be defiled with blood; see Lev. 24, 14. Compare the note on 14, 19. — καὶ οἱ μάρτυρες, κ. τ. λ., *and the witnesses laid off their garments*, that they might have the free use of their arms in hurling the stones. The law of Moses required the witnesses in the case of a capital offence to begin the work of death; see Deut. 13, 10; 17, 7. The object of the law, it has been suggested, may have been to prevent inconsiderate or false testimony. Many would be shocked at the idea of shedding blood, who would not scruple to gain a private end, or to gratify their malice, by misrepresentation and falsehood. — παρὰ τοὺς πόδας, *at his feet* for safekeeping; comp. 22, 20. Their selecting Saul for this purpose shows that he was already known as a decided enemy of the Christians. His zeal and dialectic skill in the controversy with Stephen (see on 6, 9) could not have failed to establish his claim to that character. — νεανίου, *a young man;* a designation which the Greeks could apply to a person till he was forty years old, but perhaps in common speech would rarely extend beyond the age of thirty. This term, therefore, is very indefinite, as an indication of Saul's age at the time of this occurrence. In all probability he was not far from thirty when he was converted; not much less, as the Sanhedrim would hardly have entrusted so important a commission to a mere youth (see 9, 1 sq.), and not more, as his recorded life (closing about A. D. 64) would otherwise be too short for the events of his history.[1]

V. 59. ἐπικαλούμενον, *calling upon*, viz. Christ. κύριε Ἰησοῦ just before supplies the only natural object after this participle. "That the first Christians called on Jesus," says De Wette, i. e. addressed prayer to him, "is evident from 9, 14. 21; 22, 16; comp. 2, 21; Rom. 10, 12 sq." See further, on 9, 14. — As the dying Saviour said to the Father, "Into thy hands I commend my spirit," so the dying Stephen said now to the Saviour, δέξαι τὸ πνεῦμά μου.

V. 60. μὴ στήσῃς . . . . ταύτην, *establish not this sin to them*, reckon or count it not to them (Rob. De Wet.). Christ had set an example of this duty, as well as enjoined it by precept. No parallel to this prayer of Stephen can be found out of Christian history. The Greeks expressed a dehortatory command or wish by μή with the subjunctive aorist, when the act was one not yet commenced; comp. on 10, 15. This is Hermann's rule. See Mt. § 511. 3; K. § 259. 5. — ἐκοιμήθη, *fell asleep*, died; comp. 13, 36; 1 Cor. 15, 18, etc. Heathen writers employed the verb occasionally in that sense; but its derivative, κοιμητήριον, *cemetery*, i. e. a place where the body sleeps in the hope of a resurrection, was first used by Christians. It marks the introduction of the more cheerful ideas which the gospel has taught men to connect with the grave.

CHAPTER VIII.

VERSES 1–3. *The Burial of Stephen.*

V. 1. The first sentence here would have closed more properly the last chapter. — συνευδοκῶν, *consenting*, *approving with* them, viz. the murderers of Stephen, so that he shared their guilt without

[1] For information in regard to the early life and training of the apostle Paul (a topic important to a just view of his character and history), the student may consult Dr. Davidson's Introduction to the New Testament, Vol. II. p. 122 sq.; Conybeare and Howson's Life and Epistles of St. Paul, Vol. I. p. 40 sq. (2d ed.); Selections from German Literature (Edwards and Park), p. 31 sq.; Schrader's Der Apostel Paul, Zweiter Theil, p. 14 sq.; Hemsen's Das Leben des Apostels u. s. w., erstes Kapitel; and Tholuck's Vermischte Schriften, Band II. p. 272 sq.

participating so directly in the act. In Rom. 1, 32, Paul lays it down as one of the worst marks of a depraved mind that a person can bring himself to applaud thus coolly the sins of others, and in 22, 20, he says that he himself had exhibited that mark of depravity in relation to the death of Stephen. Luke here records probably a confession which he had often heard from the lips of the apostle. For ἦν with the participle, see on 1, 10. — ἐν ἐκείνῃ τῇ ἡμέρᾳ, *on that day* (comp. 11, 19); not indefinite *at that time*, which would require the noun to be plural. The stoning of Stephen was the signal for an immediate and universal persecution. — πάντες need not be pressed so as to include every individual; see on 3, 18. Zeller clings to the letter, and then argues against the truth of the narrative from the improbability of such a panic. Many of those who fled returned, doubtless, after the cessation of the present danger. It is not to be supposed that the church which we find existing at Jerusalem after this was made up entirely of new members. — κατὰ τὰς χώρας, κ. τ. λ. They fled at first to different places in Judea and Samaria; but some of them, probably the foreign Jews, went afterwards to other countries (see v. 4 and 11, 19).

V. 2. συνεκόμισαν, *bore away together* (i. e. to the grave), joined to bury; or simply *buried*, as the force of the preposition is not always traceable in this verb (see Pape s. v.). — δέ, *now*, carries back the mind to Stephen after the digression in v. 1; not *but*, in spite of the persecution, for it was not only permitted among the Jews, but required, that the bodies of those executed should be buried. — ἄνδρες εὐλαβεῖς are pious Jews (see on 2, 5), who testified in this way their commiseration for Stephen's fate, and their conviction of his innocence. The Christians would not have been allowed to perform such an office; they, too, would have been designated as disciples or brethren. — κοπετόν, *lamentation*, as expressed in the Oriental way by clapping the hands or smiting on the breast.

V. 3. δέ, *now*, presents Saul again as the principal person; or possibly *but* (E. V.), contrasting his conduct with that of the εὐλαβεῖς. — κατὰ τοὺς οἴκους, *into the houses* one after another. The preposition marks both direction and succession. — σύρων, *dragging*, bearing off with violence; comp. 14, 19; 17, 6. See Tittm. Synm. p. 57 sq. We see the man's ferocious spirit in his manner. "Haling," in the English translation, is an old word for *hauling* or *hawling*. — τε ἄνδρας, κ. τ. λ., *not only men but women;* repeated also in 9, 2 and 22, 4 as a great aggravation of his cruelty.

VERSES 4–8. *The Gospel is preached in Samaria.*

V. 4. οἱ μὲν οὖν διασπαρέντες, *Those therefore dispersed,* taken as a substantive; comp. 1, 6. The clause is illative as well as resumptive, since it was in consequence of the persecution (v. 1) that the disciples were led to new fields of labor. — διῆλθον, *went abroad,* lit. *through,* i. e. different places. Luke intimates the circuit of their labors more fully in 11, 19.

V. 5. This is the *Philip* mentioned in 6, 5 and 21, 8; not the apostle of that name, for he remained still at Jerusalem, see v. 1. — κατελθών, *having come down,* because he journeyed from Jerusalem (v. 15); to go to that city was ἀναβαίνειν. — εἰς πόλιν τῆς Σαμαρείας, *unto the city of Samaria,* genitive of apposition (Grot. Kuin. Win. Rob.), or *a city* in that country (Olsh. Neand. De Wet. Mey.). That the capital was called *Samaria* at this time, as well as *Sebaste,* we see from Jos. Antt. 20. 6. 2. πόλιν, with that reference, may omit the article because Σαμαρείας defines it; comp. 2 Pet. 2, 6. W. § 19. 2. It would be most natural to repair at once to the chief city, and it was there that such a man as Simon Magus (see v. 9) would be most apt to fix his abode. — ὄχλοι, in v. 6, indicates a populous city. If it was not the capital, it may have been Sychar, where the Saviour preached with so much effect (Olsh.); see John 4, 5 sq. — αὐτοῖς, *unto them.* The antecedent lies in πόλιν, comp. 18, 11; Matt. 4, 23; Gal. 2, 2. W. § 67. 1. d.

V. 6. προσεῖχον, *attended,* listened with eager interest; not *believed* (Kuin.), which anticipates the result in v. 12. — ἐν τῷ ἀκούειν, κ. τ. λ., *when they heard, and saw,* etc. ἐν with the infinitive denotes here, not the cause, but the time or occasion. K. § 289. 1. 2.

V. 7. πολλῶν γάρ, κ. τ. λ., *For from many who had unclean spirits, they* (the spirits) *went forth,* etc. πολλῶν depends on ἐξ in the verb (Mey. De Wet.), comp. 16, 39; Matt. 10, 14. Some (Bng. Kuin.) make πνεύματα the subject of the verb, and supply αὐτά after ἐχόντων. The other is the more natural order. — βοῶντα, κ. τ. λ., *crying with a loud voice,* and testifying to the Messiahship of Jesus, or the truth of the gospel; comp. Mark 3, 11; Luke 4, 41. The expression would suppose the reader to be acquainted with the fuller account of such cases in the history of Christ. Some understand the cry here to have been an exclamation of rage or indignation on the part of the demons, because they were compelled to release their victims. — πολλοὶ δέ, κ. τ. λ. Here, too (see on 5, 16), ordinary diseases are distinguished from demoniacal possession.

VERSES 9–13. *Simon the Sorcerer, and his Professed Belief.*

V. 9. Σίμων. For the history of this impostor, his character, and the traditions of the church respecting him, the reader is referred to Neander's Church History, Vol. I. p. 454, or his Planting of the Church, p. 46 sq. See note on v. 24. — προϋπῆρχεν, *was there before*, i. e. the arrival of Philip, and had been for a long time, see v. 11. — μαγεύων, κ. τ. λ., states in what character and by what arts he secured so much power. — ἐξιστῶν τὸ ἔθνος, *bewitching the nation;* either because he traversed the country, or drew to himself crowds in the city where he dwelt.

V. 10. ἀπὸ μικροῦ ἕως μεγάλου, *from small unto great*, i. e. both young and old, see Heb. 8, 11; Jon. 3, 5 (Sept.). The expression has been called a Hebraism, but examples of it occur in Greek writers (Mey.). — οὗτος, κ. τ. λ., *This one is the great power of God*, i. e. through him is exhibited that power; they supposed him to perform wonders which evinced his possession of superhuman gifts. The language is similar to that in Rom. 1, 16, where the gospel is said to be δύναμις θεοῦ εἰς σωτηρίαν, i. e. an instrumentality exhibiting the power of God in the salvation of men. This is the more obvious view of the sense, and is the one commonly received. Neander would ascribe to the words a theosophic, concrete meaning. He supposes the Samaritans to have recognized Simon "as more than a man: the Great Power which at first emanated from the invisible God, and through which he created every thing else, had now appeared in a bodily form on the earth." It appears to be exacting too much from the language to understand it in that manner. λέγων εἶναί τινα ἑαυτὸν μέγαν, in v. 9 (comp. 5, 36; Gal. 2, 6), would not show that he himself carried his pretensions so far; and the people are not likely to have conceded to him more than he claimed. — The variation ἡ καλουμένη μεγάλη is well supported (Grsb. Mey. Tsch.): *which is called great*, i. e. is truly so, deserves the epithet. De Wette thinks καλουμένη a gloss, added to weaken the idea: *called great*, but not so in reality.

V. 11. ἱκανῷ χρόνῳ, *for a long time.* The dative stands for the ordinary accusative, as in 13, 20; John 2, 20; Rom. 16, 25. W. § 31. 9; S. § 106. 4. — ταῖς μαγείαις, κ. τ. λ., *they had been bewitched by his sorceries* (lit. *put beside themselves*); not *he had bewitched them* (Vulg. Eng. V.). The perfect ἐξεστακέναι, says Scholefield

(Hints, etc. p. 40), does not admit a transitive sense. See also Brüd. Concord. s. v. It was necessary that men deluded to such an extent should be reclaimed by arguments addressed to the senses; see vv. 6. 7. 17.

V. 13. ὁ δὲ Σίμων, κ. τ. λ., *And Simon also himself believed*, viz. the word preached, i. e. professed to be a disciple, and was baptized in that character. The verb describes him with reference to his supposed or apparent state, not his actual position. He may have been not wholly insincere at first, but soon showed that he had no correct views of the gospel, that he was a stranger to its power; see on v. 18. — δυνάμεις differs from σημεῖα, as explained on 2, 22. — Editors hesitate between δυνάμεις καὶ σημεῖα μεγάλα and σημεῖα καὶ δυνάμεις μεγάλας.

VERSES 14–17. *Peter and John are sent to Samaria.*

V. 14. There is no inadvertence here. The apostles had remained at Jerusalem (v. 1). — Σαμάρεια may be the name of the city or the country; see on v. 5. The application here would not control it there. Neander refers it to the country. In that case, as Philip had preached at one place only, we must regard the idea as generalized: his success there was hailed as the pledge of success in all Samaria. — πρὸς αὐτούς, *unto them* in that city, or country; the antecedent implied, as in v. 5.

V. 15. καταβάντες, *having come down*. Their imparting the Spirit was consequent on the journey hither (post hoc), but is not said to have been the object of it (propter hoc). That none but the apostles were empowered to bestow this gift, has been affirmed by some, and denied by others (see 1 Tim. 4, 14). If it was a prerogative of the apostles (who had no successors in the church), the inference would be that it ceased with the extinction of that order. The Catholics and those who entertain Catholic views appeal to this scripture as showing the inferiority of the pastor to the bishop. — προσηύξαντο, κ. τ. λ. The Samaritans had received already the converting influences of the Spirit; and hence the object of the prayer was, that their faith might be confirmed by a miraculous attestation; see on 5, 32. — ὅπως with the finite verb circumscribes the infinitive; comp. 25, 3; Matt. 8, 34 (De Wet.); better here as telic, since prayer may be viewed as a necessary condition of the gift; comp. v. 24.

V. 17. ἐπετίθουν is the imperfect of a repeated act. For the import of the symbol, see on 6, 6. — καὶ ἐλάμβανον, κ. τ. λ., *and they received the Holy Spirit* as the author of the endowments conferred on them. Among these may have been the gift of tongues (see 2. 4; 10, 46), and also that of prophesy, as well as the power of working miracles. Middleton's rule is, that the anarthous πνεῦμα denotes only some effect or actual operation of the Spirit, while τὸ πνεῦμα signifies the Divine Person in general, without reference to any particular instance or mode of operation. See Green's Gr. p. 229. The distinction affects no question of a doctrinal nature; it may agree well enough with some passages, but is purely arbitrary in its application to others. The true principle is that stated on 1, 2.

VERSES 18–24. *The Hypocrisy of Simon, and its Exposure.*

V. 18. θεασάμενος (which means *to see with interest*, or *desire*) has less external support than ἰδών. Meyer retains the former, on the principle that the more common word would displace the less common, instead of the reverse. The ambition or cupidity of Simon had slumbered for a time, but was now aroused at the sudden prospect of obtaining a power which would enable him to gratify his selfish desires, which would place at his command unbounded wealth and influence. He had seen Philip perform miracles, but had seen no instance until now, in which that power had been transferred to others. The interval between this development of his true character and his profession of the Christian faith, was probably not long. — προσήνεγκεν αὐτοῖς χρήματα, *offered to them money.* This act has originated our word *simony*, which Webster defines as "the crime of buying or selling ecclesiastical preferment, or the corrupt presentation of any one to an ecclesiastical benefice for money or reward." It is fortunate for us, that our religious institutions in this country require us to obtain our knowledge of the term from a lexicon.

V. 19. κἀμοί, *to me also*, that I may possess it like you; not *to me* as well as to others, since no example of such transfer was known to him. — ᾧ ἐάν, *upon whomsoever*, see on 2, 21. — ἐξουσίαν ταύτην refers to v. 18, *this power*, authority, which he had seen them exercise; not to the clause following. Hence ἵνα is not definitive, *to wit, that*, but telic, *in order that.*

V. 20. τὸ ἀργύριον, κ. τ. λ., *May thy money with thee* (= and thou) *perish*, lit. *be for destruction*, consigned thereto. This is the language of strong emotion; it expresses the intense abhorrence which the proposal excited in the mind of Peter. That it was not a deliberate wish, or an imprecation, is evident from v. 22, where the apostle points out to Simon the way to escape the danger announced to him. σύν σοι some take to mean *with thee* who art in the way to destruction, i. e. may thy money share the doom to which thou art devoted. But the clause contains only one verb, and it is violent to make it thus optative and declarative at the same time. — ὅτι τὴν δωρεὰν, κ. τ. λ., *because thou didst think,* deem it possible (aor., because the proposal made was the sin) *to acquire* (not passive, as in the Eng. V.) *the gift of God with money.* τὴν δωρεάν stands opposed to διὰ χρημάτων κτᾶσθαι, and hence means, that which God bestows gratuitously on those who are qualified to receive it; not that which it is *his* prerogative to give in distinction from men.

V. 21. οὐκ ἔστι . . . . κλῆρος, *Thou hast no part nor lot.* The first term is literal, the second figurative; they are conjoined in order to affirm the exclusion spoken of with more emphasis. — ἐν τῷ λόγῳ τούτῳ, *in this word,* doctrine, or gospel, which we preach (Olsh. Neand.), or *in this thing,* viz. the gift of the Spirit (Bng. Mey. De Wet.). The first sense accords better with the usage of the word, and is also stronger and more comprehensive; for if the state of his heart was such as to exclude him from the ordinary benefits of the gospel, much more must it render him unfit to recieve the higher communications of the Spirit, or to be honored as the medium of conferring them on others.

V. 22. μετανόησον . . . . ταύτης occurs *in sensu prægnanti* for *repent,* and turn *from this thy wickedness;* comp. μετάνοια ἀπὸ νεκρῶν ἔργων in Heb. 6, 1. W. § 66. 2. — For the received θεοῦ after δεήθητι, most manuscripts read κυρίου. — εἰ ἄρα . . . . καρδίας σου, *if perhaps the thought of thy heart shall be forgiven thee.* Some idea like *and thus see if,* appears to lie between the imperative, and the indicative future. See W. § 41. p. 268. Some attribute the problematical form of the expression to an uncertainty, on the part of Peter, whether the man had sincerely repented or would repent of his sin. That view assigns the qualifying effect of ἄρα to the first clause, instead of the second, where it stands. Others, more correctly, find the ground of it in the aggravated nature of the sin, or in the apostle's strong sense of its aggravated nature, leading him to doubt whether he ought to represent the pardon as certain, even if he repented. — ἡ ἐπίνοια, *the thought,* wicked purpose, a *vox media.*

V. 23. εἰς γὰρ, κ. τ. λ., *For I see that thou art in the gall of bitterness.* The gall of noxious reptiles was considered by the ancients as the source of their venom; and hence χολή, with an allusion to that fact, becomes an expressive metaphor to denote the malice or moral corruption of the wicked. Compare this with Job 20, 14; Rom. 3, 13. ῥίζα πικρίας, in Heb. 12, 15, is a different figure. πικρίας describes a quality of χολήν, and is equivalent to an adjective, *bitter gall* (see on 7, 30); so that, transferring the idea from the figure to the subject, the expression imports the same as *malignant, aggravated depravity.* — καὶ σύνδεσμον ἀδικίας, *and in the bond of iniquity*, i. e. not only wicked in principle, but confirmed in the habit of sin, bound to it as with a chain. — εἰς (lit. *unto*) belongs also to the second clause, and in both cases implies the idea of abandonment to the influence or condition spoken of.

V. 24. δεήθητε, κ. τ. λ. We may infer from Luke's silence as to the subsequent history of Simon, that the rebuke of the apostle alarmed only his fears; that it produced no reformation in his character, or his course of life. This conclusion would be still more certain, if it were true, as some maintain, that this Simon was the person whom Josephus mentions under the same name as the wicked accomplice of the procurator Felix (Antt. 20. 7. 2). Neander held at one time that they were the same, but afterwards receded from that opinion. So common a name is no proof of their identity, and it is proof against it, that this Simon, according to Justin Martyr, belonged to Samaria, while the other is said to have been a native of Cyprus.

VERSES 25–35. *Conversion of the Ethiopian.*

V. 25. οἱ μέν, viz. Peter and John; probably unattended by Philip. — εὐηγγελίσαντο (T. R.), *preached*, may state the result of their labors while they had been absent, or what took place on their return to Jerusalem. The latter view agrees best with the order of the narrative, and is required if we read ὑπέστρεφον and εὐηγγελίζοντο (Lchm. Mey. Tsch.), *were preaching*. This verb, according to a later Grecism (Lob. ad Phryn. p. 267), may take its object in the accusative, as well as the dative; comp. v. 40; 14, 15. 21; 16, 10; Luke 3, 18; Gal. 1, 9. W. § 32. 1.

V. 26. δέ answers to μέν in v. 25. — ἐλάλησε, κ. τ. λ. Philip appears to have received this direction in Samaria (v. 13), and soon after the departure of the apostles. Zeller conjectures (Theol. Jahrb. 1851) that he had come back to Jerusalem in the mean time; but the terms of the communication are against that view. — ἀνάστηθι involves an idiom explained in the note on 9, 18. — πορεύου. For the tense, see on 3, 6. — κατὰ μεσημβρίαν, *down to the south*, because in Samaria he was so far to the north of Jerusalem. This expression points out, not the direction of the road from Jerusalem to Gaza, but that in which Philip was to travel, in order to find the road. The collocation joins the words evidently to the verb, and not, as some have represented, to the clause which follows. — *Gaza* was about sixty miles southwest from Jerusalem. — αὕτη ἐστὶν ἔρημος, *This is desert.* Some refer the pronoun to Γάζαν, and, as that city was demolished a short time before the destruction of Jerusalem, they suppose that Luke by ἔρημος would describe its condition in consequence of that event. This is the opinion of Hug, Scholz, Meyer (formerly), Lekebusch, and others. But unless Luke wrote the Acts later than A. D. 64 or 65,[1] this explanation cannot be correct; for Gaza was not destroyed by the Romans till after the commencement of the Jewish war which resulted in the overthrow of Jerusalem. Most of the critics who contend for a later origin of the book derive their chief argument for it from this assumed meaning of ἔρημος. But further, even supposing Luke to have written just after the destruction of Gaza, it appears improbable that the novelty merely of the event would lead him to mention a circumstance so entirely disconnected with his history. Others refer αὕτη to ὁδόν, but differ on the question whether we are to ascribe the words to Luke or the angel. According to Bengel, Olshausen, Winer (Realw. I. p. 395), De Wette, and others, they form a parenthetic remark by Luke, who would give the reader an idea of the region which was the scene of so memorable an occurrence. I prefer this opinion to any other. According to some, the words belong to the communication of the angel, and were intended to point out to the evangelist the particular road on which he would find the eunuch. In that case it seems to me that the relative pronoun would have introduced them more naturally than αὕτη (yet see W. § 22. 4); and besides, if it were so that any one road to Gaza was known as "desert" beyond others, *Luke* may have inserted the epithet for the *reader's* information, as well as the angel for the sake of Philip. "There were several ways," says Dr. Robinson, "leading from Jerusalem to Gaza. The most frequented at the present day, although the longest, is the way by Ramleh. Anciently there appear to have been two more direct roads; one down the great Wady es-Surar by Beth-Shemesh, and then passing near Tell es-Safieh; the other through Wady el-Musurr to Betogabra or Eleutheropolis, and thence to Gaza through a more southern tract." Bibl. Res. II. p. 640; or p. 514 (ed. 1856). Another route still proceeded by the way of Bethle-

[1] See Introduction, § 5.

hem and Bethzur to Hebron, and then turned across the plain to Gaza. It passed through the southern part of Judea, and hence through a region actually called "the desert" in Luke 1, 80. This description would apply no doubt to some part of any one of the roads in question. The Hebrews termed any tract "a desert" which was thinly inhabited or unfitted for tillage. See more on v. 36. Lange[1] spiritualizes the expression: *this is desert* (morally); the angel's reason why the evangelist should seek to enlighten also this benighted region.

V. 27. Αἰθίοψ, *an Ethiopian,* may refer to the country where he resided (comp. 2, 9), or to his extraction. Hence some suppose that the eunuch was a Jew, who lived in Ethiopia, but most that he was a heathen convert to Judaism. Observe the meaning of Αἰθιόπων in the next clause. It was customary for proselytes, as well as foreign Jews, to repair to Jerusalem for worship; comp. 20, 2; John 12, 20. — εὐνοῦχος, *a eunuch* in the proper import of the word; not a minister of state, *courtier,* to the exclusion of that import, because it would then render δυνάστης superfluous. The latter term, *a state officer,* is a noun both in form and usage (De Wet. Rob.), and is not to be translated as an adjective with εὐνοῦχος (Kuin. Mey.).— Κανδάκης τῆς βασιλίσσης Αἰθίοπων, *Candace, the queen of the Ethiopians.* Ethiopia was the name of the portion of Africa known to the ancients south of Egypt, of which Meroe, a fertile island formed by two branches of the Nile, constituted an important part. Win. Realw. II. p. 439. "It is evident both from Strabo and Dio that there was a queen named Candace in Ethiopia, who fought against the Romans about the twenty-second or twenty-third year of the reign of Augustus Cæsar. (Dio calls her queen of the Αἰθίοπες ὑπὲρ Αἰγύπτου οἰκοῦντες.) It is clear also from Pliny, who flourished in the reign of the Emperor Vespasian, that there was a queen of Ethiopia named Candace in his time; and he adds, that this had been the name of their queens now for many years. It is beyond all doubt, therefore, that there was a queen of Ethiopia of this name at the time when Philip is said to have converted the eunuch. Eusebius tells us that this country continued to be governed by women even to his time." See Biscoe, p. 47. Candace was the name, not of an individual, but of a dynasty, like Pharaoh in Egypt, or Cæsar among the Romans. — ἐπὶ τῆς γάζης, *over* (as in 12, 20) *the treasure.* — προσκυνήσων, *in order to worship* proves, not that he was a Jew, but that he was not a heathen.

[1] Das apostolische Zeitalter, zweiter Band, p. 109.

V. 28. ἀνεγίνωσκε, *was reading*, aloud as we see from v. 30, and probably the Greek text, not the Hebrew, since the Septuagint was used mostly out of Palestine. It is still a custom among the Orientals, when reading privately, to read audibly, although they may have no particular intention of being heard by others.[1] It was common for the Jews to be occupied in this way, especially when they were travelling (Schöttg. Hor. Heb. II. p. 443). — It is not improbable that the eunuch had heard, at Jerusalem, of the death of Jesus, and of the wonderful events connected with it, of his claim to be the Messiah, and the existence of a numerous party who acknowledged him in that character. Hence he may have been examining the prophecies at the time that Philip approached him, with reference to the question how far they had been accomplished in the history of the person concerning whom such reports had reached him. The extraordinary means which God employed to bring the Æthiopian to a knowledge of the gospel, and the readiness with which he embraced it, authorize the belief, that in this way, or some other, his mind had been specially prepared for the reception of the truth.

V. 29. κολλήθητι τῷ ἅρματι τούτῳ, *attach thyself to this chariot*, keep near it, follow it. He heard the eunuch read for a time unobserved before he addressed him.

V. 30. ἆράγε, κ. τ. λ., *Dost thou understand then what thou readest?* γε serves to render the question more definite. The answer after ἆρα is more commonly negative; comp. Luke 18, 8. Klotz ad Devar. II. p. 180 sq.; W. § 57. 2. This is given as the rule for prose. — γινώσκεις ἃ ἀναγινώσκεις is a paronomasia (comp. 2 Cor. 3, 2) and is too striking to be accidental. Philip spoke no doubt in Greek, and would arouse the mind through the ear.

V. 31. πῶς γὰρ, κ. τ. λ., *For how could I——?* The form of the reply attaches itself to the implied negative which precedes. — ὁδηγήσῃ, *should guide*, instruct, similar to John 16, 13.

V. 32. ἡ δὲ περιοχὴ, κ. τ. λ., *Now the contents* (comp. 1 Pet. 2, 6) *of the passage* (De Wet. Mey.); not *of the Scripture* in general, *section*, because γραφῆς, being limited by the relative clause, must denote the particular place *which he was reading;* comp. v. 35; Luke 4, 21. — ἦν αὕτη, *was this*, viz. Is. 53, 7. 8, quoted almost *verbatim* from the Septuagint. — ἤχθη, *was led*, sc. עֶבֶד יְהוָֹה, *the servant of Jehovah*, or the Messiah. — καὶ ὡς ἀμνὸς, κ. τ. λ., *and as a lamp*, etc. This comparison represents the uncomplaining submission with which the Saviour yielded himself to

[1] See Jowett's Researches in Syria, p. 443.

the power of his enemies. The death of Christ was so distinctly foretold in this passage, that Bolingbroke was forced to assert that Jesus brought on his own crucifixion by a series of preconcerted measures, merely to give the disciples who came after him the triumph of an appeal to the old prophecies.[1]

V. 33. ἐν τῇ ταπεινώσει, κ. τ. λ., admits most readily of this sense: *In his humiliation*, i. e. in the contempt, violence, outrage, which he suffered, *his judgment was taken away*, viz. the judgment due to him; he had the rights of justice and humanity withheld from him. The Hebrew is מֵעֹצֶר וּמִמִּשְׁפָּט לֻקָּח, which yields essentially the same meaning: *Through violence and punishment he was taken away*, i. e. from life (De Wet.).—τὴν δὲ γενεὰν, κ. τ. λ., *and his generation who shall fully declare?* i. e. set forth the wickedness of his contemporaries in their treatment of him (Mey. De Wet. Rob.). The Hebrew sustains fully that translation. It is possible, also, to render the Greek and the original thus: *Who shall declare his posterity*, the number of his spiritual descendants or followers? The prophet in this case points, by an incidental remark, from the humiliation of Christ to his subsequent triumph, or glorification. Hengstenberg prefers the last meaning.[2]—ὅτι . . . . αὐτοῦ conforms to the first sense of the clause which precedes, better than to the second.

V. 34. ἀποκριθείς, *addressing* (see 3, 12), or *answering* in further reply to the question in v. 30 (Mey.). The passage from Isaiah is cited for the information of the reader, and this verse follows historically after v. 31.—περὶ ἑαυτοῦ, κ. τ. λ. The perplexity of the eunuch in regard to the application of the prophecy indicates that he was a foreigner, rather than a Jew. The great body of the Jewish nation understood this portion of Isaiah to be descriptive of the character and sufferings of the Messiah.[3] "The later Jews," says Gesenius, "no doubt, relinquished this interpretation, in consequence of their controversy with the Christians."

V. 35. ἀνοίξας τὸ στόμα αὐτοῦ is an imperfect Hebraism, i. e. was not peculiar to the Hebrew or Hellenistic writers, but most common in them. See W. § 3. It arises from the Oriental fondness for the minute in description, the circumstantial. The ex-

[1] Chalmers, Evidences of Christianity, Chapter VI.

[2] For a fuller view of the original passage, the reader is referred to Hengstenberg's Christology, Vol. I. p. 518 sq.; and to Professor Alexander's Commentary on Isaiah.

[3] See the proofs in Hengstenberg's Christology, Vol. I. p. 484 sq., and Schöttgen's Horæ Hebraicæ, Vol. II. p. 647 sq.

pression occurs properly before important, weighty remarks; comp. 10, 34; Job 3, 1; 32, 20. — καὶ ἀρξάμενος ἀπὸ τῆς γραφῆς ταύτης is elliptical for *and beginning from this passage*, and proceeding thence to others. W. § 66. 1. c.

VERSES 36–40. *The Baptism of the Eunuch.*

V. 36. κατὰ τὴν ὁδόν, *along* (5, 15) *the way.* — ἐπί τι ὕδωρ, *unto a certain water;* not *some*, as the genitive would follow that partitive sense. C. § 362. β. — τί κωλύει, κ. τ. λ., *What hinders* (what objection is there) *that I should be baptized?* This is the modest expression of a desire on the part of the eunuch to declare his faith in that manner, provided the evangelist was willing to administer the ordinance to him; comp. 10, 47. As De Wette remarks, the question presupposes that Philip, among other things, had instructed him in regard to the nature and necessity of baptism. As the road on which the eunuch journeyed is unknown (see on v. 26), it cannot be ascertained where he was baptized. It may interest the reader to state some of the conjectures. Eusebius and Jerome concur in saying that it took place at Bethzur (Josh. 15, 58; Neh. 3, 16), near Hebron, about twenty miles south of Jerusalem. The site has been identified, bearing still the ancient name. The water there at present issues from a perennial source, a part of which runs to waste in the neighboring fields, and a part is collected into a drinking trough on one side of the road, and into two small tanks on the other side. It was formerly objected that no chariot could have passed here on account of the broken nature of the ground; but travellers have now discovered the traces of a paved road and the marks of wheels on the stones. See Ritter's Erdkunde, XVI. 1. p. 266, and Wilson's Lands of the Bible I. p. 381. The writer found himself able to ride at a rapid pace nearly all the way between Bethlehem and Hebron. The veneration of early times reared a chapel on the spot, the ruins of which are still to be seen. Von Raumer[1] defends the genuineness of this primitive tradition. In the age of the crusaders, the baptism was transferred to Ain Haniyeh, about five miles south-west of Jerusalem. A fountain here on the hill-side, which irrigates freely the adjacent valley, is known among the Latins as St. Philip's Fountain. One of the ancient roads to Gaza passed here, but appears to have been less travelled than the others. Dr. Robinson thinks that the parties must have been nearer to Gaza at the time of the baptism, and would

[1] Palästina, von Karl von Raumer (1850), p. 411 sq.

refer the transaction to a Wady in the plain near Tell el-Hasy. Bibl. Res. II. p. 641; or p. 514 (1856).

V. 37. This verse is wanting in the best authorities. The most reliable manuscripts and versions testify against it. The few copies that contain the words read them variously. Meyer suggests that they may have been taken from some baptismal liturgy, and were added here that it might not appear as if the eunuch was baptized without evidence of his faith. Most of the recent editors expunge the verse. In regard to the passage, see Green's Developed Criticism, p. 97, and Tregelles on the Text of the N. T., p. 269. Yet the interpolation, if it be such, is as old certainly as the time of Irenæus; and Augustine in the fourth century, though he objected to a certain misuse of the text, did not pronounce it spurious. See Humphry's note here. Those who contend for the words remind us that the oldest manuscripts represent a later age, than that of these fathers. Bornemann puts them in brackets as entitled still to some weight. — τὸν υἱὸν τοῦ θεοῦ is the predicate after εἶναι.

V. 38. καὶ ἐκέλευσε, κ. τ. λ., *And he ordered* (viz. the charioteer) *that the carriage should stop*, lit. *stand;* an instructive use of the word for 9, 7. The eunuch's equipage corresponded with his rank. — καὶ κατέβησαν, κ. τ. λ., *and both went down into the water;* not here *unto it* (which εἰς may also mean) for it stands opposed to ἐκ τοῦ ὕδατος, in the next verse; besides they would have occasion to enter the stream, or pool, in order to be baptized into it; comp. ἐβάπτισθη εἰς τὸν Ἰορδάνην, *was baptized into the Jordan*, in Mark 1, 9. See Rob. Lex. p. 118. The preposition in κατέβησαν may refer to the descent from the higher ground to the water, or to the entrance into the water; but not to the descent from the chariot, for this verb corresponds to ἀνέβησαν in v. 39, *they went up*, whereas the eunuch only returned to the carriage.

V. 39. ἐκ τοῦ ὕδατος, *out of the water;* where some render *from*, which confounds ἐκ with ἀπό. — πνεῦμα, κ. τ. λ., *the Spirit of the Lord seized* (hurried away) *Philip*. The expression asserts that he left the eunuch suddenly, under the impulse of an urgent monition from above, but not that the mode of his departure was miraculous in any other respect. This last certainly is not a necessary conclusion. — ἐπορεύετο, κ. τ. λ., *for he went his way*, returned to his country, *rejoicing*. χαίρων belongs logically to a separate clause, but is put here for the sake of brevity. — Tradition says that the eunuch's name was Indich, and that it was he who first preached the gospel in Ethiopia. It is certain that Christianity existed there at an early period, but its introduction, says Neander, cannot be traced to any connection with his labors.

V. 40. εὑρέθη, κ. τ. λ., not *was* = ἦν (Kuin.), but *was found at* (lit. *unto*, from the idea of the journey thither) *Azotus*, i. e. was next heard of there, after the transaction in the desert. This place was the ancient Ashdod, a city of the Philistines, near the sea-coast. The ruins consist of a mound covered with broken pottery, and of a few pieces of marble (see Amos 1, 8). A little village not far off, called Esdud, perpetuates the ancient name.—πόλεις does not depend on the participle, but on the verb, as in v. 25. Among the towns through which he passed between Azotus and Cæsarea must have been Lydda and Joppa. Cæsarea was Philip's home. Here we find him again, after the lapse of more than twenty years, when the Saul who was now "breathing menace and murder against the disciples" was entertained by him as a Christian guest; see 21, 8.—Luke's narrative brings us frequently to *Cæsarea*. It was about sixty miles northwest from Jerusalem, on the Mediterranean, south of Carmel. It was the ancient Στράτωνος πύργος, which Herod the Great had rebuilt and named Cæsarea in honor of Augustus. It was now the residence of the Roman procurators. Its inhabitants were mostly heathen; the Jewish population was small. For an account of this city in its splendor, and in its present state of desolation, see Howson's Life and Epistles of St. Paul, Vol. II. p. 344 sq.

CHAPTER IX.

VERSES 1–9. *Christ appears to Saul on the way to Damascus.*

V. 1. δέ, *but*, turns the attention again to Saul.—ἔτι connects this verse with 8, 3.—ἐμπνέων . . . . φόνου, *breathing menace and murder;* in 26, 11, ἐμμαινόμενος. The figure is founded apparently on the fact, that a person under the excitement of strong emotion breathes harder and quicker, pants, struggles to give vent to the passion of which he is full (Wetst. Kyp. Kuin. Olsh.). πνεῖν τινος, *to breathe of something*, to be redolent, is a different expression. The genitive in this construction denotes properly that from or out of which one breathes, as the cause, source; the accusative, that which one breathes, as the substance, element. See W. § 30. 9. c; Mt. § 376. Meyer translates ἐμπνέων, *inhaling;* but ἐν in this compound was generally lost; see Tromm's Concord. s. v.—τῷ ἀρχιερεῖ. If Saul was converted in A. D. 36, *the high-priest* was Jonathan, the successor of Caiaphas (deposed in A. D. 35) and a son of Ananus, or Annas; but if he was converted in A D. 37 or 38, the high-priest was Theophilus, another son of Annas.

V. 2. ἐπιστολάς, *letters*, which were not merely commendatory, but armed him with full power to execute his object; see v. 14; 26, 12. For the apostle's age at this time, see on 7, 58. The Jews in every country recognized the Sanhedrim as their highest ecclesiastical tribunal. In 26, 10 (comp. v. 14 below), Paul says that he received his authority from the ἀρχιερεῖς, and in 22, 5, from the πρεσβυτέριον, which are merely different modes of designating the Sanhedrim; see on 4, 5. He says here that he had his commission from the high-priest; which harmonizes entirely with the other passages, since the high-priest represented the Sanhedrim in this act. On receiving Saul's application, he may have convened that body, and have been formally instructed to issue the letters. The proposal was sufficiently important to engage the attention of the entire council.—εἰς Δαμασκόν states the local destination of the letters. This ancient capital of Syria was still an important city, and had a large Jewish population. It lay northeast of Jerusalem, distant about one hundred and forty miles, making for those times a rapid journey of five or six days. The route of Saul on this expedition can only be conjectured. If the Roman roads in Syria had been opened as early as this, he went probably for the sake of despatch by the way of Bethel or Gophna to Neapolis, crossed the Jordan near Scythopolis, the ancient Bethshean (now Beisan), and proceeded thence to Gadara, a Roman city, and so through the modern Hauran to Damascus. By another track which coincided in part with the preceding, he passed along the base of Tabor, crossed the Jordan a few miles above the Sea of Tiberias (where Jacob's bridge now is), and then either ascended to Cæsarea Philippi, at the foot of Hermon, or turned more abruptly to the right, and traversed the desert as before on the east of Antilebanon. For the details, see Howson's Work, Vol. I. p. 102 sq.—πρὸς τὰς συναγωγάς, *unto the synagogues*, i. e. the officers of them, who were the ἀρχισυνάγωγος (Luke 8, 49), and the πρεσβύτεροι associated with him (Luke 7, 3). The former term was sometimes applied to them both; see 13, 15; Mark 5, 22. These rulers formed a college, whose province it was, among other duties, to punish those who deserted the Jewish faith. De Wet. Heb. Archæol. § 244. Hence it belonged to them to discipline those who joined the Christian party; or, as it was proposed in this instance, to carry them to Jerusalem, it was their duty to aid Saul in his efforts to apprehend the delinquents. — τῆς ὁδοῦ, i. e. κατ' ἐξοχήν, *of the* (well-known Christian) *way* in regard to faith, manner of life, etc.; comp. 19, 9. 23; 22, 4; 24, 14, 22. See the idea expressed more fully in 16, 17; 18, 25. W. § 18. 1. ὁδοῦ depends on ὄντας under the rule of appurtenance, property. K. § 273. 2; C. § 387.

V. 3. ἐν δὲ τῷ πορεύεσθαι, κ. τ. λ., *Now while he journeyed, it came to pass* (Hebraistic) *that he*, etc. — Δαμασκῷ depends on the verb (K. § 284. 3. 2); not the dative of the place *whither.* — περιήστραψεν αὐτὸν φῶς, *a light gleamed around him.* The preposition in the verb governs αὐτόν. In 22, 6, it is repeated, according to the rule stated on 3, 2. In 22, 6, Paul says that the light which he saw was a *powerful* light, and in 26, 13, that it exceeded the splendor of the sun at noonday. That Luke's statement is the more general one, while the intenser expressions occur in Paul's recital, is what we should expect from the truth of the history.

V. 4. πεσὼν ἐπὶ τὴν γῆν, *having fallen to the earth*, probably from the animal which he rode; see 22, 7. — ἤκουσε, κ. τ. λ. See also 22, 7; 26, 14. The necessary inference is, that Saul heard audible words, and not merely that an impression was made upon him as if he heard them. It was a part of the miracle that those who accompanied him heard the voice of the speaker, but failed to distinguish the words uttered. The communication was intended for Saul, and was understood, therefore, by him only.

V. 5. τίς εἶ, κύριε; *Who art thou, Lord?* He did not know yet that it was Christ who addressed him. Hence κύριε has the significance which belongs to it as recognizing the fact, that an angel, or perhaps God himself, was now speaking to him from heaven. To suppose it used by anticipation, i. e. as denoting him who proved to be Christ, makes it Luke's word, and is unnatural. Yet Saul's uncertainty could have been but momentary: "conscientia ipsa facile diceret, Jesum esse" (Bng.). — The remainder of the verse, as it stands in the common text, viz. σκληρὸν . . . . λακτίζειν, has been transferred to this place from 26, 14. See Green's Developed Criticism, p. 98.

V. 6. Most of the manuscripts begin this verse with ἀλλά. The sentence τρέμων . . . . ποιῆσαι (which the English translation has copied) is wanting in the best authorities. It rests chiefly upon some of the early versions. The words καὶ ὁ κύριος πρὸς αὐτόν have been derived from 22, 10. — ἀλλά occurs often before a command abruptly given; comp. 10, 20; 26, 16. W. § 53. 7; K. § 322; R. 12. — καὶ λαληθήσεταί, κ. τ. λ. It would appear from the speech before Agrippa (see 26, 16–18), that Christ may have made to Saul, at this time, a fuller communication than Luke has reported in this place. The verb here (*it shall be told thee*, etc.) does not exclude that supposition; for it may import that, on his arrival in the city, he should be confirmed in what he had now heard, or instructed further, in regard to his future labors. But some prefer to consider Paul's narrative before Agrippa as the abridged account. The message which Ananias delivered to Saul (intimated here in v. 15, but recorded more fully in 22, 14–16) was a message from Christ; and as the apostle makes no mention of Ananias in 26, 16 sq., it is very possible that he has there, for the sake of brevity, passed over the intermediate agency, and referred the words directly to Christ, which Christ communicated to him through Ananias. This would be merely applying the common maxim, *Quod quis per alium facit, id ipse fecisse putatur.* — τί σε δεῖ ποιεῖν, *what thou must do*, is the answer probably to Saul's question τί ποιήσω, *what shall I do*, recorded in 22, 9. δεῖ refers not to duty, but the divine purpose, destination; see 22, 10.

V. 7. εἱστήκεισαν ἐννεοί, *were standing* (see on 1, 10) *speechless*, having stopped instantly, overcome by amazement and terror; comp. ἔμφοβοι ἐγένοντο in 22, 9. The adjective is more correctly written ἐνεοί. W. § 5. 1. This verb often means *to stand*, not as opposed to other attitudes, but to be fixed, stationary, as opposed to the idea of motion; comp. 8, 38; Luke 5, 2. See the Class. Lexx. s. v. In this sense the passage is entirely consistent with 26, 14, where it is said that when they heard the voice *they all fell to the ground.* Plainly it was not Luke's object to say that they stood erect in distinction from kneeling, lying prostrate, and the like; but that, overpowered by what they saw and heard, they were fixed to the spot; they were unable for a time to speak or move. The conciliation which some adopt (Bng. Kuin. Bmg.) is that they fell to the ground at first, but afterwards rose up and stood. It is unnecessary to urge this view; but Zeller's objection to it that εἱστήκεισαν as pluperfect excludes a previous falling is ungrammatical. — ἀκούοντες μὲν τῆς φωνῆς, *hearing indeed the voice.* The genitive after this verb points out the source or cause of the hearing; the accusative (see v. 4), that which one hears. See the note on v. 1. In 22, 9, Paul says, in reference to the same occurrence, τὴν δὲ φωνὴν οὐκ ἤκουσαν τοῦ λαλοῦντός μοι, which we may render, *but they understood not the voice of him speaking to me.* In adding τοῦ λαλοῦντος, *who spake,* the writer shows that he had in mind the sense of φωνήν, and not the mere sound. ἀκούω, like the corresponding word in other languages, means not only *to hear*, but to hear so as *to understand.* Of the latter usage, the New Testament furnishes other clear examples. 1 Cor. 14, 2. "For he that speaketh in an unknown tongue, speaketh not unto men, but unto God; for no man understands him," — οὐδεὶς γὰρ ἀκούει; comp. v. 16, where ἀκούει passes into οἶδε. Mark 4, 33: "And with many such parables spake he the word unto them, as they were able to understand it," — καθὼς ἠδύναντο ἀκούειν. Some reckon here John 6, 60; Gal. 4, 21, and other passages. For instances of this sense in the classics, see Rob. Lex. s. v. The same usage exists in the Hebrew. One of the definitions of שָׁמַע (see Gesen. Lex. s. v.) is *to understand.* In Gen. 42, 23, it is said that Joseph's brethren "knew not that he heard them" (i. e. *understood,* in the E. V.); "for he spoke unto them by an interpreter." See also Gen. 11, 7. The English language has the same idiom. We say that a person is not heard, or that we do not hear him, when, though we hear his voice, he speaks so low or indistinctly that we do not understand him. The intelligence of the writer of the Acts forbids the idea of a palpable contradiction in the two passages. Since in 22, 9 we have φωνήν, and here in v. 7 φωνῆς, some would attribute to the genitive a partitive sense, i. e. something of the voice, or indistinctly. But the difference does not hold; for in 22, 7, Paul says of himself ἤκουσα φωνῆς, where he cannot mean that he had only a confused perception of what was said to him. Some prefer to vary the sense of φωνή, viz. *noise* or *sound* in this place, but *voice* in 22, 9. But allowing the word to admit of that distinction (see on 2, 6), it is much less common than the proposed variation in ἀκούω, and much less probable here, since the use of the verb would be varied in passages so remote from each other, whereas φωνή would have different senses in almost successive verses. — μηδένα δὲ θεωροῦντες, *but seeing no one* who could have uttered the voice. This appears to be denied of Saul's companions, in opposition to what was true of him, viz. that simultaneously with the light he had seen a personal manifestation of Christ; comp. v. 17; 22, 18. That he saw the speaker as well as heard him, we may infer from the language of Barnabas in v. 17, and that of Ananias in v. 17 and 22, 14. To the fact of his having a view of the glorified Saviour at this time, Paul alludes probably in 1 Cor. 9, 1, where he mentions his having seen the Lord as an evidence of his equality with the other apostles. See the note on 1, 3. Neander, De Wette, Meyer, Osiander, Thiersch, and others, find such an allusion in that passage.

V. 8. ἀνεῳγμένων .... αὐτοῦ, *and when his eyes were opened*, i. e. his eyelids, which he had spontaneously closed when struck with the gleaming light. This expression refers usually to the recovery of one's eyesight, as in Matt. 9, 30; John 9, 10. 20. etc.—οὐδένα ἔβλεπε, *saw no one*, i. e. of his companions, because he was now blind; or, which is a better reading, οὐδέν, *saw nothing*, and hence being unable to see at all, must be led by the hand; not *no one* from whom the voice came (Bng.), since we must have here an explanation of the next clause.

V. 9. μὴ βλέπων (subjective negative), *not seeing* as opposed to a possible idea of the reader that Saul might have regained his sight ere this; whereas οὐ (objective) in the next clause states the historical fact. W. § 55. 5. Meyer, in his last edition, recalls his remark that the negatives are interchanged here.

VERSES 10–18. *Ananias is sent to Saul, and baptizes him.*

V. 10. That *Ananias* was one of the seventy disciples is an unsupported conjecture of some of the older writers.— ὁ κύριος, i. e. Christ, see v. 17.— ἰδοὺ ἐγώ = הִנֵּנִי. This answer implies that the person hears, and waits to listen further; comp. Gen. 22, 1. 7; 27, 1; 1 Sam. 3, 8, etc.

V. 11. For ἀναστάς, see on v. 18.—ῥύμην, *street*, or more strictly *alley*, lane (comp. Luke 14, 21); = στενωπός in the later Greek. See Lob. ad Phryn. p. 40, and R. and P. Lex. s. v.—τὴν καλουμένην εὐθεῖαν, *which is called straight.* The principal street in Damascus at present runs through the city from east to west, and is remarkably straight in some parts, as well as narrow. The Oriental Christians say that this is the street in which Saul lodged. The traces of a triple colonade are reported to be found in the adjacent houses on both sides of the street, and if so they show that the present street, though not so wide, follows at least the line of an ancient street of the city. But even in that case it may be questioned whether ῥύμη would be applied to a thoroughfare adorned with works of so much splendor.—Ταρσέα, *a native of Tarsus* (22, 3), see on v. 30.—γὰρ προσεύχεται, *for he prays.* The act is then taking place, and is mentioned as a reason why Ananias might be sure of a favorable reception. He is informed of the vision also because that served in like manner to prepare the way for his visit.

V. 12. καὶ εἶδεν, κ. τ. λ., *and saw a man*, (made known to him in the vision as) *Ananias by name;* a breviloquence like that in 15, 9. — ἐπιθέντα αὐτῷ χεῖρα, *placing hand upon him*, as a sign of the benefit which he was to be the medium of communicating; comp. on 6, 6. The expression is indefinite, like that in 12, 1. Lachmann thinks the authority sufficient to read τὰς χεῖρας, as in v. 17. — ἀναβλέψῃ, *might look up*, open his eyes and see. This sense is not common out of the New Testament. It is found (a case not usually cited) at the close of Plut. de sera Num. vindicta.

V. 13. The reply of Ananias shows how fearful a notoriety as a persecutor Saul had acquired. Compare 26, 10. — ὅσα κακά, *how great evils.* — τοῖς ἁγίοις σου, *unto thy saints*, i. e. those consecrated to him, and so his. This term, as applied in the New Testament, refers to the normal or prescribed standard of Christian character, rather than the actual one. See 1 Cor. 1, 2, as compared with 1 Cor. 3, 2; 11, 21, etc. It belongs to all who profess to be disciples, and does not distinguish one class of them as superior to others in point of excellence.

V. 14. ἔχει ἐξουσίαν. Ananias may have received letters from the Christians at Jerusalem; or those who came with Saul may have divulged the object of the journey since their arrival. — τοὺς ἐπικαλουμένους τὸ ὄνομά σου, *those who call upon*, invoke in prayer, *thy name;* comp. 2, 21; 7, 59; 1 Cor. 1, 2. This participle is middle, not passive. The Greek for *those on whom thy name is called* would be like that in 15, 17. The expression here is the one which the Seventy commonly use to translate קָרָא בְּשֵׁם, a well known formula in the Old Testament signifying *to worship.* Gesenius (Lex. p. 938) says with reference to this phrase: *To call on the name of God* is to invoke his name, i. e. to praise, celebrate, worship God. Of course, we are to attach the same meaning to the words in the New Testament. Hence this language, which states a fact so characteristic of the first Christians that it fixed upon them the name of *callers upon Christ*, shows that they were accustomed to offer to him divine honor. See on 7, 59.

V. 15. σκεῦος ἐκλογῆς, *a vessel* (2 Cor. 4, 7), instrument, *of choice*, i. e. a chosen instrument. For this use of the genitive, see on 7, 30. The similar examples in Greek belong rather to poetry. It is a common idiom in Hebrew. Gesen. Heb. Gr. § 104. — βαστάσαι, *to bear*, continues the metaphor in σκεῦος (Alf.). — βασιλέων, *kings*, rulers of the highest class; comp. 17, 7; John 19, 15. Paul stood as a witness for Christ before the governors of Cyprus, Achaia, and Judea, and before Herod Agrippa and probably Nero. — υἱῶν Ἰσραήλ. The progress of the narrative will show how faithfully he executed this part of his mission. Though he was the great apostle of the Gentiles, he never ceased to preach to his countrymen.

V. 16. ἐγὼ γὰρ, κ. τ. λ., *For I will show him* by experience, will cause him to learn in the course of his life (Bng. Mey.). According to De Wette, it means that God would teach him by revelation; but this verb is not employed to denote the communication of knowledge in that manner. The statement here confirms the declaration that Saul would accomplish so much for the cause of Christ; *for* (γάρ) he was to suffer much, and his labors would be efficient in proportion to his sufferings.

V. 17. εἶπε, κ. τ. λ. The address of Ananias to Saul is reported more fully in 22, 14 sq. He salutes him as *brother* (ἀδελφέ), not as of the same stock nationally (2, 29; 21, 1; 28, 17), but as having now "obtained like precious faith" with himself. He could apply that title to Saul with confidence after having received such information in regard to the state of his mind, and the sphere of labor to which Christ had called him.—'Ιησοῦς .... ἤρχου. Luke's account of the communication to Ananias passes over this part of it. ᾗ, in this clause, *in which*, omits the preposition because the antecedent has it (a species of attraction); comp. ὃ προσκέκλημαι in 13, 2. Mat. § 595. 4. c.—καὶ πλησθῇς, κ. τ. λ., *and mayest be filled with the Holy Spirit*, i. e. receive abundantly the extraordinary gifts and qualifications which he would need as an apostle (comp. Gal. 2, 7 sq.). See the note on 1, 8.

V. 18. ἀπέπεσον .... ὡσεὶ λεπίδες, *there fell off from his eyes as if scales.* This means that he experienced a sensation as if such had been the fact. ὡσεί shows that it was so in appearance, not in reality; comp. 2, 3; 6, 15, etc. The nature of the injury which his eyes had suffered we cannot determine; but it is certain that the recovery from the injury was instantaneous and complete. We may suppose that Luke had often heard Paul relate how he felt at that moment.—ἀναστάς, *having risen up*, and (if need be) gone forth to the place of baptism; comp. Luke 4, 38 (see Rob. Lex. s. v. II. 1. a); or simply, *having made himself ready*, i. e. without delay; comp. Luke 15, 18. On this Hebraistic use of the word, see Gesen. Lex. p. 919; W. § 65. 4. c. It is impossible to infer from it that he was baptized in the house of Judas, or that he was not. Damascus at the present day abounds in water, and all the better houses have a reservoir in their court, or stand beside a natural or an artificial stream. See Robinson, Vol. III. p. 400.—λαβὼν τροφήν, *having taken food* after the fast of the three days, see v. 9.

VERSES 19–22. *The Labors of Paul at Damascus.*

V. 19. μετὰ τῶν μαθητῶν, *with the disciples*, in private intercourse with them. — ἡμέρας τινάς, *certain days*, denotes too brief a period to apply to the entire residence at Damascus (Neand. De Wet. Mey.).

V. 20. καὶ εὐθέως, *and immediately*, after the days spent in the society of the Christians there. — ἐκήρυσσε τὸν Ἰησοῦν = ἐκήρυσσε ὅτι ὁ Ἰησοῦς ἐστιν, κ. τ. λ.; see on 3, 10. Ἰησοῦς is the individual or personal name of the Saviour; and it was the apostle's object to establish the identity of Jesus with the Son of God, or the promised Messiah; comp. v. 22.

V. 21. ὁ πορθήσας, *who destroyed*, put to death; see 22, 3. — ὄνομα τοῦτο, viz. that of Jesus (v. 20). The form of the remark adapts itself to the narrative. — ὧδε, *hither*, after a verb of motion; *here* in v. 14. — εἰς τοῦτο anticipates the next clause. — For ἀρχιερεῖς, see on 4, 6. — The astonishment expressed here proceeded from the Jews, whom Paul addressed in the synagogues. Most of the Christians at Damascus must have been apprised of the change in his character before he appeared in public.

V. 22. Σαῦλος δὲ, κ. τ. λ., *But Saul was more strengthened*, i. e. in his faith, see 16, 5; Rom. 4, 20. This remark describes his state after the lapse of some time subsequent to his conversion. It is made apparently, not merely to indicate his Christian progress, but to suggest why he preached with such convincing power. — συμβιβάζων, κ. τ. λ., *proving that this one is the Christ*. οὗτος recalls Ἰησοῦν in v. 20 the more readily, because τοῦτο intervenes in v. 21.

VERSES 23–25. *The Flight of Paul from Damascus.*

V. 23. ὡς δὲ .... ἱκαναί, *Now when many days were accomplished*. At this place, probably, we are to insert the journey into Arabia, which the apostle mentions in Gal. 1, 17. So Neander, Hemsen, Meyer, and others. That Luke makes no allusion to this journey agrees with the summary character of his history generally, in relation to the early portion of Paul's life. It will be observed, he does not say that the "many days" were all spent at Damascus, but that many had elapsed since his first arrival, before the escape which took place under the circumstances narrated. Hence the language leaves us at liberty to suppose that he passed more or less of the intermediate period elsewhere. The time that Paul was absent in Arabia belongs probably to the earlier part of the ἡμέραι ἱκαναί, rather than the latter; for in Gal. 1, 17 he mentions Arabia before Damascus, as if the former country was the first important scene of his apostleship. The time which he spent in Arabia formed not improbably a large part of the three years before his return to Jerusalem; for that supposition explains best the fact that he was still so unknown there as a Christian, see v. 26. Some critics, as Olshausen, Ebrard, Sepp,[1] would place the excursion into Arabia between v. 25 and v. 26. The objection to that view is, that the apostle must then have come back to Damascus (πάλιν ὑπέστρεψα εἰς Δαμασκόν in Gal. 1, 17), in the face of the deadly hostility on the part of the Jews which had already driven him from that city.

V. 24. ἐγνώσθη τῷ Σαύλῳ, *became known by Saul*, to him. For the dative after the passive, see on 5, 9. The discovery enabled the apostle to escape the danger. — παρετήρουν τὰς πύλας, *were watching the gates*, i. e. with the aid of soldiers whom the governor placed at their disposal, so that the act of guarding the city could be ascribed to the Jews, as in this passage, or to the ethnarch, as in 2 Cor. 11, 32. The Jews at this time were influential as well as numerous at Damascus, and could easily enlist the government on their side. — διὰ τοῦ τείχους, *through the wall*, and at the same time διὰ θυρίδος διὰ τοῦ τείχους, *through a window through the wall*, as is stated in 2 Cor. 11, 33, i. e. as commonly understood through the window of a house overhanging the wall. Compare Josh. 2, 15; 1 Sam. 19, 12. Houses are built in that manner, in Eastern countries, at the present day. A wood-cut representing such a window may be seen in Howson's Work, Vol. I. p. 124.[2] — ἐν σπυρίδι, *in a basket*. That those who aided Paul's escape should have used a basket for the purpose, was entirely natural, according to the present customs of the country. It is the sort of vehicle which people employ there now if they would lower a man into a well, or raise him into the upper story of a house. See Illustrations of Scripture, p. 69.

[1] Das Leben Christi, von Dr. Joh. Rep. Sepp, Band, IV. p. 47.

[2] Possibly another explanation may be the correct one. A few steps to the left of Bab-es-Shurkeh, the gate on the east side of Damascus, I observed two or three windows in the external face of the wall, opening into houses on the inside of the city. If Saul was let down through such a window (which belongs equally to the house and the wall), it would be still more exact to interchange the two expressions; that is, we could say, as in the Acts, that he escaped "through the wall," or as in the Epistle to the Corinthians, that he escaped "through a window through the wall."

VERSES 26–31. *Paul returns to Jerusalem, and from there goes to Tarsus.*

V. 26. This is Paul's first journey to Jerusalem since his conversion, and took place in A. D. 39. See Introduct. § 6. 1. His motive for this step, as he states in Gal. 1, 18, was that he might make the acquaintance of Peter. — κολλᾶσθαι, *to associate* with them as one of their own faith. — πάντες ἐφοβοῦντο, κ. τ. λ. If Paul had spent most of the last three years at Damascus, we should suppose that the report of his labors during that time would have reached Jerusalem, and prepared the way for his more cordial reception. On the contrary, if he had been withdrawn for the most part from their knowledge, in the more retired region of Arabia, it is less surprising that they now regarded him with suspicion. The language, according to either view, it will be observed, does not affirm that they had never heard of his conversion, but that they could not readily persuade themselves that it was sincere. The sudden appearance of Voltaire in a circle of Christians, claiming to be one of them, would have been something like this return of Saul to Jerusalem as a professed disciple.

V. 27. Βαρνάβας stood high among the disciples at Jerusalem (4, 36; 11, 22). No one out of the circle of the apostles could have interposed a more powerful word in behalf of Saul. — πρὸς τοὺς ἀποστόλους, *unto the apostles*, viz. Peter and John (Gal. 1, 19). The other apostles were probably absent from Jerusalem at this time. — διηγήσατο, *related fully*, since they may have heard a report of the occurrence, but had received no definite information concerning it. He could add also his own personal testimony to the truth of what had come to their ears. — πῶς . . . . ἐπαῤῥησιάσατο. He had been himself probably a witness of Paul's zeal at Damascus; and for that reason, and because his labors there were more recent, he says nothing of the residence in Arabia. — ἐν τῷ ὀνόματι τοῦ Ἰησοῦ, *in the name of Jesus*, as the sphere of his preaching (Mey.); not in virtue of authority from him.

V. 28. ἦν μετ' αὐτῶν, *was with them*, during fifteen days, as we learn from Gal. 1, 18. — εἰσπορευόμενος καὶ ἐκπορευόμενος, *going in and going out*, i. e. in the exercise of his ministry, as results from the next clause. For the import of this Hebraism, see on 1, 21.

V. 29. πρὸς τοὺς Ἑλληνιστάς. See note on 6, 1. He addressed himself to them because he himself was a foreign Jew, and was familiar with the Greek, which they also spoke. It has been conjectured that one of the festivals may have been in progress at this time, and that these Hellenists had come to Jerusalem on that account. Compare John 12, 20. — ἐπεχείρουν, *attempted;* imperfect because they were seeking the opportunity to kill him. We are not to suppose that they had ventured as yet on any open act.

V. 30. ἐπιγνόντες δὲ οἱ ἀδελφοί, *But the brethren having ascertained,* viz. their hostile design. Paul departed in conformity with their advice. We learn from 22, 17, that another motive concurred with this: he was informed in a vision that God would have him occupy a different field of labor. Without that revelation he might have thought it best to remain, in defiance of the present danger, and notwithstanding the importunity of his friends; comp. 21, 13. It is a mark of truth that we find Luke stating the outward impulse, the apostle the inner ground. — In κατήγαγον the preposition marks the descent to the sea-coast. — For *Cæsarea,* see on 8, 40. For the route hither from Jerusalem, see on 23, 31. — καὶ ἐξαπέστειλαν, κ. τ. λ., *and they sent him forth to Tarsus.* This city was the capital of Cilicia, on the river Cydnus. It possessed at this time a literary reputation which rivalled that of Athens and Alexandria. It had received important political privileges both from Antony and Augustus, but did not enjoy the right of Roman citizenship. See the note on 22, 29. — We might conclude from the statement here, that Paul went directly to Tarsus by sea. That inference, it has been said, contradicts Gal. 1, 21, where, speaking of this journey, Paul puts Syria before Cilicia, as if he went to the latter country through the former. It is to be noticed that these two countries are always named in that order (see 15, 23. 41), and that order agrees with the land-route from Jerusalem to Cilicia, which was the one more commonly taken. Hence Paul may have adhered to that order in Gal. 1, 21, from the force of association, though in this instance he went first to Cilicia, and from there made missionary excursions into Syria. But if any one prefers, he can suppose, with De Wette, that Paul took ship at Cæsarea, and then landed again at Seleucia; or with Winer, Rückert, and others, that Syria, in the Epistle to the Galatians, included a part of the region between Jerusalem and Cæsarea. The term had sometimes that wider sense. Some have fixed on Cæsarea in the north of Palestine as the place meant here; but in that case the epithet which distinguishes the less celebrated city from the other would have been added, as in Matt. 16, 13; Mark 8, 27. — In these regions of Syria and Cilicia, Paul remained four or five years; for he went thither from Jerusalem in A. D. 39 (see on v. 26), and left for Antioch in A. D. 43 (see on 11, 26). That he was occupied during this time in laboring for the spread of the gospel, is not only to be inferred from the character of the man, but is expressly stated in Gal. 1, 21–23. Further, in the sequel of the narrative, (15, 23. 41), we find churches existing here, the origin of which is unknown, unless we suppose that they were planted by Paul's instrumentality at this time. It is not an irrelevant reflection, which Mr. Howson suggests, that during this residence of Paul in his native land "some of those Christian 'kinsmen,' whose names are handed down to us (Rom. 16, 7. 11. 21), possibly his sister, the playmate of his childhood, and his sister's son, who afterwards saved his life (23, 16 sq.), may have been gathered by his exertions into the fold of Christ." The apostle reappears next in 11, 25.

VERSES 31–35. *Peter preaches at Lydda, and heals a Paralytic.*

V. 31. αἱ μὲν οὖν, κ. τ. λ., *The churches now . . . . had peace*, i. e. rest from the persecution which they had suffered since the death of Stephen. It had continued for three years (see v. 26), if the subject of this paragraph be next in order after the preceding one. It is not certain that Luke mentions the cause of this respite. As Lardner, De Wette, and others suggest, it may have been owing to the troubles excited by the order of Caligula, to have his image set up in the temple. (Jos. Antt. 18. 8. 2–9.) The Jews may have been too much engrossed by their opposition to that measure to pursue the Christians. οὖν in that case takes up again the main thread of the history after the digression relating to Paul. Meyer makes it strictly illative from v. 3–30, as if the peace was the result of Paul's conversion and labors. But as he began to act on the side of the Christians so soon after the death of Stephen, we should then have too brief an interval for the persecution. Copies vary between ἐκκλησίαι and ἐκκλησία, but favor the latter.—Γαλιλαίας. This is our only notice of the existence of churches in that native land of the apostles.—οἰκοδομούμεναι, *being built up*, i. e. in faith and piety; see 1 Cor. 8, 1; 14, 4; 1 Thes. 5, 11, etc. It is contrary to usage to understand it of external organization. It does not refer to the increase of numbers, since that is the idea of the verb which follows. The E. V. makes this participle a verb, and separates it from its natural connection in the sentence.—πορευόμεναι = הָלַךְ, *walking;* a common Hebraism, to denote a course of conduct.—τῷ φόβῳ τοῦ κυρίου, *in the fear of the Lord,* in conformity with that state of mind; dative of rule or manner. W. § 31. 6. b. — καὶ τῇ παρακλήσει τοῦ ἁγίου πνεύματος, belongs not to πορευόμεναι, but to ἐπληθύνοντο, of which it assigns the cause: *and by the aid,* persuasive energy, (Kuin. Mey. Rob.), *of the Holy Spirit were multiplied.* That sense of παρακλήσει is not certain. De Wette: The power of consolatory discourse conferred by the Spirit on those who preached; comp. 4, 36.

V. 32. *Peter* may have left Jerusalem soon after the departure of Paul; see on v. 27. — διερχόμενον, κ. τ. λ., *passing through all* the believers in that part of the country. After πάντων supply ἁγίων (Bng. Mey. De Wet.), not τόπων (Kuin. Wiesl.); comp. 20, 25; Rom. 15, 28. The narrative assumes that the gospel had been preached here already (see 8, 44); and this was a tour of visitation. — καί, *also,* includes the saints at Lydda among the πάντων. In crossing the plain from Yafa or Joppa to Ramleh, the traveller sees a village with a tall minaret in the southeast, and on inquiring the name is told that it is Lud or Lid. It stands on the ancient line of travel between Jerusalem and Cæsarea. It is the modern representative of the Lydda in our text.

V. 33. His name may indicate that *Æneas* was a Greek, or Hellenistic Jew. He was probably a believer, as faith was usually required of those who received the benefits of the gospel. — ἐξ ἐτῶν ὀκτώ, *since eight years,* for so long a time. — κραββάτῳ, *pallet,* as in 5, 15.

V. 34. στρῶσον σεαυτῷ, *spread for thyself,* i. e. thy bed, not in future (Kuin.), but immediately (De Wet. Mey.). Others had performed that office for him hitherto. He was now to evince his restoration by an act which had been the peculiar evidence of his infirmity. The object of the verb suggests itself; it is not strictly an ellipsis.

V. 35. εἶδον αὐτόν, *saw him* after his recovery, whom they had known before as a confirmed paralytic. — πάντες may be restricted, as suggested on 3, 18. — τὸν Σάρωνα = הַשָּׁרוֹן, *the Plain.* It extended along the sea-coast from Joppa to Cæsarea, about thirty miles. Here the part nearest to Lydda appears to be meant. Some have thought (Win. Realw. II. p. 383) that Saron may designate here a village of that name. — οἵτινες ἐπέστρεψαν, κ. τ. λ., *who,* influenced by the miracle, *turned unto the Lord,* see v. 42; not *who had turned* (Kuin.). In the latter case, the import of the remark would be that the miracle was a credible one, because it was so well attested. Such an apologetic interest is foreign to Luke's manner.

VERSES 36–43. *Peter visits Joppa.*

V. 36. Ἰόππη, *Joppa* (Jon. 1, 3) was northwest from Lydda (see on v. 32), the present Japha, or Yafa, on the sea-coast.— *Tabitha* = טְבִיתָא is Chaldee, and means a *gazelle.* We may infer from it her Jewish origin. To her Greek friends she may have been known also by the other name.—καὶ ἐλεημοσυνῶν, *and* (especially) *alms*, deeds of charity; καί, explicative.

V. 37. λούσαντες, κ. τ. λ., *having washed, they placed her in the upper chamber* of the house where they were. As the limitation suggests itself, the article is omitted. W. § 19. 1. It is inserted in v. 39, because there it points back to this place. It was customary among the Hebrews for women to perform this rite; but as Luke would specify here the act rather than the agency, he employs the masculine of the participle, equivalent to the indefinite "they." W. § 27. 6.

V. 38. ἐγγύς governs Ἰόππη as an adverb. The distance between the places is ten or twelve miles. — ἀπέστειλαν. It is not said that they sent for him with any definite expectation of a miracle. It was natural that they should desire his presence and sympathy at such a time.

V. 39. εἰς τὸ ὑπερῷον, *into the upper chamber.* The body was usually kept here when for any reason the interment was delayed. See Jahn's Archæol. § 204; Win. Realw. I. p. 467. They had been waiting in this instance for the arrival of Peter. — αἱ χῆραι, *the widows,* who had been the objects of her benevolence, and who now mourned the death of their benefactress. Every one must be struck at the natural manner in which this beautiful incident is introduced. — χιτῶνας καὶ ἱμάτια, *tunics and coats,* such as were worn by men and women. The omission of the article (suggestive of a wrong sense as inserted in E. V.) shows that they presented specimens only of her industry. Some of the garments may have been worn by those present, and others have been laid up for future distribution. — ὅσα, *which all,* which so many, not = ἅ simply, *which.* — ἐποίει (imperf.), *was accustomed to make.*

V. 40. ἐκβαλὼν .... πάντας, *But having put all forth,* caused them to retire; not with violence, see Mark 5, 40; John 10, 4. The object may have been to secure himself from observation and interruption, while he prayed with fervor and agony. Elisha pursued the same course, for the same reason probably, when he restored to life the Shunamite's son; see 2 Kings 4, 33; also

Matt. 9, 25. — προσηύξατο. Peter would address his prayer to Christ; for the apostles wrought their miracles in his name; see v. 34; 3, 6. 16; 4, 10. — ἀνάστηθι, *arise*, stand erect. Peter speaks as one who felt assured that his prayer had prevailed, see Matt. 17, 20.

V. 42. ἐγένετο draws its subject from the context, viz. the miracle. — ἐπὶ τὸν κύριον, *upon the Lord*, Christ, whose gospel had been so signally attested as true.

V. 43. Peter remained here *many days*, because the place was large, and the people evinced a preparation for the reception of the word. — βυρσεῖ, *a tanner*. The more scrupulous Jews regarded such an occupation as unclean, and avoided those who pursued it. The conduct of Peter here shows that he did not carry his prejudices to that extent.

CHAPTER X.

VERSES 1–8. *The Vision of Cornelius, the Centurion.*

V. 1. ἑκατοντάρχης is often interchanged with ἑκατοντάρχος (21, 32; 22, 25, etc.). The first is the prevalent form in the later Greek. W. § 8. 1. The word has a uniform termination in some copies of the text. — σπείρης Ἰταλικῆς. Some suppose this *cohort* to have belonged to the *legio Italica*, or *Italica prima*, of which we read in Tacitus (Hist. 1. 59, 64, etc.); but the fact stated by Dio Cassius (55. 24) is overlooked, that this legion was raised by Nero, and consequently was not in existence at this period of our narrative. While no ancient writer has left any notice confirming Luke's accuracy in this passage, it so happens that an inscription in Gruter[1] informs us that volunteer *Italian* cohorts served in Syria, i. e. Italian or Roman soldiers, who enlisted of their own accord, instead of being obliged to perform military service (see Dict. of Antt. art. *Velones*). It is generally supposed that the Roman cohorts, instead of being incorporated always with a particular legion, existed often separately. It is probable that such an independent cohort was now stationed at Cæsarea,

[1] Copied in Ackerman's Numismatic Illustrations of the Narrative Portions of the New Testament, p. 34.

called the *Italian*, because it consisted of native Italians, whereas the other cohorts in Palestine were levied for the most part from the country itself. See Jos. Antt. 14. 15. 10; Bell. Jud. 1. 17. 1. Compare the note on 27, 1. It is worthy of remark, as Tholuck[1] suggests, that Luke places this *Italian* cohort precisely here. Cæsarea was the residence of the Roman procurator (see on 8, 40); and it was important that he should have there a body of troops on whose fidelity he could rely.

V. 2. εὐσεβὴς . . . . θεόν, *devout and fearing God.* All the centurions in the New Testament appear in a favorable light (Hmph.). See 27, 3; Matt. 8, 5; Luke 7, 2. The one here was a worshipper of Jehovah, but had not submitted to circumcision, or avowed publicly the Jewish faith. The opinion that he was a proselyte disagrees with v. 28. 34; 11, 1. 8; 15, 7; for those passages show that he was regarded by the Jews at this time as belonging still to a heathen community. Cornelius was one of those men, so numerous in this effete age of idolatry, who were yearning for a better worship, and under that impulse had embraced the pure theism of the Old Testament, so much superior to every other form of religion known to them. They attended the synagogues, heard and read the Scriptures, practised some of the Jewish rites, and were in a state of mind predisposing them to welcome the gospel of Christ when it was announced to them. This class of persons furnished the greater part of the first Gentile converts. — τῷ λαῷ, *the people*, viz. of the Jews; comp. v. 42; 26, 17. 23; 28, 17. Perhaps Luke 7, 5 brings to view one of the ways in which he applied his benefactions.

V. 3. ἐν ὁράματι may be understood of an inner or of an outward *vision* (Neand.). — φανερῶς, *distinctly*, applies better to a perceptive act than to an act of consciousness. εἶδεν is ambiguous in that respect. — ὡσεὶ ὥραν ἐννάτην, *about the ninth hour*, in the course of it; accusative of time how long. Bernh. Synt. p. 116. This hour was one of the Jewish hours of prayer (3, 1).

V. 4. τί ἐστι; *What is it* which is designed or desired? — For κύριε, see the remark on 9, 5. — προσευχαί and ἐλεημοσύναι, which belong to one verb here, are assigned to two verbs in v. 31. — εἰς μνημόσυνον, *for a memorial*, as such (see on 7, 21), i. e. he was now to receive evidence of his being remembered, inasmuch as God was about to open a way for his attainment of the peace of mind which he had so anxiously sought.

V. 5. *Joppa* was about thirty miles south of Cæsarea. — μετά-

[1] Die Glaubwürdigkeit der Evangelischen Geschichte, p. 174.

πέμψαι is middle, because he was to execute the act through the agency of others. K. § 250. R. 2; B. § 135. 8.—*Σίμωνα . . . . Πέτρος*. Both names are given, so as to prevent mistake as to the individual whom the messengers were to find. This, too, is the reason for describing so minutely his place of abode.

V. 6. *παρὰ θάλασσαν, by the sea-shore,* viz. that of the Mediterranean. Luke states a fact here; the ground of it we learn from other sources. The sanatory laws of the ancients, it is said, required tanners to live out of the city; "non solum ob mortua animalia, quorum usum ipsa eorum opificii ratio efflagitabat, sed etiam ob fœtidos in eorum officinis et ædibus odores et sordes.' Walch, Dissertationes, etc., Vol. I. p. 125. The convenient prosecution of their business required that they should be near the water.—*οὗτος λαλήσει σοι τί σε δεῖ ποιεῖν*, at the close of this verse, in the common text, was inserted in conformity with 9, 6; 10, 32.

V. 7. *ὡς δὲ ἀπῆλθεν, κ. τ. λ.* He despatched the messengers, therefore, on the same day, although it was so far advanced (v. 3); comp. *ἐξαυτῆς* in v. 33.—*ὁ λαλῶν* must be taken as imperfect; comp. John 9, 8 (De Wet.).—*τῶν προσκαρτερούντων αὐτῷ, of those* (sc. soldiers) *who waited upon him,* who stood ready to perform those personal services which he might require. Kuinoel's idea is that they acted as a house-sentry.—*εὐσεβῆ* accords with the description of the centurion's family in v. 2.

VERSES 9–16. *The Vision of Peter.*

V. 9. *τῇ ἐπαύριον, on the morrow,* after their departure from Cæsarea.—*ἐπὶ τὸ δῶμα, upon the house-top,* the roof which, according to the Oriental manner, was flat, or but slightly inclined. It was the place often chosen for the performance of religious duties. Jahn's Archæol. § 24. The situation does not expose one necessarily to public view. A wall or balustrade three or four feet high surrounds many of the roofs in the East, where a person may sit or kneel without being observed by others. Moses required (Deut. 22, 8) that every house should have such a protection.

V. 10. *πρόσπεινος* occurs only here. The law of analogy shows it to be intensive, *very hungry.*—*ἤθελε γεύσασθαι, desired to eat;* not *would have eaten.*—*παρασκευαζόντων δὲ ἐκείνων, While they now* (not *but*) *were preparing,* i. e. for the evening repast; see v. 9. The pronoun refers to those in the family where Peter was entertained.—*ἔκστασις* = *ἐν πνεύματι* (Rev. 1, 10), i. e. *a trance,* or *rapture,* whereby (if we may so express it) he was transported out of himself, and put into a mental state in which he could discern objects beyond the apprehension of man's natural powers. See 11, 5; 22, 17. — In the mode of instruction which God employed in this instance, he adapted himself to the peculiar circumstances in which Peter was placed. "The divine light that was making its way to his spirit revealed itself in the mirror of sensible images, which proceeded from the existing state of his bodily frame" (Neand.)

V. 11. θεωρεῖ, *beholds* with wonder (see on 4, 13). — σκεῦός τι, *a certain vessel*, receptacle, which ὡς ὀθόνην μεγάλην describes more definitely *as a great sheet.* — τέσσαρσιν . . . . γῆς, *bound by four corners* or ends (anarthrous, since the number was not definite of itself), *and* (thus) *let down upon the earth.* The conception of the scene suggested by the text is that of the sheet upheld by cords attached to its four points, and suspended from above by an unseen power. This is the common view, and, I think, the correct one. Meyer understands ἀρχαῖς of *the four corners* of heaven, i. e. east, west, north, and south, to which the four ends of the sheet were fastened. Neander inclines to that interpretation. ἀρχαῖς with such a reference would seem to demand the article, as much as the translation into English and German. — Lachmann expunges δεδεμένον καί, after A, B, C, and some other authorities; but probably the omission of the words in 11, 5 led to their omission here.

V. 12. πάντα τὰ τετράποδα, *all the quadrupeds*, i. e. as to their varieties, not individually. The text here is confused. τῆς γῆς is to be retained, no doubt, but should follow ἑρπετά (Lchm. Mey. Tsch.). — καὶ τὰ θηρία before καὶ τὰ ἑρπετά is not found in the controlling manuscripts. It is evident that the text in 11, 6 has influenced the text in this passage.

V. 13. ἀναστάς. See on 9, 18. Yet Peter may have been kneeling, or reclining, at that moment (Mey.). — θῦσον καὶ φάγε, *slay and eat*, i. e. any one of the creatures exhibited to him, without regard to the distinction of clean or unclean.

V. 14. πᾶν, preceded by the negative, is a Hebraism for οὐδέν; comp. Matt. 24, 22; Rom. 3, 20; Eph. 5, 5. The two modes of expression present the idea from different points of view. That of the Hebrews excepts *every thing* from the action of the verb; that of the Greeks subjects *nothing* to it. Gesen. Heb. Gr. § 149. 1; W. § 26. 1. — κοινόν is the opposite of ἅγιον, *common*, unholy As this sense was unusual, the more explicit ἀκάθαρτον follows.

V. 15. ἃ ὁ θεὸς ἐκαθάρισε, *What God cleansed*, i. e. declared by this symbolic act to be clean. The aorist and perfect should not be confounded here. Verbs in Hebrew have often this declarative sense; comp. Lev. 13, 3. 8. 13; 16, 30; Ezek. 43, 3; Jer. 1, 10, etc. See Gesen. Heb. Lex. s. טִהֵר. An approximating usage exists in Greek. — σὺ μὴ κοίνου, *call not thou common.* σύ is contrasted with θεός. It is not usual to insert the first or second personal pronoun as the subject of a verb, unless it be emphatic. K. § 302. 1; B. § 129. 14. The imperative is present because he was committing the prohibited act at the time. Compare the note on 7, 60.

V. 16. τοῦτο refers to the repetition of the voice, not to the vision as seen three times. Those who understand it in the latter way overlook πάλιν ἐκ δευτέρου just before. The command was reiterated, in order to impress the words more deeply on the mind of Peter.

VERSES 17–22. *The Messengers arrive at Joppa.*

V. 17. διηπόρει, *was perplexed,* uncertain. — τί ἂν εἴη, *what it might be,* signify; comp. Luke 8, 9; John 10, 6. He must have been convinced that such a revelation was not designed merely to announce the abolition of a ceremonial custom; but it was not yet evident to him how much the principle comprehended, and especially in what practical manner he was to exhibit his liberation from the scruples by which he had been bound hitherto. — ὃ εἶδε, *which he had seen;* comp. on 1, 2. — καὶ ἰδού, *then behold,* as in 1, 10. — διερωτήσαντες, a strengthened sense, *having inquired out.* The tanner was an obscure man and not to be found in a moment. — ἐπὶ τὸν πυλῶνα, *unto the gate,* which opened directly into the house or court; not *the porch,* vestibule, since the more splendid houses only had that appendage (De Wet.); comp. Matt. 26, 71.

V. 18. φωνήσαντες, sc. τινά (see v. 7), *having called* some one, or, without any object, *having called,* announced their presence. — εἰ ξενίζεται, *if he lodges.* The present tense turns the question into a direct form. The use of the two names again (v. 5) is not unmeaning. So many persons were called Simon, that the strangers must be minute in their inquiry.

V. 19. διενθυμουμένου is stronger than ἐνθυμουμένου in the common text: *earnestly considering.* The first is the better attested word. — τρεῖς after ἄνδρες should be omitted. It was added from v. 7; 11, 11.

V. 20. ἀλλά, *but,* turns the discourse to a new point; comp. 9, 6. — μηδὲν διακρινόμενος, *making no scruple,* i. e. to go with them, although they are heathen. — ἐγώ = πνεῦμα in v. 19. — ἀπέσταλκα αὐτούς, *sent them;* not perfect (E. V.).

V. 21. τοὺς ἀπεσταλμένους ἀπὸ τοῦ Κορνηλίου πρὸς αὐτόν defines ἄνδρας; and since, in the public reading of the Scriptures, a new section began here, the words were necessary in order to suggest the connection. This accounts for our finding them in a few copies. The preponderant testimony is against them.

V. 22. μαρτυρούμενος occurs, as in 6, 3. — ἐχρηματίσθη, *was divinely instructed;* comp. Matt. 2, 12. In the classics this word refers to a communication madè in reply to a question; but in the New Tetsament and the Septuagint it drops that relative sense. — ῥήματα, *words,* instruction; comp. λαλήσει σοι in v. 32. The first account of the vision (v. 4 sq.) omits this particular.

VERSES 23–33. *Peter proceeds to Cæsarea.*

V. 23. τῇ ἐπαύριον, *on the morrow* after the arrival of the messengers. — τινὲς τῶν ἀδελφῶν. They are the six men mentioned in 11, 12. We are not informed of their object in accompanying the apostle. They may have gone as his personal friends merely, or from a natural desire to know the result of so extraordinary a summons. In his defence before the church of Jerusalem (see 11, 1 sq.), Peter appealed to these brethren to confirm his statements. Some have conjectured that he may have foreseen the necessity of that justification, and took the precaution to secure the presence of those who would be acknowledged as impartial Jewish witnesses.

V. 24. τῇ ἐπαύριον, *on the morrow* after leaving Joppa; comp. v. 9. Thirty miles (see on v. 5) was more than a single day's journey in the East. It must be the truth which brings out such accuracy in these details. — For εἰς in the verb repeated before the noun, see on 3, 2. — τοὺς ἀναγκαίους φίλους, his *intimate friends.* The classical writers combine the words with that meaning (Kypk. Wetst.).

V. 25. ὡς δὲ, κ. τ. λ., *Now as it came to pass that Peter was entering, Cornelius having met him,* viz. at the door, or in the court of the house. The first interview appears to have taken place there, and then the centurion and the apostle proceeded to the room where the company were assembled; see v. 27. — ἐπὶ τοὺς πόδας, *upon the feet,* viz. of Peter, which he may have embraced at the same time; comp. Matt. 28, 9. — προσεκύνησεν, *paid reverence,* viz. by prostrating himself in the Oriental manner. Since

Cornelius acknowledged Jehovah as the true God, and must have regarded him as the only proper object of worship, it is difficult to believe that he intended this as an act of religious homage. The description of his character in v. 2 and v. 22 cannot be easily reconciled with the imputation of such a design. See more on the next verse.

V. 26. αὐτὸν ἤγειρε, *raised him up*, caused him to rise by the command addressed to him. — κἀγὼ αὐτὸς, κ. τ. λ., *I also myself am a man*, as well as you. Peter may have been surprised at such a mode of salutation from a Roman, whose national habits were so different; he had reason to fear that the centurion had mistaken his character, was exceeding the proper limits of the respect due from one man to another. He recoiled at the idea of the possibility of having a homage tendered to him, which might partake of the reverence that belongs only to God. In other words, it is more probable that Peter, in his concern for the divine honor, warned the centurion against an act which he apprehended, than that the centurion committed an act so inconsistent with his religious faith. That inconsistency is so much the less to be admitted, because Peter had just been represented in the vision so distinctly as a man. The apostles claimed no ability to know the hearts or thoughts of men, except as their actions revealed them. Compare with this conduct of Peter that of Paul and Barnabas at Lystra (14, 14 sq.). The Saviour, on the contrary, never repressed the disposition of his disciples to think highly of his rank and character. He never reminded them of the equality of his nature with their own, or intimated that the honor paid to him was excessive. He received their homage, whatever the form in which they offered it, however excited the state of mind which prompted it. This different procedure on the part of Christ we can ascribe only to his consciousness of a claim to be acknowledged as divine.

V. 27. συνομιλῶν αὐτῷ, *conversing with him* (Whl. Rob.); comp. ὁμιλεῖν in 20, 11; 24, 26; Luke 24, 14. 15. Some render *accompanying him*, which is too self-evident to be stated so formally. The first sense is peculiar to Luke. — εἰσῆλθε, *went in*, perhaps into an upper room; see on 1, 13.

V. 28. ὡς may qualify the adjective, *how*, in what degree (Mey.), or ἐστίν, *how it is* (knowledge and fact accordant). — ἀθέμιτον, *unlawful*. The Jews professed to ground this view on the laws of Moses; but they could adduce no express command for it, or just construction of any command. No one of the N. T. writers employs this word, except Peter here and in 1 Pet. 4, 3. —

κολλᾶσθαι, κ. τ. λ., *to associate with* (5, 15), *or come unto, one of another nation.* The second verb evolves the sense of the first. ἀλλόφυλοι is applied to the Philistines in 1 Sam. 13, 3–5 (Sept.), and to the Greeks in 1 Macc. 4, 12. It has been said that Luke has betrayed here an ignorance of Jewish customs; since the Jews, though they refused to eat with the uncircumcised (Gal. 2, 12), did not avoid *all* intercourse with them. But the objection presses the language to an extreme. We are to limit such general expressions by the occasion and the nature of the subject. The intercourse with the Gentiles, represented here as so repugnant to Jewish ideas, was such intercourse as had now taken place; it was to enter the houses of the heathen, partake freely of their hospitality, recognize their social equality. In accordance with this, we find κολλᾶσθαι exchanged for συνέφαγες in 11, 3; the word there may be supposed to define the word here. De Wette objects that the act of eating has not been mentioned; but it is not mentioned anywhere, and yet the subsequent accusation against the apostle alleges it as the main offence. The act was, doubtless, a repeated one; see v. 48. An instance of it may have preceded the utterance of the words here in question. Nothing would be more natural, at the close of such a journey, than that the travellers should be supplied with the means of refreshment before entering formally on the object of the visit. Considered in this light, Peter's declaration in this verse agrees entirely with that of Josephus (Cont. Ap. 2. 28): "Those foreigners (ἀλλόφυλοι) who come to us without submitting to our laws, Moses permitted not to have any intimate connections with us;" see also Ib. 2. 36. Compare John 18, 28. – καὶ ἐμοὶ, κ. τ. λ., *and* (in opposition to that Jewish feeling) *God showed me*, viz. by the vision.

V. 29. διὸ καὶ, κ. τ. λ., *Therefore I also came*, i. e. he was not only instructed, but obeyed the instruction. καί connects ἦλθον with ἔδειξε. — ἀναντιῤῥήτως = ἀναμφιβόλως, *without delay*, (Heysch.). It is a later Greek word. — τίνι λόγῳ, *with what reason*, for what object; dative of the ground or motive. W. § 31. 6. c. Peter was already apprised that Cornelius had sent for him in consequence of a revelation, but would desire naturally to hear a fuller statement of the circumstances from the centurion himself. The recital may have been necessary, also, for the information of those who had assembled.

V. 30. ἀπὸ τετάρτης ἡμέρας, κ. τ. λ., has received different explanations. (1.) *From the fourth day* (prior to the vision) *was I fasting unto this hour*, i. e. unto an hour corresponding to that which was then passing, viz. the ninth (Hnr. Neand. De Wet.). According to this view, Cornelius had been fasting four days at the time of the angel's appearance to him. (2.) *From the fourth day* (reckoned backward from the present) *unto this hour*, i. e. he was observing a fast which began four days before and extended up to the time then present. It was on the first of the days that he saw the angel. But ἤμην as past represents the fast as having terminated, and so would exclude ταύτης τῆς ὥρας. Meyer in his second edition abandons this view for the next. (3.) *From the fourth day* (reckoning backward as before) i. e. four days ago *unto this hour* in which he was then speaking (Bng. Kuin. Olsh.). The fast commenced with the day and had continued unbroken until the ninth hour, when the angel appeared. This view agrees with the number of days which had elapsed since the angel's communication, viz. four, and allows time enough for the abstinence to justify the use of νηστεύων.—ἤμην is an imperfect middle, rare out of the later Greek. W. § 14. 2. b; B. § 108. IV. 2.—καὶ τὴν ἐννάτην ὥραν, *and during the ninth hour* (accusative as in v. 3); so that (ταύτης = ἐννάτην) it was about three o'clock in the afternoon when Peter arrived at Cæsarea.—ἀνὴρ ἐν ἐσθῆτι λαμπρᾷ = ἄγγελον τοῦ θεοῦ in v. 3. See 1, 11.

V. 31. εἰσηκούσθη, *was heard* (not *is* in E. V.), and so ἐμνήσθησαν, *were* (not *are*) *remembered;* comp. also v. 4. He is assured now of the approval of his acts; the acts were approved when he performed them.—ἡ προσευχή refers more especially to his prayer at this time. But the answer to this prayer was an answer to his other prayers, since the burden of them had doubtless been, that God would lead him to a clearer knowledge of the truth, and enable him to attain the repose of mind which a conscience enlightened, but not yet "purged from a sense of evil," made it impossible for him to enjoy. Hence προσευχαί in v. 4, could be exchanged here for the singular.

V. 32. πέμψον οὖν, *Send, therefore*, because in this way he would obtain the evidence that he was approved.—μετακάλεσαι exemplifies the usage of the middle noticed on v. 5.—The verbal accuracy here as compared with v. 5, is natural. There was but one way to report the words of such a message. The angel's voice and mien had left an impression not to be effaced.

V. 33. ἐξαυτῆς agrees with the narrative in v. 7.—καλῶς ἐποίησας, *thou hast done well* (see 3 John v. 6); a common phrase expressive of the gratification which a person derives from the act of another (Wetst. Raph.). For the construction, comp. Phil. 4,

14. — ἐνώπιον τοῦ θεοῦ, *in the sight of God*, with a consciousness of his presence; and hence prepared to hear and obey his message. This is a reason why Peter should speak with freedom and confidence. "Terra bona; inde fructus celerrimus" (Bng.)

VERSES 34–43. *The Address of Peter.*

V. 34. See the remark on ἀνοίξας τὸ στόμα in 8, 35. — προσωπολήπτης is a word coined to express concretely the idea of נָשָׂא פָּנִים: *respecter of persons*, i. e. here *partial* in the way of regarding one man as better than another, on the ground of national descent.

V. 35. δεκτὸς αὐτῷ ἐστι, *is acceptable to him*, i. e. his righteousness, his obedience to the divine will, as far as it extends, is as fully approved of God, though he be a Gentile, as if he were a Jew. It is evident from καταλαμβάνομαι, that ὁ φοβούμενος αὐτὸν καὶ ἐργαζόμενος δικαιοσύνην describes the centurion's character before his acceptance of the gospel, and, consequently, that δεκτὸς αὐτῷ applies to him as a person still destitute of faith in Christ. That Peter did not intend, however, to represent his righteousness, or that of any man, prior to the exercise of such faith, as sufficient to justify him in the sight of God, is self-evident; for in v. 43 he declares that it is necessary to believe on Christ, in order to obtain "the remission of sins;" comp. also, 15, 11. The antithetic structure of the sentence indicates the meaning. ὁ φοβούμενος, κ. τ. λ., is the opposite of οὐκ προσωπολήπτης, i. e. God judges man impartially; he approves of what is excellent, in those of one nation as much as in those of another; he will confer the blessings of his grace as readily upon the Gentile who desires to receive them, as upon the Jew. In other words, since the apostle has reference to the state of mind which God requires as preparatory to an interest in the benefits of the gospel, the righteousness and the acceptance of which he speaks must also be preparatory, i. e. relative, and not absolute.[1]

V. 36. The construction is uncertain, but the most simple is that which makes λόγον depend on οἴδατε, in apposition with ῥῆμα: *The word which he sent* . . . . (I say) *ye know the thing that was done*, etc. So essentially, Kuinoel, Meyer, Winer, and others. See W. § 62. 3. Others refer λόγον to what precedes, and supply κατά or take the accusative as absolute: *the word* (viz. that God is thus impartial) *which he sent*, etc. (Bng. Olsh. De Wet.). That mode of characterizing the contents or message of the gos-

[1] Neander's remarks on this passage, in his Planting of the Christian Church, deserve attention; see the close of the first Section or Book.

pel is unusual. The structure of the sentence is no smoother in this case than in the other. A recent writer[1] has proposed to construe εὐαγγελιζόμενος as a predicate of ὁ φοβούμενος, κ. τ. λ.: *he that fears God is acceptable to him .... having announced* (to him) *as glad tidings, peace,* etc. But the participle in this position cannot be separated without violence from the subject of ἀπέστειλε, nor is the accusative in any other instance retained after this verb in the passive; comp. Matt. 11, 5; Heb. 4, 2. The construction would be correct in principle, but is not exemplified.—ἀπέστειλε, κ. τ. λ., *sent to the sons of Israel,* i. e. in the first instance, as in 3, 26; 13, 26. That priority Peter concedes to the Jews.—εἰρήνην, *peace,* reconciliation to God procured through Christ; comp. Rom. 5, 1. 10; not *union* between the Jews and Gentiles (De Wet.), an effect of the gospel too subordinate to be made so prominent in this connection. The apostle restates the idea in v. 43.—οὗτος .... κύριος, *This one is Lord of all.* πάντων is masculine, not neuter. Peter interposes the remark as proof of the universality of this plan of reconciliation. The dominion of Christ extends over those of one nation, as well as of another; they are all the creatures of his power and care, and may all avail themselves of the provisions of his grace. Compare Rom. 3, 29. 30; 10, 12.

V. 37. οἴδατε, κ. τ. λ., implies that they had already some knowledge of the life and works of Christ. The fame of his miracles may have extended to Cæsarea (see Matt. 15, 21; Mark 7, 24); or Philip, who resided there (8, 40), may have begun to excite public attention as a preacher of the gospel. Some think that Cornelius was the centurion who was present at the crucifixion of Christ (Matt. 27, 44; Mark 15, 39; Luke 23, 47), since it was customary to march a portion of the troops at Cæsarea to Jerusalem, for the preservation of order during the festivals. It is impossible to refute or confirm that opinion. Peter proceeds to communicate to them a fuller account of the Saviour's history, and of the nature and terms of his salvation.—ῥῆμα = λόγον in v. 36 (Kuin. Mey.); or *thing* (De Wet.), which is more congruous with γενόμενον, and associates *the word* with the indubitable facts on which it rested.—μετὰ τὸ βάπτισμα, *after the baptism,* i. e. the completion of John's ministry. The Saviour performed some public acts at an earlier period, but did not enter fully on his work till John had finished his preparatory mission. The difference was so slight that it was sufficiently exact

[1] In the Theologische Studien und Kritiken, 1850, p. 402 sq.

to make the beginning or the close of the forerunner's career the starting-point in that of Christ. See on 1, 22.

V. 38. Ἰησοῦν transfers the mind from the gospel-history to the personal subject of it. The appositional construction is kept up still. ἀπὸ Ναζαρέτ, *from Nazareth*, as the place of his residence; see Matt. 2, 23. — ὡς ἔχρισεν, κ. τ. λ., *how God anointed him with the Holy Spirit*, etc. See note on 1, 2, and on 4, 26. δυνάμει is defined by what follows as *power* to perform miracles. — διῆλθεν, *went from place to place*; comp. 8, 4. — ἰώμενος, κ. τ. λ., *healing those oppressed by the devil.* His triumph over this form of Satanic agency is singled out as the highest exhibition of his wonder-working power.

V. 39. ἐσμέν supplies the correct word after ἡμεῖς, but is not genuine. — ἔν τε τῇ χώρᾳ, κ. τ. λ., *both in the country of the Jews and in Jerusalem*; the capital of the nation, and its territory here opposed to each other. The Jews inhabited not only Judea, but Galilee, and a region on the east of the Jordan. — ὃν καί, *whom also*, an additional fact (Luke 22, 24) in the Saviour's history (De Wet.); showing the extent of their animosity and violence. Winer (§ 66. 3) suggests a brachylogy: *whom* (of which *also* we are witnesses) *they slew*, etc. This is too complicated. — κρεμάσαντες, *by hanging*. See note on 5, 30. Here again the E. version represents the Saviour as put to death before he was suspended on the cross.

V. 41. οὐ παντὶ τῷ λαῷ, *not unto all the people*, i. e. of the Jews; comp. on v. 2. — ἀλλὰ μάρτυσι, κ. τ, λ., *but unto witnesses before appointed by God.* The choice of the apostles is ascribed indifferently to Him, or to Christ (1, 2.) πρό in the participle represents the selection as made before Christ rose from the dead; not as purposed indefinitely before its execution. — The exception here made to the publicity of the Saviour's appearance accords with the narrative of the Evangelists; they mention no instance in which he showed himself to any except his personal followers. Paley founds the following just remarks on that representation of the sacred writers. "The history of the resurrection would have come to us with more advantage, if they had related that Jesus had appeared to his foes as well as his friends; or even if they asserted the public appearance of Christ in general unqualified terms, without noticing, as they have done, the presence of his disciples on each occasion, and noticing it in such a manner as to lead their readers to suppose that none but disciples were present. If their point had been to have their story believed, whether true or false; or if they had been disposed to present their testimony, either as personal witnesses or as historians, in such a manner as to render it as specious and unobjectionable as they could; in a word, if they had thought of any thing but the truth of the case as they understood and believed it, — they would, in their account of Christ's several appearances after his resurrection, at least have omitted this restriction. At this distance of time, the account, as we have it, is perhaps more credible than it would have been the other way; because this manifestation of the historian's candor is of more advantage to their testimony than the difference in the circumstances of the account would have been to the nature of the evidence. But this is an effect which the Evangelists could not foresee; and is one which by no means would have followed at the time when they wrote." — οἵτινες . , . . αὐτῷ, *who ate and drank with him.* See Luke 24, 43; John 21, 13. Hence they testified to a fact which they had been able to verify by the most palpable evidence. Compare the note on 1, 3. — μετὰ τὸ ἀναστῆναι αὐτὸν ἐκ νεκρῶν, *after he rose from the dead,* belongs to the clause which immediately precedes. It was after his resurrection that they had this intercourse with him. The punctuation of some editors refers the words incorrectly to v. 40.

V. 42. κηρῦξαι τῷ λαῷ, *to preach to the people,* as above. Peter alludes to the sphere of their ministry which they were directed to occupy at first; comp. 1, 8; 3, 26, etc. — ὅτι αὐτός, *that himself* and no other. W. § 22. 4. — κριτὴς ζώντων καὶ νεκρῶν, *judge of the living and dead,* i. e. of all who shall be on the earth at the time of his final appearance (1 Thess. 4, 17), and of all who have lived previously and died. For other passages which represent Christ as sustaining this office of universal judge, see 17, 31; 2 Tim. 4, 1; 1 Pet. 4, 5. Olshausen and some others, understand *the living and dead,* to be *the righteous* and *wicked;* but we are to attach to the words that figurative sense only when the context (Matt. 8, 22), or some explanatory adjunct (Eph. 2, 1), leads the mind distinctly to it.

V. 43. τούτῳ . . . . μαρτυροῦσιν, *For this one* (dat. comm.) *testify all the prophets;* comp. on 3, 24. — ἄφεσιν . . . . εἰς αὐτόν states the purport of their testimony. This clause presents two ideas: first that the condition of pardon is faith in Christ; and secondly, that this condition brings the attainment of pardon within the reach of all: *every one,* whether Jew or Gentile, *who believes on him shall receive remission of sins.* See Rom. 10, 11. For the explanation of τοῦ ὀνόματος αὐτοῦ, see on 2, 21.

VERSES 44–48. *Cornelius and others receive the Spirit, and are baptized.*

V. 44. ἔτι λαλοῦντος, *still speaking.* Hence Peter had not finished his remarks when God vouchsafed this token of his favor; see 11, 15. — τὸ πνεῦμα, *the Spirit,* i. e. as the author of the gifts mentioned in v. 46. The miracle proved that the plan of salvation which Peter announced was the divine plan, and that the faith which secured its blessings to the Jew was sufficient to secure them to the Gentile. A previous submission to the rites of Judaism was shown to be unnecessary. It is worthy of note, too, that those who received the Spirit in this instance had not been baptized (comp. 19, 5), nor had the hands of an apostle been laid upon them (comp. 8, 17). This was an occasion when men were to be taught by an impressive example how little their acceptance with God depends on external observances. — πάντας restricts itself to the Gentiles (v. 27) since they were properly *the hearers* to whom Peter was speaking, and not the Jews.

V. 45. οἱ ἐκ περιτομῆς, *they of the circumcision,* i. e. the Jewish brethren, mentioned in v. 23; comp. 11, 2; Rom. 4, 12; Col. 4, 11. — πιστοί = πιστεύοντες. See 16, 1; John 20, 27. "Verbal adjectives in τός, which have usually a passive signification, have often in poetry, and sometimes in prose, an active signification." See K. Ausführ. Gr. § 409. 3. A. 1. — ὅτι καὶ ἐπὶ τὰ ἔθνη, *that also upon the heathen,* as well as upon the Jews. The assertion is universal because this single instance established the principle.

V. 46. ἤκουον αὐτῶν, *were hearing them* while they spoke. — γλώσσαις, *with tongues* new, before unspoken by them. The fuller description in 2, 4 prepares the way for the conciser statement here.

V. 47. μήτι τὸ ὕδωρ, κ. τ. λ., *Can perhaps any one forbid the water that these should not be baptized?* The article may contrast ὕδωρ and πνεῦμα with each other, or more naturally designate the water as wont to be so applied. The import of the question is this: Since, although uncircumcised, they have believed and received so visible a token of their acceptance with God, what should hinder their admission into the church? Who can object to their being baptized, and thus acknowledged as Christians in full connection with us? As κωλύω involves a negative idea, μή could be omitted or inserted before βαπτισθῆναι. The distinction may be, that the infinitive with μή expresses the result of the hinderance; without μή, that which the hinderance would prevent. See Woolsey on the Alcestis, v. 11. *μή* after such verbs has been said to be superfluous (K. § 318. 10), or simply intensive (Mt. § 534. 3). Klotz ad Devar. (II. p. 668) suggests the correct view. See also Bernh. Synt. p. 364. — καθὼς καὶ ἡμεῖς, *as also we* received, viz. ἐν ἀρχῇ (see 11, 15), *in the beginning.*

V. 48. προσέταξε, *commanded* that the rite should be performed by others; he devolved the service on his attendants. Peter's rule in regard to the administration of baptism may have been similar to that of Paul; see 1 Cor. 1, 14. — ἐπιμεῖναι, sc. ἐπ' αὐτοῖς; comp. 28, 14.

CHAPTER XI.

VERSES 1–18. *Peter justifies himself at Jerusalem for his visit to Cornelius.*

V. 1. Peter, John and James were among *the apostles* now at Jerusalem (8, 14; 12, 2), and no doubt others. — κατὰ τὴν Ἰουδαίαν, *throughout* (comp. 15, 23) *Judea,* since *the brethren* belonged to different churches in this region; see Gal. 1, 22. — τὰ ἔθνη, *the heathen* while still uncircumcised (see v. 3).

V. 2. ὅτε ἀνέβη, *when he went up.* There is no evidence that Peter was summoned to Jerusalem to defend his conduct. He had reason to fear that it would be censured until the particulars of the transaction were known, and he may have hastened his return, in order to furnish that information. — οἱ ἐκ περιτομῆς, *they of the circumcision,* are the Jewish believers, as in 10, 45; not here a party among them more tenacious of circumcision than the others. It is implied that this tenacity was a Jewish characteristic. The narrower sense of the expression occurs in some places.

V. 3. See the remarks on 10, 28. Notice the ground of the complaint. It was not that Peter had preached to the heathen, but that he had associated with them in such a manner as to violate his supposed obligations as a Jew. Compare the note on 2, 39. We may infer that he had avoided that degree of intimacy when he himself entertained the Gentile messengers (10, 23).

V. 4. ἀρξάμενος, κ. τ. λ., *commencing,* i. e. proceeding to speak (see on 2, 4), or *beginning* with the first circumstances *he related unto them,* etc. This repetition of the history shows the importance attached to this early conflict between the gospel and Judaism.

V. 5. For the omission of τῇ before πόλει, see on 8, 5. — ὅραμα denotes here what was seen, and differs from its use in 10, 3. — τέσσαρσιν ἀρχαῖς καθιεμένην, *let down*, suspended, *by four corners*, i. e. by means of cords fastened to them. Luke abbreviates here the fuller expression in 10, 11.

V. 12. By a mixed construction, διακρινόμενον agrees with the suppressed subject of συνελθεῖν, instead of μοι. C. § 627. β.; Mt. § 536. — οἱ ἓξ ἀδελφοὶ οὗτοι, *these six men* (see 10, 23); they had, therefore, accompanied Peter to Jerusalem, either as witnesses for him, or for his own vindication, since they had committed the same offence.

V. 13. τὸν ἄγγελον, *the angel* known to the reader from the previous narrative (10, 3. 22). Those addressed had not heard of the vision, and must have received from Peter a fuller account of it than it was necessary to repeat here. — ἄνδρας has been transferred to this place from 10, 5.

V. 14. πᾶς ὁ οἶκός σου, *all thy family*. The assurance embraces them because they were prepared, as well as Cornelius, to welcome the apostle's message; comp. 10, 2. This part of the communication has not been mentioned before.

V. 15. ἄρξασθαι is not superfluous (Kuin.), but shows how soon the Spirit descended after *he began to speak*: see on 10, 44. W. § 67. 4. — ἐν ἀρχῇ, *in the beginning*, i. e. on the day of Pentecost. The order of the narrative indicates that the conversion of Cornelius took place near the time of Paul's arrival at Antioch. Some ten years, therefore (see on v. 26), had passed away since the event to which Peter alludes; comp. on 15, 7.

V. 16. ἐμνήσθην, κ. τ. λ., *And I remembered the declaration of the Lord*, i. e. had it brought to mind with a new sense of its meaning and application; comp. Matt. 26, 75; John 12, 16. The Saviour had promised to bestow on his disciples a higher baptism than that of water (see 1, 5; Luke 24, 49); and the result proved that he designed to extend the benefit of that promise to the heathen who should believe on him, as well as to the Jews. — ὡς ἔλεγεν, *how he said*. See on 1, 5.

V. 17. ἔδωκεν, *gave*, as mentioned in 10, 44. — καί, *also*, connects ἡμῖν with αὐτοῖς. — πιστεύσασιν, *having believed*, refers to both pronouns (De Wet. Mey.), i. e. they all received the same gift in the same character, viz. that of believers. Bengel (to whom Mey. assents now) limits the participle to ἡμῖν. — ἐγὼ δὲ τίς ἤμην, κ. τ. λ., combines two questions (W. § 66. 5.); *Who then was I? Was I able to withstand God?* i. e. to disregard so distinct an intimation of his will that the heathen should be recognized as worthy of all the privileges of the gospel, without demanding of them any other qualification than faith in Christ. δυνατός suggests that such opposition would have been as presumptuous and futile, as a contest between man's power and infinite power. δέ with τίς strengthens the question, as in 2 Cor. 6, 14. It is left out of some copies, but not justly.

V. 18. ἡσύχασαν, *were silent*, refrained from further opposition (v. 2); comp. 21, 14. — ἐδόξαζον expresses a continued act. The sudden change of tenses led some to write ἐδόξασαν. — ἄραγε, *therefore, then* (Matt. 7, 20; 17, 26); more pertinent here than the interrogative ἆράγε (8, 30). The accentuation varies in different editions. — For τὴν μετάνοιαν ἔδωκεν, see the note on 5, 31. — εἰς ζωήν, ecbatic, *unto life*, i. e. such repentance as secures it; comp. 2 Cor. 7, 10.

VERSES 19–24. *The Gospel is preached at Antioch.*

V. 19. οἱ μὲν οὖν διασπαρέντες, *those therefore dispersed*, recalls the reader to an earlier event in the history; see 8, 4. — ἀπὸ τῆς θλίψεως, *from* (as an effect of) *the persecution* (Whl. Win. Mey.); comp. 20, 9; Luke 19, 3. This is better than to render *since the persecution*. It is more natural to be reminded here of the cause of the dispersion, than of the time when it began. — ἐπὶ Στεφάνῳ, *upon Stephen*, on his account; comp. 4, 21; Luke 2, 20. W. § 48. c. — διῆλθον. See 8, 4. 40. — Φοινίκης. *Phœnicia* in this age lay chiefly between the western slope of Lebanon and the sea, a narrow plain reaching from the river Elutherus on the north to Carmel on the south. Its limits varied at different times. Among the Phœnician cities were Tyre and Sidon; and the statement here accounts for the existence of the Christians in those places, mentioned so abruptly in 21, 4; 27, 3. — Ἀντιοχείας. Here we have the first notice of this important city. *Antioch* was the capital of Syria, and the residence of the Roman governors of that province. It was founded by Seleucus Nicator, and named after his father, Antiochus. It stood "near the abrupt angle formed by the coasts of Syria and Asia Minor, and in the opening where the Orontes passes between the ranges of Lebanon and Taurus. By its harbor of Seleucia it was in communication with all the trade of the Mediterranean; and, through the open country behind Lebanon, it was conveniently approached by the caravans from Mesopotamia and Arabia. It was almost an Oriental Rome, in which all the forms of the civilized life of the empire found a representative." Howson, I. p. 149. See further, on 13, 4. It is memorable in the first Christian age as the seat of missionary operations for the evangelization of the heathen.

V. 20. Whether the preachers came to Antioch before the conversion of Cornelius or afterward, the narrative does not decide. Some prefer to place the arrival after his baptism, lest Peter might not seem to be the first who preached the gospel to the Gentiles. See the note on 15, 7. — δέ, *but*, distinguishes the course pursued by *certain of them*, from that of the other διασπαρέντες. The general fact is first stated, and then the exception. — Κύπριοι, i. e. Jews born in Cyprus; see 2, 5. 9. — πρὸς τοὺς Ἕλληνας, *unto the Greeks*, opposed to Ἰουδαίοις, *Jews*, in the foregoing verse. The received text has Ἑλληνιστάς, *Hellenists* (see on 6, 1) and the mass of external testimony favors that reading. Wordsworth's note[1] presents the evidence on that side in a strong light. On the contrary, the internal argument appears to demand Ἕλληνας. Some of the oldest versions and a few manuscripts support that as the original word. The majority of critics in view of this two-fold evidence decide for Ἕλληνας (Grsb. Lchm. Tsch. De Wet. Mey.). It would have been nothing new to have preached, at this time, to the Greek-speaking Jews; see, e. g. 2, 9; 9, 29. If we accept Ἕλληνας, the Greeks addressed at Antioch must have been still heathen in part, and not merely Jewish proselytes. No other view accounts for Luke's discrimination as to the sphere of the two classes of preachers. — Κυρηναῖοι. See on 2, 10.

V. 21. For χεὶρ κυρίου, comp. 4, 30; Luke 1, 66. — μετ' αὐτῶν, *with them* who preached at Antioch. The subject of discourse, both in the last verse and the next, requires this reference of the pronoun.

V. 22. ἠκούσθη εἰς τὰ ὦτα is a Hebraism, says De Wette, without any instance exactly parallel in Hebrew. — ὁ λόγος, *the report*. περὶ αὐτῶν excludes the idea that it was a communication sent from the brethren at Antioch. — ἐξαπέστειλαν derives its subject from ἐν Ἱεροσολύμοις; comp. Gal. 2, 2. — διελθεῖν, with the direction *that he should go* (comp. 20, 1); left out of some of the early versions as if unnecessary. See W. § 65. 4. d. — Βαρνάβαν. See 4, 36; 9, 27.

V. 23. χάριν τοῦ θεοῦ, *the grace*, or *favor of God*, as manifested in the conversion of the heathen. — παρεκάλει πάντας, *exhorted all*

[1] The New Testament in the Original Greek with Notes, by Chr. Wordsworth, D. D., Canon of Westminster (London 1857).

who had believed. We find him exercising here the peculiar gift for which he was distinguished; see on 4, 36. — τῇ προθέσει τῆς καρδίας, *with the purpose of the heart,* i. e. a purpose sincere, earnest.

V. 24. ὅτι ἦν, κ. τ. λ., *because he was a man good and full of the Holy Spirit,* etc. This description states why he exerted himself so strenuously to establish the converts in their faith. ἐξαπέστειλαν in v. 22 is too remote to allow us to view it as the reason why they selected him for such a service. — καὶ προσετέθη, κ. τ. λ. The labors of Barnabas resulted also in the accession of new believers.

VERSES 25. 26. *Paul arrives at Antioch, and labors there.*

V. 25. Our last notice of Paul was in 9, 30. — ἀναζητῆσαι, *in order to seek out,* find by inquiry or effort. It was not known at what precise point the apostle was laboring; see Gal. 1, 21. εὑρών indicates the same uncertainty. Barnabas would naturally direct his steps first to Tarsus, whither he would proceed by sea from Seleucia (see on 13, 4), or track his way through the defiles of the intervening mountains. Howson: "The last time the two friends met was in Jerusalem. In the period since that interview, 'God had granted to the Gentiles repentance unto life' (v. 18). Barnabas had 'seen the grace of God' (v. 23), and under his own teaching 'a great multitude' (v. 24) had been 'added to the Lord.' But he needed assistance; he needed the presence of one whose wisdom was greater than his own, whose zeal was an example to all, and whose peculiar mission had been miraculously declared. Saul recognized the voice of God in the words of Barnabas; and the two friends travelled in all haste to the Syrian metropolis."

V. 26. ἐνιαυτὸν ὅλον, *a whole year,* viz. that of A. D. 44, since it was the year which preceded Paul's second journey to Jerusalem, at the time of the famine. See on 12, 25. The apostle had spent the intervening years, from A. D. 39 to 44, in Syria and Cilicia (see on 9, 30). — συναχθῆναι, κ. τ. λ., *they came together in the church,* the public assembly, i. e. for the purpose of worship, and, as we see from the next clause, for preaching the word: *and taught a great multitude* (comp. 14, 21); many of whom, no doubt, they won to a reception of the truth. Meyer explains συναχθῆναι of the hospitality shown to the teachers, with an appeal to Matt. 25, 35. But the context which should indicate that sense, is opposed to it here. — χρηματίσαι .... Χριστιανούς, *and the disciples were first named Christians at Antioch.* Thus ten years or more elapsed after the Saviour left the earth before the introduction of this name. Its origin is left in some uncertainty. Χριστιανοί has a Latin termination, like Ἡρωδιανοί in Matt. 22, 16, and Mark 3, 6. We see the proper Greek form in Ναζωραῖος in 2, 22, or Ἰταλικός in 10, 1. Hence some infer (Olsh. Mey.) that it must have been the Roman inhabitants of the city, not the Greeks, who invented the name. The argument is not decisive, since Latinisms were not unknown to the Greek of this period. It is evident that the Jews did not apply it first to the disciples; for they would not have admitted the implication of the term, viz. that Jesus was the Messiah. It is improbable that the Christians themselves assumed it; such an origin would be inconsistent with its infrequent use in the New Testament. It occurs only in 26, 28; 1 Pet. 4, 16, and in both places proceeds from those out of the church. The καλὸν ὄνομα τὸ ἐπικληθὲν ἐφ' ὑμᾶς in James 2, 7 may be the Christian name. The believers at Antioch had become numerous; they consisted of Gentiles and Jews; it was evident that they were a distinct community from the latter; and probably the heathen, whether they were Greeks or Romans, or native Syrians, needing a new appellation for the new sect, called them Christians, because the name of Christ was so prominent in their doctrine, conversation, and worship. The term may not have been at first opprobrious, but distinctive merely.

VERSES 27–30. *Barnabas and Saul are sent with Alms to Jerusalem.*

V. 27. ἐν ταύταις ταῖς ἡμέραις, *in these days*, i. e. about the time that Paul himself came to Antioch; for it is reasonable to suppose that an interval of some extent occurred between the prediction and the famine. — προφῆται, *inspired teachers;* see on 2, 17. Agabus, at least, possessed the prophetic gift, in the strict sense of that expression.

V. 28. ἀναστάς, *having stood up*, in order to declare his message more formally. — Ἄγαβος is known only from this passage and 21, 10. — ἐσήμανε, *made known* (see 25, 27), not *intimated* merely. — λιμόν, in the later Greek, is masculine or feminine; hence some copies have μέγαν, others μεγάλην. See W. § 8. 2. 1. — μέλλειν ἔσεσθαι contains a double future, as in 24, 15; 27, 10. The reading varies in 24, 25. As one of its uses, the first infinitive in such a case may represent the act as fixed, certain; the second as future. The famine that was to take place was decreed. See

Mt. § 498. e; C. § 583. — ἐφ' ὅλην τὴν οἰκουμένην, sc. γῆν, *over all the inhabited* land, i. e. Judea and the adjacent countries, or according to some, the Roman empire. The Greek and Roman writers employed ἡ οἰκουμένη to denote the Greek and the Roman world; and a Jewish writer would naturally employ such a term to denote the Jewish world. Josephus appears to restrict the word to Palestine in Antt. 8. 13. 4. Speaking of the efforts of Ahab to find the prophet Elijah, he says that the king sent messengers in pursuit of him κατὰ πᾶσαν τὴν οἰκουμένην, *throughout all the earth* or land, i. e. of the Jews. Ancient writers give no account of any universal famine in the reign of Claudius, but they speak of several local famines which were severe in particular countries. Josephus (Antt. 20. 2. 6; Ib. 5. 2) mentions one which prevailed at that time in Judea, and swept away many of the inhabitants. Helena, queen of Adiabene, a Jewish proselyte who was then at Jerusalem, imported provisions from Egypt and Cyprus, which she distributed among the people to save them from starvation. This is the famine, probably, to which Luke refers here. The chronology admits of this supposition. According to Josephus, the famine which he describes took place when Cuspius Fadus and Tiberius Alexander were procurators; i. e. as Lardner suggests, it may have begun about the close of A. D. 44, and lasted three or four years. Fadus was sent into Judea on the death of Agrippa, which occurred in August of the year A. D. 44. If we attach the wider sense to οἰκουμένην, the prediction may import that a famine should take place throughout the Roman empire during the reign of Claudius (the year is not specified below), and not that it should prevail in all parts at the same time. So Wordsworth, Notes, p. 58. — ἐπὶ Κλαυδίου, *in* (lit. *upon*) *the reign of Claudius*. On ἐπί, in such chronological designations, see K. § 273. 4. b. The Greek idiom views the events as resting *upon* the ruler as their source or author; the English idiom as taking place *under* his guidance or auspices. — Καίσαρος after Κλαυδίου (T. R.) is not warranted.

V. 29. τῶν μαθητῶν depends by attraction on τις. The ordinary construction would be οἱ μαθηταὶ καθὼς ηὐπορεῖτό τις αὐτῶν (Mey. De Wet.): *The disciples in proportion as any one was prospered determined each of them*, etc. The apostle Paul prescribes the same rule of contribution in 1 Cor. 16, 2. For the augment in ηὐπορεῖτο, see on 2, 26. For ἕκαστος after a plural verb, see on 2, 6. — εἰς διακονίαν, *for relief*, lit. ministration, i. e. to their wants. The act here suggests the idea of its result or object. — πέμψαι sc. τὶ. — ἐν τῇ Ἰουδαίᾳ, *in Judea;* not the capital merely but other parts also, since the famine was general and believers were found in different places (see v. 1 and Gal. 1, 22).

V. 30. καί connects ἐποίησαν with ὥρισαν: they executed their determination. — πρὸς τοὺς πρεσβυτέρος, *unto the elders*, either those at Jerusalem who could easily forward the supplies to the destitute elsewhere, or those in Judea at large whom the messengers visited in person. The latter idea presents itself very readily from Ἰουδαίᾳ just before, and has also this to commend it, that Paul would have had an opportunity to preach now in that province, as mentioned in 26, 20 (see note there). — For the office of the presbyters, see on 14, 23. — Βαρνάβα is the Doric genitive; comp. 19, 14; Luke 13, 29, John I, 43, etc. W. § 8. 1; K. § 44. R. 2. — Meyer finds a contradiction between this passage and Gal. 2, 1, as if Paul could not have gone to Jerusalem at this time because he has not mentioned it in the Epistle. It is impossible to see why the reason commonly assigned for this omission does not account for it. Paul's object in writing to the Galatians does not require him to enumerate all his journeys to Jerusalem. In the first chapter there, he would prove that as an apostle he was independent of all human authority, and in the second chapter that the other apostles had conceded to him that independence. He had no occasion, therefore, to recapitulate his entire history. Examples of the facts in his life were all that he needed to bring forward. He was not bound to show how often he had been at Jerusalem, but only that he had gone thither once and again, under circumstances which showed in what character he claimed to act, and how fully the other apostles had acknowledged this claim.

CHAPTER XII.

VERSES 1. 2. *Renewed persecution at Jerusalem, and Death of James.*

V. 1. κατ᾽ ἐκεῖνον τὸν καιρόν, *about that time*, i. e. when Barnabas and Saul went to Jerusalem, as has just been related. See on v. 25. — Ἡρώδης. This *Herod* was Herod Agrippa the First, son of Aristobulus and grandson of Herod the Great. On the accession of Caligula, he received as king the former possessions of Philip and Lysanias, see Luke 3, 1; at a later period, the tetrarchy of Antipas; and in the year A. D. 41, Samaria and

Judea which were conferred on him by Claudius; so that, like his grandfather Herod, he swayed the sceptre, at this time, over all Palestine.[1] — ἐπέβαλε τὰς χεῖρας does not mean *attempted* (Kuin.), but *put forth violent hands;* comp. 4, 3; 5, 18; 21, 27. — κακῶσαι, *to oppress*, maltreat. The E. version derives "vex" from Tyndale. — ἀπὸ τῆς ἐκκλησίας, *of the church*, (lit. *from*), since the idea of origin passes readily into that of property, adherence. W. § 47. 4.

V. 2. ἀνεῖλε μαχαίρᾳ, *slew him with the sword*, beheaded him. The article fails, because the idea is general, abstract; comp. 9, 12. W. § 19. 1. On the mode of execution among the Jews, see Jahn's Archæol. § 257. Agrippa had the power of life and death, since he administered the government in the name of the Romans. See the note on 7, 59. The victim of his violence was James the Elder, a son of Zebedee and brother of John (Matt. 4, 21; 10, 2; Mark 1, 19, etc.). He is to be distinguished from James the Younger, the kinsman of the Lord (Gal. 1, 19), who is the individual meant under this name in the remainder of the history (17; 15, 13; 21, 18). The end of James verified the prediction that he should drink of his Master's cup; see Matt. 20, 23. Eusebius (2. 9) records a tradition that the apostle's accuser was converted by his testimony and beheaded at the same time with him. "The accuracy of the sacred writer," says Paley, "in the expressions which he uses here, is remarkable. There was no portion of time for thirty years before, or ever afterwards, in which there was a king at Jerusalem, a person exercising that authority in Judea, or to whom that title could be applied, except the last three years of Herod's life, within which period the transaction here recorded took place." The kingdom of Agrippa the Second, who is mentioned in 25, 13, did not embrace Judea.

VERSES 3–5. *The imprisonment of Peter.*

V. 3. ἰδὼν ὅτι ἀρεστόν, κ. τ. λ., *seeing that it is pleasing*, etc. The motive of Agrippa, therefore, was a desire to gain public favor. Josephus (Antt. 19. 7. 3) attributes to this ruler the same trait of character; he describes him as eager to ingratiate himself with the Jews. — προςέθετο, κ. τ. λ., *he apprehended still further Peter also;* an imitation of the Heb. וַיּוֹסֶף with the infinitive, comp. Luke 20, 11. 12. W. § 54. 5; Gesen. Heb. Gr. § 139. — ἀζύμων, *the days of unleavened bread*, i. e. the festival of the

[1] See Introduction, § 6. 2.

Passover, which continued seven days; and was so named because during that time no leaven was allowed in the houses of the Jews. The common text omits αἱ before ἡμέραι, which the best editors insert as well attested. It is not grammatically necessary. W. § 19. 2.

V. 4. καί, *also*, carries the mind back to συλλαβεῖν in v. 3, the idea of which πιάσας repeats. — τέσσαρσι τετραδίοις, *to four quaternions*, four companies of four, who were to relieve each other in guarding the prison. The Jews at this time followed the Roman practice of dividing the night into four watches, consisting of three hours each. Of the four soldiers employed at the same time, two watched in the prison and two before the door; or perhaps in this case (see on v. 10) were all stationed on the outside. — βουλόμενος, *meaning*, but disappointed in that purpose. — μετὰ τὸ πάσχα, *after the Passover*, i. e. not the paschal supper, but the festival which it introduced; comp. Luke 21, 1; John 6, 4. The reason for deferring the execution was that the stricter Jews regarded it as a profanation to put a person to death during a religious festival. Agrippa himself may have entertained, or affected to entertain, that scruple. — ἀναγαγεῖν αὐτόν, *to bring him up*, i. e. for trial and execution; comp. Luke 22, 66. But Herod was nearer his end than Peter. — τῷ λαῷ, *for the people* (dat. comm.), i. e. that they might be gratified with his death.

V. 5. οὖν, *therefore*, committed to such a guard. — ἐν τῇ φυλακῇ *in the prison* mentioned in v. 4. — ἐκτενής, *intent*, earnest, not *unceasing*, constant. See Luke 22, 44; 1 Pet. 4, 8. It is a word of the later Greek. Lob. ad Phryn. p. 311. All the English translators from Wiclif downward adopt the temporal sense. — ἐκκλησίας. The members of the church were so numerous, that they must have met in different companies. One of them is mentioned in v. 12.

VERSES 6–11. *The Miraculous Liberation of Peter.*

V. 6. νυκτὶ ἐκείνῃ, *in that night* preceding the day when he was to have been executed. — δεδεμένος ἁλύσεσι δυσί, *bound with two chains.* The Roman mode of chaining prisoners was adopted in this case, and was the following: "The soldier who was appointed to guard a particular prisoner had the chain fastened to the wrist of his left hand, the right remaining at liberty. The prisoner, on the contrary, had the chain fastened to the wrist of his right hand. The prisoner, and the soldier who had the care of him, were said to be tied (*alligati*) to one another. Sometimes, for greater security, the prisoner was chained to two soldiers, one on each side of him." Dict. of Antiq. art. *Catena.* Paul was bound with two chains on the occasion mentioned in 21, 33. — φύλακές τε, κ. τ. λ., *and keepers before the door* (perhaps two at one station and two at another) *were guarding the prison;* not after v. 5, *were keeping guard* (Raph. Walch).

V. 7. ἐν τῷ οἰκήματι, *in the abode = the prison.* This was an Attic euphemism which passed at length into the common dialect. — πατάξας, *having smitten,* in order to rouse him from sleep. — ἀνάστα is a second aorist imperative; comp. Eph. 5, 14. Grammarians represent the form as poetic in the earlier Greek. K. § 172. R. 5; W. § 14. 1. h. — ἐξέπεσον . . . . χειρῶν, *his chains fell off from his hands,* or *wrists.* χείρ the Greeks could use of the entire forearm, or any part of it.

V. 8. περίζωσαι. For convenience he had unbound the girdle of his tunic while he slept. The ἱμάτιον which he threw around him was the outer coat, or mantle, worn over the χιτών. There was no occasion for a precipitate flight; and the articles which he was directed to take would be useful to him. Note the transition to the present in the last two imperatives.

V. 9. ἀληθές, *true,* actual, as distinguished from a dream or vision. Peter's uncertainty arose from the extraordinary nature of the interposition; it was too strange to be credited. He was bewildered by the scene, unable at the moment to comprehend that what he saw and did was a reality.

V. 10. διελθόντες . . . . δευτέραν, *having passed through the first and second watch,* i. e. as Walch *de vinculis Petri* suggests, first through the two soldiers stationed at Peter's door (v. 6), and then through two others near the gate which led into the city. He supposes the two soldiers to whom Peter was bound (v. 6) were not included in the sixteen (v. 4), since their office would not require them to remain awake, and consequently to be changed during the night, like the others. A more common opinion is, that the *first watch* was a single soldier, before the door, and the *second* another at the iron gate, and that these two soldiers, with the two by the side of Peter, made up the quaternion then on duty. But διελθόντες, *having passed through,* suggests a plural sense of φυλακήν, and must be said loosely, if applied to a single person. This participle after ἐξελθών in v. 9 indicates a different position of *the first watch* from that of the two soldiers who guarded Peter in his cell; some have proposed that explanation. The numeral renders the article unnecessary. W. § 19. 2. That Peter passed the watch unopposed, or perhaps unobserved (see v.

18), was a part of the miracle. See on 5, 19. — ἐπὶ τὴν πύλην, κ. τ. λ. The precise situation of the prison is unknown. The *iron gate* may have formed the termination of a court, or avenue, which connected the prison with the town. De Wette, after Lightfoot, Walch, and others, thinks that the prison was in a tower between the two walls of the city, and that this was the outer gate of the tower. Others have proposed other conjectures. — αὐτομάτη is equivalent to an adverb, *spontaneously*. K. § 264. 3. c; B. § 123. 6. The gate opened without any visible cause. — προῆλθον ῥύμην μίαν, *went forward one street* or lane (9, 11). The angel accompanied him until he was beyond the reach of pursuit. — εὐθέως, *immediately*, on having come thus far.

V. 11. γενόμενος ἐν ἑαυτῷ, *having come to himself*, recovered from the confusion of mind into which he had been thrown. — ἐξαπέστειλε, *sent forth* from heaven. — ἀπὸ πάσης τῆς προσδοκίας, *from all the expectation* of the Jews who were so eager for his execution, and looking forward to it with confidence.

VERSES 12–17. *Peter repairs to the House of Mary, where some of the Believers had assembled for Prayer.*

V. 12. συνιδών, sc. τὰ γενόμενα, *having become aware* (14, 6), conscious to himself of the state of things (Whl. Alf. Mey.). Luke reminds us of this fact again (see v. 11), as if it might appear strange that Peter acted with so much deliberation. Some render *considering*, i. e. either what he should do, or where he should find an assembly of the disciples. Both the meaning and the tense of the participle favor this explanation less than the other. — Ἰωάννου . . . . Μάρκου. This *John Mark* is called simply John in 13, 5. 13; and Mark in 15, 39. He is supposed to have been the same Mark whom Peter terms his son in 1 Pet. 5, 13, i. e. in a spiritual sense, converted by his instrumentality. There is no reason for questioning his identity with the Evangelist who wrote the Gospel of Mark. See further, on v. 25. — προσευχόμενοι. One of the objects for which they were praying was the safety of Peter (v. 5).

V. 13. παιδίσκη, *a maid-servant*. Her Greek name, *Rhoda*, does not disprove her Jewish origin; see on 1, 23. The portress among the Jews was commonly a female; see John 18, 16. That the person should be known after so long a time shows how minute was Luke's information. — ὑπακοῦσαι, *to hearken*. This was the classical term signifying to answer a knock or call at the door.

V. 14. καὶ ἐπιγνοῦσα τὴν φωνήν, *and having recognized his voice* (3, 10; 4, 13). Peter may be supposed to have announced his name, or to have given it in reply to her inquiry. — ἀπὸ τῆς χαρᾶς. Nothing could be more life-like than the description of the scene which follows. Rhoda in the excess of her joy forgets to open the door, runs into the house, declares the news, while Peter is left in the street still knocking, and exposed to arrest. The passage has all the vividness of the recital of an eye-witness. Mark was undoubtedly in the house at the time, and may have communicated the circumstances to Luke at Antioch; or Luke may have obtained his information from Barnabas, who was a relative of the family; see Col. 4, 10.

V. 15. διϊσχυρίζετο, *affirmed confidently.* — ὁ ἄγγελος αὐτοῦ ἐστιν, *It is his angel,* i. e. his tutelary angel with his form and features. It was a common belief among the Jews, says Lightfoot, that every individual has a guardian angel, and that this angel may assume a visible appearance resembling that of the person whose destiny is committed to him. This idea appears here not as a doctrine of the Scriptures, but as a popular opinion, which is neither affirmed nor denied.

V. 17. κατασείσας τῇ χειρί, *having motioned with the hand downward,* as a signal that he would speak, and wished them to hear. Their joy was so tumultuous, that he could make them understand a gesture better than a word. — σιγᾶν. His object was not to prevent their being overheard, and so discovered by their enemies, but to secure to himself an opportunity to inform them how he had been liberated. — ὁ κύριος, *the Lord,* as the angel had been sent by him; see v. 7, 11. — Ἰακώβῳ. *James* is distinguished from the others on account of his office as pastor of the church at Jerusalem; see on v. 2. — καὶ ἐξελθών, *and* (probably on the same night) *having gone forth,* i. e. from the house, as the context most readily suggests; hence εἰς ἕτερον τόπον is indefinite, and may denote *unto another place,* in the city or out of it. It is most probable that he left the city for a time, as he must have foreseen (see v. 19) that vigorous efforts would be made to retake and destroy him. We find him at Jerusalem again a few years after this; see 15, 7. He may have returned even sooner than that, as Agrippa lived but a short time after this occurrence. Catholic writers and some others hold that Peter proceeded to Rome at this time, and labored for the Jews there as the apostle of the circumcision (Gal. 2, 7; 1 Pet. 1, 1). If this be true, he must then have been the founder of the church in that city, or at all events have established a relation to it personal and official, stronger than that of any other teacher. It is entirely adverse to this view, that Paul makes no allusion to Peter in his Epistle to the Romans, but writes with a tone of authority which his avowed policy, his spirit of independence (2 Cor. 10, 16), would not have suffered him to employ, had it belonged more properly to some other apostle to instruct and guide the Roman church. The best opinion from traditionary sources is that Peter arrived at Rome just before the outbreak of Nero's persecution, where he soon perished as a martyr. It is related that he was placed on the cross, at his own request, with his head downward, as if unworthy to suffer in the posture of the Master whom he had denied.

VERSES 18. 19. *Trial and Execution of the Soldiers.*

V. 18. γενομένης ἡμέρας, *when day had come.* If the soldiers to whom Peter was bound had been changed at the expiration of each watch (see on v. 10), why did they not ascertain the escape sooner? Wieseler (Chronologie u. s. w. p. 220) replies that the flight took place in the last watch not long before break of day. This is doubtful, as it would abridge so much the time allowed for the interview at the house of Mary, and for the departure from the city. The question requires no answer if Walch's opinion as stated in v. 10 be well founded. — τάραχος, *commotion,* partaking of the nature both of inquiry and alarm. The former part of the idea leads the way to the question which follows. There was reason for fear, because the soldiers in such a case were answerable for the safety of the prisoner, and, if he escaped, were liable to suffer the punishment which would have been inflicted on him. Compare 16, 27; Matt. 28, 14. στρατιώταις would include naturally the entire sixteen (v. 4), though the four who were on guard at the time of the escape had most reason to tremble for their lives. — τί ἄρα, κ. τ. λ., *what then* (syllogistical, since he was gone) *was become of Peter?*

V. 19. ἀνακρίνας, *having examined,* tried them for a breach of discipline; see 4, 9; Luke 23, 14. — We need not impute to Herod such barbarity as that of putting to death the entire detachment. φύλακας may be understood of those who were more immediately responsible for the prisoner's safety. — ἀπαχθῆναι, *to be led away,* i. e. to execution. The word was a *vox solennis* in this sense, as Lösner, Kypke, and others have shown. The Romans employed *ducere* in the same absolute way. — καὶ κατελθὼν, κ. τ. λ. Herod resided usually at Jerusalem, and went now to

Cæsarea, as Josephus informs us, to preside at the public games in honor of the Emperor Claudius.

VERSES 20–24. *Death of Herod Agrippa at Cæsarea.*

V. 20. The reader should compare the narrative of this event with that of Josephus, in Antt. 19. 8. 2. The Jewish historian has confirmed Luke's account in the most striking manner. He also makes Cæsarea the scene of the occurrence; he mentions the assembly, the oration, the robe, the impious acclamations of the people, the sudden death of Herod, and adds to the rest that his terrible end was a judgment inflicted upon him for his impiety.— θυμομαχῶν may refer to an open war or violent feeling of hostility. As Josephus makes no mention of any actual outbreak between Agrippa and the Phœnicians, the latter is probably the sense of the word here. The Phœnicians may either have apprehended a war as the result of Agrippa's anger, or they may have been threatened with an interruption of the commerce carried on between them and the Jews. — παρῆσαν πρός αὐτόν, *came unto him*, i. e. in the person of their representatives; lit. *were present*, the antecedent motion being applied. W. § 50. 4. — πείσαντες, *having persuaded*, brought to their interest. *Blastus*, judging from his name, may have been a Greek or a Roman. His influence with the king was the reason why they were so anxious to obtain his mediation. A bribe may have quickened his sympathy with the strangers. — ἐπὶ τοῦ κοιτῶνος, *over his bedchamber*, his chamberlain. His office placed him near the king's person and enabled him to hold the keys to his heart (Bmg.). — ᾐτοῦντο εἰρήνην, *desired peace*, i. e. according to the circumstances of the case, sought to avert a rupture of it, or, if it was already impaired, to effect its restoration. Their desire for this result may have been increased by the existing famine. — τὸ τρέφεσθαι, κ. τ. λ., *because their country was sustained*, etc. The Tyrians and Sidonians were a commercial people, and procured their supplies of grain chiefly from Palestine in exchange for their own merchandise. This relation of the two countries to each other had existed from early times; see 1 Kings 5, 9; Ezra 3, 7; Ezek. 27, 17.

V. 21. τακτῇ ἡμέρᾳ, *on an appointed day*, which, according to Josephus, was the 1st of August, and the second day of the public games. — ἐνδυσάμενος ἐσθῆτα, κ. τ. λ. The circmstances related by Josephus may be combined (Howson, I. p. 158) with Luke's account, as follows: "On the second day of the festival, Agrippa came into the theatre. The stone seats, rising in a great semicircle, tier above tier, were covered with an excited multitude. The king came in, clothed in magnificent robes, of which silver was the costly and brilliant material. It was early in the day, and the sun's rays fell upon the king, so that the eyes of the beholders were dazzled with the brightness which surrounded him. Voices from the crowd, here and there, exclaimed that it was the apparition of something divine. And when he spoke and made an oration to them, they gave a shout, saying, 'It is the voice of a god, and not of a man.' But in the midst of this idolatrous ostentation, an angel of God suddenly smote him. He was carried out of the theatre a dying man, and on the 6th of August he was dead." — ἐπὶ τοῦ βήματος, *upon the seat*, or *throne*, provided for him in the theatre; see on 19, 29. — ἐδημηγόρει, *spoke publicly;* because though he directed his speech to the deputies, he was heard also by the people who were present (v. 22). The Phœnicians were there as suppliants for peace, and the king's object now was to announce to them his decision. The giving audience to ambassadors and replying to them in public was not uncommon in ancient times. — πρὸς αὐτούς, *unto them*, i. e. the Tyrians and Sidonians as represented by their agents. The pronoun does not refer to δῆμος. See W. § 22. 3. 1. It was the messengers, not the Cæsareans who awaited the king's answer.

V. 22. ἐπεφώνει, *shouted thereupon*, again and again. It enhanced the eloquence no doubt, that what they had heard accorded with their wishes. In such a city, the bulk of the assembly would be heathen (see on 8, 40), and θεοῦ may be taken in their sense of the term.

V. 23. ἀνθ' ὧν, κ. τ. λ., *because he gave not glory to God*, i. e. did not repel the impious flattery, was willing to receive it. Some editors insert τήν before δόξαν. — καὶ γενόμενος, κ. τ. λ., *and having been eaten with worms, he expired.* In ascribing Agrippa's death to such a cause, Luke makes it evident that he did not mean to represent it as instantaneous. His statement, therefore, does not oppose that of Josephus, who says that Herod lingered for five days after the first attack, in the greatest agony, and then died. It is evident also for the same reason, that Luke did not consider the angel as the author of Herod's death in any such sense as to exclude the intervention of secondary causes.

V. 24. δέ, *but*, contrasts slightly the fate of Herod, the persecutor of the church, with the prosperity of the church itself. — ὁ λόγος . . . . ἐπληθύνετο, *the word of God grew*, was diffused more and more, *and increased*, i. e. (comp. 6, 1) was embraced by increasing numbers. λόγος suggests the complex idea of doctrine and disciples, and the verbs which follow divide the idea into its parts.

VERSE 25. *Barnabas and Saul return to Antioch.*

V. 25. This verse appears to be introductory to the subject of the next chapter. It was proper to apprise the reader that Barnabas and Saul returned to Antioch (see 11, 30), since the narrative of what next occurred in that city implies that they were there, and no mention has been made of their return. Paul and Barnabas made this journey to Jerusalem probably near the beginning of the year A. D. 45; for the famine commenced at the close of the preceding year (see on 11, 28), and the supplies collected in anticipation of that event would naturally be forwarded before the distress began to be severe. That the journey took place about this time results also from its being mentioned in connection with Herod's death. The two friends appear to have remained at Jerusalem but a short time, as may be inferred from the object of their mission, and still more decisively from the absence of any allusion to this journey in Gal. 2, 1 sq. — Ἰωάννην. *John* was a relative of Barnabas, as we learn from Col. 4, 10; and this relationship may have led to the present connection. He appears next in the history as their associate in missionary labors (13, 5).

CHAPTER XIII.

VERSES 1–3. *Barnabas and Saul are sent to preach to the Heathen.*

V. 1. The narrative mentions three different journeys of Paul among the heathen; the account of the first of these commences here. — τινές (probably not genuine) would indicate that those named were not all the teachers at Antioch. — In κατὰ τὴν ἐκκλησίαν the preposition may be directive as well as local: *in the church* and for its benefit. The office supplied a correspondent (κατά) want. Or the idea may be that of distribution: such teachers belonging to the different churches (comp. 14, 23), the writer's mind passes along the series to those at Antioch. — προφῆται (see on 2, 17) is the specific term; διδάσκαλοι the generic. The prophets were all teachers, but the reverse was not true. Compare the note on 14, 23. — Συμεών. *Symeon* is otherwise unknown. He was evidently a Jew, and hence in his intercourse with Gentiles (see on v. 9) was called also Niger. The latter was a familiar name among the Romans, and is a precarious reason for inferring (Alf.) that he was an African proselyte. — Λούκιος may be the *Lucius* who is mentioned in Rom. 16, 21. Some have thought that Luke, the writer of the Acts (no doubt a native of Antioch), may be intended here; but Λούκιος and Λουκιανός or Λουκᾶς are different names. See W. § 16. 4. R. 1. — Κυρηναῖος. See on 2, 10. — Μαναήν = מְנַחֵם (2 Kings 15, 14) occurs only here. — Ἡρώδου τοῦ τετράρχου. This *Herod* was the one who put to death John the Baptist; a son of Herod the Great, and an uncle of Agrippa, whose death has just been related. He was now in exile on the banks of the Rhone, but though divested of his office is called *tetrarch*, because he was best known under that title; see on 4, 6. There are two views as to the import of σύντροφος. One is that it means *comrade*, lit. *one brought up*, educated with another. It was very common for persons of rank to associate other children with their own, for the purpose of sharing their amusements and studies, and by their example serving to excite them to greater emulation. Josephus, Plutarch, Polybius, and others, speak of this ancient practice. So Calvin, Grotius, Schott, Baumgarten, and others. The more approved opinion is that it means *collactaneus*, nourished at the same breast, *foster-brother*. Kuinoel, Olshausen, Tholuck, De Wette, and others, after Walch *de Menachemo*, adopt that meaning. The mother of Manaen, according to this view, was Herod's nurse. In either case the relation is mentioned as an honorary one.

V. 2. λειτουργούντων refers here to the rites of Christian worship, as prayer, exhortation, fasting, see v. 3. 15, 14, 23. — αὐτῶν, i. e. the prophets and teachers. The participation of others in the service is not asserted, or denied. It is possible that they were observing a season of prayer with reference to this very question, What were their duties in relation to the heathen. — ἀφορίσατε δή μοι, *Separate now for me*, i. e. for the Holy Spirit The Spirit makes the revelation, selects the missionaries, assigns to them their work. The personality of the agent may be inferred from such acts. The command in this form was addressed to the associates of Barnabas and Saul, but the latter would hear the same voice pointing out to them their duty and directing them to perform the service laid upon them. — δή strengthens the command; see 15, 36; Luke 2, 15. K. § 315. 1. The verb contains the idea both of selection and consecration. —

ὅ, *unto which*, without the preposition because the antecedent has it; comp. ᾗ ἤρχον in 9, 17. — προσκέκλημαι has a middle sense. W. § 39. 3. The nature of this work, not stated here, we learn from the subsequent narrative; they were to go into foreign countries and publish the gospel to Jews and Gentiles. The great object of the mission was doubtless to open more effectually "the door of faith to the heathen."

V. 3. τότε, κ. τ. λ., *Then having fasted*, etc. This was a different fast from that spoken of in v. 2, and observed probably by the body of the church. — On ἐπιθέντες τὰς χεῖρας αὐτοῖς, see 6, 6. The act was a representative one, and though performed by a part involves the idea of a general participation. Paul was already a minister and an apostle (see Gal. 1, 1 sq., where he claims this character from the outset), and by this service he and Barnabas were now merely set apart for the accomplishment of a specific work. They were summoned to a renewed and more systematic prosecution of the enterprise of converting the heathen; see on 9, 30; 11, 20. — ἀπέλυσαν, *sent away*. That the subject of this verb includes the Antiochian Christians in general, may be argued from the analogous case in 15, 40. The brethren commended Paul to God as he departed on his second mission.

VERSES 4–12. *The Journey to Cyprus, and its Results.*

V. 4. ἐκπεμφθέντες. We may place this mission in the year A. D. 45. It does not appear that they remained long at Antioch before their departure. See the note on 12, 25. — εἰς τὴν Σελεύκειαν. *Seleucia* lay west of Antioch, on the sea-coast, five miles north of the mouth of the Orontes. It was situated on the rocky eminence, forming the southern extremity of the hilly range called Pieria. The harbor and mercantile suburb were on level ground towards the west. A village called Antakia and interesting ruins point out the ancient site. "The inner basin, or dock, (there were two ports) is now a morass; but its dimensions can be measured, and the walls that surrounded it can be distinctly traced. The position of the ancient flood-gates, and the passage through which the vessels were moved from the inner to the outer harbor, can be accurately marked. The very piers of the outer harbor are still to be seen under the water. The stones are of great size, some of them twenty feet long, five feet deep, and six feet wide; and are fastened to each other with iron cramps. The masonry of ancient Selucia is still so good, that not long since a Turkish Pacha conceived the idea of clearing out and repairing the harbor." See authorities in Howson. Those piers were still unbroken, this great seaport of the Seleucids and the Ptolemies was as magnificent as ever, under the sway of the Romans, when Paul and Barnabas passed through it on their present mission. Whether they *came down* (κατῆλθον) from the interior to the coast by land, or by water, is uncertain. The windings of the river make the distance about forty-one miles, but by land it is only sixteen miles and a half. At present, the Orontes is not navigable, in consequence of a bar at the mouth, and other obstructions; but Strabo says (16. 2), that in his time they sailed up the stream in one day. The road, though it is now mostly overgrown with shrubs, was then doubtless a well worn track like the road from the Piræus to Athens, or from Ostia to Rome. At Seleucia, the two missionaries with their companion went on board (ἀπέπλευσαν) one of the numerous vessels which must have been constantly plying between that port and the fertile Cyprus. "As they cleared the port, the whole sweep of the bay of Antioch opened on their left, — the low ground by the mouth of the Orontes, — the wild and woody country beyond it, — and then the peak of Mount Cassius, rising symmetrically from the very edge of the sea to a height of five thousand feet. On the right, in the south-west horizon, if the day was clear, they saw the island of Cyprus from the first. The current sets northerly and north-east between the island and the Syrian coast. But with a fair wind, a few hours would enable them to run down from Seleucia to Salamis; and the land would rapidly rise in forms well known and familiar to Barnabas and Mark." Howson, I. p. 169. The fact that Barnabas was a native of Cyprus (4, 36) may have induced them to give this direction to their journey.

V. 5. καὶ γενόμενοι ἐν Σαλαμῖνι, *And having arrived in Salamis.* This town was on the eastern shore of Cyprus, "on a bight of the coast to the north of the river Pediæus. A large city by the sea-shore, a wide-spread plain with corn-fields and orchards, and the blue distance of mountains beyond, composed the view on which the eyes of Barnabas and Saul rested when they came to anchor in the bay of Salamis." — ταῖς συναγωγαῖς indicates that the Jews here were numerous, since in other places where they were few they had only one synagogue; comp. 17, 1; 18, 4. This intimation is confirmed by ancient testimony. In the time of Trajan, A. D. 116, the Jews in Cyprus were so powerful that they rose and massacred two hundred and forty thousand of the Greek inhabitants (Dio Cass. 68. 32). In revenge for this slaughter, Hadrian, who was afterwards emperor, landed on the island, and either put to death or expelled the entire Jewish population. At the time of Paul's visit, many of the Cyprian Jews must have resided at Salamis, which was the seat of a lucrative commerce. — εἶχον . . . . ὑπηρέτην, *and they had also John* (see 12, 25) *as an assistant* — in what? καί, as I think, recalls most naturally κατήγγελον τὸν λόγον; and the answer would be that he assisted them in the declaration of the word. Compare 26, 16; Luke 1, 2; 1 Cor. 4, 1. But the view of most critics is different; they suppose John to have had charge of the incidental cares of the party, so as to leave Paul and Barnabas more at liberty to preach the gospel. We are not informed how long they remained at Salamis, or what success attended their labors.

V. 6. διελθόντες, κ. τ. λ., *And having passed through the whole island unto Paphos,* which was at the other end of Cyprus. The city intended here was *new* Paphos, in distinction from the old city of that name, which was several miles farther south. The distance from east to west was not more than a hundred miles. The Peutingerian Table[1] (which dates probably from the time of Alexander Severus, i. e. about A. D. 230) represents a public road as extending from Salamis to Paphos. If that road existed at this earlier period, Paul arrived at Paphos in a short time, and without difficulty. The present Baffa occupies the site of that city. — εὗρόν τινα μάγον, *found a certain Magian,* which was his professional title, since it stands for Ἐλύμας in v. 8; not *sorcerer* (E. V.), which would be opprobrious. — ψευδοπροφήτην is the narrator's term for describing him; he was a fortune-teller, but his art was an imposition. It may appear singular that a person of his character should so mislead and captivate the prudent Sergius. But the incident presents in fact a true picture of the times. At that period (I abridge Mr. Howson's paragraph here) impostors from the East, pretending to magical powers, had great influence over the Roman mind. The East but recently thrown open was the land of mystery to the western nations. Reports of the strange arts practised there, of the wonderful events of which it was the scene, excited almost fanatically the imagination both of the populace and the aristocracy of Rome. Syrian fortune-tellers crowded the capital, and appeared in all the haunts of business and amusement. The strongest minds were not superior to their influence. Marius relied on a Jewish prophetess for regulating the progress of his campaigns. Pompey,

[1] See Forbiger's Handbuch der alten Geographie, Vol. I. p. 469 sq.

Crassus, and Cæsar sought information from Oriental astrology. Juvenal paints to us the Emperor Tiberius "sitting on the rock of Capri, with his flock of Chaldæans round him." The astrologers and sorcerers, says Tacitus, are a class of men who "will always be discarded and always cherished."

V. 7. ὃς ἦν, κ. τ. λ., *who was with the proconsul Sergius Paulus.* It would not have been correct to apply this title to the governor of every Roman province, or even to the governor of the same province at different periods. It was so difficult to observe accuracy in the use of the varying titles given to Roman magistrates, that several of the classic authors of this period have, beyond all question, misapplied them in various instances. Luke was exposed to error in this passage on the right hand and on the left. On the establishment of the empire, Augustus divided the provinces into two classes. Those which required a military force he retained in his own hands, and the others he committed to the care of the Senate and the Roman people. The officers or Governors sent into the emperor's provinces were styled proprætors or legates (*proprætores, legati,* or ἀντιστράτηγοι, πρεσβευταί); those sent into the people's provinces were called proconsuls (*proconsules,* ἀνθύπατοι). Cyprus, then, must have been a senatorian province at this time, or Luke has assigned to Sergius a false title. But, further, the same province was often transferred from one jurisdiction to another. Thus, in the present instance, Augustus at first reserved Cyprus to himself and committed its administration to proprætors, or legates. Strabo informs us of that circumstance, and there leaves the matter. Hence it was supposed for a long time that Luke had committed an oversight here, or had styled Sergius proconsul without knowing the exact import of the appellation. But a passage was discovered at length in Dio Cassius (53. 12), which states that Augustus subsequently relinquished Cyprus to the Senate in exchange for another province, and (54. 4) that it was governed henceforth by proconsuls: καὶ οὕτως ἀνθύπατοι καὶ ἐς ἐκεῖνα τὰ ἔθνη πέμπεσθαι ἤρξαντο. Coins, too, have been found, struck in the reign of Claudius, which confirm Luke's accuracy. Bishop Marsh mentions one on which this very title, ἀνθύπατος, is applied to Cominius Proclus, a governor of Cyprus. It was in the reign of Claudius that Paul visited this island. For similar confirmations of our history, see on 18, 12; 19, 38. — συνετῷ, *intelligent,* discerning. It may have been his possession of this quality that prompted him to seek the acquaintance of Elymas; he may have hoped to gain from him that deeper knowledge of futurity and of the mysteries of nature which the human mind craves so instinctively. It certainly was proof of his discernment, that he was not deceived by the man's pretensions; that, on hearing of the arrival of Paul and Barnabas, he sent for them, and on the strength of the evidence which confirmed their doctrine, yielded his mind to it. — ἐπεζήτησεν, *desired earnestly*. — τὸν λόγον τοῦ θεοῦ, *the word of God*, designates the new doctrine from Luke's point of view (Mey.).

V. 8. Ἐλύμας is an Arabic word which means *the wise*. It was a title of honor, like ὁ μάγος, to which it is here put as equivalent. He was born, perhaps, in Arabia, or had lived there; and may have assumed this name in a boastful spirit, or may have received it from others, as a compliment to his skill. — ζητῶν . . . . πίστεως, *seeking to turn aside the proconsul from the faith*, i. e. from adopting it; for he was not yet a believer (see v. 12).

V. 9. ὁ καὶ Παῦλος, *the also Paul* = ὁ καὶ καλούμενος Παῦλος. ὁ is the article here, not a pronoun. W. § 18. 1. The origin of this name is still disputed. Among the later critics, Olshausen and Meyer adhere to the older view, that Paul assumed it out of respect to Sergius Paulus, who was converted by his instrumentality. But had the writer connected the name with that event, he would have introduced it more naturally after v. 12. He makes use of it, it will be observed, before speaking of the proconsul's conversion. Neander objects further, that it was customary among the ancients for the pupil to adopt the name of the teacher, not the teacher to adopt that of the pupil. There is force, too, in his remark, that, according to this view, the apostle would seem to recognize the salvation of a distinguished person as more important than that of others; for that Sergius was his first convert from heathenism, and received this honor on that account, assumes incorrectly that he had preached hitherto to none but those of his own nation. It is more probable that Paul acquired this name like other Jews in that age; who, when they associated with foreigners, had often two names, the one Jewish, the other foreign; sometimes entirely distinct, as Onias and Menelaus, Hillel and Pollio, and sometimes similar in sound, as Tarphon and Trypho, Silas and Silvanus. In like manner the apostle may have been known as Saul among the Jews, and Paul among the heathen; and, being a native of a foreign city, as Lightfoot suggests, he may have borne the two names from early life. This explanation of the origin of the name accounts for its introduction at this stage of the history.

It is here for the first time that Luke speaks directly of Paul's labors among the heathen; and it is natural that he should apply to him the name by which he was chiefly known in that sphere of his ministry. According to some, the name changes here, because Luke has followed hitherto written memoranda, in which the apostle was called Saul (Neand. Alf.). This hypothesis is unnecessary, and improbable. Luke had no need of such memoirs, as he could learn from Paul himself all that he has related of him; and further, the style of what precedes, instead of indicating a different hand, is homogeneous with that which follows. Zeller, though he denies that Luke wrote the Acts, maintains that a single author must have written it. — πλησθείς, κ. τ. λ. He was thus impelled to expose the man's wickedness, and to announce his punishment.

V. 10. δόλου, *deceit,* refers to his occupation; ῥᾳδιουργίας, *wickedness,* to his character. — υἱὲ διαβόλου, *son of the devil.* The kindredship is that of disposition, moral resemblance; see John 8, 44. The second noun is sufficiently definite to omit the article. W. § 19. 1. It has the article, however, in other passages, except 1 Pet. 5, 8, where it stands in apposition. — οὐ παύσῃ .... εὐθείας; *Wilt thou not cease to pervert,* i. e. to misrepresent, malign, *the right ways of the Lord?* viz. those which he requires men to follow, as repentance, faith, obedience. It was Christian truth, the gospel, which he opposed. Most critics prefer the interrogative form of the sentence as more forcible than the declarative. οὐ denies παύσῃ=*persist* (W. § 57. 3), and implies the ordinary affirmative answer. εὐθείας suggests possibly a contrast with the impostor's own ways, so full of deceit and obliquity.

V. 11. χεὶρ κυρίου sc. ἐστι, *hand of the Lord;* here God perhaps as the phrase is common in the Old Testament. — ἐπὶ σέ, *upon thee,* viz. i. e. for punishment; in a good sense, in 11, 21. — μὴ βλέπων states a consequence, hence μή, not οὐ. — ἄχρι καιροῦ, *until a season,* a certain time; comp. Luke 4, 13 The infliction would be temporary; either because the object (see next verse) did not require it to be permanent, or because the mildness might conduce to the man's repentance. — ἀχλὺς καὶ σκότος, *a mist and darkness,* related as cause and effect; or by degrees, first one and then the other. — ἐζήτει states his habit (imperf.) during the period of his blindness.

V. 12. ἐκπλησσόμενος .... κυρίου, *being astonished at the doctrine of the Lord,* i. e. its confirmation by such a miracle, comp. Mark 1, 27.

VERSES 13–15. *They proceed to Perga, and thence to Antioch in Pisidia.*

V. 13. ἀναχθέντες, *having put to sea,* lit. having gone up (note the etymology), because the sea appears higher than the land. Paphos was on the sea-shore, and they would embark at that place. — οἱ περὶ τὸν Παῦλον, *Paul and his companions.* περί presents the name after it as the central object of the group, see John 11, 19. W. § 53. i. Hitherto the order has been Barnabas and Saul; but from this time Paul appears in the narrative as the principal person, and Barnabas as subordinate. — ἦλθον εἰς Πέργην, *came unto Perga.* They must have "sailed past the promontories of Drepanum and Acamas, and then across the waters of the Pamphylian Sea, leaving on the right the cliffs (six hundred feet high) which form the western boundary of Cilicia, to the innermost bend of the bay of Attaleia." *Perga* was the chief city of Pamphylia, situated on the Cestrus, about seven miles from its mouth. A bar obstructs the entrance of this river at the present time; but Strabo (14. 4) says expressly that it was navigable in his day as far up as Perga. The ruins of this city are to be seen still, sixteen miles northeast of the modern Adalia, or Satalia. They consist of "walls and towers, columns and cornices, a theatre and a stadium, a broken aqueduct, and tombs scattered on both sides of the site of the town. Nothing else remains of Perga but the beauty of its natural situation, between and upon the sides of two hills, with an extensive valley in front, watered by the river Cestrus, and backed by the mountains of the Taurus."[1] — Ἰωάννης, κ. τ. λ. Why John Mark left them so abruptly is unknown. It is certain from 15, 38 (see the note there) that his reason for turning back was not one which Paul approved. He returned not to Antioch, but Jerusalem, where his home was (12, 12).

V. 14. αὐτοί, *they themselves,* unaccompanied by their former associate. — ἀπὸ τῆς Πέργης. The stay at Perga, therefore, was brief; they did not even preach there at this time; comp. 14, 25. What occasioned this singular haste? Very possibly, as Howson suggests, they arrived there in the spring of the year, and, in order to prosecute their journey into the interior, were obliged to advance without delay. "Earlier in the season the passes would have been filled with snow. In the heat of summer the weather

[1] Sir C. Fellows's "Asia Minor," pp. 190–193.

would have been less favorable for the expedition. In the autumn the disadvantages would have been still greater, from the approaching difficulties of winter." On the journey from the coast to the interior, Paul may have encountered some of the "perils of robbers" (κινδύνοις λῃστῶν) and "perils of rivers" (κινδύνοις ποταμῶν), to which he alludes in 2 Cor. 11, 26. The marauding habits of the people on the mountains which he now crossed were notorious in all ancient history. The country swarmed with banditti of the most desperate character. The physical character of the region exposed him, also, to the other class of dangers. The streams here are numerous and violent, beyond those of any other tract in Asia Minor. Torrents "burst out at the base of huge cliffs, or dash down wildly through narrow ravines." See Howson for fuller information on these points. — εἰς Ἀντιόχειαν. *Antioch*, which lay north from Perga, was on the central tableland of Asia Minor, on the confines of Pisidia and Phrygia. It was built by the founder of the Syrian Antioch. Under Augustus it rose to the rank of a colony. It was now an important city, inhabited by many Greeks, Romans, and Jews, in addition to its native population. The site of Antioch was first identified by Mr. Arundel in 1833. — τῶν σαββάτων, *of the Sabbath*, i. e. the rest season. The plural arose probably from the fact, that such a season included often more than one day. See W. § 27. 3.

V. 15. μετὰ δὲ τὴν ἀνάγνωσιν, κ. τ. λ. The practice of reading the Scriptures in this manner grew up probably during the exile. Win. Realw. II. p. 548. νόμος here designates the Pentateuch; προφῆται, the other books of the Old Testament, see Matt. 5, 17; Luke 16, 16, etc. The *Psalms* formed sometimes a third division, see Luke 24, 44. — ἀπέστειλαν, sc. ὑπηρέτην (Luke 4, 20), *the rulers of the synagogue* (see on 9, 2) *sent unto them a servant.* It may have been known that they were teachers, or, as Hemsen suggests, they may have occupied a seat which indicated that such was their office. — ἐν ὑμῖν, *in you*, in your minds; comp. Gal. 1, 16; Phil. 1, 5. — παρακλήσεως, *exhortation.* The object was to incite them to a stricter observance of the law.

VERSES 16–41. *The Discourse of Paul at Antioch.*

The topics are, first, the goodness of God to Israel, especially in having promised to send to them a Saviour, 16–25; secondly, Jesus has been proved to be this Saviour, by his death and resurrection, in accordance with the prophecies of the Old Testament, 26–37; and, thirdly, it is the duty of men to receive him in this character, since they can be saved in no other way, 38–41.

V. 16. κατασείσας τῇ χειρί (comp. on 12, 16) was the customary gesture on rising to speak. It betokened respect for the audience and a request for attention. — οἱ φοβούμενοι τὸν θεόν, *who fear God*, as in 10, 2, i. e. Gentiles who were friendly to Judaism, but uncircumcised. They occupied, it is said, a separate place in the synagogue. The contents of the address show that the Israelites greatly outnumbered that class of the hearers. This discourse deserves the more attention, as furnishing so copious an illustration of the apostle's manner of preaching to the Jews.

V. 17. ὕψωσεν, *exalted*, made them numerous and powerful. — ἐν γῇ, *in the land.* For the absence of the article, see on 7, 29. μετὰ βραχίονος ὑψηλοῦ, *with a high arm*, i. e. one raised on high, and so ever ready to protect and defend them; comp. Ex. 6, 6.

V. 18. ἐτροφοφόρησεν = ὡς τροφὸς ἐβάστασεν, *carried them as a nurse* (in the arms as it were), sustained, cared for them. The term is derived probably from Deut. 1, 31. Most of the later editors prefer this word to ἐτροποφόρησεν, *endured their manners.* It suits the connection better than the other word, since what the apostle would bring to view here is not so much the forbearance of God towards his people, as his interpositions, his direct efforts in their behalf. ἐτροφοφόρησεν is well attested also, though the evidence is not decisive.

V. 19. ἔθνη ἑπτά, *seven nations.* See their names in Deut. 7, 1. They were the principal tribes in Palestine at that time. — ἐν γῇ, anarthrous as above. — κατεκληρονόμησεν αὐτοῖς, *assigned to them as a possession;* Hellenistic for the Hiphil of נָחַל.[1] — τὴν γῆν αὐτῶν, *their land* by promise, gift; or, better, henceforth theirs and that of their descendants.

V. 20. μετὰ ταῦτα, *after these things*, viz. the conquest and occupation of the country. — ὡς ἔτεσι . . . . κριτάς, *during about four hundred and fifty years he gave judges.* For the dative, see on 8, 11. This number is the sum of the years assigned in the Old Testament to the administration of the judges from the time of Joshua to the death of Eli, added to the sum of the years during which the nation was subject to foreign oppressors. Hence it would be very natural for the Jews to speak of four hundred and fifty years as the proximate number of years during which the judges ruled. But whether the computation arose in that way, or some other, it was certainly in use among the Jews; for Jose-

[1] For the origin of such Hebraisms, see the writer's Hebrew Exercises, p. 96.

phus (Antt. 8. 2. 1) gives the time from the departure out of Egypt till the building of the temple as five hundred and ninty-two years. If we deduct from that the forty years in the wilderness, twenty-five for the administration of Joshua (Antt. 5. 1. 29, not stated in the Old Testament), forty for Saul's reign (see v. 21), forty for David's, and four under Solomon (1 Kings 6, 1), we have for the period of the judges four hundred and forty-three years, which the apostle could call, in round numbers, *about four hundred and fifty years.* It is evident, therefore, that Paul has followed here a mode of reckoning which was current at that time, and which, being a well-known received chronology, whether correct or incorrect in itself considered, was entirely correct for his object, which was not to settle a question about dates, but to recall to the minds of those whom he addressed a particular portion of the Jewish history. The Hebrews had still another computation, as appears from 1 Kings 6, 1. The time from the exodus to the building of the temple is there given as four hundred and eighty years; which (deducting the other dates as stated above) would allow but two hundred and thirty-one years for the period of the judges. In regard to such differences, see also on 7, 6. Some of the best critics read ὡς ἔτεσι τετρακοσίοις καὶ πεντήκοντα καὶ μετὰ ταῦτα. The four hundred and fifty years belong then to the preceding verse, and may be the years from the birth of Isaac when God showed that he had chosen the fathers, to the distribution of the land of Canaan. Adding together sixty years from the birth of Isaac to that of Jacob, one hundred and thirty as the age of Jacob on going into Egypt, two hundred and fifteen as the sojourn there, and forty-seven thence to the settlement of the tribes, the sum is four hundred and fifty-two. See again on 7, 6. This reading is found in the oldest manuscripts (A, B, C), and some others, and is approved by Griesbach, Lachman, Luthardt[1] Green, Wordsworth, and others. The text may have been changed to relieve the difficulty (Mey.); but it is singular that the three oldest witnesses concur in that variation. A summary decision is not to be pronounced here. — ἕως Σαμουήλ, *unto Samuel,* who is to be included probably among the judges; or ἕως may be taken as exclusive. How long he governed is not mentioned in 1 Sam. 7, 15, nor in 28, 3. The tradition (Jos. Antt. 6. 13. 5), which is not perhaps of much value, makes it twelve years. ὡς would allow us to add these years to four hundred and fifty, if any one prefers that.

[1] In Reuter's Repertorium, p. 205, Jahrgang 1855.

V. 21. κἀκεῖθεν, *and thereafter*, is here an adverb of time. — ᾐτήσαντο, *asked for themselves*, etc. See 1 Sam. 8, 5; 10, 1. — ἔτη τεσσαράκοντα, *forty years*, which agrees with Jos. Antt. 6. 14. 9. The Old Testament does not mention the length of Saul's reign.

V. 22. μεταστήσας αὐτόν, *having removed him*, i. e. from life (De Wet.); or from his office (Kuin.). The two events were coincident in point of time. Saul reigned until his death, though David was anointed as prospective king during his lifetime. — ᾧ . . . . μαρτυρήσας, *to whom* (dat. comm.) *also he testified, saying*. The dative depends on the participle. The apostle quotes the substance of 1 Sam. 13, 14, and Ps. 89, 21. This commendation is not absolute, but describes the character of David in comparison with that of Saul. The latter was rejected for his disobedience and impiety; David, on the contrary, was always faithful to the worship of Jehovah, and performed his commands as they were made known to him by revelation, or the messengers whom God sent to him.

V. 23. Jesus could not be the Messiah, unless he were descended from David. τούτου stands first in order to give prominence to his descent from that source. — κατ' ἐπαγγελίαν, *according to promise*, as made to the fathers (v. 32); not to David merely.

V. 24. Ἰωάννου. The Jews acknowledged John's authority as a prophet, and were bound, therefore, to admit his testimony. — πρὸ προσώπου (= לִפְנֵי) τῆς εἰσόδου, *before his entrance*, i. e. upon his public ministry; see Matt. 11, 10: Luke 7, 27. — βάπτισμα μετανοίας, *baptism of repentance*, i. e. such as required repentance on the part of those who received it; see 19, 4.

V. 25. ὡς . . . . δρόμον, *Now as John was finishing his course*, was near its close (De Wet. Mey.); not *while he was completing it* (Kuin. Olsh.). The forerunner was about to be imprisoned when he bore this testimony to his successor. — τίνα με, κ. τ. λ., *Whom do ye suppose that I am? I am not*, viz. the Messiah. The predicate is omitted as well known; comp. Mark 13, 6; Luke 21, 8; John 13, 19. Some critics (Calv. Raph. Kuin.) exclude the question, and render, *he whom* (τίνα = ὅντινα) *ye suppose, I am not*. This punctuation does violence to the pronoun, while the sense has no advantage over the other. See W. § 25. 1. — ἔρχεται μετ' ἐμὲ, κ. τ. λ., *comes after me*, etc. In this way he would express strongly his official and personal inferiority to Christ. It was an office of the lowest servants, not only among the Jews, but the Greeks and Romans, to bind and unbind the sandals of their masters. See Jahn's Archæol. § 123.

V. 26. ἄνδρες ἀδελφοί, *men*, at the same time *brethren*; not different classes. — ὑμῖν includes both Jews and proselytes. — τῆς σωτηρίας ταύτης, *of this salvation* which they preached (comp. 5, 20); or procured by Jesus, named in v. 23. — ἀπεστάλη, *was sent forth*, i. e. from God, the author of the word.

V. 27. γάρ confirms the implication in σωτηρίας ταύτης in v. 26, viz. that Jesus, whom Paul preached, was the promised Saviour; *for* (γάρ) he had suffered and been put to death, and so had fulfilled what was predicted of the Messiah. De Wette, Winer (§ 57. 6), and others, maintain this view of the connection. Meyer (followed by Alf.) opposes ὑμῖν in v. 26 to οἱ κατοικοῦντες here, i. e. the foreign Jews, being less guilty, had the message of salvation sent to them, which the other Jews had forfeited. This explanation arrays the passage against other passages, e. g. 2, 38; 3, 17. 26. It was not true that those who crucified the Saviour excluded themselves from the offers of the gospel. — τοῦτον .... ἐπλήρωσαν, *this one*, viz. Jesus *not having known*, failed to recognize, *and the voices of the prophets* (not having known) *they fulfilled* them, viz. the prophecies *by condemning* him to death. This is the simplest translation and the one most approved (Calv. Grot. Kuin. Hmph.). The principal English versions agree in this sense. ἀγνοήσαντες is milder than ἠρνήσασθε in 3, 13; see note there. In this case we must supply pronouns after κρίναντες and ἐπλήρωσαν, which refer to different antecedents. The construction may be harsh, but occasions no obscurity. Meyer renders: *Since they knew not this one .... they also fulfilled the voices*, etc. The Jews are usually represented as rejecting Christ because they failed to discern the import of the predictions concerning him. The thought here would be inverted somewhat: the rejection appears as the reason why they misunderstand and fulfil the prophets. De Wette construes ἀγνοήσαντες as a verb: *they knew him not, and the voices .... fulfilled.* This analysis secures more uniformity in the structure of the sentence; but such a use of the participle is infrequent. Scholefield translates: *Being ignorant of this* word, and the *voices of the prophets .... fulfilled* it *by condemning* him. He assigns in this way a nearer antecedent to τοῦτον, but must set aside the more obvious subject suggested to the mind by the context. It is not clear in what sense he would have us regard the rejection of Christ as fulfilling the word or gospel. — τὰς κατὰ, κ. τ. λ., *which are read every Sabbath*, and hence their ignorance was the more inexcusable.

V. 28. μηδεμίαν .... εὑρόντες, *although they found no cause of death*, none that justified it, see 28, 18. They charged him with blasphemy and sedition, but could not establish the accusation. See 3, 13; Matt. 27, 24; Luke 23, 22.

V. 29. ἔθηκαν has the same subject as the other verbs, see v. 27. The burial, however, was the particular act of Joseph of Arimathea and Nicodemus; see John 19, 38 sq. What the apostle would assert is that Christ had fulfilled the prophecy, which announced that he should be put to death, and rise again. It was not important that he should discriminate as to the character of the agents in the transaction. Some translate, *those who took him down placed him*, etc.. The participle in that relation to to the verb would require the article.

V. 31. τοῖς συναναβᾶσιν αὐτῷ, *those who came up with him*, i. e. the Galilean disciples who attended him on his last journey to Jerusalem. They knew, therefore, what they testified; their means of knowledge had been ample. This idea occurs in the Acts often. — νῦν, *now.* The resurrection rested not on tradition, but on the testimony of living men. The English version, after the received text, omits this particle. — πρὸς τὸν λαόν, *unto the people*, i. e. the Jews, see v 24; 10, 42, etc.

V. 32. καὶ ἡμεῖς, *and so we*, i. e. in view of these various proofs that Jesus is the Messiah; see vv. 23. 25. 27. 31. — εὐαγγελιζόμεθα has a double accusative only here. W. § 32. 4. — ἐπαγγελίαν stands in the first clause with the usual effect of that attraction; see on 3, 10.

V. 33. ἐκπεπλήρωκε, *has completely fulfilled*, stronger than ἐπλήρωσαν in v. 27; because the resurrection, considered as involving the ascension and exaltation, was essentially the finishing act in the fulfilment of the promise relating to the Messiah. — ἀναστήσας Ἰησοῦν means, as Luther, Schott, Stier, De Wette, Meyer, Hengstenberg, Tholuck and others, decide, *having raised up Jesus* from the grave; not *having brought him into existence* (Calv. Bng. Kuin. Olsh.). The mind attaches that sense to the word most readily after v. 30. It was unnecessary to insert ἐκ νεκρῶν, because the context suggests the specific meaning: comp. 2, 24. 32. ἀναστήσας, in the sense of *having raised up* merely, expresses too little for the prophecy which that event is said to have fulfilled. The original passage refers, not to the incarnation of the Messiah, but to his inauguration or public acknowledgment on the part of God as the rightful Sovereign of men. To no moment in the history of Christ would such a prediction apply with such significance as to that of his triumphant resurrection from the dead. The progression of the argument in the next verse demands this interpretation. To the assertion here that God had raised Jesus to life again, the apostle adds there that this life was one which death would invade no more. — ὡς καί, *as also*, i. e. what took place was foretold. — πρώτῳ ψαλμῷ. The second Psalm in our English version is named here the first, because in some manuscripts the Hebrews reckoned the first Psalm merely as prefatory. δευτέρῳ has much less support. — υἱός . . . . σύ (Ps. 2, 7) affirms the Sonship of the Messiah, which included his divine nature; see Rom. 1, 4. Hence γεγέννηκά σε cannot refer to the *origin* of this relationship, but must receive a figurative interpretation; either, *I have begotten thee*, brought thee into a state of glory and power such as Christ assumed after his resurrection as Mediator at the right hand of God; or, according to a familiar Hebrew usage, *I have declared, exhibited thee as begotten*, i. e. as my Son, viz. by the resurrection from the dead. The thought here is entirely parallel to that in Rom. 1, 4. As to the declarative sense of Hebrew verbs, see the note on 10, 15. — σήμερον, *to-day*, designates the precise point of time on which the prophet's eye was then fixed, viz. that of Christ's assumption of his mediatorial power, or that of his open proclamation as Messiah on the part of God when he raised him from the dead.

V. 34. ὅτι . . . . εἰς διαφθοράν, *Further* (as proof) *that he raised him up from the dead as one who would die no more.* δέ is progressive. ἀνέστησεν repeats the idea of the foregoing ἀναστήσας, for the purpose of describing this resurrection more fully: it would be followed by no return to death. ἐκ νεκρῶν does not distinguish the two words as to sense, but draws attention more strongly to the contrast between the death which he had suffered, and his exemption from death in future. μηκέτι . . . . εἰς διαφθοράν, as applied to Christ, whose body underwent no change while it remained in the grave, must be equivalent to οὐκέτι ἀποθνήσκει in Rom. 6, 9. The dissolution or corruption of the body is the ordinary consequent of death; and hence in common speech, *to return to corruption* and *to die*, or the opposite, *not to return to corruption* and *not to die*, are interchangeable expressions. Bengel saw this import of the phrase. See W. § 66. 10. The perpetuity of Christ's existence is an important truth in the Christian system. In Rom. 5, 10, Paul urges it as a ground of certainty, that, if men believe on Christ, they will be finally saved, and in Rom. 6, 9, as a pledge that, inasmuch as he "dies no more, we shall live with him;" see also John 14, 19; Heb. 7, 25, etc. This incidental agreement of the address with Paul's circle of doctrine speaks for its genuineness. — ὅτι is the sign of quotation. — δώσω . . . .

πιστά expresses the substantial sense of Is. 55, 3: *I will give to you*, perform unto you, *the holy*, inviolable *promises of David* (i. e. made to him), *the sure*. The language is very nearly that of the Seventy. One of these promises was that David should have a successor whose reign would be perpetual, the throne of whose kingdom God would establish for ever and ever; see 2 Sam. 7, 13 sq. It was essential to the accomplishment of that promise that the Messiah should be exempt from death, and hence, as Jesus had been proved to be the Messiah by his resurrection, that promise made it certain that he would live and reign henceforth, without being subject to any interruption of his existence or power.

V. 35. διὸ καί, *Therefore also*, i. e. because he was not mortal, in further confirmation of that fact. — ἐν ἑτέρῳ, sc. ψαλμῷ, viz. 16, 10. See on 2, 25 sq. The inspired declaration that the Messiah should not experience the power of death had not only been verified in his resurrection, but guarantied that he would not experience that power at any future period. — λέγει, sc. θεός, viz. through David; see v. 34; 1, 16, etc.

V. 36. γάρ vindicates the reference of the passage to Christ, since it could not apply to David. — μέν is antithetic to δέ in v. 37. — ἰδίᾳ γενεᾷ .... βουλῇ admits of a twofold translation. γενεᾷ may depend on ὑπηρετήσας: *having served his own generation* (been useful to it), *according to the purpose of God* (dative of norm or rule). Our English translators, Calvin, Doddridge, Robinson, and others, adopt this construction. Olshausen, Kuinoel, De Wette, Meyer, and others, refer βουλῇ to the participle: *having in his own generation* (dative of time), or *for it* (dat. comm.), *served the purpose, plan of God*, i. e. as an instrument for the execution of his designs; comp. v. 22. γενεᾷ, if connected with the participle, secures to it a personal object, and in that way forms a much easier expression than βουλῇ with the participle. The main idea of the clause is that David, like other men, had but one generation of contemporaries; that he accomplished for that his allotted work, and then yielded to the universal law which consigns the race to death. Some join τῇ βουλῇ with ἐκοιμήθη, which renders the remark much less significant. — καὶ προσετέθη, κ. τ. λ., *and he was added unto his fathers*. This expression recognizes the existence of the soul in a future state (Bng. Olsh. Doddr.). Gesenius says that it is distinguished expressly both from death and burial in Gen. 25, 8; 35, 29; 2 Kings 22, 20; see Lex. s. אָסַף. — εἶδε διαφθοράν, *saw corruption* as to his mortal part; comp. 2, 31.

V. 38. οὖν, illative. Jesus has been shown to be the Messiah, and he is, *therefore*, the author of pardon and salvation to those who believe on him. — διὰ τούτου belongs to ἄφεσις, rather than the verb: *through this one the forgiveness of sins* (having been procured) *is announced unto you;* comp. 10, 36; Luke 24, 47. The next verse reaffirms and amplifies the proposition.

V. 39. The sentence here depends still on ὅτι. A comma is the proper point between this verse and the last. The apostle declares now, first, that the forgiveness which Christ has procured is not partial, but extends to all the sins of the transgressor; secondly, that all men need it, since no other way of pardon remains for those who are condemned by the law; and, thirdly, since faith in Christ is the only condition annexed to it, this salvation is free to all. — καὶ ἀπὸ πάντων, κ. τ. λ., *and that from all things*, i. e. sins, *from which* (= ἀφ' ὧν by attraction) *ye were not able by the law of Moses to be justified*, etc. We cannot suppose this to mean, according to a possible sense of the words, that the gospel merely completes a justification which the law nas commenced or accomplished in part; for such an admission would be at variance with the doctrine of the New Testament in in regard to the utter inefficacy of all legal obedience to cancel the guilt of transgression, and the necessity of an exclusive reliance on the work of Christ for our justification. We must adopt a different view of the meaning. As Olshausen suggests, we may regard ὧν (= ἀφ' ὧν) after ἀπὸ πάντων, not as a supplementary clause, but as explanatory of the other, or coextensive with it, viz. *from all sins from which* (i. e. *from all* which sins) *ye were unable*, etc. In other words, the first clause affirms the sufficiency of the gospel to justify from all sins, while the second clause affirms the insufficiency of the law to the same extent, i. e. to justify from any sins; comp. Rom. 8, 3 sq. To represent this meaning to the ear, we should read ἀπὸ πάντων with an emphasis, and ὧν . . . . δικαιωθῆναι as parenthetic. Neander (Pflanzung. I. p. 195) declares himself strongly for this sense of the words. Alford's comment (similar to Meyer's) represents a different view: "Christ shall do for you all that the law could not do; leaving it for inference or for further teaching that this was absolutely *all;* that the law could do *nothing*." According to some, the apostle concedes a certain value to the rites of Judaism: they were the appointed means of obtaining the pardon of offences, which concerned the ritual merely and social or public relations. See Lange's Geschichte der Kirche, II. p. 171. This explanation rests on a false view of the nature of the Hebrew rites. As ἐν τούτῳ stands opposed to ἐν νόμῳ, it belongs to δικαιοῦται, not to πιστεύων.

V. 40. βλέπετε οὖν, *beware, therefore,* since ye are thus guilty and exposed. — μὴ ἐπέλθῃ, κ. τ. λ., *lest that spoken*, etc., lest the declaration be fulfilled, verified in your case. The mode of citing the prophecy shows that the apostle did not regard it as spoken in view of that occasion. — ἐν τοῖς προφήταις, *in the prophets,* i. e. the part of the Old Testament which the Jews so named; comp. v. 15; 7, 42; John 6, 45. See W. § 27. 2. The passage intended is Hab. 1, 5.

V. 41. The citation follows very nearly the Septuagint, and agrees essentially with the Hebrew. In the original passage the prophet refers to a threatened invasion of the Jewish nation by the Chaldeans, and he calls upon his countrymen to behold the judgment to which their sins had exposed them, and to be astonished, to tremble on account of it. Of this language the apostle avails himself, in order to warn the Jews whom he addressed of the punishment which awaited them if they rejected the message which they had now heard. Calvin: "Paulus fideliter accommodat in usum suum prophetæ verba, quia sicuti semel minatus fuerat Deus per prophetam suum Habacuc, ita etiam semper fuit sui similis." — οἱ καταφρονηταί, *ye despisers,* occurs in the Septuagint, but not in the Hebrew. The apostle could retain it, in perfect consonance with the original, because it is the incredulity of the wicked, their contempt of God's threatenings, which occasions their ruin. What suggested the word to the Seventy is uncertain. It is thought that they may have read בּוֹגְדִים, *deceitful,* proudly impious, instead of בַּגּוֹיִם, *among the heathen.* — καὶ θαυμάσατε, *and wonder,* be astonished, i. e. at the fearful, certain destruction which God prepares for his enemies. The spectacle to which the prophet directs attention here is that of the Chaldeans, mustering their hosts to march against the guilty Jews. — καὶ ἀφανίσθητε, *and perish,* unable to escape the punishment which their sins have provoked. This word elicits an idea which the Hebrew text involves, though it is not expressed there. Paul has retained it from the Septuagint. — ἔργον, κ. τ. λ., *a work* of judgment *I work,* execute. The future act is represented as present, because it was near. — The second ἔργον Paul inserts for the sake of emphasis. The copies which omit it were corrected probably after the Septuagint. — ὃ οὐ μὴ, κ. τ. λ., *which ye will not believe, though any one should fully declare it to you,* i. e. although apprised ever so distinctly of their danger, they would not heed it; they are infatuated, they cling to their delusive hopes of safety. The New Testament, like most of the later Greek, employs often the subjunctive aorist in the sense of the indicative future. W. § 56. 3; Lob. Phryn. p. 723 sq. ὅ, at the head of the clause, is a better reading than ᾧ. That the dative, however, is not a false construction, see Rom. 10, 16.

VERSES 42–49. *They preach a second time at Antioch.*

V. 42. The best editions insert αὐτῶν in place of ἐκ τῆς συναγωγῆς τῶν Ἰουδαίων in the common text, and omit τὰ ἔθνη after παρεκάλουν. — αὐτῶν must refer to Paul and Barnabas. — εἰς τὸ μεταξὺ σάββατον corresponds evidently to τῷ ἐχομένῳ σαββάτῳ in v. 44, and means *upon* (lit. *unto*, as the limit) *the next Sabbath* (Neand. Mey. De Wet.); not *during the intermediate week*, as explained by some of the older critics. μεταξύ has this sense in the N. T. here only, but belongs to the later Greek. That the apostles were not inactive during the interval, but labored in private circles, may be taken for granted.

V. 43. λυθείσης τῆς συναγωγῆς seems, at first view, superfluous after ἐξιόντων αὐτῶν. The procedure, says Neander, may have been this. As Paul and Barnabas were going out before the general dispersion of the assembly, the rulers of the synagogue may have requested that they would repeat their discourse on the next Sabbath. The people having then withdrawn, many of the Jews and proselytes followed the speakers, for the purpose of declaring their assent to what they had heard, or of seeking further instruction. — σεβομένων, sc. θεόν, not *devout* (E. V.) above others, but simply *worshippers* of Jehovah (see 16, 14) and not of idols as formerly. — τῇ χάριτι τοῦ θεοῦ, *the grace of God*, i. e. the gospel, which is the fruit of his undeserved favor.

V. 44. σχεδὸν, κ. τ. λ., *almost the entire city assembled;* where, is not stated. Paul and Barnabas on that Sabbath may have spoken to different audiences. If they both repaired to the same synagogue, the crowd must have filled not only the synagogue itself, but every avenue to it; comp. Mark 2, 2 sq.; Luke 8, 19. The hearers on this occasion were Gentiles, as well as Jews.

V. 45. ζήλου, *with indignation*, as in v. 17. — ἀντιλέγοντες is neither superfluous nor Hebraistic, but, like the participle united with its finite verb in the classics, emphasizes ἀντέλεγον (Mey.): *not only contradicting, but blaspheming.* The second participle defines the extent or criminality of the act stated by the first. W. § 45. 8.

V. 46. ὑμῖν ἦν ἀναγκαῖον, *unto you it was necessary*, because the plan of God required it; comp. on 3, 26. — πρῶτον, *first in time*, as in 3, 26. — καὶ οὐκ . . . . ζωῆς, *and ye judge yourselves not worthy of the eternal life*, viz. which we preach; see on 5, 20. This mode of speaking is not common; it rests on the just view that a man's actions may be taken as his own self-pronounced verdict as to his character and deserts. — εἰς τὰ ἔθνη, *unto the heathen* in that place. In like manner, the Jews whom they left to their doom were those at Antioch. They did not turn from the Jewish nation as such, to labor in future for the exclusive benefit of the Gentiles; see 18, 5 sq.; 19, 8 sq.

V. 47. οὕτω, *so* as they had done. — τέθεικα, κ. τ. λ. See Is 49, 6. The prophet announces there that the Messiah whom God promised to send would be the Saviour of the Gentiles as well as the Jews; that all nations would be called to share in the blessings of his kingdom. The passage is quoted to show that in turning now to the heathen they were merely carrying out the plan of God as revealed in the Old Testament (see also Is. 11, 1. 10; Rom. 9, 25 sq.); the announcement of his purpose in regard to the unrestricted design of the gospel required them as his messengers to publish it to the Gentiles.

V. 48. ἐδόξαζον . . . . κυρίου, *they glorified*, extolled, *the word of the Lord;* they expressed their joy and gratitude for the mercy which had embraced them in the plan of salvation, and had given them this opportunity to secure its benefits. We see from the next clause that they received the message as well as rejoiced to hear it. — καὶ ἐπίστευσαν . . . . αἰώνιον, *and as many as were appointed unto eternal life believed.* This is the only translation which the philology of the passage allows. So Calvin, Kuinoel, Olshausen, Usteri,[1] De Wette, Winer, Meyer, and others. In this position the demonstrative part of ὅσοι (*those who*) must be the subject of the first verb, and the relative part the subject of the second. Hence it is impossible to render *those who believed were appointed.* Some translate τεταγμένοι, *disposed*, inclined; but this term as passive, though it may signify *disposed* externally, as, e. g. drawn up in military order, was not used to denote an act of the mind. In 20, 13 the form is middle with an accusative virtually (see note there), and in 1 Cor. 16, 15 the form is active with an accusative; those cases, therefore, so unlike this are not to be cited here. Mr. Humphry, after Whitby, and others, defends still that signification, and appeals for proof of it to 2 Macc. 6, 21. The

[1] Entwickelung des Paulinischen Lehrbegriffes, p. 271 (1851).

Greek there is οἱ δὲ πρὸς τῷ παρανόμῳ σπλαγχνισμῷ τεταγμένοι, and does not mean "those who were set or bent on mercy" (Hmph.), but "those appointed for the distribution of unlawful flesh." See Wahl's Clav. Libr. Vet. Apocrph., and Biel's Lex., in LXX, s. σπλαγχνισμός. The use of τεταγμένοι in that passage not only fails to support the alleged meaning but confirms the other. εἰς ζωὴν αἰώνιον is not to be torn from its connection and joined to ἐπίστευσαν. In what sense men are appointed by God (comp. Rom. 13, 1) unto eternal life is not taught very distinctly here, but must be gathered from a comparison with other passages. For example, see Rom. 8, 28, sq.; 9, 11; Eph. 1, 4. 11; 2 Thess. 2, 13; 2 Tim. 1, 9; 1 Pet. 1, 2. The explanations of this text which have been opposed to the foregoing, are forced and unsatisfactory. Dr. Wordsworth (to give a favorable specimen) expounds it thus: Those who had set or marshalled themselves to go forward in the way to eternal life, professed their faith boldly in the face of every danger.

V. 49. διεφέρετο . . . . χώρας, *And the word of the Lord was conveyed through all the region,* i. e. in the vicinity of Antioch. This rapid extension of the gospel we must attribute in some measure to the zeal of the recent converts. Paul and Barnabas also may have visited, personally, some of the nearest places; for Luke may have passed over an interval between this verse and the next, during which the missionaries could have made such excursions.

VERSES 50–52. *They are persecuted, and depart to Iconium.*

V. 50. τὰς σεβομένας γυναῖκας. They were Gentile women who had embraced Judaism (see 17, 4), and could be easily excited against a sect represented as hostile to their faith. At Damascus, as Josephus states (Bell. Jud. 2. 20. 20), a majority of the married women were proselytes. εὐσχήμονας refers to their rank (17, 12; Mark 15, 43), as the wives of the *first men of the city.* It was the object of the crafty Jews to gain the men through the influence of the women, and thus effect the expulsion of the apostles from the city. Paul alludes to this persecution in 2 Tim. 3, 11.

V. 51. ἐπ' αὐτούς = εἰς μαρτύριον ἐπ' αὐτούς in Luke 9, 5. Shaking off the dust of the feet imported disapprobation and rejection. The act derived its significancy from the idea that those renounced in this way were so unworthy that the very dust of their land was defiling. In taking this course Paul followed the direction of Christ, given in Matt. 10, 14.—*Iconium,* to which they came next, was about forty-five miles south-east from Antioch. It was the principal city of Lyconia, situated at the foot of the Taurus. Its present name is Konieh. Leake, who approached Iconium from the mountains which separate Antioch from Philomelium, says (Travels in Asia Minor, p. 45): " On the descent from a ridge branching eastward from these mountains, we came in sight of the vast plain around Konieh, and of the lake which occupies the middle of it; and we saw the city, with its mosques and ancient walls, still at the distance of twelve or fourteen miles from us." " Konieh," says another traveller, " extends to the east and south over the plain far beyond the walls, which are about two miles in circumference. Mountains covered with snow rise on every side, excepting towards the east, where a plain as flat as the desert of Arabia extends far beyond the reach of the eye."

V. 52. οἱ μαθηταί, *the disciples*, i. e. at Antioch, where the persecution still continued; see 14, 22.—ἐπληροῦντο, κ. τ. λ., *were filled with joy and the Holy Spirit;* the relation is that of effect and author (see Gal. 5, 20). The idea suggested is, that though they were called to suffer as adherents of the new faith, they had sources of consolation opened to them which more than counterbalanced their trials.

CHAPTER XIV.

VERSES 1–7. *They preach at Iconium, but are persecuted and flee to Lystra.*

V. 1. κατὰ τὸ αὐτό, *together*, like ἐπὶ τὸ αὐτό in 3, 1; not in *the same manner*, as they were wont. — καὶ λαλῆσαι οὕτως, κ. τ. λ., *and they spake so*, viz. with this effect, *that* (ὥστε) *a great multitude*, etc. (Mey. De Wet.); not *with such power that.* οὕτως anticipates the next clause, and makes it more prominent. B. § 140. 4.—Ἑλλήνων. As the *Greeks* here were present in the synagogue, they appear to have been proselytes (comp. 13, 43), and hence were a different class from those in 13, 20.

V. 2. οἱ δὲ ἀπειθήσαντες, *But those who disbelieved*, viz. when the others believed. The present participle (ἀπειθοῦντες as in some editions) is less correct than the aorist. — ἐκάκωσαν, *rendered evil*, hostile. This sense is found in Josephus, but not elsewhere (Mey.). How the Jews produced this effect on the minds of the heathen we are not told. They sometimes alleged for that purpose that the Christians were disloyal, that they had a king of their own, and would prove dangerous to the Roman supremacy; see 18, 5-9.

V. 3. οὖν, *therefore*, i. e. because they had so much success (see v. 1), notwithstanding the opposition excited against them. Meyer regards the third and fourth verses as an inference from the first and second. "In consequence of that approbation (v. 1) and this hostility (v. 2) they preached boldly indeed for a time, but a dissension also arose among the people."—ἱκανὸν χρόνον. The entire journey was evidently a rapid one and a stay here of a few months would be comparatively *a long time*. This is our only notice respecting the time spent at the places visited on this tour.—παῤῥησιαζόμενοι ἐπὶ τῷ κυρίῳ, *speaking boldly upon the Lord*, i. e. in dependence upon him. It was their reliance on Christ that inspired them with so much courage.—The best authorities omit καί between τῷ μαρτυροῦντι and διδόντι: *who testifies by granting that*, etc.; comp. 4, 30.

V. 4. τὸ πλῆθος τῆς πόλεως, *the multitude of the city*, i. e. the Gentile population. Some of them may have favored the Christian party, without having attached themselves to it; comp. 19, 31.—ἦσαν σὺν τοῖς Ἰουδαίοις, *were with the Jews*, i. e. in sympathy, espoused their side; see 5, 17.

V. 5. ὁρμή, *impulse*, inclination; as in James 3, 4 (Mey. Alf.); not *onset*, (E. V.) because συνιδόντες would then be superfluous, and because the object of the flight was to escape an attack. *Plot*, purpose, is too strong a sense of the word.—σὺν τοῖς ἄρχουσιν αὐτῶν, *with their rulers*, i. e. those of both nations, viz. the heathen magistrates and the officers of the synagogue. Some restrict αὐτῶν to the Gentiles, others to the Jews. Here, at this distance from Jerusalem, members of the Sanhedrim could not well be meant (Rob.).

V. 6. συνιδόντες, *having become aware*, viz. of this feeling. Meyer lays no stress at present on the preposition, as if they discovered the danger as well as others.—λιθοβολῆσαι αὐτούς, *in order to stone them*. "*Once* was I stoned," says Paul, in 2 Cor. 11, 25, which was the instance mentioned in v. 19. Hence, says Paley, "had this meditated assault at Iconium been completed, had the history related that a stone was thrown, as it relates that preparations were made both by Jews and Gentiles to stone Paul and his companions, or even had the account of this transaction stopped, without going on to inform us that Paul and his companions were 'aware of the danger and fled,' a contradiction between the history and the Epistles would have ensued. Truth is necessarily consistent; but it is scarcely possible that independent accounts, not having truth to guide them, should thus advance to the very brink of contradiction without falling into it." — τῆς Λυκαονίας. The district of *Lycaonia* extends from the ridges of Mount Taurus and the borders of Cilicia, on the south, to the Cappadocian hills on the north. "It is a bare and dreary region, unwatered by streams, though in parts liable to occasional inundations. Across some portion of this plain Paul and Barnabas travelled, both before and after their residence in Iconium. After leaving the city the two most prominent objects still in view are the snowy mountains of Mount Argæus, rising high above all the intervening hills in the direction of Armenia, and the singular mass called the 'Kara-Dagh,' or 'Black Mount,' south-eastwards in the direction of Cilicia. This latter mountain is gradually approached, and discovered to be an isolated mass, with reaches of the plain extending round it like channels of the sea." Howson, I. p. 224. — Λύστραν καὶ Δέρβην. *Lystra and Derbe* were not far from the base of the Black Mountain. Their exact situation is not yet certainly known. Lystra is marked on Kiepert's map as nearly south of Iconium, about twenty miles distant; Derbe, as nearly east from Lystra, south-east from Iconium. Kiepert appears to have followed Leake's conjecture as to the site of Lystra, though no traveller speaks of any ruins at that place. Mr. Hamilton agrees with Kiepert in the position of Derbe, because it occurs on the line of a Roman road, and Divle, the modern name, resembles the ancient one. Leake, on the contrary, would place Derbe (not quite so far to the east), at Bin-bir-Kilesseh, a Turkish town, where some remarkable ruins have been found, among the rest those of numerous churches. Others, again, think that these ruins mark the site of Lystra, since they correspond better with the early ecclesiastical reputation of this city, than that of Derbe. — καὶ τὴν περίχωρον designates the country in the vicinity of the places just named. A few critics have proposed to extend the term so as to include even Galatia, and would thus assign an earlier origin to the churches in that country than it is usual to assign to them. "But περίχωρον," says Neander, "cannot denote an entire province, and still less the province of Galatia, on account of its geographical situation. Hence, the supposition that Paul preached the gospel to the Galatians on this first missionary tour is certainly to be rejected." See the note on 16, 6.

V. 7. κἀκεῖ, *and there*, viz. in those cities and the adjacent region.—ἦσαν εὐαγγελιζόμενοι, *were publishing glad tidings*, implies that they pursued their labors here for some time.

VERSES 8–13. *Paul heals a Lame Man at Lystra.*

V. 8. ἐν Λύστροις, *at Lystra;* neuter plural, as in 2 Tim. 3. 11, but feminine singular in v. 6. 21; 16, 1.—ἐκάθητο, *sat* (Mey. De Wet.), because he was lame and had never walked; others *dwelt* (Kuin. Rob.), which is Hebraistic, and rare in the New Testament.—περιπεπατήκει. Some editors write this pluperfect with an augment, others more correctly omit it. W. § 12. 9; K. § 120. R. 2.

V. 9. ἤκουε, *was hearing*, while Paul preached. The Jews at this place were probably few, as no synagogue appears to have existed here. Hence the missionaries repaired to the market, or some other place of public resort (comp. 17, 17), and there entered into conversation with such as they could induce to listen to them. The scene reminds us of the manner in which those who carry the same message of salvation to the heathen at the present day collect around them groups of listeners in Burmah or Hindostan. It was on one of these occasions, as Paul was preaching in some thoroughfare of the city, that the lame man heard him; his friends perhaps had placed him there to solicit alms (see 3, 10; John 9, 8).—ὃς ἀτενίσας, κ. τ. λ., *who looking intently upon him and seeing*, viz. from the expression of his countenance, which Paul scrutinized with such rigor. The manner in which the participles follow each other directs us to this sense. Some think that the apostle may have had, at the moment, a supernatural insight into the state of the man's heart. The language of the text contains no intimation of that nature.—πίστιν τοῦ σωθῆναι, *the faith of being healed.* The infinitive depends on the noun as a genitive construction; comp. Luke 1, 57. See W. § 44. 4. The faith so described may be faith that the Saviour, whom Paul preached, was able to heal him; or, which accords better with the mode of expression, faith such as made it proper that he should receive that benefit (see on 9, 33). The requisite degree of faith would include, of course, a persuasion of Christ's ability to bestow the favor in question. Paul may have been referring in his remarks to the Saviour's miracles of healing, in illustration of his readiness and power to bless those who confide in him.

V. 10. μεγάλῃ τῇ φωνῇ, *with a loud voice.* The article designates the voice as that of Paul (see v. 11; 26, 24), while the adjective refers to the tone with which he spoke. With the idea that his voice was a powerful one, *μεγάλῃ* would have stood between the article and noun, or after the noun with *τῇ* repeated.—*ἀνάστηθι, κ. τ. λ.* Luke makes no mention here of any direct appeal to the name of Christ before the performance of the miracle; see on 3, 6. That omission may be owing to the brevity of the record; or the tenor of Paul's discourse may have been so explicit in regard to the source of his authority, as to render the usual invocation unnecessary.—*ἥλατο*, *leaped*, sprung up, a single act. For this aorist, see W. § 15; K. § 149. R. 2. *ἥλλετο* occurs in some copies, but has no adequate support. The next verb passes to the imperfect, because it expresses a repeated act.

V. 11. *οἱ ὄχλοι, κ. τ. λ.* Their conduct shows how imperfectly they had understood the address of Paul, and the object of the miracle. They saw nothing beyond what was present and palpable; they confounded the instrument of the work with its author. *ὃ ἐποίησεν*, *what he had done;* see on 1, 2.—*Λυκαονιστί*, *in Lycaonic*, i. e. the native dialect of the province. Of the nature of this dialect, nothing is known with certainty. No relic of it remains, or at least has been identified; no description of it has been handed down to us. Those who have examined the question differ in their conclusions. According to one opinion, the Lycaonic was allied to the Assyrian; according to another, it was a corrupt species of Greek.[1] We have no reliable data for forming any opinion. Luke mentions that the Lystrians spoke in their native tongue, that we may know why the multitude proceeded so far in their design before Paul and Barnabas interposed to arrest it. In conferring with the people, they had used, doubtless, the Greek, which formed at that period an extensive medium of intercourse between those of different nations.

V. 12. *Δία, Ἑρμῆν.* They fixed upon these gods because Jupiter had a temple there, and Mercury, who appeared in the pagan mythology as his attendant, excelled in eloquence. So Ovid. Met. 8. 626:

> Jupiter huc specie mortali cumque parente
> Venit Atlantiades positis caducifer alis.

See also Hor. Od. 1. 10. 1–5. Some suggest, as a further reason for such a distribution of the parts, that Barnabas may have been an older man than Paul, and more imposing in his personal ap-

[1] Jablonsky and Gühling, who wrote dissertations on the subject, arrived at the results stated above. See Win. Realw. II. p. 37.

pearance (comp. 2 Cor. 10, 1. 10). — ὁ ἡγούμενος τοῦ λόγου, *he who leads the discourse*, is the chief speaker (comp. 14, 12).

V. 13. ὁ ἱερεύς, *the priest*, i. e. the principal one, or the one most active, at this time. The pagan worship at Lystra must have required several priests. — τοῦ Διὸς, κ. τ. λ., *of Jupiter who was before the city*, i. e. who had a statue and temple there consecrated to him. The temple of the tutelary god stood often outside of the walls. — στέμματα, *garlands*, which were to adorn the victims, and perhaps the priest and the altar (De Wet.). See Jahn's Archæol. § 401. 5. They had the garlands in readiness, but had not yet placed them on the heads of the animals. Some construe ταύρους καὶ στέμματα as = ταύρους ἐστεμμένους, *bullocks adorned with garlands* (De Wet. Rob.). With that idea the writer would have used naturally that expression. — ἐπὶ τοὺς πυλῶνας, *unto the gates* of the city (Neand. Rob. Alf. Mey. in his last ed.), since πόλεως precedes and the term is plural (as consisting of parts or being double); or less probably, of the house where the apostles lodged (Olsh. De Wet.). — ἤθελε θύειν, *would sacrifice*, but were disappointed (De Wet.), or *was about to sacrifice*, since ἐθέλω may denote an act on the point of being done. See Mt. § 498. e; C. § 583.

VERSES 14–18. *The Speech of Paul to the Lystrians.*

V. 14. ἀκούσαντες, *having heard*, i. e. a report of what was taking place, brought to them perhaps by some of the converts. — διαῤῥήξαντες τὰ ἱμάτια αὐτῶν, *having rent their garments*, i. e. according to the Jewish custom, from the neck in front down towards the girdle. See Jahn's Archæol. § 211. The Jews and other nations performed this act not only as an expression of sorrow, but of abhorrence on hearing or seeing any thing which they regarded as impious. ἱμάτια may refer to the plural subject of the verb, but more probably to their outer and inner garments; comp. Matt. 26, 65. — ἐξεπήδησαν εἰς τὸν ὄχλον, *sprang forth unto the crowd*, i. e. from the city of which we think most readily after πόλεως; or from the house, if the people had assembled in the street. ἐξ in the verb, therefore, does not settle the question in regard to ἐπὶ τοὺς πυλῶνας. The English translation, "ran in among them," rests upon εἰσεπήδησαν, now a rejected reading.

V. 15. καί connects what is said with what was in the mind: Ye are men; *and we are men like constituted with you.* Passing over the first clause, the speaker hastens at once to the main thought. ὁμοιοπαθεῖς means that they had the same nature, passions, infirmities. — εὐαγγελιζόμενοι, κ. τ. λ., *declaring to you as glad tidings*, viz. *that you should turn*, etc. This requisition that they should renounce their idols is called *glad tidings*, because it was founded on the fact that God had provided a way in the gospel in which he could accept their repentance. ὑμᾶς answers here to the dative, as in 8, 25. — ἀπὸ τούτων τῶν ματαίων, *from these vanities*, nonentities, such as Jupiter, Mercury, and the like. τούτων points back to those names. Paul and Barnabas had heard in what light the populace looked upon them. ματαίων does not require θεῶν. It is used like הֲבָלִים, אֱלִילִים, which the Hebrews applied to the gods of the heathen as having no real existence; comp. 1 Cor. 8, 4. Kuinoel renders ματαίων, *vain practices*, idolatry; which destroys the evident opposition between the term and τὸν θεὸν τὸν ζῶντα. — ὃς ἐποίησε, κ. τ. λ., *who made*, etc. This relative clause unfolds the idea of ζῶντα, *living*.

V. 16. εἴασε, *left them*, withdrew the restraints of his grace and providence; comp. on 7, 42 and 17, 30. In Rom. 1, 23, the apostle brings to view other connections of this fact. The reason why God abandoned the heathen was that they first abandoned him. — πορεύεσθαι ταῖς ὁδοῖς αὐτῶν, *to walk* (see on 9, 31) *in their own ways;* dative of rule or manner. ὁδοῖς includes belief and conduct.

V. 17. καίτοιγε . . . . ἀφῆκεν, *although indeed he left himself not without witness*. The desertion on the part of God was not such as to destroy the evidence of their dependence on him, and their consequent obligation to know and acknowledge him. The apostle's object does not lead him to press them with the full consequences of this truth. It lies at the foundation of his argument for proving the accountability of the heathen, in Rom. 1, 19 sq. See also 17, 27 sq. — ἀγαθοποιῶν, διδούς, ἐμπιπλῶν, are epexegetical of ἀμάρτυρον, but the second participle specifies a mode of the first, and the third a consequence of the second. — ὑμῖν after οὐρανόθεν is the correct reading (Grsb. Lchm. Mey.), instead of the received ἡμῖν. — τροφῆς, *with food*, including the idea of the enjoyment afforded by such fruits of the divine bounty. With that accessory idea, τροφῆς is not incongruous with καρδίας, and καρδίας ὑμῶν is not a circumlocution for ὑμᾶς (Kuin.). See W. § 22. 7. The common text has ἡμῶν, which appears in the English version.

V. 18. τοῦ μὴ θύειν αὐτοῖς states the result of κατέπαυσαν, not the object: *they hardly restrained them that they did not sacrifice to them.* See the note on 10, 47. — It is interesting to compare this speech at Lystra with the train of thought which Paul has developed in Rom. 1, 19 sq. It will be seen that the germ of the argument there may be traced distinctly here. The similarity is precisely such as we should expect on the supposition that he who wrote the Epistle delivered the speech. The diversity in the different prominence given to particular ideas is that which arises from applying the same system of truth to different occasions.

VERSES 19–28. *They proceed to Derbe; and then retrace their Way to Antioch in Syria.*

V. 19. The Jews will be found, with two exceptions, to stir up every persecution which Paul suffers; see on 19, 23. — τοὺς ὄχλους, *the crowds.* They were mostly heathen (see on v. 9); but that some Jews resided at Lystra is evident from 16, 1. — λιθάσαντες τὸν Παῦλον, *having stoned Paul.* Barnabas escapes, because his associate here and in the other cities was the prominent man. The nature of the outrage indicates that the Jews not only originated this attack, but controlled the mode of it. Stoning was a Jewish punishment. In the present instance, it will be observed, they had no scruple about shedding the blood of their victim in the city. It was otherwise at Jerusalem; see on 7, 58. An incidental variation like this attests the truth of the narrative. — νομίσαντες, κ. τ. λ., *supposing that he was dead,* intimates a mere belief as opposed to the reality. A slight accent on the first word brings this out as the necessary meaning.

V. 20. κυκλωσάντων δὲ αὐτὸν τῶν μαθητῶν, *The disciples having surrounded him.* Here we learn incidentally that their labors had not been ineffectual. Kuinoel decides too much when he says that the disciples collected around Paul in order to bury him; it may have been to lament over him, or to ascertain whether he was really dead. In that sorrowing circle stood probably the youthful Timothy, the apostle's destined associate in so many future labors and perils; see 16, 1; 2 Tim. 3, 11. — ἀναστάς, κ. τ. λ. After the expression in v. 19, we can hardly regard this as an instance of actual restoration to life. If we recognize any thing as miraculous here, it would be more justly the apostle's sudden recovery after such an outrage, enabling him to return at once to the city and on the next day to resume his journey. Paul alludes to this stoning in 2 Cor. 11, 25. The wounds inflicted on him at this time may have left some of those scars on his body to which he alludes in Gal. 6, 17 as proof that he was Christ's servant. — εἰς Δέρβην, *unto Derbe.* See on v. 6. A few hours would be sufficient for the journey hither. We have now reached the eastern limit of the present expedition.

V. 21. μαθητεύσαντες ἱκανούς, *having made many disciples* (Matt. 28, 19) as the result of the preaching mentioned in the other clause. One of the converts was probably Gaius, who is called a Derbean in 20, 4. Their labors in this city appear to have been unattended by any open opposition. Hence, in 2 Tim. 3, 11, Paul omits Derbe from the list of places associated in the mind of Timothy with the "persecutions, afflictions," which the apostle had been called to endure. Paley refers to that omission as a striking instance of conformity between the Epistle and the Acts. "In the apostolic history Lystra and Derbe are commonly mentioned together; in 2 Tim. 3, 11, Antioch, Inconium, Lystra, are mentioned, and not Derbe. And the distinction will appear on this occasion to be accurate; for Paul in that passage is enumerating his persecutions, and although he underwent grievous persecutions in each of the three cities through which he passed to Derbe, at Derbe itself he met with none. The Epistle, therefore, in the names of the cities, in the order in which they are enumerated, and in the place at which the enumeration stops, corresponds exactly with the history. Nor is there any just reason for thinking the agreement to be artificial; for had the writer of the Epistle sought a coincidence with the history upon this head, and searched the Acts of the Apostles for the purpose, I conceive he would have sent us at once to Philippi and Thessalonica, where Paul suffered persecution, and where, from what is stated, it may easily be gathered that Timothy accompanied him, rather than have appealed to persecutions as known to Timothy, in the account of which persecutions Timothy's presence is not mentioned; it not being till after one entire chapter, and in the history of a journey three or four years subsequent to this (16, 1), that Timothy's name occurs in the Acts of the Apostles for the first time." — ὑπέστρεψαν, *turned back*. Advancing still eastward from this point, they would soon have reached the well-known 'Cilician Gates,' through which they could have descended easily to Cilicia, and then have embarked from Tarsus for Antioch. They had the choice, therefore, of a nearer way to Syria; but their solicitude for the welfare of the newly founded churches constrains them to turn back, and revisit the places where they had preached.

V. 22. ἐπιστηρίζοντες, κ. τ. λ., *confirming the souls of the disciples*, not by any outward rite, but by instruction and encouragement, as we see in the next clause; comp. 15, 32. 41; 18, 23. — ἐμμένειν τῇ πίστει, *to adhere to the faith* (see 6, 7; 13, 8), i. e. of Christ or the gospel; comp. 3, 16; 20, 21, etc. — ὅτι depends on παρακαλοῦντες, which, at this point of the sentence, passes to the idea of affirming, teaching. — δεῖ may mean *it is necessary*, because such was the appointment of God (9, 16; 1 Cor. 15, 25); or because in the nature of things it was inevitable (comp. 2 Tim. 3, 12). The first is the more pertinent view, since it suggests a more persuasive motive to submission and fidelity in the endurance of trials. — ἡμᾶς, *we* who are Christians; comp. 1 Thess. 4, 17. — τὴν βασιλείαν τοῦ θεοῦ, *the kingdom of God*, i. e. the state of happiness which awaits the redeemed in heaven. The expression can have no other meaning here, for those addressed were already members of Christ's visible kingdom, and the perseverance to which the apostles would incite them has reference to a kingdom which they are yet to enter.

V. 23. χειροτονήσαντες, κ. τ. λ., *Now having appointed for them elders in every church.* χειροτονεῖν signifies properly to elect or vote by extending the hand, but also, in a more general sense, to choose, appoint, without reference to that formality. That formality could not have been observed in this instance, as but two individuals performed the act in question. When the verb retains the idea of stretching forth the hand, the act is predicated always of the subject of the verb, not of those for whom the act may be performed. Hence the interpretation *having appointed for them by their outstretched hands*, i. e. by taking their opinion or vote in that manner, is unwarranted; for it transfers the hands to the wrong persons. Whether Paul and Barnabas appointed the presbyters in this case by their own act solely, or ratified a previous election of the churches made at their suggestion, is disputed. If it be clear from other sources that the primitive churches elected their officers by general suffrage, the verb here may be understood to denote a concurrent appointment, in accordance with that practice; but the burden of proof lies on those who contend for such a modification of the meaning. Neander's conclusion on this subject should be stated here. "As regards the election to church offices, we are in want of sufficient information to enable us to decide how it was managed in the early apostolic times. Indeed, it is quite possible that the method of procedure differed under different circumstances. As in the institution of deacons the apostles left the choice to the communities themselves, and as the same was the case in the choice of deputies to attend the apostles in the name of the communities (2 Cor. 8, 19), we might argue that a similar course would be pursued in filling other offices of the church. Yet it may be that in many cases the apostles themselves, where they could not as yet have sufficient confidence in the spirit of the first new communities, conferred the important office of presbyters on such as in their own judgment, under the light of the Divine Spirit, appeared to be the fittest persons. *Their* choice would, moreover, deserve, in the highest degree, the confidence of the communities (comp. 14, 23; Tit. 1, 5); although, when Paul empowers Titus to set presiding officers over the communities who possessed the requisite qualifications, this circumstance decides nothing as to the mode of choice, nor is a choice by the community itself *thereby* necessarily excluded. The regular course appears to have been this: the church offices were intrusted to the first converts in preference to others, provided that in other respects they possessed the requisite qualifications. It may have been the general practice for the presbyters themselves, in case of a vacancy, to propose another to the community in place of the person deceased, and leave it to the whole body either to approve or decline their selection for reasons assigned. (Clem. cap. 44.) When asking for the assent of the community had not yet become a mere formality, this mode of filling church offices had the salutary effect of causing the votes of the majority to be guided by those capable of judging, and of suppressing divisions; while, at the same time, no one was obtruded on the community who would not be welcome to their hearts." Ch. Hist. (Dr. Torrey's Tr.), Vol. I. p. 189. — πρεσβυτέρους κατ' ἐκκλησίαν, *elders in every church.* The term is plural, because each church had its college of elders (see 20, 17; Tit. 1, 5); not because there was a church in each of the cities. The *elders*, or *presbyters*, in the official sense of the term, were those appointed in the first churches to watch over their general discipline and welfare. With reference to that duty, they were called, also, ἐπίσκοποι, i. e. superintendents, or bishops. The first was their Jewish appellation, transferred to them perhaps from the similar class of officers in the synagogues; the second was their foreign appellation, since the Greeks employed it to designate such relations among themselves. In accordance with this distinction, we find the general rule to be this: those who are called elders in speaking of Jewish communities are called bishops in speaking of Gentile communities. Hence the latter term is the prevailing one in Paul's Epistles. That the names with this difference were entirely synonymous, appears from their interchange in such passages as 20, 17. 28, and Tit. 1, 5. 7. It may be argued, also, from the fact that in Phil. 1, 1 and 1 Tim. 3, 1. 8 the deacons are named immediately after the bishops, which excludes the idea of any intermediate order. Other appellations given to these officers were ποιμένες, ἡγούμενοι, προεστῶτες τῶν ἀδελφῶν. The presbyters, or bishops, were not by virtue of their office teachers or preachers at the same time; nor, on the other hand, were the two spheres of labor incompatible with each other. We see from 1 Tim. 5, 17, that some of those who exercised the general oversight preached also the word; comp. also 1 Tim. 3, 2. The foregoing representation exhibits the view of Mosheim, Neander, Gieseler, Röthe, and others eminent in such inquiries. — προσευξάμενοι belongs to the following verb, not to the subordinate clause which precedes. — αὐτούς is defined by εἰς ὃν πεπιστεύκεισαν, and must refer to the believers in general, not to the elders merely.

V. 24. διελθόντες τὴν Πισιδίαν, *having passed through Pisidia.* Antioch was on the northern limit of Pisidia, and hence they traversed that district from north to south. Their journey was a descent from the mountains to the plain.

V. 25. ἐν Πέργῃ. They now preached in Perga, as they appear not to have done on their first visit; see on 13, 13. Luke's silence as to the result may intimate that they were favored with no marked success. — εἰς Ἀττάλειαν. Instead of taking ship at Perga, and sailing down the Cestrus, which they had ascended on their outward journey, they travelled across the plain to Attaleia, a seaport on the Pamphylian Gulf, near the mouth of the Catarrhactes. The distance between the two places was about sixteen miles; see on 13, 13. The founder of Attaleia was Attalus Philadelphus, king of Pergamus. It occupied the site of the modern Satalia, which Admiral Beaufort describes "as beautifully situated round a small harbor, the streets appearing to rise behind each other, like the seats of a theatre, ... with a double wall and a series of square towers on the level summit of the hill." See a view of the present town in Howson.

V. 26. ἀπέπλευσαν εἰς Ἀντιόχειαν, *sailed away unto Antioch;* though they may have disembarked at Seleucia as the town and its port are one in such designations; comp. 20, 6. — ὅθεν ἦσαν, κ. τ. λ., stands *in sensu prægnanti* for *whence, having been committed to the favor of God, they were sent forth;* see 13, 3. W. § 54. 7. — εἰς τὸ ἔργον, *for the work,* (telic) for its performance.

V. 27. ὅσα .... μετ' αὐτῶν, *how great things* (on their journey) *God wrought with them,* i. e. in their behalf (15, 4; Luke 1, 72); not *by them,* which would be δι' αὐτῶν as in 15, 12. The phrase comes from עָשָׂה עִם; comp. Josh. 2, 12; Ps. 119, 65, etc. According-ing to Meyer, μετ' αὐτῶν is = ὢν μετ' αὐτῶν, *allied with them,* which is less simple. — ὅτι ἤνοιξε, κ. τ. λ., *that he opened to the Gentiles a door of faith,* i. e. had given them access to the gospel, participation in its blessings, as well as to the Jews; not that he had opened to the apostles a door of access to the heathen. This metaphor is a favorite one with Paul (1 Cor. 16, 9; 2 Cor. 2,12; Col. 4, 3) and may have become familiar to Luke in his intercourse with him (Alf.).

V. 28. διέτριβον, κ. τ. λ. It is necessary to inquire here how long the apostle was probably absent on the tour followed by this residence at Antioch. We must be content with a somewhat vague answer to this question. The Apostolic Council at Jerusalem was held in A. D. 50 (Introd. § 6. 3); and as Paul departed on his first mission in A. D. 45 (see on 13, 3), we must divide the interval from A. D. 45 to 50 between his journey among the heathen and his subsequent abode at Antioch. The best authorities, as Anger, Wieseler, Meyer, Winer, De Wette, and others, agree in this result. How we are to distribute the intermediate years is more uncertain. It will be found that the apostle travelled more extensively during his second missionary tour than during the first; and as the limitations of time in that part of the history allow us to assign but three years, or three and a half, to that excursion, we may consider two years perhaps as sufficient for this journey. This conclusion would place the return to Antioch near the close of A. D. 47; since the apostle must have set forth somewhat late in the year A. D. 45. Compare the note on 12, 25 with that on 13, 3. Accordingly, the years A. D. 48 and 49 would be the *period not brief* (χρόνον οὐκ ὀλίγον) which Paul and Barnabas spent at Antioch between their return and the Council at Jerusalem. While they resided in that city, for the most part, they would be able, both by their own personal efforts and their supervision of the efforts of others, to extend the gospel in the regions around them.

CHAPTER XV.

VERSES 1–5. *Paul and Barnabas are sent as Delegates to Jerusalem.*

V. 1. ἀπὸ τῆς Ἰουδαίας, *from Judea,* i. e. from Jerusalem in Judea; comp. τινὲς ἐξ ἡμῶν in v. 24. It is barely possible that

Luke may include the other churches in that country. We are not to confound this party of Judaizers with those in Gal. 2, 12, who "came from James" (i. e the church over which he presided), and caused Peter to dissemble his convictions from fear of their censure. The notice in the epistle refers to a different and later event; see on 18, 23. — ἐδίδασκον, *were teaching*. They had not broached the error merely, but were inculcating it. — ὅτι ἐὰν, κ. τ. λ., *that unless ye are circumcised*, etc. This transition to the direct style gives vividness to the narrative. — τῷ ἔθει, *according to the custom*, law (see 6, 14); dative of rule or manner. — οὐ δύνασθε σωθῆναι, *ye cannot be saved*. It was this enforced submission to the rite as necessary to salvation, which made the error so fatally pernicious. (Compare the note on 16, 3). The doctrine in this form was nothing less than an utter subversion of the scheme of Christianity. It denied the sufficiency of faith in Christ as the only condition of pardon and reconciliation. It involved the feeling that circumcision was an act of merit, and that those who submitted to it acquired a virtual right to the divine favor. In a word, it substituted the law of works for the gratuitous justification which the gospel declares to be the only way in which sinners can be saved. See Gal. 5, 1, sq.

V. 2. στάσεως, *dissension* in their views; ζητήσεως, *discussion* on the points which that difference involved. — ὀλίγης belongs to both nouns (De Wet.). The adjective is not repeated because the words are of the same gender. W. § 59. 5. — αὐτούς refers to τινές in v. 1. Paul and Barnabas were the disputants on one side, and the individuals from Judea on the other. It does not appear that the Christians at Antioch took any open part in the controversy. The heresy reappeared among them at a later period, and became then so prevalent as to endanger the safety of the entire church; see Gal. 2, 11, sq. Even Barnabas, at that time, compromised the principle for which he was now so earnest. — ἔταξαν, κ. τ. λ., *they* (i. e. the brethren in v. 1) *appointed that they should go up*, etc. It appears from Gal. 2, 2, that Paul went also in compliance with a divine command. Whether the revelation was first, and the action of the church subsequent, or the reverse, it is impossible to say. It may be that Paul was instructed to propose the mission to Jerusalem; or, if the measure originated with the church, that he was instructed to approve it, and to go as one of the delegates. Either supposition harmonizes the notice in Gal. 2, 2 with this passage. — τινὰς ἄλλους, *certain others* as delegates. One of them may have been Titus, since we read in Gal, 2, 1 that he accompanied the apostle at this time. Yet perhaps συμπαραλαβὼν καὶ Τίτον, in that place, *taking along also Titus*, may indicate, that they travelled together as friends and not as official associates. The fact, too, that, being uncircumcised, he was a party in some sense to this Jewish question, may have disqualified him for such an appointment.

V. 3. οἱ μὲν οὖν προπεμφθέντες, *They having been sent forward*, i. e. attended part of the way by some of the church, as a mark of honor; comp. 20, 38; 21, 5; 3 John v. 6. The word, says Meyer, does not include the *viatica*, or supplies for the journey, unless the context point that out as a part of the service rendered, as in Tit. 3, 13. — διήρχοντο, κ. τ. λ., *passed through Phœnicia and Samaria*. See on 11, 19. As Galilee is not mentioned, they travelled probably along the coast as far south as Ptolemais (21, 7), and then crossed the plain of Esdrælon into Samaria. — τοῖς ἀδελφοῖς, *unto the brethren* in the various towns on their way. We see here the fruits of the seed which had been scattered in those regions (8, 5; 11, 19).

V. 4. ἀπεδέχθησαν, *were cordially received;* comp. 18, 27. It was not certain that, coming on such an errand, they would be greeted with entire favor. It weakens the sense to restrict it to their official recognition as messengers. This was the apostle's third visit to Jerusalem since his conversion, and was made in the year A. D. 50 (Introd. § 6. 3). — τῆς ἐκκλησίας, *the church* in general, while καί adds the prominent parts; see on 1, 14. The existence of presbyters at Jerusalem is first recognized in 11, 30. Luke does not inform us at what time, or in what manner, they were appointed. It was evidently no part of his intention to unfold any particular scheme of ecclesiastical polity. The information which he gives on that subject is incidental and imperfect. — μετ' αὐτῶν, *towards them*, in their behalf; see on 14, 27.

V. 5. ἐξανέστησαν, κ. τ. λ., *But there arose* (in the assembly at Jerusalem) *some of those from the sect of the Pharisees*. It is entirely natural that individuals of this class appear as the party who insist on circumcision. The attachment to forms, which rendered them Pharisees out of the church, rendered them legalists in it. These are the persons evidently, of whom Paul speaks so strongly in Gal. 2, 4. — αὐτούς, *them*, viz. the Gentile believers in the communication just made (v. 4). — Some regard the contents of this verse as a continuation of the report (v. 4), as if the objectors were those at Antioch, and not at Jerusalem; but in that case we should have expected καὶ πῶς or ὅτι, and *how* or *that* as the connective between ἀνήγγειλαν and ἐξανέστησαν.

VERSES 6–12 *Speech of Peter in the Assembly.*

V. 6. συνήχθησαν, κ. τ. λ. This assembly is often called the first Christian Council; but we must use some license to apply the term in that way, since a council consists properly of delegates from various churches, whereas two churches only were represented on this occasion. *The apostles and elders* are mentioned on account of their rank, not as composing the entire assembly. It is evident from v. 23, that the other Christians at Jerusalem were also present, and gave their sanction to the decrees enacted; see also v. 12, compared with v. 22. — In Gal. 2, 2, Paul states that, besides the communication which he made to the believers in a body, he had also a private interview with the chief of the apostles. That interview, we may suppose, preceded the public discussion. The object of it appears to have been, to put the other apostles in full possession of his views, and of all the facts in relation to his ministry among the heathen; so that, fortified by their previous knowledge of the case, he might have their support in the promiscuous assembly, where prejudice or misunderstanding might otherwise have placed him in a false light. — λόγου τούτου, *this matter,* subject of discussion (De Wet.); not *this expression* in v. 5 (Mey.), because the dispute had an earlier origin.

V. 7. ἀφ' ἡμερῶν ἀρχαίων, *since remote days,* a long time ago; comp. ἐν ἀρχῇ in 11, 15. The conversion of Cornelius took place during the time that Paul was at Tarsus (see on 11, 15); and the several years, so eventful in their character, which had elapsed since that period, would appear in the retrospect a long time. — ἐν ἡμῖν .... στόματός μου, *made choice among us* (the apostles) *that by my mouth,* etc., (Mey. De Wet. Win.). The subsequent clause forms the proper object of ἐξελέξατο. Some supply needlessly ἐμέ (Olsh.), and others incorrectly make ἐν ἡμῖν a Hebraistic accusative, *selected me* or *us.* See W. § 32. 3. The meaning is not necessarily that no heathen had heard or embraced the gospel till Peter preached it to them; but that it was he whom God appointed to convey the gospel to them under circumstances which showed it to be manifestly his will that they should be admitted into the church without circumcision. — For the generic ἔθνη, see on 11, 18.

V. 8. ὁ καρδιογνώστης .... αὐτοῖς, *the heart-knowing God* (who could judge, therefore, of the sincerity of their repentance and faith) *testified for them* (dat. comm.). The testimony consisted of the miraculous gifts which he imparted to them, see 10, 45. He had thus shown that ceremonial obedience was not essential to his favor; for he had granted the sign of acceptance to those who were entirely destitute of that recommendation.

V. 9. καὶ οὐδὲν .... αὐτῶν, *and made no distinction between us,* who had practised the Jewish rites, *and them,* though they were still heathen in that respect (ἄνομοι, 1 Cor. 9, 21). The next clause states how he had manifested this impartiality — τῇ πίστει .... αὐτῶν, *in that by faith he purified their hearts,* i. e. in connection with their reception of the gospel, had made them partakers of the holiness which renders those who possess it acceptable in his sight. He had bestowed this blessing as fully and freely on the uncircumcised believing Gentiles, as he had upon the circumcised believing Jews. Peter represents the purification as effected by faith, in order to deny the error which would ascribe that efficacy to circumcision or any other legal observance. The Jewish feeling was that the heathen were unclean so long as they were uncircumcised. The Spirit is the efficient author of sanctification; but faith as used here is a belief of the truth (2 Thess. 2, 13), especially of that which relates to the atonement of Christ (1 John 1, 7), and the Spirit employs the truth as the means of sanctification.

V. 10. νῦν οὖν, *Now therefore,* i. e. after such evidence that God does not require the heathen to submit to Jewish rites. — τί πειράζετε τὸν θεόν, *why do ye tempt God,* make presumptuous trial of his power and patience by demanding new proofs of his will; see 5, 9; Matt. 4, 7; 1 Cor. 10, 9. This sense is partly Hebraistic, and we must compare the verb with נִסָּה, in order to obtain the full idea. — ἐπιθεῖναι (= ἐπιθέντες) ζυγόν, *that you should place* (= by placing) *a yoke,* etc. This is a lax use of the epexegetical infinitive. W. § 44. 1. — ὃν οὔτε, κ. τ. λ., *which neither our fathers,* etc. "By this yoke," says Neander, "which Peter represents as having been always so irksome to the Jews, he certainly did not mean the external observance of ceremonies simply as such, since he would by no means persuade the Jewish Christians to renounce them. But he meant the external observance of the law, in so far as this proceeded from an internal subjection of the conscience to its power, such as exists when justification and salvation are made to depend on the performance of legal requirements. Those in this state of mind must fear lest they peril their salvation by the slightest deviation from the law; they suffer the painful scrupulosity which leads to the invention of manifold checks, in order to guard themselves, by a self-imposed constraint, against every possible transgression of its commands."

V. 11. ἀλλά marks this connection: With such an experience as to the law, we no longer expect salvation from that source; *but through the grace of the Lord Jesus believe that we shall be saved.* — κἀκεῖνοι, *also they,* viz. the heathen converts. The remark suggests its own application. If the Jews had renounced their own law as unable to benefit them, and had taken the position of the Gentiles, it was inconsistent, as well as useless, to require the Gentiles to depend on the system of the Jews. The train of thought in Gal. 2, 15 sq. is singularly coincident with this. — The reference of κἀκεῖνοι to οἱ πατέρες introduces an idea irrelevant to the subject.

V. 12. ἐσίγησε, *became silent,* recalls us to the πολλῆς συζητήσεως in v. 7. Peter's address had calmed the excitement, so that they refrained from speaking, and gave Paul and Barnabas an opportunity to be heard; comp. σιγῆσαι in the next verse. — ἤκουον (imperf.) implies a copious narration on the part of the speakers. — ἐξηγουμένων, κ. τ. λ. They gave this prominence to the miracles because these expressed so decisively God's approval of their course in receiving the heathen without circumcision. That was now the main point in question. We see from Gal. 2, 7 sq., that the narrative embraced also other topics.

VERSES 13–21. *Speech of the Apostle James.*

V. 13. The speaker is the *James* mentioned in 12, 17. Paul names him before Peter and John in Gal. 2, 9 because he was pastor of the church at Jerusalem and perhaps president of the council. — ἀπεκρίθη, *proceeded to speak* (see 3, 12); or, very properly, *answered,* since the position of the Judaistic party challenged a reply.

V. 14. Συμεών, *Symeon* (see 13, 1), as in 2 Pet. 1, 1; elsewhere Σίμων, *Simon,* after the Heb. variation שִׁימוֹן (1 Chr. 4, 20) and שִׁמְעוֹן (Gen. 29, 33). This apostle is not mentioned again in the Acts. His speech in the council is the last act of Peter which Luke has recorded. — πρῶτον, *at first,* answers to ἀφ' ἡμερῶν ἀρχαίων in v. 7. — ἐπεσκέψατο, *graciously visited,* like פָּקַד in its good sense. — ἐπὶ τῷ ὀνόματι αὐτοῦ, *after his name* (Luke 1, 9), i. e. who should be called by it, known as his people (De Wet.); comp. v. 17; Deut. 28, 10; Is. 63, 19; 2 Chr. 7, 14, etc. But the critical editions omit ἐπί, and the dative depends then on the infinitive; i. e. *for thy name,* its acknowledgment, honor.

V. 15. καὶ τούτῳ κ. τ. λ., *and with this* (not masculine, viz.

Peter, but neuter, viz. the fact just stated) *agree the words of the prophets.* As an example of their testimony, he adduces Am. 9, 11 sq.

V. 16. The citation conforms very nearly to the Septuagint.— ἀναστρέψω, κ. τ. λ., *I will return and will rebuild.* The expression implies a restoration of favor after a temporary alienation; comp. Jer. 12, 15. Some recognize here the Hebraism which converts the first of two verbs into an adverb qualifying the second: *I will again rebuild.* Meyer, De Wette, Winer (§ 54. 5), reject that explanation. It is the less apposite here, as ἀνά repeats the adverbial idea in the three following verbs. — ἀνοικοδομήσω, κ. τ. λ., *I will rebuild the tabernacle of David which has fallen,* i. e. will restore the decayed splendor of his family, to wit, in the person of his Son after the flesh (Rom. 1, 3), in the Messiah. σκηνήν represents the family as having fallen into such obscurity as to occupy the humble abode of a booth or tabernacle. The next words of the text describe the same condition still more strongly.

V. 17. ὅπως ἂν ἐκζητήσωσιν, κ. τ. λ., *that* (telic, because the Saviour must be first sent) *the rest* (lit. *those left remaining*) *of men and all the heathen may seek out the Lord.* ἄν implies that it depends on them whether the purpose will be attained or defeated. See W. § 42. 6; K. § 330. 4. *The rest of men* are the others of them besides the Jews, and these others are *all the heathen.* The last clause is explicative, not appositional. The Hebrew has *they,* i. e. the people of God, *shall possess the residue of Edom,* i. e. those of Edom reserved for mercy, *and all the* (other) *heathen.* The Seventy may have confounded some of the original words with other similar words; but the apostle followed their translation of the passage, as it contained the essential idea for which he appealed to it. The many foreign Jews who were present were familiar with the Greek Scriptures, but not the Hebrew.— ἐφ' οὓς . . . . μου, *upon whom my name has been called,* i. e. given, applied to them as a sign of their relationship to God; comp. James 2, 7. See the references on v. 14. Observe that the verb is perfect. The application of the name was future when the prophecy was uttered, and was still future to a great extent when cited at this time; but the prediction was as good as already verified, because the purpose of God made it certain. — ἐπ' αὐτούς is a Hebraism, founded on the use of אֲשֶׁר as the sign of relation (Olsh. De Wet. Mey.). Gesen. Heb. Gr. § 121. 1. The foregoing citation from Amos was pertinent in a twofold way: first, it announced that the heathen were to be admitted with the Jews into the kingdom of Christ; and, secondly, it contained no recognition of circumcision, or other Jewish ceremonies, as prerequisite to their reception. — πάντα after ταῦτα (T. R.) is not approved.

V. 18. The words here are a comment of James on the prophecy.—γνωστὰ .... αὐτοῦ, *Known from the beginning unto God are all his works.* The present call of the Gentiles, after having been so long foretold, was an evidence and illustration of the truth here asserted. Hence, the apostle would argue, if God, in extending the gospel to the heathen without requiring them to be circumcised, was carrying into effect an eternal purpose, it became them to acquiesce in it; their opposition to his plan would be as unavailing as it was criminal. — The variations of the text in this verse are numerous, but nearly all yield the same meaning. They may be seen in Griesbach, Hahn, Tischendorf, Green, and others. Lachman adheres to the common reading, with the exception of κυρίῳ for θεῷ, and ἔργον for ἔργα.

V. 19. ἐγὼ κρίνω, *I* (for my part, without dictating to others) *judge*, decide as my opinion. On ἐγώ, as thus restrictive, see W. § 22. 6. The verb affords no proof that the speaker's authority was greater than that of the other apostles; comp. 16, 4. — μὴ παρενοχλεῖν, *that we ought not to disquiet*, molest, i. e. impose on them the yoke of Jewish ceremonies; see v. 10. The infinitive includes often the idea of obligation or necessity. W. § 44. 3. b. Meyer urges the separate force of παρά, *further*, i. e. in addition to their faith, not justified apparently by usage; better in his last edition, *thereby*, along with their conversion.

V. 20. ἐπιστεῖλαι, κ. τ. λ., *that we should write to them*, direct by letter, *that they abstain.* — ἀλισγημάτων = εἰδωλοθύτων in v. 29. The parts of the victim not used in sacrifice, the heathen sold in the market as ordinary food, or ate them at feasts. The Jews, in their abhorrence of idolatry, regarded the use of such flesh as allied to the guilt of participating in idol-worship itself. See Rom. 14, 15 sq.; 1 Cor. 8, 10 sq. — καὶ τῆς πορνείας, *and from fornication* = licentiousness (Calv. Kuin. Olsh. Mey. De Wet.). Repeat ἀπό before this noun. The other practices, it will be observed, relate to things which are not sinful *per se*, but derive their character from positive law, or from circumstances. The reason, probably, for associating this immorality with such practices is, that the heathen mind had become so corrupt as almost to have lost the idea of chastity as a virtue.[1] Other senses of

[1] See Tholuck on the Nature and Moral Influence of Heathenism, in the Biblical Repository, Vol. II. p. 441 sq.

πορνεία, as idolatry, incest, marriage with unbelievers, concubinage, have been proposed. It is against any such unusual signification of the word, that it occurs again in the enactment (v. 29). The object of the decree would require it to be framed with as much perspicuity as possible, and would exclude the use of terms out of their ordinary acceptation. — καὶ τοῦ πνικτοῦ, *and from what has been strangled*, i. e. from the flesh of animals put to death in that way. The Jews were not allowed to eat such flesh, because it contained the blood; see Lev. 17, 13. 14; Deut. 12, 16, 23. — καὶ τοῦ αἵματος, *and from blood*, which the heathen drank often at their idolatrous feasts, and at other times and in various ways mingled with their food.

V. 21. This verse assigns a reason for the proposed restrictions, and that is, that the Jewish believers, being so accustomed to hear the things in question forbidden, were naturally sensitive in regard to them, and hence it was necessary, for the sake of peace and harmony, that the heathen converts should refrain from such practices. This view of the connection is the most natural one. Calvin, Hemsen, Olshausen, De Wette, Meyer, and others, agree in it. Neander follows Chrysostom, who supposes the words to explain why it was proposed to instruct the Gentiles only: the Jews had no occasion to be informed what the law required of them; *for Moses in every city*, etc. This interpretation not only turns the mind abruptly from one train of thought to another, but appears to concede more to the advocates of circumcision than the question at issue would allow. To have justified the prohibitions on such ground would be recognizing the perpetuity of the Mosaic rites, so far as the Jews were concerned; and we cannot suppose that the apostles at this time either entertained that view, or would give any direct countenance to it in the minds of others.

VERSES 22–29. *They appoint Messengers to the Churches, and send a Letter by them.*

V. 22. τότε ἔδοξε, κ. τ. λ., *Then the apostles . . . . resolved, having selected men from themselves, to send them*, etc. ἐκλεξαμένους passes into the accusative, because the object of the governing verb, ἀποστόλοις, serves at the same time as the subject of the infinitive. K. § 307. R. 2. — *Judas* is known only from this notice. His surname opposes the conjecture that he was Judas Thaddeus, the apostle. There is no proof that he was a brother of Joseph Barsabas, the candidate for the apostleship (1, 23). — *Silas* bacame Paul's associate in his second missionary tour (v. 40). For Σίλας in the Acts, we have always Σιλουανός in the Epistles. The former was his Jewish name probably, the latter his Gentile or foreign name; see on 13, 9. — ἡγουμένους, *leading*, eminent for reputation and authority (Luke 22, 26).

V. 23. γράψαντες. The nominative of a participle refers often to a preceding substantive in a different case, when that substantive forms in fact the logical subject of the clause. K. § 313. 1; W. § 64. II. 2. The impersonal expression at the head of the sentence is equivalent to a transitive verb with the dative as nominative. K. § 307. R. 5. — κατὰ τὴν Ἀντιόχειαν, κ. τ. λ., *throughout Antioch and Syria*, etc., since the brethren were in different places. We see here how extensively the Judaizers had attempted to spread their views. The scene at Antioch (v. 1) was only an example of what had occurred in many other places. As to the origin of the churches in Syria and Cilicia, see on v. 41. — χαίρειν, sc. λέγουσι. It is remarkable, says Neander, that this word, as a form of epistolary salutation, occurs only here and in James 1, 1, with the exception of 23, 26, where it is a Roman who employs it. It would account for the coincidence if we suppose that the Apostle James drew up this document. His office as pastor of the church would very naturally devolve that service on him. The occurrence of χαίρειν here and in the Epistle, Bengel, Bleek, and others, point out as an indication that the two compositions are from the same hand.

V. 24. ἐξ ἡμῶν, *from us*, which accords with v. 1. — ἐτάραξαν, *disquieted*, perplexed; see Gal. 1, 7. — λόγοις may have, as Stier thinks, a disparaging force: *with words* merely, as opposed to the truth or sound doctrine. — ἀνασκευάζοντες τὰς ψυχὰς ὑμῶν, *subverting your souls*, i. e. unsettling, removing them from the pure faith of the gospel. This clause describes the effect or tendency of the views which those who received the decrees were urged by the false teachers to adopt. — περιτέμνεσθαι, κ. τ. λ., *that ye must be circumcised, and keep the law*. For this power of the infinitive, see on v. 19. δεῖν is not to be supplied. — οἷς οὐ διεστειλάμεθα, *whom we did not command*, i. e. instruct, authorize. This declaration may be aimed at a pretence on their part that they had been sent forth by the church at Jerusalem, or at least that they represented the sentiments of that church.

V. 25. γενομένοις ὁμοθυμαδόν, *having met together* (Vulg. Neand.); but better, *having become of one mind*, unanimous (Bng. Str. Mey.). Kuinoel and De Wette are undecided. According to the latter view, the expression represents this perfect harmony as having been attained after some diversity of opinion; see v. 5. — ἐκλεξαμένους exemplifies again the construction in v. 22. — Βαρνάβᾳ καὶ Παύλῳ. This deviation from the usual order of these names since 13, 13, as De Wette remarks after Bleek, testifies to the writer's diplomatic accuracy. Paul had spent but little time at Jerusalem, and Barnabas was still a more familiar name there (comp. 9, 27), than that of the apostle to the Gentiles.

V. 26. ἀνθρώποις . . . . αὐτῶν, *men who have given up*, jeoparded, *their lives;* comp. 9, 24; 13, 50; 14, 5. 19. There was a special reason, no doubt, for this commendation of Paul and Barnabas. It would serve to counteract any attempts which the Jewish party might make, or had made, to discredit their religious views and impair their reputation as teachers.

V. 27. οὖν, *therefore*, i. e. in conformity with the conclusion in v. 25. — καὶ αὐτοὺς, κ. τ. λ., *also themselves by word announcing* (when they shall be present) *the same things*, i. e. that we now write to you (Neand. Mey. De Wet.); not *the same things* that Paul and Barnabas have taught. διὰ λόγου indicates clearly that the oral communication was to confirm the contents of the letter or the written communication. "Judas and Silas," says Stier (Reden der Apostel, I. p. 90), "should certify that the letter had actually proceeded from a unanimous resolve of the church at Jerusalem, and that Barnabas and Saul were thus honored and beloved there; they should give fuller information respecting the decrees, and answer every inquiry that might be proposed, as living epistles, confirmed by the letter and confirming it in return; and thus by their word they should restore again the harmony which those unsent members of their church had disturbed."

V. 28. ἔδοξε γάρ, *For it seemed good*, i. e. and especially how it seemed good. γάρ specifies the part of the letter which the writers had more particularly in view in τὰ αὐτά. — πνεύματι καὶ ἡμῖν = πνεύματι ἐν ἡμῖν (Olsh.). See 5, 3 and note there. The expression represents the two agencies as distinct from each other, as well as consentaneous (De Wet.). — ἡμῖν includes all (see v. 23) who took part in the action of the council. They were conscious of having adopted their conclusions under the guidance of the Spirit, and claimed for them the authority of infallible decisions. — τῶν renders ἐπάναγκες an adjective. B. § 125. 6. The things in question are said to be *necessary*, not (excepting the last of them) because they were wrong in themselves, but because the Gentile Christians were bound by the law of charity (see Rom. 14, 15) to avoid a course which, while it involved no question of conscience on their part, would offend and grieve their Jewish brethren, and lead inevitably to strife and alienation.

V. 29. ἀπέχεσθαι, to wit, *that ye abstain.* For this definitive use of the infinitive, see W. § 44. 1: C. § 623. — It is not perhaps accidental that πορνείας has here a different position from that in v. 20; see also 21, 25. — ἐξ ὧν . . . . ἑαυτούς Neander compares with ἄσπιλον ἑαυτὸν τηρεῖν ἀπὸ τοῦ κόσμου in James 1, 27. The similarity is striking, and may indicate the same hand in the two passages (see on v. 23). — εὖ πράξετε, *ye will do well,* what is right and commendable; see 10, 33; 3 John v. 6. — ἔρρωσθε, like the Latin *valete.*

VERSES 30–35. *Paul and Barnabas return to Antioch.*

V. 30. οὖν, *therefore,* since the foregoing decision was preliminary to their departure. — ἀπολυθέντες, *having been dismissed,* i. e. in all probability with religious services (v. 33; 13, 3), and perhaps with an escort for some miles on the way (v. 3). — τὸ πλῆθος, *the multitude;* see v. 12 and 6, 2. They call at once an assembly of the believers to hear their report.

V. 31. ἐπὶ τῇ παρακλήσει, *at the consolation* (lit. *upon* as the cause) furnished by the letter. They approve of what had been done; they rejoice at the prospect of so happy a termination of the dispute. Some understand παρακλήσει of *exhortation,* which certainly is not required by that sense of the verb in the next verse (Mey.), and does not accord well with the contents of so authoritative a letter.

V. 32. καὶ αὐτοὶ προφῆται ὄντες, *also themselves being prophets,* i. e. as well as Paul and Barnabas, and so competent to give the instruction needed. — παρεκάλεσαν, *exhorted,* viz. in view of the present danger, that they should rely on Christ for salvation, and not cleave to the law of works. — ἐπεστήριξαν, *confirmed,* shows the happy effect of their labors.

V. 33. μετ' εἰρήνης, *with peace;* the parting salutation (16, 36; Mark 5, 34; Luke 7, 50). The brethren took leave of them with the best wishes for their safety and welfare. Judas and Silas both returned to Jerusalem, as their commission would require, but Silas must have soon rejoined Paul at Antioch, since we find him there in v. 40. Luke has passed over that second journey.

V. 34. Griesbach, Lachmann, Tischendorf, and others, strike out this verse. Most of the manuscripts omit it, or read it variously. It is a gloss probably, supposed to be required by v. 40. If the text be genuine and Silas remained at Antioch, we must understand the plural in v. 33 as including one or more persons along with Judas, who had also come down from Jerusalem, though the narrative is otherwise silent concerning them.

V. 35. *διέτριβον.* This was the interval between the return to Antioch (v. 30), and the departure on the next missionary tour (v. 40). Some propose to insert here the scene described in Gal. 2, 11 sq.; but that such a reaction in favor of Judaism as appeared on that occasion should have taken place so soon after the decision at Jerusalem, is altogether improbable. See note on 18, 23. — *καί* adds *εὐαγγελιζόμενοι* to the other participle as epexegetical: what they taught was the glad tidings or the gospel; not instructed believers and preached to those who had not believed (Alf.). See 4, 18; 5, 42; 11, 26; 28, 31.

VERSES 36–41. *Paul and Barnabas resume their Work in different Fields of Labor.*

V. 36. *μετὰ δέ τινας ἡμέρας, Now after certain days,* denotes apparently a short period; comp. 9, 19; 16, 12. — *δή* strengthens the exhortation; see 13, 2. — *ἐπισκεψώμεθα . . . . πῶς ἔχουσι* may involve an attraction, viz. that of the subject of the last clause drawn into the first: *let us go to see . . . . how the brethren are* (W. § 66. 5); or an ellipsis: *let us visit the brethren,* and see (as in the E. V.) *how they are.* — *ἐν αἷς* is plural because *πᾶσαν πόλιν* is collective. W. § 21. 3; K. § 332. 5. — *πῶς ἔχουσι, how they are,* in the mind of Paul, would have respect mainly to their spiritual welfare.

V. 37. *ἐβουλεύσατο, determined* (see v. 5, 33; 27, 39). The feelings of Barnabas may have influenced him in this decision, more than his judgment, since he and Mark were cousins (*ἀνεψιοί*); see Col. 4, 10. *ἐβούλετο, wished,* is an ancient reading, but on the whole less approved, in part because it softens down the altercation, and may have been added for that reason.

V. 38. *ἠξίου, deemed it just,* fitting. Paul viewed the question on its ethical side and not as a personal matter. — *τὸν ἀποστάντα ἀπ᾽ αὐτῶν, who departed from them* (13, 13), in dereliction of his duty; comp. Luke 8, 13. — *τοῦτον, this one* (emphatic here), who proved so fickle.— It is pleasing to know that Mark did not forfeit the apostle's esteem so as to be unable to regain it. He became subsequently Paul's companion in travel (Col. 4, 10), and in 2 Tim. 4, 11 elicits from him the commendation that he was "profitable to him for the ministry."

V. 39. *ἐγένετο παροξυσμός, a severe contention arose.* Barnabas insisted on his purpose, Paul on his view of the merits of the case; and as neither would yield, they parted. Some writers lay all the blame on Barnabas (Bmg.), in spite of the impartiality of the text. There was heat evidently on both sides. — ὥστε .... ἀλλήλων, *so that they departed from one another.* This separation refers, not to the rupture of their friendship, but to their proceeding in different directions, instead of laboring together as heretofore. The infinitive after ὥστε is said to represent the act as a necessary or logical sequence of what precedes; the indicative as an absolute or unconditioned fact. See Klotz ad Devar. II. p. 772. It deserves to be remarked, that this variance did not estrange these brethren from their work, or occasion any permanent diminution of their regard for each other. In 1 Cor. 9, 6, which was written after this occurrence, Paul alludes to Barnabas as a Christian teacher, who possessed and deserved the fullest confidence of the churches. The passage contains fairly that implication. Even the error of Barnabas in yielding to the Jewish party (Gal. 2, 13) leads Paul to speak of him as one of the very last men (καὶ Βαρνάβας, i. e. *even he*) whom any one would suppose capable of swerving from the line of duty. And who can doubt that Barnabas reciprocated these sentiments towards the early, long-tried friend with whom he had acted in so many eventful scenes, and whom he saw still animated by the same affection towards himself, and the same devotion to the cause of their common Master? Luke does not mention the name of Barnabas again in the Acts. It is impossible to trace him further with any certainty. One tradition is that he went to Milan, and died as first bishop of the church there; another is, that, after living some years at Rome and Athens, he suffered martyrdom in his native Cyprus. The letter still extant, which was known as that of Barnabas even in the second century, cannot be defended as genuine. See Neander's Church History, Vol. I. p. 657. That such a letter, however, was ascribed to him at that early period, shows how eminent a place he occupied among the Christians of his own and the succeeding age.

V. 40. ἐπιλεξάμενος, *having chosen for himself* (comp. v. 22), not *thereupon*, viz. this disagreement. — παραδοθεὶς .... ὑπὸ τῶν ἀδελφῶν, *having been committed unto the grace of God by the brethren.* Perhaps we may infer from this remark, that the believers at Antioch took Paul's view of the point at issue between him and Barnabas. — ἐξῆλθε, *went forth*, is used of going forth as a missionary in Luke 9, 6, and in 3 John v. 7. — The departure on this second tour we may place in A. D. 51; for if Paul went to Jerusalem in the year 50 (see on 15, 4), the remainder of that year, added (if any one chooses) to the early part of the ensuing year, would suffice probably for the sojourn at Antioch indicated by τινὰς ἡμέρας in v. 36. It is impossible to be more definite than this.

V. 41. *Syria* and *Cilicia* lay between Antioch and the eastern limit of the apostle's first journey. We have had no account of the planting of any churches there, but they date undoubtedly from the period of Paul's residence in that region, mentioned in Gal. 1, 21. See 9, 30 and note there. — ἐπιστηρίζων τὰς ἐκκλησίας, *confirming the churches*, not candidates for admission to them; see 14, 22. One of these churches may have been at Tarsus, which Paul would naturally revisit at this time.

CHAPTER XVI.

VERSES 1–5. *Paul and Silas revisit the Churches and deliver the Decrees.*

V. 1. Δέρβην καὶ Λύστραν. *Derbe and Lystra* are mentioned in this order (the reverse of that in 14, 6), because the missionaries travel now from east to west. — Luke's exclamation καὶ ἰδού, *and behold*, shows how much this meeting with Timothy interested his feelings. — ἐκεῖ, *there*, viz. at Lystra. Some refer the adverb to Derbe; but that view, so far from being required by Δερβαῖος in 20, 4, is forbidden by the text there. Lystra stands nearest to ἐκεῖ, and is named again in the next verse, where Luke surely would not pass over the testimony of those who had been acquainted with Timothy from early life. Wieseler combines the two opinions by supposing that Timothy may have been a native of Lystra, but was now living at Derbe. — For the family and the early education of Timothy, see 2 Tim. 1, 5; 3, 15. Paul terms him τέκνον μου, *my son*, in 1 Cor. 4, 17, probably because he had been the instrument of his conversion; comp. 1 Cor. 4, 15; Gal. 4, 19. See the note on 14, 20. — τινός is to be erased after γυναικός. — πιστῆς, *believing*; see on 10, 45. The mother's name was Eunice. It was an instance of the mixed marriages of which Paul writes in 1 Cor. 1, 17 sq. — Ἕλληνος, *a Greek*, and still a heathen, or at all events not a proselyte in full, as otherwise the son would have been circumcised.

V. 2. ἐμαρτυρεῖτο, *was attested*, well reported of. See 6, 3; 10, 22. Supposing Timothy to have been converted during Paul's first visit to Lystra (see on 14, 20), he had now been a disciple three or four years. During this time he had exerted himself, no doubt, for the cause of Christ both in Lystra and Iconium, and had thus given proof of the piety and talents which rendered him so useful as a herald of the cross.

V. 3. σὺν αὐτῷ ἐξελθεῖν, *to go forth with him* as a preacher of the word; see 2 Tim. 4, 5.—λαβὼν . . . . αὐτόν, *having taken, he circumcised him*, either by his own hand (Mey. De Wet.), or procuring it to be done (Neand.). The Jews had no particular class of persons who performed this act. The Jewish custom, it is said, required merely that the administrator should not be a heathen. See Win. Realw. I. p. 157.—διὰ τοὺς Ἰουδαίους, κ. τ. λ., *on account of the Jews*, etc. It would have repelled the Jews from his ministry to have seen him associated with a man whom they knew to be uncircumcised. Paul took this course, therefore, in order to remove that obstacle to his usefulness. The history presents Paul here as acting on the principle stated in 1 Cor. 9, 20: ἐγενόμην τοῖς Ἰουδαίοις ὡς Ἰουδαῖος ἵνα Ἰουδαίους κερδήσω, κ. τ. λ. It was under circumstances totally different that he refused to circumcise Titus, as related in Gal. 2, 3 sq. He was then in the midst of those who would have regarded the act as ratifying their doctrine that circumcision was necessary to salvation; see on 15, 1. In the present instance he knew (that admission is due to his character for intelligence as well as consistency) that his conduct would not be misunderstood or perverted; that the believers would view it as an accommodation merely to the prejudices of the Jews, and that the Jews themselves were in no danger of supposing him to countenance the idea that their keeping the law would entitle them to the favor of God.—Other passages extend our knowledge of this transaction. Timothy was not only circumcised, but set apart to the ministry "with the laying on of the hands of the presbytery" and of the apostle, was endued with special gifts for the office (1 Tim. 4, 14; 2 Tim. 1, 6), and received at the time prophetic assurances of the success which awaited him in his new career (1 Tim. 1, 18).—ᾔδεισαν γὰρ, κ. τ. λ., *for all knew his father that*, etc. The structure of the sentence is like that in 3, 10.

V. 4. ὡς διεπορεύοντο τὰς πόλεις, *As they journeyed through the cities* on the route pursued by them. They would visit naturally all the churches in Syria and Cilicia (15, 41), and most of those on the main land, gathered during the apostle's former tour. As

Antioch and Perga were so remote from their general course, it is possible that they transmitted copies of the decrees to those places. It is not certain that the word had taken root in Perga; see on 14, 25. — *παρεδίδουν . . . . δόγματα*, *delivered* (orally or in writing) *to them the decrees to keep.* The infinitive may be telic: that they should keep them; or may involve a relative clause: which they should keep. Compare *ἃ παρέλαβον κρατεῖν* in Mark 7, 4. See W. § 44. 1. *αὐτοῖς* refers to the believers in these cities; not to the heathen converts merely (Mey.), since the decrees affected also the Jews.

V. 5. *οὖν*, *therefore*, i. e. as the result of this visit, and of the adjustment of the controversy which had divided and enfeebled the churches. — *τῷ ἀριθμῷ*, *in the number* of their members.

VERSES 6–10. *They prosecute their Journey to Troas.*

V. 6. *Φρυγίαν.* See on 2, 10. To reach *Phrygia* from Iconium or Antioch, they would direct their way to the northeast. — *Γαλατικὴν χώραν.* *Galatia* was bounded on the north by Paphlagonia and Bithynia, on the east by Pontus and Cappadocia (separated from them by the river Halys), on the south by Cappadocia and Phrygia, and on the west by Phrygia and Bithynia. Among the principal cities were Ancyra, made the metropolis by Augustus, and Pessinus. Kiepert draws the line of Paul's course, on his map, so as to include these places, on the natural supposition that he would aim to secure first the prominent towns. See on 18, 1. It is evident from the Epistle to the Galatians (see, e. g., 4, 19), that it was the apostle Paul who first preached the gospel in this country; and since he found disciples here on his third missionary tour (see 18, 23), it must have been at this time that he laid the foundation of the Galatian churches (Gal. 1, 2). Such is the opinion of the leading critics. See note on 14, 6. — *κωλυθέντες, κ. τ. λ.*, *being restrained by the Holy Spirit,* etc. The act of this participle, it will be observed, was subsequent to that of *διελθόντες* and prior to that of *ἐλθόντες* (v. 7). The course of the movement may be sketched thus. The travellers, having passed through the eastern section of Phrygia into Galatia, proposed next to preach the word in proconsular Asia (see on 2, 9). With that view they turned their steps to the southwest, and, crossing the north part of Phrygia, came down to the frontier of Mysia, the first province in Asia which they would reach in that direction. Being informed here that they were not to execute this design, they turned again towards the north and attempted to go into Bithynia, which was adjacent to Mysia. Restrained from that purpose, they passed by Mysia, i. e. did not remain there to preach, and proceeded to Troas. — This portion of the apostle's travels, though they embrace so wide a circuit, admits of very little geographical illustration. Phrygia and Galatia are parts of Asia Minor, of which the ancient writers have left but few notices and which remain comparatively unknown to the present day. We must infer from 18, 23, that Paul gained disciples in Phrygia at this time, but in what places is uncertain. Colosse was a Phrygian city, and may have received the gospel on this journey, unless it be forbidden by Col. 2, 1. The opinion of the best critics is, that the apostle includes the Colossians in that passage among those who had not "seen his face in the flesh." — τὸ πνεῦμα Ἰησοῦ, *the Spirit of Jesus*, i. e. which he sends. There is no parallel passage, unless it be Rom. 8, 9. Ἰησοῦ has been lost from some copies, but belongs to the text. The Spirit, says Reuss, appears here in a sphere of activity, made more prominent in the Acts than in all the other writings of the New Testament. "Thus, it is the Spirit who conducts Philip in the road to Gaza (8, 29), who instructs Peter to receive the messengers of Cornelius (10, 19; 11, 12), who causes Barnabas and Paul to be sent to the heathen (13, 2. 4), who directs the missionaries in the choice of their route (16, 6. 7), who urges Paul to Jerusalem (20, 22), who chooses the pastors of the churches (20, 28), etc."[1]

V. 8. παρελθόντες τὴν Μυσίαν, *having passed by Mysia*, having left it aside without remaining to preach there; comp. παραπλεῦσαι in 20, 16, and παρελθεῖν in Mark 6, 48. Wieseler (Chronologie, p. 36), Alford, Howson apparently, and others prefer this meaning here. Some render *having passed along Mysia*, i. e. the border of Mysia Minor, which belonged to Bithynia, whereas Mysia Major belonged to proconsular Asia (De Wet.) The boundary was a political one, and no distinct frontier existed, which the travellers could have had any motive for tracing so exactly. — κατέβησαν, *came down* from the inner highlands to the coast. — εἰς Τρωάδα, *unto Troas*, the name of a district or a city; here the latter, called fully Alexandria Troas, on the Hellespont, about four miles from the site of the ancient Troy. It was the transit harbor between the north-west of Asia Minor and Macedonia. Paul passed and repassed here on two other occasions (20, 6; 2 Cor. 2, 12). It is correct that Luke represents Troas here as distinct from Mysia. Under Nero, Troas and the vicinity

[1] Historie de la Theologie Chretienne, Tome second, p. 603 (Strasbourg 1852).

formed a separate territory, having the rights of Roman freedom (De Wet. Böttg.).

V. 9. καὶ ὅραμα, κ. τ. λ. Whether Paul saw this *vision* in a dream, or in a state of ecstasy (see 10, 10; 22, 17), the language does not decide. διὰ τῆς νυκτός suggests one of the conditions of the first mode, but would not be inconsistent with the other.—ἀνὴρ Μακεδών, *a man* revealed to him as *a Macedonian*; comp. 9, 12.—διαβάς, *having crossed*, i. e. the northern part of the Ægean.—βοήθησον ἡμῖν, *help us*, because the one here represented many.

V. 10. ἐζητήσαμεν, *we sought*, i. e. by immediate inquiry for a ship (Alf.). Paul had made known the vision to his associates. Here for the first time the historian speaks of himself as one of the party, and in all probablity because he joined it at Troas. The introduction would be abrupt for the style of a modern work, it is true; but, on the other hand, to have had from Luke any formal account of the manner in which he became connected with the apostle would have been equally at variance with the simplicity and reserve which distinguish the sacred writers. Nor does it account at all more naturally for this sudden use of the plural, to imagine (it is a figment purely) that Luke adopts here the narrative of another writer; for, we may just as well suppose him to speak thus abruptly in his own name, as to allow him to introduce another person as doing it, without apprising us of the change. See marginal note on p. 16.

VERSES 11–15. *Paul and his Associates arrive in Europe, and preach at Philippi.*

V. 11. εὐθυδρομήσαμεν, *we ran by a straight course.* In the nautical language of the ancients, as in that of the moderns, *to run* meant to sail before the wind, see 27, 16. Luke observes almost a technical precision in the use of such terms. His account of the voyage to Rome shows a surprising familiarity with sea-life.—εἰς Σαμοθράκην, *unto Samothrace*, which they reached the first day. This island, the present Samothraki, is about half way between Troas and Neapolis, and is the highest land in this part of the Ægean, except Mount Athos. The ordinary currents here are adverse to sailing northward; but southerly winds, though they are brief, blow strongly at times and overcome entirely that disadvantage. With such a wind, "the vessel in which Paul sailed would soon cleave her way through the strait between Tenedos and the main, past the Dardanelles, and near the eastern shore of Imbros. On rounding the northern end of this island, they would open Samothrace, which had hitherto appeared as a higher and more distant summit over the lower mountains of Imbros. Leaving this island, and bearing now a little to the west, and having the wind still (as our sailors say) two or three points abaft the beam, they steered for Samothrace, and under the shelter of its high shore, anchored for the night." See the nautical proofs in Howson. — εἰς Νεάπολιν, *unto Naples*, a Thracian city on the Strymonic gulf, the modern Cavallo. It was north-west from Samothrace, but even with a southerly wind could be reached in seven or eight hours. As the same verb describes the remainder of the journey, it might seem as if they merely touched here, but did not land, proceeding along the coast to some harbor nearer to Philippi than this. Some writers would place the port of that city further west than the present Cavallo. It is generally agreed, however, that Neapolis was the nearest town on the sea, and hence, though the distance was not less than ten miles, was identical with Philippi as to purposes of travel and trade. Cavallo is the nearest port at present, and the shore appears to have undergone no change either from recession or advance.[1]

V. 12. *Philippi* was on a steep acclivity of the Thracian Hermus, where this range slopes towards the sea, on a small stream called Gangas, or Gangitas. It was at some distance east of the Strymon, and not on that river, as some have said. The adjacent plain is memorable in Roman history, as the place where the battle was fought between the Republicans under Brutus, and the followers of Antony and Augustus. — ἥτις . . . . κολώνια, *which is the chief city of the province of Macedonia*, being *a colony*. πρώτη designates it as one of the first places there, and κολώνια explains the ground of the epithet. Augustus had sent a colony thither (see Dict. of Antt. s. *colonia*), which had conferred upon it new importance. Some understand πρώτη geographically: *first* as they entered Macedonia, which Winer calls the simplest explanation. That Neapolis lay farther east, does not clash with this view; for those who adopt it take Macedonia here in the Greek sense, which assigns Neapolis to Thrace. It is a stronger objection, that Luke would then mean Greek Macedonia here, but elsewhere the Roman province so named, i. e. Northern Greece in distinction from Achaia, or Southern Greece; see on 18, 5. Fur-

[1] My thanks are due to the Rev. Dr. Hill of Athens for inquiries in relation to this point.

ther, ἐστί indicates a permanent distinction; whereas ἦν would have been more natural to mark an incident of the journey (was *first* on their way). The proper capital of Macedonia (hence not πρώτη in that sense) was Thessalonica. If the earlier division into four parts still continued, Amphipolis was politically first in *pars prima.* "It may be added," says Akerman, "in confirmation of the words of Luke, that there are colonial coins of Philippi from the reign of Augustus to that of Caracalla." It is frequenly said, that this was the first place on the continent of Europe where the gospel was preached; but we have no certain knowledge of the origin of the church of Rome, and, very possibly, it may have been founded by some of the converts on the day of Pentecost. The church at Philippi was the first church in Europe which the apostle Paul established. — ἡμέρας τινάς, *certain days*, denotes apparently the few days which they spent there before the arrival of the Sabbath.

V. 13. Instead of the received ἔξω τῆς πόλεως, the later criticism would read ἔξω τῆς πύλης, *out of the gate.* This part of the narrative shows often the presence of the historian. — παρὰ ποτάμον, *beside a river*, viz. the Gangas. The name was unimportant, but could hardly fail to be known to Luke, who was so familiar with Philippi; see on v. 40. The river may possibly have been the more distant Strymon (Neand. Mey.); though if πύλης be the correct word, the stream intended must be a nearer one. In summer the Gangas is almost dry, but in winter or after rains may be full and swollen. — οὗ . . . . εἶναι, *where* (according to an ancient usage in that city) *was wont to be a place of prayer* (Kuin. Neand. Mey. De Wet.). The Jews preferred to assemble near the water on account of the lustrations which accompanied their worship. Neander illustrates this usage from what Tertullian says of them (De Jejun., c. 16): "per omne litus quocunque in aperto . . . . preces ad cœlum mittunt." See also Jos. Antt. 14. 10. 23. The προσευχή here appears to have been, not an edifice, but a space or inclosure in the open air consecrated to this use. The word was so well known as the designation of a Jewish chapel or oratory that it passed into the Latin language in that sense. The rendering *where prayer was wont to be made* (E. V.) does not agree easily with εἶναι. Instead of the substantive verb, the predicate would be γίνεσθαι (12, 5), or ποιεῖσθαι (1 Tim. 2, 1). — In ἐλαλοῦμεν Luke appears as one of the speakers. — ταῖς συνελθούσαις γυναιξί, *the women who came together* for prayer. The absence of a synagogue shows that the Jews here were not numerous. Those who met for prayer were chiefly women, and even some of these were converts to Judaism.

V. 14. καί τις γυνὴ, κ. τ. λ. *Lydia* was a very common name among the Greeks and the Romans. It is not surprising, therefore, that it coincided with the name of her country. Possibly she may have borne a different name at home, but was known among strangers as Lydia or the Lydian (Wetst.). She is said to have been *a seller of purple*, sc. cloths, *from Thyatira*. That city was on the confines of Lydia and Mysia; and the Lydians, as ancient writers testify, were famous for precisely such fabrics. They possessed that reputation even in Homer's time; see Il. 4. 141. An inscription, "the dyers," has been found among the ruins of Thyatira. — ἤκουεν (relative imperf.) *was hearing*, while he discoursed (14, 9; 15, 12); not when the act (διήνοιξε) took place (Alf.). — ἧς . . . . καρδίαν, *whose heart the Lord opened*, i. e. in conformity with other passages (Matt. 11, 25 sq.; Luke 24, 45; 1 Cor. 3, 6. 7), enlightened, impressed by his Spirit, and so prepared to receive the truth. — προσέχειν, *so as to attend* (ecbatic); or less obvious, *to attend* (telic).

V. 15. ὡς δὲ ἐβαπτίσθη. It is left indefinite whether she was baptized at once, or after an interval of some days. — ὁ οἶκος αὐτῆς, *her house*, family. "Here," says De Wette, "as well as in v. 33; 18, 8; 1 Cor. 1, 16, some would find a proof for the apostolic baptism of children; but there is nothing here which shows that any except adults were baptized." According to his view (in Stud. und Krit., p. 669, 1830) of the meaning of 1 Cor. 7, 14, it is impossible that baptism should have been applied to children in the primitive churches. In arguing from the case of children to that of married persons, one of whom is an unbeliever, in order to justify the continuance of the relation, "the apostle must appeal to something which lay out of the disputed case, but which had a certain similarity and admitted of an application to it. This something is nothing else than the relation which the children of Christian parents in general sustain to the Christian church, and the expression 'your children' refers to all the Corinthian Christians. The children of Christians were not yet received properly into a Christian community, *were not yet baptized*, and did not take part in the devotional exercises and love-feasts of the church; accordingly, they might have been regarded as unclean (ἀκάθαρτα), with as much reason as the unbelieving consorts could be so regarded. In this passage, therefore, we have a proof that children had not begun to be baptized in the time of the apostles." The οἶκος αὐτῆς, as Meyer remarks, consisted probably of women who assisted Lydia in her business. "When Jewish or heathen families," he says further, "became

Christians, the children in them could have been baptized only in cases in which they were so far developed that they could profess their faith in Christ, and did actually profess it; for this was the universal requisition for the reception of baptism; see, also, v. 31. 33; 18, 8. On the contrary, if the children were still unable to believe, they did not partake of the rite, since they were wanting in what the act presupposed. The baptism of children is not to be considered as an apostolic institution, but arose gradually in the post-apostolic age, after early and long continued resistance, in connection with certain views of doctrine, and did not become general in the church till after the time of Augustine. The defence of infant baptism transcends the domain of exegesis, and must be given up to that of dogmatics." Since a confession of faith preceded baptism, says Olshausen, "it is improbable in the highest degree that by 'her household' (οἶκος αὐτῆς) children of an immature age are to be understood; those baptized with her were relatives, servants, grown up children. We have not, in fact, a single sure proof-text for the baptism of children in the apostolic age, and the necessity of it cannot be derived from the idea of baptism." He says on 1 Cor. 1, 17, that "nothing can be inferred in favor of infant baptism from the word 'household' (οἶκος), because the adult members of the household (comp. 1 Cor. 16, 15), or the servants in it, may alone be meant." Neander maintains the same view of this class of passages. "Since baptism marked the entrance into communion with Christ, it resulted from the nature of the rite, that a confession of faith in Jesus as the Redeemer would be made by the person to be baptized. As baptism was closely united with a conscious entrance on Christian communion, faith and baptism were always connected with one another; and thus it is in the highest degree probable that baptism was performed only in instances where both could meet together, and that the practice of infant baptism was unknown at this period. We cannot infer the existence of infant baptism from the instance of the baptism of whole families; for the passage in 1 Cor. 16, 15 shows the fallacy of such a conclusion, as from that it appears that the whole family of Stephanus, who were baptized by Paul, consisted of adults. . . . From whom (if it belonged to the first Christian age) could the institution of infant baptism have proceeded? Certainly it did not come directly from Christ himself. Was it from the primitive church in Palestine, from an injunction given by the earlier apostles? But among the Jewish Christians circumcision was held as a seal of the covenant, and hence they had so much less occasion to make use of another dedication for their children. Could it then have been Paul that first introduced among heathen Christians this change in the use of baptism? But this would agree least of all with the peculiar Christian characteristics of this apostle. He who says of himself that Christ sent him, not to baptize, but to preach the gospel; he who always kept his eye fixed on one thing, justification by faith, and so carefully avoided everything which could give a handle or a support to the notion of justification by outward things (σαρκικά),—how could he have set up infant baptism against the circumcision that continued to be practised by the Jewish Christians? In this case, the dispute carried on with the Judaizing party, on the necessity of circumcision, would easily have given an opportunity of introducing this substitute into the controversy, if it had really existed. The evidence arising from silence on this topic has, therefore, the greater weight."[1] It may be proper to regard the decisions of such men as representing the testimony of the present biblical scholarship on this controverted subject. It is the more proper to accord to them this character, because they proceed from men whose ecclesiastical position would naturally dispose them to adopt a different view; who contend that infant baptism, having been introduced, is allowable, notwithstanding their acknowledgment that it has no scriptural warrant.—εἰ κεκρίκατε, *if ye have judged*, i. e. by admitting her to baptism, and thus declaring their confidence in her. εἰ is preferred to ἐπεί out of modesty.—πιστὴν τῷ κυρίῳ, *trusting to the Lord*, i. e. having faith in him, a believer; comp. 10, 45; 16, 1.—παρεβιάσατο ἡμᾶς, *constrained us;* not that *they* needed so much entreaty, but that *she* could not employ less in justice to her grateful feelings. Some think that they were reluctant to accept the proffered hospitality, lest they should seem to be actuated by mercenary motives. The apostle was by no means indifferent to that imputation (20, 34; 2 Cor. 12, 17. 19); but it is incorrect to say that he never showed himself unmindful of it. He was the guest of Gaius at Corinth (Rom. 16, 23), and was aided repeatedly by Christian friends, when his circumstances made it necessary (24, 23; 28, 10; Phil. 4, 15 sq.).

VERSES 16–18. *Healing of a Demoniac Woman.*

V. 16. ἐγένετο δέ, *Now it came to pass* on a subsequent day (Neand. De Wet.).—εἰς προσευχήν, *unto the place of prayer*, which

[1] Abridged from Ryland's translation. Pflanzung, u. s. w., Band I. p. 278.

may omit the article as definite, because it was the only such place there. But some editors (Grsb. Lchm.) insert τήν. — παιδίσκην . . . . πύθωνος, *a female slave* (Gal. 4, 22) *having the spirit of a pythoness*, i. e. of a diviner who was supposed to have received her gift of prophecy from Apollo. Luke describes the woman according to her reputed character; he does not express here his own opinion of the case. His view agreed no doubt with that of Paul, and what that was we learn from the sequel. To suppose him to acknowledge Apollo as a real existence would contradict 1 Cor. 8, 4. — παρεῖχε, *procured*. Winer (§ 38. 5) says, that the active is more appropriate here than the middle (comp. 19, 24; Col. 4, 1; Tit. 2, 7), because the gain was involuntary on her part. — τοῖς κυρίοις αὐτῆς, *unto her masters*. A slave among the ancients who possessed a lucrative talent was often the joint property of two or more owners. — μαντευομένη, *by divining*, was the heathen term to denote the act. Luke would have said more naturally προφητεύουσα, had he been affirming his own belief in the reality of the pretension.—The woman was in fact a demoniac (see v. 18); and as those subject to the power of evil spirits were often bereft of their reason, her divinations were probably the ravings of insanity. The superstitious have always been prone to attach a mysterious meaning to the utterances of the insane. We may take it for granted that the craft of the managers in this case was exerted to assist the delusion.

V. 17. οὗτοι, κ. τ. λ., *These men are servants*, etc. Some have supposed that she merely repeated what she had heard them declare of themselves, or what she had heard reported of them by others. But the similarity of the entire account to that of the demoniacs mentioned in the Gospels requires us to refer this case to the same class of phenomena; see Matt. 8, 29; Mark 3, 11; Luke 4, 41; 8, 28, etc. According to those passages, we must recognize the acknowledgment here as a supernatural testimony to the mission of Paul and his associates, and to the truth of the gospel which they preached.

V. 18. διαπονηθείς Hesychius defines by λυπηθείς, *being grieved*. With that sense it would refer to Paul's commiseration of the woman's unhappy condition. Taken as in 4, 2, *being indignant*, it would show how he felt to witness such an exhibition of the malice of a wicked spirit; comp. Luke 13, 16. The latter meaning directs the act of the participle to the same object as that of ἐπιστρέψας and εἶπε. It is better to preserve a unity in that respect. — τῷ πνεύματι, *to the spirit*, who is addressed here as distinct from the woman herself. The apostle deals with the case as it actually was, and his knowledge as an inspired teacher would enable him to judge correctly of its character.

VERSES 19-24. *Imprisonment of Paul and Silas.*

V 19. ὅτι ἐξῆλθεν, κ. τ. λ., *that the hope of their gain went forth*, i. e. with the exorcism (De Wet.). — ἐπιλαβόμενοι, κ. τ. λ., *having laid hold upon Paul and Silas.* Luke and Timothy may have been out of reach just at that moment (comp. 17, 5), or may have been spared because they were Greeks. — εἰς τὴν ἀγοράν. In ancient cities the seats of the magistrates were erected commonly in the markets, or near to them. — ἐπὶ τοὺς ἄρχοντας, *before the rulers*, called in the next verse στρατηγοῖς. The chief magistrates in a Roman colony were the *duumviri*, or *quatuorviri*, as the number was not always the same. They frequently took, however, the name of *prætors*, as one of greater honor, and that in Greek was στρατηγοί. It appears, therefore, that the magistrates at Philippi affected this latter title. It is worthy of notice that this is the only occasion in the Acts on which Luke applies the term to the rulers of a city. Here in a Roman colony the government would be modelled naturally after the Roman form; and the manner in which the narrative reveals that circumstance marks its authenticity.

V. 20. Ἰουδαῖοι ὑπάρχοντες, *being Jews.* They say this at the outset, in order to give more effect to the subsequent accusation. No people were regarded by the Romans with such contempt and hatred as the Jews. It is not probable that the Philippians at this time recognized any distinction between Judaism and Christianity; they arraigned Paul and Silas as Jews, or as the leaders of some particular Jewish sect.

V. 21. ἔθη, *customs*, religious practices. — οὐκ ἔξεστιν, κ. τ. λ. The Roman laws suffered foreigners to worship in their own way, but did not allow Roman citizens to forsake their religion for that of other nations. This was the general policy. But beyond that, Judaism had been specially interdicted. "It was a *religio licita* for the Jews," says Neander; "but they were by no means allowed to propagate their religion among the *Roman* pagans; the laws expressly forbade the latter, under severe penalties, to receive circumcision. It was the case, indeed at this time, that the number of proselytes from the pagans was greatly multiplied. This the public authorities sometimes allowed to pass unnoticed; but occasionally severe laws were passed anew to repress the evil." Ch. Hist. Vol. I. p. 89. Still the charge in this instance, though formally false, since they were not making proselytes to Judaism, was true substantially. It was impossible that the gospel should be preached without coming into collision with the Roman laws. The gospel was designed to subvert one system of false religion as well as another. It proposed to save the souls of men without respect to the particular government or political institutions under which they lived. The apostles, in the promulgation of their message, acted under a higher authority than that of the Cæsars; and the opposition between Christianity and heathenism soon became apparent, and led to the persecutions which the Roman power inflicted on the church in the first centuries.

V. 22. καὶ συνεπέστη, κ. τ. λ., *and the multitude rose up together against them.* The prisoners were now in the hands of the officers; hence we are not to think here of any actual onset upon them, but of a tumultuous outburst of rage, a cry on all sides for the punishment of the offenders. The magistrates hasten to obey the voice of the mob. — περιῤῥήξαντες αὐτῶν τὰ ἱμάτια, *having torn off their garments,* not their own, but those of Paul and Silas. The rulers are said to do what they ordered to be done; comp. περιέτεμεν in v. 3. It was customary to inflict the blows on the naked body. Livy (2, 5): "Missique lictores ad sumendum supplicium, nudatos virgis cædunt." — ἐκέλευον ῥαβδίζειν, *ordered to beat with rods.* The verb declares the mode as well as the act. Observe the official brevity of the expression. The imperfect describes the beating in its relation to συνεπέστη, or as taking place under the eye of the narrator. For the latter usage, see W §. 40. 3. d.; Mt. § 505. II. 1. In 2 Cor. 11, 25, Paul says that he was "thrice beaten with rods." This was one of the instances; the other two the history has not recorded. Such omissions prove that Luke's narrative and the Epistles of Paul have not been drawn from each other; that they are independent productions.

V. 23. πολλὰς πληγάς shows that no ordinary rigor would satisfy their exasperated feelings; see also v. 33. The Jewish law restricted the blows to "forty save one." The severity of the punishment among the Romans depended on the equity or caprice of the judge. In regard to the silence of Paul and Silas under this outrage, see on v. 37.

V. 24. ὅς . . . . εἰληφώς, *who having received such a command.* We need not impute to the jailer any gratuitous inhumanity; he obeyed his instructions. — εἰς τὴν ἐσωτέραν φυλακήν, *into the inner prison,* the remotest part, whence escape would be most difficult.

Some confound this prison with the dungeon, which was under ground, and would be differently described. Walch's Dissertatio *de vinculis Apostoli* Paulli treats of this passage. — καὶ τοὺς πόδας, κ. τ. λ., *and secured their feet into the block* (= *nervus*). This was an instrument for torture as well as confinement. It was a heavy piece of wood with holes into which the feet were put, so far apart as to distend the limbs in the most painful manner. Yet in this situation, with their bodies still bleeding from the effect of their recent chastisement, and looking forward to the morrow only in the expectation that it would renew their pains, they could still rejoice; their prison at midnight resounds with the voice of prayer and praise. Neander cites here Tertullian's fine remark: "Nihil crus sentit in nervo, quum animus in cœlo est."

VERSES 25-29. *An Earthquake shakes the Prison.*

V. 25. προσευχόμενοι . . . θεόν, *praying, they praised God.* Their prayers and praises were not distinct acts (hence the form of the expression), but their worship consisted chiefly of thanksgiving, the language of which they would derive more or less from the Psalms. The Hebrews were so familiar with the old Testament, especially its devotional parts, that they clothed their religious thoughts spontaneously in terms borrowed from that source. See, e. g., the songs of Mary and Elizabeth (Luke 1, 39 sq.), and of Zacharias (Luke 1, 67 sq.), and Simeon (Luke 2, 28 sq.). — ἐπηκροῶντο, *listened to them* while they sung. The imperfect describes the act; the aorist would have related it merely.

V. 26. θύραι πᾶσαι. Some ascribe this opening of the doors to the shock of the earthquake; others, more reasonably, to the power which caused the earthquake. — καὶ πάντων, κ. τ. λ., *and the chains of all*, i. e. the prisoners (see v. 28), *were loosened.* ἀνέθη is first aorist passive from ἀνίημι. B. § 108; S. § 81. I. That the other prisoners were released in this manner was, no doubt, miraculous; it was adapted to augment the impression of the occurrence, and to attest more signally the truth of the gospel. That they made no effort to escape may have been owing to the terror of the scene, or to a restraining influence which the author of the interposition exerted upon them.

V. 27. ἔμελλεν, κ. τ. λ., *was about to kill himself.* The jailer adopted this resolution because he knew that his life was forfeited if the prisoners had escaped; comp. 12, 19; 27, 42. — νομίζων . . . . δεσμίους, *supposing the prisoners to have fled*, and to be gone; infin. perfect, because the act though past was connected with the present. W. § 44. 7.

V. 28. φωνῇ μεγάλῃ, *with a voice loud;* see note on 14, 10.— μηδὲν . . . . κακόν, *do thyself no injury.* For the mode and tense, see on 7, 60. How, it has been asked, could Paul have known the jailer's intention? The narrative leaves us in doubt on that point, but suggests various possibilities. It is not certain that the prison was entirely dark (see on v. 29), and the jailer may have stood at that moment where Paul could distinguish his form; or, as Doddridge suggests, he may have heard some exclamation from him, which disclosed his purpose. The fact was revealed to the apostle, if he could not ascertain it by natural means.— ἅπαντες . . . . ἐνθάδε, *we are all here.* We do not know the structure of the prison. The part of it where the apostle was, and the position in which he sat, may have enabled him to see that no one of the prisoners had passed through the open doors; or he may have been divinely instructed to give this assurance.

V. 29. αἰτήσας φῶτα, *having called for lights,* which could be carried in the hand. The noun is neuter and in the plural, not singular (E. V.). The ordinary night-lamps, if such had been kept burning, were fastened perhaps, or furnished only a faint glimmer. φῶτα may be a generic plural, but refers more probably to the jailer's summoning those in his service to procure lights, to enable him to ascertain the condition of the prison. The sequel shows that the whole family were aroused.— προσέπεσε, *fell down,* cast himself at their feet in token of reverence; see Mark 3, 11; Luke 8, 28. He knew that the miracle was on their account.

VERSES 30–34. *Conversion of the Jailer and his Family.*

V. 30. προαγαγὼν αὐτοὺς ἔξω, *having led them forth out,* i. e. of the inner prison into another room, not into his own house; see v. 34.— τί με . . . . ἵνα σωθῶ; *What must I do in order that I may be saved.* Their answer in the next verse shows with what meaning the jailer proposed this question. It cannot refer to any fear of punishment from the magistrates; for he had now ascertained that the prisoners were all safe, and that he was in no danger, from that source. Besides, had he felt exposed to any such danger, he must have known that Paul and Silas had no power to protect him; it would have been useless to come to them for assistance. The question in the other sense appears abrupt, it is true; but we are to remember that Luke has recorded only parts of the transaction. The unwritten history would perhaps justify some such view of the circumstances as this. The jailer is suddenly aroused from sleep by the noise of the earthquake; he sees the doors of the prison open; the thought instantly seizes him,—the prisoners have fled. He knows the rigor of the Roman law, and is on the point of anticipating his doom by self-murder. But the friendly voice of Paul recalls his presence of mind. His thoughts take at once a new direction. He is aware that these men claim to be the servants of God; that they profess to teach the way of salvation. It would be nothing strange if, during the several days or weeks that Paul and Silas had been at Philippi, he had heard the gospel from their own lips, had been one among those at the river-side, or in the market, whom they had warned of their danger, and urged to repent and lay hold of the mercy offered to them in the name of Christ. And now suddenly an event had taken place, which convinces him in a moment that the things which he has heard are realities; it was the last argument, perhaps, which he needed to give certainty to a mind already inquiring, hesitating. He comes trembling, therefore, before Paul and Silas, and asks them to tell him—again, more fully—what he must do to be saved.

V. 31. καὶ σωθήσῃ, κ. τ. λ., *and thou shalt be saved and thy family.* They represent the salvation as ample; it was free not only to him but to all the members of his household who accept the proffered mercy. The apostle includes them, because, as we see from the next verse, they were present and listened with the jailer to the preaching of the gospel. As Meyer remarks, ὁ οἶκος σου belongs in effect to πίστευσον and σωθήσῃ, as well as σύ.

V. 32. καὶ ἐλάλησαν, κ. τ. λ., *and they spake to him the word of the Lord, and to all who were in his house.* This refers to the more particular instruction respecting the way of salvation, which they proceeded to give after the general direction in the preceding verse.—τοῖς ἐν τῇ οἰκίᾳ αὐτοῦ, *those in his family,* cannot embrace infants, because they are incapable of receiving the instruction which was addressed to those whom the expression designates here.

V. 33. παραλαβὼν αὐτούς, *taking them along,* says Howson correctly, implies a change of place. The jailer repaired with Paul and Silas from the outer room (see ἔξω in v. 30) to the water, which he needed for bathing their bodies.—ἔλουσεν ἀπὸ τῶν πληγῶν stands concisely for *washed* and cleansed them *from their stripes.* W. § 47, 5. b. This verb, says Dr. Robinson (Lex. N. T. s. v.), signifies to wash the entire body, not merely a part of it, like νίπτω. Trench says: "νίπτειν and νίψασθαι almost always express the washing *of a part* of the body (the hands in Mark 7, 3, the feet in John 13, 5, the face in Matt. 6, 17, the eyes in John 9, 7); while λούειν, which is not so much 'to wash' as 'to bathe,' and λοῦσθαι, or in common Greek λούεσθαι, 'to bathe one's self,' imply always, not the bathing of a part of the body, but *of the whole;* comp. Heb. 10, 23; Acts 9, 37; 2 Pet. 2, 22; Rev. 1, 5; Plato, Phæd. 115 *a*." To the same effect, see Tittm. Synm. N. T. p. 175.[1] — ἐβαπτίσθη, *was baptized.* The rite may have been performed, says De Wette, in the same fountain or tank in which the jailer had washed them. "Perhaps the water," says Meyer, "was in the court of the house; and the baptism was that of immersion, which formed an essential part of the symbolism of the act (see Rom. 6, 3 sq.)." Ancient houses, as usually built, enclosed a rectangular reservoir or basin (the *impluvium* so called) for receiving the rain which flowed from the slightly inclined roof. Some suggest that they may have used a κολυμβήθρα, or *swimming-bath,* found within the walls of the prison (Grsb. Rosnm. Kuin.). Such a bath was a common appurtenance of houses and public edifices among the Greeks and Romans. Whether the Gangas flowed near the prison so as to be easily accessible, cannot be decided. — καὶ οἱ αὐτοῦ πάντες, *and all his,* are evidently the πᾶσι τοῖς ἐν τῇ οἰκίᾳ αὐτοῦ to whom they had just preached the word, as stated in v. 32.

V. 34. ἀνεγαγών, κ. τ. λ., *having brought them up into his house,* which appears to have been over the prison. — ἠγαλλιάσατο πανοικί, *he rejoiced with all his family,* i. e. he and all his family rejoiced. — πεπιστευκὼς τῷ θεῷ, *having believed in God,* states the object or occasion of their joy (comp. 1 Cor. 14, 18). This act, like that of the verb, is predicated of the jailer's family as well as of himself.

VERSES 35–40. *They are set at Liberty, and depart from Philippi.*

V. 35. τοὺς ῥαβδούχους, *the rod-bearers* (*lictores*), who waited upon Roman magistrates and executed their orders. In the colonies they carried staves, not *fasces* as at Rome. It deserves notice that Luke introduces this term just here. Though applied occasionally to Greek magistrates as bearing the staff of authority, it was properly in this age a Roman designation, and is found here in the right place as denoting the attendants of Roman

[1] Synonyms of the New Testament (p. 216), by Richard Chevenix Trench, King's College, London (New York, 1857).

officers. — ἀπόλυσον, *release them.* The rulers did not command them to leave the city, but expected them, doubtless, to use their liberty for that purpose. It is uncertain how we are to account for this sudden change of disposition towards Paul and Silas. The magistrates may have reflected in the interval on the injustice of their conduct, and have relented; or, possibly, as they were heathen and superstitious, they had been alarmed by the earthquake, and feared the anger of the gods on accout of their inhumanity to the strangers.

V. 36. ἀπήγγειλε, κ. τ. λ., *The jailer reported these words unto Paul,* i. e. from the lictors who, therefore, did not accompany him into the prison. The same verb occurs in v. 38, of the answer which the lictors conveyed to the magistrates. — ὅτι ἀπεστάλκασιν, *that they have sent,* sc. a message, or messengers. — ἐν εἰρήνῃ, *in peace,* unmolested; see on 15, 33. The jailer anticipates their ready acceptance of the offer.

V. 37. ἔφη πρὸς αὐτούς, *said unto them,* the lictors, i. e. by the mouth of the jailer. — δείραντες, κ. τ. λ., *having scourged us publicly uncondemned, men who are Romans.* Almost every word in this reply contains a distinct allegation. It would be difficult to find or frame a sentence superior to it in point of energetic brevity. Both the *lex Valeria* and the *lex Porcia* made it a crime to inflict blows or any species of torture on a Roman citizen. "Facinus est vinciri civem Romanum, scelus verberari, prope parricidium necari." (Cic. in Verr. 5. 66). — δημοσίᾳ. It would have been a crime to have struck them a single blow, even in secret; they had been cruelly scourged in open day, and before hundreds of witnesses. — ἀκατακρίτους. The Roman laws held it to be one of the most sacred rights of the citizen that he should be tried in due form before he was condemned. "Causa cognita multi possunt absolvi; incognita quidem condemnari nemo potest." (Cic. in Verr. 1. 9). Even slaves had an admitted legal, as well as natural, right to be heard in their defence before they were punished. — Ῥωμαίους. In 22, 28, Paul says that he was "free born." In regard to the probable origin of his Roman citizenship, see the note on 22, 25. It appears that Silas possessed the same rights, but it is not known how he obtained them. At first view it may appear surprising that Paul did not avow himself a Roman at the outset, and thus prevent the indignity to which he had been subjected. "But the infliction of it," says Biscoe, "was so hasty, that he had not time to say anything that might make for his defence; and the noise and confusion were so great, that, had he cried out with ever so loud a voice that he was a Roman, he might reasonably believe that he should not be regarded. Seeing also the fury of the multitude (v. 22), it is not improbable he might think it most advisable to submit to the sentence pronounced, however unjust, in order to quiet the people, and prevent a greater evil; for he was in danger of being forced out of the hands of the magistrates, and torn in pieces. But whatever were the true reasons which induced the apostle to be silent, the overruling hand of Providence was herein plainly visible; for the conversion of the jailer and his household was occasioned by the execution of this hasty and unjust sentence." — *καὶ νῦν λάθρα, κ. τ. λ., and do they now send us forth secretly?* Some render *ἐκβάλλουσιν, thrust forth;* which is too strong (comp. 9, 40), and draws away the emphasis from *λάθρα*, to which it belongs. — *οὐ γάρ, No, certainly;* they do not dismiss us in that manner. In this use, *γέ* (resolving *γάρ* into its parts) strengthens the denial, while *ἄρα* shows the dependence of the answer on what precedes: *not according to that,* i. e. *after such treatment.* Klotz (ad Devar. II. p. 242), Winer (§ 53. 8. b), and others, adopt this analysis. — *αὐτοί, they themselves,* instead of sending their servants to us. — In asserting so strongly their personal rights, they may have been influenced in part by a natural sense of justice, and in part by a regard to the necessity of such a vindication of their innocence to the cause of Christ at Philippi. It was important that no stain should rest upon their reputation. It was notorious that they had been scourged and imprisoned as criminals; and if after their departure any one had suspected, or could have insinuated, that possibly they had suffered not without cause, it would have created a prejudice against the truth. It was in their power to save the gospel from that reproach, and they used the opportunity. It may be proper at times to allow the wicked or misguided to trample upon our individual rights and interests if they choose; but those who are "set for the defence of the gospel" owe their good name and their influence to Christ and the church, and have a right to invoke the protection of the laws against any invasion of their means of public usefulness.

V. 38. *ἀνήγγειλαν, reported back;* see on v. 36. — *ἐφοβήθησαν, were afraid.* They had cause for apprehension; comp. 22, 29. A magistrate who punished a Roman citizen wrongfully might be indicted for treason; he was liable to suffer death, and the confiscation of all his property (Grot.).

V. 39. *ἠρώτων, entreated,* begged (3, 3). This was not an unexampled humiliation for a Roman officer. Lucian mentions a case of false imprisonment in which the governor of a province not only acknowledged his error, but paid a large sum of money to those whom he had injured, in order to bribe them to be silent.

V. 40. πρὸς τὴν Λυδίαν, *unto Lydia*, whose guests they were (v. 15), and where the disciples may have been accustomed to meet. — τοὺς ἀδελφούς, *the brethren*, who had been converted at Philippi, and who formed the beginning of the church, afterwards addressed in the Epistle to the Philippians. This church was founded, therefore, about A. D. 52. We have evidence in that letter that no one of all the churches planted by Paul possessed so entirely his confidence, or exhibited the power of the gospel in greater purity. — παρεκάλεσαν, *exhorted*, viz. to be firm, to cleave to the gospel (comp. 11, 23); not *comforted*, which would be too specific for the occasion. — ἐξῆλθον, *they went forth*. The narrator, it will be seen, proceeds now in the third person, and maintains that style as far as 20, 5. Some have inferred from this, that Luke remained at Philippi until Paul's last visit to Macedonia. We find Timothy with the apostle at Berœa (17, 14), but whether he accompanied him at this time, or rejoined him afterwards, cannot be decided. See further, on 17, 10.

CHAPTER XVII.

VERSES 1–4. *They proceed to Thessalonica and preach there.*

V. 1. The place which invited their labors next was *Thessalonica*, about a hundred miles southwest of Philippi. They travelled thither on the great military road which led from Byzantium to Dyrrachium or Aulona, opposite to Brundusium in Italy. It was the Macedonian extension of the Appian way. They could accomplish the journey in three or four days (Wiesl.). — On leaving Philippi, they came first to *Amphipolis*, which was southwest, distant about thirty miles. This place was about three miles from the sea, on the eastern bank of the Strymon, which flowed almost round it, and gave to it its name. — *Apollonia*, their next station was about the same distance southwest from Amphipolis. They remained a night, perhaps, at each of these towns. — *Thessalonica* was a rich, commercial city, near the mouth of the Echedorus, on the Thermaic Gulf, about twenty-eight miles nearly west of Apollonia. It is now called *Saloniki*, having a population of seventy thousand, of whom thirty thousand are Jews. Luke's record almost reminds us of a leaf from a traveller's note book. He mentions the places in their exact order. We turn to the Itinerarium Antonini Augusti (ed. Parth. et Pind. p. 157) and read: From Philippi to Amphipolis, thirty-two miles; from Amphipolis to Apollonia, thirty-two miles; from Apollonia to Thessalonica, thirty-six miles. — ἡ συναγωγή, *the synagogue;* definite because the Jews in that region may have had but one such place of worship. W. § 17. 1.

V. 2. Here again, *according to his custom,* Paul betakes himself first to the Jews; comp. 13, 5. 14; 14. 1. εἰωθός has the construction of a noun, but governs the dative as a verb; comp. Luke 4, 16. The genitive would have been the ordinary case. W. § 31. 7. N. 2. — ἀπὸ τῶν γραφῶν, *from the Scriptures.* He drew the contents of his discourse from that source. W. § 47. p. 333.

V. 3. διανοίγων, sc. τὰς γραφάς, *opening,* unfolding their sense; comp. Luke 24, 32. — παρατιθέμενος, *propounding,* maintaining. — ὅτι τὸν Χριστὸν, κ. τ. λ., *that the Messiah must suffer,* in order to fulfil the Scriptures; comp. 3, 18; Matt. 26, 54. 56; Mark 14, 49. — καὶ ὅτι οὗτος, κ. τ. λ., *and that this one* (viz. he who was to die and rise again) *is the Messiah Jesus* (i. e. the Jesus called Messiah) *whom I announce unto you.* The scope of the argument is this: The true Messiah must die and rise again; Jesus has fulfilled that condition of prophecy, and is, therefore, the promised Messiah; comp. 2, 24 sq.; 13, 27 sq.

V. 4. τινὲς ἐξ αὐτῶν, *certain of them,* i. e. of the Jews; see v. 1. and 2. — προσεκληρώθησαν (as middle), *attached themselves to Paul and Silas* (Olsh. Whl. Rob.). This is the easier sense, and receives support from v. 34 and 14, 4, where we meet with the same thought in like circumstances. Others render *were allotted,* granted to them, as it were by divine favor. This may be the surer philological sense, and is adopted by Winer (§ 39. 2), De Wette, Meyer, and Alford. — γυναικῶν . . . . ὀλίγαι, *and of the first women* (comp. 13, 50) *not a few.* The women were evidently "devout" (σεβομένων) or proselytes (comp. 13, 50), as well as the men; so that all those mentioned as converts in this verse were won to Christianity from the Jewish faith, not from a state of heathenism. But in 1 Thess. 1, 9, Paul speaks as if many of the Thessalonian Christians had been idolaters (ἐπεστρέψατε πρὸς τὸν θεὸν ἀπὸ τῶν εἰδώλων). Hence it is possible, as Paley conjectures, that this verse describes the result of Paul's labors during the three weeks that he preached in the synagogue (v. 2); and that an interval which Luke passes over preceded the events related in v. 5-10.

During this interval the apostle, having been excluded from the synagogue by the bigotry of the Jews, may have preached directly to the heathen. Another opinion is, that he preached to the Gentiles during the week-time, while on the Sabbath he labored for the Jews in their public assemblies (Neand.).

VERSES 5–9. *The Jews accuse Paul and Silas before the Magistrates.*

V. 5. ἀπειθοῦντες before Ἰουδαῖοι (T. R.) lacks support. — τῶν ἀγοραίων, *market-loungers* (*subrostrani, subbasilicani*). Had it been in the East, where such people loiter about the gates, the term would have been inappropriate. It is instructive to observe how true the narrative is to the habits of different nations, though the scene changes so rapidly from one land to another. But why should the Jews seek such coadjutors? The reason is found in their situation: the Jews out of Judea had but little power, and must secure the aid of the native inhabitants. — Ἰάσονος. *Jason* was their host (v. 7), and also a relative of Paul, if he was the one mentioned in Rom. 16, 21. In the latter case, he must have been at Corinth when Paul wrote the Epistle to the Romans. So common a name amounts to little as proof of the relationship. — ἐζήτουν . . . . δῆμον, *sought to bring them unto the people*, and at the same time ἐπὶ τοὺς πολιτάρχας (v. 6), i. e. into the forum, where the magistrates were accustomed to try causes in the presence of the people; comp. 16, 19. They raised a mob (ὀχλοποιήσαντες) in order to arrest the offenders; but εἰς τὸν δῆμον shows that they expected the trial to take place before an orderly assembly.

V. 6. μὴ εὑρόντες, κ. τ. λ., *but not having found them, they dragged Jason and certain brethren before the city rulers.* Instead of changing their plan on failing to apprehend the leaders, they seized upon such others as fell in their way, and treated them as they had designed to treat Paul and Silas. Lange's remark is incorrect that they would have sacrificed the strangers at once to the popular fury, but must be more cautious in dealing with citizens. The ἀδελφούς appear to have been with Jason at the time of the assault; probably they were some of the Thessalonians who had believed. — οὗτοι, *these*, are Paul and Silas, since they are those whom Jason entertained. — καὶ ἐνθάδε πάρεισιν, *are present also here*, as they have been in other places, and for the same purpose. — Here and in v. 8, Luke terms the magistrates of Thessalonica *politarchs;* and his accuracy in this respect is confirmed by an inscription of that place. See Boeckh's Corpus, Vol. II. p. 53, No. 1967. The inscription, which is of the Roman times, gives a list of seven magistrates bearing this title. This is the more worthy of remark because the title is a very rare one, and might easily be confounded with that of *poliarchs,* which is another appellation of magistrates in Greek cities.[1]

V. 7. οὗτοι πάντες, *all these,* viz. Paul, Silas, and their followers. The pronoun includes more than its grammatical antecedent. — τῶν δογμάτων Καίσαρος, i. e. the Roman laws against rebellion or treason. They are said to be *the decrees of the emperor,* i. e. of each successive emperor, because they emanated from him, guarded his rights, and had the support of his authority. The reigning emperor at this time was Claudius. — βασιλέα ἕτερον, *another king,* sovereign; comp. John 19, 15; 1 Pet. 2, 13. The Greeks applied this term to the emperor, though the Romans never styled him *rex.*

V. 8. ἐτάραξαν, κ. τ. λ. The statement alarmed them, because the existence of such a party in their midst would compromise their character for loyalty, and expose them to the vengeance of their Roman masters. See on 19, 40.

V. 9. λαβόντες τὸ ἱκανόν, *having taken bail,* or *security;* said to be a law phrase adopted in Greek for *satis accipere.* What they engaged would naturally be, that, as far as it depended on them, the public peace should not be violated, and that the alleged authors of the disturbance should leave the city (Neand.). Instead of combining the two objects, some restrict the stipulation to the first point (Mey.), while others restrict it to the last (Kuin.). — τῶν λοιπῶν, *the others* who had been brought before the tribunal with Jason (see v. 6). — ἀπέλυσαν αὐτούς, *dismissed them* from custody, viz. the Thessalonians, not the missionaries who had escaped arrest.

VERSES 10–13. *Paul and Silas proceed to Berœa.*

V. 10. εὐθέως, *immediately,* on the evening of the day of the tumult. Paul and Silas had spent three or four weeks at least in Thessalonica (see v. 2), and very possibly some time longer (see on v. 4). Wieseler proposes six or eight weeks as the term of their residence in that city. Being obliged to leave so hastily, Paul was anxious for the welfare and stability of the recent con-

[1] This note is due to President Woolsey, in the New Englander, Vol. X, p 144.

verts, and departed with the intention of returning as soon as the present exasperation against him should be allayed so as to justify it (1 Thess. 2, 18). Subsequent events frustrated this purpose, and under that disappointment he sent Timothy to them to supply his place (1 Thess. 3, 2). It may be added, that while Paul was here he received supplies twice from the church at Philippi; see Phil. 4, 15. 16. From this source, and from his own personal labor, he derived his support, without being dependent at all on the Thessalonians; see 1 Thess. 2, 9; 2 Thess. 3, 8. — διὰ τῆς νυκτός, *during the night*. This secrecy indicates that they were still in danger from the enmity of the Jews; comp. 20, 3. — εἰς Βέροιαν. *Berœa*, now *Verria*, was about forty-five miles southwest of Thessalonica, on the Astræus, a small tributary of the Haliacmon. See Forbg. Handb. III. p. 1061. The modern town has six thousand inhabitants, of whom two hundred are Jews, ten or fifteen hundred Turks, and the rest Greeks.

V. 11. εὐγενέστεροι, *more noble* in their disposition. — For πάσης without the article, see on 4, 29. — τὸ καθ' ἡμέραν, *viz. from day to day*. τό particularizes the repetition or constancy of the act. W. § 20. 3. — εἰ ἔχοι ταῦτα οὕτως, *if these things* taught by Paul *were so*, as he affirmed, i. e. when examined by the Scriptures.

V. 12. Ἑλληνίδων agrees with both γυναικῶν and ἀνδρῶν. The men were Greeks as well as the women. See the note on 2, 42. — For εὐσχημόνων, see 13, 50. — ὀλίγοι may be masculine because ἀνδρῶν is the nearer word, or out of regard to the leading gender.

V. 13. καί, *also*, associates Berœa with Thessalonica. — κἀκεῖ belongs to the participle, not to the verb. They excited the populace *there also*, as they had done in Thessalonica. — Luke's narrative implies that the Jews were somewhat numerous and influential at Berœa. Coins of this city are still extant, and, unlike most other examples of ancient money, have on them no pagan figure or symbol. Akerman suggests (Num. Illustr.) in explanation of this singular fact, that the magistrates may have rejected such devices, as a concession to the feelings of the Jewish population.

VERSES 14. 15. *Paul advances to Athens.*

V. 14. πορεύεσθαι ὡς ἐπὶ τὴν θάλασσαν, *to journey as upon the sea*, i. e. as if with such a purpose. ὡς with ἐπί, εἰς, or πρός denotes design, but leaves it uncertain whether the design be executed, or professed merely. See W. § 65. 9; K. § 290. R. 2; B. § 149. Lachmann would substitute ἕως for ὡς, *as far as unto the sea*, but against the evidence. Some suppose the movement here to have been a feint; that Paul's conductors, having set out ostensibly for the sea, afterward in order to elude pursuit, changed their course, and proceeded to Athens by land (Grot. Bng. Olsh.). But in that event, they would have passed through various important places on the way, and Luke might be expected to name some of them, as he has done in v. 1. The journey by land would have been two hundred and fifty-one Roman miles (Itiner. Anton.). With a fair wind Paul and his party could have sailed from Berœa or the mouth of the Heliaemon to Athens in about three days (Wiesl.); and the probability is, that they took this more expeditious course (Win. De Wet. Wiesl. Mey.). — For an interesting sketch of the places and objects which would be seen on such a voyage, the reader is referred to Howson, I. p. 403 sq. — *Timothy* was last mentioned in 16, 1.

V. 15. οἱ καθιστῶντες, *Those who conducted*, lit. set him along on the journey whether by sea or land. — λαβόντες, *having received* before their departure, rather than *receiving* (E. V.), which might imply that they returned in consequence of the command. — ὡς τάχιστα, *as soon as possible* (K. § 239. R. 2. d), i. e. after performing the service for which they had remained. Whether they rejoined the apostle at Athens, or not, is uncertain; see on the next verse.

VERSES 16–18. *How he was affected by the Idolatry at Athens.*

V. 16. ἐκδεχομένου αὐτούς, *while he was waiting for them*, viz. Silas and Timothy. The most natural inference from 1 Thess. 3, 1, is that Timothy, at least, soon arrived, in accordance with Paul's expectation, but was immediately sent away by the apostle to Thessalonica. As Silas is not mentioned in that passage, it has been supposed that he may have failed for some reason to come at this time, or, if he came, that, like Timothy, he may have left again at once, but for a different destination; which last circumstance would account for the omission of his name in that passage of the Epistle. Our next notice of them occurs in 18, 5, where they are represented as coming down from Macedonia to Corinth; and we may suppose either that they went to that city directly from Berœa, without having followed Paul to Athens, or that they returned from Athens to Macedonia, and proceeded from there to Corinth. The latter view assumes that Luke has passed over the intermediate journey in silence. Such omissions are entirely consistent with the character of a fragmentary history like that of the Acts. Still other combinations are possible. — παρωξύνετο . . . . ἐν αὐτῷ, *his spirit was aroused in him*, comp. 15, 39; 1 Cor. 13, 5. This verb represents the apostle as deeply moved with a feeling allied to that of indignation, at beholding such a profanation of the worship due to God as forced itself upon his view on every side. — κατείδωλον means, not *given to idolatry*, but *full of idols*. The word is otherwise unknown to the extant Greek, but is formed after a common analogy, e. g. κατάμπελος, κατάδενδρος, κατάφοβος, etc. The epithet applies to the city, not directly to the inhabitants. A person could hardly take his position at any point in ancient Athens, where the eye did not range over temples, altars, and statues of the gods almost without number. Petronius says satirically, that it was easier to find a god at Athens than a man. Another ancient writer says that some of the streets were so crowded with those who sold idols, that it was almost impossible for one to make his way through them. Pausanias declares that Athens had more images than all the rest of Greece put together. Wetstein quotes Xenophon, Isocrates, Cicero, Livy, Strabo, Lucian, and others, as bearing the same testimony. Luke, therefore, has not applied this epithet at random. The Greek language offered to him a hundred other terms which would have stated what was true in relation to a heathen city; but we see that he has chosen among them all the very one which describes the precise external aspect of Athens that would be the first to strike the eye of a stranger like Paul. This mark of accuracy in the writer, those obliterate, or very nearly obliterate, who make the expression refer to the devotion of the Athenians to idolatry.[1]

V. 17. The apostle's ordinary course was to address himself exclusively at first to his own countrymen and the Jewish proselytes. At Athens he departed from this rule. — οὖν, *therefore*, i. e. being aroused by the sight of so much idolatry. The spectacle around him urges him to commence preaching simultaneously to Jews and Greeks. Some adopt a looser connection: *therefore*, i. e. being at Athens (De Wette). Some restrict οὖν to the second clause: his zeal impelled him to preach in the market. It is arbitrary to divide the sentence in that manner. — ἐν τῇ ἀγορᾷ, *in the market*, i. e. of the city; not the one in which he happened to be (Mey.). It is generally admitted that the Athenians had properly but one market,

[1] Hermann (ad Vig. p. 638, ed. 1824) turns aside to correct this error: "Κατείδωλος πόλις, Actor. Apost. 17, 16, non est, uti quidam opinantur, *simulacris dedita urbs*, sed *simulacris referta*."

although Leake has shown it to be probable, that, "during the many centuries of Athenian prosperity, the boundaries of the Agora, or at least of its frequented part, underwent considerable variation."[1] The notices of ancient writers are somewhat vague as to its course and extent; but it is agreed that the site was never so changed as to exclude the famous στοὰ ποικίλη, which, according to Forchammer's Plan, stood off against the Acropolis on the west. In this porch, as is well known, the philosophers, rhetoricians, and others were accustomed to meet for conversation and discussion; and hence it lay entirely in the course of things that some of these men should fall, as Luke states, in the way of the apostle.

V. 18. τῶν Ἐπικουρείων. The *Epicureans* were the "minute philosophers," the Greek Sadducees of the age; they admitted the existence of gods, but regarded them as indolent beings, who paid no attention to the actions or affairs of men; they had no faith in a providence, or in accountability, or in any retribution to come. Their great practical dogma was, that a wise man will make the most of all the means of enjoyment within his reach. Epicurus, the founder of the sect, had taught a higher idea of happiness; but his followers in the Roman age, and earlier still, had reduced it to the grossest sensualism. The frivolous spirit of this sect, appears perhaps in the first of the questions addressed to Paul. — τῶν Στωϊκῶν. The *Stoics* were distinguished in some respects for a more reflecting turn of mind; they extolled virtue, insisted on subjecting the passions to reason, and urged the importance of becoming independent of the ordinary sources of enjoyment and suffering. Some of the most admired characters of antiquity belonged to this school. But the Stoics were essentially fatalists in their religious views; they were self-complacent, boasted of their indifference to the world, and affected a style of morals so impracticable as to render them almost necessarily insincere or hypocritical. In Epicureanism it was man's sensual nature which arrayed itself against the claims of the gospel; in Stoicism it was his self-righteousness and pride of intellect; and it is difficult to say which of the two systems rendered its votaries the more indisposed to embrace the truth. It might have seemed to the credit of Christianity, had it been represented as gaining at least a few proselytes, in this centre of Grecian refinement, from the ranks of its scholars and philosophers; but Luke has no such triumphs to record. He relates the case as it was; the apostle was ridiculed, his message

[1] Athens and Demi, p. 217.

was treated with contempt. — συνέβαλλον αὐτῷ, *conversed* or *disputed with him* (E V., De Wet.), comp. 4, 15; not *met with him* as in 20, 14 (Bng. Mey.); since the form as imperf. applies better to a discussion, than to a single contact of the parties such as Luke mentions here. καὶ ἔλεγον agrees with either sense. — τί ἂν θέλοι, κ. τ. λ., *what would this babbler say*, does he mean to say? ἂν sharpens the taunt: if he has any meaning (Mey.). See W. § 42. 1; C. § 604. σπερμολόγος denotes strictly a seed-gatherer, and then, as used here, one who picks up and retails scraps of knowledge without sense or aim, *an idle prater*. — ξένων δαιμονίων, *foreign gods*, hitherto unknown to us. As the expression is cited from the mouth of the Greeks, we are to attach to it their sense of δαιμονίον, which was different from that of the Jews. The noun may be plural, because it refers to Jesus as an example of the class or category (see W. § 27. 2; S. § 95. 2); or it may be founded on what Paul had said to them concerning God, especially his agency in raising up Christ from the dead (comp. v. 31). The latter is the best view (De Wet.). Both Jesus and the God of whom they now heard were new to them. Many of the older critics, and some of the more recent, explain the plural as embracing ἀνάστασιν, supposing the Athenians to have understood Paul to speak of some goddess when he preached to them the resurrection. But one can hardly conceive that the apostle would express himself so obscurely on this subject as to give them any occasion for falling into so gross a mistake; and we are not authorized by any intimation in the narrative to impute to them a wilful perversion of his language.

VERSES 19–21. *Paul repairs to Mars' Hill to explain his Doctrine.*

V. 19. ἐπιλαβόμενοί τε αὐτοῦ, *and taking hold upon him*, not with violence, which would be at variance with the general spirit of the transaction, but rather by the hand, for the purpose of leading him onward; comp. 9, 27; Mark 8, 23; Luke 9, 47. — ἐπὶ τὸν Ἄρειον πάγον, *upon Mars' Hill*, i. e. the top of it; comp. 10, 9; Matt. 4, 5; 24, 16, etc. The Areiopagus, whither Paul was now brought, was a rocky eminence a little to the west of the Acropolis. See Leake's Athens, p. 165. The object of the movement was to place the apostle in a situation where he could be heard by the multitude to greater advantage. The following is Dr. Robinson's description of this important locality: "This is a narrow, naked ridge of limestone rock, rising gradually from the northern end, and terminating abruptly on the south, over against the west end of the Acropolis, from which it bears about north; being separated from it by an elevated valley. This southern end is fifty or sixty feet above the said valley; though yet much lower than the Acropolis. On its top are still to be seen the seats of the judges and parties, hewn in the rock; and towards the southwest is a descent by a flight of steps, also cut in the rock into the valley below. Standing on this elevated platform, surrounded by the learned and the wise of Athens, the multitude perhaps being on the steps and the vale below, Paul had directly before him the far-famed Acropolis, with its wonders of Grecian art; and beneath him, on his left, the majestic Theseium, the earliest and still most perfect of Athenian structures; while all around, other temples and altars filled the whole city, On the Acropolis, too, were the three celebrated statues of Minerva; one of olive-wood; another of gold and ivory in the Parthenon, the masterpiece of Phidias; and the colossal statue in the open air, the point of whose spear was seen over the Parthenon by those sailing along the gulf." Bibl. Res. I. p. 10 sq. The reader would do well to consult the admirable article on *Athens* in Smith's Dictionary of Greek and Roman Geography. He will find a Plan of that city and a view of the Acropolis restored as seen from the Areiopagus, in Mr. Howson's work. To understand the peculiar boldness and power of the speech, we must have distinctly before us the objects and scenes which met the apostle's view at the moment. — Some translate ἐπὶ τὸν Ἄρειον πάγον, *before the Areiopagus* (comp. 16, 19; 18, 12; 24, 8), and maintain that Paul was arraigned at this time before the celebrated court of that name, and underwent a formal trial on the charge of having attempted to change the religion of the state. But this opinion rests entirely upon two or three expressions, which, like the one just noticed, are ambiguous in themselves; while in other respects the entire narrative, as well as the improbability of such a procedure, testify against the idea. First, we find here no trace whatever of any thing like the formality of a legal process. Secondly, the professed object of bringing the apostle ἐπὶ τὸν Ἄρειον πάγον was to ascertain from him what his opinions were, not to put him on his defence for them before they were known. Thirdly, the manner in which the affair terminated would have been a singular issue for a judicial investigation in the highest court of Athens. And, finally, the speech which Paul delivered on the occasion was precisely such as we should expect before a promiscuous assembly; whereas, if he had stood now as an accused person before a legal tribunal, his plea has most strangely failed to connect itself, at any single point, with that peculiarity of his situation. It proves nothing in regard to the question, to show that the court of the Areiopagus had powers (that is admitted) which would have given to it jurisdiction in the case of Paul, supposing that he had been charged at this time with subverting the established worship; since the narrative on which we must rely for our information as to what was done, not only contains no evidence that the Athenians took this serious view of his doctrine, but ascribes their eagerness to hear him to a mere love of novelty; see v. 21. Calvin, Kuinoel, Neander, Winer, Olshausen, De Wette, Meyer, Baur, Doddridge, and the best critics generally, at present, reject the opinion that Paul was carried before the Areiopagus for a judicial examination. The authority of Chrysostom, among the ancient critics, stands in favor of it. A few among the Germans, as Hess, Hemsen, Scholz, follow on that side; except that some of them would say (this is true of Hemsen), that the Areiopagus was called together, not exactly to try the apostle, but to hear from him some account of his doctrine. "The process," says Wordsworth, "may have been only a preparatory inquiry, an ἀνάκρισις. They who laid hands on him, may have intended to frighten the apostle by the judicial associations of the place, and to drive him out of the city." Most of our English commentaries assume that Paul was arraigned at this time as a religious innovator. The other ambiguous expressions, which have been supposed to favor this view, will be noticed in their place. — δυνάμεθα γνῶναι, *Can we know?* Would it not have been an excess even of the Attic politeness, to have interrogated a prisoner at the bar in this manner? The object, too, of the inquiry, as defined by the accompanying terms, shows clearly that they did not regard him as occupying that position.

V. 20. ξενίζοντα, *surprising*, since the things were foreign, unheard of before. — εἰσφέρεις . . . . ἡμῶν, *thou bringest to our ears.* This phrase, drawn from common life, has an appearance of reality in this connection. — τί ἂν θέλοι. See on v. 18. τί in apposition with ταῦτα should be noticed. It is not precisely like the plural. "The singular τί," says Krüger (Gr. § 61. 8. 2), "may stand in such connections as τί ταῦτά ἐστι, when the question is, what sort of a whole, what combined result, do the particulars form?"

V. 21. The object of this verse is to explain why they addressed to him such inquiries. Their motive for proposing them was that their curiosity might be gratified. — Ἀθηναῖοι δὲ πάντες, *now all Athenians.* The omission of the article unites the characteristic more closely with the name, as its invariable attendant. K. § 246. 5. a. — *οἱ ἐπιδημοῦντες*, i. e. the foreigners permanently resident there (comp. 2, 10); *unde iidem mores*, as Bengel remarks. — *εἰς οὐδέν . . . . εὐκαίρουν*, *spent their leisure for nothing else.* This sense of the verb is a later usage. Lob. ad Phryn. p. 125. The imperfect does not exclude the continued existence of the peculiarity, but blends the reference to it with the history. See similar examples in 27, 8; John 11, 18; 18, 1; 19, 14. K. § 256. 4. a; C. 567. γ. — *καινότερον*, *newer*, sc. than before. W. § 35. 4; S. § 118. 4; K. § 323. R. 7. The comparative or the positive form of the adjective could be used in this phrase; but the former characterizes their state of mind more forcibly than the latter. Bengel has hit the point of the idiom: "Nova statim sordebant; *noviora quærebantur.*" — It is worth remarking, that this singular scene of setting up the apostle to speak for the entertainment of the people occurs, not at Ephesus, or Philippi, or Corinth, but at Athens; not only the only place, in all his journeying, where Paul met with such a reception, but just the place where the incident arises in perfect harmony with the disposition and the tastes of the people. We know, from the testimony of ancient writers, that this fondness for hearing and telling some new thing, which Luke mentions, was a notorious characteristic of the Athenians. Their great orator reproaches them with the same propensity: *βούλεσθε, εἰπέ μοι, περιϊόντες αὐτῶν πυνθάνεσθαι κατὰ τὴν ἀγοράν· λέγεταί τι καινόν;* (Philipp. I. 43). The entirely incidental manner in which the exemplification of this trait comes forth in the narrative here, bears witness to its authenticity

Outline of the Course of Thought.

The speech which Paul delivered at this time is remarkable for its adaptation, not only to the outward circumstances under which he spoke, but to the peculiar mental state of his auditors. De Wette pronounces it "a model of the apologetic style of discourse." "The address of Paul before this assembly," says Neander, "is a living proof of his apostolic wisdom and eloquence; we perceive here how the apostle, according to his own expression, could become also a heathen to the heathen, that he might win the heathen to a reception of the gospel." "The skill," says Hemsen, "with which he was able to bring the truth near to the Athenians, deserves admiration. We find in this discourse of Paul nothing of an ill-timed zeal, nothing like declamatory pomp; it is distinguished for clearness, brevity, coherence, and simplicity of representation." Dr. Robinson, speaking under the impression produced on his mind by a personal survey of the scene, says that, "masterly" as the address is, as we read it under ordinary circumstances, "the full force and energy and boldness of the apostle's language can be duly felt only when one has stood upon the spot."[1] The writer can never forget the emotions of thrilling interest, which were excited in his own mind, as he read and rehearsed the discourse, on that memorable rock. — We have first the introduction, which, in the technical language of rhetoric, is eminently conciliatory. The apostle begins by acknowledging and commending the respect of the Athenians for religion (v. 22. 23). He states next, at the close of v. 23, his design, which is to guide their religious instincts and aspirations to their proper object, i. e. to teach them what God is, his nature and attributes, in opposition to their false views and practices as idolaters. He goes on, then, in pursuance of this purpose, to announce to them, first, that God is the Creator of the outward, material universe (v. 24); secondly, that he is entirely independent of his creatures, having all-sufficiency in himself (v. 25); thirdly, that he is the Creator of all mankind, notwithstanding their separation into so many nations and their wide dispersion on the earth (v. 26); and, fourthly, that he has placed men, as individuals and nations, in such relations of dependence on himself as render it easy for them to see that he is their Creator and sovereign Disposer, and that they are the creatures of his power and goodness; and that it is their duty to seek and serve him (v. 27. 28). The ground has thus been won for the application which follows. At this point of the discourse, stretching forth his hand, as we may well suppose, towards the gorgeous images within sight, he exclaims: "We ought not, therefore, to suppose that the Deity is like unto gold, or silver, or stone, sculptured by the art and device of men" (v. 29). And that which men ought not to do, they may not safely do any longer. It was owing to the forbearance of God that they had been left hitherto to pursue their idolatry without any signal manifestation of his displeasure;

[1] Some object that the speech has been over-praised, because Paul did not succeed in bringing it to a formal close. The astonishment which one feels as he reads the address is not that the speaker was interrupted at length, when he came to announce to the Athenians the peculiar doctrines of Christianity, but that he could command their attention so long, while he bore down with such effect on their favorite opinions and prejudices, exposed their errors, and arraigned them as guilty of the grossest inconsistency and absurdity of conduct.

they were *now* required to repent of it and forsake it (v. 30), because a day of righteous judgment awaited them, which had been rendered certain by the resurrection of Christ (v. 31). Here their clamors interrupted him. It is not difficult, perhaps, to conjecture what he would have added. It only remained, in order to complete his well-known circle of thought on such occasions, that he should have set forth the claims of Christ as the object of religious hope and confidence, that he should have exhorted them to call on his name and be saved. — It will be seen, therefore, by casting the eye back, that we have here all the parts of a perfect discourse, viz. the exordium, the proposition or theme, the proof or exposition, the inferences and application. It is a beautiful specimen of the manner in which a powerful and well-trained mind, practised in public speaking, conforms spontaneously to the rules of the severest logic. One can readily believe, looking at this feature of the discourse, that it was pronounced by the man who wrote the Epistles to the Romans and Galatians, where we see the same mental characteristics so strongly reflected. As we must suppose, at all events, that the general scheme of thought, the *nexus* of the argument, has been preserved, it does not affect our critical judgment of the discourse whether we maintain that it has been reported in full, or that a synopsis only has been given. On this point opinions differ.

VERSES 22–31. *The Speech of Paul on Mars' Hill.*

V. 22. σταθείς. Paul spoke of course in the open air. A skilful hand has pictured to us the scene. "He stood on that hill in the centre of the Athenian city, and with a full view of it. The temple of the Eumenides was immediately below him, and if he looked to the east, he beheld the Propylæa of the Acropolis fronting him, and the Parthenon rising above him; and on his left the bronze colossus of Minerva, the champion of Athens, and the temple of Victory to the right; behind him was the temple of Theseus; and a countless multitude of smaller temples and altars in the Agora and Ceramicus below him." Wordsworth, p. 85. See also his "Athens and Attica," Ch. XI. — ἐν μέσῳ τοῦ Ἀρείου πάγου could be said of a place or an assembly. It is one of the ambiguous expressions adverted to above (p. 281), which leave it uncertain whether Ἀρείου πάγου is to be understood of the hill or the court assembled there. — ἄνδρες Ἀθηναῖοι. The remark just made is to be repeated here. It is the style of address which Paul would necessarily use in speaking to a concourse of Athenians; and at the same time, he might use it in speaking before judges. In the latter case, however, the Greeks oftener said ὦ ἄνδρες δικασταί. See Stalb. Plat. Apol. 17. A.—κατὰ πάντα, *in every respect*, as it were, in every possible mode of exhibition.—ὡς δεισιδαιμονεστέρους ὑμᾶς θεωρῶ, *as* (i. e. those who correspond to this character) *more religious*, sc. than others, *I see you* (De Wet. Win.). See W. § 35. 4. For the suppressed term of the comparison, see on v. 21. Josephus (Contr. Ap. 2. 11) calls the Athenians τοὺς εὐσεβεστάτους τῶν Ἑλλήνων. See other testimonies in Wetstein. δεισιδαιμονεστέρους (a *vox media*) may signify also *more superstitious*. It is improbable, as a matter of just rhetoric, that the apostle employed it in that reproachful sense at the outset of his remarks. That he used it in a good sense is evident for another reason. "He proceeds," says Neander, "to deduce their seeking after God (which he doubtless considered as something good) from this δεισιδαιμονία (comp. 25, 19), or religious propensity, so prevalent among the Athenians. He announced himself as one who would guide their δεισιδαιμονία, not rightly conscious of its object and aim, to a state of clear self-consciousness by a revelation of the object to which it thus ignorantly tended."

V. 23. καὶ ἀναθεωρῶν . . . . βωμόν, *and closely observing the objects of your religious veneration, I found also an altar.* σεβάσματα denotes, not acts of worship, devotions (E. V.), but temples, images, altars, and the like. It is a generic term, under which καί arranges βωμόν as one of the class.—ἐπεγέγραπτο (pluperf.), *had been inscribed*, includes the present, and is to be explained like the imperfect in v. 21.—ἀγνώστῳ θεῷ, *to an unknown God.* "That there was, at least, one altar at Athens with this inscription," says Meyer, "would appear as historically certain from this passage itself, even though other testimonies were wanting, since Paul appeals to a fact of his own observation, and that, too, in the presence of the Athenians themselves." But the existence of such altars at Athens is well attested by competent witnesses. Philostratus, in his Life of Apollonius (6. 2), says: σωφρονέστερον περὶ πάντων θεῶν εὖ λέγειν καὶ ταῦτα Ἀθήνησιν, οὗ καὶ ἀγνώστων θεῶν βωμοὶ ἵδρυνται, i. e. *It is more discreet to speak well of all the gods, and especially at Athens, where are erected altars also of unknown gods.* Pausanias, in his Description of Attica (1. 1), says that such altars (βωμοὶ θεῶν ἀγνώστων) existed at Phaleron, one of the harbors of Athens. It has been made a question, how we are to understand the use of the plural in these passages; whether as referring to the number of the altars on which the inscription occurred, or to the number of the gods to whom the altars were dedicated. Some have assumed the latter as the correct view; and have said that Paul has arbitrarily changed the plural into the singular, in order to accommodate the fact to his purpose; or even that the writer, by this inaccuracy, has betrayed himself as a person who had no direct knowledge of the circumstances which he professes to relate. But even if the inscription on these altars was in the plural, it does not follow that Paul may not have found one having the language which he recites. Here would be Luke's positive testimony to the fact, and that outweighs the mere silence of other writers. Such appears to be Bengel's view. Again, it would not follow that he has necessarily misrepresented the sense, admitting that he may have substituted the singular for the plural. The heathen writers often employed θεοί to convey the general idea of divine power, providence, deity, and the like.[1] With that meaning, the plural could be relinquished for the singular, or the singular for the plural, just as an individual pleased. Here the apostle might have preferred θεῷ, merely for the sake of its stricter *formal* accordance with the doctrine which he was about to advance. Kuinoel appears at a loss to decide whether the plural in the case under remark has reference to the number of the altars, or to that of the gods. Some, as Calvin and Olshausen, apparently concede that Paul deviated from the strict form of the inscription, but deny that he violated its proper import, or availed himself of any unworthy artifice. — But even the appearance of a difficulty here vanishes entirely, when we give to the language of Philostratus and Pausanias the interpretation, which is beyond any reasonable doubt the correct one. Winer states his view of the case thus: "It by no means follows from the passages (of the writers above named), that each single one of the altars mentioned by them had the inscription ἀγνώστοις θεοῖς in the plural, but more naturally that each one separately was dedicated ἀγνώστῳ θεῷ; but this singular the narrators were obliged to change into the plural, because they spoke of all those altars in a collective way. It appears, therefore, that there were several altars in different places at Athens with the inscription ἀγνώστῳ θεῷ." See his Realw. I. p. 111. Such is the decision, also, of Eichhorn, Hess, Hemsen, Meyer, De Wette, and others. It should be added that several of the older commentators render ἀγνώστῳ θεῷ, *to the unknown God*, supposing the God of the Jews, i. e. Jehovah, to be meant. Such

[1] For examples of this interchange, see the passages collected by Pfanner in his Systema Theologiæ Gentilis Purioris, p. 102, and elsewhere.

a view mistranslates the Greek, and violates all historical probability. — The precise historical origin of the altars at Athens bearing this inscription has been disputed. The conjectures are various. One is, that they were very ancient, and that it was at length forgotten to whom they had been originally built; and that the words in question were placed on them at a later period, to apprise the people that it was unknown to what gods they belonged. If that was their character, it is not easy to see what proper point of connection the apostle could have found for his remark with such a relic of sheer idolatry. Another is, that, in some time or times of public calamity, the Athenians, not knowing what god they had offended, whether Minerva or Jupiter or Mars, erected these altars so as to be sure of propitiating the right one. The same objection may be made as before; since their ignorance in this case relates merely to the identity of the god whom they should conciliate, and involves no recognition of any power additional to their heathen deities. The most rational explanation is unquestionably that of those who suppose these altars to have had their origin in the feeling of uncertainty, inherent, after all, in the minds of the heathen, whether their acknowledgment of the superior powers was sufficiently full and comprehensive; in their distinct consciousness of the limitation and imperfection of their religious views, and their consequent desire to avoid the anger of any still unacknowledged god who might be unknown to them. That no deity might punish them for neglecting his worship, or remain uninvoked in asking for blessings, they not only erected altars to all the gods named or known among them, but, distrustful still lest they might not comprehend fully the extent of their subjection and dependence, they erected them also to any other god or power that might exist, although as yet unrevealed to them. — No one can say that this explanation ascribes too much discernment to the heathen. Not to insist on other proofs, such expressions as the comprehensive address, — *At o deorum quicquid in cœlo regit* (Horat. Epod. 5. 1); the oft-used formula in the prayers of the Greeks and Romans, *Si deo, si deæ;* and the superstitious dread, which they manifested in so many ways, of omitting any deity in their invocations, prove the existence of the feeling to which reference has been made. Out of this feeling, therefore, these altars may have sprung; because the supposition is so entirely consistent with the genius of polytheistic heathenism; because the many-sided religiousness of the Athenians would be so apt to exhibit itself in some such demonstration; and, especially, because Paul could then appeal with so much effect to such an avowal of the insufficiency of heathenism, and to such a testimony so borne, indirect, yet significant, to the existence of the one true God. — Under these circumstances, an allusion to one of these altars by the apostle would be equivalent to his saying to the Athenians thus: "You are correct in acknowledging a divine existence beyond any which the ordinary rites of your worship recognize; there is such an existence. You are correct in confessing that this Being is unknown to you; you have no just conceptions of his nature and perfections." He could add then with truth, ὃν οὖν . . . . καταγγέλλω ὑμῖν, *Whom, therefore, not knowing, ye worship, this one I announce unto you.* The inverted order gives point to the declaration. ἀγνοοῦντες has the same object as the verb, and means *having no just knowledge* of him whom they worshipped; not *ignorantly*, as if they did not know whither their worship was directed. The word points back evidently to ἀγνώστῳ. Later editors read ὃ . . . . τοῦτο, instead of ὅν . . . . τοῦτον; in which case θεῷ in the inscription would be taken more abstractly as a divine power. The external evidence is not decisive. Meyer defends the common reading in his first edition, and the other in his second. The personal sense of θεῷ may have been thought to concede too much to heathenism, and so have caused the pronouns to be changed. εὐσεβεῖτε has seemed to some a strong term, as the cognate words in the New Testament always express the idea of true piety; but the term occurs further only in 1 Tim. 5, 4, and denotes there, not the exercise of piety, but of something merely kindred to it, filial reverence. It needs only a similar modification to adapt it to the use required here.

V. 24. The God whom Paul announced is the Maker of all things, and, as such, necessarily distinct from their false gods. That is the point of connection between this verse and the preceding. — οὗτος . . . . ὑπάρχων, *this one* (by his right as Creator) *being the Lord*, Sovereign, *of heaven and earth.* It was self-evident, therefore, that he was not to be confounded with any of their idols, whose existence was limited by the space which they occupied. — χειροποιήτοις, *made with hands*, is contrasted with ὁ ποιήσας . . . . ἐν αὐτῷ. — ἐν ναοῖς. The statues or images were kept in the recesses of the temple. — κατοικεῖ. The mass of the heathen in practice made no difference between the symbol and its object; the block was the god (comp. 19, 26).

V. 25. The apostle illustrates the character of the true God still further, by another contrast between him and the deities of the heathen. He is independent of his creatures; he needs nothing from them; they can earn no merit by serving him. — οὐδὲ . . . . θεραπεύεται, *and* (after a preceding negative) *he is not ministered unto by human hands*, or *hands of men*. ἀνθρωπίνων is a more correct reading, than ἀνθρώπων (T. R.). The verb here implies more than mere worship. The heathen considered it meritorious to lavish wealth on the temples and shrines of their idols; they brought to them costly gifts, and even offerings of food and drink, as if they stood in need of such things, and could be laid under obligation to their worshippers. The prayer of Chryses, priest of Apollo, in Il. 1. 37 sq., expresses the true spirit of heathenism in this respect:

> "If e'er with wreaths I hung thy sacred fane,
> Or fed the flames with fat of oxen slain,
> God of the silver bow! thy shafts employ,
> Avenge thy servant, and the Greeks destroy."

— προςδεομενος τινος, *as if needing something besides*, i. e. (note the compound) out of himself as necessary to his perfection. — αὐτὸς διδούς, *since he himself gives*. αὐτός is emphatic as opposed to the idea that his creatures are able to give to him. — τὰ πάντα, *the whole*, i. e. of the things which they enjoy. In such an expression, τά restricts the adjective to the class of objects intimated by the preceding words or the context. Some editors omit the article here. Compare Rom. 8, 32; 1 Cor. 9, 22; Phil. 3, 8, etc. But in most of these passages, too, the manuscripts fluctuate.

V. 26. ἐποίησέ τε, κ. τ. λ., *and he made of one blood every nation of men that they should dwell.* This is the more obvious view of the construction, and is the one which has been generally adopted. Yet several of the best critics (Kuin. De Wet. Mey. Alf.) regard ποιεῖν here as an instance of its use with an accusative and infinitive, like that in Matt. 5, 32; Mark 7, 37, and translate: *and he caused every nation of men* (sprung) *from one blood to dwell.* κατοικεῖν connects itself more easily in this way, it is true, with the rest of the sentence; but the facility thus gained renders the expression hard at ἐξ ἑνὸς αἵματος, so that we must supply a word to make the thought flow smoothly. The main idea beyond question is, that God has created the entire human race from a common stock; and the more prominent way, therefore, in which the translation first stated brings forward this proposition, appears to me to be a reason for preferring it. It is an objection to the other mode, that it assigns a too subordinate place to the principal thought. But why does the apostle single out thus the universal brotherhood of the race? Olshausen says it was intended as a reproof to the Athenians for their contempt of the Jews. Meyer, Neander, De Wette, and others, consider it as directed essentially against the polytheism of the heathen. If all are the children of a common parent, then the idea of a multiplicity of gods from whom the various nations have derived their origin, or whose protection they specially enjoy, must be false. The doctrine of the unity of the race is closely interwoven with that of the unity of the divine existence. This more comprehensive view of the meaning, however, does not exclude the other; since, if all nations have the same creator, it would at once occur that nothing can be more absurd than the feeling of superiority and contempt with which one affects to look down upon another. As the apostle had to encounter the prejudice which was entertained against him as a Jew, his course of remark was doubly pertinent, if adapted at the same time to remove this hinderance to a candid reception of his message. — κατοικεῖν is the infinitive of design. The various lands which the different families of mankind occupied, with all the advantages connected with their position, God had assigned to them; comp. Deut. 32, 8; Ps. 115, 16. Yea, he had proceeded from the very first with a view to their welfare. He designed, in creating men, that they should inhabit and possess the earth as their own; that they should all of them enjoy the manifold blessings allotted to them in the various places of their abode. It was to him that they were indebted for what they enjoyed, and not to accident, or their own enterprise, or the favor of some imaginary god. The remark, made as applicable to all lands, has its justification in the fact, that, notwithstanding the inequalities which diversify the condition of nations, they have severally their peculiar advantages; it is natural for every people to esteem their own country, in some respects at least, as the best.[1] But the remark was specially aimed, beyond doubt, at the feeling of self-congratulation with which the Athenians were prone to contemplate the peculiar felicity of their own position, their national renown, their past and present prosperity. This view of the meaning prepares the way for the thought which is next introduced. — ὁρίσας . . . . τῆς κατοικίας αὐτῶν, *having fixed the appointed seasons and limits of their abode.* The second participle repeats the idea of the first, not

[1] Tacitus has recognized this principle in his fine remark (Germ. § 2), — "Informem terris, asperam cœlo, *nisi si patria sit.*"

superfluously, but with the evident effect of affirming it more strongly. The approved reading is προστεταγμένους, rather than προτεταγμένους (T. R.). The apostle, by adding this, admonishes the Athenians that they, like every other people, had not only received their peculiar advantages from the common Creator, but that they could hold them only during the continuance of his good-will and favor. In assigning to the nations their respective abodes, he had fixed both the *seasons* of their prosperity and the *limits* of their territory, i. e. it was he who decided *when* and *how long* they should flourish, and *how far* their dominion should extend. We have the same idea exactly in Job 12, 23. The remark was adapted both to rebuke their spirit of self-elation, and to warn them of the danger of slighting a message from Him who had their destiny so perfectly at his command. Some explain these last words as referring to the limits which God has assigned to the lives of men individually: they have their appointed seasons and bounds, beyond which they cannot pass. But that idea lies out of the present circle of view, as the subject of discourse here relates to nations and not to individuals. It is also philologically inadmissible; since αὐτῶν can naturally refer to ἀνθρώπων only as connected with πᾶν ἔθνος. — The anti-polytheistic aim, which forms to such an extent the ground-tone of the discourse, is to be recognized perhaps, also, in this part of it. The separation of men into so many different nations might seem to oppose the idea of their common parentage; that separation itself is, therefore, represented by the apostle as having been contemplated in the divine plan. — It will be observed that what the apostle affirms in this verse as true of God is, also, intended to be denied in regard to polytheism. The conception, therefore, thus brought before the minds of his heathen auditors, was a vast one. All that power exerted in giving existence to men, controlling their destiny, exalting entire nations or casting them down, which they had parcelled out among such an infinity of gods, they are now led to concentrate in a single possessor; they obtain the idea of one infinite Creator and Ruler.

V. 27. ζητεῖν, telic, *that they should seek.* This infinitive attaches itself more particularly to the part of the sentence which commences at κατοικεῖν, and states the moral object which God had in view with reference to men, in making such provision for their convenience and happiness. It was that they might be led, by such tokens of his goodness, *to seek him*, i. e. a more perfect knowledge of him and of their obligations to him. Some, on the contrary, make the infinitive depend, almost wholly, on the clause just before, and find the connection to be this: that, excited by the proofs of his power, as manifested in the varying fortunes of nations, *they should seek*, etc. But as already explained, the controlling idea in that clause is that of the goodness of God (subject, as to its continuance, to the divine pleasure); while that of his power, as displayed in the infliction of judgments, is only incidentally involved. Again, that clause is a subordinate one, as its structure shows, and that it should break off ζητεῖν so much from the main part of the sentence would be violent. — εἰ ἄραγε .... εὕροιεν, *if perhaps they might feel after him and find him.* ψηλαφήσειαν denotes, properly, the motions of a blind man, who gropes along after an object in the dark. On the peculiar Æolic termination, see W. § 13. 2. d; K. § 116. 9; B. § 103. marg. 14. This verb is chosen, as well as the problematical form of the expression (εἰ ἄραγε), because the apostle would concede the comparative indistinctness of the light which the heathen have to guide them. — καίτοιγε, *although indeed.* This clause is added to show that the concession just made was not intended to exculpate the heathen for their estrangement from God. Although so benighted as to be compelled to grope for the object of their search, it was still within reach; they had not, after all, so far to go for a knowledge of God, that they might not find it if they would. Compare the sentiment with 14, 17, and especially with Rom. 1, 20.

V. 28. ζῶμεν καὶ κινούμεθα καί ἐσμεν, *We live and move and exist.* The different verbs present the idea on every side. We derive our existence solely from God; we depend on Him, every instant, for life, activity, being itself. Without Him we should neither continue to live, nor be such as we are, nor have been at all. From creatures thus dependent, the evidence of a Creator cannot be very deeply hidden, if they have only a disposition to seek for it. — ὡς καί, *as also*, i. e. the sentiment is not only true, but has been acknowledged. — καθ' ὑμᾶς, *among you*, i. e. Greeks in distinction from Jews; not Athenians in distinction from other Greeks. — τοῦ γὰρ καὶ γένος ἐσμέν, *For his offspring also are we.* Derivation implies dependence. The creature cannot exist apart from the Creator. The apostle brings forward the citation correctly, therefore, as parallel in sentiment to ἐν αὐτῷ .... ἐσμέν. He quotes it as an avowal that we owe our being and its preservation to a higher Power; the mythological idea of Jupiter does not enter into the meaning.[1] τοῦ stands here for the pronoun. W. § 17. 1; S. § 94. 1. The words form the first half of a hexameter, and are found in Aratus, a Cilician poet, who flourished about B. C. 270. The celebrated Hymn of Cleanthes to Jupiter (v. 5) contains almost the same words, viz. ἐκ σοῦ γὰρ γένος ἐσμέν. The same idea, variously expressed, occurs in several other Greek writers. The form of the citation the apostle took, undoubtedly, from Aratus, but says τινὲς εἰρήκασι because he would generalize the idea as if he had said, The truth is so plain that even your poetry recognizes it (see on v. 18). According to some, he uses the plural because he had in mind other passages where the thought is found; or, according to others, because he inferred that so obvious a remark must be a common one. γὰρ καί, as Meyer observes correctly, has no logical connection with Paul's speech, but is to be viewed merely as a part of the citation, which it was necessary to retain on account of the verse.

V. 29. γένος οὖν, κ. τ. λ., *Since, therefore, we are the offspring of God.* The inference drawn here is, that idolatry is supremely absurd, inasmuch as it makes that which is destitute of life, motion, intelligence, the source of these attributes to others. Compare Isa. 44, 9 sq. — In ὀφείλομεν Paul connects himself with them, and thus softens the rebuke. — χαράγματι stands in apposition with the nouns which precede, i. e. the state or form of the materials just enumerated, artificially wrought.

V. 30. The relation of this verse and the one following to the preceding verse is this: Since such is the nature of idolatry, you must *therefore* (οὖν) repent of it, because God now lays upon you his command to this effect, in view of the retributions of a judgment to come. The most important word here is ὑπεριδών. It does not occur further in the New Testament, but is found often in the Septuagint, where it signifies to neglect, which is its proper classical sense, then to despise, but especially to suffer to pass as if unnoticed, to withhold the proof of noticing a thing which is, at the same time, a matter of distinct knowledge; a frequent sense of עָלַם in Hiphil and Hithpael (see Deut. 22, 3. 4, etc.). In this last signification, the verb represents perfectly the apostle's meaning here. God had hitherto permitted the heathen to pursue

[1] No more than in the words of Milton: —

> "Fame is no plant that grows on mortal soil;
> *　*　*　*　*　*
> But lives and spreads aloft by those pure eyes,
> And perfect witness of all-judging Jove."

their own way, without manifesting his sense of their conduct, either by sending to them special messengers to testify against it, as he did to the Jews, or by inflicting upon them at once the punishment deserved. The idea is virtually the same, therefore, as that of εἴασε in 14, 16, and παρέδωκεν in Rom. 1, 24. To understand ὑπεριδών as meaning that God would not judge or punish the heathen for the sins committed in their state of idolatry, would be at variance with Paul's theology on this subject as he has unfolded it in Rom. 1, 20; 2, 11 sq. Not only so, but the repentance which the apostle now calls upon them to exercise presupposes their guilt.

V. 31. διότι, *because,* states the reason why the heathen also, as well as others, must repent; they could not, without this preparation, be safe in the day of righteous judgment which awaited them. — ἐν ἀνδρὶ ᾧ ὥρισε, *in* (the person of) *the man whom he appointed.* ἀνδρί omits the article because a definite clause follows. W. § 21. 4; S. § 89. 3. ᾧ stands, by attraction, for the accusative. — πίστιν παρασχὼν πᾶσιν, *having afforded assurance to all,* confirmation, viz. of a judgment to come. It is impossible to say just how much the apostle intended to represent as proved by the resurrection of Christ. He himself referred to it, undoubtedly, in the first place, as establishing the possibility of such a resurrection of all men from the dead as was involved in his doctrine of a general judgment; but whether he had yet developed this doctrine so far that the Athenians perceived already this bearing of the fact, is uncertain. It was enough to excite their scorn to hear of a single instance of resurrection. Again, the resurrection of Christ from the dead confirms the truth of all his claims; and one of these was that he was to be the judge of men; see John 5, 28, 29. But whether the apostle meant to extend the argument to these and other points, we cannot decide, as he was so abruptly silenced.

VERSES 32–34. *Paul is interrupted and leaves the Assembly.*

V. 32. The apostle was heard with attention until he came to speak of the resurrection; when, at the announcement of a doctrine which sounded so strangely to the ears of the Athenians, some of them broke forth into expressions of open contempt. — ἀνάστασιν νεκρῶν, *a resurrection of the dead.* Both nouns omit the article in this frequent combination, except in 1 Cor. 15, 42. W. § 19. As we do not know how much of Paul's idea the Athenians had apprehended, it is doubtful whether we are to take the plural here as generic or numerical, i. e. whether Christ merely be meant, or men in general. — ἀκουσόμεθα .... περὶ τούτου, *We will hear thee again concerning this*, viz. matter; not so naturally masc., with reference to αὐτόν in v. 31. It is disputed whether we are to understand this as said seriously, or as a courteous refusal to hear any thing further from him. The latter is the prevalent view; and so Kuinoel, Hemsen, De Wette, Meyer, Bloomfield, Howson. The manner in which Paul now left the assembly, the immediate termination of his labors at Athens, and the adversative δέ in v. 34, favor this interpretation. Such a mode of speaking, too, was entirely consonant to the Athenian character. Calvin, Grotius, Rosenmüller, Alford, are among those who impute a serious meaning to the language.

V. 33. καὶ οὕτως, *and thus*, i. e. after these events, or with such a result; comp. 20, 11; 28, 14. — ἐκ μέσου αὐτῶν, i. e. of those whom he had addressed; not from the city (comp. 18, 1).

V. 34. τινὲς δέ, *but certain* (Mey. De Wet.), appears to be contrasted, in the writer's mind, with what is stated in v. 32, respecting the effect of Paul's speech; the favorable is opposed to the unfavorable. Yet δέ may be continuative. — κολληθέντες αὐτῷ, not adhering, but *joining*, attaching themselves, *to him*. — ὁ Ἀρεοπαγίτης, *the Areopagite*, i. e. one of the judges in the court of the Areiopagus. The number of these judges varied at different times. Eusebius and other ancient writers say that this Dionysius became afterwards bishop of the church at Athens, and ended his life as a martyr. — καὶ γυνή, *and a woman*, not the wife of Dionysius, as some have said, for the article and pronoun would then have been added (comp. 5, 1); or at least the article (comp. 24, 24). It has been inferred, from her being singled out thus by name, that she was a woman of rank, but beyond this, nothing is known of her.

CHAPTER XVIII.

VERSES 1–11. *Arrival of Paul at Corinth, and his Labors there.*

V. 1. ἐκ τῶν Ἀθηνῶν. Wieseler limits the apostle's stay at Athens to fourteen days. The estimate is necessarily conjectural. It is certain that, although Paul spent the most of the two next years in Corinth and the vicinity, he did not direct his steps again to that city. On his third missionary tour, he came once more into this part of Greece, but at that time passed by Athens, certainly once and again, without repeating his visit thither. — εἰς Κόρινθον. The distance from Athens to Corinth by land is about forty-five miles. The summit of the Acropolis of the one city can be distinctly seen from that of the other. ἦλθεν does not show how Paul travelled. The voyage, says Wieseler, could be made easily in two days. A Greek seaman informed the writer that with a very fair wind he had made the passage in three hours, though on the average, in five or six hours; that in bad weather he had been five days on the way. The steamers between the Piræus and Kalimaki, the eastern port of the modern Corinth, occupy usually four hours. — *Corinth* at this period was the seat of the Roman proconsulate for Achaia, or the southern province of Greece. "In consequence of its situation," says Neander, "this city furnished a very important central point for the extension of the gospel in a great part of the Roman empire; and hence Paul remained here, as in other similar places, a longer time than was otherwise usual for him."

V. 2. Ἀκύλαν. The nominative is Ἀκύλας (v. 26). *Aquila* and *Priscilla*, or *Prisca* (Rom. 16, 3), were Roman names; and it was common for Jews to assume such names when they lived out of Palestine; see on 13, 9. That Aquila was born in Pontus harmonizes with 2, 9 and 1 Pet. 1, 1; for we see from those passages that Jews resided in that country. As we have no account of his conversion at Corinth, the probability is that Aquila embraced the gospel at Rome. So Hemsen, Olshausen, Neander, Wieseler, and others, conclude. Some allege τινὰ Ἰουδαῖον as proof that he was still unconverted (Mey. De Wet.); but he is introduced in that manner on account of what follows. The notice apprises us that he was one of the πάντας Ἰουδαίους, whom the decree banished. At this early period no distinction would be made between Jews and Jewish Christians. Aquila accompanied Paul to Ephesus (v. 18. 26), and was still there when the apostle wrote the First Epistle to the Corinthians (1 Cor. 16, 19). We find him at Rome again when Paul wrote the Epistle to the Romans (Rom. 16, 3 sq.); and at a still later period at Ephesus a second time (2 Tim. 4, 19). The nature of his business (v. 3) led him frequently to change the place of his residence. — διὰ τὸ διατεταχέναι, κ. τ. λ., *because Claudius had ordered*, etc. Luke refers unquestionably to the edict mentioned by Suetonius (Claud. c. 25): "Judæos, impulsore Chresto, assidue tumultuantes Roma expulit." Neander remarks on that passage as follows: "We might suppose that some factious Jew then living, of this name, one of the numerous class of Jewish freedmen in Rome, was intended. But as no individual so universally known as the Chrestus of Suetonius seems to have been considered by that writer is elsewhere mentioned; and as Χρίστος was frequently pronounced Χρήστος by the pagans, it is quite probable that Suetonius, who wrote half a century after the event, throwing together what he had heard about the political expectations of a Messiah among the Jews, and the obscure and confused accounts which may have reached him respecting Christ, was thus led to express himself in a manner so vague and indefinite." Church History, Vol. I. p. 49. The Roman historian does not mention the year of that expulsion, and we may suppose it to have been about A. D. 52, in accordance with our plan of chronology. προσφάτως, *lately*, shows that it was still a recent event when Paul arrived at Corinth. Some writers would identify this decree with that *De mathematicis Italia pellendis*, which Tacitus mentions (Ann. 12. 52). The *mathematici*, or as they were also called, *Chaldæi*, were banished on the ground of their aiding conspirators against the emperor by the use of their art as astrologers. Wieseler (Chronologie, p. 121 sq.) argues that the Jews may have been confounded with that class of men, and were consequently banished by the same decree. If that point were established, it would furnish a striking confirmation of the correctness of our chronology; for the edict to which Tacitus refers can be shown to have been published in A. D. 52. But it must remain uncertain whether the two events have any chronological connection with each other.

V. 3. εἰργάζετο, *wrought*, labored for his subsistence. He reminds the Corinthians of this fact in 1 Cor. 9, 6 sq. and 2 Cor. 11, 7 sq.—ἦσαν γάρ, κ. τ. λ., *for they were tent-makers as to the trade*, or (with τῇ τέχνῃ, according to Lchm. Tsch.), *in respect to the trade* (which they had). τὴν τέχνην would be a limiting accusative like τὸν τρόπον in Jud. v. 7. W. § 32. 6; K. § 279. 7. The Jews, more especially after the exile, held the mechanic arts in high estimation. It was a proverb among them that the father who neglected to bring up his son to a trade taught him to be a thief. The composition of σκηνοποιοί indicates a definite sense. It is difficult to see why some should suppose it to mean *manufacturers of tent-cloth*. It has not been shown that the usage differed from the etymology. Tent-making was a common trade in Cilicia, the native country of the apostle. A coarse species of goat's hair, called *cilicium*, was produced there in great abundance, and was much used for that purpose. A person accustomed to work on that material could work, doubtless, on any other. Paul had acquired the trade, in all probability, during his boyhood, while he lived at Tarsus.

V. 4. διελέγετο, *discoursed* (imperf.) from week to week; whereas διελέχθη (aorist), in v. 19, refers to a single occasion.—Ἕλληνας, sc. σεβομένους, i. e. Greek proselytes who attended the synagogue; comp. 13, 43; 14, 1. The apostle had not yet addressed himself to the heathen; see v. 6.

V. 5. In ὡς δὲ κατῆλθον, *Now when they came down*, ὡς is not merely temporal (Alf.), but represents the συνείχετο as immediately consequent on the arrival of the two friends. — *Macedonia* denotes here the Roman province of that name, comprising Northern Greece as distinguished from Achaia, or Southern Greece; see on v. 1. It is left uncertain, therefore, from what particular place Silas and Timothy arrived at this time. Compare on v. 16. — συνείχετο τῷ λόγῳ, *was engrossed* (lit. *held together*) *with the word* (Vulg. Kuin. Olsh. De Wet. Bmg. Rob.). The arrival of his associates relieved him from anxiety which had pressed heavily upon him (comp. 1 Thess. 3, 6 sq.); and he could now devote himself with unabated energy to his work. He had the support also of their personal coöperation. We see from 2 Cor. 1, 19, that Silas and Timothy took an active part in the proclamation of the gospel at Corinth. We see also from 1 Cor. 2, 3, where the apostle says that he was among the Corinthians "in weakness and in fear and much trembling," that he was in a state of mind to need urgently the presence and sympathy of such coadjutors. Some say it means simply that Silas and Timothy found Paul employed thus anxiously when they arrived (Mey. Alf.); but unless they had something to do with the fact, it would be unimportant whether it occurred before or after their coming: its interest in that case lay wholly in its being a part of the apostle's experience. The common text has τῷ πνεύματι after συνείχετο: *he was impelled by the Spirit*, or *by his own spirit*, his fervent zeal (comp. v. 25). The evidence decides for τῷ λόγῳ as the original word (Grsb. Mey. Tsch.).

V. 6. ἀντιτασσομένων δὲ αὐτῶν, *But they opposing themselves*, is not to be taken as explanatory of the συνείχετο (against Mey.), but as describing the conduct of the Jews occasioned by the apostle's συνείχετο. — βλασφημούντων, *blaspheming*, sc. his words, message; comp. 13, 45; 19, 9. — ἐκτιναξάμενος τὰ ἱμάτια, *shaking out his garments*, i. e. the dust upon them, as a witness against them. For the significancy of the act, see on 13, 51. — τὸ αἷμα ὑμῶν, *your blood*, i. e. the consequences of your guilt; comp. 20, 26;

Ezek. 33, 5. — ἐπὶ τὴν κεφαλήν, sc. ἐλθέτω; comp. Matt. 23, 35. — καθαρὸς ἐγώ, *I am pure*, have discharged my duty. Some point the text so as to read, *pure I henceforth will turn unto the Gentiles* (Lchm. Alf.). The two clauses utter the idea more forcibly than one, and are better suited to so grave a declaration; comp. also 20, 26 and Matt. 27, 24. On the nature of this desertion of the Jews, see on 13, 46.

V. 7. μεταβὰς ἐκεῖθεν, *having departed from there*, i. e. the synagogue (see v. 4), not from the city, or from the house of Aquila. — ἦλθεν, κ. τ. λ., *went into the house of a certain Justus*. The meaning is, not that he left Aquila and went to lodge with Justus (Alf.), but that he preached in future at the house of the latter, which was so much the more convenient because it was near the synagogue where they had been accustomed to assemble. Paul pursued precisely the same course at Ephesus; see 19, 9. — σεβομένου τὸν θεόν, *worshipping God*, describes Justus as a foreigner who had embraced Judaism, but was not yet a believer. He opened his house for the use of the Christians, because he had more sympathy with them than with the Jews. His moral position was certainly unique; and it is easy to believe that he soon exchanged it for that of a believer.

V. 8. *Crispus* was one of the few persons at Corinth whom Paul himself baptized; see 1 Cor. 1, 14. — ἐπίστευσε σὺν ὅλῳ τῷ οἴκῳ αὐτοῦ, *believed with all his house*. Here is another instance in which a whole family received the gospel; comp. 16, 15; 1 Cor. 1, 16. The Apostolical Constitutions (VII. 46) say that Crispus became bishop of Ægina. — The *Corinthians* who believed were native Greeks; not Jews at Corinth. — ἐπίστευον is imperfect, from the relation of the act to ἀκούοντες.

V. 9. δι' ὁράματος, *through a vision* as the medium of communication; a form was seen as well as a voice heard (comp. 9, 12; 16, 9; 22, 18). — μὴ φοβοῦ, *Fear not*. The form of the imperative implies that he was beginning to despond; see the note on 10, 15. — λάλει, *continue to speak*. Observe the use of the subjunctive aorist in the next verb.

V. 10. καὶ οὐδεὶς, κ. τ. λ., *and no one shall attack thee* (telic) *to injure thee*, i. e. no one shall attempt it with success (De Wet.); or ecbatic, *so as to injure thee*. The infinitive with τοῦ denotes more commonly a purpose. The Jews made an effort to destroy the apostle after this promise (v. 12 sq.), but were defeated. — διότι . . . . πολύς, *because I have much people*, i. e. many who are appointed to become such; see 13, 48, and 15, 17. Hence the activity of the apostle must have free scope until they were converted.

V. 11. ἐκάθισε, κ. τ λ., *And he abode a year and six months.* It has been questioned whether this designation of time extends merely to the arrest mentioned in v. 12 (Mey.), or embraces the entire sojourn at Corinth. "I regard the latter view," says Wieseler, (Chronologie, p. 46,) "as undoubtedly the correct one. This appears, in the first place, from the particle τε, which connects this verse in the closest manner with what precedes, and consequently with εἶπε δὲ, κ. τ. λ.: 'The Lord said, Fear not, but speak and be not silent; . . . . and *so* (W. § 53. 2) he abode a year and six months, teaching among them the word of God.' The main thought of the words which the Lord addresses to Paul in the vision (v. 9, 10) is unquestionably, 'Speak in this city, and be not silent,' and accordingly the period of time, in v. 11, during which the apostle obeys this command of Christ, must refer to the *whole* time in which he had spoken at Corinth and was not silent, i. e. must include the time until his departure. In the second place, this follows from the general nature of the statement: 'he abode there a year and six months;' comp. Luke 24, 49." Anger (p. 63) adopts the same conclusion. De Wette calls it the prevalent view, but prefers the other. — ἐν αὐτοῖς, *among them* in the city (v. 10); see on 8, 5.

VERSES 12–17. *Paul is arraigned before Gallio.*

V. 12. *Gallio* was a brother of Seneca, the celebrated moralist. His original name was Novatus. He assumed that of Gallio, out of gratitude to a distinguished rhetorician of that name, who adopted him as a son. Seneca dedicated his books *De Ira* and *De Vita Beata,* to this brother. In one of his Letters (104) he speaks of Gallio as having resided in Achaia, though he does not mention in what capacity he was there. Luke's narrative represents him as acting a part in striking harmony with his reputed character. He was known among his contemporaries as the "dulcis Gallio." He had the social qualities which make a man a general favorite. "Nemo mortalium," says Seneca, "uni tam dulcis est, quam hic omnibus." (Quæst. Nat. L. 4, Præf.) Luke's οὐδὲν τούτων ἔμελεν in v. 17 indicates the easy temper which contributes so much to personal popularity. Gallio, like his brother, was put to death by the murderous Nero. — ἀνθυπατεύοντος τῆς Ἀχαΐας, *was governing Achaia as proconsul.* This province (see on v. 1) consisted of Hellas and the Peloponnesus. Here, too, we have a striking example of Luke's accuracy. Under Tiberius (Tac. Ann. 1. 76) and Caligula, the two preceding emperors, Achaia had been an imperial province, governed by proprætors. But Claudius had restored it to the Senate (Suet. Claud. c. 25), and under that form of administration its governors were styled proconsuls. Paul was at Corinth in the reign of Claudius. Compare the note on 13, 7. — ἐπὶ τὸ βῆμα, *before the tribunal.* The βῆμα was a seat or chair from which the Roman magistrates dispensed justice. It was sometimes fixed in one place, and was sometimes movable so as to accommodate the judge wherever he might wish to hold his court.

V. 13. παρὰ τὸν νόμον, *contrary to the law,* not of the Romans, but of the Jews (comp. νόμου τοῦ καθ' ὑμᾶς in v. 15); not of both Romans and Jews (Lange), as the charge in that form demanded investigation. What Luke has stated here is a summary of the charge. That the Jews went more into detail is evident from Gallio's reply in v. 13.

V. 14. ἀδίκημα and ῥᾳδιούργημα designate the act perhaps legally and ethically: this, as an offence against morality; that, as an offence against the state or the personal rights of others. — ἂν ἠνεσχόμην ὑμῶν, *I would have suffered you,* would have listened patiently to your complaint; but the condition in the protasis not being true, he could not now do it. For ἄν with the aorist indicative in the subordinate clause, see W. § 43. 2; B. § 139. 3. 2; K. § 327. b. Gallio makes known his decision as a thing settled.

V. 15. περὶ λόγου, *concerning a doctrine.* — ὀνομάτων, *names,* because they had accused Paul of teaching that Jesus was the Messiah. — κριτὴς γὰρ, κ. τ. λ., *For I do not wish to be judge of these things.* γάρ (T. R.) is logically correct, but comes from a copyist. It was out of his province to take cognizance of such questions. The Roman laws allowed the Jews to regulate their religious affairs in their own way. Lysias (23, 29) and Festus (25, 19) placed their refusal to interfere on the same ground. — The reply which Luke attributes to Gallio has been justly cited as a mark of that candor which distinguishes the truth. A panegyrist, a dishonest narrator, says Paley, would be too jealous for the honor of his cause to represent it as treated superciliously by those of eminent rank.

V. 16. ἀπήλασεν αὐτούς, *drove them away,* dispersed them. The verb shows that they left reluctantly, but not that any violence was used. A peremptory refusal, a decisive manner would be sufficient for the purpose.

V. 17. The interpretation of this passage has influenced the text. Some of the younger manuscripts insert οἱ Ἰουδαῖοι after πάντες; as if the Jews, disappointed in their design against the apostle, attempted as their next resort to avenge themselves on one of his principal followers. But the evidence for this reading is entirely inadequate; and it is incredible, also, that Luke should mention Sosthenes merely as a ruler of the synagogue, if he had become in fact a Christian. The best authorities have πάντες without any appendage, and οἱ Ἕλληνες in the common editions must be viewed as a gloss, correct as an explanation, but textually spurious. As the Jews could have had no motive for maltreating one of their own number, πάντες must be the body of those present, such as the subalterns of the court and the Greeks whom the tumult had drawn together. *Sosthenes* was probably the successor of Crispus (v. 8), or, as Biscoe conjectures, may have belonged to another synagogue in the city. He appears to have taken an active part in the prosecution, and hence the Greeks, who were always ready to manifest their hatred of the Jews, singled him out as the object of their special resentment. In winking at this, says De Wette, Gallio may have carried his impartiality too far. If he was the Sosthenes who is called "a brother" in 1 Cor. 1, 1, he must have been converted after this, and have removed to Ephesus. The coincidence in the name is the only reason for supposing the same person to be meant in both places. — ἔτυπτον (imperf.) shows how thorough a beating Sosthenes received. It may not be wronging Gallio to suspect that he looked through his fingers and enjoyed the scene. — οὐδὲν τούτων includes most naturally the dispute between the Jews and Christians, as well as the abuse of Sosthenes. — ἔμελεν, when used as a personal verb, requires in prose a neuter subject. K. § 274. R. 1; Mt. § 348. R. 2. The indifference of Gallio is not mentioned in commendation of him, but as suggesting why the affair had such a termination. Owing to the proconsul's disposition, the Jews were unsuccessful; so far from inflicting any injury on the apostle, their attempt recoiled in disgrace and violence upon themselves.

VERSES 18–22. *Paul proceeds by the Way of Ephesus and Cæsarea to Jerusalem, and from there to Antioch.*

V. 18. ἔτι προσμείνας ἡμέρας ἱκανάς, *having remained yet many days* after the arrest. Whether the arrest took place at the end of the year and a half mentioned in v. 11, or in the course of that time, is subject, as we have seen, to some doubt. Even if the arrest was subsequent to the year and six months, the *many days* here need not be supposed to extend the sojourn at Corinth beyond a few additional months (Wiesl.). During this period the apostle planted churches in other parts of Achaia, either by his own personal labors or by the instrumentality of his converts; see 2 Cor. 1, 1. It was during this visit at Corinth, also, that Paul wrote the First and Second Epistles to the Thessalonians. That he wrote the first of them here, appears from several circumstances: first, Paul had been separated from the Thessalonians but "a short time" (1 Thess. 2, 17); secondly, Timothy and Silas were with him (1 Thess. 1, 1), as they were according to Luke (18, 5); thirdly, the apostle had been lately at Athens (1 Thess. 3. 1), and whence, also, according to our narrative (18, 1) he came directly to Corinth; and, finally, he writes to the Thessalonians as recent converts whose knowledge was very imperfect. The date of this Epistle, therefore, would be A. D. 52 or 53; see note on 18, 23. If the first Epistle was written at Corinth, the second must have been written at the same place. Timothy and Silas were still with the apostle (2 Thess. 1, 1); and as the object of the second Epistle was to correct a wrong impression made by the first (comp. 2 Thess. 2, 1 sq., with 1 Thess. 4, 16 sq., and 5, 1 sq.), the interval between the two must have been short. —ἀποταξάμενος, *having bid adieu*, which is an Alexandrian sense; see Lob. ad Phryn. p. 24. Among others, he now took leave of Silas, and perhaps of Timothy, though we find the latter with him again at Ephesus (19, 22). — εἰς τὴν Συρίαν, *unto Syria*, as his remoter destination; he embarked for Ephesus in the first instance (v. 19). — κειράμενος τὴν κεφαλήν, *having shorn the head*, most critics understand of Paul (Chryst. Calv. Neand. Olsh. Hems. De Wet. Win. Wdsth.); some of Aquila (Grot. Kuin. Wiesl. Mey.). Παῦλος is the leading subject, and the reader connects the remark spontaneously with him. It is only as an act of reflection, on perceiving that Ἀκύλας stands nearer, that the other connection occurs to the mind as a possible one. καὶ σὺν αὐτῷ Πρίσκιλλα καὶ Ἀκύλας may intervene between κειράμενος and Παῦλος, because the clause is so evidently parenthetic, and because ἐξέπλει has a tendency to draw its several subjects towards itself. It is urged for the other view, that Luke has placed the man's name after that of the woman, contrary to the natural order; but that no stress can be laid on that circumstance is clear from Rom. 16, 3 and 2 Tim. 4, 19, where the names follow each other in the same manner. Some principle of association, as possibly that of the relative superiority of Priscilla, made it customary to speak of them in that order. — ἐν Κεγχρεαῖς, *in Cenchrea*, which was the eastern port of Corinth, distant about ten miles. A church had been gathered here (Rom. 16, 1). The modern name is Kikries, a little south of Kalamaki, and, under the traveller's eye, therefore, who crosses the isthmus. — εἶχε γὰρ εὐχήν, *for he had a vow*, i. e. one resting upon him; not assumed at this time. This clause states why he shaved his head. The cutting off of the hair was a Jewish practice, and took place at the expiration of a vow, not at the commencement of it. It is an erroneous statement, therefore, that the apostle subjected himself to the vow at this time, and went to Jerusalem to obtain absolution from it. Neander would support that opinion from Jos. Bel. Jud. 2. 15; but he adopts for that purpose an interpretation of the passage which nearly all others reject. The nature of Paul's vow on this occasion is uncertain. It could not have been a strict Nazarite vow, i. e. such a vow observed in due form; for a person could absolve himself from such an obligation only at Jerusalem, where his hair, which had grown during the time that he had been a Nazarite was to be cut off and burnt as an offering in the temple (Numb. 6, 2 sq.). See Jahn's Archæol. § 395. We have no *account* of any deviation from that rule. Yet it is not unreasonable to suppose that in later times the original institution may have been relaxed or modified; that after the Jews came to be dispersed, it was held to be lawful to terminate a Nazarite vow at other places, adhering to the prescribed usages as near as the circumstances allowed. If it was not a vow of this peculiar character, it may have been of the nature of a thank-offering, and not subject to the regulations to which the Nazarite was required to conform. It must be confessed that the present knowledge of Jewish antiquities is not sufficient to clear up fully the obscurity of the passage. It contains, says De Wette, a Gordian knot still untied.

V. 19. εἰς Ἔφεσον, *unto Ephesus*, which was on the Cayster, not far from its mouth. It could be approached at that time by water, though the site of the ancient city is now two or three miles from the coast. With a favoring wind, the passage from Corinth to Ephesus could be made in two or three days. Cicero mentions that he on one occasion, and his brother Quintus on another, occupied two weeks in passing from Ephesus to Athens (ad Attic. Ep. 6, 8. 9; Ib. 3, 9); but the voyage in both instances was retarded by extraordinary delays. See further, on 28, 13. — αὐτὸς δέ, *but he himself.* This emphasis brings forward Paul again as the prominent person, after the information that his companions stayed at Ephesus. The order of statement outruns the history a little, as occurs in other cases; comp. v. 1. Luke cannot well mean that the apostle separated himself from Priscilla and Aquila, and went into the synagogue without them (Mey.). So unimportant a circumstance would not be made so prominent. Nor is it at all probable that αὐτοῦ, *there*, was opposed in the writer's mind to the synagogue as being out of the city (Alf.); for in that case some intimation like ἔξω τῆς πόλεως (see 16, 13), or at least ἐξελθών, would hardly be withheld from the reader.

V. 21. Some critics reject all in this verse from δεῖ to Ἱεροσόλυμα (Bng. Grsb. Neand. Lchm. Tsch.); others defend the clause (Olsh. De Wet. Wiesl. Mey. Bmg. Alf.). The words may be doubtful, but with the present evidence should not be separated from the text. As Meyer suggests, they may have been omitted, from not perceiving the reference of ἀναβάς in v. 22, and consequently any occasion for such haste in prosecuting the journey. — τὴν ἑορτὴν τὴν ἐρχομένην, *the coming feast.* It must have been one of the principal feasts, which Paul was so anxious to keep at Jerusalem, in all probability the Passover or Pentecost. In either case we discover here that the apostle made the journey in the spring of the year. Wieseler (p. 48) thinks that it was the later festival, Pentecost, chiefly because Paul embarked at Corinth, instead of travelling through Macedonia, as the state of navigation would have rendered expedient earlier in the season. — For ποιῆσαι, comp. ποιῶ τὸ πάσχα in Matt. 26, 18. — εἰς Ἱεροσόλυμα, *at Jerusalem;* see on 8, 40. — πάλιν, κ. τ. λ., *but I will return again*, etc. The apostle soon fulfilled that promise (19, 1).

V. 22. κατελθών, *having come down* from the sea to the land; comp. 27, 5. — *Cæsarea* was the most convenient seaport in the vicinity of Judea; see further on 8, 40. — ἀναβάς, *having gone up*, i. e. to Jerusalem (Calv. Neand. Olsh. Mey. De Wet. Wiesl.). This absolute use of the verb occasions no obscurity after the statement respecting Paul's destination in v. 21. A few have understood it as *going up* into the city above the harbor. But to mention that circumstance in addition to the arrival would give to it a singular prominence as contrasted with the general rapidity of the narrative. κατέβη, *went down*, at the close of the verse, would be inappropriate to the geographical relation of Cæsarea to Antioch (Neand.). — τὴν ἐκκλησίαν, *the church* at Jerusalem. It should be noticed that this is the *fourth* journey which Paul has made to that city since his conversion. No doubt he arrived in season to observe the feast, as nothing is said of any disappointment in that respect. — εἰς Ἀντιόχειαν. How long the apostle was absent on the tour which terminated with this return to Antioch, can only be conjectured. The year and six months at Corinth (v. 11) would be likely to constitute the greater portion of the period. Wieseler proposes six months as the time occupied between leaving Antioch and the arrival at Troas (16, 8). He would allow six months also for the apostle's labors in Europe before his arrival at Corinth. The time which this estimate allows for the Asiatic part of the tour may be too limited. The apostle visited extensively the churches in Syria and Cilicia, planted new churches in Phrygia and Galatia, and travelled very circuitously throughout his journey between Antioch and Troas. It may be safer to assign a year at least to such varied labors. According to this view, the apostle was absent on his second mission about three years; and if we place his departure early in A. D. 51, he reached Antioch again in the spring or summer of 54. Anger, Wieseler, Meyer, Winer, and others, agree in supposing Paul to have arrived at Corinth in the autumn of A. D. 52. The admission of that date fixes the main point in this part of the chronology.

VERSE 23. *Departure of Paul on his Third Missionary Tour.*

V. 23. χρόνον τινά. The time now spent at Antioch was apparently short. It was during this time, as most critics suppose, that Peter arrived here, and the scene took place between him and Paul, of which we have an account in Gal. 2, 11 sq.; see on 15, 35. Neander (Pflanzung, I. p. 351) agrees with those who insert the occurrence here. Baumgarten (II. p. 331) adds himself to the same class. The apostle's ὅτε ἦλθε in Gal. 2, 11, affords no clue to the time. We may assume that the apostle went forth again to the heathen about the beginning of the year A. D. 55. — καθεξῆς, *in successive order.* This refers, probably, not to the countries named, but to the different places in them where churches existed. In accordance with the representation on Kiepert's map, we may suppose that Paul went first to Tarsus, thence in a northwestern direction through Galatia, and then, turning to the southwest, passed through Phrygia, and so on to Ephesus. That course accounts for Luke's naming Galatia before Phrygia, instead of the order in 16, 6.

VERSES 24–28. *Apollos comes to Ephesus, and is more fully instructed in the Gospel.*

V. 24. Meyer calls this section "a historical episode." Luthardt says that it is entirely germane to the narrative: while Paul labors in Asia, another builds still further upon the foundation laid by him in Europe. — Ἀπολλώς = Ἀπολλώνιος. As a native of Alexandria, he had received probably, says Neander, "the Jewish-Grecian education, peculiar to the learned among the Jews of that city, and had acquired also great facility in the use of the Greek language." — λόγιος, *eloquent* (Olsh. De Wet. Mey.), or *learned* (Neand.). The first sense is the best, because δυνατὸς ἐν ταῖς γραφαῖς ascribes to him then a different talent, and because his superior faculty as a speaker appears to have been the reason why some of the Corinthians preferred him to Paul; see 1 Cor. 1, 12; 2, 4; 2 Cor. 10, 10. — ἐν ταῖς γραφαῖς, *in the Scriptures*. He was familiar with them, and could use them with power as a source of argument and appeal (see v. 28). This clause points out the sphere of his eloquence.

V. 25. οὗτος ἦν, κ. τ. λ., *This one was instructed in the way of the Lord*, probably by some disciple of John, who had left Judea before the Saviour commenced his public course; or possibly by John himself, whose earlier ministry Apollos may have attended. Some infer from τὰ περὶ τοῦ Ἰησοῦ that Apollos was aware that Jesus was the Messiah; but the following ἐπιστάμενος, κ. τ. λ., limits that expression, and if explained correctly below, excludes a knowledge of that fact. His ignorance in this respect was one of the defects in his religious belief, and at the same time his views of the deeper Christian doctrines must have been meagre in comparison with those possessed by the apostles. For the construction of ὁδόν, see W. § 32. 5; K. § 281. 2. — ζέων τῷ πνεύματι, *being fervent in spirit*, zealous in his disposition. It is less correct to understand πνεύματι of the Holy Spirit, since that gift appears in the New Testament as the proper fruit and seal of the Christian faith, which Apollos had not yet adopted; see Gal. 3, 2. For other places where πνεῦμα refers to the mind, comp. 19, 21; John 11, 33; 13, 21; Rom. 12, 11 (probably); 2 Cor. 2, 12. — ἀκριβῶς, *accurately* (v. 26), i. e. his doctrine was correct as far as his knowledge extended. — ἐπιστάμενος, κ. τ. λ., *knowing only the baptism of John*, which differed from that of the apostles mainly in these respects; first, that theirs recognized a Messiah who had come, and, secondly, that it was attested by the extraordinary gifts of the Spirit (19, 6). Since John, however, taught that the Saviour was about to appear, and that repentance, faith in him, and holiness were necessary to salvation, Apollos, though acquainted only with his teaching, could be said with entire truth to be *instructed in the way of the Lord*. It is not affirmed that he had submitted to John's baptism, but we suppose that from the nature of the case. That he was rebaptized, Luke does not assert; though, if we regard his moral position as analogous to that of the Johannean disciples mentioned in the next chapter, we should infer from what is related there that such was the fact. Meyer considers the cases dissimilar, and denies that Apollos was rebaptized.

V. 26. ἤρξατο, *began*, but did not preach long with such imperfect views. As soon as Aquila and Priscilla heard him, they proceeded to instruct him more fully.—παῤῥησιάζεσθαι means *to speak boldly*. He exposed their sins, required them to repent, and be prepared for the kingdom of the Messiah; comp. Matt. 3, 2 sq.—ἀκριβέστερον, *more accurately*.

V. 27. εἰς τὴν Ἀχαΐαν, *unto Achaia*, of which Corinth was the capital, see on v. 1. It was that city which he proposed to visit; comp. 19, 1; 1 Cor. 1, 12; 3, 4. What he heard from Priscilla and Aquila may have turned his thoughts to this field of labor.—προτρεψάμενοι ἔγραψαν, *they wrote and exhorted*. The participle contains the principal idea; see 1, 24. Some supply αὐτόν after προτρεψάμενος (Calv. Kuin.); but that assigns to the verb and participle different objects, and confuses the sentence. Besides, Apollos was not averse to the journey (βουλομένου), and had no need of exhortation. In 2 Cor. 3, 1, Paul alludes to this letter of commendation; or to the practice of granting such letters (συστατικαὶ ἐπιστολαί), exemplified in this case of Apollos.—συνεβάλετο, κ. τ. λ., *contributed* (as a helper) *much to those who have believed* and still believe. See W. § 40. 4. a. It is not meant that he confirmed them in their faith as Christians, but that he coöperated with them in their promulgation and defence of the truth. The next verse explains the remark.—διὰ τῆς χάριτος, *through grace*, belongs to the participle (De Wet.), not to the verb (Mey.). The natural sense is that which results from the order of the words. The doctrinal idea is that of ἡ πίστις ἡ δι' αὐτοῦ in 3, 16.

V. 28. εὐτόνως, *powerfully*.—εἶναι τὸν Χριστὸν Ἰησοῦν, *that the Messiah was Jesus*, none other than he; comp. v. 5.

CHAPTER XIX

VERSES 1–7. *Paul comes to Ephesus, and rebaptizes certain Disciples of John.*

V. 1. ἐν τῷ τὸν Ἀπολλὼ εἶναι ἐν Κορίνθῳ, *while Apollos was at Corinth.* This notice apprises us that Paul did not arrive at Ephesus till after the departure of Apollos. Ἀπολλώ (the regular genitive, see 1 Cor. 3, 4) here rejects ν in the accusative; comp. 21, 1. K. § 48. R. 1; W. § 8. 2.—τὰ ἀνωτερικὰ μέρη, *the upper parts,* in the interior as compared with the coast. The expression may be understood of the mountains on the frontier of Phrygia and Asia, which the apostle would cross on his route. — τινὰς μαθητάς, *certain disciples.* Luke ascribes to them that character (comp. πιστεύσαντες in v. 2), because, though their knowledge was so imperfect, they were sincere; they possessed the elements of a true faith, and acknowledged the name of Christ as soon as the apostle made it known to them. It is probable that they were strangers who had just arrived at Ephesus, and when the apostle found them, had not yet come in contact with any of the Christians there.

V. 2. For εἰ in a direct question, see on 1, 6. The inquiry appears abrupt, because we have so broken an account of the circumstances of the case. Undoubtedly something preceded, which led the apostle to suspect that the men entertained inadequate or mistaken views of the gospel. — πνεῦμα ἅγιον is the *Holy Spirit* here as the author of miraculous gifts, as is made evident by v. 6. — ἐλάβετε πιστεύσαντες, *Did ye receive* (note the aorist) *when ye believed?* The participle refers to the same time as the verb. — ἀλλ' ἠκούσαμεν, *But we did not hear* (when baptized) *even if there be a Holy Spirit.* A negative usually precedes ἀλλ' οὐδέ with this force (= No — on the contrary); but could be omitted with the effect of a more earnest denial. See W. § 53. 7. πνεῦμα ἅγιον must have the meaning in their reply which it had in Paul's question. Hence it is unnecessary and incorrect to supply δοθέν or ἐκχυνόμενον after ἔστι; comp. John 7, 39.

V. 3. εἰς τί, κ. τ. λ., *Unto what,* as the object of faith and confession, *therefore, were ye baptized?* — εἰς τὸ Ἰωάννου βάπτισμα should have the sense here which it has in other passages (comp. 1, 22; 10, 37; Matt. 3, 7; Luke 7, 29, etc.), viz. the baptism which John administered, or such as he administered. They may have received the rite from John himself, or from some one whom he had baptized, but who had not advanced beyond the point of knowledge at which John's ministry had left his disciples. That Apollos had baptized them is not at all probable; for the presumption is that he had left Ephesus before their arrival (see on v. 1), and because if he had not, they would have received from him more correct views, after his own better acquaintance with Christianity. The answer of the men, therefore, was not that they had been baptized unto John as the Messiah; and the idea that their error was that of adhering to him as the Messiah has no support from this expression. That some, however, at a very early period, entertained that opinion of John, is a fact well established. The Zabians, or Nazoræans, or Mendæans, as they are variously called, who were discovered in the East about the middle of the seventeenth century, are supposed to be a remnant of that sect. See Neand. Ch. Hist. Vol. I. p. 376; and Christian Review, Jan. 1855.

V. 4. μέν after Ἰωάννης, which some editors reject, is genuine (Mey. Tsch. De Wet.). The reply of Paul is apparently this: "John indeed preached repentance and a Saviour to come (as you know); but the Messiah whom he announced has appeared in Jesus, and you are now to believe on him as John directed." — τοῦτ' ἔστιν presents the adversative idea, instead of the ordinary δέ. W. § 63. I. 2. e; K. § 322, R. 4. — ἐβάπτισε governs βάπτισμα, on the principle of affinity in point of sense; comp. Luke 7, 29. W. § 32. 2; K. § 278. 1. — Χριστόν is common before Ἰησοῦς, but is unwarranted here.

V. 5. ἀκούσαντες, κ. τ. λ., *Now they* (whom Paul addressed) *having heard, were baptized.* Whether Paul himself or some assistant performed the rite, the history does not decide. Their prompt reception of the truth would tend to show that the defect in their former baptism related not so much to any positive error, as to their ignorance in regard to the proper object of faith. Some of the older writers maintained that Luke records these words as a continuation of Paul's remarks: *Now they* (whom John addressed) *having heard were baptized.* It was the object of such commentators to rescue the passage from those who appealed to it, in order to justify rebaptism. They maintained this exegesis not only against the Anabaptists, but as Baumgarten mentions, against the Catholics, who disparaged John's baptism for the purpose of exalting the Christian sacraments as distinguished from those of the first dispensation. The Council of Trent, for instance, asserted: Si quis dixerit baptismum Johannis eandem vim cum baptismo Christi habuisse, Anathema esto. (Sess. VII, de baptismo C. 1). This interpretation not only sets aside the more obvious meaning for a remote one, but palpably misstates the fact in regard to John's baptism: he did not administer it in the name of Jesus. This view of the passage may be said to be obsolete at present.

V. 6. Compare this verse with 10, 44–46. — γλώσσαις, sc. ἑτέραις (2, 4), or καιναῖς (Mark 16, 17). — For προεφήτευον, see on 2, 17.

V. 7. οἱ πάντες ἄνδρες, *all the men together*. πᾶς in this adverbial sense (= τὸ πᾶν, τὰ πάντα) occurs especially in connection with numerals. Compare 27, 35. It is rare to find the adjective with this force before the substantive. See K. A. Gr. § 489. β; Vig. ed. Herm. p. 135. — And thus those twelve men who came forward so abruptly in our history disappear as suddenly, leaving us in doubt whence they came, where they had been, and in some respects what particular phase of religious belief they represented. The episode is one of strange interest from the very fact of its suggesting so many questions, the solution of which our imperfect knowledge of the first Christian age has put beyond our reach.

VERSES 8–12. *Paul preaches at Ephesus, and confirms the Word by Miracles.*

V. 8. For ἐπαῤῥησιάζετο, *preached boldly*, see on 18, 26. — πείθων, sc. αὐτούς, *persuading them of the things*; comp. 28, 23. The first accusative specifies the aim of the act. K. § 279. 4.

V. 9. τινές, *some*, i. e. of the Jews, as results from συναγωγήν in v. 8. — τὴν ὁδόν, *the way*, i. e. of Christian belief and practice; not concretely, sect, party; comp. v. 23; 9, 2. — ἐνώπιον τοῦ πλήθους, *in the presence of the multitude*. This attempt to prevent others from believing showed how *hardened* (ἐσκληρύνοντο) they were, more fully than their own rejection of the gospel. — ἀφώρισε τοὺς μαθητάς, *separated the disciples*, i. e. from the Jews in the synagogue. — ἐν τῇ σχολῇ, *in the school*, viz. the place where he taught. This Tyrannus, otherwise unknown, was probably a teacher of philosophy or rhetoric, who occupied the apartment at other hours. Whether he rented it to the Christians, or gave them the use of it, is uncertain.

V. 10. ἐπὶ ἔτη δύο. These *two years* are exclusive of the three months mentioned in v. 8; for τοῦτο opposes expressly the preaching in the school of Tyrannus to that in the synagogue. It is probable that they are exclusive also of the time occupied by the events which took place after v. 21; for in 20, 31 Paul reminds the Ephesians that he had labored *three years* among them; so that nine months, or six months at least (if we regard τριετίαν there as a general expression), must be added to the two years and three months mentioned here. The retrospective remark in v. 20 would be a very natural one for the writer to make on the completion of a distinct period. — It was during this abode of Paul at Ephesus, and probably not long after his arrival there, that he wrote the Epistle to the Galatians. In Gal. 4, 13, Paul speaks of the *former time* (τὸ πρότερον) when he preached in Galatia; and hence (taking the expression in its strict import) he had been there twice when he wrote the Epistle. He must have written it, therefore, on this third missionary tour (at least, not before it), since he founded the Galatian churches on his second tour (see on 16, 6), and *confirmed* them on his present journey to Ephesus (see 18, 23). Further, if οὕτω ταχέως in Gal. 1, 6, refers (as, on the whole, I think it does) to the brief interval since Paul was among the Galatians, it follows that he wrote his Epistle to them during the early part of his sojourn at Ephesus. In this city Paul could obtain easily the knowledge of the Galatian heresy, which gave occasion to the letter. A partial conclusion may be drawn from another argument. If we are to place Paul's rebuke of Peter between his second and third journeys (see on 18, 23), he could not have written to the Galatians at all events *before* his departure on this tour. The foregoing data are not decisive, but furnish the best supported opinion. We may refer the Epistle to the year A. D. 56; see note on 21, 17. — ὥστε . . . . Ἀσίαν, *so that all who inhabited Asia*, viz. the Roman province of that name (2, 9). Ephesus was the capital of this province, the centre of commerce and religious worship (v. 26), to which the people resorted from all parts of the country. Hence the apostle had an opportunity to preach to a vast number, in addition to those who resided in the city; and at the same time, through the agency of those converted by him, he could have introduced the gospel into regions which he did not visit in person. It was but forty years after this that Pliny, in his celebrated letter to Trajan, says, even in reference to the more distant Bithynia: "Multi omnis ætatis, omnis ordinis, utriusque sexûs etiam, vocantu in periculum et vocabuntur. Neque enim civitates tantum, sed vicos etiam atque agros superstitionis istius contagio pervagata est."

V. 11. οὐ τὰς τυχούσας, *not casual*, i. e. uncommon, extraordinary; comp. 28, 2. As the sequel shows (v. 12), the miracles were remarkable, because they were performed without the personal agency or presence of the apostle. They were not generically different from those wrought on other occasions. —διὰ τῶν χειρῶν Παύλου, *through the hands of Paul*, not as laid upon the sick (some of the results being involuntary on his part), but through his instrumentality.

V. 12. ὥστε καί, *So that* (because God so wrought by him) *also*, i. e. among other miracles. — ἐπιφέρεσθαι, κ. τ. λ., *were carried from his body*, to which the articles had been touched for the purpose of receiving the healing power that was supposed to reside in him; see Luke 8, 46. They resorted to this course probably, because the throng was so great that the sick could not be brought directly to the apostle, or in some instances were too infirm to be removed from their houses. — σουδάρια (Lat. *sudaria*), *handkerchiefs*, lit. sweat-cloths. They had their name from the use to which they were principally applied. — σιμικίνθια, *aprons*, such as artisans and servants wore when engaged about their work. This, too, is a Latin word (*semicinctia*) which had passed into the later Greek; see on 11, 26. — It is evident from τὰς νόσους and τὰ πνεύματα that the writer made a distinction between ordinary diseases and those inflicted by evil spirits (comp. on 5, 16; 8, 7).

VERSES 13–17. *The Defeat of certain Jewish Exorcists.*

V. 13. The common text has τινὲς ἀπὸ τῶν, κ. τ. λ. The more approved reading is τινὲς καὶ τῶν, κ. τ. λ. (Grsb. Tsch. Mey.). καί joins τινές with Paul, with reference to the act in ὀνομάζειν: *they also attempted to call*, as he called. — περιερχομένων, not approbriously, *vagabond*, but *wandering* from place to place in the practice of their arts. — ἐξορκιστῶν, *exorcists;* that was their professed, reputed occupation. They appear to have regarded Paul as one of their own class, but of a higher order. They supposed he had obtained a name more potent than any employed by them, and that by means of it he could perform in reality the wonders to which they merely pretended. — ὁρκίζω ὑμᾶς τὸν Ἰησοῦν, *I adjure you by the Jesus.* For the double accusative, compare Mark 5, 7; 1 Thess. 5, 27. See W. § 32. 4; C. § 428.

V. 14. For the Doric Σκευᾶ, see on 11, 30. — ἀρχιερέως, *a chief-priest*, a priest of the higher class; see on 4, 6. — ἑπτά, *seven* The numeral is too remote from τινές to be indefinite, *several;* see on 23, 23. — οἱ τοῦτο ποιοῦντες denotes a habit. The next verse relates an instance of their practice.

V. 15. τὸ πνεῦμα, *the spirit*, viz. the one whom they were at tempting to exorcise on a certain occasion. — τὸν Ἰησοῦν γινώσκω, *the Jesus* (whom you invoke) *I know*, i. e. his authority and power; *and the Paul* (whom you name) *I know well* as the servant, messenger of God (comp. 16, 17). The article is probably significant here, though as the nouns are proper names it may be a little uncertain. — ὑμεῖς precedes τίνες, because it takes the emphasis.

V. 16. καὶ ἐφαλλόμενος, κ. τ. λ., *and the man* (impelled by the evil spirit) *leaping upon them.* — κατακυριεύσας, κ. τ. λ., *having overpowered them, was strong*, showed himself such *against them*, or *both*, viz. by tearing off their garments and beating them. ἀμφοτέρων is more correct than αὐτῶν (Grsb. Mey. Tsch.). — γυμνούς, *naked*, need not be taken in its strict sense. It could be applied to those stripped partially of their raiment; comp. John 21, 7. — ἐκ τοῦ οἴκου ἐκείνου, *from out of that house* where the transaction took place. The pronoun reveals a more definite scene in the writer's view than he has described. — In the occurrence related here, we are to recognize a special design on the part of God. It was important, says Neander, that the divine power which accompanied the gospel should, in some striking manner, exhibit its superiority to the magic which prevailed so extensively at Ephesus, and which, by its apparently great effects, deceived and captivated so many. It would have a tendency to rescue men from those arts of imposture, and prepare their minds for the reception of the truth.

Verses 18–20. *Many are converted, and confess their Sins.*

V. 18. πολλοί τε τῶν πεπιστευκότων, *And many of the believers* (convinced by such evidence); lit. *those who have believed* and still believe. The language ascribes to them a definite character, but does not decide when it began. They were probably new converts (De Wet. Alf.), as the confession made by them would be inconsistent with the life required of those who had been recognized as Christians. They were a different class, also, from those spoken of in the next verse; hence, not the jugglers themselves, but their dupes, those who had confided in them and been accessory to the wicked delusion. — ἤρχοντο (imperf.), *came* one after another. — τὰς πράξεις αὐτῶν, *their deeds*, superstitious practices (Olsh. Mey. De Wet.); not their sins in general (Kuin.). It is better to restrict the meaning in this connection, especially as with the other sense the more obvious term would be ἁμαρτίας and not πράξεις.

V. 19. ἱκανοὶ, κ. τ. λ., *And many of those who practised magic arts*, lit. *things over-wrought*, curious, recondite. — τὰς βίβλους, *the books* which contained their mysteries, i. e. magical signs, formulas of incantation, nostrums, and the like. — κατέκαιον describes them as throwing book after book into the blazing pile. — καὶ εὗρον, κ. τ. λ., *and they found* as the sum *fifty thousand* (sc. δραχμάς) *of silver money*. It was common in such designations to omit the name of the coin. See Bernh. Synt. p. 187. The *Attic drachm* passed at this time among the Jews and Romans for a *denarius*, and was worth about fifteen cents; so that the books amounted to $7,500. Some supply *shekel* as the elliptical word; which, reckoning that coin at sixty cents, would make the amount four times as great. But as the occurrence took place in a Greek city and as Luke was not writing for Jews, it is entirely improbable that he has stated the sum in their currency. All books in ancient times were expensive, and especially those which contained secrets or charms held in such estimation.

V. 20. ηὔξανε καὶ ἴσχυεν, *grew and was strong*, mighty. The first verb refers to the general extension of the gospel, the second to its influence on the conduct of those who embraced it. What precedes illustrated the remark in both respects. — This verse presents a striking coincidence as compared with 1 Cor. 16, 9. It was here at Ephesus, and about this time, that Paul wrote the First Epistle to the Corinthians. That it was written at Ephesus is certain from 1 Cor. 16, 8. But Paul visited this city only twice: the first time when he touched here on his way to Jerusalem (18, 19), and again at this present time of his prolonged residence here. He could not have written the Epistle on his first visit, because the church at Corinth so recently gathered would not answer then to the character which it bears in the Epistle, and still more decisively because Apollos who was the head of one of the parties there (1 Cor. 1, 12) did not proceed to Corinth (18, 27) till shortly before Paul's second arrival at Ephesus. Again, Paul speaks in 1 Cor. 4, 17 of having recently sent Timothy to Corinth (comp. 1 Cor. 16, 10), and here in the Acts (19, 22) Luke speaks evidently of the same event, which he represents as preparatory to the apostle's intended visit to the same place. As Paul now left Ephesus in the spring of A. D. 57 (see note on 20, 1), he wrote his First Epistle to the Corinthians a few months before his departure.

VERSES 21. 22. *The Apostle proposes to leave Ephesus.*

V. 21. A new epoch begins here, viz. that from the end of the year and three months to Paul's departure. — ταῦτα, *these things* up to this time since the arrival at Ephesus; not so naturally those relating merely to the exorcism and its effects. — ἔθετο ἐν τῷ πνεύματι, *placed in his mind*, purposed; see on 5, 4. — *Macedonia* and *Achaia* occur here also in the Roman sense. The order of the names indicates that the apostle intended at this time to have proceeded directly from Corinth to Jerusalem. An unexpected event (see 20, 3) compelled him to change his plan. — δεῖ . . . . ἰδεῖν, *it is necessary that I should see also Rome;* not in order to fulfil any revealed purpose of God, but to satisfy his own feelings. He was anxious to visit the believers there, and to preach the gospel in that metropolis of the world; see Rom. 1, 11. 14. — Paley institutes a striking comparison between this verse and Rom. 1, 13 and 15, 23–28. "The conformity between the history and the Epistle is perfect. In the first passage of the Epistle, we find that a design of visiting Rome had long dwelt in the apostle's mind; here, in the Acts, we find that design expressed a considerable time before the Epistle was written. In the history we find that the plan which Paul had formed was to pass through Macedonia and Achaia; after that, to go to Jerusalem; and when he had finished his visit there, to sail for Rome. When the Epistle was written, he had executed so much of his plan, as to have passed through Macedonia and Achaia; and was preparing to pursue the remainder of it, by speedily setting out towards Jerusalem; and in this point of his travels he tells his friends at Rome, that, when he had completed the business which carried him to Jerusalem, he would come to them, when he should make his journey into Spain." Nor is the argument to be evaded by supposing the passages to have been adjusted to each other in this manner. "If the passage in the Epistle was taken from that in the Acts, why was *Spain* put in? If the passage in the Acts was taken from that in the Epistle, why was *Spain* left out? If the two passages were unknown to each other, nothing can account for their conformity but truth."

V. 22. *Timothy* was at Corinth when last mentioned (18, 5). He would be likely to cross over to Ephesus on hearing of Paul's arrival there. But what connection is there between the apostle's sending Timothy into Macedonia and his own purpose to proceed to Achaia? We obtain an answer to that question from 1 Cor. 4, 17–19. We learn there that Timothy was not to stop in Macedonia, but to pass on to Corinth, the capital city of Achaia, and prepare the church for the approaching visit of the apostle. Thus "the narrative agrees with the Epistle; and the agreement is attended with very little appearance of design. One thing at least concerning it is certain; that if this passage of Paul's history had been taken from his letter, it would have sent Timothy to Corinth by name, or at all events into Achaia." — *Erastus* may be the person of that name in 2 Tim. 4, 20, but as he travelled with Paul, the best critics distinguish him from the Erastus in Rom. 16, 23 (Neand. De Wet. Win.). The office of the latter as "treasurer of the city" would demand his more constant presence at Corinth. — αὐτὸς . . . . Ἀσίαν, *he himself* (while they departed) *kept back unto Asia;* εἰς not *in* (De Wet. Rob.), and not *for* as dat. comm. (Win.), uncommon before a proper name, but *unto* as the direction towards which (Mey.).

VERSES 23-27. *Demetrius excites a Tumult at Ephesus.*

V. 23. As at Philippi (16, 19), so here the Greeks instigated the riot; their motive was the same — fear of losing the means of their ill-gotten wealth. See note on 14, 19. — κατὰ τὸν καιρὸν ἐκεῖνον, *about that time*, viz. that of Paul's intended departure. — περὶ τῆς ὁδοῦ, *concerning the way;* see on 9, 2.

V. 24. γάρ explains why a tumult arose. — ναοὺς ἀργυροῦς Ἀρτέμιδος, *silver shrines* (not *for* in E. V. but) *of Artemis.* These were small portable images, resembling the temple at Ephesus, and containing a figure of the goddess. The manufacture of these shrines was a lucrative business, as they were in great request; they were set up in houses as objects of worship, or carried about the person as having the supposed power to avert diseases and other dangers. They were not only sold here in Asia, but sent as an article of traffic to distant countries. *Demetrius*, it would seem, was a wholesale dealer in such shrines. He executed orders for them, and employed τεχνίταις, *artisans*, who received lucrative wages (ἐργασίαν οὐκ ὀλίγην) for their labor. — Compare παρείχετο with the active form in 16, 16.

V. 25. οὓς, κ. τ. λ., *whom having assembled and the other workmen* in his employ. The artisans performed the more delicate processes, and the ἐργάτας the rougher work. So Bengel, Kuinoel, Hemsen, and Meyer distinguish the two nouns from each other. It appears improbable that Demetrius would confine his appeal to his own men. It may be better to understand ἐργάτας of the laborers in general, who were devoted to such trades, whether they exercised them on their own account or that of some employer. — τοιαῦτα preceded by τά limits the reference to ναούς, i. e. definitely, *such things* as those; comp. Matt. 19, 14; 2 Cor. 12, 2. 3. K. § 246. 4. It is incorrect to extend the pronoun so as to include statuary, pictures, coins, and the like (Blmf.). — ἐπίστασθε, *ye know well;* see v. 15. — ταύτης refers to ποιῶν ναούς in Luke's narrative. It stands, therefore, for some equivalent term or idea in the speech of Demetrius. — εὐπορία, *prosperity*, wealth.

V. 26. Ἐφέσου, *of* or *from* (not *at*) *Ephesus* depends on ὄχλον as a genitive of possession. — Ἀσίας has, no doubt, its Roman sense. The effect ascribed here to Paul's labors agrees with the statement in v. 10. — μετέστησεν, *turned aside*, i. e. from our mode of worship. — ὅτι οὐκ, κ. τ. λ., *that they are not gods which are made by hands.* The mode of speaking illustrates the disposition of the heathen to identify their gods with the idols or temples consecrated to them; see on 17, 24. We can imagine the effect of these words on such auditors, uttered with a look or gesture towards the splendid temple within sight.

V. 27. τοῦτο τὸ μέρος, *this part*, branch of our labor (Kyp. Mey.). The idea is, that their art as silversmiths, of whatever use it might be in other respects, would soon be ruined, as to this particular application of it. — ἡμῖν, *for us* (dat. incomm.), to our detriment. Their receipts had declined perceptibly already, and at this rate would soon be cut off altogether. — ἀλλὰ καί, κ. τ. λ., *but also the temple of the great goddess Artemis* is in danger, etc. κινδυνεύει extends also into this clause and governs the following infinitive. μεγάλης was one of the special titles of the Ephesian Diana. In regard to her temple, reckoned as one of the wonders of the world, the reader will find ample details in Howson. The edifice in Paul's time had been built in place of the one burnt down by Herostratus on the night of Alexander's birth, and was vastly superior to it in size and grandeur. No ruins of it remain at present on the spot; but the traveller sees some of the columns in the Mosque of St. Sophia at Constantinople, originally a church, and in the naves of Italian Cathedrals. — εἰς ἀπελεγμὸν ἐλθεῖν, *to come into contempt* (Mey.); *in redargutionem venire* (Vulg.), i. e. *to be confuted*, rejected (De Wet.). The noun occurs only here, and its meaning must be inferred from its relation to cognate words. A result of *confutation* is shame, loss of character, and hence the expression could be used to signify that they feared lest their business should lose its credit in the public estimation. — μέλλειν, κ. τ. λ., *and also that her glory will be destroyed*, etc. The discourse here changes from the direct to the indirect, as if ἔφη or εἶπε had introduced this part of the sentence. We have a similar transition in 23, 24. See W. § 64. III. 2. τε (needlessly exchanged by some for δέ) joins the clause with what precedes, while καί adds another argument to enforce the speaker's object. — ἡ οἰκουμένη, *the world;* comp. on 11, 28. The temple at Ephesus had been built at the common expense of all the Greek cities of Asia. Pilgrims repaired thither from all nations and countries. — The speech of Demetrius deserves attention for its artful character. He takes care, in the first place, to show his fellow-craftsmen how the matter affected their own personal interests, and then, having aroused their selfishness, he proceeds to appeal with so much the more effect to their zeal for religion. His main reliance, as Calvin thinks, was upon the first: "Res ipsa clamat non tam pro aris ipsos quam pro focis pugnare, ut scilicet culinam habeant bene calentem."

VERSES 28–34. *The Mob seize two of Paul's Companions and rush to the Theatre.*

V. 28. πληρεῖς θυμοῦ, *full of wrath* against Paul and the Christians. — ἔκραζον, *continued crying.* The Greeks lived so much in the open air, Demetrius may have harangued his men in public; if in private, the rioters had now gone into the street. Perhaps they traversed the city for a time with their outcry, before executing the assault spoken of in the next verse, and swelled their number with recruits on the way.

V. 29. καὶ ἐπλήσθη, κ. τ. λ., *And the whole city was filled with tumult,* or *the tumult* if we read τῆς. The evidence for the article is not decisive. — ὥρμησαν, κ. τ. λ., *And they rushed with one accord into the theatre.* The subject of the verb here includes those who excited the disturbance and those who joined in it. They rushed to the theatre because it was the custom of the Greeks, though not of the Romans, to use their theatres for public business as well as for sports. See on 12, 21. The multitude had evidently no definite plan of action, and no definite idea of the cause of the present excitement; see v. 32. All they knew was, that some danger threatened their religion, and under that impression they hastened as with one impulse (ὁμοθυμαδόν) to the usual place of concourse for further inquiry, or for consultation. Remains of the theatre at Ephesus are still visible. Its outline can be traced, showing its dimensions to have been larger than those of any other theatre known to us from ancient times. It was built on the side of a lofty hill, with the seats rising in long succession one above another, and, like similar edifices among the ancients, was entirely open to the sky. A recent traveller judges that it was large enough to contain thirty thousand persons. The temple of Diana could be seen from it, at no great distance, across the market-place. Luke has violated no probability, therefore, in representing so many people as assembled in such a place. — συναρπάσαντες, *after having seized along* (out of the house, prior to ὥρμησαν), or (coincident with the verb), *having seized along* when they rushed. See note on 21, 7. Meyer prefers the first mode, De Wette the second. See W. § 45. 6. b. For a different explanation of σύν in the participle, see Rob. Lex. s. v. — *Gaius*, or *Caius*, who was a Macedonian, is not the one mentioned in 20, 4, or in Rom. 16, 23 and 1 Cor. 1, 15; for the former belonged to Derbe, the latter to Corinth. — *Aristarchus* was a Thessalonian (20, 4); see further, on 27, 2.

V. 30. Παύλου. Paul may have been absent from his abode at the time of the assault, as was the case at Thessalonica (17, 6). — εἰς τὸν δῆμον, *unto the people* in the theatre (v. 31). His idea may have been, that his appearance there in person, or a declaration that he was willing to have his conduct examined, would allay the tumult; comp. v. 37. His anxiety must have been the greater from his not knowing to what danger the friends who had fallen into the hands of the mob might be exposed. — οἱ μαθηταί, *the disciples*, who were, no doubt, native Ephesians. They understood their countrymen too well to encourage the apostle's inclination.

V. 31. τῶν Ἀσιαρχῶν. The *Asiarchs* were ten men (Mey.), chosen annually from the chief towns in proconsular Asia, to superintend the games and festivals held every year in honor of the gods and the Roman emperor. They were chosen from the wealthier class of citizens, since, like the Roman ædiles, they were required to provide for these exhibitions at their own expense. Those who had filled the office once, retained the title for the rest of life. One of the number acted as chief Asiarch, who resided commonly at Ephesus. The Bithyniarchs, Galatarchs, Syriarchs, were a similar class of magistrates in other provinces of Western Asia. — Akerman offers here the following just remark: "That the very maintainers and presidents of the heathen sports and festivals of a people to whom the doctrine of Christ and the resurrection was foolishness were the friends of Paul, was an assertion which no fabricator of a forgery would have ventured upon. We cannot penetrate the veil which antiquity has thrown over these events, and are only left to conjecture, either that Christianity itself had supporters, though secret ones who feared the multitude, in these wealthy Asiatics; or that, careless of the truth of what the apostle preached, they admired his eloquence, and wished to protect one whom they considered so highly gifted."

V. 32. οὖν, *therefore*, resumptive as in 9, 31; 8, 4. It puts forward the narrative from the point reached in v. 29. The two preceding verses relate to a collateral circumstance.

V. 33. ἐκ δὲ τοῦ ὄχλου, κ. τ. λ., *Now out of the crowd*, from their midst, *they*, viz. the Jews, *urged forward Alexander*. "As the Jews here lived in the midst of a numerous Greek population who viewed them with constant aversion, any special occasion roused their slumbering prejudices into open violence, and they had then much to suffer. Hence the Jews on this occasion feared that the anger of the people against the enemies of their gods — especially as many of them did not know who were really intended — would be directed against themselves, and they were anxious, therefore, that one of their number, a man by the name of Alexander, should stand forward, in order to shift the blame from themselves upon the Christians; but the appearance of such a person who himself belonged to the enemies of their gods, excited in the heathen still greater rage, and the clamor became more violent." This is the view of Neander, and is the one adopted by Kuinoel, Hemsen, Olshausen, Winer, and most others. Some, on the contrary, as Calvin, Meyer, Wieseler, understand that Alexander was a Jewish Christian, and that the Jews, who recognized him as such, pushed him forward in order to expose him to the fury of the populace. ἀπολογεῖσθαι has been said to favor this opinion; but it may refer to a defence in behalf of the Jews as well as of the Christians. The Alexander in 2 Tim. 4, 14 could hardly have been the same person; ὁ χαλκεύς may have been added there to distinguish him from this individual. — προβαλλόντων αὐτὸν τῶν Ἰουδαίων, *the Jews thrusting him forward*. The subject of this subordinate clause is the same as that of the principal clause which precedes; whereas, according to the ordinary rule, it is only when the subjects are different that the genitive absolute is employed. προβαλλόντων would have been regularly in the nominative. Exceptions like this occur in the classics. The idea of the secondary clause acquires in this way more prominence. See K. § 313. R. 2, as compared with § 312. 3.

V. 34. ἐπιγνόντες is nominative, as if ἐφώνησαν ἅπαντες had followed, instead of φωνὴ . . . . ἐκ πάντων. See W. § 63. I. 1. The expression with that change would have been more correct, but less forcible. μία ἐκ πάντων is a *callida junctura*, which will arrest the reader's attention. — ὡς ἐπὶ ὥρας, κ. τ. λ. Their unintermitted cry *for about two hours*, "*Great is Diana of the Ephesians!*" not only declared their attachment to her worship, but, according to the ideas of the heathen, was itself an act of worship; comp. 1 Kings 18, 26; Matt. 6, 7. The Mohammedan monks in India at the present time often practise such repetitions for entire days together. They have been known to say over a single syllable, having a supposed religious efficacy, until they exhaust their strength and are unable to articulate any longer.[1] — It has been remarked that the reverberation of their voices from the steep rock which formed one side of the theatre (see on v. 29) must have rendered the many-mouthed, frenzied exclamation still more terrific.

VERSES 35–40. *Speech of the City-Recorder, who quells the Uproar and disperses the Multitude.*

V. 35. ὁ γραμματεύς, *The Recorder.* In the cities of Asia Minor, as appears from notices and inscriptions, this was the title of a very important magistrate with various functions, though his more immediate province was to register the public acts and laws, or to preserve the record of them. See Win. Realw. I. p. 649. He was authorized to preside over public assemblies, and is mentioned on marbles as acting in that capacity. He stood next in rank to the municipal chief, and performed his duties during the absence or on the death of that officer. A γραμματεύς, or town-clerk, of Ephesus is often mentioned on coins of that city. See New Englander, X. p. 144. — καταστείλας τὸν ὄχλον, *having stilled the crowd,* by showing himself to them, and making a sign (13, 16) that he wished to speak. — In τίς γάρ ἐστιν, κ. τ. λ., the conjunction refers to a suppressed thought: You have no occasion for this excitement; *for what human being is there,* etc. ἀνθρώπων (comp. 1 Cor. 2, 11) and not ἄνθρωπος (T. R.) is to be read here. — ὃς οὐ, κ. τ. λ., *who does not know that the city of the Ephesians is keeper,* guardian, *of the great Diana;* and hence it was unbecoming in them to be so sensitive, as if their reputation was at stake. θεᾶς after μεγάλης (T. R.) should be omitted. νεωκόρον, lit. *temple-sweeper,* became at length an honorary title, and as such was granted to certain Asiatic cities in recognition of the care and expense bestowed by them on the temple and worship of their favorite deities. It is found on coins of Ephesus, struck about Paul's time. — τοῦ Διοπετοῦς, sc. ἀγάλματος, *the image fallen from Jupiter,* and hence so much the more sacred. There was a similar tradition in regard to a statue of Artemis in Tauris (Eurip. Iph. T. 977), and also one of Pallas at Athens (Pausan. I. 26. 6).

[1] See Tholuck's Auslegung der Bergpredigt (3d ed.), p. 328 sq.

V. 36. *τούτων, these things,* viz. the established reputation of the Ephesians for their attachment to the worship of Diana, and the well-known origin of her image. Hence the argument is two-fold: They had no reason to fear that such a people (*νεωκόρον*) could be induced to abandon a religion which so wonderful an event (*διοπετοῦς*) had signalized. — *δέον ἐστὶν ὑμᾶς, it is necessary that you,* i. e. morally, *you ought.*

V. 37. *γάρ* confirms the implication in *προπετές,* i. e. that they had acted rashly. — *τούτους* refers to Gaius and Aristarchus; see v. 29. Paul was not present. — *ἱεροσύλους, robbers of temples,* not *of churches.* It is singular that the latter translation, so incorrect, should be found in all the English versions, except Wiclif's and the Rheims, which being drawn from the Vulgate, have "sacrilegious." The temples among the heathen contained votive offerings and other gifts, and were often plundered. — *οὔτε ...... ὑμῶν, nor blaspheming your goddess.* It was the effect of Paul's preaching to undermine idolatry, and bring the worship of Artemis into contempt; but as at Athens, so here he had refrained from denunciation, opprobrium, ridicule, and had opposed error by contending for the truth. Hence the Recorder could urge that technical view of the apostle's conduct, and deny that he had committed any actionable offence. It would almost seem as if, like the Asiarchs, he was friendly at heart to the new sect.

V. 38. *οὖν, therefore,* since the men are innocent in regard to such crimes as sacrilege and blasphemy. — *σὺν αὐτῷ, with him,* i. e. his associates in the complaint against Paul (comp. 5, 17). The speaker knew of their connection with the case from something which they had done or said in the assembly, which Luke has not related. — *ἀγόραιοι,* sc. *ἡμέραι ἄγονται, court-days are kept,* observed. The days are so called because the courts were held in the forum; comp. 16, 19; 17, 5. It is contended by some, that this adjective should be marked as proparoxytone in this sense, but as circumflex when used as in 17, 5. See W. § 6. 2. The distinction is a doubtful one. — *καὶ ἀνθύπατοί εἰσιν, and there are proconsuls.* The plural is generic (comp. Matt. 2, 20), as but one such officer presided over a province. The coins of Ephesus show that the proconsular authority was fully established there in the reign of Nero. Akerman gives the engraving of one which has the head of that emperor on the obverse; and on the reverse, a representation of the temple of Diana, with the words: (Money) *of the Ephesians, Neocori, Æchmocles Aviola, Proconsul.* — *ἐγκαλείτωσαν ἀλλήλοις, let them implead each other,* is a technical phrase.

V. 39. They were a mob, and could transact no public business. — εἰ δέ τι, κ. τ. λ., *But if ye make any demand* (stronger than the simple verb) *concerning other things* than those of a private nature. — ἐν τῇ ἐννόμῳ ἐκκλησίᾳ, *in the lawful assembly* which this is not. "Legitimus cœtus est qui a magistratu civitatis convocatur et regitur." (Grot.)

V. 40. γάρ justifies the intimation in ἐννόμῳ as to the character of the present concourse. — κινδυνεύομεν. They were in danger of being called to account by the proconsul. The Roman government watched every appearance of insubordination or sedition in the provinces with a jealous eye. Thousands were often put to death in the attempt to suppress such movements. It was a capital offence to take any part in a riotous proceeding. The speaker's hint, therefore, was a significant one. — στάσεως depends on περί, not on the verb. The accent on περί is not drawn back, though its noun precedes (B. § 117. 3), because an adjective phrase follows. — μηδενὸς αἰτίου ὑπάρχοντος explains, not why they were liable to be arraigned, but how seriously it would terminate if the affair should take that direction. — περὶ οὗ, *in virtue of which.* — This speech is the model of a popular harangue. Such excitement on the part of the Ephesians was undignified, as they stood above all suspicion in religious matters (v. 35. 36); it was unjustifiable, as they could establish nothing against the men (v. 37); it was unnecessary, as other means of redress were open to them (v. 38. 39); and, finally, if neither pride nor justice availed anything, fear of the Roman power should restrain them (v. 40).

CHAPTER XX.

VERSES 1–6. *Paul proceeds a second time to Greece, and returns from there to Troas.*

V. 1. μετὰ δὲ τὸ παύσασθαι τὸν θόρυβον, *Now after the tumult had ceased.* This clause shows that Paul left Ephesus soon after the disturbance, but furnishes no evidence, says Neander, that his departure was hastened by it. We may conclude that Paul "tarried at Ephesus until Pentecost," pursuant to his intention expressed in 1 Cor. 16, 8; and consequently, that he left that city in the spring or summer of A. D. 57 or 58. Compare the note on 18, 23 with that on 19, 10. — Before taking leave of

Ephesus, we must notice another event which Luke has not recorded, but which belongs to this part of the history. In 2 Cor. 12, 14 (written on the way to Greece), the apostle says: ἰδού, τρίτον τοῦτο ἑτοίμως ἔχω ἐλθεῖν πρὸς ὑμᾶς, *Behold, this third time I am ready to come unto you.* The connection decides that τρίτον belongs to ἐλθεῖν. It cannot refer to a third intention merely to visit the Corinthians; for he is saying that, as he had "not been burdensome to them" hitherto when he was among them, so in his present visit he would adhere to the same policy. Again, in 2 Cor. 13, 1, he says: τρίτον τοῦτο ἔρχομαι. Here it is expressly said, that the apostle was now on the point of making his third journey to Corinth. The correct interpretation of 2 Cor. 1, 15. 16 presents no obstacle to this construction of the passages here referred to. The sixteenth of these verses explains the fifteenth. The apostle has reference in v. 16 to a journey to Corinth which he had purposed, but had failed to execute; viz. a journey into Macedonia by the way of Corinth, and then a return to Corinth from Macedonia; and in v. 15 he says that this plan would have secured to the Corinthians "a second benefit" (δευτέραν χάριν) in connection with the tour proposed, i. e. the benefit of his presence, not once merely, but a second time. There is every reason to suppose, therefore, that Paul had been at Corinth twice when he wrote his Second Epistle to the church in that city. So conclude, among others, Michaelis, Schrader, Bleek, Lücke, Schott, Anger, Rückert, Credner, Neander, Olshausen, Meyer, Wieseler, Osiander, Howson. But where in Luke's narrative are we to insert this second journey to Corinth? Of the different answers given to this question, I regard that as the most satisfactory which places the journey within the period of Paul's residence of three years at Ephesus. It would have been easy for him to have crossed over from the one city to the other at any time; and, considering the urgent reasons for such a visit furnished by the condition of the Corinthian church, one would think that he could hardly have refrained from availing himself of the opportunity. As his stay there was probably very brief, and unattended by any important event, Luke has made no mention of it. Schrader, Rückert, Olshausen, Meyer, Wieseler, Howson, and others, intercalate the journey at this point. Neander suggests that Paul, at the commencement of this missionary tour, may have extended his travels before his arrival at Ephesus so far as to have included Greece. Anger, Schott, and some others, think that Paul's second visit to Corinth may have been a return to that city from some excursion which he made into the neighboring regions during the year and a half of his first sojourn at Corinth (18, 1 sq.). — ἀσπασάμενος, *having embraced* them. How many tears of affection must have been shed! How many prayers must have been offered for each other and for the cause of Christ! From such hints as those in v. 37. 38 and in 21, 5. 6, we can call up to ourselves an image of the scene. They must have parted with a presentiment at least that the apostle was now taking his final leave of Ephesus; see v. 25. 38. — ἐξῆλθε, κ. τ. λ., *went forth to go into Macedonia.* The direction which the apostle took we learn from 2 Cor. 2, 12. 13. He proceeded to Troas, where he had expected to meet Titus, whom he had sent to Corinth in order to ascertain the effect of his First Epistle to the church in that city. It was his intention, apparently, to remain and labor for a time at Troas, in case the information for which he was looking should be favorable. But not finding Titus there, and being unable to endure a longer suspense, he embarked at once for Macedonia. On his arrival there he met with Titus, and was relieved of his anxiety; see 2 Cor. 7, 6.

V. 2. τὰ μέρη ἐκεῖνα, *those parts,* i. e the region of Macedonia. — παρακαλέσας αὐτούς, *having exhorted them,* viz. the believers; see on 16, 40. The expression shows that he now revisited the places where he had preached on his first visit here, viz. Philippi, Thessalonica, Berœa. It was here and now that Paul wrote his Second Epistle to the Corinthians. That he wrote the letter in Macedonia is evident from 2 Cor. 9, 2. 4. He speaks there of his boasting to the churches of Macedonia of the liberality of the Corinthians, and of the possibility that some of the Macedonians would accompany him to Corinth. See, also, 2 Cor. 7, 5. The apostle, now, as far as we know, was in that country only three times. When he was there first he had not yet been at Corinth at all (16, 11) and when he passed through that province on his last return to Jerusalem (v. 3 below), he was going in the opposite direction, and not advancing to Corinth, as stated in the Epistle. He wrote the Second Epistle to the Corinthians, therefore, on this second journey through Macedonia, in the summer probably, or early autumn of A. D. 58; see note on 21, 17. — In Rom. 15, 19, Paul speaks of having published the gospel *as far as to Illyricum,* which was a country on the west of Macedonia. It was at this time, probably, that he penetrated so far in that direction. It could not have been on his first visit to Macedonia (16, 12 sq.); for the course of his journey at that time is minutely traced in the Acts from his landing at Philippi to his leaving Corinth. He moved along the eastern side of the peninsula, and was kept at a distance from Illyricum. When he passed through Macedonia next (v. 3), he had already written the Epistle to the Romans. Lardner pronounces this geographical coincidence sufficiently important to confirm the entire history of Paul's travels. — εἰς τὴν Ἑλλάδα, *unto Greece*, which stands here for Ἀχαΐα (18, 12; 19, 21), as opposed to Macedonia. Wetstein has shown that Luke was justified in that use of the term. Paul was proceeding to Corinth, the capital of the province; comp. Rom. 16, 1.

V. 3. The *three months* spent here preceded the summer of this year; see v. 6. The stay was thus brief because the apostle was anxious to return to Jerusalem (v. 16). The Jewish plot was contemporaneous with his leaving, but did not occasion it. — ποιήσας is anacoluthic for ποιήσαντι; see 19, 24. — It was just before his departure from Corinth, that Paul wrote the Epistle to the Romans. That it was written at Corinth admits of being proved by several distinct arguments. One is that Paul was the guest of Gaius at the time (Rom. 16, 23), and Gaius, as we learn from 1 Cor. 1, 14, was one of the converts at Corinth whom Paul baptized. Again, he commends to the Roman Christians Phœbe, a deaconess of the church at Cenchrea (see on 18, 18), who was on the point of proceeding to Rome (Rom. 16, 1), and was probably the bearer of the letter. Further, the apostle's situation as disclosed in the Epistle agrees with that in the Acts at this time. Thus, he was on the eve of departing to Jerusalem (Rom. 15, 25), was going thither with contributions for the Jewish believers (Rom. 15, 25. 26), and after that was meditating a journey to Rome. The date of the Epistle, therefore, was the spring of A. D. 58 or 59. — μέλλοντι, κ. τ. λ., *as he is about to embark for Syria*, with the intention of going directly to Jerusalem; see also 19, 21. The effect of the conspiracy was to change his route, but not to cause him to depart prematurely. He came with the design of passing only the winter there; see 1 Cor. 16, 6. — ἐγένετο, κ. τ. λ., *it was thought best that he should return through Macedonia.* The infinitive depends on γνώμη as a sort of appositional genitive. The expression indicates that he took this course as the result of advice or consultation. How his journeying by land rather than by sea would enable him to escape the machinations of the Jews is not perfectly clear. The opinion that he was waiting to have the navigation of the season reopen, but was compelled to hasten his departure before that time, is certainly incorrect; for it is said he was on the point of embarking when the conspiracy of the Jews was formed or came to be known. It is possible that the Jews intended to assault him on his way to the ship, or else to follow and capture him after having put to sea. Hemsen's conjecture (Der Apostel Paulus, u. s. w., p. 467) is, that he had not yet found a vessel proceeding to Syria, and that his exposure at Corinth rendered it unsafe for him to remain, even a few days longer, until the arrival of such an opportunity.

V. 4. συνείπετο αὐτῷ, *followed him*, formed his party. This could be said, though they did not travel in company all the time. The verb belongs to all the names which follow, but agrees with the nearest. — The best manuscripts read Πύῤῥου after Σώπατρος, sc. υἱός; genitive of kindredship (see on 1, 13). This addition distinguishes *Sopater* perhaps from *Sosispater* in Rom. 16, 21, since they are but different forms of the same name (Win.). — Θεσσαλονικέων is a partitive genitive. — *Aristarchus* was mentioned in 19, 29. The *Gaius* in that passage must be a different person from the one here, since they belonged to different countries. This Gaius is probably the individual of this name to whom the apostle John wrote his Third Epistle. Some critics (Kuin. Olsh. Neand.) would point the text, so as to make Gaius one of the Thessalonians, and join Δερβαῖος with Τιμόθεος. But that division not only puts καί out of its natural place, but disagrees with 16, 1, where Timothy appears as a native of Lystra.—*Secundus* is otherwise unknown.—Luke supposes *Timothy's* origin to be familiar to the reader, and so passes it over (De Wet. Mey.). — *Tychicus* is named in Eph. 6, 21; Col. 4, 7; Tit. 3, 12, and 2 Tim. 4, 12. He was one of the most trusted of Paul's associates. — *Trophimus*, who was an Ephesian, appears again in 21, 29, and 2 Tim. 4, 20. He and probably Aristarchus (27, 2) went with the apostle to Jerusalem. The others may have stopped at Miletus, since the language in v. 13 intimates that the party kept together after leaving Troas. Consequently, ἄχρι τῆς Ἀσίας would state the destination of the majority of the travellers, and would be consistent with the fact that two of them went further.

V. 5. οὗτοι, *these*, viz. the seven mentioned in v. 4, not the two named last. It is entirely arbitrary to limit the reference of the pronoun. — προελθόντες, *having gone forward* from Corinth in advance of Paul and Luke. It is barely possible that they shipped at once for Troas; but it is more probable that they journeyed through Macedonia, both because συνείπετο suggests a common route of the parties, and because Sopater and the others may have been sent thither to finish the alms-collection, which Paul had commenced.—ἡμᾶς, *us*. Luke resumes here the first person plural, which has not occurred since 16, 17. See the remarks on 16, 40.

V. 6. ἡμεῖς, *we*, must include the writer of the narrative, Paul, and possibly others, in distinction from those who had gone forward to Troas. As Timothy was one of those who preceded the apostle, it is evident that he and the writer of the narrative were different persons. Tholuck, Lange,[1] Ebrard, and others, pronounce this passage sufficient of itself to disprove the hypothesis that Timothy, not Luke, wrote the portions of the Acts in which the historian speaks as an eye witness. — ἐξεπλεύσαμεν ἀπὸ Φιλίππων, *we sailed forth from Philippi*, i. e. from its harbor on the coast; see note on 16, 12. — μετὰ τὰς ἡμέρας τῶν ἀζύμων, *after the days of unleavened bread*, the festival of the Passover (see on 12, 3), which no doubt they observed, not in the Jewish spirit any longer, but with a recognition of Christ as the true Paschal Lamb; see John 1, 36 and 1 Cor. 5, 7. Some think that they remained at Philippi for the sake of the celebration (Mey.); but we must view that as an inference altogether, since Luke mentions the Passover only in its chronological relation to the voyage. Calvin suggests as the motive for remaining that Paul would find the Jews more accessible to the truth during the season of such a solemnity. — ἄχρις ἡμερῶν πέντε, *unto five days*, as the limit reached; they were so long on the way. The passage on the apostle's first journey to Europe occupied two days only; see 16, 11. Adverse winds or calms would be liable, at any season of the year, to occasion this variation. — ἡμέρας ἑπτά, *seven days*, may be indefinite, *a week's time* (comp. 21, 4; 28, 14). They arranged it so as to bring a Sabbath within the time spent there. If the number be exact, then they arrived just at the close of the week, since they left the day after the Sabbath (v. 7).

VERSES 7–12. *Paul preaches at Troas, and administers the Sacrament.*

V. 7. ἐν τῇ μιᾷ τῶν σαββάτων, *on the first day of the week;* not on *one of the Sabbaths*, Jewish festivals, which overlooks the article, and not on *the one of them* next after their arrival, since that would imply that they passed more than one such festival here, contrary to Luke's statement that they left on the day following. In the New Testament εἷς stands generally for πρῶτος in speaking of the days of the week; see Matt. 28, 1; Mark 16, 2; John 20, 19, etc. W. § 37. 1. It is an imitation of the ordinal sense of אֶחָד. See Gesen. Heb. Gr. § 118. 4. The passages just cited, and also Luke 24, 1; John 20, 1, and 1 Cor. 16, 2 show that *week* is one of the senses of σάββατα. The Jews reckoned the day from evening to

[1] Das Leben Jesu nach den Evangelien dargestellt, Erstes Buch, p. 251.

morning, and on that principle the evening of *the first day of the week* would be our Saturday evening. If Luke reckons so here, as many commentators suppose, the apostle then waited for the expiration of the Jewish Sabbath, and held his last religious service with the brethren at Troas, at the beginning of the Christian Sabbath, i. e. on Saturday evening, and consequently resumed his journey on Sunday morning. But as Luke had mingled so much with foreign nations and was writing for Gentile readers, he would be very apt to designate the time in accordance with their practice; so that his evening or night of *the first day of the week* would be the end of the Christian Sabbath, and the morning of his departure that of Monday. Olshausen, Neander, De Wette, Meyer, and most other critics, recognize here a distinct trace of the Christian Sabbath in that early age of the church. See also 1 Cor. 16, 2, and Rev. 1, 10. It is entirely immaterial, of course, to the objects of the day or the validity of the apostolic example, whether the first Christians began their Sabbath in the Jewish way, on Saturday evening, or at midnight, a few hours later. "Since the sufferings of Christ," says Neander, "appeared as the central point of all religious experience and life, since his resurrection was considered as the foundation of all Christian joy and hope, it was natural that the communion of the church should have specially distinguished the day with which the memory of that event had connected itself." But the introduction of the Sabbath was not only in harmony with Christian feeling, but, as we have good reason to believe, was sanctioned and promoted by the special authority of the apostles. "It is in the highest degree probable," says Meyer, "that the observance of the Sabbath rests upon apostolic institution; since the gospel was extended among the heathen who had not been accustomed to the Jewish Sabbath, it was natural and necessary that the apostles should instruct them in regard to such a day, on account of the importance of the resurrection of Christ; and this supposition is an indispensable one, in order to account for the very early and general celebration of the Christian Sabbath." In support of the last remark, this author refers to Justin Martyr, who, born at the beginning of the second century, says (Apol. II.) that the Christians of his time, "both in the cities and the country, were accustomed to assemble for worship on the day called Sunday" (τῇ τοῦ ἡλίου λεγομένῃ ἡμέρᾳ).—συνηγμένων ἡμῶν, *we being assembled;* not τῶν μαθητῶν, the received reading, which our version follows. The latter term may have been inserted to provide an antecedent for αὐτοῖς. The use of the pronoun is like that in 8, 5.—For κλάσαι ἄρτον, see on 2, 42. 46.

V. 8. ἦσαν δὲ λαμπάδες ἱκαναί, *Now there were many lamps;* and hence the fall of the young man was perceived at once. So Meyer explains the object of the remark. But that relation of the circumstance to the rest of the narrative is not clearly indicated. It has much more the appearance of having proceeded from an eye witness, who mentions the incident, not for the purpose of obviating a difficulty which might occur to the reader, but because the entire scene to which he refers stood now with such minuteness and vividness before his mind. The moon was full at the Passover (v. 6), and after the lapse now of somewhat less than three weeks, only appeared as a faint crescent in the early part of the night (Hws.).—ἐν τῷ ὑπερῴῳ, *in the upper room,* which, as appears from the next verse, was on the third story. See note on 1, 13.—οὗ ἦμεν συνηγμένοι, *where we were assembled.* In the received text the verb is ἦσαν, *they were,* which accords with the variation in the last verse.

V. 9. ἐπὶ τῆς θυρίδος, *upon the window,* the seat of it. "It will be recollected that there were no windows of glass; and the window here mentioned was a lattice of joinery, or a door, which on this occasion was set open on account of the heat from the many lights and the number of persons in the room. It should be observed that the windows of such places in general reached nearly to the floor; they would correspond well to what our word 'window' signified originally, viz. *windore, wind-door,* i. e. a door for the admission of wind or air."[1]—καταφερόμενος ὕπνῳ βαθεῖ, *being overcome with deep sleep.*—κατενεχθεὶς ἀπὸ τοῦ ὕπνου, *having been borne down from* (the effect of) *the sleep* into which he had sunk. This second participial clause states a result of the condition described by the first.—ἔπεσεν. The window projected (according to the side of the room where it was situated) either over the street, or over the interior court; so that in either case he fell from the third story upon the hard earth or pavement below.—ἤρθη νεκρός, *was taken up dead;* which it is entirely foreign to any intimation of the context to qualify by adding "in appearance," or "as they supposed."

V. 10. ἐπέπεσεν, κ. τ. λ., *fell upon him, and having embraced him,* after the example of Elisha in 2 Kings 4, 34. As in that instance, so in this, the act appears to have been the sign of a miracle.—μὴ θορυβεῖσθε, *do not lament,* which, according to the Oriental habit and the import of the word, they were doing with loud and passionate outcry; comp. Matt. 9, 23; Mark 5, 39. See on 10, 15.—

[1] Illustrated Commentary, Vol. V. p. 206.

ἡ γὰρ ψυχὴ . . . . ἐστιν, *for his life is in him*, which he could say whether he perceived that it was not extinct, or had been restored.

V. 11. τὸν ἄρτον, *the bread* already spoken of in v. 7. The article which the T. R. omits, belongs here (Tsch. Lchm. Mey.). The fall of Eutychus had delayed the communion, which Paul now proceeds to administer. — γευσάμενος, *having eaten*, because probably they connected a repast with the sacrament; see on 2, 42. — ἐφ' ἱκανόν may refer to the time occupied in the entire service; or, more naturally in this connection, to the remainder of the night after the preceding interruption.— ἄχρις αὐγῆς, *until day-break*, about five o'clock, A. M., at that season (Alf.). — οὕτως, *thus*, after these events; comp. 17, 33; 28, 14. — ἐξῆλθεν, *went forth*, i. e. on his journey. Yet the term may not exclude a brief interval between the religious services and his departure, and during that time the vessel could weigh anchor and start for Assos (see on v. 13).

V. 12. ἤγαγον, *brought him* into the assembly (Hems. Mey.), not to his home. The subject of the verb is indefinite. This circumstance is supplementary to what is stated in v. 11; not subsequent to it in point of time.— ζῶντα, *living*, which suggests as its antithesis that he had been dead; or, at least, that such was their belief. — παρεκλήθησαν, *were consoled*, viz. by his restoration to them. Some understand it of the effect of Paul's discourse; which is incorrect, as that is not here the subject of remark.— οὐ μετρίως, *not a little*, very much. Observe the litotes.

VERSES 13-16. *They prosecute the Journey to Miletus.*

V. 13. ἡμεῖς, *we*, viz. the writer and the other companions of the apostle. — προελθόντες, *having gone forward*, though from the circumstances of the case, it could not have been long first. They may have left as soon as the assembly broke up, while Paul still remained a short time (see on v. 11); or, in order to reach Assos in good season, may have left even before the conclusion of the service. *They* spent the entire week at Troas as well as Paul (see v. 6), and hence could not have preceded him before the end of that time. — εἰς τὴν Ἄσσον, *unto Assos*, which was a coast-town in Mysia, south of Troas. — ἐκεῖθεν, *from there*, because the writer has his mind, not on their arrival, but the subsequent departure or progress. — οὕτω γὰρ, κ. τ. λ., *for so* (that they should take him at that place) *he had arranged for himself;* the passive in the sense of the middle. W. § 39. 3. — μέλλων refers to his intention. — πεζεύειν. This foot-journey, according to the best evidence, was about twenty miles. A paved road extended from Troas to Assos; so that starting even as late as seven or eight o'clock, A. M., Paul could have reached Assos in the afternoon. A friend of the writer, a native of Greece, stated that he himself had travelled on foot between the two places in five hours. The distance by sea is about forty miles. His object, it is conjectured, may have been to visit friends on the way, or to have the company of brethren from Troas, whom the vessel was not large enough to accommodate.

V. 14. ὡς συνέβαλεν ἡμῖν, *as he met with us*, seems to imply that he found them already there. — εἰς τὴν Ἄσσον, *at Assos*, lit. *unto*, because the preceding verb implies the idea of the journey thither on the part of Paul. *Mitylene*, where they appear to have stopped over night, was on the east side of Lesbos, the capital of that island. The distance from Assos by sea was thirty miles; so that the voyage hither from Troas was an easy one for a day. Castro, the present capital, stands on the site of the ancient city. The name of the island is now Metilino or Metelin, a corruption of Mitylene.

V. 15. τῇ ἐπιούσῃ, *on the following day*, the second from Troas. —ἀντικρὺ Χίου, *opposite to Chios*, the modern Scio, south of Lesbos. The language intimates that, instead of putting into the harbor, they lay off the coast during the night.— τῇ δὲ ἑτέρᾳ, κ. τ. λ., *and upon the next day* (the third from Troas) *we put along unto Samos.* This island is still further down the Ægean. At one point it approaches within six miles of the mainland. It retains still the ancient name. They may have touched here, but as appears from the next clause did not stop long.— καὶ μείναντες ἐν Τρωγυλλίῳ, *and having remained at Trogyllium*, which was their next night-station, since *on the following day*, being the fourth, they arrived at Miletus. Trogyllium most commentators suppose to be the promontory and the town of that name in southern Ionia, opposite Samos where it is nearest to the shore. There was also an island of the same name on the coast of this promontory (Strab. 14. 636), which, says Forbiger (Handb. II. p. 170), was unquestionably the Trogyllium intended in this passage. The apostle would have been nearer to Ephesus, at Trogyllium on the mainland, than he was at Miletus; but a better harbor or greater facility of intercourse may have led him to prefer the more distant place for his interview with the elders. — *Miletus* was on the confines of Caria, twenty-eight miles south of Ephesus, and just below the mouth of the Meander. They reached here on the fourth day from Troas, hence either on Wednesday or Thursday, some doubt existing (see on v. 7) as to the day of the week when they sailed from Troas.

V. 16. The external testimony requires κεκρίκει, instead of ἔκρινε (Grsb. Lchm. Mey.): *For he had determined to sail past Ephesus*, which explains why they had left that city at the north; they were opposite to it when at Samos. As it depended on his decision whether they stopped or proceeded, Paul and his friends had evidently some control of the vessel. The number being so great, they may have chartered the craft (as is very common in the Levant at present); at all events they must have had sufficient influence with the captain to induce him to consult their wishes. — ὅπως . . . . ἐν τῇ Ἀσίᾳ, *that it might not happen to him*, i. e. that he might avoid inducements, *to spend time in Asia.* He might have gone to Ephesus and returned during the time that he remained at Miletus; but he feared to trust himself there lest the importunity of friends or the condition of the church might detain him too long, or even lead him to alter his purpose. — ἔσπευδε γάρ, κ.τ.λ., *for he was hastening, if it were possible for him*, etc. More than three of the seven weeks between the Passover and Pentecost had elapsed already. One had expired before they left Philippi; they were five days on their way to Troas, remained there seven days, and were four days on the way to Miletus. — For πεντηκοστῆς, see on 2, 1. — γενέσθαι implies motion, and takes after it εἰς.

VERSES 17–35. *The Address of Paul to the Ephesian Elders at Miletus.*

V. 17. His subject is fidelity in the ministerial office; first, as illustrated in his own example; and secondly, as required of those whom the Spirit has called to this office. In v. 18–21 he reminds his hearers of his conduct while he lived among them; in v. 19–25 he informs them that he is about to be separated from them to meet no more on earth; and in v. 26–35 he charges them to be watchful for the safety of the flock which had been intrusted to them, and was to be exposed in future to so many dangers. — πρεσβυτέρους = ἐπισκόπους (v. 28). Compare the note on 14, 23. Our English translators render the latter term "overseers" in v. 28, contrary to their usual practice. "The E. V.," says Mr. Alford very candidly, "has hardly dealt fairly in this case with the sacred text; since it ought there as in all other places to have been 'bishops,' that the fact of *elders* and *bishops* having been originally and apostolically synonymous might be apparent to the ordinary English reader, which now it is not." — Luke speaks only of the Ephesian elders as summoned to meet the apostle at

Miletus; but as the report of his arrival must have spread rapidly, it could not have failed to draw together others also, not only from Ephesus, but from the neighboring towns where churches had been established. See on v. 25.

V. 18. ὑμεῖς is emphatic; see on 10, 15. — ἀπὸ πρώτης .... Ἀσίαν, *from the first day I came unto Asia*, we are to connect with πῶς .... ἐγενόμην, *how I conducted* (Kuin. De Wet.); not with ἐπίστασθε, *ye know* (Mey.). As was to be foreseen, Meyer corrects himself here in his last edition. — The duration of the period (πάντα χρόνον) is stated in v. 31. The position of τόν before πάντα is exceptional, as in Gal. 5, 14, and 1 Tim. 1, 16. See K. § 246. 5. β.

V. 19. μετὰ πάσης ταπεινοφροσύνης, *with all*, the utmost (see on 4, 29), *lowliness of mind*, humility; its opposite is ὑψηλὰ φρονεῖν (Rom. 12, 16). Compare Phil. 2, 3 and 1 Pet. 5, 5. This use of πᾶς, says Tholuck,[1] is eminently Pauline; comp. Eph. 1, 3. 8; 4, 2; 6, 18; 2 Cor. 12, 12; 1 Tim. 3, 4; 2 Tim. 4, 2; Tit. 2, 15; 3, 2. — δακρύων, *with tears* of solicitude for their salvation; see v. 31. Compare 2 Cor. 2, 4 and Phil. 3, 18. πολλῶν before δακρύων in the common text should be dropped (Grsb. Mey. Tsch.). — πειρασμῶν, *trials*, persecutions which he suffered from his countrymen. Luke has not spoken distinctly of these Jewish machinations at Ephesus; but in 19, 9 he describes a state of feeling on the part of the Jews, which must have been a prolific source of hostility both to the person of the apostle and to the objects of his ministry. That his situation there was one of constant peril we see from 1 Cor. 15, 31. 32; 16, 9; and 2 Cor. 1, 8–10.

V. 20. ὡς οὐδὲν, κ. τ. λ., depends still on ἐπίστασθε (v. 18), but illustrates at the same time the intervening πῶς ἐγενόμην: *how* (not *that*) *I kept back nothing of the things expedient*, i. e. out of regard to men's censure or their favor. How perfectly this remark harmonizes with Paul's character we have proof in such passages as 2 Cor. 4, 2; Gal. 1, 10; 1 Thess. 2, 4. — τοῦ μὴ ἀναγγεῖλαι, κ. τ. λ., *that I should* or *might* (telic, as if in denial of the possibility that he could mean to preach less than the entire truth) *not announce unto you and teach you*, viz. the things expedient for them. But both clauses contain a negative idea, and the rule stated on 10, 47 may apply here: he withheld nothing from them, that *he should* (as the effect of such withholding) *not announce*

[1] "Die Reden des Apostels Paulus in der Apostelgeschichte, mit seinen Briefen verglichen," in the Studien und Kritiken, 1839, p. 305 sq. I have drawn several of the notes on this address from that instructive Article.

and teach. In other words, the infinitive states not the object of ὑπεστειλάμεν as before, but a consequence of the suppression if unhindered. See W. § 44. 4. Compare v. 27 below. — δημοσίᾳ, *in public*, as in the synagogue (19, 8), or in the school of Tyrannus (19, 9). — κατ' οἴκους, *in houses*, private assemblies.

V. 21. τὴν εἰς τὸν θεὸν μετάνοιαν, *the repentance* (which is meet) *in respect to God*, i. e. exercised towards him as especially wronged by transgression. See Ps. 51, 4. De Wette supposes a breviloquence, as in 8, 22: *repentance* (with a return) *unto God.* Compare 26, 20. The first sense agrees best with the use of εἰς in the next clause. "In God the Father," says Olshausen, "lies expressed the idea of the strict righteousness, to which the repentance directs itself, in Christ the idea of the compassion to which the faith has reference." — "It appears," says Tholuck, "to belong to the peculiarities of the apostle that he in particular appeals so often to his blameless manner of life. The occasion for this lies sometimes in the calumnies of his enemies, as when he says in 2 Cor. 1, 12: 'For our boasting (καύχησις) is this, the testimony of our conscience, that in simplicity and godly sincerity, not with fleshly wisdom, but by the grace of God, we have had our conversation in the world, and more especially among you.' The eleventh chapter shows what adversaries he had in view in this self-justification. But often these appeals spring only from that just confidence with which he can call upon others to imitate him, as he himself imitates the Saviour. Thus in 1 Cor. 11, 1 he cries: 'Be ye followers of me, even as I also am of Christ;' and in Phil. 3, 17: 'Brethren, be followers together of me, and mark them who walk so as ye have us for an ensample.' Such personal testimonies are not found in the other Epistles of the New Testament, nor are they frequent in the writings of other pious men; on which account we are authorized to consider their occurrence in this discourse (v. 18–21) as a mark of its historical character."

V. 22. δεδεμένος τῷ πνεύματι, *bound in the spirit*, i. e. his own, in his mind, feelings (19, 21); constrained by an invincible impulse or sense of duty (Hnr. Kuin. De Wet. Rob.), so as to be indifferent to danger on the one hand (v. 23), and perhaps immovable under any remonstrance or appeal on the other (21, 13). The expression may be compared with our mode of speaking when we say "bound in good faith, in conscience," and the like. Some understand πνεύματι of the Holy Spirit: urged by his influence or command (Calv. Kypk. Wdsth.). But that meaning is the more doubtful here, because τὸ ἅγιον in the next verse appears to be added to distinguish that πνεῦμα from this.

The sense *bound in the spirit*, i. e. viewing himself as already in chains, a prisoner in imagination, though not yet in body (Chrys. Grot. Bng. Hws.), anticipates the sequel of the sentence, and is too artificial where all the rest is expressed with so much simplicity. Meyer's first explanation was *bound on the Holy Spirit* (Rom. 7, 2; 1 Cor. 7, 27), i. e. dependent on him; but I am pleased to see that in his last edition he defends the first of the views given above.

V. 23. πλὴν, sc. εἰδώς, *but knowing*. — κατὰ πόλιν, *from city to city*, as he pursued the present journey. — διαμαρτύρεταί μοι, *testifies fully to me*, not by an inward revelation (for why should he have received that κατὰ πόλιν?), but through the prophetic announcement of others. Luke has not recorded the instances; they may have occurred at Philippi, at Troas, at Assos. He mentions two such communications which were made to Paul after this; see 21, 4. 11. The common text leaves out μοι, which belongs after the verb. — μένουσιν, *await me*, not wherever he went, but at Jerusalem. πορεύομαι εἰς Ἱερουσαλήμ determines the place. — Paley compares this verse with Rom. 15, 30, which Epistle the apostle had just written at Corinth. He there entreats the Roman Christians "to strive together with him in their prayers to God for him, that he might be delivered from them who believed not in Judea." The two passages, therefore, "without any resemblance between them that could induce us to suspect that they were borrowed from one another, represent the state of Paul's mind, with respect to the event of the journey, in terms of substantial agreement. They both express his sense of danger in the approaching visit to Jerusalem; they both express the doubt which dwelt upon his thoughts concerning what might there befall him."

V. 24. οὐδενὸς λόγον ποιοῦμαι, *I make account of nothing*, i. e. which I may be called to suffer. On the contrary, as he says in 2 Cor. 12, 10: "I take pleasure in infirmities, in reproaches, in necessities, in persecutions, in distresses, for Christ's sake." Another reading draws the two clauses of the common text into one: ἀλλ' οὐδενὸς λόγου ποιοῦμαι τὴν ψυχὴν τιμίαν ἐμαυτῷ, *but of no account do I esteem my life worthy for myself.* The construction is less simple than the other, and may have given place to it on that account (Tsch. Mey. Alf.). — ὡς τελειῶσαι τὸν δρόμον μου, *thus* (i. e. with this aim, to wit) *in order to finish my course.* That he should shrink from no danger, that he should be willing to offer up his life for the sake of the gospel, he regarded as due to his office, as essential to his character as an approved minister of Christ. ὡς strengthens merely the telic force of the construction

It occurs with the infinitive here only (unless we add 17, 14), and in the phrase ὡς ἔπος εἰπεῖν (Heb. 7, 9). W. § 44. 1. Alford refers ὡς to τιμίαν, held not his life *so precious as to finish*, etc. But he must arbitrarily insert for that purpose the correlative "so," and even then translates the common reading only and not the one received into his text. — Some critics (Lchm. Mey. Tsch.) omit μετὰ χαρᾶς after δρόμον μου. It is wanting in several important authorities. — διαμαρτύρασθαι . . . . τοῦ θεοῦ defines in what the διακονία consisted. The infinitive may depend on the verbal idea involved in that noun (De Wet.): (commanding or requiring) *that I should testify fully*, etc.; or it may follow as epexegetical. — In the sublime language of this verse we hear distinctly the voice of the man who, on approaching the end of his career, could say: "I am now ready to be offered, and the time of my departure is at hand. I have fought a good fight; I have finished my course, I have kept the faith. Henceforth there is laid up for me a crown of righteousness, which the Lord, the righteous judge, shall give me at that day" (2 Tim. 4, 6–8). Compare also Phil. 2, 17.

V. 25. καὶ νῦν resumes the thought in v. 22. — οἶδα expresses, not an apprehension or a presentiment, but a conviction. γὰρ οἶδα τοῦτο (T. R.) has more against it than for it. Paul's οἶδα having been fulfilled, Zeller sees evidence of the *post eventum* character of the word in that agreement. — ὅτι οὐκέτι, κ. τ. λ., *that ye shall see no more*, etc. If Paul's Roman captivity closed with his death, he certainly never saw the Ephesian elders after this interview. "Nor, if we suppose him to have been liberated, can any contradictory result be urged on that ground, since the traditions of the fathers decide nothing in regard to the journeys of the apostle between his supposed liberation and his second captivity." (Mey.) It has been proposed to emphasize πάντες, as if some of them at least might hope to renew their intercourse with him; but that qualification is inconsistent with v. 37. 38. — ἐν οἷς διῆλθον, *among whom I went about*, may intimate a wider circuit of labor than that furnished by a single city. The apostle either addressed those who had come from different churches in the region (see on v. 17), or at this point of the discourse recognized those before him as representatives of these churches. Some understand διῆλθον to describe Paul's labors in various parts of Ephesus, or the visits which he made to the houses of the presbyters. The expression favors the wider view, says Neander, but is not inconsistent with the other.

V. 26. διό, *therefore;* since it was proper for him to close his ministry with such a testimony. — μαρτύρομαι = μαρτυρέω, *I testify*, declare as a witness, as in Gal. 5, 3, and Eph. 4, 17, and occasionally in the classics (Pape Lex., s. v.). It means properly *obtest*, call to witness, with the accusative of a person. — ὅτι καθαρὸς, κ. τ. λ. See on 18, 6. The expression is peculiar to Paul's speeches. In this clause εἰμί may have been displaced from the text (Grsb. Lach. Mey.).

V. 27. οὐ γὰρ, κ. τ. λ., *For I shrunk not back* (while among you) *that I should not declare unto you.* Compare on v. 20. — τὴν βουλὴν τοῦ θεοῦ, *the plan of God* as to the way of saving men, unfolded in the gospel.

V. 28. προσέχετε οὖν, κ. τ. λ., *Take heed, therefore,* (since in future the responsibility will rest on you,) *unto yourselves* (that ye be faithful), *and unto all the flock* (that they be kept from error). Here Paul speaks just as he writes in 1 Tim. 4, 16. — ἐν ᾧ, *in which,* since the bishops made part of the flock, while they had the direction of it. — τὸ πνεῦμα ἔθετο may refer to their having been chosen under the direction of the Spirit (13, 2; 14, 23), or to their having been qualified for their office by the Spirit (1 Cor. 12, 8). — ποιμαίνειν includes the idea not only of instruction, but of government and of supervision in general; comp. 1 Pet. 5, 2. See the note on 14, 23. — τὴν ἐκκλησίαν τοῦ κυρίου, or θεοῦ, *the church of the Lord* or *God.* The reading here is disputed. The external testimony preponderates in favor of κυρίου, and most of the recent critics accept that as the original word, as Griesbach, Lachman, Bornemann, Tischendorf, Meyer, Tregelles. Some, as Bengel, Rinck, Scholz, Mill, Alford, decide for θεοῦ. The internal argument is claimed on both sides. It is said that θεοῦ agrees best with the usage of Paul, since in his Epistles ἐκκλησία τοῦ θεοῦ occurs eleven times, ἐκκλησία τοῦ Χριστοῦ once, but never ἐκκλησία τοῦ κυρίου. It is replied to this, that the uncommon expression is more likely to have been exchanged for the ordinary one than the reverse.[1] Wordsworth inclines to θεοῦ, mainly for internal reasons. See Humphry's note on the other side. The variations τοῦ κυρίου θεοῦ, τοῦ θεοῦ καὶ κυρίου, and τοῦ κυρίου καὶ θεοῦ are too slightly supported to require notice. — ἣν περιεποιήσατο, *which he* (redeemed and thus) *obtained for himself* (as a possession); comp. ἵνα λυτρώσηται ἡμᾶς ἀπὸ πάσης ἀνομίας, καὶ καθαρίσῃ ἑαυτῷ λαὸν περιούσιον (Tit. 2, 14); and λαὸς εἰς περιποίησιν (1 Pet. 2, 9). — διὰ τοῦ

[1] For a view of the testimonies in the case, see Davidson's Lectures on Biblical Criticism, p. 175 sq. He adopts τοῦ κυρίου as the probable reading. Green (p. 111) comes to the same conclusion.

ἰδίου αἵματος represents the atonement as consisting preëminently in the sacrifice and death of Christ. See Matt. 20, 28; Rom. 3, 24; Eph. 1, 7; 1 Tim. 2, 6; Heb. 9, 12; 13, 12, etc.

V. 29. τοῦτό gives prominence to the following clause; comp. 9, 21. — εἰσελεύσονται is said of those who should come to them from other places. — μετὰ τὴν ἄφιξίν μου, not *after my decease* (De Wet.), but *my departure.* μετὰ τὴν ἄπιξιν (Ion. for ἄφιξιν) τὴν εἰς Θήβας occurs in Herod. 9. 17. — λύκοι βαρεῖς, *violent,* rapacious, *wolves,* which represent here, not persecutors, but false teachers; see v. 30, and Matt. 7, 15. These men would be as far from corresponding to their professed character as guardians of the flock, as fierce wolves are unlike the faithful shepherd.

V. 30. ἐξ ὑμῶν αὐτῶν, *from you yourselves,* i. e. from their own community; not necessarily from the number of those present. — That the danger which Paul announced was realized, we learn from the Epistles to Timothy (see especially 2 Tim. 2, 17) and from Rev. 2, 2. The latter passage shows that some of these false teachers, in order to strengthen their influence, laid claim to the authority of apostles.

V. 31. διὸ γρηγορεῖτε, *Therefore watch;* since their vigilance should be equal to the dangers which threatened them. — μνημονεύοντες, κ. τ. λ., *remembering,* etc. How they should *watch,* with what constancy and solicitude, they had been taught by his own example. — τριετίαν, *the space of three years,* may be a proximate expression, but must come nearer to *three* years than *two.* See the note on 19, 10. In Rev. 2, 2. 3, we have an interesting proof that the apostle's admonition was not in vain. "Thou hast tried them," it is said of the church at Ephesus, "who say that they are apostles and are not, and hast found them liars; .... and for my name's sake hast labored and hast not fainted."

V. 32. παρατίθεμαι, κ. τ. λ., *I commend you to God and to the word of his grace,* i. e. in this connection, to the power of this word as the instrumentality which God employs for the religious confirmation and security of his people. — ἀδελφοί fails in so many copies as to be doubtful. — τῷ δυναμένῳ it is best to refer to θεῷ as the principal word (Calv. Bng. Mey. De Wet.); not to λόγῳ (Hnr. Kuin.). — ἐποικοδομῆσαι, *to build up further,* is Pauline, but has less support here than οἰκοδομῆσαι. "This term reminds us of Eph. 2, 20, and can be taken only in the sense of that passage. Remarkable, also, is the expression κληρονομία ἐν τοῖς ἡγιασμένοις πᾶσιν. Here πάντες gives prominence to the idea of a great company of the holy, and reminds us again of Eph. 3, 18. The expression, 'an inheritance among the sanctified,' i. e. participation in the spiritual blessings which exist among them, is likewise peculiarly Pauline, and occurs further only in the words of Paul in 26, 18 and in Eph. 1, 18." (Thol.)

V. 33. He warns them against avarice, against a sordid spirit. — ἐπεθύμησα, *coveted* when he was with them; not perf. as in E. V. — ἱματισμοῦ, *raiment.* The wealth of the Orientals consisted in part of costly garments; they trafficked in them or kept them in store for future use. See Ez. 2, 69; Neh. 7, 70; Job 27, 16; 2 Kings 5, 26. This fact accounts for the allusion to the destructive power of the moth, as well as rust, in Matt. 6, 19 and James 5, 2.

V. 34. καὶ τοῖς οὖσι μετ' ἐμοῦ is an instance of varied construction: *and to* (the wants of) *those with me.* W. § 63. II. 1. Those referred to here are Timothy, Erastus, Luke, and others, who traversed sea and land with the apostle, attached to him as personal friends and still more as friends of the cause which they served. — αἱ χεῖρες αὗται, *these hands,* which we may suppose him to have held up to view as he spoke, and which may have been marked with traces of the toil to which they were inured. See the note on 17, 10 and 18, 3. — This allusion to the apostle's habit of manual labor while he was at Ephesus accords remarkably with 1 Cor. 4, 11. 12. Luke has said nothing of it in his narrative of Paul's residence in that city (19, 1 sq.). But in the above-named passage of the Epistle, which Paul wrote just before his departure from Ephesus, we find him saying: "*Unto this present hour* .... we labor, working with our own hands." Nothing could be more undesigned than this agreement. "It is manifest that, if the history in this passage had been taken from the Epistle, this circumstance, if it appeared at all, would have appeared in its *place,* that is, in the direct account of Paul's transactions at Ephesus. The correspondence would not have been effected, as it is, by a kind of reflected stroke, that is, by a reference in a subsequent speech to what in the narrative was omitted. Nor is it likely, on the other hand, that a circumstance which is not extant in the history of Paul at Ephesus, should have been made the subject of a fictitious allusion, in an Epistle purporting to be written by him from that place; not to mention that the allusion itself, especially in time, is too oblique and general to answer any purpose of forgery whatever." Paley.

V. 35. πάντα, not *all things* as the object of ὑπέδειξα (E. V., Hmph.), but adverbial, *in all ways,* i. e. by doctrine and by example; comp. 1 Cor. 10, 33; Eph. 4, 15. — οὕτω κοπιῶντας, *so laboring,* viz. as I have done. — δεῖ ἀντιλαμβάνεσθαι τῶν ἀσθενούντων, *that you ought to assist the weak*, feeble, i. e. the poor, whom this mode of designation contrasts with the rich, who are strong, powerful (Chrys. Kuin. Olsh. De Wet. Rob. Hws.). The examples in Wetstein sanction this meaning of ἀσθενούντων. See also Rob. Lex. s. v. But the stricter sense of the word (4, 9; 5, 15; Matt. 25, 39, etc.) is entirely appropriate: *the weak*, i. e. those unable in consequence of physical infirmity to labor for their own support. The apostle would enforce here the duty of industry and self-denial, in order to procure the means of relieving those who are disabled by any cause from taking care of themselves. He holds up to them his own example, his diligence in labor, his disinterestedness, as worthy of their imitation. Compare 2 Thess. 3, 7 sq. — Others understand ἀσθενούντων of the *weak* in their religious faith or principles. The apostle's object as they argue, was to exhort the elders to maintain themselves by their own labor, out of regard to those who would not appreciate their claim to support, who would take offence at the appearance of anything like a mercenary spirit in their teachers. So Calvin, Bengel, Neander, Meyer, Tholuck, and others. It is alleged that this interpretation is necessary, in order to make the cases parallel; that, as Paul labored for his own support, so the object of their labor must be the same. But οὕτω κοπιῶντας does not require that sort of correspondence. Instead of the same application of the fruits of his industry, the οὕτω may refer equally well to the *manner* and *spirit* of his labor, i. e. to his assiduity in it, and his benevolence, which he would have them imitate, though the class of persons to be benefited in the two cases was different. The positive objections to this exegesis are first, that the language is too mild, as understood of such illiberality; secondly, that some word or the context should define ἀσθενούντων, qualified by τῇ πίστει in Rom. 14, 1 sq., and in effect by τῇ συνειδήσει in 1 Cor. 8, 9 (compared with v. 7); and, thirdly, that it destroys the opposition between the giving of personal favors and the reception of them, as contemplated in the words of Christ. The use of τῶν ἀσθενῶν in 1 Thess. 5, 14 weakens, it is true, the second objection. It may be added, that Paul, although he waived his own right to a maintenance from those to whom he preached, was remarkable for the decision with which he asserted that right in behalf of others; comp. Rom. 15. 27; 1 Cor. 9, 13. 14; Gal. 6, 6; 1 Tim. 5, 17. 18. See also the Saviour's rule on this subject in Luke 10, 7. Hence, if the explanation under remark were correct, it would array the author of the speech against the Epistles. It would justify Zeller's objection, that the true Paul after representing his own assumption of the expenses of his support (for example, in 1 Cor. 9, 1–27) as unprescriptive and voluntary, would not so forget himself as to impose his example in that respect upon the Ephesian teachers as one which they must follow. — ὅτι αὐτός, *that he himself.* Our English translation overlooks the emphasis. — μακάριον . . . . λαμβάνειν, *It is more blessed to give, than to receive.* The Evangelists have not recorded this saying of Christ. It comes down to us here as an interesting specimen of the many such words that fell from his lips and were treasured up in the memory of the first disciples, but which no similar application has rescued from oblivion. It will be noticed that Paul alludes to the remark as familiar to his hearers. — The best authorities read μᾶλλον διδόναι instead of the inverse order. — Nothing is wanting to attest the Pauline origin of this Miletian speech. It agrees with Paul's history, reflects Paul's character, bears the stamp of Paul's style. This last point deserves a fuller illustration. The following examples show the linguistic affinity between the discourse and the apostle's writings. δουλεύειν τῷ κυρίῳ, θεῷ or Χριστῷ occurs in v. 19 above; six times in Paul, elsewhere only in Matt. 6, 24 and Luke 16, 13. ταπεινοφροσύνη is found only in v. 19, five times in Paul, and once in Pet. 5, 5; ὑποστέλλω in v. 20. 27, and in Gal. 2, 12; τὸ συμφέρον in v. 20, once in Heb. 12, 20, and three times in the First Epistle to the Corinthians; διακονία in v. 24, and twenty-two times in Paul; μαρτύρομαι in v. 26, and in Gal. 5, 3 and Eph. 4, 17; φείδομαι in v. 29, in 2 Pet. 2, 4, and seven times in Paul; νουθετεῖν in v. 31, and seven times in Paul; κοπιᾶν in v. 35, in Paul on the contrary thirteen times; and the hortatory γρηγορεῖτε in v. 31, elsewhere only in 1 Cor. 16, 13. See Lekebusch, Composition der Apostelgeschichte, p. 339.

VERSES 36–38. *Paul prays with the Elders, and embarks again.*

V. 36. θεὶς τὰ γόνατα, *having kneeled* (7, 60; 9, 40). This was the attitude in prayer which prevailed among the early Christians, except on the Sabbath and during the seven weeks before Pentecost, when they generally stood. They regarded the latter posture as the more appropriate one for the expression of gratitude, and adopted it, therefore, on joyful occasions (Hmph.). It cannot be shown that the distinction was observed at this early period.

V. 37. The scene here is a touching one; the simplicity of Luke's description heightens the effect of it. We feel instinctively that the eye must have seen what the pen has portrayed in so natural a manner. — καὶ ἐπιπεσόντες . . . . Παύλου, *and having fallen upon the neck of Paul.* In the same manner Joseph manifested his strong affection for Benjamin his brother (Gen. 45, 14), and for Jacob his father (Gen. 46, 29), after their long separation from each other. It was in accordance with Oriental manners. — κατεφίλουν, *kissed tenderly* (compound) and (imperf.) *again and again.* The Evangelist uses this word to describe the affected earnestness of the traitor's kiss (Matt. 26, 49).

V. 38. ᾧ εἰρήκει, *which he had spoken* (pluperf.); dative by attraction. — ὅτι is declarative. — θεωρεῖν = θεάομαι (Tittm. de Syn. p. 120), *behold*, contemplate. It suggests the idea of the interest and affection with which they looked upon that countenance for the last time. The writer's tact in using this word of the Ephesians, but ὄψεσθε of Paul in v. 25, should be noticed. — προέπεμπον, κ. τ. λ., *they sent him forward*, escorted him, *unto the ship.* See the note on 15, 3, and the illustration on 21, 5. It is implied that the roadstead where the vessel lay, was at some distance from the town. The site of Miletus, though originally on the coast, has gradually receded till it is now ten miles from the sea. It must have lost its maritime position long before the apostle's time, though not so far inland then as at present.

CHAPTER XXI.

VERSES 1–6. *They continue the Voyage to Tyre.*

V. 1. ὡς δὲ ἐγένετο, κ. τ. λ., *When now it came to pass that we put to sea.* The construction is like that in v. 5. Luke certainly as one of the ἡμᾶς, Trophimus (21, 29), and Aristarchus (27, 2), accompanied Paul to Jerusalem. As the others who belonged to the company (20, 4) are not mentioned again, the probability is (*ex silentio*) that they proceeded no further. Some suppose that Timothy went at this time from Miletus to Ephesus, and assumed or resumed the oversight of the church there. — ἀποσπασθέντας ἀπ' αὐτῶν, *having departed from them* (De Wet. Rob.); less probably, *having torn ourselves away* (Chrys. Kuin. Mey.). Usage weakened the etymological sense, and in Luke 22, 41 an emphasis appears to me out of place. — εὐθυδρομήσαντες, *having run straight*, shows that the wind was in their favor; see on 16, 11. — Κῶ is for Κῶν, like Ἀπολλώ in 19, 1. *Cos* was about forty miles from Miletus; directly south, and could have been reached in six hours.

It was one of the smaller islands of the Archipelago, on the Carian coast, between the promontories, on which stood Cnidus and Halicarnassus. Its present name is *Stanchio*, which has arisen from a slurred pronunciation of ἐς τὰν Κῶν, like Stambul from ἐς τὰν πόλιν. — Having rounded Cape Crio, the ancient Triopium, they turned their prow eastward, and sailed along the southern shore of Asia Minor. *Rhodes* was at the entrance of the Ægean, on the coast of Caria. The celebrated colossus was prostrate at this time, having been overthrown by an earthquake. — *Patara* was a coast-town of Lycia, at some distance from the left bank of the Xanthus. "Now its port is an inland marsh, generating poisonous malaria, and the mariner sailing along the coast would never guess that the sand-hills before him blocked up the harbor into which St. Paul sailed of old."[1] Patara was best known for its celebrated oracle of Apollo, which, in the height of its authority, had almost rivalled that of Delphos. How near to it in the person of these wayfaring men was now brought the power which was to subvert that great delusion of heathenism! How soon after this could it be said, in the words of Milton's Hymn on the Nativity of Christ:

> "The oracle's are dumb,
> No voice or hideous hum
> Runs through the arched roof in words deceiving.
> Apollo from his shrine
> Can no more divine,
> With hollow shriek the steep of Delphos leaving.
> No nightly trance or breathed spell
> Inspires the pale-eyed priest from the prophetic cell."

V. 2. The party take now another vessel. We are not informed of the reason for this measure. The vessel which had brought them thus far may have been adapted only to sailing along the shore, or they may have engaged the use of it (see on 20, 16) only until they should find an opportunity like the present. — διαπερῶν, *crossing over* just as they arrived. This particularity is as graphic "as if taken from a journal written during the voyage." The present participle denotes often an appointed or approaching act; comp. v. 3; 27, 6. W. § 45. 1. b.

V. 3. ἀναφανέντες δὲ τὴν Κύπρον, *And having had a view of Cyprus*, lit. *having had it brought up to sight*, made visible to us above the horizon. The language is that of an eye-witness, and of one familiar with the phraseology of seamen, who are accustomed to

[1] Travels in Lycia by Spratt and Forbes, Vol. I. p. 31.

speak of *raising* the land when they approach it. The opposite expression is ἀποκρύπτειν γῆν; see Krüg. on Thucyd. 5. 65; Stalb. on Prot. 338. A. The corresponding Latin words, says Mr. Humphry, are *aperire* and *abscondere* (Virg. Æn. 3. 275, 291). Some render, *being shown Cyprus,* having it pointed out to us in the distance (Rob.); but the composite form indicates a more specific sense. This verb, which in the active governs a dative and accusative, retains the latter in the passive. W. § 39. 1; K. § 281. 3.— καταλιπόντες αὐτήν, *having left it behind.* — εὐώνυμον, *on the left,* is an adjective, not an adverb. K. § 264. 3. a. They passed, therefore, to the south of the island. They must have had a fair wind to enable them to take that course. The view of Cyprus must have carried back the apostle's mind to the days which he and Barnabas had spent there in the missionary work. — ἐπλέομεν εἰς Συρίαν, *we sailed unto Syria,* refers to the voyage to Tyre; for in the Roman age Syria included Phœnicia (Win.), of which Tyre was the commercial emporium. For its present state, see Rob. Bibl. Res. III. p. 392 sq. The most important ruins lie at present beneath the sea. It was with melancholy interest that I looked down upon them through the calm waters, in the long twilight which closed the tenth of May, 1852. — ἐκεῖσε γὰρ, κ. τ. λ., is best taken as brachylogical: *for* having come *thither the ship was unlading* (i. e. about to unlade) *the cargo.* See W. § 45. 5. This use of the participle coincides essentially with that in v. 2; see further Matt. 26, 28; Luke 22, 19. Some understand ἐκεῖσε of the conveyance of the freight from the ship to the town; *for thither* (after the arrival) *was the ship unlading the cargo* (Mey. De Wet.). The writer would not be likely to specify so minute a circumstance. ἐκεῖσε is not to be confounded with ἐκεῖ. The clause assigns the reason (γάρ) for their stopping at this port. The voyage from Patara to Tyre need not have exceeded two days, if the wind was fair and the vessel in a good condition. The distance is three hundred and forty geographical miles.[1]

V. 4. καὶ ἀνευρόντες τοὺς μαθητάς, *and having found out the disciples* who lived there; because being strangers they must make inquiry. The English version overlooks both the preposition and the article. The gospel had been preached here at an early

[1] The writer embarked at Beirut (on the coast to the north of Tyre) at half-past six o'clock, P. M.; the next day at ten o'clock, we arrived off against Larnica on the Island of Cyprus, and on the following night, at two o'clock, A. M., came to anchor in the harbor of Rhodes. This was very nearly the apostle's track, except in the inverse order. An ancient vessel, under circumstances entirely favorable, would almost equal the speed of a Levant steamer.

period; see on 11, 19. The Saviour had performed some of his miracles in the vicinity of Tyre and Sidon; see Matt. 15, 21; Mark 7, 24. — ἐπεμείναμεν. See on 10, 48. — ἡμέρας ἑπτά, *seven days*, may be indefinite, as was remarked on 20, 6. We cannot doubt that they occupied the time spent here in making known the word, and in consulting for the welfare of the Tyrian church. — οἵτινες . . . . εἰς Ἱερουσαλήμ, *who said to Paul through the Spirit that he should not go up unto Jerusalem*, i. e. if he had any regard to his own safety or personal welfare, or to their affectionate solicitude on his account; comp. παρεκαλοῦμεν, κ. τ. λ., in v. 12. They were informed by the Spirit that bonds and afflictions awaited the apostle at Jerusalem; but it was not revealed to them as the will of God that he should desist from his purpose to proceed thither.

V. 5. ὅτε . . . . ἐξαρτίσαι. See the first clause in v. 1. — τὰς ἡμέρας, *the days* named in v. 4. — προπεμπόντων, κ. τ. λ., *all sending us forward*, etc. See on 20, 38. — ἕως ἔξω τῆς πόλεως, *till out of the city*, quite out of it, beyond the suburbs, where they could be alone and undisturbed. — ἐπὶ τὸν αἰγιαλόν, *upon the beach*. The word denotes a smooth shore as distinguished from one precipitous or rocky; comp. 27, 39. Luke manifests an autoptic accuracy here. A level, sandy beach extends for a considerable distance on both sides of the site of the ancient Tyre. — Modern missionary life presents its parallels to the scene so briefly sketched in this verse. The following extract occurs in the journal of a college friend, whose field of labor is in the region of Paul's birth-place. Speaking of his departure with his family from Aintab for a temporary absence, the missionary says: "More than a hundred of the converts accompanied us out of the city; and there, near the spot where one of our number had once been stoned, we halted, and a prayer was offered amid tears. Between thirty and forty escorted us two hours further, on horses and mules, singing hymns as we proceeded on our way. Then another prayer was offered, and, with saddened countenances, and with weeping, they forcibly broke away from us. It really seemed as though they could not turn back."[1]

VERSES 7-16. *From Tyre they proceed to Ptolemais, and thence to Cæsarea and Jerusalem.*

V. 7. ἡμεῖς . . . . εἰς Πτολεμαΐδα, *Now we, completing* (thereby) *the voyage, came down from Tyre to Ptolemais.* When the par-

[1] Rev. B. Schneider, in the Missionary Herald, Vol. xlviii. p. 201, (1852).

ticiple and the verb combined thus are both in the past tense, the act of the participle may be antecedent to that of the verb or simultaneous with it. The sense must decide this ambiguity. — ἀπὸ Τύρου in this position belongs to the verb, not to πλοῦν (E. V.). Their arrival at Ptolemais terminated the sea part of their journey. The distance is a moderate day's journey by land. A vessel with a good breeze would make the run in a few hours. This city was the ancient Accho (Judg. 1, 31), still called Akka by the Arabians, and Acre or St. Jean d'Acre by Europeans. It is on the Mediterranean, at the north angle of a bay which bears the same name, and sweeps in the form of a semicircle towards the south, as far as Mount Carmel. The graceful curve of the bay appears to great advantage from the top of that mountain. — τοὺς ἀδελφούς, *the brethren* who were there; see on v. 4.

V. 8. They now travelled by land. Issuing from the south-eastern gate, in ten minutes they would cross the Belus, now the Nahmen, then for three hours would proceed along the beach with the surf breaking at their feet, at the base of Carmel would ford the mouth of the Kishon (El-Mukatta), and turning that headland, follow the line of the coast to Cæsarea. The distance hither from Akka is about forty miles. — The received οἱ περὶ τὸν Παῦλον after ἐξελθόντες is untenable. A church reading began here, and a more definite subject than ἡμεῖς was needed to suggest the connection. The gloss has passed into our English translation. — εἰς Καισάρειαν. This is the third time that Paul has been at *Cæsarea.* He was there on his journey from Jerusalem to Tarsus (9, 30), and again on his return to Antioch from his second missionary progress (18, 22). — Φιλίππου. See on 8, 40. — τοῦ εὐαγγελιστοῦ. This title appears to have been given to those who had no stated pastoral charge, but travelled from place to place and preached as they had opportunity. See Eph. 4, 11; 2 Tim. 4, 5. — τοῦ ὄντος τῶν ἑπτά, *who was of the seven* (E. V.), recalls Philip as already known to us in another capacity; see 6, 5. But the best critics reject τοῦ, and ὄντος becomes then ambiguous: either causal, *since he was of the seven* (De Wet. Alf.), or simply historical as in the other case. See Green's Gr. p. 190. It is improbable that the office merely influenced Paul, and so much the less, since according to this view it would be the inferior office which Philip no longer held and not his present one. ὄντος follows the tense of the other verbs, and is past. W. § 45. 1. Philip, as an Evangelist, had relinquished his service at Jerusalem; perhaps the occasion for it had been only temporary.

V. 9. τούτῳ, κ. τ. λ., *Now this one had four daughters,* etc. Luke mentions the fact as remarkable, and not as related in any way to the history. It is barely possible that they too (see v. 10) foretold the apostle's approaching captivity.

V. 10. ἐπιμενόντων ἡμέρας πλείους, *remaining several days* (comp. 13, 31; 27, 20), a longer time than in the other places on the way. Having travelled rapidly since he left Miletus, and being now within two days of Jerusalem, the apostle had no occasion to hasten his journey; see 20, 16. — Ἄγαβος has been mentioned in 11, 28. He cannot well be a different person, as some have thought; for not only his name, but office (προφήτης), and residence (ἀπὸ τῆς Ἰουδαίας) are the same in both instances. Whether he had heard of Paul's arrival and came to Cæsarea on that account (Bmg.), must be left undecided.

V. 11. δήσας . . . . πόδας. The prophet performed the act on himself, not on Paul. The pronoun should be αὑτοῦ, not αὐτοῦ. Many of the best manuscripts read ἑαυτοῦ. — οὕτω . . . . Ἰουδαῖοι, *So shall bind at Jerusalem the Jews.* The Romans put the apostle in chains, but they did it at the instigation of the Jews. — Agabus, like the ancient prophets, accompanied his prediction with a symbolic act, which served to place the event foretold more vividly before them; the scene, being thus acted out before their eyes, was rendered present, real, beyond what any mere verbal declaration could possibly have made it.

> "Segnius irritant animos demissa per aurem
> Quam quæ sunt oculis subjecta fidelibus, et quæ
> Ipse sibi tradit spectator."

Examples similar to this are frequent in the Old Testament; see 1 Kings 22, 11; Is. 20, 1 sq.; Jer. 13, 1 sq.; Ezek. 4, 1 sq., etc.

V. 12. ἡμεῖς, *we*, viz. the writer, Trophimus, Aristarchus (see on 20, 4), and possibly others. — οἱ ἐντόπιοι restricts itself to the Christians of the place.

V. 13. τί ποιεῖτε is the language of remonstrance: *What are you doing that you weep*, etc. The same mode of expression occurs in Mark 11, 5. — ἐγὼ γάρ, κ. τ. λ. Their opposition was not only painful to him (συνθρύπτοντές μου τὴν καρδίαν), but was useless; *for* (γάρ) he was not to be shaken in his purpose (De Wet.); or, which agrees better with ἑτοίμως ἔχω, their distress was unnecessary; *for* he deemed it a privilege, not a hardship, to suffer in the cause of Christ; comp. 5, 41.

V. 15. The text fluctuates here, but ἐπισκευασάμενοι has decidedly the best support: *having packed up our baggage*, having placed it upon the beasts of burden; comp. ἐπισκευασάμενοι ὑποζύγια in Xen. Hell. 7, 2. 18. This is ever an important item in Eastern travelling, and it was natural that Luke, a companion of the journey, should mention it. If the alms which they were carrying to Jerusalem (24, 17) consisted in part of raiment or provisions, the loading and unloading would require more than ordinary attention. Another reading is ἀποσκευασάμενοι, *having packed away our baggage*, i. e. at Cæsarea, where they left it, or at least the superfluous part of it (Olsh.). The reason for such a step is not obvious. If it was their sea-luggage and unnecessary for the rest of the way, it is surprising that they did not leave it at Ptolemais, where they ended the voyage. Some insist that, if we adopt this word rather than the other, we may obtain from it the same meaning: *having packed our baggage away*, i. e. from the place where they had stored it, in order to carry it with them (Mey. De Wet.): that appears to me a forced interpretation. παρασκευασάμενοι and ἀποταξάμενοι are explanatory variations. — "The English version," says Mr. Humphry, "uses the word 'carriage' in the sense of 'things carried,' baggage, as in Judges 18, 21 and 1 Sam. 17, 22. Cranmer has 'took up our burdens,' and the Geneva version 'trussed up our fardels.'" — For the route "in going up" to Jerusalem, see on 23, 31.

V. 16. συνῆλθον, sc. τινές, which governs μαθητῶν; comp. John 16, 17. W. § 64. 4. — ἄγοντες . . . . Μνάσωνι stands by attraction for ἄγοντες παρὰ Μνάσωνα παρ' ᾧ ξενισθῶμεν, *bringing us to Mnason with whom we should lodge* (Olsh. Mey. De Wet.). His relation to them as their host was more important to them than his name, and presents itself first, therefore, in the order of statement. Μνάσωνι could depend possibly on ἄγοντες, *bringing us to Mnason* (W. § 31. 5); but the construction is hard. Some render *bringing Mnason*, i. e. with them from Cæsarea; which attributes to them an improbable act, while it leaves the dative equally irregular. — ἀρχαίῳ μαθητῇ = μαθητῇ ἀπ' ἀρχῆς, *an ancient* (not an *aged*) *disciple*, i. e. who had long been such. He may have been converted on the day of Pentecost (comp. ἐν ἀρχῇ in 11, 15), or have been a personal follower of Christ.

VERSES 17–26. *Paul assumes a Vow, to conciliate the Jewish Believers.*

V. 17. The apostle arrives now at Jerusalem for the *fifth* time since he left it on his persecuting errand to Damascus. It is the last recorded visit that he ever made to the Jewish capital. His present return could not have taken place later than the spring of A. D. 59; since we must reserve two years for his imprisonment at Cæsarea (24, 27), and two for his imprisonment at Rome, before we come to A. D. 64. See Introduction, § 6. 5. If we fix upon this limitation on that side, we have then four years as the term of the apostle's third missionary excursion, which we may distribute as follows. He left Antioch about the beginning of A. D. 55 (see on 18, 23), and reached Ephesus in the spring of that year. Here he spent about three years (20, 31), and proceeded to Macedonia in the spring of A. D. 58 (see on 20, 1). He was occupied here and in other parts of Northern Greece during the summer and autumn of that year (see on 20, 2), and arrived at Corinth early in the following winter. Having spent the next three months in that city (20, 3), he returned to Macedonia and embarked for Syria in the spring of A. D. 59. Or, our scheme of chronology admits of a slightly different combination. If we suppose two years and six months or nine months to exhaust τριετίαν in 20, 31, we may assign Paul's return to Jerusalem to the spring of the preceding year, viz. that of A. D. 58. The apostle may have left Antioch on his third tour sufficiently early in A. D. 54 (see on 18, 22) to have spent several months at Ephesus before Pentecost in A. D. 55; and he could then have completed the two remaining years of his residence in that city, at Pentecost in A. D. 57. The advantage of this computation would be, that it frees us from the necessity of crowding the two years of the apostle's Roman captivity so near the year A. D. 64 — ἀσμένως .... ἀδελφοί, *the brethren received us gladly.* This may refer to the more private friendly greetings which preceded the interview on the next day. Luke may have been struck with this cordiality the more, because Paul and his friends as preachers to the heathen had reason to apprehend some coldness. See the note on 15, 4, and Rom. 15, 31. The interview would be likely to take place in the house of Mnason, but οἱ ἀδελφοί is too general to be understood merely of him and his family.

V. 18. The notice here relates to a more public reception. — τῇ ἐπιούσῃ, *on the following day* after their arrival. — σὺν ἡμῖν, *with us*, viz. Luke and Paul's other companions. It was now probably that the gifts of the foreign churches were delivered up to the almoners. — Ἰάκωβον. This is *James* the Younger, who presided over the church at Jerusalem; comp. 12, 17. As no one of the other apostles is mentioned in this part of the narrative, it is probable that they were either not living or were laboring in foreign lands. — πρεσβύτεροι. The pastor and *the presbyters* are named as the principal persons (see 15, 6), not as excluding others.

V. 19. ἀσπασάμενος αὐτούς, *having embraced them.* He had performed the same act of courtesy on his preceding visit to them; see 18, 22.—διὰ τῆς διακονίας αὐτοῦ, *through his ministry* in the course of his recent journey.

V. 20. πόσαι μυριάδες, *how many myriads,* stands for a large but indefinite number, *what multitudes.* Compare 1 Cor. 4, 15 and 14, 19.—ζηλωταὶ τοῦ νόμου, *zealots for the law;* an objective or causative genitive (comp. Gal. 1, 14). K. § 265. 2. b.

V. 21. ὅτι ἀποστασίαν διδάσκεις, κ. τ. λ., *that thou dost teach apostasy from Moses,* etc. Neander presents the following just view of the transaction related here. "This accusation against Paul was certainly false in the form in which it was alleged; for he opposed the external observance of Judaism only so far as the justification and sanctification of men were made to depend upon it. It was his principle, that no one should abandon the national and civil relations in which he stood at the time of his conversion, except for important reasons; and in accordance with this principle he allowed the Jews to adhere to their peculiarities, among which was the observance of the Mosaic law (1 Cor. 7, 18). But it could not fail to happen that those who entered into Paul's ideas of the relations of the law to the gospel, and were thus freed from their scrupulous regard for the former, would be led into a freer line of conduct in this respect, and individuals might carry this disposition further than Paul desired. It may be that such instances gave occasion to the charge that he pursuaded the Jewish Christians to release themselves from the law. It is indeed true, that, when it was once admitted that circumcision avails nothing as a means of obtaining an interest in the kingdom of God, this rite must, sooner or later, fall away of itself. But Paul would not hasten this result by any arbitrary or violent act; he would leave it to be the work of time, and would have no one break away capriciously from the relations in which he has been called to be a Christian. Hence, without deviating from the principles of strict sincerity, he could repel that accusation of the Jewish zealots. He was far from entertaining the hatred against Judaism, and the ancient theocratic nation, with which his violent opponents charged him. In conformity with the principle avowed in his Epistles, viz. that he became a Jew to the Jews, as he became a heathen to the heathen and weak to those who were weak, he declared himself ready to do what James proposed to him, in order to refute that accusation. He consented to refute it by taking part in the Jewish worship in a mode which was highly esteemed by pious Jews."

V. 22. τί οὖν ἐστι; *What, therefore, is it?* viz. which the occasion requires; comp. 1 Cor. 14, 15. 16. — πάντως .... συνελθεῖν, *It is entirely necessary* (inevitable) *that a multitude* (viz. of the Jewish Christians) *should come together,* i. e. around Paul as he appeared in their public assemblies, in the temple and elsewhere, in order to watch his conduct and see whether their suspicions of him were just. It is not meant that the church would assemble in a body for the purpose of consultation (Calv. Grot.); for with that idea we should have had τό before πλῆθος (comp. 4, 32; 15, 12. 30). Nor does the language intimate that Paul's advisers apprehended any violent outbreak on the part of the Jewish Christians (Kuin.); the subsequent riot which led to his apprehension originated not with them, but with the unbelieving Jews (comp. v. 27).

V. 23. ὅ σοι λέγομεν, *which we say to thee,* viz. James and the elders; for the subject of this verb must be the same as that of εἶπον in v. 20. The narrative does not allow us to separate James from the others; as if he merely acquiesced in the proposal while the responsibility of suggesting it lay wholly with them (against Hws.). — The ἄνδρες τέσσαρες were certainly Jews, and may be supposed from the relation implied in εἰσὶν ἡμῖν to have been also Jewish believers. — εὐχὴν ἔχοντες ἐφ' ἑαυτῶν, *having a vow upon themselves,* which as appears from every circumstance of the description, must have been a Nazarite vow. This vow bound those who assumed it to let the hair grow, to abstain from intoxicating drink, and in other respects to maintain a life of ascetic rigor (Numb. 6, 2 sq.). It was left to their option how long they continued such a vow; though it seems to have been customary among the Jews of this period to extend it at least to thirty days (Jos. Bell. Jud. 2. 15. 1). "When the time specified in the vow was completed, the Nazarite offered a ram of a year old for a burnt-offering, a sheep of the same age for a sin-offering, a ram for a thank-offering, a basket of unleavened cakes, and a libation of wine. His hair was shaven off at the gate of the sanctuary, and cast into the fire where the thank-offering was burning. He offered as a wave-offering to God, the shoulders of the thank-offering and two cakes, which were both given to the priest." Jahn's Archæol. § 395.

V. 24. τούτους παραλαβών, *these taking with thyself,* as associates in the vow. — ἁγνίσθητι σὺν αὐτοῖς, *purify thyself with them;* enter upon the same course of abstinence and religious consecration. Howson understands ἁγνίσθητι of the ordinary ablutions before entering the temple; but in that case σὺν αὐτοῖς loses its signifi-

45

cance, since the apostle's purification would have no more relation to them than to any other Jews. — καὶ δαπάνησον ἐπ' αὐτοῖς, *and spend upon them*, incur expense on their account. "As, in some instances, the Nazarites had not sufficient property to enable them to meet the whole expense of the offerings, other persons who possessed more defrayed the expense for them, or shared it with them, and in this way were made parties to the vow." The Jews looked upon it as an act of special merit to assist a Nazarite in this manner. Josephus relates (Antt. 19. 6. 1) that Agrippa the First, on his arrival at Jerusalem after having obtained the sovereignty of Palestine, paid the expense of numerous indigent Nazarites who were waiting to be released from their vows. He intended it as a thank-offering for his good fortune. — καὶ γνώσονται πάντες, *and all shall know* by this act. γνῶσι and γνώσωνται, *all may know* (E. V.), are grammatical corrections, founded on the false view that this clause depends on ἵνα. — καὶ αὐτός, *also thyself*, as well as other Jews.

V. 25. περὶ δὲ τῶν πεπιστευκότων ἐθνῶν, *But* (as we are both aware) *in regard to the Gentiles who have believed*, etc. — ἡμεῖς, *we*, i. e. the apostles and Christians at Jerusalem; for the adoption of the decree was properly their act (comp. 15, 22), and not that of Paul and the other delegates from Antioch who submitted to them the question which the decree settled (15, 1). The object of the reminiscent remark in this verse was to obviate any scruple that Paul might feel, lest the proposed measure should interfere with the liberty of the Gentile converts. — εἰ μὴ φυλάσσεσθαι, κ. τ. λ. See the note on 15, 20.

V. 26. παραλαβών refers to his connecting himself with the men (v. 24), while ἁγνισθείς defines the nature of the connection. — τῇ ἐχομένῃ ἡμέρᾳ, *on the following day* after his interview with James, and the third since his arrival at Jerusalem (v. 18). — σὺν αὐτοῖς belongs certainly to ἁγνισθείς (see v. 24) and perhaps to εἰσῄει; not, in the latter case, necessarily because he now took them to the temple in order to absolve them at once from their vow (Hws.), but because it may have been important that they should be present when he declared his intention to assume their expenses. — διαγγέλλων . . . . ἁγνισμοῦ, *announcing*, viz. to the priests (εἰς τὸ ἱερόν suggests the persons) *the completion* (lit. *filling out*) *of the days of the purification*; in other words, making known the interval (viz. seven days) between this declaration and the end of the vow and the bringing of the necessary offerings. So essentially Stier, Kuinoel, De Wette, Meyer, Wordsworth, and others. τοῦ before ἁγνισμοῦ defines *the purification* as that referred to in σὺν αὐτοῖς ἁγνισθείς; hence that of those associated in the act, not that of the men merely and not that of Paul merely (both mistakes have been made). The convenience of the priests may have required this notification to enable them to prepare for the concluding ceremony at the temple. Others (as Wiesl.) explain ἐκπλήρωσιν of the actual expiration of the days during which the men's vow was to continue. Such a view leaves no time for the apostle's partnership with them, and thus conflicts both with σὺν αὐτοῖς ἁγνισθείς, and with εὗρόν με ἡγνισμένον ἐν τῷ ἱερῷ in 24, 18. The apostle's arrest (v. 27) was subsequent to his present appearance in the temple, and at the time of the arrest, as we see from the words just quoted, he was still observing his part of the vow. —ἕως οὗ, κ. τ. λ., *until the offering* (known as necessary) *was brought.* This clause depends naturally on διαγγέλλων, κ. τ. λ., and as it formed a part of the notice which Paul gave in the temple (hence *oratio directa*) would have naturally the subjunctive (*until it should be brought,* as in 23, 12. 21; 25, 21), instead of the indicative. It may be an instance, as Meyer suggests, in which the direct form of the announcement glides over into the past of the narrative. See K. Ausfh. Gr. § 846. Some carry back the clause to εἰσῄει εἰς τὸ ἱερόν as elliptical: *went into the temple* and staid there *until the offering was brought.* In that case we must pass over the nearer point of connection for a remoter one, and must even insert the word in the text which renders that connection possible. Further, it is improbable that Paul lodged two or three days in the temple; and yet as he speaks of himself as there on the day of the riot, in order to bring the final offerings (24, 18), it would follow on this view of the subject that he had remained there from his first repairing to the temple till that time. The true emphasis of ὑπὲρ ἑνὸς ἑκάστου lies in the fact that Paul was to be answerable for the expenses of the offering of *each one;* not (as Hws.) that he would remain in the temple until *each one's* offering was presented.

VERSES 27–30. *Paul is seized by the Jews, and dragged from the Temple.*

V. 27. ὡς δὲ ἔμελλον, κ. τ. λ., *Now as the seven days were about to be completed,* i. e. in all probability the seven days announced to the priests as the limit to which the vow of the Nazarites would extend, and as the period also of the apostle's partnership in that consecration. This is the readiest explanation and the one to which most critics assent (Bng. Kuin. Olsh. Mey. De Wet.

Alf.). Neander's idea is that their vow embraced only seven days in all, and that Paul joined them on the last of these days. Against that construction stands the inference from εὐχὴν ἔχοντες ἐφ' ἑαυτῶν in v. 23, that the vow had been resting on them for a considerable time before the apostle's connection with them, and, also, that ἵνα ξυρήσωνται τὴν κεφαλήν (v. 24) would signify very little if the ceremony was to take place at the expiration of a single week. — Wieseler (p. 105) has revived the opinion of some of the older interpreters, viz. that *the seven days* were those observed as the feast of Pentecost. His arguments are mainly two: first, as obviating an objection, that this meaning suggests itself readily enough after the information (20, 16) that Paul was hastening to keep the Pentecost at Jerusalem; and, secondly, that the reckoning of the twelve days between his arrival there and his subsequent trial at Cæsarea demands this explanation. Howson adopts the same view. But the article before ἑπτὰ ἡμέραι recalls quite irresistibly *the days of the purification* just spoken of, and the twelve days mentioned in 24, 11 may be computed in different ways (see note there), and hence though compatible with that theory do not establish it. Above all, the assumption that the Jews observed Pentecost as a hebdomadal festival is too uncertain to be made the basis of an explanation. The law of its institution prescribed but one day though the later Jews, it would seem, added a second. Win. Realw. I. p. 243. — οἱ ἀπὸ τῆς Ἀσίας Ἰουδαῖοι, *the Jews from Asia,* i. e. the province of that name where Paul had resided so long (20, 31). Some of them may have been from Ephesus, who would recognize Trophimus (v. 29) as a fellow-townsman. The Jews here, the authors of this riot, were not believers and hence not of the class of Jews whom the apostle expected to conciliate.

V. 28. βοηθεῖτε, *help,* i. e. to apprehend him, or to wreak vengeance on him. — ἔτι τε καί, *and further also;* comp. 2, 26. It is one of Luke's peculiar phrases. — Ἕλληνας may be the plural of the class or category, because what Paul had done in the case of one, he might be said in point of principle to have done for many; or it may have been an exaggeration for the purpose of increasing the tumult. — εἰς τὸ ἱερόν, *into the temple,* i. e. the part of it interdicted to foreigners. The outer court or inclosure was called the court of the Gentiles, and could be entered by them without profanation. The second court, or that of the Israelites, was surrounded with marble pillars, on which, as Philo states, was inscribed in Latin and Greek: "On penalty of death let no foreigner go further."

V. 29. ἦσαν προεωρακότες, *had seen before*, on some previous occasion; or possibly, *had seen away*, at a distance (Mey.). In this compound the preposition refers elsewhere to the future (out of question here) or to space, not to past time (R. and P. Lex.). The retrospective sense lies so near to the use of πρό, and occurs so readily here, that we need not scruple to admit it. — For *Trophimus*, see on 20, 4. He was a foreigner (Ἐφέσιον), and not a Jew from Ephesus. — ὃν ἐνόμιζον, κ. τ. λ., *whom they were supposing*, etc. They had seen Trophimus in the city with him, and from that rushed to the conclusion that he had brought Greeks into the temple. "Zelotæ *putantes*," says Bengel, "sæpe errant."

V. 30. εἷλκον . . . . ἱεροῦ, *they dragged him out of the temple*, so as not to pollute it with blood (Olsh. Mey. De Wet.). They had determined already to kill him. Bengel conjectures (whom Bmg. follows) that they wished to prevent him from taking refuge at the altar. But the Mosaic law restricted the right of asylum to those who had been guilty of accidental murder; see Ex. 21, 13. 14. — ἐκλείσθησαν αἱ θύραι, *the doors* (of the second court) *were closed*, probably by the Levites, who had the care of the temple; see the note on 4, 1. They may have feared that the crowd would return, or some new disturbance arise.

VERSES 31–40. *The Roman Commander rescues Paul from the Hands of the Jews.*

V. 31. ζητούντων δὲ αὐτὸν ἀποκτεῖναι, *Now while they are seeking to kill him;* they were beating him for that purpose (see v. 32). But as the onset had been sudden, and they were not furnished with weapons, some delay intervened. It was nothing in all human appearance but that momentary delay, that saved now the life of the apostle. The Roman officer had time to appear and snatch him from impending death. — ἀνέβη, κ. τ. λ., *a report went up to the chiliarch of the cohort;* see his name in 23, 26. It was but the work of a moment to convey to him the information. He had his station in the castle of Antonia, which was on a rock or hill at the northwest angle of the temple-area. The tower at the southeast corner of the castle "was seventy cubits high, and overlooked the whole temple with its courts. The fortress communicated with the northern and western porticos of the temple-area, and had flights of stairs descending into both; by which the garrison could at any time enter the court of the temple and prevent tumults." Bibl. Res. I. p. 432. During the festivals it was customary to keep the troops in readiness to suppress the riots which were so liable to occur at such times (comp. on 10, 37). See Jos. Antt. 20. 5. 3; Bell. Jud. 5. 5. 8.—The Turkish garrison stands at present very nearly on the site of the old castle. The traveller obtains his best view of the court of the Haram or mosque of Omar, the ancient temple-area, from the roof of this garrison.

V. 32. ἑκατοντάρχους, *centurions*, each with his proper complement of men. The chiliarch ordered out a force sufficiently large to intimidate all opposition.—κατέδραμεν ἐπ' αὐτούς, *ran down upon them.* To that despatch Paul was indebted for his escape; note also ἐξαυτῆς. This verb corresponds to ἀνέβη in v. 31—οἱ δὲ ἰδόντες, κ. τ. λ., *Now when they saw the chiliarch,* etc. They knew the consequences too well to run the risk of a collision with the Roman troops. See on 19, 24.

V. 33. δεθῆναι ἁλύσεσι δυσί, *to be bound with two chains,* i. e. to have his arms fastened to two soldiers, one on each side of him. The mode was described in the note on 12, 6.—τίς ἂν εἴη, *who he might be,* since his name and rank were uncertain.—καὶ τί ἐστι πεποιηκώς, *and what he has done.* The form of the inquiry presupposes that he had committed some crime. W. § 41. 4. c. He put the question to the crowd, as the responsive clamor shows in the next verse.

V. 34. εἰς τὴν παρεμβολήν, *into the garrison* or *barracks;* not the *castle* as a whole (E. V.), but the part of it assigned to the soldiers.

V. 35. ἐπὶ τοὺς ἀναβαθμούς, *upon the stairs* which led up to the castle. On arriving here, the crowd pressed on Paul so as to awaken the fear of some outrage or treachery. Some think that he was lifted off his feet by the throng, and then taken and carried up the stairs.—συνέβη, κ. τ. λ., *it happened that he was borne* (in their arms or on their shoulders) *by the soldiers.* συνέβη is not superfluous. ἐβαστάζετο alone would have pointed out less distinctly the peril of his situation, as evinced by their adopting such a precaution.

V. 36. Now was heard again the shout which thirty years before surrounded the prætorium of Pilate, "Away with him, away with him" (Hws.). αἶρε is imperative present because ἠκολούθει (imperf.) represents the cry as a continued one; see 22, 22. Compare ἆρον in John 19, 15, where the aorist precedes.

V. 37. Ἑλληνιστὶ γινώσκεις; *Dost thou know Greek?* The adverb stands in the place of the object (comp. οὕτω in 20, 13), and λαλεῖν is not to be supplied (Kuin.); comp. τοὺς Συριστὶ ἐπισταμένους in Xen. Cyr. 7. 5. 31, and in Latin *Græce nescire* (Mey. De Wet.).

V. 38. οὐκ ἄρα, κ. τ. λ., *Art thou not therefore the Egyptian?* i. e. as I supposed. οὐ indicates an affirmative answer with reference to the speaker's former state of mind. W. § 57. 3. The commander, on being addressed in Greek, concludes that he is mistaken; for it was notorious (it would seem) that the Egyptian was unable to speak that language. He could not have drawn that inference solely from his Egyptian origin, for the Greek was now spoken more or less in almost every country. — Of this Egyptian impostor, Josephus has given two different accounts which need to be reconciled with each other, as well as with Luke. In his Bell. Jud. 2. 13. 5, he relates that a juggler (γόης), whom he also denominates ὁ Αἰγύπτιος, having procured for himself the reputation of a prophet, led a great multitude of about thirty thousand men out of the desert to the Mount of Olives, and promised them that the walls of Jerusalem would fall down at his command; but Felix fell upon them, the Egyptian fled μετ' ὀλίγων, with a small number, most of his followers were slain or taken prisoners, and the rest of the crowd (τὸ λοιπὸν πλῆθος) dispersed. In his Antt. 20. 7. 6 (he wrote this work later than his Jewish War), he states that this Egyptian came to Jerusalem, that he persuaded the populace to go out with him to the Mount of Olives, where he would exhibit to them the wonder before mentioned; and then he speaks of the attack of Felix, and in that connection says merely that *four hundred* of the Egyptian's people were slain, and *two hundred* were taken captive, without any further addition. "Here now," says Tholuck (Glaubwürdigkeit, p. 169), "Josephus has in all appearance contradicted himself in the most glaring manner; for in one case the Egyptian brings the people from the desert to the Mount of Olives, in the other, from Jerusalem; in the one case the greater part of thirty thousand people are slain or taken prisoners; in the other, the number of the slain amounts to only four hundred, that of the prisoners to only two hundred. This example serves to illustrate an important rule of criticism, so often violated by sceptical writers in relation to the Bible; and that is, that, if the general credibility of an historian be acknowledged, we are bound to reconcile an apparent difference by interpretation or combination. The application of this principle here enables us to view the matter thus. The man had at first a band of *sicarii*, and a rabble had also attached themselves to him; these people he leaves behind on the Mount of Olives, and leads thither out of Jerusalem an additional crowd, so that the entire multitude might amount to about thirty thousand men. As usually happens in such cases, curiosity merely had drawn together most of them. Only a smaller company belonged to the train of his followers, and among these were the *sicarii*, the attack of the Romans was directed properly against these, of whom Felix slew four hundred, and made two hundred prisoners. With a small number, i. e. *with the four thousand of whom Luke speaks*, he escaped into the desert; the remaining mass, i. e. τὸ πλῆθος, of which the first passage of Josephus speaks, dispersed. In this, or in a similar way, the Jewish historian may be reconciled with himself, and with the writer of the Acts." — εἰς τὴν ἔρημον, *into the desert*, viz. between Egypt and Palestine, as he came from that direction. — τοὺς τετρακισχιλίους, *the four thousand*. The event was so recent that the precise number was still known. The same Felix was procurator of Judea at this time; see 23, 24. — σικαρίων, *assassins*, a Latinism. They received their name from the Roman *sica*, a curved dagger adapted by its form to be concealed beneath the clothes; they could use it for striking a fatal blow, in a crowd, without being observed.

V. 39. ἐγὼ .... Ταρσεύς, as analyzed by Meyer, contains two clauses: *I am indeed* (μέν) not the Egyptian, but *a Jew from Tarsus*. δέ below can hardly be antithetic. — Κιλικίας depends on πόλεως; not in apposition with an implied genitive in Ταρσεύς (E. V.). — οὐκ ἀσήμου, *not unnoted;* on the contrary, says Josephus (Antt. 1. 6. 1), the most important city of all Cilicia. Many of the coins of Tarsus bear the title of *Autonomous* and *Metropolis*. See on 9, 30.

V. 40. Παῦλος ἑστὼς, κ. τ. λ. "What nobler spectacle," exclaims Chrysostom, "than that of Paul at this moment! There he stands bound with two chains, ready to make his defence to the people. The Roman commander sits by, to enforce order by his presence. An enraged populace look up to him from below. Yet in the midst of so many dangers, how self-possessed is he, how tranquil!" — τῇ Ἑβραΐδι διαλέκτῳ, *in the Hebrew dialect*, i. e. in the Syro-Chaldaic or Aramæan, as in John 5, 2; 19, 13. See on 6, 1. In that language, if he was not more intelligible to most of his hearers, he could at least "speak more directly to the hearts of the people."

CHAPTER XXII.

VERSES 1–21. *Paul's Speech on the Stairs of the Castle.*

V. 1. As we examined Luke's account of Paul's conversion (9, 1–18) in connection with this address, it will be sufficient for the most part to refer the student to the notes there, so far as the two narratives coincide. I subjoin Mr. Humphry's introductory paragraph. "Though the subject-matter of this speech has been related before, it assumes here a fresh interest from the manner in which it is adapted to the occasion and the audience. The apostle is suspected of disaffection to the Mosaic law. In order to refute this charge, he addresses them in Hebrew; he dwells on his Jewish education, and on his early zeal for the law; he shows how at his conversion he was guided by Ananias, a man devout according to the law, and of good report among the Jews at Damascus, and how he subsequently worshipped in the temple at Jerusalem. So far they listen to him; but he no sooner touches on the promulgation of the gospel among the heathen (v. 21) than he is interrupted, and his fate would probably have been the same as Stephen's, had he not been under the protection of the Roman captain."—For ἀδελφοὶ καὶ πατέρες, see on 7, 2. Some of the rulers mingled with the crowd, whom Paul knew personally or recognized by some badge of office. Here too (1, 16) ἄνδρες is complimentary and belongs with that force to both nouns. —μου depends not on ἀκούσατε (comp. 1, 4), but on ἀπολογίας.

V. 3. The common rule would place μέν after γεγεννημένος. It stands out of its place now and then in the best writers. W. § 61. 5. The opposition lies evidently between Paul's foreign birth and his education at Jerusalem.—Κιλικίας depends not on πόλει understood, but on Ταρσῷ under the rule of possession. W. § 30. 2. —Critics point this sentence differently. Many of the older commentators, whom Meyer follows, place the comma after Γαμαλιήλ, instead of ταύτῃ, so as to bring a participle at the head of the several clauses. This division promotes the rhythm at the expense of the sense. The comma should be put undoubtedly after ταύτῃ (Grsb. Lchm. De Wet.). Tischendorf follows this punctuation in his second edition. παρὰ τοὺς πόδας Γαμαλιήλ, *at the feet of Gamaliel*, is appropriate to πεπαιδευμένος, but not to ἀνατεθραμμένος; the latter having respect to his physical growth or progress to manhood, the former to his professional training. ἀνατεθραμμένος ἐν τῇ πόλει ταύτῃ, *having been brought up in this city*, forbids the supposition that Paul was an adult when he went to reside at Jerusalem. Compare, also, 26, 4. He must have removed thither from Tarsus in his boyhood or early youth. It is surprising that Eichhorn and Hemsen should maintain, in opposition to such evidence, that Paul did not enter the school of Gamaliel until the thirtieth year of his age. See note on 7, 58. *To be taught at one's feet* was a proverbial expression among the Jews, founded on the fact that in their schools the teachers, whether they stood or sat, occupied a higher place than the pupils. Schöttg. Hor. Hebr. p. 477.—κατὰ ἀκρίβειαν = κατὰ τὴν ἀκριβεστάτην αἵρεσιν in 26, 5. Paul had been a Pharisee, and in his zeal for Judaism had surpassed all the adherents of that sect who had been students with him under Gamaliel (see Gal. 1, 13).—πατρῴου νόμου = νόμου τῶν πατέρων; comp. τῷ πατρῴῳ θεῷ in 24, 14.—θεοῦ is like the genitive in 21, 20.

V. 4. ταύτην τὴν ὁδόν (19, 23), stands concisely for *those of this way;* comp. 9, 2.—ἄχρι θανάτου, *unto death*, not the aim merely (Grot. Mey.), but result of his persecution. The facts in the case justify the strongest sense of the expression; see v. 20 and 26, 10.—ἄνδρας, κ. τ. λ. See on 8, 2.

V. 5. ὡς καὶ . . . . μοι, *as also the high-priest testifies* (= is witness) *for me;* i. e. the ἀρχιερεύς at that time (see on 9, 1), who was known to be still living. Some construe the verb incorrectly as future.—πρὸς τοὺς ἀδελφούς = πρὸς τὰς συναγωγάς in 9, 2; i. e. unto the Jewish rulers of the synagogue whom Paul recognizes as brethren (as in v. 1), to show that he was not hostile to his countrymen or alienated from them (21, 28); comp. Rom. 9, 1 sq.—ἐπορευόμην, *was journeying;* not *went* (E. V.).—ἄξων . . . . ὄντας, *in order to bring also those there*, lit. *thither*, because the speaker's mind passes from where he is to them; not the emigrants *thither* (Mey. Alf.), since the Jews had resided there too long to be viewed in that light.—ἵνα τιμωρηθῶσιν, *that they might be punished*, viz. by imprisonment (v. 4; 8, 3), by stripes (v. 19; 26, 11), or by death (v. 4; 8, 1).

V. 6. ἐγένετο, κ. τ. λ., *But it happened to me as I journeyed* (the participle as imperfect) *that*, etc.—μοι πορευομένῳ is not an instance of the dative absolute, but depends on ἐγένετο; comp. v. 17. W. § 31. 2. R. 2.—περὶ μεσημβρίαν, *about mid-day.* See on 9, 3. That he should have had such a vision (φῶς ἱκανόν) at such an hour made it the more impossible that he should be deceived.—For περί in περιαστράψαι repeated before ἐμέ, see on 3, 2.

V. 7. ἔπεσα, which is changed in some copies to ἔπεσον, is an

Alexandrian form; comp. Gal. 5, 4. W. § 13. 1. a. Transcribers have probably altered this termination to the second aorist in some other passages, as John 6, 10; Heb. 3, 17; Rev. 7, 11. For ἔπεσα in the classics, see K. § 154. R. 2; B. § 114.

V. 9. οἱ σὺν ἐμοὶ ὄντες = οἱ συνοδεύοντες αὐτῷ in 9, 7 (comp. 26, 14). So those might be described who happened to be travelling with Saul in the same caravan; but the common view is more correct, that they are the men who accompanied him as his assistants. He would need the aid of others to enable him to convey his prisoners in safety to Jerusalem (v. 5). — τὴν δὲ φωνὴν οὐκ ἤκουσαν, *but the voice of him who spoke to me they understood not.* For this translation, see the remarks on 9, 7.

V. 11. ὡς δὲ οὐκ ἐνέβλεπον, *As now I saw not,* i. e. any thing; here only without an object. — ἀπὸ τῆς δόξης τοῦ φωτὸς ἐκείνου, *from the glory,* splendor, *of that light,* which was "above the brightness of the sun;" see 26, 13. "The history (9, 9) mentions simply the fact of his blindness, but the apostle states its cause, as an eye-witness would naturally do." Birks, p. 328.[1]

V. 12. εὐσεβής is the authorized word, not εὐλαβής. "The historian (9, 10) calls Ananias a disciple; but the apostle 'a devout man according to the law, having a good report of all the Jews who dwelt there.' Such a description was admirably suited to his immediate object, to conciliate his audience in every lawful way. How consistent it was with the other account appears from 21, 20, in the words of James: 'Thou seest, brother, how many thousands of Jews there are who believe, and *they are all zealous of the law.*'" Birks, p. 329. — κατοικούντων, sc. ἐν Δαμασκῷ. — ἐπιστάς, *standing near,* in order to place his hands upon him; comp. 9, 17. — The recapitulation here omits the vision to Ananias, related so fully in the history (comp. 9, 10 sq.). The circumstances of that event were unimportant to the apostle's defence, and would have made his commission to the Gentiles needlessly prominent at this stage of the address.

V. 13. ἀνάβλεψον, *look up* and see; and so in the next clause, ἀνέβλεψα εἰς αὐτόν, *I looked up upon him.* We are to think of Paul as sitting there blind, and Ananias as standing before him (Mey). The verb does not vary its meaning, but suggests in the first instance what it asserts in the second. The involved idea prevails over the direct one in such a use as that in 9, 12.

V. 14. ὁ θεὸς τῶν πατέρων ἡμῶν, *the God of our fathers,* is another of

[1] Horæ Apostolicæ, by the Rev. T. R. Birks, late Fellow of Trinity College, Cambridge (London 1850).

"those conciliatory touches which mark a real discourse." — προεχειρίσατο, κ. τ. λ., *appointed* (destined, as in 3, 20) *thee to know his will,* not as to the way of saving men (i. e. βουλήν in 20, 27), but as to what he was to do and suffer in his future sphere of labor; comp. 9, 15. 16. — καὶ ἰδεῖν. See the last remark on 9, 7. — τὸν δίκαιον, as in 3, 14; 7, 52.

V. 15. ὅτι ἔσῃ . . . . ἀνθρώπους, *for thou shalt be a witness for him unto all men.* This is the reason why Christ had revealed himself to Paul; comp. Gal. 1, 16. πάντας ἀνθρώπους takes the place of ἐθνῶν καὶ βασιλέων, υἱῶν τε Ἰσραήλ in 9, 15. The more guarded phraseology here evinces the tact of the speaker. Paul would keep back for the present the offensive εἰς ἔθνη which when uttered at length (v. 21) was the last word that the bigoted Jews would bear from him. — The idea of our English "martyr" was not attached to μάρτυρ or μάρτυς till a later period. We see the word in its progress to that signification in v. 20 and Rev. 17, 6. Towards the close of the second century it had become so honorable a title, that the Christians at Lyons who had been condemned to suffer torture or death, fearful that they might waver in the moment of extremity, refused to be called "martyrs." "This name," said they, "properly belongs only to the true and faithful Witness, the Prince of Life; or, at least, only to those whose testimony Christ has sealed by their constancy to the end. We are but poor, humble confessors, i. e. ὁμόλογοι." (Euseb. Hist. 5. 2). — ὧν instead of ἅ, which the verb requires, arises from the suppressed ἐκείνων after μάρτυς.

V. 16. ἀναστάς stands opposed to μέλλεις, i. e. *without delay;* see on 9, 18. — βάπτισαι, *be baptized,* or, with a stricter adherence to the form, *have thyself baptized* (De Wet.). One of the uses of the middle is to express an act which a person procures another to perform for him. W. § 38. 3; K. 250. R. 2. This is the only instance in which the verb occurs in this voice, with reference to Christian baptism. In the analogous case (1 Cor. 10, 2) the reading is ἐβαπτίσαντο or ἐβαπτίσθησαν. — καὶ ἀπόλουσαι τὰς ἁμαρτίας σου, *and wash* (bathe) *away thy sins.* This clause states a result of the baptism, in language derived from the nature of that ordinance. It answers to εἰς ἄφεσιν ἁμαρτιῶν in 2, 38, i. e. submit to the rite in order to be forgiven. In both passages baptism is represented as having this importance or efficacy, because it is the sign of the repentance and faith which are the conditions of salvation. Compare ἀπελούσασθε in 1 Cor. 6, 11. The sort of outward washing expressed by this verb has been noticed on 16, 33. Hence there can be no question as to the mode of baptism in this instance; for if it be maintained that βάπτισαι is uncertain in its meaning, a definition is added in ἀπόλουσαι which removes the doubt. — ἐπικαλεσάμενος τὸ ὄνομα αὐτοῦ supplies essentially the place of ἐπὶ τῷ ὀνόματι Ἰησοῦ Χριστοῦ in 2, 38; see the note on that clause. τοῦ κυρίου after ὄνομα has much less support than αὐτοῦ. The pronoun can refer only to Christ; comp. on 9, 14.

V. 17. For this journey to Jerusalem, see on 9, 10. — ἐγένετο governs μοι as in v. 6. — In προσευχομένου μου the construction changes to the genitive absolute. On account of this intervening clause, με accompanies γένεσθαι, though ἐγένετο has the same logical subject (see on 15, 23). W. § 44. 3. — On ἐκστάσει, see 10, 10. Some, as Schott, Wieseler, and others, would identify this "ecstasy" with the vision to which Paul alludes in 2 Cor. 12, 2; and would establish by this coincidence the date of the composition of that Epistle. But as the apostle had so many similar revelations in the course of his life, and as the character of this vision is so unlike that described in 2 Cor. 12, 2, the conjecture that they are the same must be pronounced vague and improbable.

V. 18. ἐν τάχει, *quickly*, accords with Gal. 1, 18. On this first visit Paul remained at Jerusalem but fifteen days, and received this command probably on one of the last of them. In that passage of the Epistle the apostle says nothing respecting this vision in the temple, as it was sufficient for his object to mention the reason for this journey thither and the brevity of his stay. — διότι . . . . περὶ ἐμοῦ, *because they* (viz. his unconverted countrymen) *will not receive thy testimony*, i. e. although he should continue to declare it to them. See the note on 9, 30.

V. 19. εἶπον, κ. τ. λ. The apostle states the reason here why he supposed Jerusalem to be his proper field of labor. His history as a converted blasphemer and persecutor was notorious in that city; the testimony of such a man might be expected to have more weight among those who had witnessed the change in his character, than among those to whom his previous life was unknown.

V. 20. μάρτυρός σου, *thy witness*, not "martyr" (E. V.); see on v. 15. — καὶ οὐτός, *then* (see on 1, 10) *I myself*. — In respect to συνευδοκῶν, see the note on 8, 1. τῇ ἀναιρέσει αὐτοῦ the critical editions of the text omit, or put in brackets. It is probably an addition from 8, 1. — On φυλάσσων, κ. τ. λ., see 7, 58.

V. 21. πορεύου is present, because he was to obey at once. He proceeded to Syria and Cilicia (9, 30 and Gal. 1, 21), and remained there three or four years before his arrival at Antioch (see on 9, 30). As he was ordered to leave Jerusalem because

God would send him to the Gentiles, we may infer (though this is not the common opinion) that he preached to heathen as well as Jews during his sojourn in those regions. See note on 13, 3. — "Paul relates this vision to show," as Alford remarks, "that his own inclination and prayer had been, that *he might preach the gospel to his own people;* but that it was by the imperative command of the Lord himself that he went to the Gentiles."

VERSES 22–29. *Paul pleads his Roman Citizenship, and escapes the Torture.*

V. 22. ἤκουον, *continued to hear.* — ἄχρι τούτου τοῦ λόγου, *unto this word,* viz. that God would send him to the heathen. — αἶρε is present because it was a repeated cry; see on 21, 37. — For τόν with τοιοῦτον, *the one such as he,* see on 19, 25. — οὐ γὰρ καθῆκεν αὐτὸν ζῆν, *for it was not fit he should live;* imperfect because he had forfeited life long ago. W. § 41. 2. Meyer refers the past tense to the chiliarch's interference; he ought not to have rescued the man, but should have left him to his fate. Some copyists, stumbling apparently at the imperfect, wrote καθῆκον or καθήκει.

V. 23. ῥιπτούντων τὰ ἱμάτια means, not *throwing off their garments* as a preparation for stoning Paul (Grot. Mey.), for he was now in the custody of the Roman captain; but *throwing them up,* tossing them about, as a manifestation and an effect of their incontrollable rage. Their *casting dust into the air* was an act of the same character. This mode of demonstrating their feelings was suited also to inflame the populace still more, and to impress the tribune with the necessity of conceding something to their demands. Sir John Chardin, as quoted by Harmer,[1] says that it is common for the peasants in Persia, when they have a complaint to lay before their governors, to repair to them by hundreds, or a thousand, at once; they place themselves near the gate of the palace, where they suppose they are most likely to be seen and heard, and there set up a horrid outcry, rend their garments, and throw dust into the air, at the same time demanding justice.

V. 24. ἐκέλευσεν, κ. τ. λ. It is not surprising that the chiliarch gave this order. He had been unable to follow Paul's address on account of his ignorance of the language; and witnessing now this renewed outburst of rage, he concludes that the prisoner must have given occasion for it by some flagrant offence, and determines, therefore, to extort a confession from him. — εἰπὼν .... αὐτόν, *directing that he should be examined by scourges.* The plural

[1] Observations, Vol. IV. p. 203.

refers to the blows or lashes of the scourge. It was proposed to torture him into an acknowledgment of his supposed crime. — ἵνα ἐπιγνῷ, *that he might ascertain.* — οὕτως ἐπεφώνουν αὐτῷ, *were so crying out against him;* not *cried out* (E. V.).

V. 25. ὡς δὲ προέτειναν αὐτὸν τοῖς ἱμᾶσιν has received two different explanations. Some, as De Wette, Meyer, Robinson, render: *But as they* (sc. the soldiers, see on v. 29) *stretched him forth for the thongs*, i. e. for the scourge, which consisted sometimes of two or more lashes or cords. They placed the apostle in an upright posture, so as to expose him more fully to the blows, or caused him to lean forward in order to receive them more effectually. The stripes, it will be remembered, were inflicted on the naked back (see 16, 22). Others translate, *they stretched him forth with the thongs*, against a block or pillar, i. e. bound him to it with them, preparatory to his being scourged. The article in this case would designate *the thongs* as those which it was customary to use on such occasions. Böttger (Schauplatz, p. 84), who advocates the view last stated, deduces a strong confirmation of it from v. 29. It is said that the chiliarch feared when he ascertained that Paul was a Roman citizen, because he *had bound him;* but that fear could not relate to the command in 21, 33, for he kept Paul in chains until the next day (v. 30), and Felix left him still in that condition at the expiration of his term of office (24, 27). It was not contrary to the Roman laws for a magistrate to bind a criminal or suspected person for safe-keeping, although he was known to be a Roman citizen; and hence it is difficult to see what can be meant by δεδεκώς in v. 29, unless it be the binding connected with the scourging to which the commander had ordered Paul to be subjected. That was an outrage which was not to come near the person of a Roman even after condemnation; the infliction of it on the part of a judge or magistrate exposed him to the severest penalty. (Wdsth. concurs in this view.) Several critics (e. g. Kuin. Olsh.) render προέτειναν, *delivered*, consigned, i. e. to the scourge, which is too vague for so specific a term. — πρὸς τὸν ἑστῶτα ἑκατόνταρχον, *unto the centurion standing there*, having charge of the inquisition. It was the custom of the Romans to commit the execution of such punishments to that class of officers; comp. Mark 15, 39. — καὶ ἀκατάκριτον, *and* (that too) *uncondemned*, without previous trial; see on 16, 37.

V. 26. ὅρα, rendered *take heed* in the English version, Griesbach and others omit, after decisive authorities. It was added apparently to give more point to the caution. — ὁ γὰρ, κ. τ. λ., *for this man is a Roman.* It may excite surprise that the centurion believed Paul's word so readily. We have the explanation of this in the fact, that a false claim of this nature was easily exposed, and liable to be punished with death. (Suet. Claud. c. 25.) It was almost an unprecedented thing that any one was so foolhardy as to assert the privilege without being entitled to it.

V. 27. λέγε μοι, κ. τ. λ. He asks the question, not from any doubt of Paul's veracity, but in order to have the report confirmed from his own lips, and at the same time to elicit an explanation of so unexpected a fact. The inquiry indicates his surprise that a man in Paul's situation should possess a privilege which he himself had procured at such expense.

V. 28. πολλοῦ κεφαλαίου, *for a great sum.* It has been inferred from this circumstance, and from his name, that Lysias was a Greek. It was very common under the emperors to obtain the rights of citizenship in this way. Havercamp says in a note on Josephus (Antt. 1. p. 712), that a great many Jews in Asia Minor were Roman citizens at this time, who had purchased that rank. It did not always require great wealth to procure it. A few years earlier than this, in the reign of Claudius, "the rights of Roman citizenship were sold by Messallina and the freedmen, with shameless indifference, to any purchaser, and it was currently said that the Roman *civitas* (Dict. of Antt. s. v.) might be purchased for two cracked drinking-cups." — καί, *also,* connects the fact of his freedom with its origin. — γεγέννημαι, sc. Ῥωμαῖος, i. e. he had inherited his rights as a Roman citizen. In what way the family of Paul acquired this distinction is unknown. Many of the older commentators assert that Tarsus enjoyed the full privileges of citizenship, and that Paul possessed them as a native of Tarsus. But that opinion (advanced still in some recent works) is certainly erroneous. The passages in the ancient writers which were supposed to confirm it are found to be inconclusive; they prove that the Romans freed the inhabitants of Tarsus from taxation, allowed them to use their own laws, and declared their city the metropolis of Cilicia; but they afford no proof that the Romans conferred on them the birthright of Roman citizenship. Indeed, the opinion to that effect, could it be established, so far from supporting Luke's credibility, would bring it into question; for it is difficult to believe that the chiliarch, after being told that Paul was a citizen of Tarsus (21, 39), would have ordered him to be scourged, without any further inquiry as to his rank. It only remains, therefore, that Paul's father, or some one of his ancestors, must have obtained Roman citizenship in some one of the different ways in which foreigners could obtain that privilege. It was conferred often as a reward for fidelity to the Roman interest, or for distinguished military services; it could be purchased, as was mentioned above; or it could be acquired by manumission, which, when executed with certain forms, secured the full immunities of freedom to the emancipated. In which of these modes the family of Paul became free can only be conjectured. Some adopt one supposition, some another. Nothing is certain beyond the fact that Paul inherited his citizenship.

V. 29. οἱ μέλλοντες are soldiers who aided the centurion (v. 25). Luke does not mention the command of Lysias, which caused them to desist so promptly. — ἐπιγνοὺς ὅτι Ῥωμαῖός ἐστι, *having ascertained that he is a Roman.* "Illa vox et imploratio, 'Civis Romanus sum,' quæ sæpe multis, in ultimis terris, opem inter barbaros et salutem tulit,"[1] proved itself effectual, also, in this instance. — ὅτι .... δεδεκώς, *because he had bound him.* Those who understand this of his having ordered him to be chained in 21, 33, must suppose that his present fear was very transient. ἔλυσεν in v. 30 shows that Paul was kept in chains during the night.

VERSE 30. *Paul is examined before the Sanhedrim.*

V. 30. For the use of τό before the interrogative clause, see on v. 21. — τί κατηγορεῖται παρὰ τῶν Ἰουδαίων, *why he is accused on the part of the Jews,* not directly or formally, but, in point of fact, by their persecution of him, their clamor for his death. παρά is a more exact preposition for this sense (W. § 47. p. 327) than ὑπό, which has taken its place in some manuscripts. Some have joined παρὰ τῶν Ἰουδαίων with γνῶναι τὸ ἀσφαλές, as if it could not follow a passive verb. — ἀπὸ τῶν δεσμῶν after ἔλυσεν expands the idea, and was added to the text probably for that purpose. It is destitute of critical support. — καταγαγὼν τὸν Παῦλον, *having brought down Paul* from his prison in the castle (see on 21, 31) to the lower place where the Sanhedrim assembled. According to Jewish tradition, that body transferred their sittings at length from Gazith, an apartment in the inner temple (see on 6, 13), to a room on Mount Zion, near the bridge over the Tyropœon. It was here probably that the council met at this time; for Lysias and his soldiers would not have presumed to enter the sacred part of the temple. The Romans conceded to the Jews the right of putting any foreigner to death who passed the forbidden limits; comp. on 21, 28. See Lewin, II. p. 672.[2]

[1] Cic. in Verr. Act. 2. 5. 57.

[2] The Life and Epistles of St. Paul, by Thomas Lewin of Trinity College, Oxford (1851).

CHAPTER XXIII.

VERSES 1–10. *Paul's Speech before the Jewish Council.*

V. 1. πάσῃ συνειδήσει ἀγαθῇ, *with all good conscience;* or, more strictly, *consciousness*, i. e. of integrity and sincerity. See on 20, 21.—πεπολίτευμαι τῷ θεῷ, *I have lived unto God*, i. e. for his service and glory; dative of the object (see Rom. 14, 18; Gal. 2, 19). The verb refers to his conduct in all respects; not specially to his political or civil relations. Compare ἀξίως τοῦ εὐαγγελίου πολιτεύεσθε in Phil. 1, 27.—ἄχρι ταύτης τῆς ἡμέρας, *unto this day*, from the time that he became a Christian. As his conduct before his defection from Judaism was not in question now, he had no occasion to speak of that part of his life, though he could claim in some sense to have acted conscientiously even then (see 26, 9).

V. 2. ὁ ἀρχιερεὺς Ἀνανίας. This *Ananias* is to be distinguished from the Annas, or Ananus, of whom we read in 4, 6; Luke 3, 2, and John 18, 13. He is unquestionably, says Winer (Realw. I. p. 57), the son of Nebedæus, who obtained the office of high-priest under the procurator Tiberius Alexander, in the year A. D. 48, and was the immediate successor of Camydus or Camithus (Jos. Antt. 20. 5. 2). He filled this office also under the procurator Cumanus, but, having been implicated in a dispute between the Jews and the Samaritans, he was sent by the Syrian proprætor to Rome, in A. D. 52, in order to defend himself before the Emperor Claudius. The subsequent history of Ananias is obscure. He either lost his office in consequence of this journey, or, which is more probable (Jos. Antt. 20. 6. 3), he was acquitted, and continued to officiate as high-priest until he was superseded by Ismael, son of Phabi, just before the departure of Felix from Judea. In the latter case, says the same writer, he was the actual high-priest at the time of the occurrence related here, and is called ἀρχιερεύς on that account, and not because he had formerly held the office, or because he occupied it during a vacancy.—τοῖς παρεστῶσιν αὐτῷ, *those who stood near to him;* not members of the council, or spectators, but the ὑπηρέται, the servants in attendance; see on 4, 1.—τύπτειν αὐτοῦ τὸ στόμα, *to strike his mouth.* The mouth must be shut that uttered such a declaration. It was not to be endured that a man arraigned there as an apostate from the religion of his fathers should assert his innocence. This mode of enjoining silence is practised in the East at the present day. "As soon as the ambassador came," says a traveller in Persia, "he punished the principal offenders by causing them to be beaten before him; and those who had spoken their minds too freely, he smote upon the mouth with a shoe." He relates another instance: "'Call the Ferasches,' exclaimed the king; 'let them beat the culprits until they die.' The Ferasches appeared and beat them violently; and when they attempted to say anything in their defence, they were struck on the mouth."[1]

V. 3. τύπτειν . . . . ὁ θεός, *God shall smite thee.* The apostle declares in terms suggested by the outrage that God would punish the author of the brutal insult; he does not imprecate vengeance on him, or predict that he would die by violence. As Ananias was killed by an assassin (Jos. Bell.Jud. 2. 17. 9), some have supposed Paul's language to prefigure such an end. — τοῖχε κεκονιαμένε, *thou whited wall,* i. e. hypocrite, because, as stated in the next clause, he did one thing while he professed another. For the origin of the expression, see Matt. 23, 27. The Jews painted their sepulchres white, so as not to defile themselves by coming unexpectedly in contact with them; hence they were fair to the eye while they were full of inward corruption. Jahn's Archæol. § 207. — καὶ σὺ κάθῃ, *And dost thou sit?* etc. The verb is a later form for κάθησαι. Lob. ad Phryn. p. 358. καί conforms here to its use in questions designed to bring out the inconsistency of another's views or conduct. Compare Mark 4, 13; Luke 10, 29. K. § 321. R. 1. — κρίνων με κατὰ τὸν νόμον, *judging me according to the law,* states what was true of him in theory, παρανομῶν, *transgressing the law,* what was true in point of fact.

V. 5. οὐκ ᾔδειν, *I did not know* at the moment, bear in mind (Bng. Wetst. Kuin. Olsh. Wdsth.). Compare the use of this verb in Eph. 6, 8; Col. 3, 24. Some understand that Paul *did not know,* was ignorant, that Ananias was now the high-priest; a possible ignorance, certainly, since he had been absent from the country so long, and the high-priest was changed so frequently at that period. On the contrary, if the high-priest presided on such occasions or wore an official dress, Paul could tell at a glance who that dignitary was, from his position or his costume. But this view is liable to another objection; it renders the apostle's apology for his remark irrelevant, since he must have perceived from the presence of Ananias that he was at least one of the rulers of the people, and entitled to respect on account of his

[1] Morier's Second Journey through Persia, pp. 8, 94.

station. Others think that Paul spoke ironically, meaning that he did not know or acknowledge such a man as high-priest (Mey. Bmg.). The sarcasm so covertly expressed would not have been readily understood, and the appeal to Scripture in that state of mind, becomes unmeaning, not to say irreverent. — γὰρ γέγραπται connects itself with an implied thought: Otherwise I should not have so spoken; *for it is written,* viz. in Ex. 22, 28. The passage applies to any civil magistrate, as well as to the high-priest. Paul admits that he had been thrown off his guard; the insult had touched him to the quick, and he had spoken rashly. But what can surpass the grace with which he recovered his self-possession, the frankness with which he acknowledged his error? If his conduct in yielding to the momentary impulse was not that of Christ himself under a similar provocation (John 18, 22. 23), certainly the manner in which he atoned for his fault was *Christ-like.*

V. 6. γνοὺς δὲ, κ. τ. λ. Neander: "In order to secure the voice of the majority among his judges, Paul availed himself of a measure for promoting the triumph of the truth which has been oftener employed against it, — the *divide et impera* in a good sense; in order to produce a division in the assembly, he addressed himself to the interest for the truth which a great part of his judges acknowledged, and by which they really approached nearer to him than the smaller number of those who denied it. He could say with truth that he stood there on trial because he had testified of the hope of Israel, and of the resurrection of the dead; for he had preached Jesus as the one through whom this hope was to be fulfilled. This declaration had the effect of uniting the Pharisees present in his favor, and of involving them in a violent dispute with the Sadducees. The former could find no fault with him. If he said that the spirit of a deceased person, or that an angel, had appeared to him, no one could impute that to him as a crime; what he meant by this, and whether what he alleged was true or not, they did not trouble themselves to decide." — περὶ ἐλπίδος, κ. τ. λ., *for hope's sake and* (that) *a resurrection of the dead* (Mey. De Wet.), i. e. by hendiadys, *the hope of the resurrection* (Kuin. Olsh.). The first mode of stating it analyzes the grammatical figure.

V. 7. ἐγένετο στάσις, *there arose a dissention,* difference of views respecting Paul's case; see on 15, 2. — As the effect of this difference, ἐσχίσθη τὸ πλῆθος, *the multitude was divided,* took opposite sides.

V. 8. μὴ εἶναι . . . . πνεῦμα, *that there is no resurrection, nor angel or spirit.* See Mark 12, 18. μηδέ adds a second denial to the first, while μήτε expands this denial into its parts. See W. § 55. 6. Josephus confirms this statement as to the belief of the Sadducees. In one place (Bell. Jud. 2. 8. 14) he says, that "the Sadducees reject the permanence or existence of the soul after death, and the rewards and punishments of an invisible world;" and in another place (Antt. 18. 1. 4), that "the Sadducees hold that the souls of men perish with their bodies." The Talmudists and other Jewish writers make the same representation. — τὰ ἀμφότερα, *both,* i. e. according to the above analysis, a resurrection and the reality of spiritual existences, whether angels or the souls of the departed. Josephus belonged to the sect of the Pharisees, and he represents their opinion to have been, "that souls have an immortal vigor, and are destined to be rewarded or punished in another state according to the life here, as it has been one of virtue or vice; that the good will be permitted to live again (i. e. in another body on the earth), and that the wicked will be consigned to an eternal prison." (Antt. 18. 1. 3.) "There was a variety of opinions concerning the resurrection," says Biscoe, "among the Pharisees, or traditionary Jews. In this account of it, which resembles the heathen idea of transmigration, Josephus, as I apprehend, has given us that which comes nearest to his own belief, or which he was inclined to have the Greek philosophers understand to be his own. For he is accused by learned men, and certainly not without reason, of sometimes accommodating the Jewish revelation to the sentiments of the heathen, or bringing it as near to what was taught by them as might be."

V. 9. οἱ γραμματεῖς, κ. τ. λ., *the scribes of the party of the Pharisees contended,* disputed violently. They appear as the champions of their party, because they were the men of learning, and accustomed to such debates. — εἰ δὲ πνεῦμα, κ. τ. λ., *but if a spirit spoke to him, or an angel* ——; undoubtedly, a designed aposiopesis. A significant gesture or look towards the Sadducees expressed what was left unsaid: that is not an impossible thing, the matter then assumes importance, or something to that effect. See W. § 64. II. For other examples of aposiopesis, see Luke 19, 42 and 22, 42. Some maintain that the sentence is incomplete, because the remainder was unheard amid the tumult that now ensued. The common text supplies μὴ θεομαχῶμεν as the apodosis; but the testimonies require us to reject that addition. It was suggested, probably, by θεομάχοι in 5, 39.

V. 10. μὴ διασπασθῇ ὁ Παῦλος ὑπ' αὐτῶν, *lest Paul should be pulled in pieces by them,* as the parties struggled to obtain possession of him; their object being on the one side to protect him, and on the other to maltreat or kill him. — τὸ στράτευμα, *the soldiery*, some of the troops stationed in the castle; see v. 27. — Observe the collateral τε after ἄγειν, since the rescue and the conveyance to the garrison are parts of the same order.

VERSES 11–15. *A Conspiracy of the Jews to slay Paul.*

V. 11. ὁ κύριος, i. e. Christ. — θάρσει, *be courageous still.* The tense is present. Though he had not begun to despond, he was on the eve of trials which would expose him to that danger. — Παῦλε in the T. R., which the E. V. retains, is to be struck out. — εἰς Ἱερουσαλήμ and εἰς Ῥώμην involve an ellipsis like that noticed on 8, 40. — δεῖ, *is necessary*, because such was the purpose of God; comp. 27, 24. Paul had long cherished a desire to see Rome (19, 21; Rom. 1, 13); but as far as we know, he was now assured for the first time that such was to be his destiny

V. 12. ποιήσαντες συστροφήν, *having formed a combination* (Mey. Rob.), which συνωμοσίαν in v. 13 defines more precisely. — οἱ Ἰουδαῖοι, *the Jews*, since this party of them manifested the Jewish spirit; see the last remark on 4, 1. τινὲς τῶν Ἰουδαίων is an unapproved reading.

V. 14. τοῖς ἀρχιερεῦσι καὶ τοῖς πρεσβυτέροις, *the chief-priests and the elders*, i. e. those of these classes who were hostile to Paul, the Sadducee members of the council (Mey. De Wet.). This limitation suggests itself without remark, after the occurrence which has just been related. — ἀνεθεματίσαμεν ἑαυτούς, *we cursed ourselves.* The expression points to some definite ratification of the atrocious oath. The reflexive of the third person (see v. 12) may follow a subject of the first or second person. K. § 303. 8; B. § 127. n. 5.

V. 15. σὺν τῷ συνεδρίῳ, *with the Sanhedrim*, i. e. in the name of that body, as if it was their united request. — αὔριον has been added to the text in some copies, because it occurs in v. 20. — ἀκριβέστερον, *more exactly* than on the former trial. — πρὸ τοῦ ἐγγίσαι αὐτόν, *before he has come near*, i. e. to the place of assembly. Their plan was to kill him on the way; see v. 21. — τοῦ ἀνελεῖν depends on ἕτοιμοι as a genitive construction. W. § 44. 4. — It would be difficult to credit the account of such a proceeding, had Luke related it of any other people than the Jews. Here, as Lardner suggests (Credibility, I. p. 224), are more than forty men who enter into a conspiracy to take away Paul's life in a clandestine manner; and they make no scruple to declare it to the council, relying upon their approbation. It is clearly implied that these teachers of religion, these professed guardians of the law, gave their assent to the proposal; they had nothing to object, either to so infamous a design, or to the use of such means for accomplishing it. But, out of place as such a passage would be in any other history, it relates a transaction in perfect harmony with the Jewish opinions and practices of that age. A single testimony will illustrate this. Philo, in speaking of the course to be pursued towards a Jew who forsakes the worship of the true God, lays down the following principle: "It is highly proper that all who have a zeal for virtue should have a right to punish with their own hands, without delay, those who are guilty of this crime; not carrying them before a court of judicature, or the council, or, in short, before any magistrate; but they should indulge the abhorrence of evil, the love of God, which they entertain, by inflicting immediate punishment on such impious apostates, regarding themselves for the time as all things, senators, judges, prætors, sergeants, accusers, witnesses, the laws, the people; so that, hindered by nothing, they may without fear, and with all promptitude, espouse the cause of piety." Josephus mentions a similar combination against the life of Herod into which a party of the Jews entered on account of the religious innovations which they charged him with introducing. (Antt. 15. 8. 1–4.)

VERSES 16–22. *The Plot is disclosed to the Roman Commander.*

V. 16. ὁ υἱὸς τῆς ἀδελφῆς, *the son of his sister.* Whether the family of this sister resided at Jerusalem, or the nephew only, does not appear from the narrative. His anxiety for the safety of Paul may have arisen from a stronger interest than that prompted by their relationship to each other. See the note on 9, 30. He was not a bigoted Jew at all events; for in that case he would have allowed no tie of blood, no natural affection to interfere with the supposed claims of his religion. — εἰσελθὼν, κ. τ. λ., *having entered into the castle*, whence it appears that his friends, as afterward at Cæsarea (24, 23), had free access to him. Lysias may have been the more indulgent, because he would atone for his fault in having bound a Roman citizen. — τὴν ἐνέδραν, *the ambush* which the Jews were preparing.

V. 18. ὁ δέσμιος shows that Paul was still bound, i. e. by a chain to the arm of a soldier. — ἔχοντά τι λαλῆσαί σοι, *since he has something to say to thee;* comp. ἔχει γὰρ, κ. τ. λ., in v. 17.

V. 21. ἐνεδρεύουσι, *lie in wait,* which they were doing inasmuch as their plot was already so mature; comp. ἐνέδραν ποιοῦντες in 25, 3. — τεσσαράκοντα, sc. ἀνδρῶν, as in v. 13. — ἕτοιμοί εἰσι, sc. τοῦ ἀνελεῖν αὐτόν; comp. v. 15. — προσδεχόμενοι τὴν ἀπὸ σοῦ ἐπαγγελίαν, *awaiting the* (expected) *promise from thee.* ἐπαγγελία has this constant sense in the New Testament.

V. 22. Note the change to the direct style in ὅτι ταῦτα ἐνεφάνισας πρός με. W. § 63. II. 1. Compare Luke 5, 14. The opposite change occurs in v. 24.

VERSES 23–30. *The Letter of Lysias to Felix.*

V. 23. δύο τινὰς τῶν ἑκατοντάρχων, *some two or three of the centurions;* not *one or two* (Hws.), from the nature of the expression and because less than two would be an inadequate command for so large a force. Though it is not said expressly, the inference is that these officers were to take charge of the expedition, as well as prepare for it. τὶς joined with numerals renders them indefinite; comp. δύο τινὰς τῶν μαθητῶν in Luke 7, 19. W. § 25. 2. b; K. § 303. 4. — στρατιώτας, *soldiers,* who, as they are distinguished from the other two classes named, must be the ordinary, heavy-armed legionaries. — δεξιολάβους occurs only here and in two obscure writers of the iron age. "Its meaning," says De Wette, "is a riddle." The proposed explanations are these: παραφύλακες, military lictors who guarded prisoners, so called from their taking the right-hand side (Suid. Bez. Kuin.); *lancers* (Vulg. E. V.); a species of light-armed troops (Mey.), since they are mentioned once in connection with archers and peltasts. Codex A reads δεξιοβόλους, *jaculantes dextra* (Syr.). See De Wette's note here. — ἀπὸ τρίτης ὥρας, *from the third hour,* i. e. nine o'clock with us; it being implied that they were to march at that hour as well as be ready.

V. 24. κτήνη τε παραστῆσαι, *and that they should provide beasts of burden,* as two or more would be needed for relays, or for the transportation of baggage. The discourse changes at this point from the direct to the indirect; comp. on 19, 27. — ἵνα ἐπιβιβάσαντες, κ. τ. λ., *that having mounted Paul* (on one of them) *they might convey him in safety unto Felix.* διά in the verb refers to the intermediate space, not to the dangers through which they were to pass; comp. 18, 27; 27, 44; 1 Pet. 3, 20. — *Felix* was the procurator of Judea, having received this office from the Emperor Claudius, probably in the autumn of A. D. 52 (Win. Ang. Mey.). He was originally a slave, was a man of energy and talents, but avaricious, cruel, and licentious. Tacitus (Hist. 5. 9) has drawn his character in a single line: "Per omnem sævitiam ac libidinem jus regium servili ingenio exercuit." See further, on 24, 3. 24.

V. 25. γράψας belongs to the subject of εἶπεν in v. 23. — περιέχουσαν τὸν τύπον τοῦτον, *containing this outline*, draught, i. e. a letter to this effect. The Roman law required that a subordinate officer, in sending a prisoner to the proper magistrate for trial, should draw up a written statement of the case. The technical name of such a communication was *elogium*.

V. 26. κρατίστῳ is an honorary epithet; see on 1, 1. — ἡγεμόνι stands in the New Testament for the more specific ἐπίτροπος (comp. Matt. 27, 2). — χαίρειν. Compare the last remark on 15, 23.

V. 27. τὸν ἄνδρα is the object of ἐξειλόμην, which αὐτόν repeats on account of the distance of the noun from the verb; comp. τούτων in 1, 22. — μέλλοντα ἀναιρεῖσθαι, *on the point of being killed*; not *should have been* (E. V.). — σὺν τῷ στρατεύματι, *with the military* (see v. 10). — μαθὼν ὅτι Ῥωμαῖός ἐστι, *having learned that he is a Roman*, which is stated as a reason why Lysias was so prompt to rescue him. It was not until after he had taken Paul into his custody that he ascertained his rank; but, as was not unnatural, he wished to gain as much credit as possible in the eyes of his superior. This deviation from truth, says Meyer, testifies to the genuineness of the letter. Some resolve μαθών into καὶ ἔμαθον, as if he learned the fact that Paul was a Roman citizen after his apprehension. The Greek of the New Testament affords no instance of such a use of the participle. See W. § 46. 2. Luke with his inquisitive habits (see his Gospel 1, 1) would find an opportunity to copy the letter during his abode of two years at Cæsarea.

V. 28. βουλόμενος, κ. τ. λ., *Wishing to know* or *ascertain* (γνῶναι and ἐπιγνῶναι are both found) *the crime* (not *charge*), of which at this stage of the affair Paul was supposed to be guilty. The weaker sense of αἰτίαν (Hws.) makes ἐνεκάλουν repetitious. — δι' ἥν, κ. τ. λ., *on account of which they were accusing him*, not formally, but by their continued outcry, as Luke has related. — κατήγαγον αὐτόν, *I brought him down* in person, as he must be present to gain the desired information; see on 22, 30.

V. 29. περὶ ζητημάτων τοῦ νόμου αὐτῶν, *concerning questions of their law*. See the note on 18, 15. — As θανάτου and δεσμῶν denoted the highest and lowest penalties of the law, the idea is that Paul had no crime alleged against him that required his detention or punishment (Böttg.). Every Roman magistrate before whom the apostle is brought declares him innocent.

48

V. 30. The writer falls out of his construction here. He says μηνυθείσης at the beginning of the sentence, as if he would have added τῆς μελλούσης; but in the progress of the thought adds μέλλειν, as if he had commenced with μηνυσάντων . . . . ἐπιβουλὴν, κ. τ. λ. The idea of the thing disclosed gives place to that of the persons who disclose it. W. § 63. I. — ὑπὸ τῶν Ἰουδαίων after ἔσεσθαι the recent editors omit (Tsch. De Wet. Mey.). — ἔπεμψα, *I sent;* since the future act would be past on the reception of the letter (comp. Phil. 2, 28; Philem. 11). W. § 41. 5. 2. — ἐπὶ σοῦ, *before thee.*

VERSES 31–35. *Paul is sent to Felix at Cæsarea.*

V. 31. ἀναλαβόντες, *having taken up*, answers to ἐπιβιβάσαντες in v. 24. — διὰ τῆς νυκτός, *during the night*, which would include the hours from nine o'clock, P. M. (v. 23) to six, A. M. — εἰς τὴν Ἀντιπατρίδα, *unto Antipatris*, which was about thirty-eight miles from Jerusalem, on the route to Cæsarea. It was built by Herod the Great, on the site of a place called Caphar Saba, and was named by him Antipatris, in honor of his father Antipater. See Jos. Antt. 16. 5. 2; Bell. Jud. 1. 21. 9. The modern Kefr Sâba, about ten miles from Lud, the ancient Lydda, stands no doubt on the same spot.[1] It is an instance, like Ptolemais (21, 7), in which the original name regained its sway, on the decline of the power which imposed the foreign name. The Romans had two military roads from Jerusalem to Antipatris; a more southerly one by the way of Gibeon and Beth-horon, and a more northerly one by way of Gophna. Bibl. Res. II. p. 138. If Paul's escort took the latter as the more direct course, they would arrive at Gophna about midnight, and at day-break would reach the last line of hills which overlooked the plain of Sharon. Antipatris lay on a slight eminence, at a little distance from the base of these hills. To perform this journey in the time allowed, would require them

1 See the account of a visit to Kefr Sâba by the late Dr. Smith, in the Bibliotheca Sacra, 1843, p. 478 sq. "It is a Muslim village, of considerable size, and wholly like the most common villages of the plain, being built entirely of mud. We saw but one stone building, which was apparently a mosque, but without a minaret. No old ruins, nor the least relic of antiquity, did we anywhere discover. A well by which we stopped, a few rods east of the houses, exhibits more signs of careful workmanship than anything else. It is walled with hewn stone, and is fifty-seven feet deep to the water. The village stands upon a slight circular eminence, near the western hills, from which it is actually separated, however, by a branch of the plain." Raumer (Palästina, p. 132, 3d ed.) and Ritter (Erdkunde, XVI. p. 571) suppose Antipatris to have been at this place.

to proceed at the rate of about four miles an hour. As those who conducted Paul had a good road (traces of the old Roman pavement are still visible), they could accomplish a forced march of that extent, in nine hours. Strabo says that an army, under ordinary circumstances, could march from two hundred and fifty to three hundred stadia in a day, i. e. an average of about thirty miles. Forbiger (Handb. der Geog. p. 551) gives a table of the various distances of a day's journey among the ancients. Some understand ἤγαγον διὰ τῆς νυκτός to mean that they *brought him by night*, in distinction from the day; in which case they could have occupied two nights on the road. It is suggested that the escort may have proceeded to Nicopolis the first night, which was twenty-two Roman miles from Jerusalem, and, remaining there the next day, have arrived at Antipatris the night following. Biscoe, Meyer,[1] Kuinoel, and others, adopt this opinion. In this case τῇ ἐπαύριον in v. 32 must denote *the morrow* after the arrival at Antipatris on the second night, instead of *the morrow* after leaving Jerusalem, as the text would more obviously suggest. If it be thought necessary, we may consider διὰ τῆς νυκτός as applying only to the greater part of the journey. It would be correct to speak of the journey, in general terms, as a journey by night, although it occupied two or three hours of the following day. This view, which Winer maintains (Realw. I. p. 65), allows us to assign twelve hours to the march, and the rate of travelling would then be a little more than three miles the hour.

V. 32. ἐάσαντες, κ. τ. λ. The remaining distance to Cæsarea was not more than twenty-five miles. They were now so far from the scene of danger that they could with safety reduce the escort. Whether they had orders to do this or acted on their own discretion, we are not told. They commenced their return to Jerusalem on *the morrow*, but after so hurried a march would travel leisurely, and may have occupied two days on the way.

V. 34. ὁ ἡγεμών appears in the common text, without sufficient reason — ἐπερωτήσας, κ. τ. λ., *having asked from what province he is.* He makes the inquiry, perhaps, because the letter stated that Paul was a Roman citizen.

V. 35. διακούσομαί σου, *I will hear thee fully.* Observe the compound. The expression exhibits a singular conformity to the processes of Roman law. The rule was, *Qui cum elogio* (see on

[1] J. A. G. Meyer in his Versuch einer Vertheidigung und Erläuterung der Geschichte Jesu und der Apostel aus Griechischen und Römischen Profanscribenten (p. 461).

v. 25) *mittuntur, ex integro audiendi sunt.* The governor of a province was not to give implicit credit to the document with which a prisoner was sent to him; he must institute an independent examination of the case for himself. See Böttger, Beiträge, u. s. w., II. p. 8. — ἐν τῷ πραιτωρίῳ τοῦ Ἡρώδου, *in the prætorium of Herod*, i. e. in the palace built by him at Cæsarea, and now occupied as the residence of the Roman procurators. Paul was confined in some apartment of this edifice, or within its precincts. See Win. Realw. II. p. 324.

CHAPTER XXIV.

Verses 1–9. *Tertullus accuses Paul before Felix.*

V. 1. As to *Ananias*, see on 23, 2. — μετὰ δὲ πέντε ἡμέρας, *Now after five days*, i. e. in popular usage, on the fifth since Paul's departure from Jerusalem (Kuin. Mey. De Wet.); not since his capture there, or since his arrival at Cæsarea. The escape from the Jewish conspiracy is nearest to the mind here after what has been related; and further, according to Roman usage, a case referred like this should be tried on the third day, or as soon after that as might be possible (comp. 25, 17). See Böttger, II. p. 9. The reckoning in v. 11 admits of this decision. — μετὰ τῶν πρεσβυτέρων, *with the elders*, i. e. the Sanhedrists, represented by some of their number. τινῶν is a gloss. — ῥήτορος Τερτύλλου. As the people in the provinces were not acquainted with the forms of Roman law, they employed advocates to plead for them before the public tribunals. *Tertullus* was one of this class of men, and may have been a Roman or a Greek. It is not certain, that "the proceedings before Felix were conducted in Latin. In ancient times the Romans had attempted to enforce the use of Latin in all law courts, but the experiment failed. Under the Emperors trials were permitted in Greek, even in Rome itself, as well in the senate as in the forum, and it is unlikely that greater strictness should have been observed in a distant province." Lewin, II. p. 684. — ἐνεφάνισαν, κ. τ. λ., *informed the governor against Paul*, lodged their complaint. "The beginning of any judicial action," says Geib, "consisted in the formal declaration on the part of the accuser, that he wished to prosecute a particular person on account of a certain crime." [1]

[1] Geschichte des Römischen Criminal-processes, p. 115.

V. 2. κληθέντος αὐτοῦ, *he having been called,* after information of the case had been given (ἐνεφάνισαν), but before the charges against him were produced. The Roman law secured that privilege to the accused; see 25, 16. Nothing could be more unstudied than this conformity to the judicial rule. — ἤρξατο κατηγορεῖν, *proceeded to accuse.* Tertullus insisted on three charges; viz. sedition (κινοῦντα στάσιν), heresy (πρωτοστάτην τῶν Ναζωραίων), and profanation of the temple (ὃς καὶ, κ. τ. λ.); see on v. 5. 6.

V. 3. In this verse the participial clause forms the object of ἀποδεχόμεθα; comp. εὐχαριστῶ τῷ θεῷ πάντων ὑμῶν μᾶλλον γλώσσαις λαλῶν in 1 Cor. 14, 18. W. § 46. 1. a. Translate, *That we enjoy much peace through thee, and* (the benefit of) *many* (sc. πολλῶν) *excellent deeds performed for this nation by thy prudence, we acknowledge, with all gratitude.* Most critics transfer the idea of πολλῆς to κατορθωμάτων (De Wet. Mey. Rob.), which term refers to the general measures of his administration. The speaker employs the first person plural, because he identifies himself with his clients. — πάντη τε καὶ πανταχοῦ some join with γινομένων: *both in every way and everywhere* (Rob.); others with ἀποδεχόμεθα, and render, *both always and everywhere;* not merely now and here (De Wet. Mey.). The first is the surer sense of πάντη. The best editors write this word without iota subscript. W. § 5. 4. e. — The language of Tertullus is that of gross flattery. History ascribes to Felix a very different character. Both Josephus and Tacitus represent him as one of the most corrupt and oppressive rulers ever sent by the Romans into Judea. He deserved some praise for the vigor with which he suppressed the bands of robbers by which the country had been infested. The compliment had that basis, but no more.

V. 4. ἵνα . . . . ἐγκόπτω, *But that I may not hinder,* weary, *thee too much,* I will be brief, i. e. in what he proposes to advance. ἐπὶ πλεῖον refers, not to the few words of his preamble (Mey.), as if that was beginning to be tedious, but to his subsequent plea. — ἀκοῦσαι ἡμῶν συντόμως, *to hear us briefly,* where the adverb qualifies the verb. It is unnecessary to supply λεξόντων after ἡμῶν.

V. 5. The sentence is irregular. We should have expected ἐκρατήσαμεν αὐτόν at the beginning of the apodosis; but instead of that the writer says ὃν καί, influenced apparently by ὃς καί in the clause which precedes. W. § 46. 2. — γάρ, *namely:* the case is as follows (comp. 1, 20). — λοιμόν, *pest,* like our use of the word. — κινοῦντα . . . . Ἰουδαίοις, *exciting disturbance unto all the Jews,* i. e. among them and to their detriment. The latter idea occasions the use of the dative. The charge is, that he set the Jews at variance with one another; not that he excited them to rebel against the Romans. — Ναζωραίων occurs here only as a term of reproach (Olsh.); see on 2, 22.

V. 6. ὃς . . . . βεβηλῶσαι, *who also attempted*, etc. See 21, 28. — The entire passage καὶ κατά . . . . ἐπὶ σέ (v. 6-8) is of doubtful authority. It is rejected by Griesbach, Bengel, Mill, Lachmann, Tischendorf, De Wette, and others. Manuscripts of the first class omit the words, and others contain them with different variations. "If they are genuine," says Meyer, "it is difficult to see why any one should have left them out; for κατὰ τὸν ἡμέτερον νόμον ἠθελήσαμεν κρίνειν would be no more offensive in the mouth of the advocate who speaks in the name of his client, than the preceding ἐκρατήσαμεν. The indirect complaint against Lysias in v. 7 was entirely natural to the relation of the Jews to this tribune, who had twice protected Paul against them." It is urged for the words that their insertion answers no apparent object, and that they may have been dropped accidentally (Wdsth.). — ἠθελήσαμεν, κ. τ. λ., *we wished to judge*, etc. We obtain a very different view of their design from 21, 31; 26, 21.

V. 7. In μετὰ πολλῆς βίας, *with much violence*. Tertullus misstates the fact. The Jews released Paul without any struggle, on the appearance of Lysias; see 21, 32. — ἐπὶ σέ, *before thee*.

V. 8. παρ' οὗ would refer to Paul, if we exclude the uncertain text which precedes; but more naturally to Lysias, if we retain it (comp. v. 22). — ἀνακρίνας may be used of any judicial examination. It is impossible to think here of a trial by torture, since both Paul and Lysias were exempt from it in virtue of their rank as Roman citizens. It was illegal at all events to have recourse to this measure. See Howson's note, II. p. 322.

V. 9. συνεπέθεντο, κ. τ. λ., *And the Jews also assailed him at the same time*, viz. by asserting that the charges were true. This is a better reading than συνέθεντο, *assented*, agreed, though we have that word in 23, 20.

VERSES 10-23. *Paul's Defence before Felix.*

V. 10. ἐκ πολλῶν ἐτῶν, *since many years*. As Felix became procurator probably in A. D. 52 (see on v. 24), he had been in office six or seven years, which was comparatively a long time, at this period when the provincial magistrates were changed so rapidly. Some of them exceeded that term of service, but a greater number of them fell short of it. Before his own appointment as procurator, he had also governed Samaria for some years, under Cumanus, his predecessor. See Hertz. Encycl. IV. p. 354. — ἔθνει depends on κρίτην as dat. comm., *judge for this nation,* since the relation existed ideally for their benefit. B. § 133. 2. h; W. § 31. 2. Paul avoids the usual λαός and says ἔθνος, because he is speaking to a foreigner; see, also, v. 17. — εὐθυμότερον, *more cheerfully* (T. R.); or εὐθύμως, *cheerfully* (Tsch.); the former more correct since the comparative as less obvious was liable to be displaced.

V. 11. δυναμένου σου γνῶναι, *since you are able to know,* i. e. by inquiry; or, ἐπιγνῶναι (Tsch.), *to ascertain.* Paul adds this as another reason why he was encouraged to reply. The subject lay within a narrow compass. Felix could easily ascertain how the prisoner had been employed during the time in which he was said to have committed the crimes laid to his charge. — The common text inserts ἢ before δεκαδύο, which the later editions omit. See on 4, 22. The best mode of reckoning the *twelve days* is the following: First, the day of the arrival at Jerusalem (21, 17); second, the interview with James (21, 18); third, the assumption of the vow (21, 26); fourth, fifth, sixth, and seventh, the vow continued, which was to have been kept seven days (being interrupted on the fifth); eighth, Paul before the Sanhedrim (22, 30; 23, 1–10); ninth, the plot of the Jews and the journey by night to Antipatris (23, 12. 31); tenth, eleventh, twelfth, and thirteenth, the days at Cæsarea (24, 1), on the last of which the trial was then taking place. The number of complete days, therefore, would be twelve; the day in progress at the time of speaking not being counted. The *five days* mentioned in v. 1 above agree with this computation, if, as suggested there, we reckon the day of leaving Jerusalem as the first of the five, and that of the arrival at Cæsarea as the last. So essentially Wetstein, Anger, Meyer, De Wette, and others. Some, as Kuinoel, Olshausen, would exclude the days spent at Cæsarea, and extend the time assigned to the continuation of the vow. But εἰσί μοι (note the tense) evidently represents the days as reaching up to the present time. According to Wieseler's hypothesis, that Paul was apprehended on the second day of the vow, the αἱ ἑπτὰ ἡμέραι in 21, 27 form no part of the series. He distributes the time as follows: two days on the journey from Cæsarea to Jerusalem (21, 15); third, interview with James; fourth (πεντηκοστή), seizure of Paul in the temple; fifth, the session of the Sanhedrim; sixth, the departure by night to Cæsarea; seventh, the arrival at Cæsarea; twelfth (five days after that), the journey of Ananias from Jerusalem (24, 1); and thirteenth, his arrival at Cæsarea, and the trial of Paul. — ἀφ' ἧς is abbreviated for ἀπὸ τῆς ἡμέρας ἧς. — προσκυνήσων, *in order to worship*, i. e. in the temple; which was an object entirely different from that imputed to him. For this use of the future participle, see B. § 144. 3.

V. 12. The grammatical analysis here requires attention. The first οὔτε extends to ὄχλοι, and ἤ, *or* (not *nor*), connects merely the participial clauses, not εὗρον expressed with that verb repeated. Before the second and third οὔτε we are to insert again εὗρον .... ὄχλου; so that both acts, the having disputed and the having excited a tumult, are denied with reference to the temple, the synagogues, and the city. — The διαλεγόμενον was not in itself censurable, but in this instance he could urge that he had not even had any religious discussion during the few days in question. — ἐν ταῖς συναγωγαῖς, *in the synagogues* at Jerusalem, where they were numerous; see on 6, 9. — κατὰ τὴν πόλιν, *throughout the city*, up and down the streets (Alf.); not excluding διαλεγόμενον, but refering especially to ἐπισύστασιν.

V. 14. Having replied to what was falsely alleged, he states now (δέ adversative) what was true in the case. — ὅτι κατὰ τὴν ὁδὸν, κ. τ. λ., *that according to* (those of) *the way* (9, 2; 19, 9, etc.) *which* (not *in which*) *they call a sect* (αἵρεσιν, with a shade of reproach) *so* (i. e. after their mode) *I worship*, etc. This appears to me more simple than to make οὕτω prospective: *so*, viz. *by believing all things*, etc. (Mey. De Wet.). — κατὰ τὸν νόμον, *throughout the law*, in all the books of Moses; see on 13, 15.

V. 15. ἐλπίδα .... θεόν, *having a hope in reference to God*, i. e. founded on him, since his word and his promise furnish the only basis of such a hope. — ἣν καὶ, κ. τ. λ., *which also these themselves entertain, that it is appointed there shall be* (see on 10, 28) *a resurrection of the dead*, etc. αὐτοὶ οὗτοι are the Jews present, viewed as representatives of the nation. Hence most of his accusers here were Pharisees, and the breach between them and the Sadducees (23, 7) had been speedily repaired. νεκρῶν in T. R. lacks the requisite support (Lchm. Tsch.). — δικαίων τε καὶ ἀδίκων, *not only of the just* (those accepted as such by faith), *but of the unjust*. The resurrection of the wicked in order to be punished is as clearly taught here, as that of the righteous to be rewarded. The apostle represents this hope as the prevalent Jewish faith. Comp. 26, 7. "The Sadducees," says Biscoe, (p. 68) "were so few in number, that they were not worthy of his notice by way of exception. Josephus expressly tells us, 'that they were a few men only of the chief of the nation' (Antt. 18. 1. 4); that they prevailed only with the rich to embrace their sentiments, and that the common people were all on the side of the Pharisees (Ib. 13. 10. 6)."

V. 16. ἐν τούτῳ, *therefore* (comp. John 16, 30), i. e. in anticipation of such a day. — καὶ αὐτός, *also I myself*, as well as others who exemplify the proper effect of this doctrine. It is impossible, the apostle would argue, that he should entertain such a persuasion, and yet be guilty of the crimes imputed to him. — ἀσκῶ, *I strive*, exert myself. — ἀπρόσκοπον, *blameless*, lit. not made to stumble, preserved from it, and hence unoffended. The term is passive here, as in Phil. 1, 10, but active in 1 Cor. 10, 32.

V. 17. The defence here (δέ metabatic) goes back to the specification in v. 6. — δι' ἐτῶν πλειόνων, *after several years*, i. e. of absence. It was now A. D. 58 or 59. He had made his last visit to Jerusalem in the year A. D. 54 or 55. — ἐλεημοσύνας ποιήσων, *in order to bring alms* which he had collected in the churches of Macedonia and Achaia, for the relief of the believers at Jerusalem; see Rom. 15, 25. 26; 1 Cor. 16, 1–4; 2 Cor. 8, 1–4. This allusion is very abrupt. It is the first and only intimation contained in the Acts, that Paul had been taking up contributions on so extensive a plan. The manner in which the Epistles supply this deficiency, as Paley has shown, furnishes an incontestable proof of the credibility of the New Testament writers. — προσφοράς depends loosely on ποιήσων: and while there I was making or would have made, *offerings;* which after the information in 21, 26 we naturally understand of those that he engaged to bring in behalf of the Nazarites. They are not *the oblations* which were made during the feast of Pentecost; since no connection would exist then between προσφοράς and the purification spoken of in the next verse.

V. 18. ἐν οἷς, *in which*, the business of the offerings. For this use of the pronoun, comp. 26, 12. — εὗρον . . . . ἐν τῷ ἱερῷ, *they*, sc. the Jews, *found me purified as a Nazarite in the temple*. ἡγνισμένον must have this sense here, since it points back so evidently to 21, 24. 26. — οὐ μετὰ ὄχλου, *not with a mob*, as Tertullus had given out (v. 5), but conducting himself altogether peaceably. — He now retorts this charge of a riot upon the true authors of it. τινὲς δὲ ἀπὸ τῆς 'Ασίας 'Ιουδαῖοι, *but certain Jews from Asia* — it is they who excited a tumult, not I. The verb could be omitted (a true picture of the speaker's earnestness) because it suggests itself so readily from θορύβου, and because the details of the affair have been related at such length (21, 27). The common text omits δέ and makes τινές the subject of εὗρον. This is incorrect, as δέ must be retained. Our English translation is founded on the omission of this particle.

V. 19. οὓς ἔδει, *whom it became to be present;* imperfect because they should have been there already (comp. καθῆκεν in 22, 22). The instigators of the riot were the persons to testify how it arose. — εἴ τι ἔχοιεν, *if they might have anything;* a possibility purely subjective, and hence optative.

V. 20. ἢ αὐτοὶ οὗτοι, *or* (since the proper witnesses are not here) *let these themselves* (see v. 1. 15) *say what crime they found.* With εἰ in the T. R. we must read *if they found any*, etc. (E. V.); but εἰ is unauthorized.

V. 21. ἢ περὶ μιᾶς ταύτης φωνῆς, *No other offence than* (that) *concerning this one expression.* The sentence is framed as if τί ἄλλο ἀδίκημα had preceded (Mey. De Wet.). The Sadducees might object to his avowal of a belief in the resurrection, but the rest of his countrymen would esteem that a merit and not a crime. — ἧς ἔκραξα, *which I cried;* an attracted genitive, instead of the accusative, which this verb would properly take as having a kindred sense. In Matt. 27, 50, and Mark 1, 26, φωνῇ after the same verb denotes the instrument of speech, not, as here, what was spoken. See W. § 24. 1.

V. 22. αὐτούς, *them*, viz. both parties like ὑμᾶς just below. — ἀκριβέστερον εἰδὼς τὰ περὶ τῆς ὁδοῦ, *knowing the things in regard to the way* (the Christian sect) *more accurately*, i. e. than to give a decision against Paul (comp. 25, 10), or than the complaint against him had taken for granted. "Since Felix," says Meyer, "had been already procurator more than six years, and Christianity had spread itself, not only in all parts of Judea, but in Cæsarea itself, it is natural that he should have had a more correct knowledge of this religion than the Sanhedrists on this occasion had sought to give him; hence he did not condemn the accused, but left the matter in suspense." Other explanations of the comparative are the following: *knowing the case more accurately*, i. e. as the result of the present trial (which would have been a reason for deciding it, instead of deferring it); *knowing it more accurately* than to postpone it, i. e. (a remark of Luke) Felix should have acquitted Paul at once (which brings a severe reflection on his conduct into too close connection with the account of his lenity in the next verse); and, finally, *knowing the case more exactly*, i. e. (joined with what follows) when I thus know it, after hearing the testimony of Lysias, judgment shall be given. This last sense is out of the question, because it disregards utterly the order of the words, as well as the proper meaning of διαγνώσομαι, *I will know fully*, not *will decide.*

V. 23. The τῷ before ἑκατοντάρχῃ, designates *the centurion* as the one who had charge of Paul, and perhaps other prisoners (see 27, 1; 28, 16); whether he belonged to Cæsarea or had come from Jerusalem. This officer is not necessarily the one who had conducted the troops from Antipatris (23, 32) in distinction from the one who returned, since τῷ admits of the other explanation, and since δύο τινάς in 23, 23 leaves the number indefinite. Hence as the article does not identify the centurion, the inference to that effect (Blunt,[1] p. 323 and Birks, p. 344) is not to be urged as a proof of the verity of the history. — τηρεῖσθαι αὐτόν, not middle, *to keep him* (E. V.), but *that he should be kept as a prisoner*, be guarded. — ἔχειν τε ἄνεσιν, *and should have respite* or *alleviation*, i. e. be treated with indulgence, and not subjected to a severe captivity. One of the favors which he received is mentioned in the next clause. — The grammatical subject changes before κωλύειν of which καί (note τέ between the other verbs) admonishes the reader. — ὑπηρετεῖν, *serve him*, minister to his wants. — ἢ προσέρχεσθαι is doubtful, and may be borrowed from 10, 28.

VERSES 24–27. *Paul testifies before Felix and Drusilla.*

V. 24. παραγενόμενος, *having come*, not to Cæsarea, after a temporary absence, but to the place of audience; comp. 5, 21; 25, 23. — σὺν Δρουσίλλῃ . . . . Ἰουδαίᾳ, *with Drusilla, his wife, being a Jewess*, which would imply that she still adhered to the Jewish religion. This Drusilla was a younger daughter of Agrippa the First, who was mentioned in 12, 1 sq., and a sister of Agrippa the Second, who is mentioned in 25, 13. We turn to Josephus (Antt. 20. 7. 1 sq.) and read the following account of her: "Agrippa gave his sister Drusilla in marriage to Azizus, king of the Emesenes, who had consented to be circumcised for the sake of the alliance. But this marriage of Drusilla with Azizus was dissolved in a short time after this manner. When *Felix was procurator for Judea*, he saw her, and, being captivated by her beauty, persuaded her to desert her husband, transgress the laws of her country, and marry himself." "Here," as Paley observes, "the public station of Felix, the name of his wife, and the circumstance of her religion, all appear in perfect conformity with the

[1] Undesigned Coincidences in the Writings of the Old and New Testaments by Rev. J. J. Blunt, London 1847.

sacred writer." The fate of this woman was singular. She had a son by Felix, and both the mother and the son were among those who lost their lives by the eruption of Mount Vesuvius, in A. D. 79. — Luke does not inform us why Felix summoned Paul to this conference. We may infer from the presence of Drusilla, that it was on her account. In all probability it was to afford her an opportunity to see and hear so noted a leader of the Christian sect.

V. 25. περὶ δικαιοσύνης, *concerning justice*, which the conduct of Felix had so outraged. Tacitus (Ann. 12. 54) draws this picture of him as a magistrate: "Relying upon the influence of his brother at court, the infamous Pallas, this man acted as if he had a license to commit every crime with impunity." — καὶ ἐγκρατείας, *and self-control*, especially continence, chastity. Here we have another and double proof of the apostle's courage. At the side of Felix was sitting a victim of his libertinism, an adultress, as Paul discoursed of immorality and a judgment to come. The woman's resentment was to be feared as well as that of the man. It was the implacable Herodias and not Herod, who demanded the head of John the Baptist. — ἔμφοβος γενόμενος, *having become alarmed.* — τὸ νῦν ἔχον, *as to what is now*, for the present (Kyp. De Wet. Mey.). The construction is that of an adverbial accusative. K. § 279. R. 10. — Place a comma or colon, not a period, at the end of the verse.

V. 26. ἅμα καὶ ἐλπίζων, *at the same time also* (that he gave this answer) *hoping.* The participle connects itself with ἀπεκρίθη (comp. 23, 25), and is not to be taken as a finite verb. — ὅτι χρήματα, κ. τ. λ., *that money will be given to him by Paul*, i. e. as an inducement to release him. — ὅπως λύσῃ αὐτόν (T. R.), *that he might loose him* (E. V.), suggests a correct idea, but is not genuine. Felix had conceived the hope that his prisoner would pay liberally for his freedom. He may have supposed him to have ample resources at his command. He knew that his friends were numerous, and had been informed (see v. 17) that they were not too poor or too selfish to assist one another.

V. 27. διετίας δὲ πληρωθείσης, *Two years now having been completed*, i. e. since Paul's imprisonment at Cæsarea. — ἔλαβε διάδοχον ὁ Φῆλιξ Πόρκιον Φῆστον, *Felix received Porcius Festus as successor.* Luke wrote first, or we might suspect him of having copied Josephus who says, Πορκίου δὲ Φήστου διαδόχου Φήλικι πεμφθέντος (Antt. 20. 8. 9). As to the year in which this change in the procuratorship took place, see Introd. § 6. 4. — θέλων . . . . τοῖς Ἰουδαίοις, *and wishing to lay up favor for himself with the Jews*, to make himself popular among them; which was the more important at this time, as they had a right to follow him to Rome, and complain of his administration if they were dissatisfied with it. His policy was unsuccessful; see Introd. § 6. 4. An act like this, on leaving such an office, was not uncommon. Thus Albinus, another corrupt procurator of Judea, having heard that Gessius Florus had been appointed to succeed him, liberated most of the state prisoners at Jerusalem, in order to conciliate the Jews. — κατέλιπε, κ. τ. λ., *left Paul behind chained*, still a prisoner, instead of setting him at liberty. I correct my former note here in view of Mr. Howson's suggestion. As we are not to infer from ἄνεσιν in 24, 23 that Paul was freed from his chains, δεδέμενον does not mean that he was rebound after a temporary release. Wieseler (p. 380) has shown that the *custodia libera* was granted only to persons of rank, and hence Paul could not have enjoyed that favor, as is proved, also, by his subjection to the surveillance of the centurion. Meyer has changed the note in his last edition to agree with this view. According to De Wette, Felix loaded Paul again with the chains which he had removed. Lange (II. p. 326), speaks of the *custodia libera* as exchanged now for the *custodia militaris*.

CHAPTER XXV.

VERSES 1–5. *Festus refuses to bring Paul to Jerusalem.*

V. 1. οὖν, *therefore*, since he was the successor of Felix. — "The new procurator," says Mr. Lewin (II. p. 699), "had a straightforward honesty about him, which forms a strong contrast to the mean rascality of his predecessor. He certainly did not do all the justice that he might have done; but allowing somewhat for the natural desire to ingratiate himself with the people of his government, his conduct, on the whole, was exemplary, and his firmness in resisting the unjust demands of the Jews cannot fail to elicit our admiration." — μετὰ τρεῖς ἡμέρας, *after three days*, i. e. on the third, which allows him one day for rest between his arrival at Cæsarea and his departure for Jerusalem.

V. 2. If ὁ ἀρχιερεύς (T. R.) be correct, this *high-priest* must have been Ismael, son of Phabi, who succeeded Ananias (Jos. Antt. 20. 8. 8). Two years have elapsed since the trial before Felix (24, 1 sq.), at which Ananias was so active. Instead of the singular, some read οἱ ἀρχιερεῖς (Lchm. Tsch.), which was introduced probably to agree with v. 15 (De Wet. Alf.).— οἱ πρῶτοι, *the first men*, are the *chief-priests and the elders* in v. 15, except that the ἀρχιερεύς mentioned separately here would be one of the ἀρχιερεῖς there. — παρεκάλουν, as imperfect, shows their importunity.

V. 3. αἰτούμενοι χάριν, κ. τ. λ., *asking for themselves a favor against him*, viz. *that he would send for him*, etc. — ἐνέδραν ποιοῦντες, *making an ambush*, arranging for it; see 23, 21. They anticipated no obstacle to their plan, and may have already hired their assassins and pointed out to them the cave or rock whence they were to rush forth upon their victim. Compare the note on v. 16.

V. 4. ἀπεκρίθη, *answered*, viz. to their second request (see note on v. 16). — τηρεῖσθαι, κ. τ. λ., *that Paul was kept as a prisoner at* (lit. *unto*) *Cæsarea*, as the Jews were aware; and hence as the governor was about to proceed thither, it would be more convenient to have the trial at that place. The English version, viz. *that Paul should be kept*, conveys the idea of a too peremptory refusal. So decided a tone would have given needless offence. τηρεῖσθαι announces a fact rather than a purpose. — εἰς Καισάρειαν (more correct than ἐν with the dative) opposes tacitly his being kept back *unto Cæsarea* to his removal thence; not unlike εἰς Ἀσίαν in 19, 22.

V. 5. οἱ δυνατοὶ ἐν ὑμῖν, *the powerful among you*, your chief men; not those who are able, who may find it easy or possible to perform the journey (Calv. Grot. E. V.). Their attendance at the trial was imperative, and the magistrate would not speak as if they were to consult their convenience merely in such a matter. Kuinoel has shown that Ἰουδαίων οἱ δυνατοί was common among the Jews as a designation of their rulers; see Jos. Bell. Jud. 1. 12. 4; 2. 14. 8 and elsewhere. Compare, also, 1 Cor. 1, 26 and Rev. 6, 15. Howson, after Meyer, renders *those who are competent*, are authorized to act as prosecutors, but without offering any proof of that absolute use of the term. — φησί should stand before ἐν ὑμῖν, not after it (T. R.).

VERSES 6–12. *Paul appeals from Festus to Cæsar.*

V. 6. διατρίψας, κ. τ. λ., *Having now spent not more than eight or ten days*, i. e. having returned speedily, as he had intimated (ἐν τάχει in v. 4). Instead of οὐ πλείους ὀκτὼ ἢ δέκα (Grsb. Tsch. Mey.) as above, the received text (and so E. V.) reads πλείους ἢ δέκα, *more than ten days*, as if Festus (δέ, adversative, *but*) had not fulfilled his word (v. 4). — τῇ ἐπαύριον = τῇ ἑξῆς in v. 17.

V. 7. περιέστησαν, *stood around him*, not the tribunal (Kuin.); comp. περὶ οὗ σταθέντες in v. 18. — Most manuscripts omit κατὰ τοῦ Παύλου after φέροντες. Tischendorf writes καταφέροντες; but others defend the simple participle. — The *heavy charges* (βαρέα αἰτιώματα) as the defence of the apostle shows (v. 8), were heresy, impiety, and treason; comp. 24, 5. 6.

V. 9. ἐκεῖ . . . . ἐπ' ἐμοῦ, *there to be judged* (viz. by the Sanhedrim) *before me*, i. e. in his presence, while he should preside (Mey. De Wet. Wiesl.), and perhaps confirm or reject the decision. There are two views as to the import of this proposal. One is, that Festus intended merely to transfer the trial from Cæsarea to Jerusalem; and the other is, that he wished to change the jurisdiction in the case, to surrender Paul to the Jews, and allow them to decide whether he was innocent or guilty. The explanation last stated agrees best with the intimations of the context. The reply of the apostle (ἐπὶ τοῦ βήματος . . . . κρίνεσθαι in v. 10), and the fact that he proceeds at once to place himself beyond the power of Festus, would appear to show that he regarded the question (θέλεις, κ. τ. λ.) as tantamount to being deprived of his rights as a Roman citizen.

V. 10. ἐπὶ τοῦ βήματος, κ. τ. λ., *before the tribunal of Cæsar am I standing*, am under Roman jurisdiction since Festus was the representative of the emperor. The answer of Festus, *unto Cæsar hast thou appealed, unto Cæsar shalt thou go* (v. 11), is founded on the apostle's subsequent Καίσαρα ἐπικαλοῦμαι, and is not proof (Wdsth.) that Paul viewed himself as "already standing in his own resolve before *Cæsar's* judgment-seat." — οὗ . . . . κρίνεσθαι, *where I ought to be judged* (present), to be having my trial; as matter of right (δεῖ), not because it is God's will (comp. v. 24 and 24, 19). — ὡς καὶ σὺ κάλλιον ἐπιγινώσκεις, *as also thou perceivest better*, i. e. than to make such a proposal; comp. 24, 22. W. § 35. 4. Such a comparative is very convenient as suggesting something which it might be less courteous to express (Wdsth). After hearing the charges against Paul, and his reply to them, Festus knew that the prisoner was entitled to be set free, instead of giving him up to a tribunal where his accusers were to be his judges. The temporizing Roman confesses in v. 18 that Paul was right in imputing to him such a violation of his convictions.

V. 11. εἰ οὖν ἀδικῶ, *if therefore I am unjust*, guilty, i. e. in consequence of past wrong-doing. The verb expresses here the result of an act, instead of the act itself. See W. § 40. 2. c. γάρ in the common text (*for* in E. V.) is incorrect. The clause is illative with reference to the assumption (v. 9) that the Jews might find him guilty. Some combine the present and past in ἀδικῶ, and render *if I have done and am doing wrong.* See K. § 255. R. 1.— καὶ ἄξιον . . . . τι defines the degree of guilt. If it was such that he deserved to die, he was willing to die. — εἰ οὐδέν ἐστιν ὧν = εἰ οὐδέν ἐστι τούτων ἅ.

V. 12. συλλαλήσας μετὰ τοῦ συμβουλίου, *having spoken with the council,* i. e. the assessors or judges (πάρεδροι, *consiliarii*) who assisted him at the trial. It was customary for the proconsul, or his substitute, to choose a number of men whose office it was to aid him in the administration of justice. The proconsul himself presided, but was bound to consult his assessors, and to decide in accordance with the views of the majority. See Geib's Geschichte, p. 243 sq. The subject of consultation in this instance, doubtless, was whether the appeal should be allowed or refused. Writers on Roman law inform us that the provincial magistrates had a certain discretionary power in this respect. An appeal to the emperor was not granted in every case. It was necessary to consider the nature of the accusation, and also the amount of evidence which supported it. Some offences were held to be so enormous as to exclude the exercise of this right; and when the crime was not of this character, the evidence of guilt might be so palpable as to demand an immediate and final decision. — Καίσαρα ἐπικέκλησαι is declarative (not a question as in E. V.) and repeats Paul's last word before the consultation, for the purpose of attaching to it the verdict. — ἐπὶ Καίσαρα πορεύσῃ, *unto Cæsar shalt thou go,* be sent, announces the ready conclusion in regard to the present appeal. I perceive no severity in this answer (Bng.), beyond that of the abrupt official form. The prisoner is told that the government would carry out his appeal, and take measures to convey him to Rome; see on 27, 1.

VERSES 13–22. *Festus confers with Agrippa concerning Paul.*

V. 13. ἡμερῶν, κ. τ. λ., *certain days being past* since the appeal. —Ἀγρίππας ὁ βασιλεύς. This *Agrippa* was a son of the Agrippa whose tragical end has been related in 12, 20–24. At his father's death, as he was considered too young to succeed him on the throne, Judea was committed again to the government of procurators. He passed his early life at Rome. In A. D. 50, on the death of Herod, his uncle, he received the sovereignty of Chalcis, and in A. D. 53 the dominions of Philip, and Lysanias (Luke 3, 1), at which time he assumed the title of king. In the year A. D. 55 Nero added to his possessions a part of Galilea and Perea. He died, after a reign of nearly fifty years, in A. D. 100. It will be observed that, although Luke in this passage styles Agrippa a king, he does not style him king of Judea; whereas, in speaking of his father (12, 1 sq.), he not only applies to him this title, but mentions an instance of his exercise of the regal power at Jerusalem. The facts stated above show how perfectly this distinction conforms to the circumstances of the case. — Βερνίκη. *Bernice* was the eldest daughter of Agrippa the First, and a sister of Drusilla (24, 24). She was noted for her beauty and her profligacy. Luke's accuracy in introducing her at this stage of the history is worthy of remark. After a brief marriage with her first husband, she became the wife of Herod, her uncle, king of Chalcis, and on his death remained for a time with Agrippa her brother. She was suspected of living with him in a criminal manner. Her third marriage with Polemon, king of Cilicia, she soon dissolved, and returned to her brother, not long before the death of the Emperor Claudius. She could have been with Agrippa, therefore, in the time of Festus, as Luke represents in our narrative. Her subsequent connection with Vespasian and Titus made her name familiar to the Roman writers. Several of them, as Tacitus, Suetonius, and Juvenal, either mention her expressly or allude to her. — ἀσπασόμενοι τὸν Φῆστον, *in order to salute Festus.* It was their visit of congratulation. Agrippa, being a vassal of the Romans, came to pay his respects to this new representative of the power on which he was dependent.

V. 15. ἐνεφάνισαν, *informed*, i. e. judicially, brought accusation; comp. v. 2; 24, 1. — αἰτούμενοι . . . . δίκην, *asking for themselves justice against him.* The idea of condemnation lies in κατ' αὐτοῦ, not in δίκην. Tischendorf decides against καταδίκην.

V. 16. In v. 3 the request of the Jews was that Paul might be brought to Jerusalem; and in that case the accusers and the accused would have met face to face. Hence the reply of Festus here, in order to warrant his objection, must relate to a different proposal, viz. that he would condemn Paul at once (see v. 24) and in his absence. On his declaring that as a Roman magistrate he could not be guilty of such injustice, the Jews, as it would seem, changed their tactics. If it was so that the parties must confront each other, they asked then that he would summon the prisoner to Jerusalem and have him tried there. But this second request was a mere pretence. They knew the weakness of their cause too well to await the result of a trial, and wanted only to secure an opportunity to waylay and kill the apostle on the road. The two proposals may have been made at different times; so that in the interval they could have begun the ambuscade (as intimated in v. 3), believing that though baffled in their first attempt they could not fail in the second. — ὅτι .... Ῥωμαίοις, *that it is not a custom for Romans*, if it was for Jews. The article (E. V.) obscures the opposition. — ἄνθρωπον (as generic) declares the rule to be universal. The claim to this impartiality was a *human* right in the eye of the Roman law. — εἰς ἀπώλειαν after ἄνθρωπον (T. R. and hence E. V.) is unapproved.

V. 18. περὶ οὗ, *around whom*, belongs to σταθέντες (comp. v. 7), not to ἐπέφερον, *against whom* (E. V.). The antecedent of οὗ is ἄνδρα, not the remoter βήματος. — αἰτίαν, sc. τούτων. — ὧν (= ἅ by attraction) ὑπενόουν, *which I was suspecting*, i. e. some capital offence, as treason, murder, or the like.

V. 19. περὶ τῆς ἰδίας δεισιδαιμονίας, *concerning their own religion;* not *superstition*. Compare the note on δεισιδαιμονεστέρους in 17, 22. Agrippa was known to be a zealous Jew, and Festus would not have been so uncourteous as to describe his faith by an offensive term. ἰδίας refers not to the subordinate οὗ, *his own*, viz. Paul's, but to κατήγοροι, the leading subject. — περί τινος Ἰησοῦ, κ. τ. λ., *concerning a certain Jesus*, etc. As to Luke's candor in recording this contemptuous remark, see note on 18, 15.

V. 20. ἀπορούμενος, *perplexed*, uncertain, as Festus may have said with truth, but could not honestly assign as the motive for his proposal; see v. 9 above. — εἰς τὴν περὶ τούτου ζήτησιν, *in regard to the dispute concerning this one*, viz. Jesus (v. 19); not *this matter;* as if it were neuter. But the best reading is περὶ τούτων, *concerning these things*, viz. in relation to their religion and the resurrection of Jesus.

V. 21. τοῦ δὲ Παύλου, κ. τ. λ., *But Paul havivg appealed* (and so demanded) *that he should be kept* in Roman custody, instead of being tried at Jerusalem. — εἰς τὴν τοῦ Σεβαστοῦ διάγνωσιν, *with a view to the examination of Augustus*. The Senate conferred this title on Octavius in the first instance; but it was given also to his successors. — ἐκέλευσα .... αὐτόν, *I commanded that he should still be kept* (infinitive present) at Cæsarea. In τηρηθῆναι just before, the time is entirely subordinate to the act. — ἕως οὗ πέμψω αὐτόν, *until I shall send him* (T. R.); but the surer word is ἀναπέμψω, *shall send up* (Lchm. Tsch. Mey.); comp. Luke 23, 7. 11. Festus would intimate that he was waiting only until a vessel should sail for Italy.

V. 22. ἐβουλόμην καὶ οὐτός, *I myself also could wish*, i. e. were it possible. The Greeks employed the imperfect indicative to express a present wish which the speaker regarded, or out of courtesy affected to regard, as one that could not be realized. Compare Rom. 9, 3; Gal. 4, 20. W. § 41. 2; S. § 138. 3; K. § 259. R. 6. It is less correct to understand the wish as one long entertained.

VERSES 23–27. *Paul is brought before Agrippa.*

V. 23. μετὰ πολλῆς φαντασίας, *with much pomp*, display, which consisted partly in their personal decorations (comp. 12, 21), and partly in the retinue which attended them. — εἰς τὸ ἀκροατήριον, *unto the place of audience*, which the article represents as the customary one (Olsh.), or as the one to which they repaired on this occasion (Mey.). — σὺν τοῖς χιλιάρχοις, *with the chiliarchs*, the commanders of the cohorts stationed at Cæsarea, which were five in number (Jos. Bell. Jud. 3. 4. 2). Compare the note on 27, 1.

V. 24. The procurator could say πᾶν τὸ πλῆθος τῶν Ἰουδαίων, *all the multitude of the Jews*, because he had reason to know that the Jewish rulers (v. 2. 15) who had demanded the death of Paul represented the popular feeling. Meyer suggests that a crowd may have gone with them to the procurator and enforced their application by clamoring for the same object. — ἐνέτυχόν μοι, *interceded* (in its bad sense here) *with me*, against him. A genitive or dative may follow this verb. — Some manuscripts read ζῆν αὐτόν, and others αὐτὸν ζῆν; and so, in the next verse, some read θανάτου αὐτόν, and others αὐτὸν θανάτου. Such transpositions, which have no effect on the sense, show how unimportant are many of the various readings of the sacred text. — ἐπιβοῶντες, *crying against* him, etc.; see on v. 15. — μηκέτι. A qualification like this in a negative sentence requires a compound, containing the μή or οὐκ which precedes. K. § 318. 6; B. § 148. 6. — ἔκρινα, *I decided*, viz. at the time of the trial when he appealed. The perfect (E. V.) is less accurate than the aorist.

V. 26. περὶ οὗ, κ. τ. λ., *Concerning whom I have nothing sure*, definite, *to write to the sovereign.* In such cases of appeal it was necessary to transmit to the emperor a written account of the offence charged as having been committed, and also of all the judicial proceedings that may have taken place in relation to it. Documents of this description were called *apostoli*, or *literæ dimissoriæ.* — κυρίῳ is the Greek for *dominus.* The writer's accuracy should be remarked here. It would have been a mistake to have applied this term to the emperor a few years earlier than this. Neither Augustus nor Tiberius would allow himself to be called *dominus*, because it implied the relation of master and slave. The appellation had now come into use as one of the imperial titles. — σχῶ τι γράψω, *may have what* (future) *I shall write;* not τι γράψαι (T. R.), *what to write* (E. V.). Some repeat ἀσφαλές after τι (Mey.), which is not necessary. Meyer leaves out the ellipsis in his new edition.

V. 27. ἄλογον γάρ μοι δοκεῖ, *For it appears to me absurd.* It was illegal, too; but Festus thinks of the act as being a violation, not so much of the law, as of the propriety which dictated the law. — πέμποντα, sc. τινὰ, κ. τ. λ., *that any one* (De Wet.) *sending a prisoner should not also signify the charges* (not *crimes*) *against him.* Some would make πέμποντα the subject of σημᾶναι, without any ellipsis. K. § 238, R. 2. e. Some supply ἐμέ as the subject. It is more forcible in such a case to state the general rule or principle which controls the particular instance. — Josephus (Bell. Jud. 2. 14. 1) describes Festus as a reasonable man, who was not destitute of a regard for justice and the laws, and who approved himself to such of the Jews as were willing to submit to any foreign rule. What Luke relates of him shows him to be worthy of this encomium.

CHAPTER XXVI.

VERSES 1–23. *Paul's Speech before Agrippa.*

V. 1. This speech of the apostle is similar to that which he delivered on the stairs of the castle (22, 1 sq.). The main topic is the same in each, viz. the wonderful circumstances of his conversion; but in this instance he recounts them, not so much for the purpose of asserting his personal innocence, as of vindicating the divine origin of his commission, and the truth of the message proclaimed by him. So far from admitting that he had been unfaithful to Judaism, he claims that his Christian faith realized the true idea of the religion taught in the Old Testament. On the former occasion, "he addressed the infuriated populace, and made his defence against the charges with which he was hotly pressed, of profaning the temple and apostatizing from the Mosaic law. He now passes by these accusations, and, addressing himself to a more intelligent and dispassionate hearer, he takes the highest ground, and holds himself up as the apostle and messenger of God. With this view, therefore, he paints in more striking colors the awful scene of his conversion, and repeats more minutely that heavenly call which was impossible for him to disobey (v. 19), and in obeying which, though he incurred the displeasure of his countrymen (v. 21), he continued to receive the divine support (v. 22)." Humphry, p. 192. — ἐπιτρέπεταιι . . . . λέγειν. It is Agrippa who gives the permission to speak, because as he was the guest on this occasion and a king, he presides by right of courtesy; comp. 21, 40. — ἐκτείνας τὴν χεῖρα, *having stretched forth the hand*, is the same as κατασείσας τῇ κειρί in 13, 16 (comp. 21, 40), and κατασείσας τὴν χεῖρα in 19, 33. The gesture was the more courteous, because the attention asked for was certain from the known curiosity of the hearers. On the arm which Paul raised hung one of the chains, to which he alludes in v. 29.

V. 2. ὑπὸ Ἰουδαίων, *by Jews*, without the article (comp. 22, 30) because he would represent the accusation as purely *Jewish* in its character. The best manuscripts omit τῶν before the proper name. — βασιλεῦ. For Agrippa's claim to the title, see on 25, 13. — Some copies place ἐπὶ σοῦ after μακάριον, others after ἀπολογεῖσθαι. The first is the best position, because it secures a stronger emphasis to the pronoun (Grsb. Tsch.). — The object of ἥγημαι is the same as the subject, but the latter, which is more prominent, controls the case of μέλλων. This verb is perfect, *have thought*; not *think* (E. V.). Paul distinguishes the tenses in Phil. 3, 7. 8.

V. 3. μάλιστα, *especially*, rendered *namely* in the older versions (Tynd. Cran. Gen.) states why Paul was so eminently fortunate; not how much Agrippa knew. — γνώστην ὄντα σε, *since thou art expert*, lit. *a knower*. The accusative is anacoluthic, instead of the genitive (Mey. Win. Rob.). W. § 32. 7. Some explain it as an instance of the accusative absolute; but we have no clear example of that construction in the New Testament. ὀφθαλμούς in Eph. 1, 18, has been cited as an example of it, but stands really in apposition with πνεῦμα, or depends on δῴη. Beza's unauthorized εἰδώς (whence "knowing" in E. V.) obviates the irregularity. The Rabbinic writers [1] speak of Agrippa as having excelled in a knowledge of the law. As the tradition which they follow could not have flowed from this passage, it confirms the representation here by an unexpected agreement. — κατὰ Ἰουδαί-

[1] Sepp gives the testimonies in his Das Leben Christi, Vol. IV. p. 138.

ους, *among Jews*, of whom we are led to think as existing in different places. W. § 53. d. — διό, *therefore*. In the presence of such a judge, he proposes to speak at length, and requests a patient hearing.

V. 4. οὖν, *therefore*, i. e. encouraged thus he will proceed. The apostle enters here on his defence — ἐκ νεότητος, *from youth*. See on 22, 3. — ἀπ' ἀρχῆς, *from the beginning*, refers to the same period of his life, but marks it more strongly as an early period. It will be observed that, while the apostle repeats this idea in the successive clauses, he brings forward in each case a new circumstance in connection with it. He states, first, *how long* the Jews had known him; secondly, *where* they had known him so long (ἐν τῷ ἔθνει μου ἐν Ἱεροσολύμοις); and, thirdly, *what* (ὅτι κατὰ τὴν ἀκριβεστάτην αἵρεσιν, κ. τ. λ.) they had known of him so long and in that place.

V. 5. προγινώσκοντές με, *knowing me before* (i. e. the present time). — ἐὰν θέλωσι μαρτυρεῖν, *if they would be willing to testify*, as he had not the confidence in their honesty to expect. — ὅτι κατὰ τὴν ἀκριβεστάτην αἵρεσιν, *that according to the strictest sect* in regard both to doctrine and manner of life. See 22, 3. Josephus describes this peculiarity of the Pharisees in similar language: εὐσεβέστερον εἶναι τῶν ἄλλων καὶ τοὺς νόμους ἀκριβέστερον ἀφηγεῖσθαι (Bell. Jud. 1. 5. 2). ὅτι reaches back to ἴσασι.

V. 6. καὶ νῦν, *and now*, compares his present with his former position. If his rigor as a Pharisee had been a merit in the eyes of the Jews, his hope as a Christian was merely that of the true Israel, and should as little be imputed to him as a crime. — τῆς πρὸς τοὺς πατέρας ἡμῶν ἐπαγγελίας γενομένης, *of the promise* (i. e. of a Messiah) *made unto our fathers* (Kuin. Olsh. De Wet. Mey.). The same expression occurs in Paul's discourse at Antioch (13, 32), where it is said that God fulfilled *the promise*, or showed it to be fulfilled, by raising up Jesus from the dead. See the note on that passage. Compare 28, 20. — εἰς ἥν, *unto which*, viz. the promise, its accomplishment. This is the natural antecedent and not the remoter ἐλπίδι. — δωδεκάφυλον (= ταῖς δώδεκα φυλαῖς in James 1, 1) exists only here, but is formed after the analogy of other compounds from δώδεκα. The Jewish nation consisted of those who were descended from the twelve tribes; which fact justifies the expression historically, though the twelve tribes had now lost their separate existence. — ἐν ἐκτενείᾳ, *with earnestness*. See on ἐκτενής in 12, 5. The noun is a later Grecism. Lob. Phryn. p. 311. Such forms help us to fix the age of the New Testament writings. — νύκτα καὶ ἡμέραν λατρεῦον, *worshipping night and day*. This was a phrase which denoted habitual worship, especially as connected with fasting and prayer. See Luke 1, 75; 2, 37; 18, 1; 1 Thess. 5, 17; 1 Tim. 5, 5.

V. 7. περὶ ἧς ἐλπίδος ἐγκαλοῦμαι, *concerning which hope I am accused.* The apostle means to say, that he was accused of maintaining that this hope of a Messiah had been accomplished in Jesus, and had been accomplished in him because God raised him from the dead. The presence of the latter idea in the mind of the apostle leads to the interrogation in the next verse.—'Αγρίππα after βασιλεῦ has decisive evidence against it — ὑπὸ Ἰουδαίων, *by Jews,* is reserved to the end of the sentence, in order to state more strongly the inconsistency of such an accusation from such a source. Here, too, the article (E. V.) weakens the sense, and is incorrect.

V. 8. τί is printed in some editions as a separate question: *What? Is it judged incredible?* Other editions connect τί with the verb: *Why is it judged incredible?* Griesbach, Kuinoel, De Wette, Howson, and others, prefer the first mode; Knapp, Hahn, Meyer, Tischendorf, and others, prefer the second mode. The latter appears to me more agreeable to the calm energy of the apostle's manner. "It is decisive against the other view," says Meyer in his last edition, "that τί *alone* was not so used; the expression would be τί γάρ, τί οὖν, or τί δέ." The examples of τί as interrogative in Rom. 3, 3. 9; 6, 15 and Phil. 1, 18 agree with this criticism. — ὑμῖν extends the inquiry to all who were present. The speaker uses the singular number when he addresses Agrippa personally; see v. 2. 3. 27. — εἰ ὁ θεὸς, κ. τ. λ., *if God raises the dead;* where εἰ is not for ὅτι, but presents the assertion as one that the sceptic might controvert. — ἐγείρει is present because it expresses a characteristic act. The resurrection of Jesus was past, but illustrated a permanent attribute or power on the part of God.

V. 9. This verse is illative, with reference to the preceding question. ἐγὼ μὲν οὖν, *I indeed, therefore,* i. e. in consequence of a spirit of incredulity, like that of others. — ἔδοξα ἐμαυτῷ, *I seemed to myself,* thought. The pronoun opposes his own to another and higher judgment. This same act in which Paul gloried at the time, appeared to him as the crime of his life after he became a Christian. In 1 Cor. 15, 9 he declares that he "was the least of the apostles, that he was not meet to be called an apostle, because he persecuted the church of God." — πρὸς τὸ ὄνομα Ἰησοῦ, *against the name of Jesus;* comp. πρός in Luke 23, 12. — πολλὰ ἐναντία, *many things hostile.*

V. 10. ὃ refers to the collective idea in πολλὰ ἐναντία. — καὶ connects ἐποίησα with ἔδοξα. — καὶ πολλοὺς, κ. τ. λ., adds the facts in illustration of what was stated in general terms. — τῶν ἁγίων, *the saints*, is no doubt a chosen word here. It does not occur in Luke's account of the apostle's conversion (9, 1 sq.). Paul himself avoids it in his speech to the Jews (22, 4 sq.) who were so sensitive in regard to any claim of merit in behalf of the Christians. "But here before Agrippa, where there was no such need of caution, the apostle indulges his own feelings, by giving them a title of honor which aggravates his own guilt." Birks, p. 327. — ἐγώ, emphatic. The imprisoning was the speaker's act. —The common text omits ἐν before φυλακαῖς, *I shut up unto prisons*, which would be an instance of the local dative sometimes found after verbs compounded with κατά. See Bernh. Synt. p. 243. But Griesbach, Tischendorf, and others, allege good authority for reading ἐν φυλακαῖς, which would be the ordinary construction; comp. Luke 3, 20. — παρὰ τῶν ἀρχιερέων. See the note on 9, 2. — ἀναιρουμένων .... ψῆφον, *and as they* (which refers to ἁγίων as a class, not to all those imprisoned) *were put to death, I brought or cast my vote against them*, i. e. encouraged, approved the act (Bng. Kuin. De Wet. Mey.); comp. συνευδοκῶν in 22, 20. Some insist on the literal sense of the phrase, and infer from it that Paul was a member of the Sanhedrim, and voted with the other judges to put the Christians to death. But the Jews required, as a general rule, that those who held this office should be men of years; and Paul at the time of Stephen's martyrdom, could hardly have attained the proper age. It is said, too, on the authority of the later Jewish writers, that one of the necessary qualifications for being chosen into the Sanhedrim was that a man should be the father of a family, because he who is a parent may be expected to be merciful; a relation which, from the absence of any allusion to it in the apostle's writings, we have every reason to believe that he never sustained. The expression itself affords but slight proof that Paul was a voter in the Sanhedrim. ψῆφος, a stone used as a ballot, like our "suffrage," signified also opinion, assent, and accompanied various verbs, as τιθέναι and καταφέρειν, as meaning to think, judge, sanction, with a figurative allusion only to the act of voting. Plato uses the term often in that sense. See R. and P. Lex., p. 2576. — αὐτῶν agrees with the intimation of other passages (8, 3; 9, 1; 22, 4), that Stephen was not the only victim whose blood was shed at this time.

V. 11. καὶ κατὰ πάσας, κ. τ. λ., *and punishing them often throughout all the synagogues* in the different places where he pursued his work of persecution. See 22, 19. "The chief rulers of the synagogues," says Biscoe (p. 81), "being also the judges of the people in many cases, especially those which regarded religion (comp. on 9, 2), chose to give sentence against offenders, and see their sentence executed in the synagogue. Persons were always scourged in the presence of the judges (Vitr. de Synag. Vett. p. 177). For punishment being designed 'in terrorem,' what more likely to strike the mind with awe, and deter men from falling into the like errors, than to have it executed in their religious assemblies, and in the face of the congregation? Our Lord foretold that his disciples should be scourged in the synagogues (Matt. 10, 17; 23, 34), and we learn here that Paul was an instrument in fulfilling this prediction, having beaten them that believed in every synagogue." — ἠνάγκαζον βλασφημεῖν, *I was constraining them* (i. e. urged them by threats and torture) *to blaspheme*, viz. Jesus, or the gospel; comp. 13, 45; James 2, 7. The imperfect states the object, not the result of the act. That, among the many who suffered this violence, every one preserved his fidelity, it would be unreasonable to affirm. We learn from Pliny's letter to Trajan (Lib. X. 97), that heathen persecutors applied the same test which Saul adopted, for the purpose of ascertaining who were truly Christians. "Propositus est libellus sine auctore, multorum nomina continens; qui negarent se esse Christianos aut fuisse, quum præeunte me deos appellarent et imagini tuæ (quam propter hoc jusseram cum simulacris numinum adferri) thure ac vino supplicarent, præterea maledicerent Christo; *quorum nihil cogi posse dicuntur qui sunt revera Christiani.*" — ἕως καὶ εἰς τὰς ἔξω πόλεις, *as far as even unto foreign cities*, as those would be called which were out of Judea. Among these Luke and Paul single out Damascus, because a train of such events followed the apostle's expedition to that city.

V. 12. ἐν οἷς καί, *in which also*, while intent on this object; comp. ἐν οἷς in 24, 18. καί, so common in Luke after the relative, some of the best copies omit here.— ἐξουσίας and ἐπιτροπῆς strengthen each other; he had ample power to execute his commission.

V. 13. ἡμέρας μέσης, *at midday*. "μέση ἡμέρα, pro meridie communis dialecti est, at μέσον ἡμέρας, aut μεσημβρία (22, 6) elegantiora." See Lob. ad Phryn. p. 55. — κατὰ τὴν ὁδόν, *along the way* (Mey. Rob.); not *on the way* (De Wet.). — For με after περιλάμψαν, see on 9, 3. — For τοὺς σὺν ἐμοὶ πορευομένους, *those journeying with me*, see on 22, 9.

V. 14. πάντων . . . . εἰς τὴν γῆν, *And we all having fallen down upon the earth*, from the effect of terror, not as an act of reverence; comp. 9, 4; 22, 17. In regard to the alleged inconsistency between this statement and εἱστήκεισαν in 9, 7, see the note on that passage. — σκληρόν σοι πρὸς κέντρα λακτίζειν, *It is hard for thee to kick against goads.* The meaning is, that his opposition to the cause and will of Christ must be unavailing; the continuance of it would only bring injury and ruin on himself. Wetstein has produced examples of this proverb from both Greek and Latin writers. Euripides (Bacch. v. 791) applies it as here: θυμούμενος πρὸς κέντρα λακτίζοιμι, θνητὸς ὢν θεῷ. Terence (Phorm. 1. 2. 27) employs it thus: "Num quæ inscitia est, Advorsum stimulum calces?" Plautus (4. 2. 55) has it in this form: "Si stimulos pugnis cædis, manibus plus dolet." The Scholiast on Pind. Pyth. 2. 173 explains the origin of the expression: ἡ δὲ τροπὴ ἀπὸ τῶν βοῶν· τῶν γὰρ οἱ ἄτακτοι κατὰ τὴν γεωργίαν κεντριζόμενοι ὑπὸ τοῦ ἀροῦντος, λακτίζουσι τὸ κέντρον καὶ μᾶλλον πλήττονται. The same or a similar proverb must have been current among the Hebrews, though this is the only instance of it found in the Scriptures. The common plough in the East at present has but one handle. The same person, armed with a goad six or eight feet long, holds the plough and drives his team at the same time. As the driver follows the oxen, therefore, instead of being at their side as with us, and applies the goad from that position, a refractory animal of course would kick against the sharp iron when pierced with it. In early times the Greeks and Romans used a plough of the like construction.

V. 16. εἰς τοῦτο prepares the mind for what follows; see on 9, 21. — γάρ shows that the command to arise was equivalent to assuring him that he had no occasion for such alarm (v. 14); the object of the vision was to summon him to a new and exalted sphere of effort. — προχειρίσασθαί σε ὑπηρέτην, *to appoint thee as a minister*, call him to his destined work. The antecedent purpose must be sought in the nature of the act, rather than in the verb. See on 3, 20. — Understand τούτων after μάρτυρα as the attracting antecedent of ὧν. — ὧν τε ὀφθήσομαί σοι is an unusual construction. The best solution is, that ὧν stands for ἅ, as a sort of explanatory accusative (K. § 279. 7): *as to which*, or = δι' ἅ, *on account of which* (Mey.), *I will appear unto thee.* See W. § 39. 3. 1. Many commentators assign an active sense to ὀφθήσομαι: *which I will cause thee to see* or *know.* This use of the verb has no warrant either in classic or Hellenistic Greek.

V. 17. ἐξαιρούμενος . . . . ἐθνῶν, *delivering thee from the people*, i. e. of the Jews (see on 10, 2), *and the heathen.* For this sense of the participle, see 7, 10; 12, 11; 23, 27. Such a promise was conditional from the nature of the case. It pledged to him the security which he needed for the accomplishment of his work until his work was done. Some render ἐξαιρούμενός σε, *selecting thee*, so as to find here the idea of σκεῦος ἐκλογῆς in 9, 15 (Kuin. Hnr. Rob. Hws.). This interpretation would suit τοῦ λαοῦ, but, as De Wette and Meyer remark, it is inappropriate to τῶν ἐθνῶν. Paul was not one of the heathen, and could not be said to be chosen from them. — εἰς οὕς, *unto whom*, refers to both the nouns, which precede. — The correct text inserts ἐγώ before σέ, and omits νῦν. — ἀποστέλλω is present, *I send*, because his ministry is to begin at once.

V. 18. It is important to obseve the relation of the different clauses to each other. ἀνοῖξαι ὀφθαλμοὺς αὐτῶν, *to open their eyes*, states the object of ἀποστέλλω. — τοῦ ἐπιστρέψαι, *that they may turn*, derives its subject from αὐτῶν. The verb is intransitive (see v. 20; 14, 15); not active, *in order to turn them* (E. V.). This clause states the designed effect of the illumination which they should receive. — τοῦ λαβεῖν, κ. τ. λ., *that they may obtain forgiveness of sins*, expresses the direct object of the second infinitive and the ultimate object of the first. — For κλῆρον ἐν τοῖς ἡγιασμένοις, *an inheritance among the sanctified*, see the note on 20, 32. — πίστει τῇ εἰς ἐμέ, *by faith on me*, our English translators and some others join with ἡγιασμένοις; but the words specify evidently the condition by which believers obtain the pardon of sin and an interest in the heavenly inheritance. ἡγιασμένοις is added merely to indicate the spiritual nature of the κλῆρον.

V. 19. ὅθεν, *whence*, accordingly, i. e. having been so instructed, and in such a manner. οὐκ ἐγενόμην ἀπειθής, *I proved not disobedient*, affirms the alacrity of his response to the call more strongly than if the mode of expression had been positive, instead of negative. ἀπειθής attaches itself to the personal idea of ὀπτασίᾳ, and demands that element in the meaning of the word. The service required of him and so promptly rendered evidently was that he should preach the gospel to Jews and Gentiles (v. 17). It is impossible to reconcile such intimations with the idea that the apostle after this remained for years inactive in Arabia, or spent the time there in silent meditation and the gradual enlargment of his views of the Christian system. I cannot agree with Dr. Davidson, that "Paul was not a preacher of the gospel in Arabia, but went through a process of training there, for the purpose of preaching it." See his Introduction, II. p. 80. — τῇ οὐρανίῳ ὀπτασίᾳ, *the heavenly vision*, manifestation of the Saviour's person;

comp. Luke 1, 22; 24, 23; 2 Cor. 12, 1. See the note on 9, 7.

V. 20. τοῖς ἐν Δαμασκῷ πρῶτον, *to those in Damascus first*, as stated in 9, 20, and implied in Gal. 1, 17. — Ἱεροσολύμοις with ἐν repeated, *in Jerusalem;* hardly *unto* as a direct dative (Mey.). — εἰς πᾶσαν, κ. τ. λ., *and unto* (i. e. with a union of the local idea with the personal, the inhabitants of) *all the region of Judea;* comp. ἀπήγγειλαν εἰς τὴν πόλιν in Luke 8, 34. Meyer extends τοῖς from the other clause into this: *and unto those throughout all the region.* But in his last edition he gives up this analysis and approves the other. — The apostle during his labors in Syria and Cilicia, after his first visit to Jerusalem, was as yet unknown in person to the churches of Judea. See Gal. 1, 22. Hence he must have preached there, as intimated in this passage, at a later period. He could have done so when he went thither at the time of the famine (see on 11, 30) or while he was at Jerusalem between his first and second mission to the heathen (18, 22). — ἄξια τῆς μετανοίας ἔργα, *deeds worthy of repentance*, such as showed that they were changed in heart and life. Zeller charges that Paul would not have spoken so, because his doctrine was that of justification by faith alone. The answer is that in Paul's system good works are the necessary evidence of such faith, and further, that πίστει τῇ εἰς ἐμέ above (v. 18) shows that he adhered fully on this occasion to his well-known doctrinal view. — πράσσοντας deserts the case of ἔθνεσιν and agrees with αὐτούς as the suppressed subject of the verbs.

V. 22. ἐπικουρίας . . . . θεοῦ, *Having therefore obtained assistance from God;* since exposed to such dangers in the fulfilment of his ministry (ἐπειρῶντο διαχειρίσασθαι in v. 21) he must otherwise have perished. The assistance was an inference (οὖν) from his present safety. — μαρτυρόμενος μικρῷ τε καὶ μεγάλῳ, *testifying to both small and great* (Rev. 11, 18; 13, 16; 19, 5); not *young and old* (8, 10). The phrase admits either sense, but the more obvious distinction here is that of rank, not of age. The grace of God is impartial; the apostle declared it without respect of persons. It is uncertain whether this is the correct participal or the received μαρτυρούμενος. The latter would mean *attested,* approved, *both by small and great* (Bretsch. Mey.); comp. 6, 3; 10, 22; 16, 2. It is objected that the sense with the latter reading is impossible, because Paul was so notoriously despised and persecuted by Jews and heathen (Alf.). But the meaning might be that though not openly approved he had received that verdict at the bar of their consciences; he had not failed to commend himself and his doctrine to every man's better judgment. The avowal would imply no more than Paul affirms to be true of all who preach faithfully the system of truth which he preached; see 2 Cor. 4, 2. Some render μαρτυρούμενος as middle, *bearing witness*, instead of passive; but confessedly without any example of that use. Knapp, Hahn, Tischendorf, Baumgarten, and others, approve of μαρτυρόμενος. It has no less support than the other word, and affords an easier explanation.

V. 23. This part of the sentence attaches itself to λέγων rather than to μελλόντων γίνεσθαι. — εἰ παθητὸς ὁ Χριστός, *if the Messiah can suffer* (*passibilis* in Vulg.), not so much as a possibility of his nature, as one of the conditions of his office, i. e. would be appointed or allowed to suffer, and so could be subject to infirmity, pain, death. Verbals in τός express possibility and correspond to Latin adjectives in *ilis*. B. § 103. N. 2. The apostle, as I understand, approaches the question on the Jewish side of it, not on the Christian; and that was, whether the Messiah, being such as many of the Jews expected, *could suffer;* not whether *he must suffer*, in order to fulfil the Scriptures. εἰ presents the points as questions which he was wont to discuss. Many of the Jews overlooked or denied the *suffering* character of the Messiah, and stumbled fatally at the gospel because (their σκάνδαλον) it required them to accept a *crucified* Redeemer. Some make εἰ = ὅτι, *that*, i. e. the sign of a moderated assertion. — ὁ Χριστός, *the Messiah* as such; not a personal name here.— πρῶτος ἐξ ἀναστάσεως νεκρῶν = πρωτότοκος ἐκ τῶν νεκρῶν in Col. 1, 18. If Moses and the prophets foretold that the Messiah would suffer, die, and rise from the dead, it followed that Jesus was the promised Saviour of men, and the author of eternal life to those who believe on him. The apodosis (μέλλει καταγγέλλειν, κ. τ. λ.) depends logically on the protasis (εἰ παθητός, εἰ πρῶτος, κ. τ. λ.).

VERSES 24–29. *The answer of Paul to Festus.*

V. 24 ταῦτα refers more especially to the words last spoken (Mey.), and not in the same degree to the entire speech (De Wet.). The idea of a resurrection, which excited the ridicule of the Athenians (17, 32), appeared equally absurd to the Roman Festus, and he could listen with patience no longer. It is evident that τούτων in v. 26 has reference to ἐξ ἀναστάσεως νεκρῶν in v. 23, and the intermediate ταῦτα would not be likely to turn the mind to a different subject. — ἀπολογουμένου may be present, because Festus interposed before Paul had finished his defence

(Mey.). — μεγάλῃ τῇ φωνῇ. See on 14, 10. The "loud voice" was the effect of his surprise and astonishment. — μαίνῃ, *thou art mad*, which he says earnestly, not in jest (Olsh.), because it really appeared to him that Paul was acting under an infatuation which could spring only from insanity (Neand. Mey. De Wet.). Bengel: "Videbat Festus, naturam non agere in Paulo; gratiam non vidit." — τὰ πολλὰ γράμματα admits of two senses: *the many writings* which thou readest (Kuin. Mey. Hws.), or *the much learning* which thou hast or art reputed to have (Neand. De Wet. Alf.). The latter is the more natural idea (as Meyer now holds), and may have been suggested to the mind of Festus from his having heard that Paul was distinguished among the Jews for his scholarship. It is less probable that he was led to make the remark because he was struck with the evidence of superior knowledge evinced in Paul's address. It was able and eloquent, but would not be characterized as learned in any very strict sense of the term.

V. 25. οὐ μαίνομαι, κ. τ. λ., *I am not mad*, etc. This reply of Paul is unsurpassed as a model of Christian courtesy and self-command. Doddridge takes occasion to say here, that, "if great and good men who meet with rude and insolent treatment in the defence of the gospel would learn to behave with such moderation, it would be a great accession of strength to the Christian cause." — κράτιστε, *most excellent*, as in 23, 26. — ἀληθείας, *of truth*, as opposed, not to falsehood (his veracity was not impeached), but to the fancies, hallucinations, of a disordered intellect. — σωφροσύνης is the opposite of μανία, i. e. *a sound mind.*

V. 26. ἐπίσταται . . . . ὁ βασιλεύς, *For the king knows well concerning these things*, viz. the death and resurrection of Christ. The apostle is assured that Agrippa has heard of the events connected with the origin of Christianity, and could not deny that they were supported by evidence too credible to make it reproachful to a man's understanding to admit the reality of the facts. — πρὸς ὃν καὶ παῤῥησιαζόμενος λαλῶ, *unto whom also* (i. e. while he has this knowledge and on that account) *I speak boldly*, without fear of contradiction. — ἐν γωνίᾳ, *in a corner*, secretly (litotes); on the contrary, at Jerusalem, the capital of the nation. The expression was current in this sense (Wetst.). — τοῦτο = τούτων just before. The plural views the circumstances in detail, the singular as a whole. See the note on 5, 5.

V. 27. πιστεύεις, κ. τ. λ. As Agrippa professed to believe the Scriptures, which foretold that the Messiah would rise from the dead, he was bound to admit that there was nothing irrational or improbable in the apostle's testimony concerning an event which accomplished that prophecy.

V. 28. ἐν ὀλίγῳ (sc. χρόνῳ) .... γενέσθαι, *In a little time* (at this rate) *you persuade me to become a Christian* (Wetst. Raph. Kuin. Neand. De Wet. Rob.). It was not uncommon in Greek to omit χρόνος after this adjective. Wetstein, Raphel (Anott. II. p. 188), and others, have produced decisive examples of this ellipsis. By taking ἐν ὀλίγῳ as quantitative, instead of temporal, Meyer brings out this sense from the expression: *With little*, i. e. trouble, effort, *you persuade me to become a Christian;* in other words (said sarcastically), You appeal to me as if you thought me an easy convert to your faith. This would be, no doubt, the correct explanation, if, with Meyer, Tischendorf, and others, we adopt ἐν μεγάλῳ as the correct reading in Paul's reply, instead of ἐν πολλῷ; but the testimony for the common text outweighs that against it (Neand. De Wet.). It is held, at present, to be unphilological to translate ἐν ὀλίγῳ, *almost* (Bez. Grot. E. V.). The Greek for that sense would have been ὀλίγου, ὀλίγου δεῖ, or παρ' ὀλίγον. The translation of the common version appears first in the Geneva version. Tyndale and Cranmer render: "Somewhat thou bringest me in mind for to become a Christian." Agrippa appears to have been moved by the apostle's earnest manner, but attempts to conceal his emotion under the form of a jest.

V. 29. εὐξαίμην ἂν τῷ θεῷ, *I could pray to God*, i. e. if I obeyed the impulse of my own heart, though it may be unavailing. For ἂν with the optative, see W. § 41. 1. b; B. § 139. m. 15. — καὶ ἐν ὀλίγῳ καὶ ἐν πολλῷ, *both in a little and in much time.* We may paraphrase the idea thus: "I could wish that you might become a Christian *in a short time*, as you say; and if not in a short time, *in a long time.* I should rejoice in such an event, could it ever take place, whether it were sooner or later." If we read ἐν μεγάλῳ, the words would then mean, *whether by little effort or by great;* whether he was to be converted with ease or difficulty. — παρεκτὸς τῶν δεσμῶν τούτων, *except these chains*, which were hanging upon his arms as he made his defence. See note on 12, 6. Though separated from his keepers, he must wear still the badges of his condition. Hess writes (II. p. 459) as if the soldiers were present and Paul was bound to them. Some have taken the language as figurative: *except this state of captivity.* The literal sense is not inconsistent with an occasional Roman usage. Tacitus mentions the following scene as having occurred in the Roman Senate (Ann. 4. 28): "Reus pater, accusator filius (nomen utrique Vibius Serenus) in senatum inducti sunt. Ab exilio retractus et tum *catena* vinctus, orante filio. At contra reus nihil infracto animo, obversus in filium *quatere* vincla, vocare ultores deos," etc.

VERSES 30–32. *Agrippa pronounces Paul innocent.*

V. 30. The best authorities read ἀνέστη τε without καὶ ταῦτα εἰπόντος αὐτοῦ. — ὁ is repeated before βασιλεύς and ἡγεμών, because they are the titles of different persons. — οἱ συγκαθήμενοι αὐτοῖς, *those who sat with them*, are the military officers and magistrates who were mentioned in 25, 23. The parties are named as rising and leaving the hall in the order of their rank.

V. 31. ἀναχωρήσαντες, *having retired*, withrawn from the place of audience (see 25, 23); not apart simply in the same room. — ἐλάλουν πρὸς ἀλλήλους, *talked with one another*. The object of the conference was to ascertain Agrippa's opinion in regard to the merits of the case. For οὐδὲν θανάτου ἄξιον ἢ δεσμῶν, *nothing worthy of death*, etc., see on 23, 29. — οὐδὲν πράσσει, *does nothing* in that he holds such opinions, pursues such a course. See W. § 40. 2. c. It is not an instance of the present for the perfect (Kuin.).

V. 32. ἀπολελύσθαι ἐδύνατο, *could have been* (not *could be*) *released*, i. e. at any previous time since his apprehension, before his appeal to Cæsar. It will be seen that both verbs are in the past tense. As the appeal had been accepted, it could not be withdrawn, even with the consent of the parties. The procurator had now lost the control of the case, and had no more power to acquit the prisoner than to condemn him (Böttg. Grot.). — One effect of Agrippa's decision may have been that Festus modified his report, commended Paul to the clemency of the court at Rome. See on 28, 16.

CHAPTER XXVII.

VERSES 1–5. *Paul embarks at Cæsarea for Rome, and proceeds as far as Myra.*

V. 1. ὡς, *as*, presents ἐκρίθη as immediately antecedent to παρεδίδουν. — ἐκρίθη relates to the time of departure, not to the original purpose that Paul should be sent; see 25, 21. — τοῦ ἀποπλεῖν is a lax use of the telic infinitive; the conception being that the decision took place with a view to the sailing. W. § 44. 4. b. — ἡμᾶς, *us*, includes the historian as one of the party; last used in 21, 18. — παρεδίδουν, *proceeded to deliver* (imperfect as related to ἐκρίθη), or, *delivered*, as a series of acts. The plural subject of the verb refers to those who acted in this case under the command of the procurator. — ἑτέρους, *other*, i. e. additional, *prisoners*, not different in character from Paul, viz. heathen, as Meyer supposes. Luke uses that term and ἄλλος indiscriminately; see 15, 35; 17, 34. — The statement here, that not only Paul, but certain other prisoners, were sent by the same ship into Italy, implies, as Paley remarks after Lardner, that the sending of persons from Judea to be tried at Rome was a common practice. Josephus confirms this intimation by a variety of instances. Among others, he mentions the following, which is the more pertinent as it took place about this time. "Felix," he says (Life, § 3), "for some slight offence, *bound and sent to Rome* several priests of his acquaintance, honorable and good men, to answer for themselves to Cæsar." — σπείρης Σεβαστῆς, *of the Augustan cohort.* It is well established that several legions in the Roman army, certainly the 2d, 3d, and 8th, bore the above designation. No ancient writer, however, mentions that any one of these was stationed in the East. Some critics suppose, notwithstanding the absence of any notice to this effect, that such may have been the fact, and that one of the cohorts belonging to this legion, and distinguished by the same name, had its quarters at Cæsarea. The more approved opinion is, that it was an independent cohort, assigned to that particular service, and known as the Augustan or imperial, because, with reference to its relation to the procurator, it corresponded in some sense to the emperor's life-guard at Rome.[1] It may have taken the place of the Italian cohort, which was mentioned in 10, 1; or, very possibly, as Meyer suggests, may have been identical with it. The two names are not inconsistent with this latter opinion. *Augustan* may have been the honorary appellation of the cohort, while it was called *Italian* by the people, because it consisted chiefly of Italians or Romans. The other four cohorts at Cæsarea, as stated by Josephus (Antt. 20. 8. 7; 19. 9. 2), were composed principally of Cæsareans, or Samaritans. Hence, again, some explain σπείρης Σεβαστῆς as meaning *Sebas-*

[1] Such exceptions to the general system occur under every military establishment. Speaking of that of England at a certain period, Mr. Macaulay says that "a troop of dragoons, which did not form part of any regiment, was stationed near Berwick, for the purpose of keeping the peace among the moss-troopers of the border."

tenean or *Samaritan cohort*, since the city of Samaria bore also the Greek name Σεβαστή in honor of the Emperor Augustus. But in that case, as Winer (Realw. II. p. 338), De Wette, Meyer, and others decide, we should have expected Σεβαστηνῶν, instead of Σεβαστῆς, or an adjective equivalent in sense, formed like Ἰταλική in 10, 1. Wieseler (p. 391) has proposed another view of the expression. It appears that Nero organized a body-guard, which he denominated Augustani (Suet. Ner. 20. 25) or Augustiani (Tac. Ann. 14. 15). The critic just named thinks that Julius may have been a centurion in that cohort, whose station of course was at Rome; and that, having been sent to the East for the execution of some public service, he was now returning to Italy with these prisoners under his charge. But that guard, as Wieseler himself mentions, was organized in the year A. D. 60; and, according to his own plan of chronology in the Acts, it was in that very year that Paul was sent from Cæsarea to Rome. This coincidence in point of time leaves room for a possibility that the centurion may have left his post of duty thus early, but encumbers the supposition with a strong improbability. Mr. Howson admits the force of this objection. The Roman discipline, says Meyer, would have given the procurator no claim to the service of such an officer.

V. 2. πλοίῳ Ἀδραμυττηνῷ, *a vessel of Adramyttium*, which was a seaport of Mysia, on the eastern shore of the Ægean Sea, opposite to Lesbos. It was on a bay of the same name, and was then a flourishing city. Pliny speaks of it as one of the most considerable towns in that vicinity. No antiquities have been found here except a few coins. — Some critics prefer μέλλοντι to the common μέλλοντες (Grsb. Mey. Tsch.), though it is doubtful whether the latter should be relinquished (De Wet.). — πλεῖν τοὺς κατὰ τὴν Ἀσίαν τόπους, *to sail the places along* (the coast of) *Asia*, i. e. touch at them here and there on the way to their port. This intransitive verb may govern an accusative, after the analogy of πορεύεσθαι ὁδόν and the like. K. 279. R. 5. See Krüg. Gr. § 46. 6. 3. Some regard τόπους as the place *whither* (Win. De Wet.), which confounds the incidental delays with the end of the voyage. A few copies have εἰς after πλεῖν, which was inserted, no doubt, to render the construction easier. As Myra was one of the places where the ship stopped, *Asia* here may denote Asia Minor. Luke's prevalent use of the term restricts it to the western countries washed by the Ægean. — It would appear that they embarked in this Adramyttian ship because they had no opportunity at this time to sail directly from Cæsarea to Italy. " The vessel was evidently bound for her own port, and her course from Cæsarea thither necessarily led her close past the principal seaports of Asia. Now, this is also the course which a ship would take in making a voyage from Syria to Italy; they would, therefore, be so far on their voyage when they reached the coast of Asia, and in the great commercial marts on that coast they could not fail to find an opportunity for proceeding to their ulterior destination."[1] The opportunity which they expected presented itself at Myra (v. 6). — Ἀριστάρχου. This is the *Aristarchus* named in 19, 29; 20, 4. Our English translators speak of him, very strangely, as "*one* Aristarchus," as if he were otherwise unknown. That he accompanied Paul to Rome appears also from Philem. 24; Col. 4, 10; which Epistles the apostle wrote while in that city. In the latter passage he terms Aristarchus συναιχμάλωτος, which, if taken literally, would lead us to suppose that he too had been apprehended and was now sent as a prisoner to Rome. But in Philem. 24 he is called merely συνεργός, and hence it is more probable that he went with the apostle of his own accord, and that he received the other appellation merely as a commendatory one, because by such devotion to him he had thus made Paul's captivity as it were his own. This is the general opinion of critics. We have every reason to suppose that Luke also went as the voluntary companion of the apostle.

V. 3. κατήχθημεν εἰς Σιδῶνα, *we landed at Sidon,* the modern Saida. This city had anciently one of the finest harbors in the East, and was celebrated at this time for its wealth and commerce. It was the rival of Tyre; see 21, 3. The vessel stopped here perhaps for purposes of trade. They must have sailed quite near to the shore, and the views on land which passed under their notice were, first, the mountains of Samaria in the background, then the bold front of Carmel, the city of Ptolemais with the adjacent plain of Esdrælon, the hills about Naza-

[1] "The Voyage and Shipwreck of St. Paul," etc. By James Smith, Esq., of Jordanhill, F. R. S., etc. London, 1848 and 1856. I have availed myself freely of the illustrations of this valuable treatise in the commentary on this chapter and the next. No work has appeared for a long time that has thrown so much light upon any equal portion of the Scriptures. The author is entirely justified in expressing his belief, that the searching examination to which he has subjected the narrative has furnished a new and distinct argument for establishing the authenticity of the Acts. It would occasion too much repetition to quote this work in a formal manner. I am indebted to Mr. Smith for nearly all the quotations from English travellers and for most of the explanations which involve a knowledge of nautical matters.

reth,[1] and perhaps the heads of Gilboa and Tabor, the white cliffs of Cape Blanco or Ras el-Abiad, Tyre with its crowded port, and the southern ridges of Lebanon. — Saida is now the seat of a flourishing mission from this country, with an outpost at Hasbeiya near the foot of Mount Hermon. — The distance from Cæsarea to Sidon was sixty-seven geographical miles. As they performed the voyage in a single day, they must have had a favorable wind. The prevailing winds now in that part of the Mediterranean, at the period of the year then arrived, are the westerly;[2] and such a wind would have served their purpose. The coast line between the two places bears N. N. E. The season of the year at which Paul commenced the voyage is known from v. 9. It must have been near the close of summer, or early in September. — φιλανθρώπως . . . . χρησάμενος. It is interesting to observe that the centurion manifested the same friendly disposition towards the apostle throughout the voyage. See v. 43; 28, 16. It is not impossible that he had been present on some of the occasions when Paul defended himself before his judges (see 24, 1; 25, 23), and that he was not only convinced of his prisoner's innocence, but had been led to feel a personal interest in his character and fortunes. — τοὺς φίλους, *the friends*, believers in that place. Sidon was a Phœnician city; and, as we learn from 11, 19, the gospel had been preached in Phœnicia at an early period. See on 21, 4. The narrative presupposes that Paul had informed the centurion that there were Christians here. — πορευθέντα agrees with the suppressed subject of τυχεῖν; comp. 26, 20. K. § 307. R. 2. It is corrected in some manuscripts to πορευθέντι, agreeing with αὐτῷ, implied after ἐπέτρεψε.

V. 4. ὑπεπλεύσαμεν, κ. τ. λ., *we sailed under Cyprus because the winds were contrary.* It is evident from the next verse that they left this island on the left hand and passed to the north of it, instead of going to the south, which would have been their direct

[1] From Neby Ismail on the hill behind Nazareth, I could see distinctly Mount Carmel with its foot running out into the sea, the entire sweep of the bay from Carmel to Akka, the plain of Akka and the town itself, with glimpses of the Mediterranean at other points up and down the coast between the opening hills. It is not certain that Tabor can be made out at sea, though the sea can be distinguished as a blue line along the edge of the horizon from the summit of Tabor.

[2] An English naval officer, at sea near Alexandria, under date of July 4th, 1798, writes thus: "The wind continues to the westward. I am sorry to find it almost as prevailing as the trade winds." Again, on the 19th of the next month, he says: "We have just gained sight of Cyprus, nearly the track we followed six weeks ago, so invariably do the westerly winds prevail at this season."

course in proceeding from Sidon to Proconsular Asia. The reason assigned for this is, that the winds were adverse to them. Such would have been the effect of the westerly winds which, as before stated, prevail on that coast at this season, and which had favored their progress hitherto. It may be supposed, therefore, that, these winds still continuing, they kept on their northern course after leaving Sidon, instead of turning towards the west or northwest, as they would have done under favorable circumstances. It is entirely consistent with this view that they are said to have *sailed under Cyprus*, if we adopt the meaning of this expression which some of the ablest authorities attach to it. Wetstein has stated what appears to be the true explanation as follows: "Ubi navis vento contrario cogitur a rectu cursu decedere, ita ut tunc insula sit interposita inter ventum et navem, dicitur ferri *infra* insulam." (Nov. Test. II. p. 637.) According to this opinion, ὑπό in the verb affirms merely that the ship was on that side of the island from which the wind was blowing, i. e. to use a sea phrase, on the lee side. It decides nothing of itself with respect to their vicinity to the island; though, from the nature of the case, it would not be natural to speak of *sailing under a land*, or being *on the lee of it*, unless the land was somewhere near, rather than remote. In this instance they passed within sight of Cyprus, since that island was visible from the Syrian coast. See the note on 13, 4. Many commentators, on the other hand, render ὑπεπλεύσαμεν τὴν Κύπρον, *we sailed near Cyprus*, as it were *under* its projecting shore. In this case they must have had a different wind from that supposed above, in order to enable them to cross from the coast of Palestine to that of Cyprus; but having gained that position, they must then have gone around to the north of that island, in accordance precisely with the other representation.

V. 5. τὸ πέλαγος τὸ κατὰ τὴν Κιλικίαν καὶ Παμφυλίαν, *the sea along Cilicia and Pamphylia*, i. e. the coast of those countries. The Cilician Sea extended so far south as to include even Cyprus. That pass the Greeks called also *Aulon Cilicium.*[1] The Pamphylian Sea lay directly west of the Cilician. Luke says nothing of any delay in these seas, and the presumption is that the voyage here was a prosperous one. This agrees perfectly with what would be expected under that coast at that season of the year. Instead of the westerly winds which had been opposed to them since their departure from Sidon, they would be favored now by

[1] Hoffmann's Griechenland und die Griechen, Vol. II. p. 1385.

a land breeze[1] which prevails there during the summer months, as well as by a current which constantly runs to the westward along the coast of Asia Minor.[2] Their object in standing so far to the north was no doubt to take advantage of these circumstances, which were well known to ancient mariners. — Μύρα τῆς Λυκίας. *Myra* was in the south of Lycia, two or three miles from the coast (Forbg. Handb. II. p. 256). The vicinity abounds still in magnificent ruins, though some of them, especially the rock tombs, denote a later age than that of the apostle.[3] The ancient port of Myra was Andriaca, which was identified by Captain Beaufort at the bay of Andraki, "where the boats trading with the district still anchor, or find shelter in a deep river opening into it."

VERSES 6–12. *Incidents of the Voyage from Myra to Crete.*

V. 6. πλοῖον Ἀλεξανδρῖνον πλέον, *an Alexandrian ship about sailing.* The participle describes a proximate future, as in 21, 2. 3, etc. This ship was bound directly for Italy, having a cargo of wheat, as we learn from v. 38. See the note there. Egypt at this time, it is well known, was one of the granaries of Rome; and the vessels employed for the transportation of corn from that country were equal in size to the largest merchant-vessels of modern times. Hence this ship was able to accommodate the centurion and his numerous party, in addition to its own crew and lading. Josephus states (Life, § 3) that the ship in which he

[1] M. de Pagés, a French navigator, who was making a voyage from Syria to Marseilles, took the same course, for which he assigns also the reason which influenced probably the commander of Paul's ship. "The winds from the west," he says, "and consequently contrary, which prevail in these places in the summer, forced us to run to the north. We made for the coast of Caramania (Cilicia) in order to meet the northerly winds, and which we found accordingly."

[2] "From Syria to the Archipelago, there is a constant current to the westward." — Beaufort's Description of the South Coast of Asia Minor, p. 39. Pococke found this current running so strong between Rhodes and the continent, that it broke into the cabin windows even in calm weather. — Description of the East, Vol. II. p. 236.

[3] "The village of Dembra (the Turkish name of the modern Myra) occupies a small part of the site of the ancient city of Myra. The acropolis crowns the bold precipice above. — We commenced the ascent to the acropolis, at first exceedingly difficult, until we found an ancient road cut out of the rock, with steps leading to the summit. The walls of the acropolis are entirely built of small stones with mortar. We saw no remains of any more substantially or solidly built structures; but it is evidently the hill alluded to by Strabo, upon which 'Myra is said to have been situated.'" — Spratt and Forbes, Vol. I. p. 132.

was wrecked in his voyage to Italy contained six hundred persons. Myra was almost due north from Alexandria; and it is not improbable that the same westerly winds which forced the Adramyttian ship to the east of Cyprus drove the Alexandrian ship to Myra. The usual course from Alexandria to Italy was by the south of Crete; but when this was impracticable, vessels sailing from that port were accustomed to stand to the north till they reached the coast of Asia Minor, and then proceed to Italy through the southern part of the Ægean. See the proofs of this statement in Wetstein. The Alexandrian ship was not, therefore, out of her course at Myra, even if she had no call to touch there for the purposes of commerce. It may be added, that "the land breeze on the Cilician coast appears to be quite local, and consequently might enable Paul's ship to reach Myra, although the prevalent wind did not admit of the ships in that harbor proceeding on their voyage." — This vessel must have reached Myra in August or early in September, according to v. 9 below. That an Alexandrian wheat ship now should have been here, just at this time, suggests a coincidence which may be worth pointing out. At the present day, the active shipping season at Alexandria commences about the first of August. The rise of the Nile is then so far advanced that the produce of the interior can be brought to that city, where it is shipped at once and sent to different parts of Europe. At the beginning of August in 1852, as I saw it stated in the circular of a commercial house at Alexandria, there were twelve vessels then taking on board grain cargoes, just received from Upper Egypt. Thus it appears that the Alexandrian ship mentioned by Luke may have left Egypt not only after the grain harvest of the year had been gathered (it is ripe at the end of March), but just at the time when cargoes or the earliest cargoes of that kind could be obtained there; and, further, that the ship would have had, after this, just about the time requisite for reaching Myra, when Paul's ship arrived at the same place. — ἐνεβίβασεν ἡμᾶς εἰς αὐτό (a *vox nautica*), *he put us on board of it*. It will be noticed that Luke employs such terms with great frequency, and with singular precision. He uses, for example, not less than thirteen different verbs which agree in this, that they mark in some way the progression of the ship, but which differ inasmuch as they indicate its distance from the land, rate of movement, direction of the wind, or some such circumstance. With the exception of three of them, they are all nautical expressions.

V. 7. ἐν ἱκαναῖς δὲ ἡμέραις βραδυπλοοῦντες. The distance from

Myra to Cnidus is not more than a hundred and thirty geographical miles. They occupied, therefore, "many days" in going a distance which with a decidedly fair wind they could have gone in a single day. We must conclude from this, that they were retarded by an unfavorable wind. Such a wind would have been one from the northwest, and it is precisely such a wind, as we learn from the Sailing Directions for the Mediterranean, that prevails in that part of the Archipelago during the summer months. According to Pliny, it begins in August, and blows for forty days. Sailing vessels almost invariably experience more or less delay in proceeding to the west in this part of the Mediterranean at that season of the year. But with northwest winds, says Mr. Smith, the ship could work up from Myra to Cnidus; because, until she reached that point, she had the advantage of a weather shore, under the lee of which she would have smooth water, and, as formerly mentioned, a westerly current; but it would be slowly and with difficulty. μόλις refers evidently to this laborious progress, and not (E. V.) to the fact of their having advanced barely so far. — Κνίδον. *Cnidus* was the name both of a peninsula on the Carian coast, between Cos on the north and Rhodes on the south, and of a town on the Triopian promontory which formed the end of this peninsula. It is the town that is intended here. It was situated partly on the mainland, and partly on an island, with which it was connected by a causeway, on each side of which was an artificial harbor (Forbg. Hand. II. p. 221). "The small one," says Captain Beaufort, "has still a narrow entrance between high piers, and was evidently a closed basin for triremes. The southern and largest port is formed by two transverse moles; these noble works were carried into the sea at the depth of nearly a hundred feet. One of them is almost perfect, the other, which is more exposed to the southwest swell, can only be seen under water."[1] — μὴ προσεῶντος ἡμᾶς τοῦ ἀνέμου, *the wind not permitting us unto* it, i. e. to approach Cnidus, to take shelter in the harbor there, which would have been their first preference. They adopted, therefore, the only other alternative which was left to them. προσεάω does not occur in the classics. πρός cannot well mean *further*, as some allege, since they would have had no motive to continue the voyage in that direction, even if the weather

[1] Caramania, or a Brief Description of the South Coast of Asia Minor, p. 76. "Few places bear more incontestable proofs of former magnificence. The whole area of the city is one promiscuous mass of ruins; among which may be traced streets and gateways, porticos and theatres."

had not opposed it.[1] — ὑπεπλεύσαμεν τὴν Κρήτην κατὰ Σαλμώνην, *we sailed under* (i. e. to the leeward of) *Crete against Salmone*, a promontory which forms the eastern extremity of that island, and bears still the same name. An inspection of the map will show that their course hither from Cnidus must have been nearly south. The wind drove them in this direction. It has been said that they avoided the northern side of Crete, because it furnished no good ports; but such is not the fact. Soudra and Longa Spina are excellent harbors on that side of the island. Having passed around Salmone, they would find a northwest wind as much opposed to them in navigating to the westward as it had been between Myra and Cnidus; but, on the other hand, they would have for a time a similar advantage: the south side of Crete is a weather shore, and with a northwest wind they could advance along the coast, until they reached that part of it which turns decidedly towards the north. Here they would be obliged to seek a harbor, and wait until the wind changed. The course of movement indicated by Luke tallies exactly with these conditions.

V. 8. μόλις τε παραλεγόμενοι αὐτήν, *and with difficulty coasting along it*, viz. Crete, not Salmone, since the former, though not so near, is the principal word. Besides, Salmone was not so much an extended shore as a single point, and at all events did not extend so far as the place where they stopped. This participle is a nautical word. — εἰς τόπον . . . . λιμένας, *unto a certain place called Fair Havens.* No ancient writer mentions this harbor, but no one doubts that it is identical with the place known still under the same name, on the south of Crete, a few miles to the east of Cape Matala. This harbor consists of an open roadstead, or rather two roadsteads contiguous to each other, which may account for the plural designation. It is adapted, also, by its situation, to afford the shelter in northwest winds which the anchorage mentioned by Luke afforded to Paul's vessel. Nautical authorities assure us, that this place is the farthest point to which an ancient ship could have attained with northwesterly winds, because here the land turns suddenly to the north. — ᾧ . . . . Λασαία, *near to which was the city Lasæa.* The vicinity of this place ap-

[1] Mr. Smith supposes that the winds did not permit their proceeding on their course, and in his second edition (p. 76) urges against me the authority of Admiral Penrose as maintaining the same view. It is not claimed that the Greek word is at all decisive, but that the nautical reason demands their interpretation. It does not become me to urge my opinion on such a point in opposition to that of experienced navigators. One would say as a critic that προσεῶντος in such proximity to κατὰ τὴν Κνίδον would have naturally the same local direction.

pears to be mentioned because it was better known than Fair Havens. In the first edition I wrote that all trace of Lasæa was supposed to be lost. Since then an English traveller in Crete reports that the name is applied by the natives to the site of an ancient town on the coast, about five miles east of Fair Havens. Two white pillars, masses of masonry and other ruins occur on the spot.[1] Here ἐγγύς governs ᾧ as an adverb. ἦν, *was*, incorporates the notice with the history without excluding the present. Compare 17, 21. 23. K. § 256. 4. a.

V. 9. ἱκανοῦ δὲ χρόνου διαγενομένου, *Now a long time having elapsed*, i. e. since the embarkation at Cæsarea. The expression is to be taken in a relative sense. On leaving Palestine they expected to reach Italy before the arrival of the stormy season, and would have accomplished their object had it not been for unforeseen delays. — ὄντος ἤδη ἐπισφαλοῦς τοῦ πλοός, *the navigation being now unsafe*, i. e. at this particular period of the year. πλοός is a later Greek form for πλοῦ. W. § 8. 2. b; S. § 22. 2. — διὰ τὸ καὶ, κ. τ. λ., *because also the fast was now past*. καί adds this clause to the one immediately preceding, in order to fix more precisely the limits of the ἤδη there, by informing us how far the season was advanced. See W. § 53. 3. c. — τὴν νηστείαν denotes *the fast* κατ' ἐξοχήν, which the Jews observed on the great day of expiation, which fell on the tenth of the month Tisri, about the time of the autumnal equinox. See Lev. 16, 29; 23, 27. Jahn's Archæol. § 357. Philo also says that no prudent man thought of putting to sea after this season of the year. The Greeks and Romans considered the period of safe navigation as closing in October, and recommencing about the middle of March. Luke's familiarity with the Jewish designations of time rendered it entirely natural for him to describe the progress of the year in this manner. It was not on account of the storms merely that ancient mariners dreaded so much a voyage in winter, but because the rains, prevailed then, and the clouds obscured the sun and stars on which they were so dependent for the direction of their course. See the note on v. 20. — παρῄνει, *exhorted* them, viz. to remain here and not continue the voyage. It is not stated in so many words that this was his object, but it may be inferred from the argument which he employs, and from the representation in the next two verses, that they renewed the voyage in opposition to his advice. See also v. 21.

[1] Mr. Smith inserts an interesting account of this discovery (p. 262) in his edition of 1856.

V. 10. θεωρῶ, *I perceive*, have reason to think. This verb expresses a judgment which he had formed in view of what they had already experienced, as well as the probabilities of the case, looking at the future. The revelation which he afterward received respecting their fate, he announces in very different terms; see v. 23. He may be understood as declaring his own personal conviction, that, if they now ventured to sea again, the ship would certainly be wrecked, and that among so many some of them at least would lose their lives. None lost their lives in fact, and hence Paul could not speak as a prophet here. The apostles were not infallible, except in their sphere as religious teachers.— In ὅτι μετὰ ὕβρεως, κ. τ. λ., we have a union of two different modes of expression. The sentence begins as if μέλλει ὁ πλοῦς was to follow, but on reaching that verb the construction changes to the infinitive with its subject, as if ὅτι had not preceded. See W. § 63. 2. c. Such variations are so common, even in the best writers, that they are hardly to be reckoned as anacoluthic. — μετὰ ὕβρεως καὶ πολλῆς ζημίας, *with violence* (lit. *insolence*, i. e. of the winds and waves) *and much loss*. The second noun states an effect of the first, which is applied here in a sort of poetic way, like our "sport" or "riot" of the elements. Kuinoel quotes τό τε καῦμα καὶ τὴν ἀπὸ τῶν ὄμβρων ὕβριν ἀπομαχόμενα in Jos. Antt. 3. 6. 4, as showing this sense. Horace has the same idea in his "ventis debes ludibrium" (Od. 1. 11. 14). To render the words *injury* and *loss* does violence to the first of them, and makes them tautological. Some have relied for this meaning on Pind. Pyth. I. 140; but the poet is speaking, says Professor Vömel,[1] not of a shipwreck, but a sea-fight, and ὕβρις is used there in its strictest sense. Meyer understands it of the *rashness*, the presumption, which they would evince in committing themselves again to the deep. If we assume that meaning here, we are to retain it naturally in v. 21; and it would be there a term of reproach, which we should not expect the apostle to employ in such an address.

V. 11. ἑκατοντάρχης. In regard to the termination, see on 10, 1. — τῷ κυβερνήτῃ, *the steersman*, whose authority in ancient ships corresponded very nearly with that of the captain in our vessels. — τῷ ναυκλήρῳ, *the owner*, to whom the ship belonged. The proprietor, instead of chartering his vessel to another, frequently went himself in her, and received as his share of the profit the money paid for carrying merchandise and passengers. The

[1] Of the Gymnasium at Frankfort on the Maine. In his Programme for 1850, he inserts a translation of this chapter of the Acts, with some critical remarks.

owners of the cargo hired the captain and the mariners. — τοῖς ὑπὸ τοῦ Παύλου λεγομένοις changes the object of the verb (ἐπείθετο) from that of a person to a thing. Compare 26, 20.

V. 12. ἀνευθέτου, *not well situated*, inconvenient. The harbor deserved its name undoubtedly (see v. 8), for many purposes, but in the judgment of those to whose opinion it was most natural that the centurion should defer, it was not considered a desirable place for wintering (πρὸς παραχειμασίαν). The question was not whether they should attempt to proceed to Italy during the present season, but whether they should remain here in preference to seeking some other harbor where they might hope to be more secure. In this choice of evils, the advice of Paul was that they should remain here; and the event justified his discernment.[1] — οἱ πλείους, *the majority*. Their situation had become so critical, that a general consultation was held as to what should be done. — κἀκεῖθεν, *also from there*, as they had sailed previously from other places, see v. 4. 6; ἐκεῖθεν (Lchm.) is less correct. — εἰς Φοίνικα, *unto Phœnix*, which must have been a town and harbor in the south of Crete, a little to the west of Fair Havens; comp. on v. 13. The palm-trees in that region are supposed to have given occasion to the name. Strabo mentions a harbor with this name on the south of Crete, and Ptolemy mentions a town called Phœnix, with a port which he terms Phœnicus. On the contrary, Stephanus Byzantinus calls the town Phœnicus, which Hierocles, again, calls Phœnice. See Hoffm. Griechenland, II. p. 1334. The best way to harmonize these notices is to suppose that the different names were, at times, applied promiscuously to the town and the harbor. It is uncertain with what modern port we are to identify the ancient Phœnix. Anapolis, Lutro (unless the places differ merely as town and harbor), Sphakia, Franco Castello, Phineka, have each been supposed to be that port. — εἴπως δύναιντο, *if by any means they might be able*, etc. Those who advise the step consider it perilous. — λιμένα τῆς Κρήτες βλέποντα κατὰ Λίβα καὶ κατὰ

1 Paul's dissent from the general opinion has appeared to some very singular; for the bay at Fair Havens, open to nearly one-half of the compass, was ill adapted, it was thought, to furnish a permanent shelter. But recent and more exact observations establish the interesting fact that "Fair Havens is so well protected by islands and reefs, that though not equal to Lutro, it must be a very fair winter harbor; and that considering the suddenness, the frequency, and the violence with which gales of northerly wind spring up, and the certainty that if such a gale sprung up in the passage from Fair Havens to Lutro (Phœnix), the ship must be driven off to sea, the prudence of the advice given by the master and owner was extremely questionable, and that the advice given by St. Paul may possibly be supported even on nautical grounds." Smith, p. 88 (1856).

Χῶρον, *a harbor looking towards Lips and towards Corus*, i. e. the points from which the winds so called blew, viz. the southwest and the northwest. The intermediate point between these winds is west; so that the harbor would have faced in that direction, while the opposite shores receded from each other towards the south and north. This mode of employing the names of the winds is a constant usage in the ancient writers to designate, as we say, the points of the compass. Such is the general view of the meaning of this expression, and there can be no doubt of its correctness. — Mr. Smith (p. 80) maintains that the Phœnix of Luke is the present Lutro. That harbor, however, opens to the east. To reconcile Luke's statement with this circumstance, he understands κατὰ Λίβα καὶ κατὰ Χῶρον to mean *according to the direction* in which those winds blew, and not as is generally supposed, *whence* they blew. "Now this is exactly the description of Lutro, which looks or is open to the east; but having an island in front which shelters it, it has two entrances, one looking to the northeast, which is κατὰ Λίβα, and the other to the southeast, κατὰ Χῶρον." But it is unsafe to give up the common interpretation for the sake of such a coincidence; it rests upon a usage of the Greek too well established to justify such a departure from it. This mode of explaining κατὰ Λίβα involves, I think, two incongruities: first, it assigns opposite senses to the same term, viz. *southwest* as the name of a wind, and *northeast* as the name of a quarter of the heavens; and, secondly, it destroys the force of βλέποντα, which implies certainly that the wind and the harbor confronted each other, and not that they were turned from each other. Mr. Smith adduces κατὰ κῦμα καὶ ἄνεμον from Herod. 4. 110; but the expression is not parallel as regards either the preposition or the noun. κατά denotes there conformity of motion, and not of situation where the objects are at rest, and ἄνεμος does not belong to the class of proper names, like Lips and Corus, which the Greeks employed in such geographical designations. "There is a passage in Arrian," he says, "still more apposite to this point. In his Periplus of the Euxine, he tells us that, when navigating the south coast of that sea, towards the east, he observed during a calm a cloud suddenly arise, which was driven before the east wind. Here there can be no mistake; the cloud must have been driven to the west." But to translate κατ' εὖρον in that manner assumes the point in dispute. The context presents no reason why we should not adopt the ordinary sense of such phrases; viz. *towards the east*, i. e. the cloud appeared in that quarter. In this expression, therefore, *Eurus* would denote the point from which the east wind blows, and not whither.[1]

VERSES 13–16. *A Storm rages, and drives the Vessel to Claude.*

V. 13. ὑποπνεύσαντος δὲ Νότου, *Now when a south wind blew moderately.* After passing Cape Matala, the extreme southern point of Crete, and only four or five miles to the west of Fair

[1] The writer published some remarks on Mr. Smith's explanation of κατὰ Λίβα καὶ κατὰ Χῶρον in the Bibliotheca Sacra, 1850, p. 751. Mr. Smith has had the kindness to address to me a letter, stating some additional facts ascertained since the publication of his work on "The Voyage and Shipwreck of Paul." In this letter he reaffirms his view of the expression referred to, and calls my attention again to the passage in Arrian, as conclusive in support of his position. A distinguished Hellenist (Professor Felton of the University at Cambridge) has favored me with the following remarks on that passage: — "It is true that the cloud of which Arrian speaks was borne towards the west; but that is not expressed by κατ' εὖρον, but must be inferred from the circumstances of the case. The course of the voyage they were making was eastward; after a calm, during which they used their oars alone, 'suddenly a cloud springing up broke out nearly east of us' (ἄφνω νεφέλη ἐπαναστᾶσα ἐξεῤῥάγη κατ' εὖρον μάλιστα), and brought upon them a violent wind. The wind, of course, was an easterly wind, because it made their further progress towards the east slow and difficult. But the navigator in the phrase κατ' εὖρον is speaking of the direction in which he saw the cloud, not in which the cloud was moving. If he had been simply describing the direction in which the cloud was moving, as Herodotus is describing the motion of the ship (and not the direction in which the ship is seen from another point), then κατ' εὖρον would mean *with the Eurus* or *before the Eurus*. . . . . If a person is floating on the wind, or driven by the wind, if he is in motion according to the wind, then of course his direction is determined by that of the wind. But if he is at rest, and looking according to the wind, he is looking where the wind is the most prominent object; that is, he is facing the wind, as Arrian's crew were facing the cloud and the wind, and not turning his back upon it." — As this question has excited some interest, it may be well to mention how it is viewed in works published since the preceding note was written. Humphry (1854) says (p. 202) that Mr. Smith's passages are not quite conclusive as to βλέποντα κατὰ Λίβα. He supposes Phœnix to be the modern Phineka which opens to the west, and thus adopts the common explanation of the phrase. Alford (1852) agrees with Smith that κατὰ Λίβα and similar combinations denote *whither* and not *whence* the winds blow, but intimates a purpose to fortify his ground against objections in a future edition. Howson (II. p. 400) would admit an instance of that usage in Jos. Antt. 15. 9. 6 (*sic*), but says that the other alleged proofs are untenable or ambiguous. He mediates between the two opinions by suggesting that the point of view (βλέποντα) is from the sea and not the land; so that κατὰ Λίβα would have its usual meaning and yet the harbor open towards the east, like Lutro. Wordsworth (p. 120) has a copious note on this question. He reviews the arguments on both sides, and sums up with the result that we should "not abandon the ancient interpretation;" or, at all events, should "suspend our decision till we have more complete topographical details for forming it."

Havens, the coast turns suddenly to the north; and hence, for the rest of the way up to Phœnix, a south wind was as favorable a one as they could desire. — δόξαντες τῆς προθέσεως κεκρατηκέναι, *thinking to have gained their purpose*, regarding it as already secured. It was somewhat less than forty miles from Fair Havens to Phœnix. With a southern breeze, therefore, they could expect to reach their destination in a few hours. — ἄραντες, sc. τὰς ἀγκύρας, *having weighed.* — ἆσσον παρελέγοντο τὴν Κρήτην, *they coasted along Crete nearer*, sc. than usual, i. e. quite near. This clause, as we see from the next verse, describes their progress immediately after their anchorage at Fair Havens. It applies, therefore, to the first few miles of their course. During this distance, as has been suggested already, the coast continues to stretch towards the west; and it was not until they had turned Cape Matala that they would have the full benefit of the southern breeze which had sprung up. With such a wind they would be able just to weather that point, provided they kept near to the shore. We have, therefore, a perfectly natural explanation of their proceeding in the manner that Luke has stated.

V. 14. μετ' οὐ πολύ, *After not long*, shortly; comp. 28, 6. The tempest, therefore, came upon them before they had advanced far from their recent anchorage. They were still much nearer to that place than they were to Phœnix. It is important to observe this fact, because it shows what course the ship took in going from Crete to Claude. — ἔβαλε κατ' αὐτῆς ἄνεμος τυφωνικός, *a typhonic wind struck against it*, i. e. the ship. ἔβαλε may imply ἑαυτόν, or be intransitive. Luke employs αὐτῆς, because the mental antecedent is ναῦς, which actually occurs in v. 41, though his ordinary word is πλοῖον. It would be quite accidental, which of the terms would shape the pronoun at this moment, as they were both so familiar. See W. § 47. 5. k. κατά takes the genitive, because the wind was unfriendly, hostile, as in the Attic phrase κατὰ κόῤῥης τύπτειν. Bernh. Synt. p. 238. Some critics, as Kuinoel, De Wette, Meyer, refer αὐτῆς to Κρητήν, and render *drove* us or the ship *against it.* Similar is the Geneva version: "There arose agaynste Candie a stormye wynd out of the northeast." But how can we understand it in this way, when we are told in the next verse that they yielded to the force of the wind, and were driven by it towards Claude, which is southwest from Fair Havens? We must discard that view, unless we suppose that the wind in the course of a few minutes blew from precisely opposite quarters. Luther refers αὐτῆς to προθέσεως: *struck against it*, defeated their purpose. Tyndale lived for a time with the German Reformer, at Wittenberg, and took his translation perhaps from that source: "Anone after ther arose agaynste ther purpose a flawe of wynd out of the northeaste." The Greek expression is awkward for such an idea and is unsupported by proper examples. Some recent commentators refer αὐτῆς as before to the island, but vary the preposition: *struck down from it*, viz. Crete, i. e. from its mountains, its lofty shores (Alf. Hws. Hmph. Wdsth.). κατά admits confessedly of this sense; but does the verb? Was it used of winds unless the object *struck* was added or implied after it? And if the *striking* was in the writer's mind here and led to the choice of this particular verb, how can κατ' αὐτῆς (i. e. the ship) fail to be this object? It is questionable whether "to strike down" as said of a wind, and "to blow, come, rush down," are convertible terms; and unless they are so, κατέβη in Matt. 8, 23, ἐγένετο in Matt. 7, 24, and γίνεται in Mark 4, 37 do nor bear specially on the case. In the Greek Thesaurus (Paris ed., II. p. 90) it is said of βάλλειν: "Feriendi significatione dicitur de sole, luce, vento, voce et quovis sonitu *ad corpus aliquod accedente*." ἔβαλλον occurs of winds in Il. 23, 217, but with the accusative of the object struck.[1] — τυφωνικός describes the wind with reference to the whirling of the clouds occasioned by the meeting of opposite currents of the air. Pliny (2. 48), in speaking of sudden blasts, says that they cause a vortex which is called "typhoon;" and Aulus Gellius (19. 1) mentions certain figures or appearances of the clouds in violent tempests, which it was customary to call "typhoons." This term is intended to give us an idea of the fury of the gale; and its name, Εὐρακύλων as the word should most probably be written, denotes the point from which it came, i. e. *Euroaquilo*, as in the Vulgate, *a northeast wind*. This reading occurs in A and B, which are two of the oldest manuscripts, and in some other authorities. It is approved by Grotius, Mill, Bengel, Bentley, De Wette, and others. Lachmann inserts it in his edition of the text. εὐρακύλων, says Green (p. 117), "which simply Grecises *Euroaquilo*, demands the preference among the various shapes of the name." The internal evidence favors that form of the word. A northeast storm accounts most perfectly for the course of the ship, and for the means employed to control it, mentioned or intimated in the sequel of the narrative. The other principal readings are Εὐροκλύδων (T. R., Tsch.), compounded of εὖρος and κλύδων, *Eurus fluctus excitans*, or, as De Wette thinks

[1] This criticism may not be useless if it should serve to elicit further inquiry before discarding the common view. My means do not allow me to treat the subject more fully at present.

more correct, *fluctus Euro excitatus;* and Εὐρυκλύδων, from εὐρύς and κλύδων, *broad wave.* It appears, therefore, that the gentle southern breeze with which they started changed suddenly to a violent north or northeast wind. Such a sudden change is a very common occurrence in those seas. An English naval officer, in his Remarks on the Archipelago, says: "It is always safe to anchor under the lee of an island with a northern wind, as it dies away gradually; but it would be extremely dangerous with southerly winds, as they almost invariably shift to a violent northerly wind.

V. 15. συναρπασθέντος, *being seized,* caught by the wind.—ἀντοφθαλμεῖν, *to look in the face,* withstand. It is said that the ancients often painted an eye on each side of the prow of their ships. It may not be easy to determine whether the personification implied in this mode of speaking arose from that practice, or whether the practice arose from the personification.—ἐπιδόντες, sc. τὸ πλοῖον, *giving up* the vessel to the wind. Some supply ἑαυτούς as the object of the participle, in anticipation of the next verb. The idea is the same in both cases.—ἐφερόμεθα, *we were borne,* not hither and thither, but at the mercy of the wind, the direction of which we know from the next verse.

V. 16. νησίον . . . . Κλαύδην, *Running under a certain small island called Claude.* This island Ptolemy calls Claudos. It bears now the name of Gozzo. As the gale commenced blowing soon after the departure from Fair Havens, the ship, in order to reach Claude, must have been driven to the southwest. Their course, had they been near Phœnix at the commencement of the storm, would have been due south. The effect which the wind produced shows what the direction of the wind was; it must have been from the north or northeast, which agrees, as we have seen, with the probable import of the name which Luke has employed to designate the wind. ὑποδραμόντες implies, first, that they went before the wind (see on 16, 11); and secondly, according to the view suggested on v. 4, that they passed Claude so as to have the wind between them and that island, that is, since the direction of the wind has been already determined, they went to the southeast of it instead of the north. That they approached near to the island at the same time, may be inferred from their being able to accomplish the object mentioned in the next clause. Others infer their vicinity to the island from the preposition, which they take to mean *under* the coast; but as in the other case, they suppose that this was the southern coast, from the direction in which such a wind must have driven the ship.—μόλις

. . . . τῆς σκάφης, *we were able with difficulty to secure the boat.* Luke includes himself, perhaps not from sympathy merely, but because he took part in this labor. The preservation of the boat was important, as affording the last means of escape; see v. 30. They may have begun already to have forebodings of the result. Those expert in maritime affairs say, that, while a vessel is scudding before a strong gale, her boat cannot be taken on board or lashed to the side of the vessel (see on v. 32) without extreme danger. Hence it is probable, that, when on the southern side of Claude, they were sheltered somewhat against the storm, and were able to arrest the progress of the ship sufficiently to enable them to accomplish this object. Yet the sea even here was still apparently so tempestuous as to render this a difficult operation. It may have added to the difficulty, that the boat, having been towed more than twenty miles through a raging sea, could hardly fail to have been filled with water. They had omitted this precaution at the outset because the weather was mild, and they had expected to be at sea but a few hours. It will be observed that Luke has not stated why they found it so difficult to secure the boat. We are left to conjecture the reasons.

VERSES 17–20. *They undergird and lighten the ship, but despair of safety.*

V. 17, βοηθείαις ἐχρῶντο, *they used helps,* i. e. ropes, chains, and the like, for the purpose specified in the next clause, viz. *that of undergirding the ship.* Most scholars take this view of the meaning, and it is doubtless the correct one. De Wette would extend βοηθείαις so as to include other similar expedients: *they used helps,* of which ὑποζωννύντες τὸ πλοῖον was an example. βοηθείαις cannot denote the *services* of the passengers, as some have said; for we have no such limiting term annexed as that sense of the expression would require. The "helps" here are the ὑποζώματα, which Hesychius defines as "cables binding ships round the middle." It is probable that ships were occasionally undergirded with planks; but that could only be done in the harbor, and was a different thing from performing the process at sea. But how, the question arises next, were the cables applied so as to accomplish the proposed object? Falconer, in his Marine Dictionary, describes the mode of undergirding ships, as practised in modern navigation, in the following terms: "To frap a ship (*ceintrer un vaisseau*) is to pass four or five turns of a large cable-laid rope round the hull or frame of a ship, to support her in a great storm, or otherwise, when it is apprehended that she is not strong enough to resist the violent efforts of the sea. This expedient, however, is rarely put in practice." In ancient times it was not uncommon to resort to this process. The larger ships on their more extended voyages carried with them ὑποζώματα, or ropes for undergirding, so as to be prepared for any emergency which might require them. The Attic arsenals kept a supply of them always on hand for public use. This mode of strengthening a ship at sea, although not adopted so often as it was anciently, is not unknown in the experience of modern navigators. In 1815, Mr. Henry Hartley was employed to pilot the Russian fleet from England to the Baltic. One of the ships under his escort, the Jupiter, was frapped round the middle by three or four turns of a stream-cable. Sir George Back, on his return from his Arctic voyage in 1837, was forced, in consequence of the shattered and leaking condition of his ship, to undergird her. The Albion, a British frigate, in 1846, encountered a hurricane on her voyage from India, and was under the necessity of frapping her hull together to prevent her from sinking. To these more recent instances many others of an earlier date might be added.[1] The common representation in regard to the ancient mode of applying the *hypozomata* to a ship makes it different from the modern usage. Boeckh's view is the one followed in most of the recent works. According to his investigations, the ropes, instead of being passed under the bottom and fastened on deck, "ran in a horizontal direction around the ship from the stern to the prow. They ran round the vessel in several circles, and at certain distances from one another. The length of these *tormenta*, as they are called in Latin, varied accordingly as they ran around the higher or lower part of the ship, the latter being naturally shorter than the former. Their number varied according to the size of the ship."[2] Mr. Smith, in his Dissertation on the Ships of the Ancients (p. 173 sq.), controverts the foregoing opinion, as being founded on a misapprehension of the passages in the ancient writers which have been supposed to

[1] Some suppose that Horace alludes to this practice in Od. 1. 14. 6: — "Sine funibus Vix durare carinæ Possint imperiosius Æquor." I was once explaining this passage to a college class, according to that view, when one of the members who had been at sea stated that he himself had assisted in such an operation on board a vessel approaching our own coast.

[2] This is quoted from the Dictionary of Greek and Roman Antiquities, Art. *Ships*. The account rests on Boeckh's authority. The writer of the article on *Navis* in Pauly's Real-Encycklopädie der classischen Alterthumswissenschaft, follows the same authority.

prove it. He maintains that the cables, instead of being applied lengthways, were drawn around the middle at right angles to the ship, and not parallel to it.[1] The other mode, he says, "must have been as impracticable as it would have been unavailing for the purpose of strengthening the ship." Luke states a fact simply in relation to this matter; he does not describe the mode. The question, therefore, is one of archæological interest merely; it does not affect the writer's accuracy. — μὴ εἰς τὴν Σύρτιν ἐκπέσωσι, *lest they should be stranded upon the Syrtis.* The verb literally means *to fall out*, i. e. from the sea or deep water upon the land or rocks; comp. v. 26. 29. Syrtis Major is here meant, which was on the coast of Africa, southwest from Crete. This gulf was an object of great dread to mariners on account of its dangerous shoals. The other Syrtis was too far to the west to have been the one to which they would feel exposed in their present situation. Some have taken Σύρτιν to denote a *sand-bank* near Claude; but as any such bank there must have been comparatively unknown, the writer with that allusion would more naturally have left out the article. — χαλάσαντες τὸ σκεῦος, *having lowered the sail.* σκεῦος is indefinite, and may be applied to almost any of the ship's appurtenances, as sails, masts, anchors, and the like. Many have supposed it to refer here to the mast, or, if there was more than one in this case, to the principal mast; but it would seem to put that supposition out of the question, that according to all probability the masts of the larger sailing ships among the ancients were not movable, like those of the smaller vessels, but were fixed in their position, and would require to be cut away; a mode of removal which the accompanying participle shows could not have been adopted in the present instance. The surprising opinion of some, that σκεῦος is the anchor, is contradicted by the following οὕτως ἐφέροντο. Of the other applications of the word, the only one which the circumstances of the ship at this juncture naturally suggest is, that it refers to the sail. It is not certain how we are to take the article here. It leads us to think most directly perhaps of the large, square sail, which was attached to the principal mast. The ancients had vessels with one, two, and three masts.[2] τό would then point out that sail by way of emi-

[1] The mode of executing this manœuvre, as I am informed, or at least one mode, is to sink the ropes over the prow, and then draw them towards the middle of the ship, fastening the ends on deck.

[2] See Pauly's Real-Encyklopädie der classischen Alterthumswissenschaft, Vol. V. p. 463.

nence. The presumption is, that, if the ship carried other sails, as cannot well be doubted, they had taken them down before this; and now, having lowered the only one which they had continued to use, they let the vessel "scud under bare poles." This is the general view of the meaning. It would follow from this, that the wind must have changed its direction before they were wrecked on Melita; for some thirteen days elapsed before that event, during which the storm continued to rage; and within that time, had they been constantly driven before a northeast wind, they must have realized their fear of being stranded on the African coast.—But an eastern gale in the Levant, at this season of the year, is apt to be lasting; the wind maintains itself, though with unequal violence, for a considerable time, in the same quarter. Professor Newman, of the London University, states the following fact[1] in his own experience: "We sailed from Larnica in Cyprus in a small Neapolitan ship with a Turkish crew, on the 2d of December, 1830. We were bound for Latika, in Syria,—the course almost due east,—but were driven back and forced to take refuge in the port of Famagousta, the ancient Salamis. Here we remained wind-bound for days. Owing to our frequent remonstrances, the captain sailed three times, but was always driven back, and once after encountering very heavy seas and no small danger. It was finally the first of January, if my memory does not deceive me, when we reached the Syrian coast." It was probably such a gale which Paul's ship encountered, that is, a series of gales from the east, but not a constant hurricane; for the seamen were able to anchor and to let down their boat, and a part of the crew to attempt to escape in it to the shore. If, then, we assume that the wind blew from the same point during the continuance of the storm, we must suppose that they adopted some precaution against being driven upon the African coast, which Luke does not mention, although his narrative may imply it. The only such precaution, according to the opinion of nautical men, which they could have adopted in their circumstances, was to *lie-to*, i. e. turn the head of the vessel as near to the wind as possible, and at the same time keep as much sail spread as they could carry in so severe a gale. For this purpose, they would need the principal sail; and the sail lowered is most likely to have been the sail above it, i. e. the topsail, or *supparum*, as the Romans termed it. By the adoption of these means they would avoid the shore on which they were

[1] Mentioned in Mr. Smith's letter, alluded to on p. 422.

so fearful of being cast, and drift in the direction of the island on which they were finally wrecked. τό, according to this supposition, would refer to the sail as definite in the conceptions of the writer, or as presumptively well known to the reader. — οὕτως ἐφέροντο, *thus* (i. e. with the ship undergirded, and with the mainsail lowered; or, it may be, with the topsail lowered and the stormsail set) *they were borne on*, at the mercy of the elements. Here closes the account of the first fearful day.

V. 18. σφοδρῶς δὲ χειμαζομένων ἡμῶν, *Now we being violently tempest-tost.* — τῇ ἑξῆς, *on the following day*, i. e. after their attempt to reach the port of Phœnix. The night brought to them no relief. The return of day disclosed to them new dangers. The precaution of undergirding had accomplished less than they hoped. It was evident that the ship must be lightened or founder at sea. Their next step, therefore, was to try the effect of this measure. — ἐκβολὴν ἐποιοῦντο, *proceeded to throw overboard*, is one of the sea-phrases which Julius Pollux mentions as used by the ancients to denote the lightening of a ship at sea. The noun omits the article, because they cast out only a part of what the vessel contained. We are not told what it was that they sacrificed at this time; it may have been their supernumerary spars and rigging, and some of the heavier and more accessible articles of merchandise with which the ship was laden. It appears from v. 38 that the bulk of the cargo consisted of wheat, and they reserved that until the last. The seamen in the vessel in which Jonah embarked had recourse to the same expedient. "There was a mighty tempest in the sea, so that the ship was like to be broken. Then the mariners were afraid, and cried every man unto his god, and cast forth the wares that were in the ship into the sea, to lighten it of them" (Jon. 1, 4. 5).

V. 19. τῇ τρίτῃ. The *third day* arrives and the storm has not abated. They are obliged to lighten the ship still more. This renewed necessity appears to indicate that the ship was in a leaking condition, and that the danger from this cause was becoming more and more imminent. It was one of the great perils to which ancient vessels were exposed. Their style of architecture was inferior to that of modern vessels; they were soon shattered in a storm, "sprang leaks" more easily, and had fewer means for repairing the injury. "In the accounts of shipwrecks that have come down to us from ancient times, the loss of the ship must, in a great number of instances, be ascribed to this cause. Josephus tells us that, on his voyage to Italy, the ship sunk in the midst of the Adriatic Sea (βαπτισθέντος γὰρ ἡμῶν τοῦ πλοίου κατὰ μέσον τὸν Ἀδρίαν). He and some of his companions saved themselves by swimming; the ship, therefore, did not go down during the gale, but in consequence of the damage she sustained during its continuance. One of St. Paul's shipwrecks must have taken place under the same circumstances; for he tells us, a day and a night I have been in the deep (2 Cor. 11, 25), supported no doubt on spars or fragments of the wreck. In Virgil's description of the casualties of the ships of Æneas, some are driven on rocks, others on quicksands; but

> 'laxis laterum compagibus *omnes*
> Accipiunt inimicum imbrem, rimisque fatiscunt.'

The fact, that the ships of the ancients were provided with *hypozomata* or cables ready fitted for undergirding, as a necessary part of their stores, proves how liable they were to such casualties." It is easy to see, therefore, what must have been the fate of Paul's ship had they not discovered land so providentially; she must have foundered at sea, and all on board have perished.— αὐτόχειρες . . . . ἐῤῥίψαμεν, *we cast out with our hands the furniture of the ship*, such as tables, beds, chests, and the like (Mey. De Wet. Lng. Alf. Wdsth.). The self-inflicted loss in this case (αὐτόχειρες), which affected so much the personal convenience of each one, showed how urgent was the danger. Yet σκευήν is a very doubtful word. Some understand it of the masts, yards, sails, and other equipments of the ship similar to these. With this interpretation, we must regard the term as applying to that class of objects in a general way; for we see from v. 29 that they retained at least some of their anchors, and from v. 44 that, at the last moment, they had boards and spars at command to assist them in reaching the shore. According to some again, as Wetstein, Kuinoel, Winer, σκευήν denotes the baggage of the passengers. αὐτόχειρες is more significant with that sense, but πλοίου as genitive of the container, *the baggage on board the ship*, is very harsh. τὴν σκεύην means, says Smith, "the mainyard, an immense spar, probably as long as the ship, and which would require the united efforts of passengers and crew to launch overboard. The relief which a ship would thus experience, would be of the same kind as in a modern ship, when the guns are thrown overboard." — Some read ἐῤῥίψαμεν, some ἔῤῥιψαν. Tischendorf retains the former, as in T. R. Meyer is too positive that the first person betrays its origin in αὐτόχειρες.

V. 20. μήτε . . . . ἐπικειμένου, *Now neither sun nor stars shining upon* us *for many days, and a storm not slight pressing upon* us.

Observe the force of the compounds. The absence of the sun and stars increased their danger, since it deprived them of their only means of observation. The Greeks and Romans, in the most improved state of navigation among them, were reluctant to venture out to sea beyond the sight of land. During the day they kept the high lands on shore, or some island, in view, to direct them; and at night depended for the same purpose on the position, the rising and setting of different stars. Dict. of Antt., Art. *Ship*. The *many* or *several days* include, probably, the three days which have been mentioned, but how many of the eleven days which followed (v. 27) before the final disaster is uncertain. We do not know how long the interval was between Paul's address and that event. The expression would be inappropriate, however, unless it comprehended the greater part of them. — λοιπόν, *for the future*, thenceforth. They relinquish now their last hope of escape; destruction seemed to be inevitable. In their condition they must have felt that their only resource was to run the vessel ashore. But the state of the weather rendered it impossible for them to distinguish in what direction the shore lay; and thus they were unable to make the only further effort for their preservation which was left to them. In judging of the dangers which menaced them, we must take into account the state of the vessel, as well as the violence of the storm. — περιῃρεῖτο means *was utterly taken away*. — τοῦ σώζεσθαι depends on ἐλπίς as a genitive construction; comp. 14, 9.

VERSES 21–26. *The Apostle cheers them with the Hope of Deliverance.*

V. 21. πολλῆς ἀσιτίας denotes *much abstinence* as to time and degree, i. e. both long continued and severe, but not entire; see on v. 33. This abstinence was not owing to their want of provisions (see v. 36), but was the effect, in part at least, of their fears and dejection of mind (see v. 22. 36); and in part, also, of the difficulty of preparing food under such circumstances, and of the constant requisition made upon them for labor. "The hardships which the crew endured during a gale of such continuance, and their exhaustion from labor at the pumps, and hunger, may be imagined, but are not described." — ἔδει μέν, κ. τ. λ., *you ought* (past as a violated duty) *having obeyed me*, because the counsel was wise, not authoritative as from an apostle. — ἀνάγεσθαι is present because they were still at sea. Note the aorist which follows. — Paul recalls to mind their former mistake in disregarding his advice, not to reproach them, but in order to show his claim to their confidence with reference to the present communication. μέν is unattended here by any responding δέ. — κερδῆσαί τε τὴν ὕβριν ταύτην καὶ τὴν ζημίαν, *and to have escaped* (lit. *gained*) *this violence and loss;* see on v. 10. *Lucrari* was used in the same manner. An evil shunned is a gain as well as a good secured. As ὕβριν refers to something actually suffered, it cannot mean *harm* to their persons (Hws.); for the exemption from such injury of which Paul assures them in the next verse and still more emphatically in v. 34, applies undoubtedly to the whole voyage.

V. 22. πλὴν τοῦ πλοίου, There shall be no loss *except of the ship.* This limitation qualifies, not the entire clause which precedes, but only ἀποβολὴ οὐδεμία ἔσται, which we are to repeat before the words here. μόνον would have marked the connection more precisely. See W. § 66. 1. e. As to the rest, compare the remarks on θεωρῶ in v. 10.

V. 23. παρέστη. Whether *the angel* appeared to the apostle in a vision or a dream, the mode of statement does not enable us to decide. See on 16, 9. — ταύτῃ τῇ νυκτί, *this night* just passed, or that which was passing. Most think it probable that Paul did not communicate the revelation to those in the ship until the return of day. — οὗ εἰμι, *whose I am,* to whom I belong as his property; in other words, whose servant I am. — ᾧ καὶ λατρεύω, *whom also I worship,* to whom I offer religious service and homage. This verb refers to external acts of worship, and not to a religious life in general, except as the latter may be a concomitant of the former.

V. 24. Καίσαρί σε δεῖ παραστῆναι, *thou must stand before Cæsar.* See on 23, 11. To remind the apostle of this still unfulfilled purpose of God, was the same thing as to assure him that he would escape the present danger. — κεχάρισται . . . . σοῦ, *God has given to thee all those who sail with thee.* They should be preserved for his sake. No one supposes the declaration here to affirm less than this. Many think that it implies also that Paul had prayed for the safety of those in the ship with him; and that he receives now the assurance that his prayer in their behalf has prevailed. "For I hope," says Paul in Philem. v. 22, "that through your prayers I shall be given unto you." Such is the view of Calvin, Bengel, Olshausen, De Wette, Lange, and others. Bengel remarks here: "Facilius multi mali cum paucis piis servantur, quam unus pius cum multis reis perit. Navi huic similis mundus."

V. 25. πιστεύω, κ. τ. λ. It is evident from v. 32 that the apostle had acquired a strong ascendency over the minds of the passengers in the ship, if not of the others. He could very properly, therefore, urge his own confidence in God as a reason (γάρ) why they should dismiss their fears (εὐθυμεῖτε), so far at least as the preservation of their lives was concerned.

V. 26. εἰς νῆσόν τινα, *upon some island.* More than this was not revealed to him. Paul was as ignorant of the name of the place where they were wrecked as the rest of them; see v. 39. — δέ opposes what they must suffer to what they would escape. — δεῖ in such a communication may represent the event as not merely certain, but certain because it was fixed by the divine purpose. — ἐκπεσεῖν, *be cast away.* Se the remark on v. 17.

VERSES 27–32. *The Discovery of Land; and the frustrated Attempt of the Mariners to desert the Ship.*

V. 27. τεσσαρεσκαιδεκάτη νύξ, *the fourteenth night* since their departure from Fair Havens. — διαφερομένων ἡμῶν ἐν τῷ Ἀδρίᾳ, *as we were borne through* (sc. the waters, comp. v. 5) *in the Adriatic.* They may have been driven hither and thither, or onward in one direction; the participle is indefinite. Mr. Smith's calculation assumes a uniform drift towards Melita. It has been said that the modern Malta lies too far south to be embraced in the sea so designated. The statement is erroneous. In its restricted sense, the Adriatic was the sea between Italy and Greece; but in a wider sense it comprehended also the Ionian Sea around Sicily, near which was Melita. (Forbg. Handb. II. p. 19; Win. Realw. I. p. 23.) The later Greek and Roman writers, as Biscoe has shown, gave the name to the entire sea as far south as Africa. — ὑπενόουν . . . . χώραν, *the mariners suspected that some land was approaching them.* As Mr. Smith remarks, Luke uses here the graphic language of seamen, to whom the ship is the principal object, whilst the land rises and sinks, nears and recedes. The narrator does not state on what ground they suspected their vicinity to the land. It was, no doubt, the noise of the breakers. This is usually the first notice of their danger which mariners have in coming upon a coast in a dark night. This circumstance furnishes reason for believing that the traditionary scene of the shipwreck is the actual one. It is impossible to enter St. Paul's Bay from the east without passing near the point of Koura; and while the land there, as navigators inform us, is too low to be seen in a stormy night, the breakers can be heard at a considerable distance, and in a northeasterly gale are so violent as to form on charts the distinctive feature of that headland. On the 10th of

August, 1810, the British frigate Lively fell upon these breakers, in a dark night, and was lost. The quartermaster, who first observed them, stated, in his evidence at the court-martial, that at the distance of a quarter of a mile the land could not be seen, but that he saw the surf on the shore. — The distance from Claude to the point of Koura is 476.6 miles. Luke's narrative allows a fraction over thirteen days for the performance of this voyage. It must have occupied a day, or the greater part of a day, to have reached Claude after they left Fair Havens (see v. 13–16). According to the judgment of experienced seamen, "the mean rate of drift of a ship circumstanced like that of Paul" (i. e. working its way in such a direction in a gale of moderate severity, against a northeast wind) would be thirty-six and a half miles in twenty-four hours. "Hence, according to these calculations," says Mr. Smith (p. 122 sq.), "a ship starting late in the evening from Claude, would, by midnight on the fourteenth, be less than three miles from the entrance of St. Paul's Bay. I admit that a coincidence so very close as this is, is to a certain extent accidental; but it is an accident which could not have happened had there been any great inaccuracy on the part of the author of the narrative with regard to the numerous incidents upon which the calculations are founded, or had the ship been wrecked anywhere but at Malta."

V. 28. βραχὺ δὲ διαστήσαντες. κ. τ. λ. There was but a short distance, it will be observed, between the two soundings; and the rate of decrease in the depth of the water, viz. first, *twenty fathoms*, and then *fifteen*, is such as would not be found to exist on every coast. It is said that a vessel approaching Malta from the same direction finds the same soundings at the present day. — ὀργυιά, *fathom*, (from ὀρέγω, to stretch,) σημαίνει τὴν ἔκτασιν τῶν χειρῶν σὺν τῷ πλάτει τοῦ στήθους. Etym. Magn.

V. 29. εἰς τραχεῖς τόπους, *upon rough*, i. e. rocky, *places*. Their apprehension arose, not from what they saw, but from what they had reason to fear in a dark night on an unknown coast. The alarm was well founded; for "the fifteen fathom depth here is as nearly as possible a quarter of a mile only from the shore, which is girt with mural precipices, and upon which the sea must have been breaking with great violence." — ἐκ πρύμνης . . . . τέσσαρας, *having cast out four anchors from the stern*. "To anchor successfully in a gale of wind, on a lee shore, requires holding-ground of extraordinary tenacity. In St. Paul's Bay, the traditionary locality of the shipwreck, the anchorage is thus described in the Sailing Directions: — 'The harbor of St. Paul is open to easterly and northeast winds. It is, notwithstanding, safe for small ships, the ground, generally, being very good; and while the cables hold there is no danger, *as the anchors will never start.*'" The ancient vessels did not carry, in general, so large anchors as those which we employ; and hence they had often a greater number. Athenæus mentions a ship which had eight iron anchors. Paul's ship, as we see from the next verse, had other anchors besides those which were dropped from the stern. One object of anchoring in that way was to arrest the progress of the ship more speedily. No time was to be lost, as they knew not that they might not founder the next moment upon the shoals where the breakers were dashing. Had they anchored by the bow, we are told, there was reason for apprehending that the vessel would swing round and strike upon the rocks. The ancient ships were so constructed that they could anchor readily by the prow or the stern, as circumstances might require. Another advantage of the course here taken was that the head of the vessel was turned towards the land, which was their best position for running her ashore. That purpose they had no doubt formed already. "By cutting away the anchors (τὰς ἀγκύρας περιελόντες), loosing the bands of the rudders (ἀνέντες τὰς ζευκτηρίας), and hoisting the artemon (ἐπάραντες τὸν ἀρτέμονα), all of which could be done simultaneously, the ship was immediately under command, and could be directed with precision to any part of the shore which offered a prospect of safety." — The English ships of war were anchored by the stern in the battle of Copenhagen and rendered very effective service in that position. Mr. Howson mentions the singular fact that Lord Nelson stated after the battle that he was led to adopt that plan, because he had just been reading this twenty-seventh chapter of the Acts. — ηὔχοντο ἡμέραν γενέσθαι, *they desired that day might come.* The remark is full of significance. In the darkness of the night they could not tell the full extent of the dangers which surrounded them. They must have longed for returning day on that account. In the mean time it must have been difficult to preserve a vessel which had been so long tempest-tost from sinking. Their only chance of escape was to strand the ship as soon as the light enabled them to select a place which admitted of it. It is evident that every moment's delay must have been one of fearful suspense, as well as of peril to them.

V. 30. τῶν δὲ ναυτῶν, κ. τ. λ. This ungenerous attempt of the seamen to escape confirms the remark before made, that the ship was probably in so shattered a state, as to render it uncertain whether it could outride the storm until morning. They may have had another motive for the act. The shore might prove to be one on which they could not drive the vessel with any hope of safety; and they may have deemed it more prudent to trust themselves to the boat, than to remain and await the issue of that uncertainty. — χαλασάντων τὴν σκάφην, *having lowered down the boat*, which they had previously hoisted on board; see v. 16. 17. — ἐκ πρώρας, *from the prow*, since it was nearer thence to the shore, and was there only that they could pretend to need anchors, the stern being already secure. — ἀγκύρας ἐκτείνειν, not *to cast out* (E. V.), but *stretch out anchors*. The idea of extending the cables runs into that of carrying out and dropping the anchors. Favored by the darkness, and under color of the pretext assumed, they would have accomplished their object, had not Paul's watchful eye penetrated their design.

V. 31. εἶπεν . . . . στρατιώταις. Paul addressed himself to *the centurion and the soldiers*, because the officers of the ship were implicated in the plot, or, in consequence of the general desertion, had no longer any power to enforce their orders. The soldiers are those who had charge of the different prisoners (v. 1), subject probably to the command of the centurion who had the particular care of the apostle. — οὗτοι, *these*, viz. the mariners. — ὑμεῖς σωθῆναι οὐ δύνασθε, *you cannot be saved*. The pronoun is emphatic. The soldiers were destitute of the skill which the management of the ship required. It could not be brought successfully to land without the help of the mariners. This remark of Paul proves that the plan to abandon the vessel was not confined to a portion of the crew, but was a general one.

V. 32. ἀπέκοψαν τὰ σχοινία τῆς σκάφης, *cut off the ropes of the boat*, which fastened it to the vessel; not those by which they were lowering it as that was already done (v. 30). The short sword of the soldiers furnished a ready instrument for the summary blow. — εἴασαν αὐτὴν ἐκπεσεῖν, *let it fall off* (i. e. from the side of the vessel), go adrift. The next billow may have swamped the frail craft.

VERSES 33–35. *Paul assures them again that their Lives would be saved.*

V. 33. ἄχρι . . . . γίνεσθαι, *Now until it should be day*, i. e. in the interval between the midnight mentioned in v. 27 and the subsequent morning. — σήμερον is appositional in sense with ἡμέραν. — προσδοκῶντες, *waiting* for the cessation of the storm (De Wet.).

— ἄσιτοι διατελεῖτε, *ye continue fasting*, where the adjective supplies the place of a participle. W. § 45. 4. — μηδὲν προσλαβόμενοι, *having taken nothing*, adequate to their proper nourishment, no regular food during all this time; see v. 21. "Appian," says Doddridge, "speaks of an army, which, for twenty days together, had neither food nor sleep; by which he must mean, that they neither made full meals nor slept whole nights together. The same interpretation must be given to this phrase." The apostle's language could not be mistaken by those to whom it was addressed. Compare v. 21.

V. 34. τοῦτο . . . . ὑπάρχει, *for this* (viz. that they should partake of food) *is important for your preservation.* For πρός with this sense, see W. § 47. 5. f. They would have to submit to much fatigue and labor before they reached the shore, and needed, therefore, to recruit their strength. — οὐδενὸς . . . . πεσεῖται, *For there shall not a hair fall*, etc. This was a proverbial expression, employed to convey an assurance of entire safety. See 1 Kings 1, 52; Luke 21, 18.

V. 35. ἄρτον, *bread.* This word, by a Hebraistic usage, often signifies *food* in the New Testament; but κλάσας, which follows, appears to exclude that sense here. Yet the present meal had no doubt its other accompaniments; the bread only being mentioned because that, according to the Hebrew custom, was broken and distributed among the guests after the giving of thanks. The apostle performed, on this occasion, the usual office of the head of a Hebrew family. Olshausen expresses the fanciful opinion, as it seems to me, that the Christians among them regarded this act as commemorative of the Lord's Supper, though the others did not understand Paul's design. The language employed here, it is true, more frequently describes that ordinance, but it is used also of an ordinary meal; see Luke 24, 30.

VERSES 36–38. *They partake of Food and again lighten the Ship.*

V. 36. εὔθυμοι δὲ γενόμενοι πάντες, *Having all now become cheerful.* It is not accidental that the writer makes this remark in connection with προσελάβοντο τροφῆς. In their despair they had lost their inclination to eat; but the return of hope brought with it a keener sense of their wants, and they could now think of satisfying their hunger. See on v. 21. 33. — καὶ αὐτοί, *also themselves* as well as he. The apostle had set them the example (ἤρξατο ἐσθίειν), and they all followed it.

V. 37. The emphatic πάντες in v. 36 leads the writer to specify the number. — *αἱ πᾶσαι ψυχαί, all the souls together.* For this adverbial use of *πᾶς*, see the note on 19, 7. For this use of *ψυχαί*, see on 2, 41. — *διακόσιαι ἑβδομήκοντα ἕξ, two hundred and seventy-six.* The number of persons on board shows that the vessel must have been one of the larger size. In the reign of Commodus, one of the Alexandrian wheat ships was driven, by stress of weather, into the Piræus, and excited great curiosity on the part of the Athenians. Lucian visited this vessel, and has laid the scene of one of his Dialogues (*πλοῖον ἢ εὐχαί*) on board of her. From the information furnished by him it has been estimated that the keel of this ship was about one hundred feet in length, and that she would measure between eleven and twelve hundred tons. Her dimensions, therefore, although inferior to those of many modern vessels, "were quite equal to those of the largest class of modern merchantmen." Luke's ship was engaged in the same commerce (being, to use Lucian's language, *μίαν τῶν ἀπ' Αἰγύπτου εἰς Ἰταλίαν σιταγωγῶν*); and we have no reason to be surprised at her containing such a number of men. See further, on v. 6.

V. 38. *ἐκούφιζον τὸ πλοῖον.* Among the nautical terms of Julius Pollux, we find *κουφίσαι τὴν ναῦν*; see on v. 18. Luke states merely the fact, that *they lightened the ship* again (it is the third time), but gives no explanation of it. The object may have been to diminish the depth of water which the ship drew, so as to enable them to approach nearer to the shore before striking. It has been conjectured, also, that the vessel may have been leaking so fast that the measure was necessary in order to keep her from sinking. — *ἐκβαλλόμενοι τὸν σῖτον, casting out the wheat* or *grain,* corn, since the term has frequently that wider sense. As suggested on v. 18, we are to understand here that they threw into the sea the grain which constituted the cargo, or the bulk of the cargo, which the ship carried. The fact that the ship belonged to Alexandria is presumptive proof that she was loaded with grain, since that was the principal commodity exported from Egypt to Italy. The explicit notice here, that they lightened the ship by throwing the grain into the sea, harmonizes with that presumption, and tends to confirm it. Some have thought that *σῖτον* may denote the ship's provisions; but these would have consisted of various different articles, and would not naturally be described by so specific a term as this. The connection, which has been said to favor the opinion last stated, agrees equally well with the other. Having their hopes revived by the spectacle of Paul's undisturbed serenity, and by his animating address, and being reinvigorated after so long a fast by the food of which they had partaken, they were now in a condition both of mind and body to address themselves to the labors which their safety required. This view, therefore, places their lightening of the ship in a perfectly natural connection with the circumstances related just before. In addition to this, as Hemsen urges, their remaining stock of provisions, after so protracted a voyage, must have been already so reduced that it could have had little or no effect on the ship, whether they were thrown away or retained. — Mr. Blunt (p. 326) has very properly called attention to the manner in which the narrative discloses to us the nature of the ship's cargo. In the fifth verse we are informed that the vessel "into which the centurion removed Paul and the other prisoners at Myra belonged to *Alexandria*, and was *sailing into Italy*. From the tenth verse we learn that it was a merchant-vessel, for mention is made of its *lading*, but the nature of the lading is not *directly* stated. In this verse, at a distance of some thirty verses from the last, we find, by the merest chance, of what its cargo consisted. The freight was naturally enough kept till it could be kept no longer, and then we discover for the first time that it was *wheat;* the very article which such vessels were accustomed to carry from Egypt to Italy. These notices, so detached from each other, tell a continuous story, but it is not perceived till they are brought together. The circumstances drop out one by one in the course of the narrative, unarranged, unpremeditated, thoroughly incidental; so that the chapter might be read twenty times, and their agreement with one another and with contempory history be still overlooked."

VERSES 39–44. *The Shipwreck. Those on board escape to the Shore by swimming, or on Fragments of the Vessel.*

V. 39. τὴν γῆν οὐκ ἐπεγίνωσκον, *they recognized not the land,* within view. The day has dawned, and they could now distinguish it. It has appeared to some surprising that none of those on board should have known a place with which those at least who were accustomed to the sea might be expected to have been so well acquainted. The answer is, that the scene of the shipwreck was remote from the principal harbor, and, as those who have been on the spot testify, distinguished by no marked feature which would render it known even to a native, if he came unexpectedly upon it. The Bay, so justly known as St. Paul's Bay, is at the northwest extremity of the island, and is formed by the main shore on the south, and the island of Salmonetta on the north. It extends from east to west, two miles long and one broad at the entrance, and at the inner end is nearly land-locked on three sides. It is several miles north of Valetta, the famous rock-bound harbor of Malta.[1] — κόλπον . . . . αἰγιαλόν, *they perceived a certain inlet*, creek, *having a shore*, one open or smooth (see on 21, 5), on which they could run the ship with a hope of saving their lives. "Luke uses here the correct hydrographical term." The remark implies that the coast generally was unsafe for such an attempt. The present conformation of the coast on that side of Malta confirms Luke's accuracy in this particular. The shore there presents an unbroken chain of rocks, interrupted at only two points. — εἰς ὃν . . . . πλοῖον, *into which they determined, if they could, to thrust forth* (i. e. from the sea), to drive ashore, *the ship*. For ἐξῶσαι from ἐξωθέω, see W. § 15; K. § 165. 7. The wind must have forced them to the west side of the bay, which is rocky, but has two creeks. One of these, Mestara Valley, has a shore. The other has no longer a sandy beach, but must have had one formerly, which has evidently been worn away by the action of the sea. The vessel grounded (v. 41) before they reached the point on shore at which they aimed, though they may have entered the creek.

V. 40. καὶ τὰς ἀγκύρας . . . . θάλασσαν, *and having entirely cut away the anchors they abandoned them unto the sea.* On this force of the preposition in περιελόντες, comp. περιῃρεῖτο in v. 20. It has been referred to the position of the anchors as being around the ship; but they had all been dropped from the stern (v. 29), and as the strain would be mainly in one direction, they would not be likely to be found on different sides of the vessel. Our English translators followed the Vulgate in their inaccurate version of this clause. — ἅμα . . . . πηδαλίων, *at the same time having unfastened the bands of the rudders.* Most of the ancient vessels were furnished with two rudders. No sea-going vessel had less than two, although small boats and river craft, such as those on the Nile, were sometimes steered by one. The πηδάλια were more like oars or paddles than our modern helm. They were attached to the stern, one on each quarter, distinguished as the right and the left rudder. In the larger ships the extremities of the rudders were joined by a pole, which was moved by one man and kept the rudders always parallel. See Dict. of Antt., Art. *Guber-*

[1] Smith's chart of St. Paul's Bay is copied in Howson, with the necessary explanations. I had the gratification of a hurried visit to this locality on my way to Alexandria. It appeared to me to fulfil every condition of the narrative, as the scene of the apostle's shipwreck.

naculum. When a vessel was anchored by the stern, as was the case here, it would be necessary to lift the rudders out of the water and to secure them by bands. These bands it would be necessary to unfasten when the ship was again got under weigh. ἀνέντες is the second aorist participle in the active from ἀνίημι. K. § 180. See on 16, 26. — ἐπάραντες . . . . τῇ πνεούσῃ, sc. αὔρᾳ, *having hoisted the foresail to the wind.* ἀρτέμων has been taken by different writers as the name of almost every sail which a vessel carries, e. g. mainsail, topsail, jib, etc. We have no ancient definition of the term which throws any certain light upon its meaning. It passed into some of the modern languages, where it is variously applied, but occurs in no ancient Greek author out of Luke's account of this voyage. Most commentators, without any attempt to substantiate their opinion, put it down as the "mainsail." The nautical argument is said to be in favor of the foresail, i. e. the sail attached to the mast nearest the prow; or if there was but one mast, fixed to a spar or yard near the prow. "As the ancients depended for speed chiefly upon one principal sail, an appendage or additional sail at the bow of the ship was required for the purpose of directing the vessel when in the act of putting about; for, although there could be no difficulty in bringing the ship's head to the wind with the great sail alone, a small sail at the bow would be indispensable for making her 'pay off,' that is, bringing her head round; otherwise she would acquire stern-way, and thereby endanger the rudders, if not the ship itself." The vessels on coins and in other ancient representations exhibit a sail of this description. With this sail raised, it is said that a ship situated like that of Paul would move towards the shore with more precision and velocity than with any other. "A sailor will at once see that the foresail was the best possible sail that could be set under the circumstances."

V. 41. περιπεσόντες δὲ εἰς τόπον διθάλασσον, *having fallen into a place having two seas.* This has been supposed by many commentators to have been a concealed shoal or sand-bank, formed by the action of two opposite currents. In the course of time such a bank, as is frequently the case at the mouth of rivers or near the shore, may have been worn away,[1] so that the absence of any such obstruction there at the present time decides nothing against that supposition. It has also been understood to have been a tongue of land or promontory, against the shores of which

[1] For examples of this, see Lyell's Principles of Geology, p. 285 sq. (8th ed., 1850).

the sea beat strongly from opposite quarters. It is not stated that any projection exists there now, to which Luke's description, if explained in that manner, would apply. Mr. Smith is of the opinion that τόπος διθάλασσος may refer to the channel, not more than a hundred yards in breadth, which separates the small island Salmonetta from Malta; and which might very properly be called a place where "two seas meet," on account of the communication which it forms between the sea in the interior of the bay and the sea outside. He would place the scene of the shipwreck near that channel, and, according to the representation on his map, a little to the north of the place to which tradition has generally assigned it. The creek near here, at present without a beach (see v. 39), may be the one which they attempted to enter. The final shock now ensues. — καὶ ἡ μὲν πρώρα, κ. τ. λ., *And the prow, sticking fast, remained immovable, but the stern was broken by the violence of the waves.* "This is a remarkable circumstance, which, but for the peculiar nature of the bottom of St. Paul's Bay, it would be difficult to account for. The rocks of Malta disintegrate into extremely minute particles of sand and clay, which, when acted upon by the currents, or surface agitation, form a deposit of tenacious clay; but in still water, where these causes do not act, mud is formed; but it is only in the creeks where are no currents, and at such a depth as to be undisturbed by the waves, that the mud occurs. In Captain Smyth's chart of the bay, the nearest soundings to the mud indicate a depth of about three fathoms, which is about what a large ship would draw. A ship, therefore, impelled by the force of a gale into a creek with a bottom such as has been described, would strike a bottom of mud into which the fore part would fix itself and be held fast, whilst the stern was exposed to the force of the waves." — Meyer defends τῶν κυμάτων with good reason against Tischendorf and others.

V. 42. It is the soldiers who initiate this scheme; since they only and not the mariners were interested in the fate of the prisoners. — βουλή, *plan*, resolution, not *counsel* merely; comp. βουλήματος below. — ἵνα τοὺς δεσμώτας ἀποκτείνωσι, *that they should kill the prisoners*, defines βουλή, and circumscribes the declarative or supplementary infinitive. W. § 44. 8; S. § 162. 3. 2. Meyer after Fritzsche never admits this use, but insists on ἵνα as telic even here. — Of the rigor with which those were liable to be punished who were charged with the custody of prisoners, if the latter escaped from them in any way, we have had proof in 12, 19 and 16, 27.

V. 43. It will be recollected that, according to the Roman custom, each of the prisoners was chained to a particular soldier, who was his keeper. As to the relation of these soldiers to the centurion, see on v. 31. — ἐκώλυσεν αὐτοὺς τοῦ βουλήματος, *restrained them from their purpose.* Thus it happened again (see v. 24) that Paul's companions were indebted to their connection with him for the preservation of their lives. τέ connects this clause with the next, because of their co-ordinate relation to βουλόμενος. — ἀποῤῥίψαντας has a reciprocal sense. — ἐξιέναι, *to go forth,* not from the ship, which is the force of ἀπό in the participle just before, but from the sea ἐπὶ τὴν γῆν.

V. 44. τοὺς λοιποὺς is the subject of ἐξιέναι, repeated from the preceding clause. — ἐπὶ σανίσιν, *upon boards,* such probably as were in use about the ship, but not parts of it, which would confound this clause with the next. — ἐπί τινων τῶν ἀπὸ τοῦ πλοίου, *upon some of the pieces from the ship,* which they themselves tore away or which the surge had broken off. Most critics distinguish the two expressions in this manner. Kuinoel renders σανίσιν, *tables.* A few understand that term of the permanent parts of the vessel, and τινων ἀπὸ τοῦ πλοίου of such things as seats, barrels, and the like which were floating away from the wreck. But articles of this description they would be likely to have lost, or to have thrown into the sea before this time. — οὕτως, *thus,* i. e. in the two ways that have been mentioned. — διασωθῆναι, *were saved.* This was not the first peril of the kind from which the apostle had been delivered. In 2 Cor. 11, 25, he says, "thrice I suffered shipwreck, a night and a day have I spent in the deep;" and he recorded that statement several years before the present disaster.

CHAPTER XXVIII.

VERSES 1–10. *Their Abode during the Winter at Melita.*

V. 1. ἐπέγνωσαν, κ. τ. λ., *they ascertained* (by intercourse probably with the inhabitants) *that the island is called Melita.* That this was the modern Malta cannot well be doubted. An island with the same name, now Meleda, lies up the Adriatic on the coast of Dalmatia, which some have maintained to be the one where Paul was wrecked. Bryant defended that opinion. It is advocated still in Valpy's Notes on the New Testament. The argument for that opinion founded on the name Adriatic has been already refuted in the remarks on 27, 27. It has also been alleged for it, that no poisonous serpents are found at present on Malta. Mr. Smith mentions Coleridge (Table Talk, p. 185) as urging that difficulty. The more populous and cultivated state of the island accounts for the disappearance of such reptiles. Naturalists inform us that these animals become extinct or disappear as the aboriginal forests of a country are cleared up, or as the soil is otherwise brought under cultivation. See note on v. 3. It would be difficult to find a surface of equal extent in so artificial a state as that of Malta at the present day. The positive reasons for the common belief as to the place of the shipwreck are, that the traditional evidence sustains it; that Malta lies in the track of a vessel driven by a northeast wind; that the reputed locality of the wreck agrees with Luke's account; that the Alexandrian ship in which they reëmbarked would very naturally winter there, but not at Meleda; and that the subsequent course of the voyage to Puteoli is that which a vessel would pursue in going from Malta, but not from the other place. Malta is sixty miles from Cape Passero, the southern point of Sicily, and two hundred miles from the African coast. It is farther from the main land than any other island in the Mediterranean. It is seventeen miles in length, nine miles in its greatest breadth, and sixty miles in circumference. It is nearly equi-distant between the two ends of the Mediterranean. Its highest point is said to be six hundred feet above the level of the sea.

V. 2. οἱ δὲ βάρβαροι. The inhabitants are called *barbarians* with reference to their language, which was not that either of the Greeks or Romans; not because they were rude and degraded. It is strange that Coleridge should say that the Melitæans cannot be meant here because they were highly civilized. These islanders belonged to the Phœnician race, and spoke a Semitic dialect, most probably the Punic, i. e. the Phœnician as spoken by the people of Carthage. "The Hebrew language," in its widest extent, says Hupfeld, "was the language not merely of the Hebrews, but of the other nations that inhabited *Canaan*, or *Palæstina*, especially of the Phœnicians, so renowned as a commercial people in the ancient world, and of the Carthaginians descended from them. This is proved especially by the proper names of the Canaanites in the Bible, and of the Phœnicians and Carthaginians in the classic writers, which are all formed in the Hebrew manner, and also by the remains of the Phœnician and the Punic language on Phœnician monuments and in the classics, so far as these have been as yet deciphered."[1] The Greeks and Romans who settled on the island at different times never introduced to any great extent their language or customs. — οὐ τὴν τυχοῦσαν. See on 19, 11. — προσελάβοντο, *received to themselves*, or to their regard; comp. Rom. 14, 1 (De Wet.); not to their fire (Mey.). — διὰ τὸν ὑετὸν τὸν ἐφεστῶτα, *on account of the rain which came upon* us (De Wet. Rob.); the *present rain* (Wetst. E. V.). They would suffer the more from this inclement weather after so much exposure and fatigue. This remark in regard to the rain and cold disproves the assumption of some critics that it was a Sirocco wind, i. e. from the southeast, which Paul's ship encountered. That wind does not continue to blow more than two or three days, and is hot and sultry even as late as the month of November.

V. 3. συστρέψαντος .... πλῆθος, *Now Paul having collected a great number* (a heap) *of dry sticks*, such as would naturally be found among the rocks around the shore. — ἔχιδνα, *a viper*. The Greeks applied this term to that reptile in distinction from other serpents, as is evident from Aristot. Lib. I. c. 6: ἀλλ' οἱ μὲν ἄλλοι ᾠοτοκοῦσιν ὄφεις, ἡ δ' ἔχιδνα μόνον ζωοτοκεῖ. Vipers are the only viviparous serpents in Europe. It was remarked above that the viper is unknown in Malta at the present day. "No person," says Mr. Smith, "who has studied the changes which the operations of man have produced on the Fauna (animals) of any country, will be surprised that a particular species of reptiles should have disappeared from that of Malta. My friend, the Rev. Mr. Landsborough, in his interesting excursions in Arran, has repeatedly noticed the gradual disappearance of the viper from that island since it has become more frequented. Mr. Lyell,[2] in quot-

[1] It has been frequently asserted that the ancient Punic is the basis of the language spoken by the native Maltese of the present day. That opinion is incorrect. Malta, at the time of the Saracen irruption, was overrun by Arabs, from whom the common people of the island derive their origin. The dialect spoken by them is a corrupt Arabic, agreeing essentially with that of the Moors, but intermixed to a greater extent with words from the Italian, Spanish, and other European languages. The Maltese language approaches so nearly to the Arabic that the islanders are readily understood in all the ports of Africa and Syria. Gesenius first investigated thoroughly this dialect in his Versuch über die maltesische Sprache, etc. (Leipzig 1810). He has given the results of this investigation in his Article on *Arabien* in Ersch and Gruber's Encyklopädie. In his History of the Hebrew Language, he remarks that, although the ancestral pride of the Maltese themselves may dispose them to trace back their language to the old Punic, yet it contains nothing which is not explained far more naturally out of the modern Arabic, than as the product of so ancient a tongue.

[2] Principles of Geology (7th ed.), p. 655.

ing the travels of Spix and Martius in Brazil, observes: 'They speak of the dangers to which they were exposed from the jaguar, *the poisonous serpents*, crocodiles, scorpions, centipedes, and spiders. But with the increasing population and cultivation of the country, say these naturalists, these evils will gradually diminish; when the inhabitants have cut down the woods, drained the marshes, made roads in all directions, and founded villages and towns, man will, by degrees, triumph over the rank vegetation and the noxious animals.'" — ἐκ τῆς θέρμης, *from the heat*, the effect of it (De Wet.); or (less appropriate to the noun) from the place of it, as explained by Winer (§ 47. 5. b.) and others. But the best manuscripts read ἀπό (Lchm. Tsch. Mey.), and the sense then is (comp. 20, 9; Luke 19, 3), *on account of the heat.* The viper had evidently been taken up among the sticks which Paul had gathered; and, as may be inferred from ἐπιθέντος ἐπὶ τὴν πυράν, had been thrown with them into the fire. This latter supposition is required by the local sense of ἐκ τῆς θέρμης, and is entirely consistent with the causal sense. The viper was probably in a torpid state, and was suddenly restored to activity by the heat. It was now cold, in consequence both of the storm and the lateness of the season (v. 2); and such reptiles become torpid as soon as the temperature falls sensibly below the mean temperature of the place which they inhabit. Vipers, too, lurk in rocky places, and that is the character of the region where the incident occurred. They are accustomed, also, to dart at their enemies, sometimes several feet at a bound; and hence the one mentioned here could have reached the hand of Paul as he stood in the vicinity of the fire.[1] — Instead of ἐξελθοῦσα (T. R.), *having come forth*, the more descriptive διεξελθοῦσα (Tsch. Mey.), represents the viper as *having come forth* (from the fire) *through* the sticks among which it was taken up. — καθῆψε, *fastened itself*, in the sense of the middle. This reflexive use of the active occurs only here, which accounts for καθήψατο, as read in some copies.

V. 4. ὡς δὲ, κ. τ. λ., *Now as the barbarians saw the animal hanging from his hand*, to which it clung by the mouth. Aristotle also uses θηρίον of the viper. That it was "venomous" (E. V.) results, not from this mode of designation, but from ἔχιδνα. Luke does not say expressly that Paul was bitten; but the nature of the reptile, the leap, the clinging to his hand, leave us to infer that

[1] For the information in this note concerning the habits of the viper, I am indebted chiefly to Professor Agassiz of Cambridge.

with almost entire certainty. Those who stood near and witnessed the occurrence supposed evidently that such was the fact. That he should have escaped being bitten under such circumstances would have been hardly less miraculous than that the ordinary effect of the poison should have been counteracted. We seem to be justified, according to either view, in regarding his preservation as a fulfilment of the promise of Christ in Mark 16, 17. 18. On the form of κρεμάμενον, see K. § 179. 5. — φονεύς .... οὗτος, *this man is a murderer.* They perceived from his chain, perhaps, or some other indication, that Paul was a prisoner. The attack of the viper proved to them that he must have committed some atrocious crime. φονεύς points, not to a specific offence, but to the class of offenders to which they supposed he might belong. — ἡ δίκη ζῆν οὐκ εἴασεν, *justice suffered not to live.* Observe the past tense. They consider his doom as sealed. Vengeance, in their view, had already smitten its victim.

V. 5. ἔπαθεν οὐδὲν κακόν, *suffered no evil.* This statement agrees with the supposition either that he had not been bitten, or that the poison had produced no effect upon him.

V. 6. αὐτὸν μέλλειν πίμπρασθαι, *that he would be inflamed* (lit. *burn*), since inflammation is attended with heat. — καταπίπτειν ἄφνω νεκρόν, *that he would suddenly fall down dead.* Sudden collapse and death ensue often from the bite of serpents. Shakspeare speaks as a naturalist when he says of the asp-bitten Cleopatra,

> "Trembling she stood, and on the sudden dropped."

— μηδὲν ἄτοπον, *nothing bad,* injurious; in a moral sense, in Luke 23, 41. — μεταβαλλόμενοι may take after it τὴν γνώμην or omit it. — θεὸν αὐτὸν εἶναι, *that he was a god.* Bengel: "Aut latro, inquiunt, aut deus; sic modo tauri, modo lapides (14, 13. 19). Datur tertium; *homo* DEI."

V. 7. περὶ τὸν τόπον ἐκεῖνον, *around that place,* the one where they were wrecked. Tradition places the residence of Publius at Citta Vecchia, the Medina of the Saracens; which, though in the centre of Malta, is but a few miles from the coast (see on v. 1). — τῷ πρώτῳ τῆς νήσου. There can be no doubt that *Publius* is called *the first* (or chief) *of the island* because he was the Roman governor. Melita was first conquered by the Romans during the Punic wars, and in the time of Cicero (4 Ver. c. 18) was annexed to the prætorship of Sicily. The prætor of that island would naturally have a legate or deputy at this place.

The title πρῶτος, under which he is mentioned here, has been justly cited by apologetic writers, as Tholuck, Ebrard, Krabbe, Baumgarten, Lardner, Paley, Howson, as a striking proof of Luke's accuracy. No other ancient writer happens to have given his official designation; but two inscriptions, one in Greek and the other in Latin, have been discovered in Malta, in which we meet with the same title employed by Luke in this passage.[1] It is impossible to believe that Publius, or any other single individual, would be called the *first man* in the island, except by way of official eminence. It will be observed that the father of Publius was still living, and during his lifetime he would naturally have taken precedence of the son, had the distinction in this case been one which belonged to the family.[2] — ἡμᾶς ἐξένισεν,

[1] "The one in Greek is supposed to form a votive inscription by a Roman knight, named Aulus Castricius, 'first of the Melitans' (πρῶτος Μελιταίων), to the emperor. The Latin inscription, on the pedestal of a column, was discovered at Citta Vecchia, in excavating the foundation of the Casa del Magistrato, in 1747."

[2] I have allowed this note to remain as it stood in the other edition, as it represents the general opinion of scholars respecting the official rank of Publius. Yet it is possible that they have erred in assigning this precise import to the title. I insert with thanks for the suggestion the following criticism of President Woolsey on this point: "The best information which we can obtain respecting the situation of Malta at the time of Paul's visit, renders it doubtful, to say the least, whether the interpreters are in the right as it regards the station of Publius. In a Greek inscription of an earlier date we find mention made of two persons holding the office of *archon* or magistrate in the island. A later inscription of the times of the Emperors may be translated as follows: 'Lucius Pudens, son of Claudius, of the tribe Quirina, a Roman eques, first [πρῶτος, as in Acts] and patron of the Melitaeans, after being magistrate and having held the post of flamen to Augustus, erected this.' Here it appears that the person named was still chief man of the island, although his magistracy had expired. From this inscription and others in Latin found at Gozzo, it is probable that the inhabitants of both islands had received the privilege of Roman citizenship, and were enrolled in the tribe Quirina. The magistracy was, no doubt, that of the Duumvirs, the usual municipal chief officers. The other titles correspond with titles to be met with on marbles relating to towns in Italy. Thus the title of *chief* corresponds to that of *princeps* in the colony of Pisa, and is probably no more a name of office than the title of *patron*. For no such officer is known to have existed in the colonies or in the *municipia*, and the *princeps coloniæ* of Pisa is mentioned at a time when it is said that owing to a contention between candidates there were no magistrates." — The difference does not affect the value of the alleged proof of the narrator's accuracy; for in either case the term is a Roman title, and is applied by Luke to a person who bears it at the right time and in the right place. Indeed, the appellation of *prince* or *patron* would be more striking than that of *magistrate*, inasmuch as the range of its application is narrower, and a writer who was not stating the truth would be more liable to introduce it under circumstances that would render it inadmissible.

entertained us, viz. Luke, Paul, Aristarchus (27, 2), and no doubt the noble-hearted Julius; not the entire two hundred and seventy-six (Bmg.), as so indiscriminate a hospitality would be uncalled for and without any sufficient motive.

V. 8. πυρετοῖς. The plural has been supposed to describe the fever with reference to its recurrent attacks or paroxysms. This is one of those expressions in Luke's writings that have been supposed to indicate his professional training as a physician. See also 12, 23; 13, 11; and especially the comparison (ὁ ἱδρὼς αὐτοῦ ὡσεὶ θρόμβοι αἵματος καταβαίνοντες) in his Gospel (22, 44). It is correct to attach to them that significancy. No other writer of the New Testament exhibits this sort of technical precision in speaking of diseases. The disorder with which the father of Publius was affected was dysentery combined with fever. It was formerly asserted that a dry climate, like that of Malta, would not produce such a disorder; but we have now the testimony of physicians resident in that island, that it is by no means uncommon there at the present day.

V. 10. οἳ καί, *who also*, on their part, i. e. while they came and were healed of their maladies. — πολλαῖς τιμαῖς ἐτίμησαν ἡμᾶς, *honored us* (viz. Paul and his companions) *with many honors*, courtesies. They were entertained with a generous hospitality, and distinguished by marks of special regard and kindness. Some render τιμαῖς *rewards* or *presents;* but the next clause appears to limit their reception of the favors in question to the time of their departure and to the relief of their necessary wants. It is certain that they did not, even then, accept the gifts which were proffered to them as a reward for their services; for that would have been at variance with the command of Christ in Matt. 10, 8.

VERSES 11–16. *Prosecution of the Journey to Rome.*

V. 11. μετὰ τρεῖς μῆνας. The *three months* are the time that they remained on the island. They were probably the months of November, December, and January. The season may have admitted of their putting to sea earlier than usual. The arrival at Melita could not have been later than October, for a brief interval only lay between the fast (27, 9) and the beginning of the storm (27, 27). — ἐν πλοίῳ παρακεχειμακότι. Luke does not state why this vessel had wintered here. It is a circumstance which shows the consistency of the narrative. The storm which occasioned the wreck of Paul's vessel had delayed this one so long, that it was necessary on reaching Melita to suspend the voyage until spring. This vessel had been during the winter at Valetta, which must always have been the principal harbor of Malta. — παρασήμῳ Διοσκούροις, *with the sign Dioscuri,* or *distinguished by Dioscuri,* i. e. having images of Castor and Pollux painted or carved on the prow, from which images the vessel may have been named. This use of figure-heads on ancient ships was very common. See Dict. of Antt., Art. *Insigne.* Castor and Pollux were the favorite gods of seamen, the winds and waves being supposed to be specially subject to their control. It is of them that Horace says (Od. 1. 12. 27–32):

> "Quorum simul alba nautis
> Stella refulsit,
> Defluit saxis agitatus humor;
> Concidunt venti, fugiuntque nubes,
> Et minax (quod sic voluere) ponto
> Unda recumbit."

See, also, Od. 1. 3. 2. παρασήμῳ may be a noun or an adjective. The former appears to have been most common in this application. The other construction is easier as regards the dative, and is preferred by De Wette.

V. 12. Συρακούσας, *Syracusæ.* This city, the capital of Sicily, on the southeastern coast of that island, was about eighty miles north from Melita. It was built partly on the adjacent island of Ortygia, and from that circumstance, or as others say because it included at length several villages, may have received its plural name. The modern Siracusa or Siragossa occupies only a part of the ancient city, viz. Ortygia (Forbg.). — ἐπεμείναμεν. They may have stopped here for trade, or in the hope of a better wind.

V. 13. περιελθόντες, *having come around* or *about.* The sense of the preposition it is impossible to determine with certainty. One supposition is, that it refers to their frequent alteration of the ship's course; in other words, to their tacking, because the wind was unfavorable. So Smith, Howson, and others, explain the word. Mr. Lewin thinks that "as the wind was westerly, and they were under the shelter of the high mountainous range of Etna, they were obliged to stand out to sea in order to fill their sails, and so come to Rhegium by a circuitous sweep."[1] Another view is, that they were compelled by the wind to follow

[1] "I was informed by a friend many years ago, that when he made the voyage himself from Syracuse to Rhegium, the vessel in which he sailed took a similar circuit for a similar reason." Lewin, II. p. 736.

closely the sinuosities of the coast, to proceed circuitously. De Wette says, which is much less probable, that they may have gone *around* Sicily, or the southern extremity of Italy. — εἰς Ῥήγιον, *unto Rhegium*, now Reggio, which was an Italian seaport, opposite to the northeastern point of Sicily. Here they remained a day, when the wind, which had been adverse since their leaving Syracuse, became fair, and they resumed the voyage. The steamers between Naples and Malta touch at Messina, and Reggio appears in full view on the Italian side. If Paul passed here in February (v. 11 above), the mountains on the island and on the main land were still covered with snow, and presented to the eye a dreary aspect. — ἐπιγενομένου νότου, *a south wind having arisen on* them; comp. the compound participle in v. 2, and in 27, 20. The dative of the person is often expressed after ἐπί with this force; see Herod. 8. 13. — δευτεραῖοι, *on the second day*; comp. John 11, 39. This adverbial use of the ordinals is classical. K. § 264. 3. b. — εἰς Ποτιόλους. *Puteoli*, now Pozzuoli, was eight miles southwest from Neapolis, the modern Naples. It derived its name from the springs (*putei*) which abound there, or from the odor of the waters (*a putendo*).[1] Its earlier Greek name was Δικαιάρχεια. It was the principal port south of Rome. Nearly all the Alexandrian and a great part of the Spanish trade with Italy was brought hither. The seventy-seventh Letter of Seneca gives a lively description of the interest which the arrival of the corn-ships from Egypt was accustomed to excite among the inhabitants of that town. A mole with twenty-five arches stretched itself into the sea, at the entrance of this bay, alongside of which the vessels as they arrived cast anchor for the delivery of their freight and passengers. Thirteen of the piers which upheld this immense structure, show their forms still above the water, and point out to us as it were the very footsteps of the apostle as he passed from the ship to the land. — The voyage from Rhegium to Puteoli, which the Castor and Pollux accomplished in less than two days, was about one hundred and eighty miles. The passage, therefore, was a rapid one; but as examples of the ancient rate of sailing show, not unprecedented. Herodotus states that a ship could sail seven hundred stadia in a day, and six hundred in a night, i. e. thirteen hundred in twenty-four hours, which would be at the rate of about one hundred and fifty English miles a day. Strabo says, that a voyage could be made from Sammo-

[1] As examples, travellers will recollect the Grotto del Cane near Cumæ, and the Baths of Nero at Baia.

nium to Egypt in four days, reckoning the distance at five thousand stadia, or about five hundred and seventy-three miles. This would be sailing one hundred and forty-three miles in twenty-four hours, or six miles an hour. Pliny mentions several voyages which would be considered very good in modern times. He says that the prefects Galerius and Babilius arrived at Alexandria, the former on the seventh, the latter on the sixth day, after leaving the Straits of Messina. He states, also, that passages were made, under favorable circumstances, from the Straits of Hercules to Ostia, in seven days; from the nearest port of Spain, in four; from the province of Narbonne, in three; and from Africa, in two. Probably the most rapid run mentioned by any ancient writer is that of Arrian, in his Periplus of the Euxine, who says that "they got under way about daybreak," and that by midday they had come more than five hundred stadia; that is, more than fifty geographical miles, which is at least eight miles an hour.[1] The mean of the foregoing examples is seven miles an hour; and if we suppose that the Castor and Polux sailed at that rate, the passage would have required only about twenty-six hours. This result agrees perfectly with Luke's account; for he states that they left Rhegium on one day and arrived at Puteoli on the next. Their course, it will be observed, was nearly due north, and they were favored with a south wind.

V. 14. ἐπ' αὐτοῖς, *with* (lit. *upon*) *them;* comp. 21, 4. The local idea blends itself with the personal. See W. § 48. c. — ἡμέρας ἑπτά, *a week;* see on 20, 6. They had an opportunity to spend a Sabbath with the Christians there. The centurion granted this delay, not improbably, in order to gratify the wishes of Paul. After such events, the prisoner would have a power over his keeper well nigh unbounded. In the mean time, the news of the apostle's arrival would travel to Rome, and thus prepare the way for what we read in the next verse. — καὶ οὕτως, κ. τ. λ., *and so*, after the interval thus spent, *we went unto Rome;* not *came* unless the remark be proleptic. The incidents in v. 15 occur on the way thither. On leaving Puteoli, Julius and his party would proceed naturally to Capua, about twelve miles, the nearest point for intersecting the Appian Way. The distance from Capua to Rome by this road was about one hundred and twenty-five miles.[2]

[1] I have relied for these statements, partly on Forbiger, and partly on Biscoe and Smith.

[2] Mr. Howson's map of this journey to the city will enable the reader to follow the apostle's course very distinctly.

V. 15. Two companies of the Christians at Rome went forth to meet the apostle; but separately and at different times. Hence the advanced party reached *Appii Forum*, about forty miles from Rome, before Paul appeared; the later party met him at *Tres Tabernæ*, which was thirty miles from Rome. (Itiner. Antonin.) Other estimates (Itiner. Hieros.) place Appii Forum a few miles nearer to Rome. This town was named from Appius Claudius Cæcus, who built the Appian Way. It lay on the northern border of the Pontine Marshes, at the end of the canal which extended thither from a point a few miles above Anxur or Terracina. Horace (Sat. 1. 5. 4) speaks of Appii Forum as "full of boatmen," who were engaged in forwarding passengers over this canal, a distance of twenty miles. The Appian Way ran near the canal, and it would depend on circumstances unknown to us, whether the centurion travelled in one mode or the other. Strabo mentions that night-travellers (as in the case of Horace) usually preferred the boat. The present Locanda di Foro Appio, a wretched inn, marks probably the site of Appii Forum. It is almost the only human shelter in the midst of a solitude enlivened once by incessant commerce and travel. — *Tres Tabernæ*, as appears from one of Cicero's letters to Atticus (2. 12), must have been near where the cross-road from Antium fell into the Appian Way. It is thought to have been not far from the modern Cisterna, the bulk of which lies on the traveller's left in going from Rome to Naples, under the shadow of the Volscian Hills. — οὓς . . . . θάρσος, *whom Paul seeing gave thanks to God and took courage.* He may have met a few of the Roman Christians in foreign lands, but was a stranger to nearly all of them except in name, and would approach the city with the natural anxiety of one who had yet to learn what feelings they entertained towards him. Such a cordial reception, such impatience to see him and welcome him to their hearts, would scatter all his doubts, and thrill his bosom with gratitude and joy. The church at Rome contained heathen converts as well as Jewish. The apostle of the Gentiles would see a special cause for encouragement and thanksgiving, in the presence of such witnesses of the success of the gospel in the great metropolis.

V. 16. As Paul travelled on the Appian Way, he must have entered Rome through the Capenian Gate, not far from the modern Porta San Sebastiano. — ὁ ἑκατόνταρχος . . . . στρατοπεδάρχῃ, *the centurion delivered the prisoners to the commander of the camp*, i. e. the prætorian camp, where the emperor's body-guard was quartered. See Phil. 1, 13. This camp or garrison had been built by Sejanus, the favorite of Tiberius, in the vicinity of the *Porta Nomentana* (Win.). The exact spot is known to be that within the projection, at the northeast corner of the present city-wall. Nearly all critics at present, as Olshausen, Anger, De Wette, Meyer, Wieseler, suppose this officer, i. e. the *præfectus prætorio*, to be meant here. The prisoners who were sent to Rome from the provinces were committed to his custody. There is a difference of opinion in regard to the article. The command of the prætorian guard was originally divided between two prefects, but during the reign of Claudius, Burrus Afranius, a distinguished Roman general, was appointed sole *præfectus prætorio*, and retained this office as late certainly as the beginning of A. D. 62. On his death the command was committed again to two prefects, as it had been at first, and this continued to be the arrangement until a late period of the empire. The time of Paul's arrival at Rome could not have been far from A. D. 62, as admits of being shown by an independent calculation (see Introd. § 6. 5). Wieseler (p. 86) supposes τῷ στρατοπεδάρχῃ to refer to Burrus, as sole prefect at that time, and he urges the expression as a reason for assigning the apostle's arrival to A. D. 62, or the year preceding. It is very possible that this view is the correct one. It would furnish a striking coincidence between Luke's narrative and the history of the times. Yet, in speaking of *the prefect*, the writer may have meant the one who acted in this particular case, the one who took into his charge the prisoners whom the centurion transferred to him, whether he was sole prefect or had a colleague with him; comp. 24, 23. De Wette assents to Meyer in this explanation of the article. The expression, as so understood, does not affirm that there was but one prefect, or deny it. — τῷ δὲ Παύλῳ, κ. τ. λ., *But it was permitted to Paul* (i. e. by the prefect to whom he had been consigned) *to dwell by himself*, instead of being confined with the other prisoners. This was a favor which the Roman laws often granted to those who were not suspected of any very serious offence. The centurion, who had already shown himself so friendly to the apostle, may have interceded for him; or the terms in which Festus had reported the case (see on 26, 32) may have conciliated the prefect. In the use of this liberty, Paul repaired first to the house of some friend (v. 23), and afterwards rented an appartment for his own use (v. 30). — σὺν τῷ φυλάσσοντι αὐτὸν στρατιώτῃ, *with the soldier who guarded him*, and to whom he was fastened by a chain. Different soldiers relieved each other in the performance of this office. Hence, as Paul states in Phil. 1, 13, he became, in the course of time, personally known to a great number of the prætorian soldiers, and through them to their comrades. The notoriety which he thus acquired served to make his character as a prisoner for the sake of the gospel more widely known, and thus to aid him in his efforts to extend the knowledge of Christ. To this result the apostle refers in Phil. 1, 12 sq.

VERSES 17–22. *Paul has an Interview with the chief Men of the Jews at Rome.*

V. 17. μετὰ ἡμέρας τρεῖς, *after three days*, on the third from his arrival; comp. 25, 1. The apostle's untiring activity is manifest to the last.—τῶν Ἰουδαίων are the unbelieving *Jews*, not the Jewish Christians. Their *first* men would be the rulers of the synagogue, or would include them. — ἐναντίον governs the dative here, as in 1 Thess. 2, 15; comp. 26, 9. — ποιήσας, *though I had done*. — ἐξ Ἱεροσολύμων, *from Jerusalem*, whence he had been sent to Cæsarea. — εἰς τὰς χεῖρας τῶν Ῥωμαίων, *into the hands of the Romans*, viz. Felix and Festus, who represented their countrymen. The remark refers to them, as is evident from ἀνακρίναντες in the next verse.

V. 19. ἀντιλεγόντες, *objecting*, describes very mildly the opposition of the Jews to the apostle's acquital. ἀδελφοί, λαῷ, πατρῴοις, Ἰσραήλ, which follow so rapidly breathe the same conciliatory spirit. Such expressions show how self-forgetting Paul was, how ready to acknowledge what was common to his opponents and himself. — ἠναγκάσθην ἐπικαλέσασθαι Καίσαρα, *I was compelled to appeal unto Cæsar;* as his only resort in order to save himself from assassination or judicial murder; comp. 25, 9 sq. — οὐχ ὡς, κ. τ. λ., *not as having* (i. e. because I had) *anything* (as the motive for this appeal) *to charge against my nation*, viz. before the emperor. The apostle would repel a suspicion which he supposed it not unnatural for the Roman Jews to entertain; or, possibly, would deny an imputation with which the Jews in Palestine had actually aspersed him (Wiesl.). Paul says *my nation* (ἔθνους μου) and not *people* (see λαῷ above), because Καίσαρα just before distinguishes the Romans and the Jews from each other.

V. 20. διὰ ταύτην οὖν τὴν αἰτίαν, *On this account, therefore*, viz. that his feelings towards the Jews were so friendly. — παρεκάλεσα ὑμᾶς ἰδεῖν, *I called*, invited, *you that I might see* you. Some supply ἐμέ as the object of ἰδεῖν, which destroys the unity of the sentence. — ἕνεκεν . . . . Ἰσραήλ, *for on account of the hope of Israel*

i. e. the hope of a Messiah which the nation entertained; comp. 26, 6. This clause is coördinate with the one which precedes. It states an additional reason why he had sought the present interview. — τὴν ἅλυσιν ταύτην περίκειμαι, *I am compassed with this chain*, have my arm bound with it. So, also, when the apostle wrote in Phil. 4, 4, "Rejoice in the Lord always; and, again, I say, rejoice," he was manacled as a felon, and was liable at any moment to be condemned to the wild beasts or the block. The construction is similar to that of the accusative after passive verbs; comp. περίκειται ἀσθένειαν in Heb. 5, 2.

V. 21. ἡμεῖς οὔτε γράμματα, κ. τ. λ., *We received neither letters*, etc. This statement refers to their having received no official information, either written or oral, in regard to the circumstances under which Paul had been sent to Rome. Some have supposed the Jews to be insincere in this declaration, as if it was improbable that they should have been uninformed in regard to so important an event. But we have no sufficient reason for calling in question their veracity. The Palestine Jews could hardly have foreseen the issue to which the case was so suddenly brought; and hence, before the apostle's appeal, would have deemed it unnecessary to apprise the Jews at Rome of the progress of the trial. It is barely possible that they could have forwarded intelligence since the appeal had taken place. Paul departed for Italy evidently soon after he had appealed, and must have availed himself of one of the last opportunities for such a voyage which the season of the year allowed. Having spent the winter at Melita, he had proceeded to Rome at the earliest moment in the spring; so that in the ordinary course of things he must have arrived there in advance of any ship that might have left Palestine after the reopening of navigation. — Repeat ἀπὸ τῆς Ἰουδαίας after παραγενόμενος. — τὶς τῶν ἀδελφῶν, *any one of the brethren*, of our countrymen, i. e. as a special messenger, as a complainant.

V. 22. ἀξιοῦμεν δὲ παρὰ σοῦ ἀκοῦσαι, *But* (though in the absence of such information we offer no complaint) *we deem it proper* (Mey. Rob.) *to hear from thee;* comp. 15, 38. The verb may also mean *we desire* (De Wet. E. V.), but is less common in that sense. — περὶ μὲν γὰρ τῆς αἱρέσεως ταύτης, *for concerning this sect* of which Paul was known to be an adherent; and as that circumstance (γάρ) was not in his favor, they intimate that he was bound to vindicate himself from the reproach of such a connection. The Jews, it will be observed, in their reply to the apostle, abstain from any allusion to the Christians at Rome; indeed, they might have expressed themselves in the same manner had

58

no church existed there at this time, or had they been entirely ignorant of its existence. To understand them, however, as affirming that they had heard of the sect only by report, that they possessed no personal knowledge of any who were connected with it, is certainly unauthorized. Baur[1] proceeds on this false assumption, and then represents the passage as inconsistent with the Epistle to the Romans, which was written several years before this, and exhibits to us a flourishing church in the Roman metropolis. Zeller says the same thing. The peculiarity in the case is not by any means that the Jews denied that they were acquainted with those who held the Christian faith, but that they avoided so carefully any reference to the fact; what they knew was matter of general notoriety (πανταχοῦ ἀντιλέγεται); they decline the responsibility of asserting anything on the ground of their own personal knowledge. Various explanations have been given of this reserve on the part of the Jews. Olshausen's hypothesis is, that the opposition between the Jewish Christians and the Jews had become such, before Claudius banished the latter from Rome, as to separate them entirely from each other; and consequently that the Christians there remained in fact unknown to the Jews who returned to Rome after the decree of banishment ceased to be in force. This view is improbable, and has found no supporters. The opinion of many of the older critics, to which Tholuck[2] also has returned, is that the πρῶτοι τῶν Ἰουδαίων affected to be thus ignorant in regard to the Roman Christians; that they wished to deceive the apostle, and uttered a direct falsehood when they told him that they had received no information concerning him from the Palestine Jews. The best account of this peculiarity, it appears to me, is that which Philippi has suggested in his recent Commentary on the Epistle to the Romans.[3] The situation of the Jews at Rome, after their recent banishment by Claudius, was still critical and insecure. It was very important for them to avoid the displeasure of the government; to abstain from any act or attitude that would revive the old charge against them of being quarrelsome or factious. They saw that Paul was regarded with evident favor by the Roman officers; they had heard from him that the procurator would have acquitted him, but the obstinate Jews had compelled

1 Paulus, der Apostel, sein Leben und Wirken, seine Briefe und seine Lehre, p. 368 sq.

2 Commentar zum Briefe Pauli an die Römer (1842), p. 14.

3 Commentar über den Brief Pauli an die Römer, von Friedrich A. Philippi (1848), p. xv.

him to appeal to Cæsar. Having had no intelligence from Judea, they might fear that their countrymen there had gone too far, and had placed it in the power of Paul to use the circumstance to the disadvantage of the Jewish cause at Rome. Hence they considered it advisable for the present to conciliate the apostle, to treat him mildly, to keep out of sight their own relations to the Christian sect. They say what was true. No special and express information had been forwarded to them respecting his person and the occurrence mentioned by him, and they knew that the sect had everywhere an evil name. But they suppress their own view in regard to the Christian faith, as something they do not consider it necessary and expedient to avow, and, out of fear of the Roman magistrates, would draw as little attention as possible to their hostile position towards the Christians.

VERSES 23–29. *His Second Interview with the Jews.*

V. 23. ταξάμενοι δὲ αὐτῷ ἡμέραν, *Now having appointed for him a day*, at his own suggestion perhaps, since by leaving it to them to designate the time he would be more sure of their presence. — εἰς τὴν ξενίαν, *unto his lodging*. The term implies (Hesych.) that it was a place where he was entertained as a guest (comp. Philem. 22); and those critics are right who distinguish it from the "hired house" mentioned in v. 30. The apostle, at first, as would be natural, was received into some one of the Christian families at Rome; but after a time, for the sake of greater convenience or independence, he removed to apartments which would be more entirely subject to his own control. That Aquila (Rom. 16, 3) became his host again as he had been at Corinth (18, 3) is not impossible. — πλείονες, *more* than on the former occasion. — πείθων . . . . Ἰησοῦ, i. e. *and persuading them of the things concerning Jesus*. For the double accusative, see on 19, 8. Here, too, the act of the participle refers to the speaker's aim or object, without including the result. It may be inferred from what follows, that the greater part of those whom Paul addressed withstood his efforts to win them to the truth; comp. v. 25.

V. 24. οἱ μέν and οἱ δέ distribute the Jews into opposite parties. The proportion which the convinced bore to the unbelieving we must gather from the drift of the narrative.

V. 25. ἀσύμφωνοι δὲ ὄντες πρὸς ἀλλήλους, *And being discordant among one another*. This variance they may be supposed to have evinced by an open declaration of their different views, by the expression of dissent and objection on the part of those who disbelieved. — εἰπόντος τοῦ Παύλου ῥῆμα ἕν, *Paul having said one word,* at the time of their departure (De Wet.); not as the occasion of it (Mey.). It was *one* final, significant word, as opposed to many words; comp. Luke 20, 3. — διὰ Ἠσαΐου, *through Isaiah.* See on 2, 16.

V. 26. λέγον, viz. Isa. 6, 9 sq., cited according to the Seventy. The passage is quoted also in Matt. 13, 14 sq. and John 12, 40. — For the Hebraistic ἀκοῇ ἀκούσετε, see the note on 4, 17. — οὐ μὴ συνῆτε may express the future result with more certainty than the future indicative. See on 13, 41. — For βλέποντες βλέψετε, see on 7, 34.

V. 28. οὖν, *therefore,* i. e. since they are so hardened and incorrigible. — ὅτι . . . . σωτήριον, *that to the Gentiles the salvation was sent,* i. e. by God in the coming of the apostle to Rome. — αὐτοί, *they* (emphatic), although they are heathen. — καὶ ἀκούσονται, *also will hear* it, viz. the message of this salvation. The object of the verb is implied in ἀπεστάλη. καί connects the reception with the offer of the gospel. — Our eyes trace here the last words in Luke's record, which fell from the lips of Paul. It is remarkable that they are precisely such words. The apostle of the Gentiles points again to his commission to preach to all nations, and declares that the heathen, to whom he was sent shall accept the Saviour whom the Jews disowned.

V. 29. This verse in the common text repeats what has been said in the eighteenth verse. It appears to be not genuine. Its principal witnesses are G H, the Ethiopic, and some of the later fathers. It is wanting in A B E, the Syriac, and the best Latin authorities. Leading critics, as Mill, Lachmann, Tischendorf, Green, reject the verse.

VERSES 30. 31. *The Condition of the Apostle during his Captivity.*

V. 30. ἔμεινε διετίαν ὅλην, *remained two whole years,* i. e. in the state mentioned, with the evident implication that at the end of that time his condition changed. Some critics deny the correctness of this inference; but the better opinion affirms it. Had the apostle been still in confinement, the writer would have employed more naturally the present tense or the perfect (*remains* or *has remained*) instead of the aorist. The reader's conclusion is, that the two years completed the term of the apostle's captivity, and that when Luke penned the sentence, the prisoner was either at liberty or else was no longer living. Lekebusch

(p. 415) pronounces this view an inevitable one. See on next verse. — The διετίαν ὅλην would bring the narrative down to A. D. 64. Some months lay between the commencement of this year and the outbreak of Nero's persecution. See Introd., p. 27. — ἐν ἰδίῳ μισθώματι, *in his own hired house*, i. e. hired at his own expense. In the bosom of a Christian church, the apostle could not have been destitute of the means of providing for such an expense. We learn, also, from Phil. 4, 14. 18, that during this captivity Paul received supplies from the church at Philippi. — ἀπεδέχετο, in its special sense, *received gladly*, because it afforded him such joy to preach the Gospel; comp. 15, 4; 18, 27.

V. 31. διδάσκων, sc. αὐτούς. The construction is similar to that in v. 23. — ἀκωλύτως, *without molestation* on the part of the Roman government.[1] According to the Roman laws, a citizen under arrest, in ordinary cases, could give security or bail, and thus enjoy his personal liberty until he was brought to trial. The freedom granted to Paul was so ample, that one might almost suppose that he was permitted to exercise that right; but it is rendered certain by Phil. 1, 13. 16, that he continued to be guarded by a Roman soldier. — Among the friends with Paul during this confinement who have been mentioned in our narrative, were Luke, Timothy, Epaphras, Mark, Aristarchus, and Tychicus. The interruption of his personal intercourse with the

[1] Agrippa the First was imprisoned in early life, at Rome. The account of his captivity confirms so entirely Luke's account of the manner in which Paul was treated as a Roman prisoner, (so unlike our modern usages,) that it may not be amiss to mention some of the circumstances. We obtain the information from Josephus (Antt. 18. 6. 5 sq.). Agrippa, on being arrested, was committed to Macro, the prætorian prefect, and confined in the prætorian camp. He was there kept under a guard of soldiers, to one of whom he was chained (called his συνδετός). A particular centurion had the oversight of the prisoner and the soldiers who guarded him. But the condition of those confined in this manner depended very much on the character of those who had the immediate charge of them. The soldiers who watched Agrippa treated him, at first, with great severity. Hence Antonia, a sister-in-law of Tiberius and a friend of Agrippa, interceded with Macro and induced him to appoint a guard known to be of a milder disposition. The situation of Agrippa was now improved. His friends who had been excluded from him, were permitted to visit him and to supply his necessary wants (comp. 24, 23). But during this time, about six months, he was still confined in the prætorian camp. On the death of Tiberius the mode of his captivity was changed again. Caligula ordered him to be removed from the prætorium to the house which he had occupied before he was bound. Here he was still guarded as a prisoner, but was subject to so much less restraint that his condition was one of comparative liberty. His captivity, in this last form of it, was doubtless like that of Paul during the two years that he "dwelt in his own hired house" at Rome.

churches caused the apostle to address them by letter, and thus the restraint on his liberty proved the means of opening to him a sphere of activity, which has given him access to all nations, which makes him the contemporary of every age. As nearly all critics allow, he wrote during this captivity his Epistles to the Ephesians, the Colossians, the Philippians, and Philemon. — It must suffice to allude merely to the subsequent history of the great apostle. I cannot hesitate to agree with those who believe that Paul on being brought to trial under his appeal to the emperor was acquitted, and, casting aside his chains, went forth to labor again for the spread of the gospel. We see from his letters written while he was a captive that he was expecting to regain his liberty. See, for example, Phil. 1, 25; 2, 23. 24; Philem. v. 22. Even if Paul entertained this belief as a matter of judgment merely, and not in the exercise of a faith warranted by a special revelation, we must allow at all events that he had good means for forming a correct opinion of his prospects, and should be supposed, therefore, to have realized his hope, and not to have been condemned, contrary to such manifest intimations of a different result. The journeys and labors indicated in the Pastoral Epistles make the supposition of an interval between a first and second imprisonment important if not indispensable as a means of reconciling Luke's account with this part of the apostle's correspondence. The facts mentioned in the letters to Titus and Timothy have no natural place in the portion of Paul's history recorded in the Acts. The style, too, and the circle of ideas in these Epistles indicate a later period in the life of the writer and in the progress of the churches, than that of the conclusion of Luke's narrative. Finally, the historical testimony, as derived from the earliest sources, asserts a second Roman captivity in the most explicit manner. Clemens, the disciple and companion of Paul, affirms that the apostle before his martyrdom travelled "to the boundary of the West," an expression which the Roman writers in that age applied to the Trans-Alpine countries; and the Canon of Muratori (A. D. 170) represents "a journey into Spain," as a well-known event in Paul's history. Eusebius states the common belief of the early churches, in these words: "After defending himself successfully it is currently reported that the apostle again went forth to proclaim the gospel, and afterwards came to Rome a second time, and was martyred under Nero." — Hints in the Epistles and traditions supply all that is known or conjectured respecting this last stage of the apostle's ministry. It is supposed, that on being liberated (writers do not agree as to the precise order), he visited again parts of Asia Minor and Greece; went to Crete and founded or more probably strengthened the churches there; made his long-contemplated journey to Spain; wrote his First Epistle to Timothy, and his Epistle to Titus; after several years of effective labor, was apprehended again as a leader of the Christian sect; was brought a second time as a prisoner of Christ to Rome; was tried there and condemned to suffer death. His Roman citizenship exempted him from the ignominy of crucifixion, and hence, according to the universal tradition, he was beheaded by the axe of the lictor. The same testimony places his martyrdom in the year A. D. 68, the last year of Nero's reign. It was in the daily expectation of this event that he wrote the last of his Epistles, the second to Timothy. It is in that Epistle, written as the aged servant of Christ looked back to his trials all surmounted, forward to the hour when he should soon "be forever with the Lord," yet amid his own joy still mindful of the welfare of others, that we hear his exultant voice: "I am now ready to be offered, and the time of my departure is at hand. I have fought a good fight, I have finished my course, I have kept the faith. Henceforth there is laid up for me a crown of righteousness, which the Lord, the righteous judge, shall give me at that day; and not to me only, but unto all them also that love his appearing."

ABBREVIATIONS.

NAMES OF WRITERS ABBREVIATED IN THE NOTES.

THE works of those referred to in the following list are mostly Commentaries, and may be presumed to be well known. The titles of some of those which are less common have been given at the foot of the page where they occur for the first time.

Alf.	Alford.	Hnr.	Heinrichs.
Ang.	Anger.	Hws.	Howson.
Bez.	Beza.	Krüg.	Krüger.
Blmf.	Bloomfield.	Kuin.	Kuinoel.
Bmg.	Baumgarten.	Kyp.	Kypke.
Bng.	Bengel.	Lchm.	Lachmann.
Böttg.	Böttger.	Light.	Lightfoot.
Bretsch.	Bretschneider.	Lng.	Lange.
Brud.	Bruder.	Mey.	Meyer.
Calv.	Calvin.	Neand.	Neander.
Chryst.	Chrysostom.	Olsh.	Olshausen.
De Wet.	De Wette.	Raph.	Raphael.
Doddr.	Doddridge.	Rob.	Robinson
Ebr.	Ebrard.	Schöttg.	Schöttgen.
Forbg.	Forbiger.	Str.	Stier.
Frtz.	Fritzsche.	Suid.	Suidas.
Gesen.	Gesenius.	Thol.	Tholuck.
Grot.	Grotius.	Tsch.	Tischendorf.
Grsb.	Griesbach.	Vitr.	Vitringa.
Hems.	Hemsen.	Wetst.	Wetstein.
Heng.	Hengstenberg.	Wdsth.	Wordsworth.
Hertz.	Hertzog.	Whl.	Wahl.
Hesych.	Hesychius.	Wiesl.	Wieseler.
Hmph.	Humphry.	Win.	Winer.

OTHER ABBREVIATIONS.

Cranm.	Cranmer's Version of N. T.	T. R.	Received Greek Text.
E. V.	Common English Version.	Vulg.	Vulgate N. Testament.
Genv.	Geneva Version.	Wicl.	Wiclif's Version.
Tynd.	Tyndale's Version.		

INDEX I.

The following Index is intended to exhibit the contents of the Notes as distinguished for the most part from the contents of the History.

A.

B.

C.

D.

E.

F.

G.

H.

I.

J.

K.

O.

P.

Q.

R.

S.

T.

U.

V.

W.

Y.

Z.

INDEX II.

THE following are the Contents of the History, with the chapters and verses, and the pages of the Commentary on which the sections may be found.

GOULD AND LINCOLN'S WORKS.

Thesaurus of English Words and Phrases. So classified and arranged as to facilitate the expression of ideas, and assist in literary composition. New and improved edition. By PETER MARK ROGET. Revised and Edited, with a List of Foreign words defined in English, and other additions, by B. SEARS, D.D., Pres. of Brown University. 12mo, cloth, $1.50.

A work which enables a writer to seize upon just the right word for his purpose.

Visits to European Celebrities. By WILLIAM B. SPRAGUE, D.D. 12mo, cloth, $1.

A Series of graphic and life-like Personal Sketches of many of the most distinguished men and women of Europe; and the novel attraction of a *fac-simile of the signature* of each of the persons introduced.

The Plurality of Worlds. A NEW EDITION. WITH A SUPPLEMENTARY DIALOGUE, in which the Author's Reviewers are reviewed. 12mo, cloth, $1.

This masterly production will now have an increased attraction in the addition of the Supplement, in which the author's reviewers are triumphantly reviewed.

Macaulay on Scotland. A Critique from the "Witness," edited by HUGH MILLER. 12mo. 25 cts.

Chambers' Cyclopædia of English Literature. The choicest productions of English Authors, from the earliest to the present time. Connected by a Critical and Biographical History. Two octavo vols. of 700 pages each, with upward of 300 elegant Illustrations. Embossed cloth, $5.

Let the reader open where he will, he can not fail to find matter for profit and delight. The selections are gems,—infinite riches in a little room: in the language of another, "*A whole English Library fused into one Cheap Book.*"

Chambers' Home Book; or, Pocket Miscellany. Containing a Choice Selection of Interesting and Instructive Reading, for the Old and Young. Six volumes, 16mo, cloth, $3.

This is fully equal, and in some respects superior, to either of the Chambers' other works.

Chambers' Miscellany of Useful and Entertaining Knowledge. With Elegant Illustrative Engravings. Ten volumes. Cloth, $7.50.

Cyclopædia of Anecdotes of Literature and the Fine Arts. A Choice Selection of Anecdotes of the various forms of Literature, of the Arts, of Architecture, Engraving, Music, Poetry, Painting, and Sculpture, and of the most celebrated Literary Characters and Artists of different Countries and Ages, etc. By KAZLITT ARVINE. Numerous Illustrations. 725 pages, octavo, cloth, $3.

The choicest collection of anecdotes ever published. It contains 3040 anecdotes, 350 fine illustrations, and such is the wonderful variety, as to afford an inexhaustible fund of interest for every class of readers.

The Hallig; or, the Sheepfold in the Waters. A Tale of Humble Life on the Coast of Schleswig. From the German of Biernatzski, by Mrs. GEORGE P. MARSH. 12mo, cloth, $1.

The Excellent Woman. as described in the Book of Proverbs. With an Introduction by Rev. W. B. SPRAGUE, D.D., containing twenty-four splendid Illustrations. 12mo, cloth, $1; cloth, gilt, $1.75; extra Turkey, $2.50.

Knowledge is Power. A View of the Productive Forces of Modern Society, and the Results of Labor, Capital, and Skill. By CHAS. KNIGHT. Numerous Illustrations. American Edition. Revised, with Additions. 12mo, cloth, $1.25.

☞ This is emphatically a book for the people. It contains an immense amount of important information, which everybody ought to possess.

Works of John Harris, D.D.
THE GREAT TEACHER, 85cts.
THE GREAT COMMISSION, $1.
THE PRE-ADAMITE EARTH, $1.
MAN PRIMEVAL, $1 25.
PATRIARCHY; OR, THE FAMILY, $1.25.
SERMONS ON SPECIAL OCCASIONS, $1.

Works of Hugh Miller.
MY SCHOOLS AND SCHOOLMASTERS, $1.25.
OLD RED SANDSTONE, $1.
FOOTPRINTS OF THE CREATOR, $1.
FIRST IMPRESSIONS OF ENGLAND, $1.
TESTIMONY OF THE ROCKS, $1.25.

Works of William R. Williams, D.D.
LECTURES ON THE LORD'S PRAYER, 85 cts.
RELIGIOUS PROGRESS, 85 cts.
MISCELLANIES, $1.25.

Works of Peter Bayne.
CHRISTIAN LIFE, SOCIAL AND INDIVIDUAL, $1.25.
ESSAYS IN BIOGRAPHY AND CRITICISM, 1ST SERIES, $1.25.
" " " 2ND SERIES, 1.25.

Works of W. K. Tweedie, D.D.
GLAD TIDINGS, 63 cts.
A LAMP TO THE PATH, 63 cts.
SEED TIME AND HARVEST, 63 cts.

Works of John Angel James.
THE MARRIAGE RING, 75 cts.
THE CHURCH MEMBER'S GUIDE, 33 cts.
THE CHURCH IN EARNEST, 40 cts.
CHRISTIAN PROGRESS, 31 cts.

Philip Doddridge; his Life and Labors. By JOHN STOUGHTON, D.D., author of *Spiritual Heroes*, etc., and an INTRODUCTORY CHAPTER by Rev. JAMES G. MIALL, author of *Footsteps of our Forefathers*, etc. With beautiful Illumined Title Page, Frontispiece. etc. 16mo, cloth, 60 cts.

Life and Character of James Montgomery. Abridged from the recent London Edition. By Mrs. H. C. KNIGHT, author of *Lady Huntington and her Friends*. Fine Likeness and beautifully illustrated title page. 12mo, cloth, $1.25.

This is an original biography prepared from the abundant, but ill-digested materials contained in the *seven octavo volumes* of the London edition.

Extracts from the Diary and Correspondence of the late Amos Lawrence. Edited by his son WM. R. LAWRENCE, M.D. With elegant portraits of Amos and Abbot Lawrence, an engraving of their Birthplace, and an Autograph page of Handwriting. One large octavo volume, cloth, $1.50; also, royal 12mo edition, cloth, $1.

Dr. Grant and the Mountain Nestorians. By Rev. THOMAS LAURIE, his surviving associate in that Mission. With a Likeness, Map of the Country, and numerous Illustrations. Third edition revised and improved. 12mo, cloth, $1.25.

☞ A most interesting memoir of a most remarkable man.

☞ In addition to works published by themselves, they keep an extensive assortment of works in all departments of trade, which they supply at Publishers' prices. ☞ They particularly invite the attention of Booksellers, Traveling Agents, Teachers, School Committees, Librarians, Clergymen, and professional men generally, to whom a liberal discount is uniformly made, to their extensive stock. ☞ To persons wishing copies of Text-books for examination, they will be forwarded, per mail or otherwise, on the reception of one half the price of the work desired. ☞ Orders from any part of the country attended to with faithfulness and dispatch.

IMPORTANT WORKS.

KITTO'S POPULAR CYCLOPÆDIA OF BIBLICAL LITERATURE. Condensed from the larger work. By the Author, JOHN KITTO, D.D., author of *Pictorial Bible; History of Palestine; Scripture Daily Readings*, etc. Assisted by JAMES TAYLOR, D.D., of Glasgow. With *over five hundred Illustrations*. One volume, octavo, 812 pp., cloth, $3.

This CYCLOPÆDIA is designed to furnish a DICTIONARY OF THE BIBLE, while at the same time it answers the place of a COMMENTARY, embodying the products of the best and most recent researches in biblical literature, in which the scholars of Europe and America have been engaged. The work, the result of immense labor and research, is, by universal consent, pronounced the best work of its class extant. It is not only intended for *ministers* and *theological students*, but is also particularly adapted to *parents, Sabbath-school teachers, and the great body of the religious public*.

A condensed view of the various branches of Biblical Science comprehended in the work.

1. BIBLICAL CRITICISM.—Embracing the History of the Bible Languages; Canon of Scripture; Literary History and Peculiarities of the Sacred Books; Formation and History of Scripture Texts.

2. HISTORY.—Proper Names of Persons; Biographical Sketches of prominent Characters; Detailed Accounts of important events recorded in Scripture; Chronology and Genealogy of Scripture.

3. GEOGRAPHY.—Names of Places; Description of Scenery; Boundaries and Mutual Relations of the Countries mentioned in Scripture, so far as necessary to illustrate the Sacred Text.

4. ARCHÆOLOGY.—Manners and Customs of the Jews and other nations mentioned in Scripture; their Sacred Institutions, Military Affairs, Political Arrangements, Literary, and Scientific Pursuits.

5. PHYSICAL SCIENCE.—Scripture Cosmogony and Astronomy, Zoology, Mineralogy, Botany, Meteorology.

In addition to numerous flattering notices and reviews, personal letters from *more than fifty of the most distinguished Ministers and Laymen of different religious denominations in the country* have been received, highly commending this work as admirably adapted to ministers, Sabbath-school teachers, heads of families, and *all* Bible students.

The following extract of a letter is a fair specimen of individual letters received from *each* of the gentlemen whose names are given below:—

"I have examined it with special and unalloyed satisfaction. It has the rare merit of being all that it professes to be; and very few, I am sure, who may consult it, will deny that, in richness and fulness of detail, it surpasses their expectation. Many ministers will find it a valuable auxiliary; but its chief excellence is, that it furnishes just the facilities which are needed by the thousands in families and Sabbath-schools who are engaged in the important business of biblical education. It is, in itself, a library of reliable information."

W. B. Sprague, D.D., Pastor of Second Presbyterian Church, Albany, N. Y.—J. J. Carruthers, D.D., Pastor of Second Parish Congregational Church, Portland, Me.—Joel Hawes, D.D., Pastor of First Congregational Church, Hartford, Ct.—Daniel Sharp, D.D., late Pastor of Third Baptist Church, Boston.—N. L. Frothingham, D.D., late Pastor of First Congregational Church (Unitarian), Boston.—Ephraim Peabody, D.D., Pastor of Stone Chapel Congregational Church (Unitarian), Boston.—A. L. Stone, Pastor of Park Street Congregational Church, Boston.—John S. Stone, D.D., Rector of Christ Church (Episcopal), Brooklyn, N. Y.—J. B. Waterbury, D.D., Pastor of Bowdoin Street Church (Congregational), Boston.—Baron Stow, D.D., Pastor of Rowe Street Baptist Church, Boston.—Thomas H. Skinner, D.D., Pastor of Carmine Street Presbyterian Church, N. Y.—Samuel M. Worcester, D.D., Pastor of the Tabernacle Church (Congregational), Salem.—Horace Bushnell, D.D., Pastor of Third Congregational Church, Hartford, Ct.—Right Reverend J. M. Wainwright, D.D., Trinity Church (Episcopal), N. Y.—Gardner Spring, D.D., Pastor of the Brick Church Chapel, Presbyterian Church, N. Y.—W. T. Dwight, D.D., Pastor of Third Congregational Church, Portland, Me.—E. N. Kirk, Pastor of Mount Vernon Congregational Church, Boston.—Prof. George Bush, author of *Notes on the Scriptures*, N. Y.—Howard Malcom, D.D., author of *Bible Dictionary*, and President of Lewisburg University.—Henry J. Ripley, D.D., author of *Notes on the Scriptures*, and Prof. in Newton Theo. Ins.—N. Porter, Prof. in Yale College, New Haven, Ct.—Jared Sparks, Edward Everett, Theodore Frelinghuysen, Robert C. Winthrop, John McLean, Simon Greenleaf, Thomas S. Williams,—and a large number of others of like character and standing of the above, whose names can not here appear.

HISTORY OF PALESTINE, from the Patriarchal Age to the Present Time; with Introductory Chapters on the Geography and Natural History of the Country, and on the Customs and Institutions of the Hebrews. By JOHN KITTO, D.D. With upward of *two hundred Illustrations*. 12mo. cloth, $1.25.

A very full compendium of the geography and history of Palestine, from the earliest era mentioned in Scripture, to the present day; not merely a dry record of boundaries, and the succession of rulers, but an intelligible account of the agriculture, habits of life, literature, science, and art, with the religious, political, and judicial institutions of the inhabitants of the Holy Land in all ages. The descriptive portions of the work are increased in value by numerous wood-cuts. A more useful and instructive book has rarely been published.—*N. Y. Commercial.*

Whoever will read this book till he has possessed himself thoroughly of its contents, will, we venture to say, read the Bible with far more intelligence and satisfaction during all the rest of his life.—*Puritan Recorder.*

Beyond all dispute, this is the best historical compendium of the Holy Land, from the days of Abraham to those of the late Pasha of Egypt, Mehemet Ali.—*Edinburgh Review.*

☞ In the numerous notices and reviews the work has been strongly recommended, as not only admirably adapted to the *family*, but also as a text book for *Sabbath and week-day schools.*

A TREATISE ON BIBLICAL CRITICISM; Exhibiting a Systematic View of that Science. By SAMUEL DAVIDSON, D.D., of the University of Halle. Revised and enlarged edition, two elegant octavo volumes, cloth, $5.

These volumes contain a statement of the *sources* of criticism, such as the MSS. of the Hebrew Bible and Greek Testament, the principal versions of both, quotations from them in early writers, parallels,—every thing, in short, is discussed, which properly belongs to the *criticism* of the text, comprehending all that comes under the title of *General Introduction*, in Introductions to the Old and New Testaments.

GOULD & LINCOLN, Publishers, Boston.

www.ingramcontent.com/pod-product-compliance
Lightning Source LLC
LaVergne TN
LVHW020922110826
845150LV00004B/740